Biological Bases of

CLINICAL ANXIETY

Biological Bases

— OF —

Clinical Anxiety

Barry N. Burijon

W. W. NORTON & COMPANY

New York • London

NOTICE
The author has made every attempt to summarize accurately and concisely a mul-
titude of references. However, readers should note that medical knowledge
changes with the times, that interpretations of studies and other factual data may
vary, and that the distillation of material from other sources necessitates the omis-
sion of certain details appearing in the original.

DRUG DOSAGES
The author and publisher have exerted every effort to ensure that the drug selection and dosage suggested in this text are in accord with current recommendations and practice at the time of publication. However, in view of ongoing research, changes in government regulations, and the constant flow of information
relating to drug therapy and drug reactions, readers are urged to check drug pack-
age inserts for changes in indications and dosage and for added warnings and pre-
cautions. This is particularly important when the recommended agent is a new or
infrequently used drug.

Library of Congress Cataloging-in-Publication Data

Burijon, Barry N.
  Biological bases of clinical anxiety / Barry N. Burijon.
      p.   ; cm.
Includes bibliographical references and index.
ISBN-13:978-0-393-70469-3
ISBN-10:0-393-70469-6
1. Anxiety disorders. I. Title.

RC531.B87 2006
616. 85'22—dc 22   2006040979

W. W. Norton & Company, Inc., 500 Fifth Avenue, New York, N.Y. 10110
www.wwnorton.com

W. W. Norton & Company Ltd., Castle House, 75/76 Wells St., London W1T 3QT
1 3 5 7 9 0 8 6 4 2

Dedicated to the honorable memory of
Dr. Robert F. Woodward

Contents

Acknowledgments

W RITING A SCIENTIFIC TEXT is a collaborative task. Grateful acknowledgment is extended to the editors at Norton Professional Books who assisted in this writing endeavor. Special thanks to the following reviewers and redactors: Drs. Brian G. Burijon, Stanley N. Furman, Gary W. Boggus, Angelina Espinosa-Guanzon, John L. Griffin, Paul Capriotti, and Kathleen M. Powis. Additional support was provided by Jonathan L. Moore, Stephani D. Moore, Joshua L. M. Pittman, and Kimberly A. Jackson. I am deeply grateful to those who have helped in this process, as well as those who have taught me so much over the years.

Preface

ALMOST AS DIVERSE as the unique experiences and expression of symptoms, the causes of anxiety are complex and varied. Seldom does a single cause create these overwhelming feelings, and rarely does a single intervention provide complete relief. Instead, theorists integrate diverse elements—genetics, neuroanatomy, biochemistry, personality traits, cultural and social mores, learning, development, cognition—into cohesive paradigms that capture the essence of each syndrome. Clinical anxiety includes distinctive genetic, neurobiological, psychological, and interpersonal dysfunctions that impede peak performance, impair daily routines, or burden other realms of human functioning. Clinical practice must identify and target all variables for comprehensive intervention. Given this basic premise, I have written this manuscript. The focus is on biological foundations of clinical anxiety. Integrated throughout is a biopsychosocial paradigm that assimilates neurobiological bases, development, psychological factors, and social variables. Within the context of neurobiological sciences, I discuss each syndrome, reviewing empirical studies and outcomes. Treatment models and recommendations from empirical research are provided.

Science progresses rapidly. Because clinical medicine evolves and advances in both understanding and application, there is always a need to update knowledge of contemporary treatments. Useful as a reference text, a resource manual, or an overview of current research, this book provides the very latest in both theory and practice within the field of clinical anxiety. As treating professionals—and lifelong students—we must strive to continually improve the quality of services provided to those in need. I hope that you can incorporate the data delineated herein to enhance patient care and treatment intervention.

Biological Bases of

CLINICAL ANXIETY

CHAPTER 1

Biological Bases of Anxiety:
An Introduction

I N THE COURSE OF human development, the affective components of fear and anxiety have served adaptive functions in alerting individuals of impending harm. **Stress** is a psychobiological process characterized by alterations in emotional, behavioral, and physiological functions. Any process that threatens control, self-esteem, and overall well-being can be described as stressful. Stress can be conceptualized as a perceptual process of viewing demands that exceed adaptive capacity, resulting in multifaceted changes in cognition, emotion, intrapsychic psychology, and biology. **Stressors** are any perceived stimuli that place demands on functioning, precipitating negative physiological, emotional, cognitive, or behavioral responses to environmental stimuli that are threatening or are perceived as threatening. The *alarm reaction* — the initial reaction to stressor stimuli — prompts heightened arousal and mobilization of resources to react to danger adaptively. Associated features may include increased heart rate and respirations, dry mouth, tinnitus, hypervigilance, autonomic hyperarousal, brooding and worrying, or insomnia. *Fear*, the emotional response to perceived threat, alerts the body and improves both physical and mental performance (Yerkes & Dodson, 1908).

Increased arousal within the body and somatic components bring about changes in mood, thought, behavior, and biophysiology (Barlow, 2002; Mc-Naughton & Gray, 2000). Involving emotion, cognition, and behavior, *anxiety*, fear's pathological counterpart, includes disturbances of mood, thought, behavior, and physiological activity (*hyperarousal*). Both arousal and the subjective association of anxiety are somatic responses that involve complex neurocircuits and multiple neurochemical components. The term *clinical anxiety* refers to any form of anxiety that impedes optimal functioning while causing significant distress. The degree to which clinical anxiety is experienced is based on numerous factors, such as the person's background capabilities and the nature of the perceived threat. As a general premise, those with clinically diagnosed anxiety conditions exhibit a labile nervous system associated with chronic overarousal and slow habituation. Epidemiological catchment studies indicate that 19% of males and 31% of females will develop some form of dysfunctional anxiety during their lifetime (Cloitre, Yonkers, et al., 2004; De Jong, Moser, An, & Chung, 2004). Table 1.1 lists the physiological symptoms of anxiety.

Although universally ubiquitous among diverse cultures, the expression of clinical anxiety often differs according to societal mores, norms, and motifs (Higgins, 2004; Kiropoulos, Klimidis, & Minas, 2004). Other cultures often use distinct means of both defining and describing the experience of anxiety (Zvolensky, Kotov, Antipova, & Schmidt, 2003). Freud (1901, 1936) used the German word *angst* to describe anxiety as dread, fearful apprehension, and experiential anguish (Zvolensky et al., 2003). Psychoanalytic views are linked to the German *trieb*, a term roughly translated as "instinct," thereby emphasizing the biological basis of anxiety. The French *anxiété* describes anxiety by emphasizing its negative physiological features. Culturally determined forms of anxiety are known as *koro* and *pa-leng* in Southeast Asian cultures, *heart distress* in Iran, *susto* in Latin America, and *shinkeishitu* in Japan (Gallagher, 2001; Luo, Fones, Thumboo, & Li, 2004; Thakker & Ward, 1998). Across cultures, contemporary definitions include com-

TABLE 1.1.
Physiological Symptoms of Anxiety

Area	Symptoms
Cardiovascular	Uncomfortable awareness of the heart (palpitations), tachycardia (increased heart rate), chest pain
Gastrointestinal	Lump in the throat, difficulty swallowing, nausea, emesis, diarrhea, stomach cramps
General	Tension, nervousness, fatigue, hyperarousal, insomnia or hypersomnolence, hot or cold sensations
Musculoskeletal	Muscle pains, tremor, spasms
Neurological	Vertigo (dizziness), lightheadedness, deficits in attention and concentration, blurred vision, numbness or tingling in mouth or extremities, tinnitus (ringing in the ears), disequilibrium
Respiratory	Shortness of breath, chest pain, increased frequency of respirations, choking sensation

mon themes of specific characteristics (phobias) and diffuse characteristics (nervousness, worry), symptomatic feelings of anxiety (usually the predominant symptom), and avoidant behavior (e.g., attempts to elude dreaded precipitants; Bhagwanjee, Parekh, Paruk, Peterson, & Subedar, 1998; Kirmayer, 1991).

DIAGNOSTIC NOMENCLATURE

Substantial differences in the conceptualization of anxiety are seen across cultures, theoretical paradigms, and biogenic emphases. Clinical syndromes, psychological constructs, and diverse classification systems (*taxonomies*) are used to define diagnostic criteria (Follette & Houts, 1996). Appropriate diagnosis and treatment are often confounded by atypical presentations, comorbidities, and multiple somatic complaints, often leading to great effort and expense in identifying the cause of "unexplained" features (Haslam, 2003). For example, symptoms may be a normal response to stressful life events, a precursor of an anxiety disorder, a symptom of another psychological syndrome such as depression, or secondary to a medical condition (Brambilla et al., 2004; Kendler, Hettema, Butera, Gardner, & Prescott, 2003). More precise *nosology* permits greater specificity in sample composition, patient description, etiology, and prognostic outlook, facilitating communication, treatment, and research of these syndromes (Katerndahl & Ferrer, 2004; McWilliams, 1994). Both the *International Classification of Diseases* (ICD-10; World Health Organization, 1992) and the *Diagnostic and Statistical Manual of Mental Disorders* (DSM-IV-TR; American Psychiatric Association, 2000) utilize a combination of theoretical models, hierarchical categorization, and both classic and prototypic criteria (Andrews & Slade, 2002; Slade & Andrews, 2001). Classification includes both theoretical and pragmatic considerations, reflecting historical and contemporary views and sorting dimensional nomenclature descriptively. By the use of clearly defined parameters, accurate diagnoses of clinical anxiety can be made by competent professionals who have a thorough understanding of its etiology, signs, symptoms, impact, and treatments (Kim, Min, & Yu, 2004; Shelton, 2004).

Prior to 1980, descriptive nomenclatures utilized Freud's (1901) model of *psychoses* and *neuroses*. The term *psychosis* refers to any syndrome or clinical disease that inhibits veridical perception of reality whereas *neurosis* refers to dystonic, distressing symptoms, relatively enduring and chronic, but with the individual's reality-testing abilities intact (Masling & Bornstein, 1994). Neurotic symptoms represent prelogical and preverbal fears that cannot be resolved through rational thought. Instead, their formative conflicts must be identified, understood, and worked through via emotional exploration, experience, and maturation. Anxiety was presumed to be the cause of all "neuroses," and two subtypes—anxiety neurosis and phobic neurosis—were identified. Over time, as with other prominent psychoanalytic terms and in an effort to provide atheoretical nosology, these terms were dropped from diagnostic nomenclature. Further, by conceptualizing psychological disorders as biological diseases and illnesses, initial models failed to clearly define observable behaviors that were part of clinical disorders, as well as describe other defining and differentiating features of specific syndromes. For example, sociologically and psychologically based etiologies were excluded in the medical model, and thus excluded from early diagnostic systems. With the development of behavioral, social learning, and humanistic theories, the early nosologic system needed revision to include various diverse paradigms. Taxonomies developed that incorporated these and other variables in describing clinical conditions and guiding their research. Reorganized, redefined, and providing operational criteria for anxiety disorders, the *DSM*, first published in 1952, uses a multiaxial model to include diverse areas of functioning: clinical syndromes, developmental characteristics, personality traits/disorders, medical conditions relevant to psychological functioning, psychosocial stressors, and a description of global functioning via a well-defined rating scale. The *DSM-IV-TR*'s description of each anxiety syndrome provides an agreed-upon, defined language for communication, creates a universally understood description of a syndrome's symptomatic features, and spurs theoretical conceptualization and empirical research (Natelson, 2004; Sarbin, 1997).

Anxiety disorders are mental conditions characterized by chronic and debilitating fear with attempts to elude anxiety-provoking stimuli. Diagnostic criteria are based on the patient's experience and expression of anxiety, which impedes or prevents usual functioning, often due to autonomic hyperarousal, subjective nervousness, or avoidant behavior. Each unique manifestation of anxiety combines two chief criteria: subjective agitation (nervousness, autonomic hyperarousal) and avoidant behavior (any means or activity targeted to reduce or elude anxiety-producing situations). Individual anxiety disorders have considerable symptomatic overlap in their presumed causes and expressions; common malfunctioning neurocircuits within the brain may account for overlap of symptoms (Roy-Byrne & Wagner, 2004). A comprehensive knowledge of the unique symptoms of each clinical syndrome provides a greater understanding of patient functioning, prognosis, and outcomes (Armstrong & Earnshaw, 2004; Smith et al., 2004).

PREVALANCE OF ANXIETY

Clinical anxiety has become a problem of epidemic proportions that requires intervention. For both children and adults, anxiety disorders are the single most common psychiatric condition, affecting 13–18% of the population (Brown, Campbell, Lehman, Grisham, & Mancill, 2001; Zimmerman & Chelminski, 2003). More than 30 million Americans are affected by an anxiety disorder per year, and their friends, families, and community also suffer (Rapaport, Clary, Fayyad, & Endicott, 2005; Sansone, Hendricks, Gaither, & Reddington, 2004). Lifetime prevalence studies estimate that 15–25% of the American adult population can be expected to have an anxiety disorder during their lives (Pelissolo et al.,

2002). As a group, anxiety disorders are the most common psychological condition in patients seeking professional care (Harman, Rollman, Hanusa, Lenze, & Shear, 2002). Some estimates suggest that as much as a fourth of the population will, at some point in their lives, experience symptoms of clinical anxiety that would merit professional diagnosis (Quilty, Van Amerigen, Mancini, Oakman, & Farvolden, 2003). Women are more likely than men to report feeling anxious (Huber & Henrich, 2003; Hughes, Feldman, & Beckham, 2005). Yet because all individuals experience anxiety in life (albeit at different levels), those who experience clinical anxiety may find their symptoms are discounted or minimized when they seek treatment, even though the emotions generated from stress, fear, and anxiety can considerably impair well-being (Heilig, 2004). Most child and adult patients do not receive appropriate care for their anxiety, even though effective models are available (Rodriguez, Weisberg, et al., 2004; Young, Klap, Sherbourne, & Wells, 2001). Many individuals who could benefit from treatment for clinical anxiety are not being reached, and those who do get treatment often receive inadequate interventions (Pollack, 2004; Salzman, 2004). Table 1.2 summarizes the epidemiology of anxiety disorders.

Using the *DSM-IV-TR*'s broad-based criteria, anxious individuals are between three and five times more likely to seek medical care and six times more likely than others to be hospitalized for a psychiatric disorder (Lepine, 2002; McLaughlin, Geissler, & Wan, 2003). Increased utilization of medical services by patients with anxiety disorders has been described in numerous epidemiologic studies, yet substantial numbers of practitioners in diverse disciplines are still undertrained and underprepared to adequately provide comprehensive clinical interventions (Issakidis, Sanderson, Corry, Andrews, & Lapsley, 2004). Compared to others, individuals with diagnosable anxiety disorders are more likely to repeatedly (six or more times) see primary-care physicians or seek care in a hospital emergency room (Mendlowicz & Stein, 2000). It is not uncommon for anxiety probands to present to general practitioners with vague, often unexplained, symptoms and undergo costly diagnostic workups that can include unnecessary lab tests, imaging scans, or consultations with specialists—or unnecessary, wrong, or inadequate medical intervention (Lipsitz & Schneider, 2000; Merritt, 2000). Unwarranted medical services may be provided in an attempt to offer some sort of assistance (Katon & Walker, 1998). Other costs include 31% for psychiatric treatment, 10% in occupational/workplace costs, 3% in mortality expenses, and 2% for pharmaceutical interventions (Lecrubier, 2001a, 2001b). Conservative estimates suggest that anxiety disorders cost the United States between $40 and $50 billion each year—almost a third of mental health treatment expenses—due to repeated and ineffectual use of healthcare services (Heuzenroeder et al., 2004). Obsessive-compulsive disorder alone costs Americans an estimated $8.4 billion in social and economic losses (Besiroglu, Cillis, & Askin, 2004). Widespread prevention, early intervention, effective therapies, equal access to clinical services, ongoing research, and comprehensive treatments are essential to reducing the societal costs and effects of anxiety (Amick et al., 1998; Harter, Conway, & Merikangas, 2003).

TABLE 1.2.
Anxiety Disorders: Epidemiology (Lepine, 2002)

Disorder	Approximate USA Number Affected (percentage)	Prominent Symptoms and Characteristics	Male/Female Ratio	Usual Age of Onset
Generalized anxiety disorder (GAD)	4 million (2.8%)	Free-floating nervousness that impedes usual functioning	Twice as common in females than males	0–20 yr
Obsessive-compulsive disorder (OCD)	3.3 million (2.3%)	Repetitive thought processes that lead to ritualized behaviors in an attempt to reduce underlying anxiety	Equally common among males and females; about 50% are firstborn children	3–25 yr; onset slightly earlier in males than females
Panic disorder (PD)	2.4 million (1.7%)	Intense, acute fear experienced as brief terror or fear of impending doom	Twice as common in females as males	15–35 yr
Posttraumatic stress disorder (PTSD)	5.2 million (3.6%)	A "reliving" of a trauma mixed with avoidant behaviors and anxiety secondary to the event	Women are more likely than men to develop PTSD following trauma	Varies by experience and environmental exposures
Specific phobia (SP)	11 million (8%)	An intense, unrealistic fear of a specific object or event	Twice as common in females than males	Varies

CLINICAL ANXIETY: PARADIGMS

To understand the complexity of anxiety, a comprehensive model is needed. This model must include diverse variables, including biological, psychological, cognitive, social, and behavioral factors. For example, some individuals are susceptible to stress produced by negative life events because of constitutional factors, relatively low social support, or some combination of personality and cognitive dispositions. Temperament, genetics, and biological functioning, in addition to psychological and social factors, guide human experience and can potentiate anxiety (Fowles, 2001; Talbot, 2004). Cohesive models comprehensively incorporate all relevant variables, factors, and research findings. The *biopsychosocial model* conceptualizes clinical disorders as a combination of three basic factors: *physiology* (e.g., biology, genetic inheritance, etc.), *psychology* (e.g., learning, cognitive styles, personality traits), and *social variables* (e.g., social support, depth and level of interpersonal relationships). At the core of this model is a biological vulnerability to stress, most likely genetically transmitted, which may manifest across numerous neurobiological systems (Degroot & Treit, 2004).

ETIOLOGY

The following list includes several potential anxiety etiologies:

- Genetic factors; inherited predispositions, prenatal development
- Personality-based traits (e.g., anxiety sensitivity); temperament
- Autonomic reactivity
- Neurobiological diatheses (e.g., neuroanatomy, biochemistry)
- Endocrine functioning; neurochemistry
- Comorbid medical and psychiatric syndromes
- Medications, drugs
- Environmental stress, daily hassles, ongoing antagonisms
- Hostile, cold, detached social relationships, particularly within the family
- Learning, psychological development, and prior conditioning
- Family background
- Current social support systems
- Lack of appropriate coping and adaptation skills
- Stunted emotional growth and maturation
- Cognitive processes; attribution styles

Perhaps the easiest symptoms to link with biological bases are those associated with clinical anxiety, particularly motivational systems based on the brain's management of neurochemistry, hormones, and perception relative to avoidance of threat. From Hippocrates (400 BCE) to contemporary views, scientists have hypothesized that a complex combination of physiological variables together influence functioning. *Constitutional factors* predispose individuals to specific mental disorders. Such features may include biologically-based personality traits, neurobiologically based medical conditions, or "nonspecific" biological factors. Vulnerability diathesis may be activated by aversive, stressful life events (Sundet, Skre, Okkenhaug, & Tambs, 2003). The predisposition can itself be environmentally caused or inherited. Hypothetical environmentally caused diatheses could include such factors as brain injury caused by prenatal hypoxia or autonomic hyperactivity stemming from years of child abuse, imprisonment, or torture. Incorporating neuroanatomy, intercell communication, biochemical actions and effects, and other neuronal processes, diverse theories delineate causes and effective treatments for anxiety, with subsequent intervention targeting aberrant processes (Kent & Rauch, 2003). The procedural, vulnerability, and kindling effects of neurochemistries support biopsychosocial models of clinical anxiety that delineate a general genetic predisposition. This is coupled with early stresses at crucial phases of development, resulting in a phenotype that is neurobiologically vulnerable and has a lowered overall threshold for coping with additional stress exposure. Diverse anxiety syndromes subsequently evolve upon this foundational vulnerability.

The vast majority of research in neuropsychiatry, biophysiological causes of psychopathology, and biochemical treatments of anxiety focuses on neuronal makeup and action (Shinnick-Gallagher, McKernan, Xie, & Zinebi, 2003). Greater understanding of neuroanatomy, pharmacology, and neurochemistry, as well as advances in brain imaging, have led to greater understanding of the body's response to stress. The brain initiates a sequence of cell firing, arousal, and biochemical release that heightens the body's ability to cope. The "normal" stress response is a complex biochemical and neurohormonal process, releasing catecholamines, serotonin, endogenous opioids, and hormones from the hypothalamus, pituitary, and adrenals (Coplan, Pine, Papp, & Gorman, 1997; Davidson, 1998). Mobilization increases oxygen and energy resources available to the tissues, boosts circulation so that resources can be moved through the body more quickly, and provides for waste-product release, tactile sensitivity, surface protection, and quick repair of tissue damage. Neural circuits increase alertness, focus attention, and redirect targeted behavior. Heightened arousal increases energy production and usage, alters electrolyte and fluid balance, and stimulates the autonomic nervous system (Kinzig et al., 2003). The pathophysiology of anxiety is caused by an aberrance of noradrenergic, serotonergic, GABAergic, and dopaminergic neural systems as well as abnormal chemoreceptor reactivity.

Whether specifying neurotransmitter or anatomical pathways, biological correlates of clinical anxiety implicate multiple systems, pathways, and processes (Kikuchi et al., 2005; Sapolsky, 1996). This biologically-based predisposition can be due to genetics, brain circuits, neurotransmitters, or brain functionality, involving multiple systems, pathways, and processes (Eley et al., 2003). **Neurobiological variables** include genetics, anatomy, the structure and functioning of nerve cells, neurological and endocrine processes, or any other biochemical activity. Neurobiological paradigms have flourished from "diathesis-stress" models to complex, comprehensive theories involving genetics, biochemistry, neuroanatomy, and endocrinology (Kandel, 1999). For example, genetic variables may be activated via cerebral lesions within the striatum (Kalin, 2004). Some studies suggest that generalized anxiety disorder (GAD) and panic disorder (PD) have separate genetic diatheses; others propose that they share a common genetic basis that defines the disorders on a continuum (Hettema, Neale, & Kendler, 2001). Physiological attributes in clinical anxiety are generally linked to hyperarousal of the sympathetic nervous system, but some theories implicate other potential neurobiological markers (Pickering, 1997). The etiology of clinical symptoms may be produced by the structural size or shape of certain brain regions or the chemicals that inhibit or enable neurons to function. The brain's specific neural pathways facilitate the experience and expression of certain emotions, such as fear, rage, and aggression (Lang, Bradley, & Cuthbert, 1998).

Many aspects of clinical anxiety can be attributed to biochemical dysfunction throughout the brain. **Biochemical theories** implicate aberrant enzymatic or metabolic processes as precipitants to or causative of clinical disorders. The distribution of various biochemicals is heterogeneous throughout the brain because different regions are dominated by distinct nerve types, receptors, and metabolites. For example, **epinephrine**, an excitatory substance that fuels the sympathetic nervous system by increasing glucose in the blood, is released by the adrenal glands as part of the body's response to stress-provoking stimuli.

Although the functioning of the nervous system is familiar to readers, it is worthwhile at this point to review it due to its foundational relationship to biological theories of anxiety (Cannistraro & Rauch, 2003). Basic elements consist of the **central nervous system (CNS)**, comprised of the brain and spinal cord; the **peripheral nervous system (PNS)**, which connects the brain and spinal cord to other parts of the body; and the connections that occur between CNS neurons and other groups of nerve cells within the central or peripheral nervous systems, sensory receptors, or muscles. As the body's most important organ, the brain regulates all somatic functions, consumes 30% of intake calories, and amasses 2% of body weight. The spinal cord relays information to and from the brain. The major function of the PNS is to carry information to and from the CNS. Peripheral nerves can carry sensory information toward or away from the CNS. **Spinal nerves** enter and exit from the spinal cord; **cranial nerves** enter and exit the brain directly.

The PNS consists of two subsystems: **somatic** (transmits information from sense organs to CNS to voluntary skeletal muscles) and **autonomic** (controls smooth muscles of the blood vessels, digestive system, glands, and cardiac muscles). The **autonomic nervous system (ANS)** relays messages to and from the body's internal organs and monitors breathing, heart rate, and digestion. The ease with which an individual's ANS is aroused is directly correlated with level and intensity of anxiety, depending on multiple factors such as genetics, heritability, and cognitive appraisal of the environmental stimuli (Liu, Bertram, Perides, McEwen, & Wang, 2004). The ANS contains two counteractive, antagonistic subdivisions: the **sympathetic nervous system (SNS)**, the adrenergic part that excites and arouses the body; and the **parasympathetic nervous system (PNS)**, the cholinergic system responsible for deceleration of metabolism and general calming within the body. When threat is perceived, the SNS stimulates some organs and inhibits others; when the potential danger is over, the PNS inhibits various bodily functions, causing an overall calming effect by slowing metabolism and lowering blood pressure.

In general, studies have shown that, compared to controls, anxious individuals have less flexible PNSs and this may contribute to prolonged experiences of anxiety when hyperarousal occurs (Schell, Marshall, & Jaycox, 2004). Gray (1976) proposed that the nervous system has subsystems that serve different functions, such as arousal and inhibition. Complex human responses (e.g., feeling anxious) involve multiple functions, regions, and processes. Individual differences in anxiety stem from differences (genetically determined) in the activation of the ***behavioral inhibition system***. Gray's (1982) theory postulates a behavioral inhibition system as hindering behavior in certain anxiety-provoking situations (e.g., novel or aversive incidents).

Along with constitutional factors, the biopsychosocial model implicates ***psychological***, ***environmental***, and ***learning*** variables. Basic biological makeup is innate and present at birth, but key developmental factors can be changed by life experiences (Andersson, et al, 2003). Child and adolescent research has shown that critical periods exist for the development of certain brain functions. Traumatic stress may have negative effects on the development of biologically based stress systems, as well as on brain development (Darnaudery, Dutriez, Viltart, Morley-Fletcher, & Maccari, 2004). Stressful environmental events, undesirable or traumatic experiences, irritants, chronic stressors, and so on combine with vulnerability factors to increase or decrease an individual's propensity for a given condition (Andrade & Guimaraes, 2003; Dadds & Roth, 2001; Kudryavtseva, Gerrits, Avgustinovich, Tenditnik, & Van Ree, 2004). For example, extensive research has shown a correlation between psychopathology and repeated exposure to cold (punitive), critical communication (Asarnow, Thompson, Hamilton, Goldstein, & Guthrie, 1994). Finally, ***protective factors***, such as coping skills, intelligence, personality traits and characteristics, benevolent and supportive social relationships, access to resources, and morale, serve to neutralize diathesis stress variables. Repeatedly, research has shown that such factors as strong social support, adequate problem-solving skills can serve as "buffers" against psychological malaise (Atanackovic, Kroger, Serke, & Deter, 2004).

Table 1.3 lists the factors just described and includes examples of each.

Vulnerability **+** *Precipitant* **−** *Protectants* **=** *Symptoms*

To understand the causes of anxiety, combine vulnerabilities with psychological and social factors, subtract protective variables. Therein lies likelihood of symptoms.

TABLE 1.3.
The Biopsychosocial Model

Factor	Examples
Constitutional	Genetics, physiology, neurobiology, biochemistry, neuroanatomy
Psychology	Negative life events, traumatic experiences, learning and contingency history, cognitive processes, social perception and cognition
Environmental	Stressors, chronic irritants, ongoing "hassles," negative social interactions (e.g., "expressed emotion")
Protective	Strong social support, secure attachment, intelligence, coping and problem-solving skills, spirituality, temperamental characteristics (e.g., sociability), extraversion, internal locus of control, optimism, positive self-esteem, supportive family/marital environment, "good genes" (absence of inherited diatheses)

Researchers continue to explore relationships among key variables to develop stronger models for each disorder and greater effectiveness of interventions. Theorists integrate diverse factors—genetics, traits, cultural and social mores, learning, development, and cognition—into cohesive paradigms that capture the essence and nature of clinical anxiety, incorporating idiographic, physiological, cognitive, emotional, interpersonal, and behavioral aspects for each disorder (Fox, Henderson, Marshall, Nichols, & Ghera, 2004). Biobehavioral models began in the 1960's (e.g., Pitts's 1969 Lactate Panicogenesis theory) and have evolved into complex, multifactorial conceptualizations. Other theories have developed from the utility (effectiveness) of antianxiety medications, advanced tomography, and burgeoning ability to identify and quantify genetic links (Aylward et al., 1996). Clinical response to effective medications has led researchers to alternative models and better understandings of clinical anxiety.

TREATMENTS

Ultimately, researchers seek to use theoretical conceptualizations of diverse pathologies to develop, revise, and improve treatment programs (Doyle & Pollack, 2003). Effective treatments for clinical anxiety include medication, psychotherapy, herbal interventions, exercise, relaxation training, bibliotherapy, and a host of "nontraditional" therapies (e.g., acupuncture, autogenic training, meditation, Hammond, 2005). Given the multifactorial nature of the biopsychosocial model of conceptualizing disorders, effective intervention can occur within any factor or stage—biology, psychology, or sociology—or include all three (Kjernisted & Bleau, 2004). Ideally, interventions can combine known etiologies from each stage model to facilitate timely, targeted relief. Theory and clinical technique must be interwoven to provide the best possible treatment. Although medical intervention can control physiological symptoms, counseling and psychotherapy is recommended for long-term relief and protection against relapse; combined models may have synergistic effects (Kaufman & Charney, 2000).

Medications

Today, medical sciences can provide safe, effective treatments for most psychopathologies, and drug therapies are the most commonly used medical intervention for clinical anxiety. In their interaction with specific biological systems, drugs can have profound effects on behavior due to their impact on how neurons communicate with each other (Bourin & Hascoet, 2001). The brain, central and peripheral nervous systems, biochemical hormones and endocrinology, and all other somatics are prime targets for the actions of psychoactive agents (Kent, Mathew, & Gorman, 2002). Drugs are designed to alter the functioning of diverse regions of the brain and subsequently have various behavioral effects (Caccia, 2004). Generally, most affect chemical neurotransmitters: amino acids, acetylcholine, catecholamines, indoleamines, histamine, or neuroactive peptides. Psychotropic agents affect the central nervous system (CNS), influencing thought processes, emotion, and human behavior. The specific mechanisms through which medications "work" are diverse, affecting anatomical substrates, neural circuits, or other processes involved in psychological and behavioral effects.

Anxiolytics are used to reduce tension, calm the subjective experience of anxiety, and decrease somatic hyperarousal. Multiple mechanisms produce anxiolytic effects; compounds with vastly different spectrums of biochemistry can have similar antianxiety effects. Numerous classes of prescription drugs, such as anticonvulsants, antidepressants, antipsychotics, and antihypertensives, can be used to reduce symptoms (Allgulander, Hirschfeld, & Nutt, 2002). Benzodiazepines, buspirone, clonidine, antihistamines, propranolol, and all antidepressants have, to varying degrees, anxiolytic effects. **Hypnotics** are sedatives that induce drowsiness or sleep. **Antidepressants** are used to reduce the symptoms of a mood disorder, usually by blocking the reuptake of catecholamines (Chen, Holschneider, Wu, Rebrin, & Shih, 2004; Hindmarch, 2002). Six distinct classes of antidepressant medications exist: tricyclics (TCAs) and heterocyclics; selective serotonin reuptake inhibitors (SSRIs); atypical agents that act on postsynaptic receptors; monoamine oxidase inhibitors (MAOIs); atypical antidepressants (bupropion, mirtazepine); and serotonin and norepinephrine reuptake inhibitors (SNRIs). Antipsychotic medications were first developed to treat schizophrenia, usually through dopaminergic antagonism. In addition, many drugs not intended primarily as psychoactive can also affect mood and behavior.

Prescriptions for psychotropic medications to treat anxiety disorders have substantially increased over time (Haapasalo-Pesu, Saarijarvi, & Sorvaniemi, 2003). The choice of medication is based on scientific support, the unique manifestation of symptoms, previous response to treatments, medical condition, and the potential impact of pharmacokinetics and pharmacodynamics in precipitating side effects (Castrogiovanni, Iapichino, Pacchierotti, & Pieraccini, 1998). Although current treatments for clinical anxiety consistently show effectiveness, some patients continue to experience low-grade symptoms or significant side effects from medical regimens. Thus, in contemporary practice, pharmacotherapy provides only one component of a comprehensive regimen including psychoeducation, counseling, and other psychosocial interventions (Table 1.4).

TABLE 1.4.
Biopsychosocial Treatments

Intervention	Target
Pharmacological approaches	Reduction of physiological symptoms
Psychoeducational interventions	Improved medication compliance, improved coping and adaptation skills (via the teaching of novel responses), relaxation, mastery of cognitive restructuring techniques
Psychological interventions	Mastery of thought-stopping and cognitive techniques, reduction of overall anxiety (via counseling), working through of latent conflicts, strengthening the self (via increased insight and clarification)
Social interventions	Improved interpersonal relationships and clarification of boundaries of responsibility, enhanced social support (to prompt treatment compliance and reduce hopelessness), heightened emotional intimacy within interpersonal relationships (to enhance therapy gains)

Psychotherapy

Psychotherapy is an interpersonal process used by trained professionals to change cognitions, behaviors, and feelings (Strupp, 1973). Combining elements from dynamic, behavioral, cognitive, humanistic, existential, interpersonal, and Gestalt paradigms, modern psychotherapies can provide comprehensive treatment for multifaceted symptoms of clinical anxiety, with outcomes equaling or exceeding those of drug regimens (Karpiak & Benjamin, 2004). *Psychosocial interventions* include any therapies that focus on psychological or social functioning, personality, cognitive and emotional factors, and interpersonal interactions (Meares, 2004). Inasmuch as learning and experience is based on changes in neural networks, cognitive functioning, or biochemical processes, the brain can be significantly influenced through effective counseling and behavioral interventions (Frey, Mabilde, & Eizirik, 2004; Orosco et al., 2004). Psychosocial interventions can enhance comprehensive treatment regimens that may include both pharmacologic and psychotherapeutic interventions (Kuzma & Black, 2004).

   Group therapy is unique in behavioral sciences and psychotherapies; with multiple interactive exchanges, participants are able to establish and maintain interpersonal relationships with peers that can facilitate characterological growth and development. Group therapy is particularly effective in addressing interpersonal issues by providing (1) the opportunity to establish growth-enhancing relationships by creating a rich and special environment for personal change; (2) therapeutic processes that occur via interactions within the group, which mimic "usual" interpersonal interactions (outside of group) that either foster or impede psychological functioning; and (3) multiple group focuses and themes that lend the process of group therapy to be applicable to most psychiatric conditions, psychological symptoms of distress or illness, and enhancement of relationships (Gallagher, Rabian, & McCloskey, 2004). Several important therapeutic factors can be defined: mutual support, group cohesiveness, inspiration fueled by hope (lessening of demoralization), and identification with other group members experiencing similar plights. Group therapy can be very effective in reducing anxiety (Kobayashi et al., 2005).

TYPES OF GROUP THERAPY

Groups can be organized or defined by the various functions or purposes for which they are developed:

- *Structured* (skills-building, theme-oriented)
- *Interpersonal* (general process, relationship-oriented)
- *Intrapersonal* (analytic, object-relations, self-psychology)

TABLE 1.5.
General Strategies for Reducing Anxiety

Hyperarousal	Avoidant Behavior
• Modify thought processes (don't catastrophize, overgeneralize, etc.), make sure symptoms are not worsened by patients' seeing them as "terrible, overwhelming, catastrophic" • Develop strong attachments to peers and close friends; learn to *trust* • Mature in ability to process and resolve emotions, identify and distinguish among fine shades of feelings and resolve them before they reach uncomfortable levels • Mediate physiological symptoms via relaxation, deep breathing, or guided imagery • Enhance problem-solving skills to reduce situational stress and tension • Revise self-talk and "automatic" cognitive processes; after to positive, life-affirming mantras • Improve self-esteem, sense of mastery, and overall feeling of competence • Break down anxiety-provoking situations into manageable parts • When feeling overwhelmed, allow short rest periods to recover and get thoughts, feelings, and reactions back on track • Concentrate on good health; maintain appropriate diet (without stimulants) and exercise • Promote positive "buffer" variables such as a set of positive attitudes regarding the expectation of responding adaptively to stress (hardiness) • Reduce overall tension and *anxiety sensitivity* (general cognitive beliefs that certain somatic symptoms will likely lead to harm or malaise)	• Break down anxiety-provoking situations into manageable parts • Reward successive approximations of target behavior • Seek support of close friends • For dreaded situations, schedule a few tasks to complete each day until all are finished • Reinforce effort; be persistent until all tasks are conquered • Ask for help to complete situations that bring stress, anxiety, or difficulty, allowing others who are better able to resolve such situations to help

Originally conceived from small case studies and anecdotal evidence, effective *individual psychotherapies* have evolved secondary to advances in the understanding of biological maturation, emotion and motivation, psychological and cognitive development, and interpersonal theory (e.g., Stern, 1985). Nonmedical paradigms and theoretical conceptualizations have evolved from the three major schools of applied psychology: (1) *psychoanalytic and dynamic theories*, (2) *cognitive and behavioral views* ("second force"), and (3) *humanistic-existential paradigms*. Change comes about in different ways for different psychotherapies: through insight in psychoanalysis, through extinction and relearning in behavior therapies, and through application of necessary and sufficient conditions (e.g., empathy, unconditional positive regard, and genuineness) in humanistic models. Table I.6 reviews the bases for each general model.

Dynamic Theories. The term *psychodynamic* (or *dynamic*) refers to traditional psychoanalytic theory as well as neo-Freudian models that understand overt behavior as the result of a complex interaction of unconscious, preconscious, and conscious motives. All dynamic theories are based on Freud's original psychoanalysis, each being a variation of his initial psychosexual model. Throughout his practice of medicine, alone and also with his colleague Josef Breuer, Freud observed that physiologically healthy individuals often became psychologically or physically sick because of conflict and distress experienced early in life. Clinical practice, combined with anecdotal evidence, yielded four basic premises: (1) behavior is determined largely by unconscious and preconscious drives; (2) personality is comprised of three basic parts—the id, ego, and superego—each important in motivating behavior; (3) human behavior seeks to maximize instinctual pleasure while minimizing intrapsychic guilt; and (4) behavior is a product of both biological and social facets (Maddi, 2001). Central concepts include unconscious motivation of behavior, a three-factor theory of personality (id, ego, superego), stage development (progressing until fixated), defense mechanisms (ego functioning used to reduce anxiety), and a novel, "talking" therapeutic intervention. Central to all dynamic theories is the concept of conflict—whether intrapsychic, sociopersonal, or interpersonal—that promotes anxiety As a general conflict theory, the role of intrapsychic motivation in psychodynamic models is paramount. Continuous, dynamic conflict between the desire to gratify biologically based instincts ("metabolic reduction of tension") and internalized moral values that generate tension. *Intrapsychic conflict*, occurring whenever an avowed goal is frustrated by contradictory or unknown motivations that determine behavior, generates anxiety that then alerts the ego of (potential) impending doom (Gillett, 1996). Freud (1936) proposed three main variants of anxiety: *realistic* (experienced when the individual is in danger of being harmed), *moral* (a threat from the internal world of the superego, such as guilt, shame, or fear of punishment), and *neurotic* (fear of being overwhelmed by the id). The ego defends against the experience and expression of anxiety by using defense mechanisms to reduce it. The rigid and extreme use of primitive defenses fosters anxiety neurosis. Table 1.7 outlines the central concepts in psychoanalysis.

TABLE 1.6.
Treatments

Model	Emphases	Representative Theorists	General View of Anxiety
Behavioral	Learning, conditioning, contingencies	Bandura, Eysenck, Lazarus, Skinner, Wolpe	Results from learning, skills deficits, or conditioning
Cognitive; cognitive-behavioral	Thought content and processes, beliefs, values	Beck, Ellis, Meichenbaum	A product of maladaptive thoughts, irrational thinking, or illogical reasoning
Interpersonal	Relationships and the experiences from past relationships integrated into a worldview	Kiesler, Klein, McWilliams, Strupp, H. S. Sullivan, Winnicott	Results from interpersonal dysfunction, ingrained styles of relating socially, or rigid adherence to internalized models
Medical	Biological variables, including genetics, biochemistry, neuroanatomy, structure and function of physiology ("organic factors")		Results from impaired brain functioning, most likely due to neurotransmitters and their effects on how the brain communicates with the body
Phenomenology	Subjective, personal experience of the individual	Maslow, May, Perls, Rogers	An inevitable aspect of life (existentialism), resulting from conditions of worth, or due to impaired contact with self and others
Psychodynamic	Conflict, including unconscious motivation, instinctual wishes, intrapersonal and interpersonal factors, personality traits	Freud, Horney, Jung, Winnicott	A symptom of underlying emotional conflicts, impaired interpersonal relationships, or immaturity of personality

As developmental models, dynamic paradigms focus on maturation from primitive (infantile) ineffectual functioning to more advanced adaptations. From childhood on, all individuals struggle with a sense of insecurity, *basic anxiety*, resulting from perceived abandonment by parents, isolation from others, or help-lessness in a hostile and uncaring world (Horney, 1937). For all human func-tions, particularly interpersonal and intrapsychic structure, the centrality of emo-tional life provides order and cohesion to identity. Developmentally, when affect attunement is needed, a failure of validation, reflection, and verbalization cre-ates a mounting state of tension, incompetence, or vulnerability within the self system. If self-object experiences fail to engage emotion or lack defining attune-ment, an arrest in development occurs that later interferes with the transition be-tween affect and feeling. Subsequent defenses, such as disavowal and withdrawal, seek to separate the emotional aspects of functioning from all other realms. A vi-cious cycle occurs when the individual tries to constrict emotionality while si-multaneously being unable to do so. This conflict becomes experienced as a gen-eral level of arousal conflict with the subjective feeling of chronic anxiety.

Clinical anxiety is viewed in psychoanalytic theory as resulting from the ego's partial failure to adequately cope with stressor stimuli, defined as either internal (e.g., instinctual drives) or external (e.g., impending harm), resulting from inade-quate defense mechanisms, delayed or impeded emotional development and maturation, or fixation within a primitive psychosexual stage (Luborsky, 1996). Self theorists have redacted Freud's theory of signal anxiety to view generalized anxiety as the self system's warning of potential disintegration (Kohut, 1971, 1977). Conscious awareness of the self system as perceiving and acting promotes reflection and protects against disintegration. If conscious awareness fails to re-store cohesion, a state of overstimulation occurs—seeking to enlist the support and assistance of others to enter the self system and restore order. Chronic failure of the self to reduce overstimulation and restore structure (coherence, order, etc.) produces anxiety. When pervasive and generalized, this experience phenomeno-logically feels similar to a state of alarm. Other revisions focus on perceived losses—relationships, contacts, identity, self-esteem, and so on—that contribute to ongoing conflict (Bond & Perry, 2004; Shear, Cooper, & Klerman, 1993).

Psychodynamic theories view anxiety as the overt manifestation of intrapsy-chic conflict or ineffectual defenses, resulting from inadequate defenses or over-reliance on certain defense mechanisms. Freud viewed birth as the prototypic anxiety situation that caused the infant to be flooded with experience without the ability to control it. After the development of the ego (throughout the first year), anxiety becomes a signal of impending overstimulation. *Signal anxiety* re-flects the ego's failure to mobilize resources to avert potential danger. When bombarded with stimuli, the ego fears being overwhelmed with helplessness and subsequent regression to infantilism. The ego copes by unconsciously blocking impulses (conflicts) or distorting them to a more acceptable form via defense mechanisms, thus allowing the ego to discharge id energy while not facing its motivation. When this underlying turmoil overwhelms the ego, anxiety becomes

TABLE 1.7.
Central Concepts in Psychoanalysis

Concept	Definition
Defense mechanisms	Created by the self system [or ego] to minimize anxiety, defenses ease conflict between demands of instincts and societal norms by striking a compromise between them.
Id, ego, superego	Personality comprises three distinct components that are continuously in conflict: id, ego, and superego. The id, present at birth, is the "genetic template" comprised of drives (physiological, biological) and wishes (the psychological part). The ego becomes differentiated for facilitating *reality principle* functioning—substituting external reduction through internal fantasy and mediating expression of impulses and behavior. The superego is a portion of the mind, differentiated from the ego, that contains the traditional values and taboos of society as interpreted for the child by its parents.
Pleasure principle	Human behavior is motivated to maximize pleasure and minimize pain. The id seeks to maximize biologically based pleasurable, sensual sensation.
Psychosexual stages (oral, anal, phallic, genital, latency)	In development a person passes through an orderly series of stages or phases. In each, sexual instincts focus on a different body area: first the mouth, then the anus, then the genitals. Subsequent personality types are based on modes of pleasure and focus of gratification.
Reality principle	Ego functioning that satisfies instinctual needs (wishes) through reality-based, socially acceptable, and "reasonable" means.
Therapeutic intervention	Free association, dream analysis, paraplexes (slips of the tongue), processing transference, catharsis, working-through, "making the unconscious conscious."
Unconscious motivation	Behavior is determined by underlying (unconscious) conflicts.

part of conscious awareness (Meissner, 1988). Revisionists implicate other variables—personality traits, disturbances in relationships, difficulties with defining and tolerating emotions, losses, unconscious conflicts about separation, anger, and sexuality—as key precipitants to anxiety (Kelly, 1997; Masling & Bornstein, 1993, 1996; Silverstein, 1999).

   Object-Relations. Psychodynamic theory has evolved, and generally has moved away from understanding behavior as motivated by instinctive drives to emphasizing relationship-oriented underpinnings. As analytic theory continued to change and evolve in the twentieth century, the British school—Klein (1932), Fairbairn (1954), and Winnicott (1965)—became more influential. These neoanalytic theories grew as a corrective attempt to invest interpersonal relations with a more significant role in personality development (Masling & Bornstein, 1994). *Object-relations theory* integrates the concepts of human psychic development with organization, behavior, and interpersonal relationships. An *object* is any person with whom an individual relates, the mental image of the primary caregiver other. *Selfobject experiences* in psychodynamic theory are all interactions between an individual and others, especially early caregivers, leading to an internalization of each important interpersonal experience (Shapiro, 1989). For example, Fairbairn (1954) viewed the relationship between an individual and others—not instinctual gratification (a la Freud)—as the source of personality development. Collectively, object-relations theories can be conceptualized as "applied developmental psychology" with particular emphasis on Bowlby's (1969) attachment theory. Social attachments and bonding with others are primary determinants of personality. Through *introjection* the experiential selfobject event becomes established and structured within the psyche. Perceptually influential, object representations act as templates for ongoing relationships (Anisman, Zaharia, Meaney, & Merali, 1998; Huot, Gonzalez, Ladd, Thrivikraman, & Plotsky, 2004).

   Object-relations theorists view the early interactions (from birth through the first year) as creating an "organizing experience" (Hedges, 1994) through which all subsequent relationships are conceived, experienced, and understood. Through the interpersonal relationships with caregivers, an infant learns how to structure and define his or her internal world. Emotional health is reflected by the ability to sustain cooperative, intimate relationships with others. In contrast, psychopathology is viewed as a disturbance in the inner, intrapsychic organization that manifests in interpersonal styles. Impaired selfobject relationships early in life color and distort subsequent capacity to engage in authentic, sustaining relationships (Basch, 1981).

   Ego Psychology. *Ego psychology* was originally a revision of traditional psychoanalysis by Anna Freud (1946), Erikson (1950), and Hartmann (1950, 1964). Their modification placed more emphasis on ego functioning and less prominence on instinctual, biological processes. Erikson viewed psychological health as a successful negotiation of ongoing life conflicts, beginning with the initial trust versus mistrust at birth to ego integrity versus despair in old age. The degree to which the ego can adaptively cope and autonomously function with minimal conflict represents the individual's potential for normality. On the other hand, when conflict becomes excessive, when life stages are not adequately negotiated, or when fixation in one developmental stage impedes further maturation, the individual will experience psychological distress and, subsequently, feel anxious.

Self Psychology. Another interpersonal theory, Kohut's (1971, 1977) ***self psychology*** views psychopathology as "incohesive or fragmented" self-concepts. Like object-relations theorists, Kohut viewed everyone as requiring age-appropriate selfobject experiences from infancy to the end of life; all humans organize such experiences as "symbolic representations of the original self-evoking experiences" (Kohut, 1971) and use them to foster and strengthen the self. The neonate is born with certain potentials that are biological; however, the interaction with the environment evokes some of these potentials and brings them into development, whereas others are left to atrophy or are destroyed. Self psychology focuses on the intrapsychic experience of individuals shaped by selfobject experiences, their need throughout the lifespan, and their maturation. Anxiety results from fear of fragmentation, decompensation, or annihilation of the self system.

Psychodynamic Interventions. Dynamic treatments (Table 1.8) focus on emotional maturation, transference, clarification and interpretation, and working through within an atmosphere of empathic reflection and understanding (Auld & Hyman, 1991; Cashdan, 1988; Strupp, 1993). Within the therapeutic relationship, the trained therapist clarifies and brings meaning to the emotional and psychological functioning of the patient within an empathic ambience. Freud defined empathy as "feeling oneself into another." Consistent, prolonged empathy fosters understanding of internal workings (feelings, emotions, thoughts), the environment (important cues, external stressors), and their interaction. The experience of feeling respected, accepted, and understood promotes growth. Initially, the empathic interaction between child and caregiver is both a verbal and nonverbal event that provides the ambience of being understood. As the caregiver provides empathic responses, the child experiences understanding and the safety to explore emotion. It is through this process that individuals become stronger and more cohesive in their sense of self. This same developmental process occurs throughout therapy. A person's sense of self is enhanced by the knowledge that another individual understands his or her inner experience. As the experience becomes integrated into the self, the individual becomes more able to empathically relate to others. Ultimately, the goals of interventions include the promotion of development and maturation, insight into latent emotion, and the fostering of ***ego strength*** (the ability of an individual to maintain the coherence and structure of identity during times of stress). Eloquent, com-

TABLE 1.8.
Psychodynamic Interventions

Technique	Description
Clarification	Verbalization of emotional attunement through the empathic reflection of the therapist. Therapist provides description of patient's emotional processes that in turn are integrated by the patient to facilitate the understanding of his or her own emotional processes; includes confrontation of resistances and defense mechanisms.
Interpretation	Verbalizing the meaning or emotional defense that prevents expression of the affect. The purpose of an interpretation is to "make the unconscious conscious"; insight occurs as the patient makes links between material and the emotional defenses that prevent experience and expression of affect. When there is too much motivation of the id, the ego becomes strengthened to defend against those impulses ("where id is, let ego be"); through therapy, the defense mechanisms that distort reality are interpreted to allow the emotional conflict to surface from unconscious, to preconscious, to conscious awareness.

prehensive, and creative, psychodynamic theories provide the most complete (relative to all other models) view of clinical anxiety, its causes, and effective treatments (Luborsky, 1996).

Behaviorism. Beginning in the early 1900's with John Watson (1913, 1916), behavioral models were the first the break away from traditional psychoanalytic theories in favor of an alternative, more concrete perspective of human functioning. Watson's dissatisfaction with Freudian trait theory, its conceptualization of the unconscious, and its emphasis on sexual and instinctual motives prompted him to advocate the changing of psychology's focus to measuring (and shaping) overt, observable functioning. Based on Pavlov's (1927) experiments with dogs, *behaviorism* applies specific techniques that employ psychological (especially learning) principles to constructively change human behavior. Reinforcement and learning produce both normal, adaptive functioning as well as dysfunctional, problematic behaviors. Not only a conceptualization of human functioning, behaviorism provides a philosophical worldview based on rationalism, principles of learning, and deterministic reinforcement models (Eysenck, 1957, 1967, 1968; Wolpe & Lazarus, 1969). Table 1.9 lists the central concepts in behaviorism.

TABLE 1.9.
Central Concepts in Behaviorism

Concept	Definition
Acquisition	Learning of a response based on the pairing of the conditioned and unconditioned responses.
Classical conditioning	Process by which an individual learns to associate stimuli, based on the theories of Pavlov (1927). A learning-through-association process takes place when a neutral stimulus is paired repeatedly with a stimulus that already evokes a response. After sufficient pairings, the formerly neutral stimulus will evoke the response when presented alone.
Contingency management	Controlling of reinforcements, both positive and negative, to influence and guide behavior.
Extinction	Loss of the conditioned response to bring about the formerly acquired response.
Learning	Developmental process of change in the individual as a result of experience or practice, modeling, role play, or vicarious practice.
Modeling	Observation and gradual imitation of a target individual who exhibits desirable behavior.
Operant conditioning	Training of an individual to perform an instrumental response to gain reward or avoid punishment.
Rehearsal	Practicing target behaviors.
Shaping	Rewarding successful approximations of desired behaviors.
Systematic desensitization	Extinction process where the patient is presented a conditioned stimuli (e.g., phobic object) in the absence of a reinforcer (aversive stimulation).

Behaviorism "proper" foundationally rests on scientific learning theory. In the early part of the 20th century, Pavlov began studying the digestive system in dogs, particularly the salivary response. Putting food powder in a dog's mouth and then measuring salivation, Pavlov quickly noticed that the dogs' responses became paired with other stimuli (such as past experience). The dogs began to salivate merely when he walked into the room, before they were given the food powder. Pavlov (1927) called this a *conditioned reflex*, later amended to a *conditioned response* (**CR**), because it was based on past experience. *Classical* *conditioning* is the process by which an individual learns to associate stimuli, a learning-through-association process that takes place when a neutral stimulus is paired repeatedly with a stimulus that already evokes a response. After sufficient pairings, the formerly neutral stimulus evokes the response when presented alone. *Operant conditioning* is the training of an individual to perform a response to gain reward or avoid punishment. Behavior that is rewarded is likely to be repeated in the future (Thorndike, 1913). *Acquisition* refers to the learning of a response based on the pairing of the conditioned and unconditioned responses. *Learning theories* stress the importance of the context in which behavior takes place, the capacity of the individual to learn from experience, and the nature of its learning and reinforcements. All learning theories utilize classical and operant conditioning models, *shaping* (the process of rewarding successful approximations of the desired target behavior until it is correctly learned), and *modeling* (the acquisition of novel behavior through observation and imitation) as key interventions.

Although changing and evolving over time, all behavioral models share common foundational beliefs: the concentration on behavior itself (instead of its presumed underlying cause); the notion that both adaptive and dysfunctional behaviors are acquired via learning (and that learning principles can effectively modify human functioning); the rejection of traditional trait theory, an emphasis on current here-and-now behavior; and a rigorous reliance on empirical research to support the efficacy of applications and outcomes. Learning and past contingencies are understood to be the primary causes of behavior. Table 1.10 lists common behavioral interventions.

Attribution Theory. Just as dynamic models evolved from Freud's initial psychoanalytic conceptualization, so too have adaptations and revisions sprouted from the tree of "radical" behaviorism. Redactors of traditional behaviorism incorporate cognitive and social factors (e.g., Bandura, 1988; Leary, 1957; Sullivan, 1953, 1954). Following World War II, social psychologists began researching the interaction between personality dispositions (e.g., traits) and the situation or environment in which they were expressed. Theories evolved out of Lewin's (1935, 1951) initial work but were more fully developed in the attribution theories of Heider (1958), Jones and Davis (1965), Kelley (1971), and Weiner (1974). Table I.11 lists central concepts in attribution theory.

Social Perception/Cognition. Social perception/cognition research showed that behavior is greatly influenced by schematic "mental frameworks" that influence how individuals structure, organize, and interpret information (Asch, 1946; Cialdini, 2001; Forsyth, 1995). Kelly's (1955) theory of *personal constructs* organizes these cognitive schemas into abstractions and generalizations, derived from concrete experience, to capture, structure, or organize ongoing experiences and events. The mind is perpetually engaged in a process of construing reality, creating tentative hypotheses that are confirmed or disconfirmed by future experi-

TABLE 1.10.
Behavioral Interventions

Technique	Description
Assertiveness training	Assertive behavior is interpersonal behavior that involves the honest and relatively straightforward expression of thoughts and feelings, in a socially appropriate way, that takes into account the feelings and welfare of others.
Aversion therapy	Application of painful stimulus creates aversion to target behavior.
Contingency management	Controlling the reinforcers of behavior such that anxiousness and avoidance are no longer positively reinforced; instead, novel (adaptive) behaviors are rewarded so that their frequency increases.
Exposure	Structured and consistent exposure-based exercises.
Fixed roles	Behaving "as if" anxiety or nervousness are not factors in functioning, so that over time fearful responses are extinguished.
Flooding	Full-intensity exposure, through the use of imagery, to an object that triggers a symptom.
Implosion therapy	A form of desensitization that involves repeated exposure to a highly feared object until counter-conditioning occurs via extinction of the fear response.
Participant modeling	The use of modeling in which the therapist guides the patient through exercises through which the target behavior is modeled by the therapist and repeated by the patient.
Relaxation	The basic premise is that muscle tension is in some way related to anxiety, and that an individual will experience a marked reduction in felt anxiety if tense muscles can be relaxed to the point where they become flaccid (Borkovec & Costello, 1993).
Response prevention	Preventing target behavior by distraction, persuasion, or redirection of activity.
Self-control procedures	Behavioral techniques that emphasize an active, coping response on the part of the individual who exerts his or her control in a problematic situation.

(continues)

TABLE 1.10.
(Continued)

Technique	Description
Self-efficacy expectations	A fear-reduction technique in which efficacy information is transferred to the patient through actual performance accomplishments, vicarious learning, verbal persuasion, or changes in physiological arousal.
Shaping	Reinforcement of gradual approximations of target behavior.
Systematic desensitization	Conditioned pairing of relaxation with stimuli that previously provoked anxious response.
Thought-stopping	Breaks the habit of fear-inducing anticipatory thoughts; patient learns to stop unwanted thoughts by saying the word *stop* and then focusing attention on achieving calmness and muscle relaxation.
Thought-switching	Individuals learn to replace negative thoughts with positive ones until positive thoughts become strong enough to overcome the anxiety-provoking ones.

ence. Subsequent revisions by Epting (1984), Niemeyer (1985a, 1985b), and Bannister (1985; Bannister & Mair, 1988) applied this model to anxiety by suggesting that symptoms occur when an individual's construct system no longer accurately describes experience. Diffuse nervousness (e.g., GAD) results when personal constructs no longer work, novel experience occurs, and the construct system does not adapt. Experiences cannot be dealt with by existing cognitive structures and constructs.

Social Learning Theory. **Social learning theory** (Bandura, 1965; Bandura & Kupers, 1964) modified behavioral paradigms by integrating **vicarious learning** — learning by observing others. The theory states that learning can take place not only without previous reinforcement, but also without any response, through imitation, modeling, or observation. The process of observational learning incorporates inherited temperaments, skills and talents, perceptions, expectations, and intention as key elements in governing behavior. Anxious distress and other symptoms of psychopathology are largely the result of impaired expectations of efficacy. Successful treatments for reducing anxiety increase an individual's sense of self-efficacy and competence in mastering feared situations. Alternatively, Rotter's (1954, 1966, 1967) model emphasized the role of **locus of control** —

TABLE 1.11.
Central Concepts in Attribution Theory

Concept	Description
Attribution cube theory (Kelley, 1971)	Attribution based on three sources of covariation data: distinctiveness across objects, consistency across time and places, and (to a lesser extent) consensus among people.
Commonsense psychology (Heider, 1958)	The more stable dispositional structures that cause behaviors and events are identified and used in a naïve, commonsense kind of manner to make theories of attribution.
Correspondent inference theory (Jones & Davis, 1965)	Attributions correspond with beliefs that an action matches a person's disposition/traits.
Three-dimensional model (Weiner, 1974)	Attributions consider locus (internal-external), stability (stable-unstable), and controllability (controllable-uncontrollable).

a personality trait that motivates the projection of reinforcements onto oneself (internal) or environment (external)—in behavior. Seligman's (1968, 1970; Abramson, Seligman, & Teasdale, 1978; Alloy, Peterson, Abramson, & Seligman, 1984) theory of *learned helplessness* conceptualizes anxiety/depression as resulting from repeated failures that are then generalized to expectations about self and others. When individuals believe that important events in their lives are largely uncontrollable, they experience dysfunctional symptoms and distress. Thus, therapeutic intervention can impart a high expectation for success in dealing with and adapting to the environment, which often leads to improved coping and outcome (*learned optimism*).

Integration of Learning Theory With Cognitive Psychology. Fueled by the influence of the cognitive revolution of the 1960's, second force therapeutic models integrated learning theories (Pavlov, 1927; Hull, 1943; Skinner, 1953, 1974; Watson, 1913) with cognitive psychology (e.g., Beck, 1976, 1991; Ellis, 1962, 1971, 1972, 1973; Kelly, 1955; McClelland, 1951, 1961; Meichenbaum, 1974, 1977, 1985; Lazarus, 1971, 1976). The *cognitive perspective* understands an individuals' *interpretation* of social situations as strongly shaping behavior; unique perception, interpretation, and assignment of meaning to a situation or experience influences subsequent emotional and behavioral reactions. Preconceptions, or "scripts," about certain types of situations therefore guide interpretation of behavior. Cognitive *schemas* are stereotyped or integrated memories that influence perception, unconscious, or conscious thought—the thought structures that hold core beliefs. *Cognitions* can include repetitive images, ideas, or doubts. *Automatic thoughts* are discrete sentences, negative in nature, that a person processes quickly or without conscious awareness and that influence behavior, interaction, or attributions. Central to cognitive models is the belief that thinking/thought processes precede and cause emotional response; affect is always a consequence of some form of cognitive appraisal (Beck, 1976, 1991; Beck & Emery, 1985). Unrealistic expectations and attitudes, represented as cognitive schemata, predispose an individual to the experience of psychological distress (Safran & Segal, 1990). McClelland's (1951) theory defined expectancies as cognitive units—that is, what one *believes* will be the content and timing of events in the future. Individuals seek to minimize large discrepancies between expectation and occurrence and maximize small discrepancies between expectation and occurrence. The greater the discrepancy between expectation and occurrence, the more intense is organismic tension, and anxiety ensues. Table 1.12 lists common cognitive errors.

Cognitive and Cognitive-Behavioral Theories. Emphasizing the connection between thought and affect, *cognitive* and *cognitive-behavioral therapies* (*CBT*) assume that maladaptive or dysfunctional cognitions, thoughts, or assumptions precipitate emotional distress. Cognitive distortions—such as selective perception, magnification, personification, overgeneralization, catastrophizing, and dichotomous thinking—are regarded as the cause of anxiety (Beck & Clark, 1988; Williams, Shahar, Riskind, & Joiner, 2005). Major theories parallel the particular emphases of idiographic paradigms. Beck's *cognitive triad* implicated a set of cognitions associated with subjective malaise: negative thoughts about self, ongoing experience, and the future (Beck, 1976). Another paradigm, Ellis' (1962, 1971) *rational emotive therapy*, delineated certain *irrational beliefs* that precipitate emotional turmoil. Meichenbaum's (1977) *stress inoculation training* taught patients anxiety management skills—breathing retraining, relaxation, thought-stopping, cognitive restructuring, and guided self-dialogue—through instruction, role playing, and modeling within the clinical session. Novel behaviors and managed arousal responses generalize to other situations and environments.

Collectively, some common themes emerge. First, anxious distress and other symptoms of psychopathology are considered to be largely the result of impaired efficacy expectations. Second, conditioning and contingencies play key roles. Third, successful treatments for reducing anxiety increase an individual's sense of self-efficacy and competence in mastering feared situations. All effective behavioral treatments include either imagined or in vivo exposure to feared stimuli. Techniques that decrease baseline anxiety, such as relaxation and social skills training, are used to reduce symptoms and facilitate overall functioning

TABLE 1.12.
Common Cognitive Errors

Error	Description
Catastrophizing	Anticipation of extreme negative or adverse outcomes
Jumping to conclusions	Accepting an arbitrary (often quickly ascertained) interpretation of an incident without rational exploration or understanding of its likelihood or omitting significant factors in the cognitive processes
Magnification	Abstracting a detail out of context and missing the significance for total situation
Mind reading	Making arbitrary inferences/assumptions about others without actually finding out their perceptions, cognitions, or views
Overgeneralization	Unjustified generalization based on limited data (or a single case)
Personalization	Making egocentric interpretations of surrounding events and stimuli that may or may not pertain to oneself
Polarized thinking	Thinking in extremes; thinking in "always" and "nevers" or all-or-nothing interpretations of situations
Selective perception	Concentrating or attending to only negative aspects of situations while ignoring positive features

(Hughes, 2002). Exposure of some type, combined with the provision of adequate social support, as well as preventing action tendencies and redirecting attention away from negative affect, will be involved in any successful treatment (Abramowitz, Foa, & Franklin, 2003; Scapillato & Manassis, 2002). Studies on the efficacy of time-limited behavioral and cognitive-behavioral therapies for clinical anxiety have consistently shown their effectiveness, but the study of long-term gains (defined as the lack of relapse) have yielded mixed results (Floyd et al., 2002; Kessler, 1996; Parker, Buckmaster, Schatzberg, & Lyons, 2004; Shear et al., 2002).

Existentialism/Humanism. In the mid-20th century, a growing emphasis of integrating existentialism, humanism, and philosophy developed among theorists. Dissatisfied with Freud's negative view of humanity, they sought to understand human functioning in a positive, progressive light, regarding human beings as having unlimited ability to choose their own direction. Intensely individualistic, these models are *idiographic*—approaches that involve the intensive study of an individual using his or her subjective, personal experience (May, 1967, 1969; Sartre, 1947, 1956; Pollich, 1952).

Existential psychology employs phenomenological analysis to view mental disorders as an individual's failure to successfully confront the basic aspects of life, such as initiative, responsibility, and freedom of choice (Bugenthal, 1976; Frankl, 1963, 1965, 1969). *Humanistic models*, the "human potential movement," view all individuals as having the potential for growth and development and, given adequate circumstances, as "naturally" or inherently inclined to maximize actualized functioning. *Phenomenology*, the study of the subjective experiences of an individual, seeks to describe an individual's immediate experience with the purpose of understanding it rather than explaining, predicting, or controlling behavior (Keen, 1970; Rogers, 1955). The subjective reference frame an individual uses to experience reality becomes the primary source, motivation, and meaning of perceptual, emotional, and developmental growth (Daldrup, Engle, Holiman, & Beutler, 1994). Inherently good and driven toward self-actualization, the self becomes a complex amalgam of identity, experience, subjective awareness, and contact with the environment.

These models, blending philosophy and psychology, are based on the foundational belief in *free will*, that humans have the unique ability to choose without limitation within their environment and thus directly guide their future. Humanity is free to make life meaningful by the choices, decisions, and responsibilities involved in guiding the direction of individual lives. Freedom makes choices meaningful, making individuals uniquely responsible for their decisions, actions, and life direction. Learning about one's feelings, personal values, and priorities—one's unique meaning in life—is a central feature in these paradigms. Often concerned with the positive aspects of life, such as self-actualization, humanistic models believe in the basic goodness of humanity, the intrinsically positive nature of all people, and the inherent push toward growth and actualization in all individuals (May, 1981).

Individuals determine for themselves the goals, pathways, and directions of their existence (*self-determination*). How individuals structure their lives determines psychological adjustment or aberrance. *Ontological anxiety* is the real pain and fear involved in choosing and guiding the unknown future. When individuals cease to look at themselves honestly and acceptingly, and distort their essence, they begin to feel anxious. The process of denying thoughts, emotions, and behaviors eventually precipitates anxiety and impedes fulfilling ultimate human potential. *Ontological guilt* refers to the stifling sense of missed opportunity involved in choosing the status quo, inaction, or having an impotent response to functioning. Subsequent emptiness follows due to inauthenticity and alienation. *Existential choice* involves being able to affirm value in spite of confirmation or disconfirmation from others. Anxiety occurs when people stop looking at themselves honestly and acceptingly and instead deny and distort their thoughts, emotions, and behaviors. Defensive postures, such as complacency, ultimately serve to make individuals extremely anxious and incapable of fulfilling their potential as human beings (*self-actualization*). **Authenticity** involves accepting the painful state of affairs inherent in living and finding the courage to persist in the face of ontological anxiety and to choose the uncertain future.

Influenced heavily by the existential philosophy of Sartre, Kierkegaard, Camus, and Tillich, humanistic approaches to the understanding and treatment of anxiety disorders conceptualize psychological distress as being caused by self-deception in which individuals hide and shirk life's responsibility. Traditional existential theories view anxiety as an inevitable condition of life, combining the fears of human finitude, meaninglessness in life, separation or isolation from others, with the uncertainty of outcome (Bugenthal, 1965, 1976; Kierkegaard, 1954; May, 1977). Freedom and responsibility inherently breed anxiety, which occurs when people stop looking at themselves honestly and acceptingly and instead deny and distort their true thoughts, emotions, and behaviors. Defensive postures ultimately serve to make individuals extremely anxious and incapable of fulfilling their potential. Awareness of one's mortality threatens meaningfulness of one's life, creating a sense of "existential terror." Self-esteem, acceptance of a cultural worldview, is an "anxiety buffer" that reduces this sense of fear. Existentialists believe that the fear of death is the fundamental anxiety of all living creatures. Psychologically, death means nonbeing or retreat from experience. To avoid such, individuals may fuse with others or use inauthentic modes of behaving that are based on false, incongruent parts of the self. Drive motivation affects perceptions and explanations, feelings and evaluations, and behavior (including thoughts, feelings, and actions), with the purpose of maximizing belongingness, understanding, interactional efficacy, benevolence, and self-esteem.

Maslow's Hierarchy of Needs. The self provides a sense of wholeness and unity to identity, organizing perception and behavior. Inherently good and driven towards self-actualization, the self is initially biologically based but over time and through development becomes a complex amalgam of identity, experience, subjective awareness, and contact with the environment (Keen, 1970). Maslow's (1968) theory views the self as organizing needs hierarchically, with progressive levels requiring greater and greater self-actualizing needs. Once such basic biological needs as food, water, oxygen are met, the needs for safety, love, and esteem emerge and seek gratification. Focusing almost exclusively on the positive side of human experience, Maslow believed needs vary in their immediacy and force, and as a general rule more primitive, basic needs become powerfully demanding. As deficiency needs become satiated, growth needs emerge and motivate fulfillment. **Self-actualization** refers to the inherent striving of an individual to fulfill his or her full capacities, to function at the highest level, or to become the "best self" possible (Maslow, 1970).

Client-Centered Therapy Although originally trained in psychoanalysis, Carl Rogers radically broke from Freudian theory based on his clinical experiences (mainly with schizophrenic patients), observations from animal behavior, and philosophy. In client-centered theory, each individual has an innate drive (*within* the individual) for self-actualization (to become a fully functioning person). According to Rogers (1942), individuals are born with a natural inclination to be friendly, cooperative, and constructive, ultimately drive to maximize inherent abilities, but insufficiencies in environments precipitate a sense of uneasiness and global anxiety. Self-actualization is limited by *facticity*, the biological and social limits on the possibilities of personal experience. The term *congruence* refers to harmony between the conscious self and the totality of the person's unconscious feelings and experiences. *Authenticity* is the habitual presentation of oneself in a congruent manner. *Openness to experience*, the opposite of defensiveness, refers to the willingness to try new experiences and be amenable to experiential learning.

Roger's (1951, 1959) *client-centered therapy* combines unconditional positive regard and empathy within the treatment process, theorizing that all psychological distress can ultimately be traced to conditions of worth (Hart & Tomlinson, 1970). All of life is based on the need for **unconditional positive regard**, a need for acceptance, love, and approval from others. Each individual has an innate drive for self-actualization, to maximize functioning, and to evolve into a heightened sense of effectiveness. Experiences that promote the actualizing tendency of the self are naturally sought out, whereas those that hinder growth and development are avoided. Denial and perceptual distortion impede the normal process of self development (Rogers, 1969). Maladjustment occurs whenever an individual lives a preconceived role for his or her life, becomes defensive and closed to novelty, lacks warmth and unconditional positive regard (for both self and others), or develops incongruence within the self (Joseph, 2004). Regardless of manifestation, all forms of clinical anxiety result from internalizing conditions of worth, imbalance, incongruent living, or lack of organismic trusting, secondary to (1) the experience of conditional regard, (2) a discrepancy between actual experience and self-regard, or (3) defensiveness that limits full functioning (Hill & Nakayama, 2000). Cautious about moralistic problem-solving approaches, client-centered therapists provide warmth, positive regard, and unconditional acceptance during treatment to promote the individual's inherent drive for actualization (Rogers, 1987). Foundational therapeutics include (1) *organismic trusting*, the tendency, ability, and fortitude to believe in and feel safe in valuing self and others; (2) *openness to experience*, being receptive to newness of life, particularly in experiencing feelings and emotions; and (3) *warmth and genuineness*, honest, empathic care for self and others.

Gestalt Therapy. In the late 1940s Fritz Perls and his daughter Laura founded **gestalt therapy** (Perls, Hefferline, & Goodman, 1951). This theory emphasizes the creative, meaningful components that comprise personality as a whole, integrating mind and body, as well as spirituality, into holistic functioning (Passons, 1975). *Gestalt* is the German word for a complete pattern or configuration.

Health and dysfunction are experienced physiologically, psychologically, and spiritually. The awareness of self—its manifestations, sense of wholeness, and provision of unity to identity—organizes perception and behavior. Each person exists in the context of the total environment. What the individual attends to is related to organismic need and need reduction. Needs arise and recede progressively as they receive attention and are satisfied (Polster & Polster, 1973; Baker, 1978). Behaviors will be directed toward satisfying the dominant need.

Awareness is the perceptual flow of figures in a lively progression as determined by needs. In the process of forming complete gestalten, that of which a person is aware becomes an ordering principle (Perls, 1969). Adequate functioning of awareness dictates the realm of health for the individual, and awareness itself can be curative. Individuals possess a set amount of energy that can be subdivided between awareness of internal and external stimuli. When energies are expended in rehashing the past, becoming concerned about the future, or any other non-present-moment event, awareness of the interaction between self and environment is limited (Korb, Gorrell, & DeRiet, 1989). In general, psychopathology occurs whenever an individual lacks of the awareness of personal experience—of not knowing or understanding it, or of being in a state of self-deception (Gardner, 1993).

In gestalt theory, the main source of psychological symptoms is **unfinished business**—any past relationships or intrapsychic conflicts that remain unresolved (Zanker, 1994). By holding onto unfinished experiences or avoiding their closure, a person invests energy and emotional reserves in sustaining the incompleteness, leaving little energy for encountering new situations and assimilating continuing experiences. Unfinished business, anxiety, depression, fears, phobias, and other symptoms are a result of *impaired contact* with the present moment. Table 1.13 pesents the gestalt view of ill health.

Contact is the essential quality of healthy functioning in making appropriate relationships between self, others, and the environment (Table 1.14). Five pathological processes can block healthy contact—introjection, projection, retroflection, deflection, and confluence—by impeding organismic self-regulation, blocking energy, distorting perception, or falsifying an individual's sense of self in relationship to others. Incomplete experiences, particularly unfinished relationships or intrapsychic conflicts, hamper experiencing the here-and-now (Silverstein & Uhlhaas, 2004). Anxiety evolves from impaired contact, lack of trust in organismic functioning, shirking responsibility, attempts to live in the future instead of being aware of the present moment, imbalance, environmental manipulation, or "stage fright" in accepting life's responsibilities and fluctuating needs (Greenberg & Malcolm, 2002).

Gestalt interventions focus on present-moment contact, awareness, and experience of self and environment, seeking to interactively integrate remnants of unfinished business in the here-and-now. Change occurs primarily through increased awareness and completion of unfinished gestalten. The patient becomes aware of personal responsibility, generates energy and contact to mobilize completion of

TABLE 1.13.
Gestalt View of Ill Health

Term	Description
Anxiety	Living in the future instead of the present; lack of trust in organismic functioning; "stage fright"
Disturbances in contact	Anything that prevents healthy contact in the present here-and-now moment, such as introjection, retroflection, deflection, or confluence
Imbalance	Identifying with one polarity at the expense of its opposite; rigidity; overcontrol
Incomplete gestalten	Unfinished experiences that cloud figure-ground; unresolved conflict
Manipulation	Any action that uses energies to obtain and maintain support from environment rather than from the self; avoidance of generating internal support

unfinished experiences, within an awareness of "now." Healthy contact between patient and therapist, defined as "unitary interfunctioning," is the vital foundation of successful growth and clinical treatment (Perls et al., 1951). Disturbances in contact (e.g., confluence) must be lifted within the therapeutic process to enable ongoing organismic functioning. *Classic experiments*, gestalt interventions, are

TABLE 1.14.
Gestalt Disturbances in Contact

Defense	Description
Confluence	Denying personal experience by "melding into the environment"
Deflection	Turning aside from healthy contact; displacing energy off-target
Introjection	Accepting something without reflection or awareness of internal functioning; "swallowing something whole"
Projection	Attributing to others or the environment one's own personal traits, attitudes, behaviors, etc.
Retroflection	Redirecting energy from healthy contact within the environment onto the self

efforts to both clarify and own (i.e., accept responsibility for) the psychological closure of what is experienced. Change occurs via completion of unfinished gestalten, acceptance of personal responsibility, restoration of balance and harmony among affective needs, or integration of figure-ground awareness within the here-and-now (Engle & Holiman, 2004). Overall, gestalt therapy seeks to help individuals restore healthy contact and awareness between self and others.

SUMMARY

A complex psychological construct including physiological, cognitive, emotional, and social factors, anxiety includes a sense of apprehension, with associated fear, that mobilizes an individual to escape or avoid danger. Anxiety's symptomatic features are initiated and mediated by multiple biological systems, integrating neuroanatomical, biochemical, and interactive functions to promote adaptive coping. When prolonged and interfering with daily functioning, anxiety can become incapacitating with negative impact, unpleasant experience, and accompanying despair. Etiological and treatment models for anxiety disorders include biological, psychological, and social factors (Barr et al., 2003; Jorm, Christensen, Griffiths, Rodgers, & Blewitt, 2004). Genetic vulnerability, added neurobiological dysfunction, and affective and psychological variables combine to create symptoms (Clement, Calatayud, & Belzung, 2002). Effective intervention regimens combine patient education, psychotherapy, and psychopharmacology. Practitioners alter techniques depending on course of treatment, and combinations of techniques are often used to facilitate effective interventions (Golden, 2004; Jorm et al., 2004).

CHAPTER 2

Behavioral Neuroanatomy and Biochemistry

R ESEARCH HAS CONSISTENTLY shown that neurobiological, genetic, and inherited factors predispose some individuals to pathological conditions. From the days of *phrenology*, the study of bumps on the head and their relationship to traits (Gall, 1835), to application of today's advanced data-analytic techniques, such as path analyses and structural equation modeling, the medical model continues to evolve and provide a better understanding of the physiological factors in anxiety. Aggregating available outcome data from efficacious treatments, known central and peripheral neurotransmitter and endocrine abnormalities, and the effects of chemical challenges, theories can generate hypotheses and testable theories of etiologies and mechanisms involved for each unique anxiety condition.

Most biological theories of anxiety focus on the brain, delineating how biochemicals inhibit or excite specific parts of the body, or the way in which neurotransmitters regulate nerve cell communication (Gorman, Hirschfeld, & Ninan, 2002). In the brain, there are millions of *neurons* and *glia*. *Astrocytes* are glial cells that surround and support nerve cells. *Microglia* are small glial cells that process and remove diseased or dying remnants of cells from nerve tissue. Nerve cells consist of three major parts: *soma* (cell body, containing the nucleus), *dendrites* (information-collecting areas), and *axons* (emanate from cell to carry information to other neurons via the synapse; carry electrical impulses). *Action potential* is the biochemical means through which an electrical signal is sent from the cell body, down the axon, to the terminal endings. Axons branch at their end forming *terminal buttons*. Substances can be transported along the axon either away from (*anterograde transport*) or toward (*retrograde transport*) the cell body. Axons making similar connections travel together in tracts of fiber bundles. The space between the nerve ending of one cell and the dendrite of another, the *synapse*, is the site of neural communication among various nerve cells. **Synaptic transmission** is the process through which nerve impulses go from one cell to another. Nerve cells have idiographic identities secondary to membrane makeup and overall function, specialized to receive, conduct, and transmit information. Generally, neurons exist in functional populations that form layers of similarly acting nerve cells, located together or in identifiable sequences of tracts throughout the CNS. **Neural networks** are interconnected nerve cells that form specific circuits recurring within a given brain structure or across structures. Complex connections occur between CNS neurons and other groups of nerve cells within the central or peripheral nervous systems, sensory receptors, or muscles. Diverse anxieties share malfunctioning neuronal circuits — accounting for overlapping symptoms and comorbidities. Biological factors can contribute to clinical anxiety at many levels: genetic vulnerabilities, constitutional liabilities, brain dysfunction and neuroplasticity, or neurotransmitter and hormonal imbalances throughout the body (Charney, 2003; Gordon & Hen, 2004).

BEHAVIORAL GENETICS

Anxiety disorders show significant familial aggregation. Anxiety disorders may be inherited genetically with the tendency to contract these illnesses rising when other blood relatives show the same syndrome. Lifetime prevalence rate of anxiety are around 15% in first-degree relatives of probands compared to 0% to 5% of controls (Hettema, Neale, et al., 2001). Further, the risk of siblings of anxiety disorders in siblings of probands with unaffected parents is between 8% and 15% but rises to 25% with one affected parent and to 40% with two affected parents (Bernstein, Borchardt, & Perwien, 1996; Quick, 2003).

Genetic Transmission of Traits

If inherited, symptomatic features of a condition have higher probabilities of development in biological relatives. Genetics direct chemical transformations in the human brain and underlie idiographic variability. Advances in understanding and mapping the human genome suggest that genetic determinants play a major role in the etiology of clinical anxiety (Ahsan, Hodge, Heiman, Begg, & Susser, 2002; Yalcin et al., 2004).

Chromosomal abnormalities — irregularities in the chromosomal structure — can be assessed (even prior to birth), making it possible to predict effects on development and behavior (Enoch, Xu, Ferro, Harris, & Goldman, 2003; Kelleu, Bratt, & Hodge, 2003). Although basic genetic material is fixed and passed to the individual from kin, its expression can vary dramatically. Genetic influences on behavior involve many genes, each having small effects. In addition, there are environmental influences on genes (Boehm, Reed, McKinnon, & Phillips, 2002; Gorwood, 2004).

Studies of genetically transmitted factors in anxiety disorders have pointed to a general diathesis for anxiety rather than for a specific disorder (Conti, Jirout, Breen, Vanella, Schork, & Printz, 2004; Larsen, Elfving, & Wiborg, 2004). Genes are significant sources of vulnerability to and variation in the habituation, acquisition, and extinction of fear. Genetic influences on complex behaviors do not fit a deterministic model of a single-gene effect that operates independently of other genes or environmental influences (Kendler et al., 1995; Krezel, Dupont, Krust, Chambon, & Chapman, 2001). The term *pleiotropy* refers to the possibility of a single gene influencing multiple syndromes or traits. Single genetic variations have been seen in both mood and anxiety disorders, suggesting substantial overlap, with as many as 80% of patients sharing comorbidities (Gorwood, 2004). Kendler, Neale, Kessler, Heath, and Eaves (1992) found significant genetic influences for both anxious and depressive symptomatology, with effect sizes ranging from .33 to .46.

Genes may act as nonspecific risks that, when coupled with individual-specific, nonshared environmental variables, prompt specific anxiety syndromes (Ansorge, Tanneberger, Davies, Theuring, & Kusserow, 2004). Phenotypic and genetic heterogeneity of symptoms pose unique difficulties in locating susceptibility genes (Meira-Lima et al., 2004). Further research is needed to identify consistent patterns and their relationship to clinical anxiety. Clearly delineating these genetic variables may facilitate the development of idiographic protocols for individualizing treatments.

Factors involved in the fear process, particularly serotonin and other transporter genes, demonstrate moderate heritability, with estimates ranging from 35 to 45% (Assal et al., 2004). Genetic variations and variations in transporters, particularly those associated with neurotransmitter functions, have been of primary interest. Researchers have identified a specific gene related to emotional lability or anxiety (Sen, Villafuerte, et al., 2004). A functional promoter polymorphism in the serotonin receptor gene has been associated with anxiety-related personality traits (C. P. Jacob et al., 2004). A promoter polymorphism in the human 5HT transporter gene is related to neural circuit engagements deep within the amygdala and is involved in mediating emotional processes (Gillespie et al., 2004; Hariri et al., 2002). Although serotonin receptor genes are implicated in both mood and anxiety disorders, their specific mechanisms and corresponding receptors have yet to be clarified (Mundo, Zai, Lee, Parikh, & Kennedy, 2001). Meta-analytic studies between polymorphisms of the serotonin transporter gene and trait anxiety have revealed consistent links among temperament, neuroticism, and trait anxiety (Hariri & Weinberger, 2003; Schinka, Busch, & Robichaux-Keene, 2004). Further, recent research has linked downregulation expression of the corticotropin-releasing factor gene within the central nucleus of the amygdala and trait anxiety (Hwang, Stewart, Zhang, Lumeng, & Li, 2004; Licinio et al., 2004).

Although genetic linkage analyses can identify genomic locations harboring vulnerable loci for genetically induced syndromes, the heritability and genetics of clinical anxiety are difficult to specify precisely because traits often are influenced by an interaction of many genes (***polygenetic transmission***). Strategies of subtyping and endophenotyping based on brain mechanisms may be able to isolate specific genetic vulnerabilities (Fehr et al., 2000; Hettema, Neale, et al., 2001).

Confounding genetic predispositions with subsequent behavioral expressions of specific syndromes may derive from many factors, including prenatal development, environmental stressors, early experiences, and learning (Arnold, Zai, & Richter, 2004). Some studies have shown significant links with identifiable genetics, whereas others (investigating the same theories) have not (Comings, Gonzalez, Cheng Li, & MacMurray, 2003; Eaves et al., 1999; Grabe et al., 2004; Lewejohann et al., 2004). The inability to rule out potential confounds makes interpretations unclear. Research methodologies have largely utilized small samples (e.g., miniscule discriminative power), inadequate controls, and inappropriate analyses to definitively link certain genetics with anxiety subtypes (Huppert, Franklin, Fon, & Davidson, 2003). Other investigations have used nonparametric techniques for analyses (e.g., Urraca, Camarena, Gomez-Caudillo, Esmer, & Nicolini, 2004), which are inherently less accurate and less powerful and omitted family-wise error rate corrections (e.g., Zhang, Steiner, Hamilton, Hicks, & Poulter, 2001), or contain a host of other research maladies (Borkovec & Cadstongway, 1998; Bradley et al., 2004). Further studies, with refined methodologies, are needed.

BRAIN ORGANIZATION

Genes largely determine brain structure and function, as well as all other physiological characteristics, which in turn create a vulnerability or predisposition for certain pathologies (Kassed & Herkenham, 2004). Some inherited influences directly affect the development of the brain and central nervous system; subtle deficiencies in brain function are implicated in many psychopathologies (Ely, 1997; Nobler et al., 2000). Human brains vary considerably in size, shape, and functional activity (Haier, 1998). Fluid movement within the brain is mediated by the ***blood-brain barrier***. The term ***brain organization*** refers to the specific architecture of neural networks and higher-order structures involved in cognitive responses. Localization of function results from specific inputs, outputs, processes, and biochemistries within brain subsections. Higher levels are generally more implicated in abstract, cognitive, and voluntary functions. The highest levels, located in the cerebral cortex, mediate consciousness, voluntary control, and planning of action. Complex behaviors (e.g., motor movement, emotion) are carried out at different levels of the nervous system. Emotional subcomponents of specific anxiety syndromes may be linked to regional brain activation. Distinct brain regions can be subdivided anatomically: ***hindbrain*** (the brain stem: cerebellum, pons, medulla), *midbrain* (tectum, tegmentum), and *fore-brain* (cerebral hemisphere, corpus callosum, thalamus, hypothalamus).

The Outer Brain

Engulfed in *cerebrospinal fluid*, the outer layer of the brain is composed of the highly convoluted *cerebral cortex*, with the *cerebral white matter* interconnecting with lower regions. Lying on the surface of the right and left cerebral hemispheres, the cerebral cortex is composed of six sublayers—containing about 70% of the neurons in the brain—that are involved in cognitive processing. Primary pathways of the cerebral cortex contain visual, auditory, and somatosensory information and project into the occipital, temporal, and parietal lobes, respectively. Posterior cerebral cortex regions are associated with sensory processes, active in receiving, processing, and storing data. Anterior portions are linked to motor functions. Both left and right hemispheres of the brain are involved in the experience and expression of emotion, albeit in different ways. The right hemisphere is more implicated in negative emotional processes, such as fear and anxiety, and the left is more involved in "positive" experiences, such as joy and elation (Clement & Chapouthier, 1998; Garraghty, Churchill, & Banks, 1998). Table 2.1 lists the different functions of the left and right hemispheres. The *corpus callosum* and *hippocampal commissures* connect and provide communication between left and right hemispheres.

The Brain Stem

The brain controls sensorimotor and integrative functions that underlie sensation and perception, thought, emotion, motivation, and behavior. Arousal is mediated primarily by the *brain stem* and the core of the cerebral hemispheres. The spinal cord merges into the brain to form the *medulla oblongata*. This lowest division of the brain, the *medulla*, is similar in makeup to the spinal cord and controls basic bodily processes (e.g., breathing). At the core of the medulla is the *central* and *periventricular gray matter*, clusters of cell bodies that surround the central canal and form the *tegmentum*. Surrounding this region of gray matter is the *reticular formation*, the brain portion that controls arousal and alertness. On both sides of the reticular formation, the *pons* regulates sensory and motor nuclei with the medulla. Several prominent nuclei, the *nucleus gracilis* and *nucleus cuneatus*, carry touch, pressure, and other sensory information from the skin and body. Located between the medulla and midbrain, neurons from these nuclei project both to the limbic system and to the cortex.

The *locus coeruleus* (LC) is a dense cluster of neurons, located in the pons, containing 50% to 70% of all noradrenergic neurons. Its projections extend throughout the cortex, limbic system, and brain stem. Encompassing distinct nuclei expressing diverse excitatory biochemicals, the LC, mediates heightened

TABLE 2.1.
Functions of the Two Hemispheres of the Brain

Left Hemisphere	Right Hemisphere
Expressive speech	Spatial orientation
Receptive language	Simple language comprehension
Language (general)	Nonverbal ideation
Complex motor functions	Picture and pattern sense
Vigilance	Performancelike functions
Paired-associate learning	Spatial integration
Liaison to consciousness	Creative associative thinking
Ideation	Facial recognition
Conceptual similarities	Sound and environmental recognition
Temporal analysis	Nonverbal paired-associate thinking
Analysis of detail	Tactile perception
Math	Gestalt perception
Writing	Pictograph processing
Calculation	Intuitive problem-solving
Finger naming	Humorous thinking
Right-left orientation	Simultaneous processing
Sequential processing	

awareness, alertness, vigilance, and the actions of the autonomic nervous system. Panic, anxiety, and fear are controlled by changes in norepinephrine metabolism in the LC, which is particularly vulnerable due to its lack of a protective blood-brain barrier (Berridge & Waterhouse, 2003). Chronic exposure to stress results in long-term alterations in LC firing and noradrenergic effects (e.g., turnover of noradrenalin innervation)—particularly affecting sensitivity of neurons to excitatory inputs. Hindbrain regions within the periaqueductal gray and LC provide integrated neural circuits that orchestrate somatic and cardiovascular changes associated with anxiety (Adamec, Blundell, & Burton, 2003; Singewald & Sharp, 2000). Both the brain stem and hypothalamus function to relay anxiety to the rest of the body.

The Fore Brain

The ***thalamus*** acts as a switching station that conducts signals from the body up to the relevant parts of the higher brain and down from the higher brain to the lower brain and spinal cord. Anterior portions extend to the cingulate gyrus; dorsal medial regions of the thalamus extend into the dorsal lateral prefrontal cortex

(Abrams, Johnson, Hollis, & Lowery, 2004; Carlini et al., 2004). Thalamic regions act as a relay station for stimulus processing and its integration with emotion, serving as a gateway of sensory input to the higher parts of the cerebral cortex. Within the basal forebrain, the *caudate nucleus* controls motor movement. Active in the conversion of perception into cognitive schemata, these brain regions (and functioning) provide a feedback circuit for controlling and interpreting sensory input. Beginning in the orbital region, just above the eyes, this communication pathway regulates primitive aggression, violent and destructive behaviors, sexuality, and bodily excretion.

The Prefrontal Cortex

The front third of the brain, the *prefrontal cortex*, regulates focus, forethought, impulse control, organization, planning, judgment, and insight. The ventral prefrontal cortex is connected to the limbic system by cingulate and anterior lobes. Numerous animal and human brain imaging studies have shown the frontal cortex and medial temporal lobes to be involved in fear and anxiety (Deacon, Penny, & Rawlins, 2003). Lesions, dysfunction, or dampened activity of the prefrontal cortex have been associated with anxiety, deficits in attention span, impulsivity, disorganization, or lack of empathy for others (Santini, Ge, Ren, Pena de Ortiz, & Quirk, 2004).

The Frontal, Temporal, Parietal, and Occipital Lobes

The brain can be organized hierarchically, subdividing the cerebral cortex into four functional lobes. Each lobal region is important to overall brain functioning and how the body responds to stress.

The *frontal lobe* is located behind the forehead and controls motor functioning. Frontal lobe disorders produce changes in motor activities, intelligence, personality, and language; decreased cerebral blood flow has been associated with apathy, indifference, inattention, and lack of perseveration (Hoehn-Saric et al., 1991). Lezak, Howieson, Loring, Hannay, and Fischer (2004) describe how right frontal lobe impairment can manifest in any (or all) of the following symptoms: compulsive or indiscriminant hypersexuality; hyperirritability regarding trivial slights; anxiety and phobic responses; paranoid concerns that generalize widely; depression or irritated euphoric periods; preoccupation with religion, cosmology, or philosophy; extensive but unproductive writing, drawing, or lecturing; preoccupation with details; circumstantiality and verbosity; and viscosity (a tendency to prolong social encounters).

The *temporal lobe* includes the auditory projection area and is involved in memory. Common symptoms associated with left temporal lobe dysfunction include aggression, hypersensitivity to slights (possibly present in social phobia), and emotional instability (Satishchandra et al., 2003).

The *parietal lobe* includes somatosensory projection areas involved in perception. The parietal cortex contains visual, tactile, and auditory inputs, with the left parietal lobe more involved in verbal processing and the right parietal region more involved in visual-spatial processing. The posterior parietal region, involved in memory and attention, has been linked to dementia processes (Rodriguez et al., 2004).

The *occipital lobe* controls visual projection and sight. Lesions in the occipital cortex are associated with agnosia, alexia, and hallucinations.

The Limbic System

Emphasizing its importance and functionality, some researchers consider the *limbic system* as a "fifth lobe" of the brain (Joseph, 1998). Buried within the cerebellum, the limbic system is a complex nucleic tract that includes portions of the hypothalamus, septum, hippocampus, amygdala, and cingulate gyrus. Related brain regions include portions of the reticular activating system, orbital frontal and inferior temporal lobes, and parts of the thalamus. The limbic system controls both visceral and physical expressions of emotion, and the roles of the amygdala and hippocampus in clinical anxiety continue to be the target of theory and research (McEwen, 2000; McEwen & Magarinos, 1997). Functional deficiency of certain neurotransmitters (e.g., GABA) within the limbic system are linked to diffuse nervousness (Brawman-Mintzer & Lydiard, 1997). Additional functions include mediating sensory information, setting emotional tone, bonding, emotionally charging memories, and guiding libido. Structures in the limbic forebrain regulate attention, environmental scanning, and arousal. Anatomical connections between the hippocampus, amygdala, and hypothalamus—particularly their deficiency in inhibiting or suppressing arousal—have been implicated in the body's response to fear (Breiter et al., 1996). Certain somatic aspects of anxiety, such as increased heart rate and blood pressure, are regulated by subcortical regions within the limbic system, although other nonlimbic functions are also involved (Muller, Pfeil, & Von Den Driesch, 2003). As vital parts to the limbic system, both the hippocampus and amygdala play key roles in the initiation, experience, and regulation of emotion.

The Hypothalamus

Facing potential danger, the body begins an "emergency reaction" that progresses through discrete stages (Selye, 1956, 1976). Stressful stimuli prompt physiological reactions mediated by the *hypothalamus*, a functional region of the forebrain that maintains homeostasis. Fully functional at birth, the hypothalamus governs primitive emotion as well as eating, drinking, sexual behavior, and metabolism. The emotional states elicited by the hypothalamus are phylogenetically primitive (i.e., archaic in evolutionarily terms), being diffuse, undirected, and unrefined (MacLean, 1990); these emotional states are short-lived, diffuse, and often unrelated to the external environment. For example, destruction of the medial portion produces primitive savagery—what K. G. Bailey (1987) called "phylogenetic regression." Higher-order emotional reactions, such as love, grief, and desire, require other limbic regions and parts of the cortex.

The *arcuate nucleus* releases endogenous opiates within the limbic system. Intimately involved in all aspects of biochemical functions, the hypothalamus regulates endocrine, hormonal, and autonomic processes. The medial hypothalamus regulates parasympathetic processes (e.g., reduced heart rate, improved peripheral circulation), whereas the lateral hypothalamus mediates sympathetic activity (e.g., increased heart rate, increased blood pressure). Both the hypothalamus and hippocampus within the limbic system are vulnerable to damage upon repeated exposure to stressful stimuli, suggesting a possible pathogenic role in posttraumatic states (Garcia, 2002). Therein, the hypothalamus sends hormonal messengers to the pituitary gland, which then signals the adrenal glands to produce certain biochemicals (Seeman, 1997).

The Amygdala

Whereas the hypothalamus regulates primitive (almost reflexive) emotion, the *amygdala* mediates higher-order affect (Davis & Shi, 1999). Located in the temporal lobe, the amygdala contains two almond-shaped neural clusters active in the discrimination of emotion and motivation. Medial and lateral portions are rich in opiate receptors. Biological drives transmitted from the hypothalamus to the amygdala prompt active scanning and evaluation of the environment for gratifying stimuli (Suzuki, Lumeng, McBride, Li, & Hwang, 2004). Neurons in the amygdala monitor sensory stimuli and stimulate emotional and behavioral responses, particularly those involved in the expression of fear (Kalin, Shelton, & Davidson, 2004; Walker, Toufexis, & Davis, 2003). Active in triggering environmental scanning and vigilance, the amygdala arouses stimulus detection, the fear response, subsequent anxiety, and overall arousal (Amaral, 2002, 2003). Nerve cells within the amygdala are responsive to facial cues and other environmental factors (J. B. Rosen, 2004), causing some researchers to propose that the amygdala functions as a protective "brake" on engagement of objects while an evaluation of potential threat is carried out. Continual stimulation of the amygdala produces fear and rage responses (Jatzko, Schmitt, Kordon, & Braus, 2005); serotonin reuptake inhibition within the central nucleus of the amygdala exerts an anxiolytic effect (Groenink, Joordens, Hijzen, Dirks, & Olivier, 2000). Anatomical connections between the hippocampus, amygdala, and hypothalamus are involved in the body's response to fear (Fredrikson & Furmark, 2003). The amygdala is a neural substrate for emotions, particularly those involve in the body's response to stress, providing a fear-based neural circuit through connecting with and mediating the hippocampus and medial prefrontal cortex (Wallace, Stellitano, Neve, & Duman, 2004). The amygdala assigns meaning to incoming stimuli by integrating memory images with emotions associated with those memories, thus guiding subsequent emotional behavior (Rauch, Shin, & Wright, 2003). Amygdala N-methyl-D-aspartate (NMDA) receptors trigger neural changes that support fear learning and the loss of fear that accompanies extinction (Bertoglio & Carobrez, 2003). This circuit may play a key role in the pathogenesis of panic.

The Basal Ganglia

Buried within the cerebral hemispheres are three large nuclei: the *caudate nucleus, putamen,* and *globus pallidus.* Collectively, these nuclei form the **basal ganglia,** which regulate motor movement and emotion, linking voluntary and automatic actions for self-regulation, survival, or basic functions (e.g., eating, drinking). Once considered important only for motor functioning, the basal ganglia are now known to be involved in the mental functions of cognitive processing of experiences, and integration of feelings, thoughts, movements, and executive functions, mediating motivation and fine motor activity (Nolte, 2002). In anxiety, the basal ganglia have been implicated in symptom modulation, regulating the brain's "idle," and operationally implicated in OCD (Benkelfat et al., 1995). Hyperactivity within the right basal ganglia heightens baseline "rev" and fosters tension, chronic anxiety (i.e., GAD), avoidant behavior, and a pessimistic outlook on the future (Harkany et al., 2003). When overactive, the left basal ganglia seem to prompt internal feelings of tension and anxiety, panic, or inadequate integration of emotion and somatic response (Zink, Pagnoni, Martin-Skurski, Chappelow, & Berns, 2004). In OCD probands, dysfunction of the basal ganglia may lead to inappropriate release of fixed-action patterns and subsequent compulsive rituals (Cavedini et al., 2003). The **striatum,** consisting of the caudate nucleus and putamen, is activated by exposure to stimuli, particularly when unexpected or potentially harmful, as in clinical anxiety (Spano et al., 2004). Multilayered, the **cingulate gyrus** interconnects with the neo-cortex, amygdala, and hippocampus, modulating emotion, visual imagery, and affective regulation (Gundel, O'Connor, Littrell, Fort, & Lane, 2003). This brain structure helps govern decision-making, attention, motivation, and novel problem-solving. Its anterior regions, heavily innervated by serotonergic fibers, mediate the shifting of attention and cognitive flexibility, and if dysfunctional may lead to deficits in tasks involving controlled attentional processing and spontaneous behavioral reactions (Papageorgiou & Rabavilas, 2003). As a central mediator among amygdala, basal ganglia, mesolimbic dopaminergic neurocircuits, mediodorsal thalamus, and the prefrontal cortex, the **nucleus accumbens** may play a modulatory role in information flow (Sena et al., 2003). If impaired, imbalanced information flow from the amygdala could prompt anxious and obsessive-compulsive symptoms (Joel, Doljansky, Roz, & Rehavi, 2005).

The Hippocampus

The ***hippocampus***, a cortical structure in the medial temporal lobe, is involved in memory, information-processing, novel learning, and behavioral arousal (Adolphs, Tranel, & Damasio, 1998; Kunzle, 2004). This region mediates transfer of short-term and incidental memories into long-term storage and recall—a vital aspect of posttraumatic stress disorder (Bannerman et al., 2004; McHugh, Deacon, Rawlins, & Bannerman, 2004). Highly sensitive to neurotoxic effects of repeated stress, hippocampal atrophy may result from exposure to trauma and be involved in PTSD, depression, and some personality traits (Scaccianoce et al., 2004; Weber & Reynolds, 2004). Mental maps and other forms of memory aids seem to be stored within the hippocampus, implicating its functionality in diverse anxiety conditions (Franconi et al., 2004). Its developmental formation is vulnerable to damage from brain dysfunction, such as seizures, ischemia, or blunt trauma (Sheline, Mittler, & Mintun, 2002). When the hippocampus is overstimulated, individuals become confused, easily distracted, and anxious (Massana et al., 2003). Dysfunction within the hippocampus has been linked with many neuropsychiatric conditions, including schizophrenia and clinical anxiety, which are characterized by nonmnemonic deficits in processing and responding to sensory input (Bast & Feldon, 2003; Miller & O'Callaghan, 2003; Yasuno et al., 2004). Alterations of synaptic efficacy in the hippocampus, lateral septum, and medial prefrontal cortex have been linked to both depression and anxiety (Alves, Pinheiro, Motta, Landeira-Fernandez, & Cruz, 2004). Table 2.2 outlines the functions of the previously mentioned brain regions, as well as the conditions and treatments associated with these.

CENTRAL NERVOUS SYSTEM COMMUNICATION

In addition to structural variables, *functionality* of specific brain regions can precipitate symptoms of clinical anxiety. Emotion involves multiple neurocircuits and neural systems, including the orbitofrontal cortex, lateral prefrontal cortex, anterior cingulate gyrus, and several limbic entities. The control of emotional behavior may be not only localized to brain regions but also related to cell communication, cellular respiration, neurotransmitter functioning within specific sections, or hormonal regulation (Lasaite, Bunevicius, Lasiene, & Lasas, 2004). Knowing the ways through which neurons communicate among themselves is essential to understanding clinical anxiety.

In the eighteenth century, the discovery of electricity spurred subsequent theories explaining interneuron communication, the existence of electrical potential across cell membranes, and basic electrical properties of neurons. Communication among neurons is ***electrochemical***. Electrical activity within the nervous system results from the uneven distribution of ***ions*** (electrically charged particles) across the membranes of nerve cells. Cell membranes are ***semiperme-***

TABLE 2.2.
Behavioral Neuroanatomy

Region/Part	Presumed Functions	Dysfunction	Associated Conditions	Treatments	Medications
Anterior cingulate	Changing of attention, flexibility, cooperation, cognitive shifting	Chronic worry, brooding, obsessive and compulsive trends, oppositional and defiant tendencies, argumentativeness, inflexibility	Obsessive-compulsive disorder (OCD), anxiety, oppositional-defiant disorder, PTSD, PMS	Serotonin agonists or reuptake inhibitors, hypericum, relationship and affect modulation counseling	SSRIs, SNRIs, SAMe, atypical antipsychotics
Basal ganglia	Regulation of emotion and level of excitement, controls smooth muscle movements, mediates behavior	Irritability, brooding, angst, fear of the future, overall tension	Anxiety, OCD, PTSD, movement disorders	Valerian root, biofeedback, cognitive therapy, hypnosis, meditation, assertiveness training, conditioning	Benzodiazepines, antidepressants, propranolol, possibly buspirone

Cerebellum	Motor control, posture, gait, higher-order reasoning, cognitive integration	Impulsivity, tremor, slowed thought and speech	Movement disorders, possibly learning disabilities	Cognitive-behavioral therapy, biofeedback, relationship counseling	Unclear
Limbic system	Emotion and motivation, pleasure and pain, appetite and circadian rhythms, fight-or-flight response	Anger, rage, amotivation, loss of libido, negativity	Depression, anxiety, intermittent explosive disorder, possibly cyclothymia	Medications to increase NE, DA, SE, SAMe, L-tyrosine, phenylalanine	Antidepressants (TCA, SSRI, SSNI, MAOI)
Parietal lobe	Spatial sensation and perception, visual mapping, tactile recognition, visual tracking	Dyslexia, dyscalculia; impaired sense of direction, denial of illness; impaired writing, reading, or math ability; poor constructional ability; impaired hand-eye coordination	Learning disabilities, Balint syndrome, loss of sense of direction	Cognitive restructuring, cognitive remapping techniques	Unclear

(continues)

TABLE 2.2.
(Continued)

Region/Part	Presumed Functions	Dysfunction	Associated Conditions	Treatments	Medications
Prefrontal cortex	Emotional control, focus, insight, organization, empathy for others, judgment	Short attention span, impulsivity, disorganization, lack of insight into self and others	ADHD, depression, dementia, psychosis, antisocial personality disorder	Organizational help, L-tyrosine; higher protein diet; biofeedback, medications that increase DA	CNS stimulants, bupropion, possibly venlafaxine
Temporal lobe	Language expression and receipt, learning, auditory processes, emotional stability, scanning and understanding environmental cues	Deficits in memory, headaches, hyper-religiosity, seizures, aggression, anxiety	Anxiety, dissociation, depression, epilepsy, possibly autism	GABA agonists, guided imagery on positive experiences, sleep, dietary changes	Anticonvulsants

able, meaning that small particles can pass through, whereas it is progressively more difficult for larger particles to pass through. *Active transport* is the metabolic process of molecules being transferred across a cell membrane. If the membrane potential reaches discharge threshold, the neuron produces an impulse that propagates down the axon. In the nervous system, electrical activity is *propagated*, meaning that it occurs much more slowly than conduction, with a maximum rate of approximately 100 meters per second.

Electrical Activity

The electrical activity within the nervous system is powered by an uneven distribution of charged particles flowing across the membranes of nerve cells. Neurons act like tiny batteries in which the inside of the cell is negatively charged and the outside is positively charged. An electrical voltage (*potential*) results from differential distribution of various ions on the two sides of the membrane. In the resting state, the membrane of the nerve cell is highly permeable to potassium (but not sodium) ions. When the nerve cell is at rest, not conducting action potentials, voltage (-70 mV) across the cell membrane is termed *resting membrane potential* because the electrical ions exist both inside and outside of nerve cells and are not equally distributed across the cell membrane. More *sodium* (Na+, positively charged) is present outside the neuron than inside it. *Potassium* (K+, another positively charged ion) is highly concentrated inside nerve cells and less so outside.

Concentration differences are maintained by the *sodium-potassium pump*, which keeps sodium outside and potassium inside the cell. The combination of negatively charged ions on the inside and positively charged ions on the outside creates a *difference* of 70 millivolts (mV) across the cell membrane. If excitation is sufficient to reduce the membrane potential to about -50 mV, the membrane permeability for positive sodium ions changes. By the *process of diffusion*, potassium ions leak out of the cell and create a charge imbalance across the membrane that produces the resting membrane potential. This influx of ions raises the potential until it becomes positive, changes the membrane potential, and signals across the cell axon. Changes in cell membrane permeability allow sodium to cross the membrane via structural changes (opening and closing of channels). Impulses can be transported along the axon either away from (*anterograde transport*) or toward (*retrograde transport*) the cell body. The process of *induction* involves the generation of action potentials by nerve cells that, because of the specialized cell membrane, can travel or propagate down the axon of the cell to remote destinations. Alternating action potential and the release of neurotransmitters (to bridge the physical gap of the synapse) occurs.

Secretion of neurotransmitters by presynaptic neurons creates *excitatory* (**EPSP**) and *inhibitory* (**IPSP**) postsynaptic potentials in postsynaptic nerve cells. The voltage across the membrane changes toward (excitatory) or away from (inhibitory) the **threshold** (the stimulus sufficient intensity to produce a response) for initiation of an action potential. Synaptic potentials are graded—that is, they depend for their size upon the number of synapses active within a short period of time. The action potential, on the other hand, is an all-or-nothing response. The **all-or-nothing principle** states that in neural transmission, once the electrical impulse reaches a certain level of intensity, it fires and moves down the axon, remaining at the same strength throughout transmission. If the threshold is not reached, no action potential occurs. **Kindling** is the progressive increase in neural excitability with repeated stimulation. A system that was initially barely responsive to a low-dose stimulus can ultimately spontaneously discharge secondary to aggregate stimulation (Kellett & Kokkinidis, 2004). The term **allostatic load** refers to the elevated or intensified activities of physiologic systems that lead to "wear and tear" or subsequent biogenic dysfunction. Thus, hormones associated with the body's response to stress promote adaptation in the short term but, with repeated activation, can prompt somatic changes that can lead to disease (McEwen, 2003).

Neurochemistry

Neurons receive excitatory and inhibitory inputs from other neurons and integrate these into creating signals. For an impulse to pass from one neuron to another, it must have a way of bridging the synaptic gap. When conducted to the ending of the presynaptic cell, a nerve impulse causes release of **neurotransmitters** into the **synaptic gap** (space between neurons). The cell that releases the transmitter is described as the **presynaptic cell**, whereas the responding cell is termed the **postsynaptic cell**. **Biosynthesis** is the process through which the neuron produces neurotransmitters. The effect of specific neurotransmitters differs depending on the site of release, its pre- and postsynaptic mediation. Neurotransmitters diffuse across the gap, attach to receptors on the membrane of the postsynaptic neuron, and produce electrical changes in the postsynaptic nerve cell. Corresponding receptors are located on or inside the neuron, glia, and other cells. Neurotransmitters facilitate or inhibit arousal and neuronal firing, either by raising or lowering membrane potential of the postsynaptic cell, by fitting into the receptor sites of postsynaptic neurons. **Receptor theories** emphasize the processes and functions of specific neurotransmitters and corresponding target receptors. **Autoreceptors** are presynaptic neuron receptors that mediate activity by responding to their own neurotransmitters. **Denervation supersensitivity** refers to an enhanced sensitivity of neurons to a neurotransmitter following the destruction of presynaptic neurons. When higher levels of neurotransmitters are present, the brain needs fewer receptors because the transmitter floods existing targets (Holmes, Kinney, et al., 2003; Jones, Duxon, & King, 2002). Increasing the amount of neurotransmitters available within clefts may cause the number of receptors to decrease and allow neurons to "respecialize," that is, take on alternative functions (Fehr et al., 2000; Harvey, Oosthuizen, Brand, Wegener, & Stein, 2004).

CLINICAL ANXIETY: BIOCHEMISTRY

Exploration of the relationship between neurotransmitters and the body's response to stress has been the chief focus of biological theories of clinical anxiety. The electrical action potential that changes the permeability of membranes is itself a biochemical process. It requires structural changes (such as the opening and closing of gates/channels) to occur and sequences of action potentials to prompt both electrical and biochemical changes. The physical gaps at the synapses separating nerve cells from each other are far too extensive to propagate action potential conduction among neurons. Thus, neurotransmitters serve as chemical messengers that influence the membrane of the next neural tract. An alternation between propagated action potentials and the release of neurotransmitters within synaptic gaps makes possible and facilitates intercell communication. Understanding how neurotransmitters are inactivated (rendered ineffective) following release is vital to linking their activity with mood (Haller, Varga, Ledent, & Freund, 2004). Inactivation of neurotransmitters occurs either by *chemical degradation* (e.g., by specific enzymes) or *reuptake*, a process in which the neurotransmitter is taken up again by the synaptic terminal. Norepinephrine, serotonin, and dopamine are mostly pumped back (*reuptake*) into the presynaptic neuron (Harmer, Shelley, Cowen, & Goodwin, 2004).

Neurotransmitters

Synthesized from the amino acids tyrosine, tryptophan, and phenylalanine, neurotransmitters are manufactured by various cell groups in the brain and secreted onto postsynaptic targets by means of terminals in synaptic contact with postsynaptic cells. Unique neurons have idiographic mechanisms that selectively bring precursor molecules from the bloodstream into cell bodies. Each cell type generates specific enzymes that produce biosynthetic changes. A single neurotransmitter can have different effects depending on its function, processes, and postsynaptic targets (Drevets, 1998). Further specificity occurs by having receptors for different portions of the transmitter molecule. Once inside, precursor molecules undergo enzyme-mediated changes that lead finally to the formation of neurotransmitters (Posserud et al., 2004).

Generally, a biochemical is defined as a neurotransmitter when it (1) is manufactured by the presynaptic neuron; (2) is released in response to electrical stimulation; (3) has a physiological effect in the postsynaptic cell; and (4) has certain mechanisms that it enable it to terminate an effect. Additionally, other biochemicals can affect transmission.

Second messenger systems link postsynaptic receptor activation on the dendrite to the firing of voltage-dependent channels along the nerve fiber. Current research suggests that some receptor-mediated second-messenger changes independent of "traditional" neurotransmitters (e.g., serotonin) occur in select anxiety disorders (Gross et al., 2002; Haddjeri & Blier, 2001).

Biogenic amines are substances that facilitate impulse transmission. Derived from precursor proteins (most from *preopiomelanocortin*, POMC), **peptide neurotransmitters** can also affect nerve cell functioning and govern hunger, thirst, libido, and emotion. **Neurotrophins** are proteins that support, differentiate, and affect the functioning of neurons within the nervous system (Altar, 1999).

Nerve Growth Factor

Nerve growth factor (NGF) was the first neurotrophin identified, but thereafter **brain-derived neurotrophic factor (BDNF)**, **neurotrophin-3 (NT-3)**, and other substances were discovered (Hall, Dhilla, Charalambous, Gogos, & Karayiorgou, 2003). Neurotrophins function as "retrograde factors" that contribute to the stabilization of synaptic contacts (Ashe & Aramakis, 1998). **Neuromodulators** influence nerve cells by either enhancing or inhibiting impulse transmission, functioning secondary to specific receptor types and neuronal substrates. Overall, a complex interaction of over 200 neurotransmitters, polypeptides, and neuromodulators within the brain is involved in clinical anxiety (De Kloet, 2003; Lapin, 2003; Linden et al., 2002). Key substances have been identified and targeted in clinical interventions.

Acetylcholine

Acetylcholine (Ach), the dominant neurotransmitter of the PNS, generally stimulates the firing of neurons and contraction of muscles. Cholinergic neurons synthesize acetylcholine within the axon from **choline** and **acetyl-coenzymeA**. In cholinergic neurons, the acetyl portion of the CoA molecule is removed and attached to choline to form acetylcholine, a process promoted by the enzyme **choline-acetyltransferase**. After its synthesis, acetylcholine is stored in synaptic vesicles. Secreted by the vagus nerve and nerves within most internal organs, acetylcholine is recognized at many different synapses throughout the body and brain; for example, its depletion within the hippocampus is associated with impaired memory (Jacobson & Sapolsky, 1991). Most cholinergic neurons lie in the reticular formation and basal forebrain. Acetylcholine fibers are heavily concentrated in the limbic and forebrain regions. Cholinergic neurons in the septum send axons through the fornix to the hippocampus; cholinergic neurons in the caudate nucleus terminate on other caudate cells. In the developing brain, catecholamines and other hormones modulate the developmental processes of neuronal migration, differentiation, and synaptic proliferation.

Two types of cholinergic receptors exist: **muscarinic**, which target organs of the parasympathetic division of the autonomic nervous system (ANS), and **nicotinic**, those associated with the autonomic nervous system, ganglia, and neuromuscular junctions (Yoo, Lee, Loh, Ho, & Jang, 2004). These divisions are particularly important in clinical anxiety, as acetylcholine has an excitatory effect at neuromuscular junctions and either an excitatory or inhibitory function within the brain (LeDoux, 1998). Choline is transported into cholinergic neurons by an active uptake mechanism. Once acetylcholine produces its effect on the post-synaptic cell, it is removed rapidly from the synapse. Chemical breakup occurs via the enzyme *acetylcholinesterase*, released at the synapse, by breaking down acetylcholine into choline and acetate. The choline produced by the metabolism of ACh is taken up by the axon terminal and reused to make new acetylcholine. *Anticholinergics* are drugs that specifically interfere with the activity of neurons that release acetylcholine.

Monoaminergic Function

Brain *monoaminergic* function has been implicated in the pathogenesis of many psychiatric disorders. The monoamines most relevant to clinical anxiety include *indoleamines* and *catecholamines*, both of which are implicated in mood, emotion, and other somatics. Indoleamines (each with an indole portion, C_8H_7N) are monoamines containing an indole portion, such as *serotonin, histamine*, and *tryptamine* (Rizk, Curley, Robertson, & Raber, 2004). An essential amino acid, *tryptophan* is a precursor for the synthesis of serotonin (known to be associated with anxiety) and melatonin. Tryptophan is metabolized into niacin, melatonin, and serotonin and has relaxing and calming effects. Formed from the precursor tryptophan and catalyzed by tryptophan hydroxylase, serotonin (5HT) is synthesized by adding a hydroxyl group to the fifth carbon atom of the tryptophan benzene ring, resulting in its byproduct, *5-hydroxyindoleacetic acid (5-HIAA)*.

Serotonin cannot cross the bloodbrain barrier, and thus most of its synthesis occurs within the central nervous system. Within the brain, serotonergic nuclei line the midline and raphe regions of the pons and upper brain stem. The raphe medianus nucleus innervates the limbic system and the dorsal raphe innervates the neostratum, cerebral cortex, cerebellum, and thalamus. Essential for both vascular and nonvascular smooth muscle contraction, serotonin is actively involved in platelet aggregation, regulation of mood, and anxiety (Sodhi & Saunders-Bush, 2004). Serotonin is a potent modulator of the physiological responses involved in clinical anxiety, and its role in clinical therapeutics has provided great success (Hariri & Weinberger, 2003). Serotonergic neurons located in the locus coeruleus, paragigantocellularis, and median raphe nucleus may be involved in anxiolytic effects (De Paula-Soares & Zangrossi, 2004). Its primary action, inhibition, is caused by an increase in K+ conduction. Synthesized by a tetrahydrobiopterin-dependent reaction, serotonin is catalyzed by *aromatic L-amino acid decarboxylase*. Identified serotonin receptors are coupled to G-proteins that affect adenylate cyclase or phospholipase C (Groenink, Van Bogaert, Van der Gugten, Oosting, & Olivier, 2003). *Melatonin,* derived from serotonin by the *N-acetyltransferase* enzyme within the retina and pineal gland, inhibits secretion of dopamine and gamma-aminobutyric acid (Becker et al., 2004; Delagrange et al., 2003). It is a natural relaxant and sleep aid.

Serotonin

Serotonin is implicated in all anxiety disorders, as well as depression, and is a vital neurotransmitter within the brain. Its organization within the brain (which contains only 2% of the body's serotonin) parallels that of norepinephrine, with distinct cell clusters scattered throughout the brain stem and with more caudal neurons sending their axons into the spinal cord and rostral neurons projecting into the midbrain and forebrain. Dense clusters of serotonergic pathways are located in the amygdala, rectus gyrus of the frontal lobe, and both inferior and superior gyri of the temporal lobe. Each of these circuits may have unique effects in clinical anxiety, and all are being researched to better understand their putative roles (Bantick et al., 2004). Specific serotonergic nuclei modulate brainstem structures implicated in anxiety, such as the locus coeruleus and the nucleus paragigantocellularis. Dense ascending pathways project into the amygdala, the "fear" section of the limbic system, and multiple 5-HT1A receptors are found within the dorsal raphe nuclei, hippocampus, lateral septum, frontal cortex, and the dorsal horn of the spinal cord. The anxiolytic effects of 5-HT1A partial agonists result primarily from an interaction with presynaptic 5-HT1A receptors, resulting in a regulation of hyperactive serotonergic neurotransmission. This neurotransmitter also functions to mediate the septohippocampal system that inhibits behavioral responses (Assal et al., 2004).

Catecholamines

Endogenously produced, **catecholamines** (each with a catechol portion, $C_6H_6O_2$) are dihydroxyphenethylamine compounds synthesized from amino acid precursors found in every cell within the body. The activation of the body's

---

SYNTHESIS OF SEROTONIN

Tryptophan
↓ tryptophan hydroxylase
5-hydroxytryptophan
↓ aromatic amino acid
↓ decarboxylase
5-hydroxytryptamine (serotonin)

Serotonin has been implicated in numerous anxiety disorders, and its synthesis is important to know in understanding its origin, effect, and excretion. Its precursor, tryptophan, is not manufactured in the body and must be obtained from the diet.

response to stress is in part due to the effects of cathecholamines' activation of the brain stem and locus coeruleus via pathways extending to the cerebral cortex, limbic regions, and spinal cord. High levels of catecholamines in the blood prompt increases in heart rate, blood pressure, and blood sugar (Rasmusson, Vythilingam, & Morgan, 2003).

Tyrosine is a simple amino acid secreted by the liver and synthesized. Within the body, the majority of tyrosine is incorporated into proteins (such as serving as a precursor to dopamine and norepinephrine); the rest is catabolized for energy production or converted into catecholamines (Degroot & Nomikos, 2004). *Tyrosine hydroxylase* enzymatically converts tyrosine into L-dopa, which is then transformed into dopamine via decarboxylase.

Dopamine (DA) is implicated in numerous psychological conditions, such as Parkinson's disease (degeneration of nigro-neostriatal pathway), attention disorders (deficit), and schizophrenia (excess) (Hameg et al., 2003). Both norepinephrine and dopamine are excitatory neurotransmitters that increase motor activity, behavioral arousal, and wakefulness. Activating central and peripheral nervous systems, dopamine serves as a general stimulant, enhancing alertness, heart rate, and respiration.

Dopamine's postsynaptic effects are due to cyclic AMP. Most dopaminergic nerve cells are in the ventral midbrain, sending axons rostrally to the caudate nucleus and putamen within the basal ganglia. This region, known as the *nigro-neostriatal pathway*, contains about 70% of the brain's dopamine (Laakso et al., 2003). Adrenergic neurons are scattered throughout the brain, with caudal axons descending into the spinal cord. Rostral adrenergic groups extend toward the midbrain and forebrain, including the hypothalamus, cerebral cortex, locus coeruleus, and hippocampus (Moore & Bloom, 1979). Dopaminergic receptors in the amygdala mediate the formation and retention of fear associations (Greba, Gifkins, & Kokkinidis, 2001). Dopaminergic neurons within the ventral tegmental area are involved in fear arousal, and antianxiety medications may "work" by blocking receptors there (Szabo & Blier, 2002). Geneticists have identified dopaminergic alleles that differ between those with an active behavioral inhibition system (BIS) and those without, linking biological process variables (e.g., dopaminergic activity) with inheritance (e.g., the location of a particular gene) (Benjamin et al., 1997).

Within the adrenal medulla, dopamine is converted to norepinephrine and epinephrine. *Norepinephrine* (NE) excites alertness and wakefulness—actively involved in the neural mechanisms in sensitization and fear conditioning. Its effects are exerted through contact with beta-adrenergic receptors, and its main sites of function are throughout the sympathetic nervous system (SNS). Two major groups of noradrenalin cell bodies exist, each ascending into separate brain regions. Most noradrenergic neurons are located in the locus coeruleus (in the midbrain) and pons, projecting throughout the cerebral cortex, hippocampus, amygdala, thalamus, and hypothalamus. The second tract of NE fibers arise from neurons in the lateral tegmental area. Norepinephrine's byproduct, *3-methoxy-*

SYNTHESIS OF CATECHOLAMINES

Tyrosine
↓ tyrosine hydroxylase

DOPA

↓ DOPA
↓ decarboxylase (L-aromatic amino acid decarboxylase)

Dopamine (DA)

↓ dopamine
β-hydroxylase

Norepinephrine (NE)

↓ phenylathanolamine-N-methyltransferase

Epinephrine

↓ bound to ATP and chromagranin A

Catecholamines, particularly dopamine and norepinephrine, have been implicated in numerous anxiety disorders, and their synthesis is important to know in understanding their origins, effects, and excretions.

4-hydroxyphenylglycol (MHPG), is associated with mood (Yoshimura, Nakamura, Shinkai, & Ueda, 2004). Synthesized by enzymatic steps in the adrenal medulla from tyrosine, norepinephrine is synthesized via methylation to epinephrine. **Epinephrine** stimulates the sympathetic nervous system and is released by the adrenal glands in response to anxiety. As a neurotransmitter, epinephrine is confined primarily to the medulla and caudal brain stem. Its effects are mediated through associated receptors called **adrenoceptors**.

COGNITIVE AND EMOTIONAL FUNCTIONING

In the brain, both serotonin and norepinephrine are associated with cognitive and emotional transmission. Catecholamine receptors are imbedded in the plasma membrane of the neuron, and their release is controlled by neuronal activity, biochemical and other feedback loops, as well as degradative enzymes contained within the cell terminal. Many receptors that respond to catecholamines have been identified, particularly epinephrine, norepinephrine, and dopamine.

Adrenergic receptors, which include alpha and beta sites, are adrenergic sites within the CNS that respond to epinephrine or norepinephrine (or related compounds). *Beta adrenergic receptors*, located throughout the nervous system, are stimulated by norepinephrine to increase blood pressure and heart rate (key responses to perceived stressors). *Dopaminergic receptors* have been identified at many sites, and those within the ventral tegmental area (VTA) are particularly involved in the body's response to fear. The three major CNS dopamine pathways are *nigrostriatal* (extra pyramidal actions), *tuberoinfundibular* (endocrine actions, increased prolactin), and *mesolimbic* (antipsychotic actions). Some catecholamine neurons extend from the limbic system and discharge neurotransmitters in the frontal cortex, prompting "vigilance" tasks involved in fight-or-flight responses (Arinami et al., 1996; Bremner, 1999, 2003b). Catecholamines are removed from the synaptic cleft by reuptake. All catecholamine neurotransmitters are inactivated by *monoamine oxidase* (*MAO*) and *catechol-O-methyltransferase* (*COMT*). When MAO interacts chemically with molecules of norepinephrine, it removes the nitrogen, or amine, component by oxidation and destroys its effectiveness as a neurotransmitter. In the axon terminal, MAO destroys any catecholamines not stored in synaptic vesicles. Serotonin-induced release of dopamine also has antidepressant effects (Dremencov et al., 2004).

Amino Acids

Amino acids are fundamental building blocks of proteins (used in protein synthesis) consisting of an organic acid combined with an amino (NH_2) group. Amino acids are formed in all neurons as part of the normal energy cycle, and although many serve as precursors for neurotransmitter synthesis, some function as neurotransmitters themselves.

Glutamate (glutamic acid) and *aspartate* (aspartic acid) are strong excitants; *gamma-aminobutyric acid* (*GABA*) and *glycine* are inhibitory (Javitt, 2004). Glutamatergic nerves cells are found predominantly within the cerebral cortex, sending axons to the neostriatum and subcortical regions (Carlsson, Calsson, & Nilsson, 2004). Glutamate metabotropic-2 receptor agonists block fear learning when fused into the amygdala (Baptista, Martin-Fardon, & Weiss, 2004; Campisi et al., 2003; Walker & Davis, 2002).

Metabotropic glutamate (*mGlu*) receptors mediate the intracellular metabolic effects of glutamate by coupling to secondary messenger systems (Lipsky & Goldman, 2003). Eight such receptors (mGlu1-mGlu8) have been identified and cloned according to their amino acid sequencing and second-messenger coupling (Walker, Rattiner, & Davis, 2002). Down regulation of amygdaloidal cholecystokinin (B) receptor binding prompts anxious behavior (Abramov et al., 2004). Selective modulators of glutamate activity may have anxiolytic effects (Klodzinska et al., 2004). Potent blockade of NMDA and glutamatergic receptors induces anxiolytic effects (Martinez et al., 2002). High concentrations of aspartate are located in the thalamus and spinal cord. Glutamate activates *nitric oxide* synthesis, whereas GABA may inhibit both glutamatergic and nitrergic transmission (Calixto, Vandresen, de Nucci, Moreno, & Faria, 2001; Weitzdoerfer et al., 2004). The exact role of nitric oxide synthesis in neuronal toxicity is unclear, but its regulation by glutamate and GABA may be involved in stress-related hippocampal degeneration. (Maccari et al., 2003; Malhotra, Murphy, & Kennedy, 2004).

Gamma-Aminobutyric Acid (GABA)

Gamma-aminobutyric acid (GABA) inhibits neuronal firing, reduces the body's state of excitability, and alleviates the overall experience of anxiety. GABA transporter inhibition induces anxiolytic like behavior in mice (Schmitt, Luddens, & Hiemke, 2002). GABA reduces excitatory glutamate and aspartate by gating calcium ions into the interior of neurons, decreasing the likelihood of internal action potential (Shinnick-Gallagher et al., 2003; Sickle, Xiang, & Tietz, 2004). GABA-containing neurons are found throughout the brain, from the brain stem to the cerebral cortex, most acting as interneurons (Zarrindast, Bakhsha, Rostami, & Shafaghi, 2002). Prime sites for these combinations have been mapped throughout the limbic system, hypothalamus, and the basal ganglia—brain regions active in anxiety and mood regulation (Bonavita et al., 2003; Kaufmann, Humpel, Alheid, & Marksteiner, 2003). GABA is distributed widely throughout the brain (with some estimates as high as 40% of all brain synapses), but the precise site or sites of its inhibitory effects remain unclear (Leslie, Shaw, McCabe, Reynolds, & Dawson, 2004).

GAT-1 transporter is the primary GABA transporter that causes the reuptake of GABA into presynaptic nerve cells and glia, resulting in the termination of postsynaptic neural action (Stahl, 2004a, 2004b). GABA is known to bind to at least three different types of receptors: **GABA(A)** (regulating neuronal excitability with accompanying changes in mood), **GABA(B)** (mediating slower inhibitory potentials involved in mood and pain), and **GABA(C)** (unclear) (Marowsky, Fritschy, & Vogt, 2004). Constructed in subunits, active GABA(A) receptors contain (at least) two alpha, two beta, and a gamma or delta subunit; only those with a gamma subunit interact and respond to benzodiazepines (G. M. Sullivan, Kent, & Coplan, 2000). All benzodiazepines primarily effect the GABA(A) receptors, which also contain chloride ion channels, and from which GABA binds to increase the efficacy of certain impulses (Rudolph & Mohler, 2004). Because GABA(A) receptors mediate chloride channels, benzodiazepines regulate the flow of chloride ions into nerve cells. The effectiveness of this class of drugs depends on the subunit compositions of the GABA(A) receptor complexes to which they bind. Benzodiazepines bind to a subunit cleft of GABA(A) receptor surfaces located between alpha and gamma subunits (Moroz, 2004). Another inhibitory amino acid, *glycine*, is found predominantly in the spinal cord, pons, and medulla.

SYNTHESIS OF GABA

Glutamic Acid
↓ glutamic acid hydroxylase
GABA

GABA has been implicated in numerous anxiety disorders, particularly GAD.

Peptides

When chained together, amino acids form **peptides** (proteins of less than 100 amino acids), such as *substance P, Leu-enkephalin,* and Met-*enkephalin* (Patel, Roelke, Rademacher, Cullinan, & Hillard, 2004; Thoenen, 1995). **Neuropeptides** are combinations of amino acids that function as neurotransmitters or neuromodulators (Table 2.3). Comprised of three peptides and a four to five G-protein-coupled receptor (**Y receptors**), neuropeptides serve as auxiliary neurotransmitters stored by the neurons, alone or with others, or with the principal neurotransmitters whose action they support or inhibit (Landgraf, 2001).

Among neuropeptides are **endorphins** and **enkephalins**, powerful endogenous analgesics (Arevalo, De Miguel, & Hernandez-Tristan, 2001; Asakawa et al., 1998). Linked to pain control, these naturally secreted opiates reduce pain, increase pleasure, and precipitate a feeling of euphoria (Maier, Laudenslager, & Ryan, 1985; Manzanares, Uriguen, Rubio, & Palomo, 2004). Within the amygdala, **substance P** and neurokinin-1 receptors (NK1) mediate the effects of opiates and control anxiety-related behaviors through activation of neurokinin receptors (Adell, 2004; Gadd, Murtra, De Felipe, & Hunt, 2003). NK-1 receptors are scattered throughout the locus coeruleus, and their antagonism has antidepressive effects. In addition to mediating wakefulness and general arousal, **neuropeptide S** may modulate anxiety through its effect in the locus coeruleus (Commons & Valentino, 2002; Xu et al., 2004). Particularly within the amygdala, **neuropeptide Y (NPY)**, **corticotrophin-releasing factor (CRF)**, and **urocortin I (UcnI)** mediate neuroanatomical structures implicated in clinical anxiety, potentially acting as endogenous agonists affecting learning and anxiety (Carpenter et al., 2004; Holmes, Heilig, Rupniak, Steckler, & Griebel, 2003; Jedema & Grace, 2004).

NPY is involved in regulating circadian rhythms, body temperature, and neuroendocrine secretion, mediating limbic functionings involved in clinical anxiety (Balasubramaniam, 2002; Redrobe, Dumont, Herzog, & Quirion, 2003). NPY has been further implicated in the pathophysiology of eating disorders, seizures, diabetes, hypertension, and intestinal disorders (Hartz et al., 2004; Sajdyk, Shekhar, & Gehlert, 2004).

TABLE 2.3.
Neurotransmitters and Selected Neuropeptides

Transmitter	Neuropeptide
Acetylcholine	Substance P
Dopamine	Cholecysokinin, neurotensin
GABA	Somatostatin, cholecystokinin
Norepinephrine	Enkephalin, neurotensin
Serotonin	Substance P, enkephalin

Known G-protein coupled receptor subtypes are denoted as Y1 to Y6 (Alcalay, Giladi, Pick, & Gozes, 2004). Decreased NPY-1 binding sites within the hippocampus and hypothalamus are associated with animal models of anxiety (Carvajal, Vercauteren, Dumont, Michalkiewiz, & Quirion, 2004; Gilligan & Li, 2004). CRF systems are major mediators of stress-induced endocrine, autonomic, immune, and behavioral processes, mediating the body's response to stressful stimuli by modulating the activity of the hypothalamic-pituitary-adrenal axis and limbic circuits (Erel, Arborelius, & Brodin, 2004; Sorensen, Lindberg, Wortwein, Bolwig, & Woldbye, 2004; Thomas, Pernar, Lucki, & Valentino, 2003). Increased CRF in the amygdala may contribute to impaired corticosterone secretion (Risbrough, Hauger, Roberts, Vale, & Geyer, 2004). CRF, particularly its corresponding receptor 1 subtype, may act as a neuromodulator of neurophysiological symptoms of anxiety (Arborelius, Owens, Plotsky, & Nemeroff, 1999; Heilig, 2004; Zorrilla & Koob, 2004).

Vasopressin and *oxytocin*, synthesized in the hypothalamus and released by the pituitary, are involved in mood regulation (Alescio-Lautier, Paban, & Soumireu-Mourat, 2000; Amico, Mantella, Vollmer, & Li, 2004). Vasopressin binds plasma membrane receptors and activates cAMP regulation (Wigger et al., 2004).

Cholecystokinin, an abundant anxiogenic neuropeptide linked with limbic-hypothalamic-pituitary-adrenal arousal, modulates anxiety-related responses within the amygdala (Horinouchi et al., 2004). Vital to pancreatic amylase secretion, CCK has an antagonistic role with GABA within the brain (Bourin, Malinge, Vasar, & Bradwejn, 1996). *Cholecystokinin (A)* receptors are plentiful in the peripheral nervous system, but some CCK (A) receptors are found within the CNS. *Cholecystokinin (B)* receptors in the basolateral amygdala are involved in anxiety-related somatic responses (Hernandez-Gomez, Aguilar-Roblero, & Perez de la Mora, 2002; Rotzinger & Vaccarino, 2003). Ingestion of CCK-B agonists prompts the release of adrenocorticotropin and cortisol that activate the hypothalamic-pituitary-adrenal axis (Brown, Varghese, & McEwen, 2004; Netto & Guimaraes, 2004). Antagonism of CCK-B receptors attenuates the fear response (Bale & Vale, 2004; Penalva et al., 2002; Wunderlich, Raymond, DeSousa, Nobrega, & Vaccarino, 2002). Table 2.4 lists the previously mentioned neurotransmitters, along with their usual effects and known receptors.

TABLE 2.4.
Neurotransmitters

Neurotransmitter	Description	Usual Effect (Derivation)	Known Receptors
Acetylcholine (ACh)	Usually stimulates firing of neurons	Excitatory or inhibitory (*choline*)	Muscarinic [M1, M2, M3, M4], nicotinic
Adenosine	Usually has depressive effects on behavior; precursor of cAMP	Inhibitory (ATP)	P1 [A1, A2], P2
Dopamine (DA)	Involved in the control of voluntary muscle and motor movement	Excitatory (*tyrosine*)	DA-1, DA-2, DA-3, DA-4, DA-5, DA-6
Endorphins, enkephalins	Natural opiates that stimulate the firing of neurons; mediate pleasure and control of pain	Inhibitory (*endogenous*)	μ, δ, k
Epinephrine (adrenaline)	Increases blood pressure, release of sugar by the liver, and overall arousal	Excitatory (*tyrosine*)	Alpha, beta
Gamma-aminobutyric acid (GABA)	Linked with GAD	Inhibitory	GABA-A, GABA-B, GABA-C,
Glutamate	Excitotoxicity, learning and memory	Excitatory or inhibitory (*glutamate acid*)	AMPA, kainite, NMDA, AP4, ACPD

(continues)

TABLE 2.4.
(Continued)

Neurotransmitter	Description	Usual Effect (Derivation)	Known Receptors
Glycine	Found primarily in interneurons	Inhibitory (*serine*)	Chloride ion channel similar to GABA receptors
Histamine	An amino acid prominent in the hypothalamus; prominent in mast cells; mediates allergic response	Inhibitory or excitatory due to cyclic AMP (*histidine*)	H-1, H-2, H-3
Nitric oxide	May serve as neurotransmitter or interneuron second messenger	Unclear (*arginine*)	NMDA receptor subtype of glutamate
Norepinephrine (NE), noradrenalin	Implicated in the control of alertness and wakefulness	Excitatory (*tyrosine*)	Alpha, beta
Serotonin (SE)	Implicated in the regulation of sleep and depression	Inhibitory (*tryptophan*)	5-HT1 [5-HT1A, 5-HT1B, 5-HT1D, 5-HT1E, 5-HT1F], 5-HT2 [5-HT2A, 5-HT2B, 5-HT2C], 5-HT3, 5-HT4, 5-HT5 [5-HT5A, 5-HT5B], 5-HT6, 5-HT7

SUMMARY

From early models to contemporary paradigms, research has shown significant and substantial biological bases for anxiety (Andreasen, 1997; Gray & McNaughton, 1996, 1998). Multiple pathways, processes, and interactions among numerous somatic systems are involved in generating and sustaining symptoms. Aggregately, various genetic studies suggest an inherited vulnerability to anxiety that when coupled with stressors, personality variables, and coping skills produces specific symptoms (Bernstein et al., 1996). Neuroanatomical bases of clinical anxiety implicate the amygdala, hippocampus, basal ganglia, or striatum. Biochemical studies have focused on the role of gamma-aminobutyric acid (GABA), serotonin, norepinephrine, epinephrine, and possibly dopamine. By studying levels of plasma proteins, indoleamines, catecholamines, antibodies, hemolytic plasma, carbohydrate metabolism, hormone levels, inorganic and organic ions, and other potential biochemical processes, we can formulate specific models for the causes of and treatments for clinical anxiety (Antoni et al., 2000).

CHAPTER 3

Psychopharmacology: Understanding Basic Medical Treatments

THE SYMPTOMS OF CLINICAL anxiety can be reduced by a wide variety of agents (Aricioglu & Altunbas, 2003; Lamberty, Falter, Gower, & Klitgaard, 2003; Lecrubier, 2001b). Compounds useful for treating clinical anxiety include both herbal substances and complex drug therapies, often combining multiple agents that augment comprehensive treatments (Thase & Trivedi, 2002). Technological, conceptual, and theoretical advances in the behavioral sciences, neurochemistry, and molecular biology, from the 1960s to the present, have further added to interest in psychotropics (Maddock et al., 2004). The need for more effective, rapidly acting medications—without adverse side effects—continues to be a primary concern regarding ongoing pharmaceutics. A comprehensive understanding of their theoretical underpinnings, empirical research, and pragmatic interventions is needed for providing competent, effective treatments.

Emotional, cognitive, and behavioral effects have linked specific classes of drugs with unique effects on perception, sensation, intermediation, and behavioral outputs (Kendall, Safford, Flannery-Schroeder, & Webb, 2004; Nutt, 2005). Early research on drug therapies was largely limited to those that would soothe, calm, or induce sleep, making it easier to manage behavioral functioning of patients with severe psychopathology.

The oldest agent used to reduce anxiety is alcohol. *Ethanol* (e.g., alcoholic beverages), a CNS depressant, is the most commonly used anxiolytic agent, modifying receptor membranes while increasing their affinity for GABA (Knapp, Overstreet, Moy, & Breese, 2004). Chronic alcohol ingestion alters biochemistry (particularly NMDA) within the brain and affects lateral and basolateral neurons within the amygdala (Floyd, Jung, & McCool, 2003). At high doses, ethanol can also open the chloride channel within the receptor independent of

GABA (Crawford, 2004; Kushner, Abrams, & Borchardt, 2000). Illicit drugs, such as cannabis, LSD, and heroin, can effectively subdue symptoms but they build tolerance and have side-effect profiles/toxicities that preclude their formal use as anxiolytics (Hayry, 2004; Post, 2004). Table 3.1 lists the medications used to treat anxiety. The rest of the chapter is devoted to describing these medications and their effects in more detail.

BARBITURATES

First introduced in the early twentieth century, **barbiturates** (CNS depressants) were used extensively as sedatives, hypnotics, and anxiolytics. Their presumed mechanism of action involves the GABA receptor channel, enhancing the effect of GABA on corresponding receptors (Coupey, 1997). Barbiturates may also inhibit the release of calcium ions into presynaptic vesicles, potentially reducing neurotransmitter release or effect (Sramek, Zarotsky, & Cutler, 2002). In contemporary practice, barbiturate use in clinical practice has almost ceased, due to potentially life-threatening side effects and susceptibility to abuse. Barbiturates and related classes of drugs can be lethal in cases of overdose, causing coma, respiratory depression, and subsequent mortality. Effective psychotropic treatment of clinical anxiety began with sedative-hypnotics in the mid-twentieth century when **meprobamate** was introduced as a "nonbarbiturate" anxiolytic. Originally, meprobamate was touted as a nonsedating anxiolytic; further research has shown it to be a mild barbiturate with similar effects to other CNS depressants. Further, both meprobamate and barbiturates have a very low toxicity-to-therapeutic-effect ratio, making them extremely difficult to monitor and regulate, with potentially serious complications when withdrawn. They also induce hepatic enzymes that create a need for increased dosings.

CNS STIMULANTS

Following the development of **benzedrine** in 1937, researchers began to explore the possible therapeutics of using amphetamine-based stimulants to treat obesity, attention deficits, and behavior disorders. **Amphetamines**, CNS stimulants (Table 3.2), indirectly precipitate the release of norepinephrine, dopamine, and serotonin from nerve terminals. In general, amphetamines enter nerve terminals by inward transport via monoaminergic transporters or lipophilic diffusion. Indirect effects include mediation of neurotransmitter transporters and fostering the efflux of monoamines into the synaptic clefts. Originally used in inhalers for the treatment of nasal congestion, the misuse of these agents spread, and they became readily abused.

Psychostimulants, amphetamine-based agents with excitatory effects on heart rate and respiration, are primarily used in the treatment of attention disorders, narcolepsy, or mood disorders (particularly in the elderly). Their primary effects

TABLE 3.1.
Medical Interventions for Anxiety

Drug Class	Presumed Mechanisms of Action
Anticonvulsants	Uncertain, but may inhibit electrical stimulation; may increase frequency with which GABA activates receptors, thus enhancing GABA to cause a flux of chloride ions into neurons.
Antihistamines	Block histamine type 1 receptor; some (e.g., cimetidine) block H-2 receptor, but their use is generally in gastrointestinal indications.
Atypical antidepressants	*Venlafaxine* blocks the reuptake of both serotonin and norepinephrine; *nefazodone* blocks serotonin reuptake and blocks the serotonin receptor that tends to cause increased anxiety and sleeplessness; *mirtezapine*, a unique piperazinoazepine, blocks presynaptic alpha-2 auto and hetero adrenoceptors, increasing norepinephrine and serotonergic transmission, and may also block 5-HT2 and 5-HT3 receptors, minimizing serotonergic side effects.
Barbiturates	Enhance the activity of GABA on GABA sites, thus increasing its inhibitory actions; may also inhibit the entry of calcium ions into presynaptic nerve terminals, thus potentially reducing neurotransmitter release.
Benzodiazepines	Augment antianxiety action of GABA-stimulated chloride system; increase affinity of the GABA receptors for GABA; relieve anxiety by a three-stage model: (1) chloride channel closes; (2) GABA binds to receptors and ion channel opens; (3) benzodiazepine molecules bind to receptors and enhance opening of chloride ion channel.
Beta-blockers	Alpha-adrenergic receptor agonists that may cause a decrease in neurotransmitter amount released from presynaptic nerve terminals; decreases central adrenergic outflow secondary to stimulation of central receptors.
Buspirone	Unlike the benzodiazepines, buspirone has no effect on GABA receptors; instead, it acts as an agonist on 5-HT1 receptors.

(continues)

TABLE 3.1.
(Continued)

Drug Class	Presumed Mechanisms of Action
MAO inhibitors	When MAO interacts chemically with molecules of norepinephrine, it removes the nitrogen, or amine, component from it by oxidation and destroys its effectiveness as a neurotransmitter—MAO inhibitors block this destructive activity of the enzyme MAO and thereby stop the destruction of norepinephrine; the result is a heightened level of norepinephrine activity causing depressive symptoms to abate.
Antipsychotics	These drugs have the basic pharmacological property of inhibiting dopaminergic neurotransmission; aripiprazole is a partial agonist at DA-2 receptors in hyperdopaminergic sites, a functional agonist at DA-2 receptors in hypodopaminergic environments, and has a moderate affinity for H-1 receptors.
SSRIs	Selectively inhibit reuptake of serotonin within the synaptic clefts.
Tricyclics, heterocyclics, tetracyclics	Multiple actions: (1) block reuptake (at presynaptic terminal axon vesicles) of both norepinephrine and serotonin; and (2) increase sensitivity of the postsynaptic receptors for both neurotransmitters. Drug actions increase the levels of norepinephrine and serotonin in brain neural transmission. Antidepressant drugs also block acetylcholine receptors; inhibit reuptake mechanism for norepinephrine and the indoleamine 5-HT (serotonin). These drugs create an increase in the concentration of these transmitters at the synaptic cleft by limiting their reuptake by the presynaptic neuron.

include catecholaminic—particularly dopaminergic (signaling its release) and noradrenergic—agonism via CNS stimulation, prompting wakefulness, alertness, elevation of mood and self-esteem, and increased overall arousal. The first formal psychotropic stimulant was introduced in 1948, when **dextroamphetamine** (*Dexedrine®*) was created as a safer alternative to "street" stimulants. It was used widely in the treatment of obesity and narcolepsy. In 1954, **methylphenidate** (*Ritalin®*) was marketed to treat "hyperkinetic impulse disorder." Other

TABLE 3.2.
CNS Stimulants

Name	Half-life	Preparations	Usual Adult Daily Dosage	Notes
d-amphetamine (*Dexedrine®*, *Dexedrine Spansules®*)	2–4 hr; longer for spansules	Tablets: 5 mg; Spansule: 5, 10, 15 mg; Elixir 5 mg/5 ml	5–40 mg	May have therapeutic effect in OCD as an augmentation to traditional SE regimens
d-methamphetamine hydrochloride (*Desoxyn®*)	4–5 hr	5 mg tablets	5–40 mg	CNS stimulant with high potential for abuse; infrequently used
Dexmethylphenidate (*Focalin®*, *Focalin XR®*)	3 hr; 6–8 hr XR capsule	2.5, 5, 10 mg tablets; 5, 10, 20 mg XR capsules	5–20 mg	d-threo enantiomer of methylphenidate
Dextroamphetamine salts (*Adderall®*, *Adderall XR®*)	6–8 hr; longer for XR	5, 7.5, 10, 12.5, 15, 20, 30 mg tablets; 10, 20, 30 mg XR capsules	5–60 mg	A mixture of amphetamine salts; graded onset and duration of effect
Magnesium pemoline (*Cylert®*)	12 hr	Tablets: 18.75, 37.5, 75 mg; Chewable tablets: 37.5 mg	37.5–75 mg	May have DA action; infrequently used, secondary to possible liver damage when used over time (ranging from reversible liver function increases to liver failure)
Methylphenidate (*Ritalin®* *Ritalin SR®* *Ritalin LA®*, *Concerta®*, *Metadate CD®*, *Metadate ER®*)	1–3 hr; longer for sustained release	Tablets: 5, 10, 20 mg; SR tablets: 10, 20 mg; LA tablets: 20, 30 40 mg; Concerta: 18, 27, 36, 54 mg	10–60 mg	Inhibits DA and NE reuptake transporters; DA reuptake inhibitor
Modafinil (*Provigil®*)	About 15 hr	100, 200 mg	100–200 mg	Indicated as a wakefulness promoting agent; other applications being researched (e.g., ADHD)

stimulant agents include **d-methamphetamine** (*Desoxyn*®), **pemoline** (*Cylert*®), **modafinil** (*Provigil*®), and various mixed compounds (e.g., dextroamphetamine salts). Theory proposed that hyperactivity was the result of a lag in developmental maturation in the CNS. Other paradigms have proposed dopaminergic deficiency or decreased dopaminergic receptor sites. Psychostimulants are used to enhance prefrontal cortex activity and prevent prefrontal cortex dysfunction during attention and concentration (Alban, Hopson, Ly, & Whyte, 2004). Decrements in the predicted growth, weight, and height rate have been reported in some child patients using CNS stimulants over time. Careful physician monitoring is recommended. Some studies suggest that psychostimulants can effectively augment treatment regimens in some anxiety conditions, whereas others suggest that they can exacerbate symptoms (Joffe, Swinson, & Levitt, 1991; Owley, Owley, Leventhal, & Cook, 2002). Further research is needed to clarify their role in successful interventions in anxiety disorders.

ANTICONVULSANTS AND MOOD STABILIZERS

In 1949, the Australian physician John Cade discovered **lithium**, a metallic mineral salt, which may act to stabilize catecholamine receptors, alter sodium ion activity and calcium-mediated intracellular processes by enhancing GABA activity, or delay norepinephrine-sensitive adenylate cyclase (Montezinho et al., 2004). Lithium may block second-messenger systems, thus reducing the responsiveness of neurons to muscarinic, cholinergic, and alpha-adrenergic stimulation. A steady state is usually achieved within 5 to 7 days. Noting its sedating effect, Cade used lithium to treat bipolar mania. In usual daily dose of 900 to 1800 mg/day (blood levels of between 0.6 and 1.2 µg/ml are within therapeutic range), lithium is effective in 70% of bipolar patients (Lepkifker et al., 2004). Side effects, such as hand tremor, diaphoresis, dyspepsia, diarrhea, polyuria, and TSH are common. Excreted primarily by the kidneys, adequate renal function is essential to avoid toxic accumulation. A nonmetabolized salt, lithium toxicity can occur from excessive doses of the drug, decreased fluid or food intake, diuretics, or GI dysfunction, with 33% to 45% of patients discontinuing lithium therapy due to side effects (Muzina & Calabrese, 2005).

The successful use of *anticonvulsants* in the treatment of depression and bipolar disorders has spurred interest in their use for anxiety, either as monotherapy or in combinations of medical regimens (Barry, Lembke, & Bullock, 2004; Ketter, Wang, Nowakowska, & Marsh, 2004). With proven efficacy in treating mood disorders, researchers continue to explore the possible application of anticonvulsants in clinical anxiety, particularly in panic, social phobia, and OCD (Erzegovesi, Cavallini, & Cavedini, 2001; Gelenberg & Pies, 2003). All anticonvulsants can precipitate somulence, vertigo, orthostatic hypotension, nausea, or chronic fatigue. Table 3.3 lists anticonvulsants and mood stabilizers.

TABLE 3.3.
Anticonvulsants and Mood-Stabilizers

Name	Presumed Action	Half-life	Preparations	Usual Adult Daily Dose	Notes
Carbamazepine (*Tegretol*®, *Carbatrol*®, *Equetrol*®)	Unclear; may decrease kindling effect of electrical firings of neurons in the limbic system; may inhibit voltage-gated sodium channels	12–17 hr; longer for sustained release	100, 200, 300 mg tablets & 100 mg/ 5 ml elixir 200, 400 mg XR	400–1600 mg	Structurally similar to imipramine; requires active blood-level monitoring (5–12 μ/ml); initial lab work including CBC with differential and liver enzymes needed; R/O blood dyscrasias and liver disease; can self-metabolize over time
Clonazepam (*Klonopin*®, *Klonopin Wafers*®)	Potentiates 5-HT; binds to GABA-chloride receptor complex facilitating GABA effect	30–40 hr	0.5, 1, 2 mg tablets; 0.125, 0.25, 0.5, 1 mg wafers	1–15 mg	Long-acting benzodiazepine, often used in benzodiazepine withdrawal or agitation; can induce depression in doses over 1.5 mg qd
Gabapentin (*Neurontin*®)	Unclear; may be chemically related to GABA	5–7 hr	100, 300, 400, 600, 800 mg	300–3600 mg	Binds to alpha(2)delta-1 and alpha(2)delta-2 regulatory subunits of gated calcium channels; broad therapeutic range

(*continues*)

73

TABLE 3.3.
(Continued)

Name	Presumed Action	Half-life	Preparations	Usual Adult Daily Dose	Notes
Lamotrigine (*Lamictal*®)	Unclear; may affect sodium channels that affect glutamate and aspartate; may have inhibitory effect on SE receptors	1–5 hr	25, 100, 125, 200 mg	50–500 mg	Blocks use-dependent voltage-gated sodium channels; may also inhibit N- and P/Q-type calcium channels; slow titration needed to avert Steven-Johnson
Lithium carbonate (*Lithobid*®, *Eskalith*®)	Unclear; may stabilize catecholamine receptors; reduces responsiveness of neurons to muscarinic, cholinergic, and alpha-adrenergic stimuli	8–35 hr (sustained release available)	300, 450 mg	400–2400 mg	For bipolar disorder, therapeutic levels achieved 0.6–1.2 mEq/l; periodic blood work is needed to monitor kidney and liver functioning; may delay NE-sensitive adenylate cyclase; regular thyroid panels (TSH)
Levetiracetam (*Keppra*®)	Unclear; may reduce Ca^{2+} current within HVACC	6–8 hr	250, 500, 750 tablets; 100 mg/mL solution	1000–3000 mg	Atypical anticonvulsant

Oxcarbazepine (*Trileptal*®)	May reduce kindling within the brain; may block sodium channels	2–9 hr	150, 300, 600 mg tablets; 300 mg/ml syrup	600–1200 mg	BID dosing; no blood monitoring required
Tiagabine hydrochloride (*Gabitril*®)	Unclear; a selective GABA reuptake inhibitor; a selective inhibitor of the GABA reuptake transporter GAT-1	7–9 hr	2, 4, 12, 16, 20 mg	4–56 mg	BID dosing; recent black box warning of first onset seizure activity
Topiramate (*Topamax*®)	Unknown; may inhibit electrical stimulation; may increase frequency with which GABA activates receptors; inhibits carbonic anhydrase isoenzymes; reduces GABA-A receptor depolarization	21 hr	15, 25, 100, 200 mg	50–400 mg	Blood level monitoring not required; may impair memory and appetite; slow titration needed to avert Steven-Johnson syndrome

(continues)

75

TABLE 3.3.
(Continued)

Name	Presumed Action	Half-life	Preparations	Usual Adult Daily Dose	Notes
Valproic acid (*Depakote®*)	Unclear; may potentiate GABA effects thus reducing electrical and biochemical activities of neurons and corresponding receptors; antikindling effect; histone deacetylase inhibitor; may enhance GABA activity by down regulation of GAT-1 and GAT-3 transporters	5–20 hr	250, 500 mg capsules & 250 mg/5 ml	750–4000 mg	Requires initial lab workup including CBC with differential and liver functions; has therapeutic plasma level (50–100 μ/ml) or 40–120 mg/ml)

Carbamazepine *(Tegretol®)*, a medication that requires careful monitoring to avoid toxicity, may stabilize mood by decreasing the kindling effect of neurons and their activity deep within the limbic system (Okada et al., 2002). Its anticonvulsant effect occurs primarily in the temporal lobe (complex partial) and amygdaloid regions, and it is effective in inhibiting seizures kindled from repeated stimulation therein (Parada & Soares-da-Silva, 2002). Carbamazepine may also block voltage-dependent sodium channels and inhibit high frequency action potentials (Ghelardoni, Tomita, Bell, Rapoport, & Bosetti, 2004). Its chief metabolite is produced in the liver with a half-life of 5 to 8 hours. Blood dyscrasias can develop suddenly. Inducing its own hepatic metabolism, ongoing carbamazepine therapy requires regular CBC and platelet counts and monthly (or PRN if hepatitis symptoms appear) LFTs. It renders reduced efficiency of oral contraceptives and has been remarketed as *Carbatrol®* and *Equetro®*. Its derivative, *oxcarbazepine* *(Trileptal®)*, also presumably reduces kindling actions but prompts a different metabolism. Compared to carbamazepine, hepatic enzyme induction is considerably less with oxcarbazepine.

Gabapentin *(Neurontin®)* has GABA ergic properties through binding to alpha(2) delta-1 and delta-2 subunits of voltage gated calcium channels (Marais, Klugbauer, & Hofmann, 2001). Although only approved for the treatment of epileptic seizures, gabapentin has been used in chronic pain, bipolar disorder, attention deficit, and anxiety, providing mixed and inconsistent results in efficacy (De-Paris et al., 2003). Many clinicians believe that both gabapentin and *levetiracetam* *(Keppra®)* have unclear or ineffectual psychotropic properties (Maneuf et al., 2003).

Lamotrigine *(Lamictal®)* may affect sodium channels that affect glutamate and aspartate, having an inhibitory effect on SE receptors (Hahn, Gyulai, Baldassano, & Lenox, 2004). Its inhibition of sodium channels is increased by depolarization of neurons (Cronin, O'Reilly, Duclohier, & Wallace, 2003).

Tiagabine *(Gabitril®)* is a selective GABA reuptake inhibitor (Borden et al., 1994). A potent selective inhibitor of the principal neural GABA transporter (GAT-1), tiagabine slows the reuptake of synaptically released GABA and prolongs inhibitory postsynaptic potentials.

Topiramate *(Topamax®)* may inhibit electrical stimulation and increase the frequency with which GABA activates receptors, thus enhancing GABA to cause a flux of chloride ions into neurons (Yatham, 2004). It inhibits CA isoenzymes and reduces GABA-A receptor depolarization (Herrero, Del Olmo, Gonzalez-Escalada, & Solis, 2002). It has been used within migraine and weight-loss protocols.

Valproic acid (VPA; Depakote®) is used extensively in the treatment of clinical anxieties, particularly adjunctive to other regimens (Citrome et al., 2004). Similar to carbamazepine, valproic acid produces anticonvulsant, antikindling, and GABA effects by blocking voltage-dependent sodium channels and high-frequency action potentials (Gaillard, Zeffiro, Fazilat, DeCarli, & Theodore, 1996; Loscher, 2002). Its excretion occurs as glucuronide within the urine, feces, and air. Scattered studies suggest that valproic acid may reduce attacks in panic disorder (Leiderman, Balish, Bromfield, & Theodore, 1991). For scattered or mixed symptoms, valproic acid may be the first choice among anticonvulsants due to its low CNS side effects and wide therapeutic window. Mood stabilizing anticonvulsant agents can calm focal areas of increased activity, enhance mood stability, and calm irritability, stabilizing temporal lobe functioning (Okada et al., 2002).

ANTIPSYCHOTICS

The use of *reserpine*, which depletes brain catecholamines by interfering with intraneuronal storage of dopamine and norepinephrine, and *phenothiazines* to "tranquilize" psychiatric patients led to the development of antipsychotic medicines, beginning with *chlorpromazine* and evolving to contemporary second generation "atypical" agents (SGAs). Although the exact mechanisms of action remain unknown, most researchers believe that antipsychotics block DA-2 receptors, although newer compounds may also affect other dopamine receptors and other neurotransmitters (Keefe et al., 2004). They may reduce the level of dopamine in the brain, decrease receptor sensitivity to it, or do both (Reznik et al., 2004). Most have inactive metabolites. These drugs effectively treat the symptoms of schizophrenia, psychoses in depressive and bipolar disorders, and other CNS dysfunctions (Meltzer, Arvanitis, Bauer, & Rein, 2004). Low doses of antipsychotics may quell anxiety (Lindenmayer et al., 2004). FDA-approved indications include the following: (1) eliminating or reducing the intensity of psychotic experiences, albeit delayed 1–2 weeks from the start of treatment; (2) decreasing agitation or acute inability to modulate affect; (3) sedation; (4) preventing relapse of psychotic disorders; or (5) treating mood disorders with accompanying psychotic features (Trichard et al., 1998). In general, typical antipsychotics are more effective in treating the "positive" (e.g., hallucinations) than "negative" (e.g., blunted affect) symptoms of schizophrenia (Tamminga, 2003). Unfortunately, these medications can produce dramatic unwanted effects, such as Parkinsonian like symptoms, dystonias, akathisia, and other extrapyramidal effects (Alexopoulos, Streim, Carpenter, & Docherty, 2004). These side effects are common and almost unavoidable at higher drug dosages, particularly if the medication is taken over extended periods of time (Findling, Aman, Eerdeken, Derivan, & Lyons, 2004). Drug dependency or tolerance does not occur. Instead, antipsychotics' primary disadvantages include troublesome side effect profiles and potential for toxicity (neuromalignant syndrome).

Advances in research technology and biochemistry have developed atypical antipsychotic compounds to effectively target the symptoms of schizophrenia and other psychoses, without the troublesome side effect profiles of older phenothiazines (Bernado et al., 2001; Fountoulakis, Nimatoudis, Iacovides, & Kaprinis, 2004). Although originally contraindicated for transient states, the advent of atypical antipsychotics has increased their use in clinical anxiety (S. H. Kennedy & Lam, 2003; Sharma, 2003). For example, some researchers believe that the augmentation of effective treatments for OCD includes the addition of low-dose antipsychotics, particularly in treatment-resistant cases (Denys, De Geus, Van Megen, & Westenberg, 2004a; Sareen et al., 2004). Although atypical antipsychotics improve upon the problematic anticholinergic effects of older medicines, they are expensive, and cost may preclude use in some patient populations (Correll, Leucht, & Kane, 2004; Loebel, Botts, & Felman, 1998).

Atypical antipsychotics share the common feature of higher affinity for 5-HT2 receptors than for DA-2 receptors, but they vary considerably in clinical and pharmacological properties (Hermann, Mamdani, & Lanctot, 2004; Lieberman, 2004; Markianos, Hatzimanolis, Lykouras, & Christodoulou, 2002).

Table 3.4 outlines predictors of antipsychotic efficacy.

Table 3.5 lists side effects that may occur with antipsychotic treatment.

Aripiprazole (*Abilify*®) modulates dopaminergic activity, functioning as an antagonist at DA-2 receptors in hyperdopaminergic regions and as an agonist at DA-2 receptors in hypodopaminergic circuits (Aihara et al., 2004). Additionally, aripiprazole may also have an antagonistic activity at 5-HT2A receptors, with ancillary effects on alpha-1 adrenergic and histamine receptors.

Clozapine (*Clozaril*®) differs from older phenothiazines in its mechanisms of action and side-effect profile. Exhibiting both serotonergic and dopaminergic (D2) antagonism, clozapine has minimal extrapyramidal side effects, essentially no risk of subsequent tardive dyskinesia, minimal prolactin increase, effectiveness with "negative" schizophrenic symptoms, and empirically based efficacy in treatment-refractory populations (Kapur & Seeman, 2001).

Olanzapine (*Zyprexa*®) can effectively treat manic episodes and is useful as a hypnotic (Bymaster et al., 1997; Weiss, Potenza, McDougle, & Epperson, 1999). Further, olanzapine does not reduce cerebral blood flow (Gonul, Kula, Sofuoglu, Tutus, & Esel, 2003).

Quetiapine (*Seroquel*®) usually does not precipitate the weight gain seen in the use of other antipsychotics (Gunasekara & Spencer, 1998).

TABLE 3.4.
Predictors of Antipsychotic Efficacy

Positive Prognosis	Negative Prognosis
Acute onset with short duration of illness	Long duration with chronic symptoms
Anxiety, tension, mood issues	Blunted affect
Common themes within delusions	Lack of cohesion or relationship among delusions
Later age of onset of symptoms	Early-age onset
Positive premorbid functioning	Negative premorbid history

TABLE 3.5.
Side Effects of Antipsychotics

Akathisia	Intense restlessness and agitation; generally, patients experience great discomfort in the limbs and continually move their arms and legs in an effort to relieve it; mimics the symptoms of anxiety
Anticholinergic effects	Dry mouth, slurred vision, urinary retention, impotence, constipation
Antinorepinephrine effects	Orthosatatic Hypertension (sudden decreases in blood pressure when the patient stands up abruptly)
Dystonia	Involuntary muscle contractions that cause bizarre and uncontrollable movements of the face, neck, tongue, and back (due to reduction of dopamine synaptic activity in the substantia nigra)
Extrapyramidal motor effects	Syndrome that includes severe muscular tremor postural or while resting, muscular rigidity (particularly in flexors), and bradykinesia (disability in initiating or sometimes arresting movement); expressionless face; shuffling gait
Antipsychotic malignant syndrome	Rapidly developing (within hours to 1–2 days) muscular rigidity and cogwheeling, fever, confusion, hypertension, sweating, and tachycardia; hyperthermia (oral temperature of at least 38.0° C in the absence of another known etiology); severe extrapyramidal effects characterized by two or more of the following: lead-pipe muscle rigidity, pronounced cogwheeling, sialorrhea, oculogyric crisis, retrocollis, opisthotonos, trismus, dysphagia, choreiform movements, festinating gait, and flexorextensor posturing, autonomic dysfunction characterized by two or more of the following: hypertension (at least 20-mm rise in diastolic pressure above baseline), tachycardia (at least 30 beats/minute), prominent diaphoresis, and incontinence
Pseudoparkinsonism	Rigidity, resting tremor, flat affect, bradykinesia
Sedation	Chronic sleepiness; hypersomnia; impaired focus, concentration

(continues)

TABLE 3.5.
(Continued)

Tardive dyskinesia	Syndrome that includes progressively worsening twitchlike movements (earlier, of face and tongue, then in arms and shoulders; later, over entire body with face twitching relentlessly and with tongue darting in and out of the mouth) that are virtually continuous during waking hours but cease during sleep, and later symptoms including unsteady gait, rocking back and forth at the hips, and gasping irregularity of breathing. TD usually does not appear until after a patient has been taking antipsychotics for many years.

Risperidone (*Risperdal®*) is generally well-tolerated, does not usually cause the movement disorders (e.g., tardive dyskinesia) seen with long-term use of older antipsychotics, and does not usually cause the mental dulling of phenothiazines (Barnes & McPhillips, 1998; Foster & Goa, 1998; Ngan, Lane, Ruth, & Liddle, 2002). Its utility in augmenting OCD treatments has been well-established (Hollander, Baldini-Rossi, Sood, & Pallanti, 2003; Lane, Lin, Huang, Chang, Hsu, & Chang, 2004).

Ziprasidone (*Geodon®*) has potent agonism of 5-HT1A receptors, antagonism of 5-HT1D receptors, and blocks the reuptake of norepinephrine (Mamo et al., 2004; Wilner, Anziano et al., 2002). In contemporary practice, novel antipsychotics are increasingly used in the treatment of clinical anxiety, either as monotherapy or complementary augmentations of existing regimens (Carson & Kitagawa, 2004; Nemeroff, 2004).

ATYPICAL ANXIOLYTICS

The success of phenothiazines to dissipate acute fears and reverse some schizophrenic symptoms has led researchers to develop "milder" agents that could allay less pathological symptoms without the drawbacks of antipsychotics. The use of *antihistamines* in clinical anxiety began in the 1940s, when histamine antagonists were found in many medications. Their main indications include allergic reactions, sedation, antipsychotic-induced dystonias, agitation and aggression, diffuse anxiety, or poor affect modulation (e.g., angry outbursts). Blockade of histaminic receptors is associated with drowsiness and weight gain. Sedating antihistamines have scattered anxiolytic effects but often produce hypersomulence. Both *diphenhydramine* and *hydroxyzine*, the most commonly used antihistamines in mental health applications, have been used as anxiolytics, but their efficacy

TABLE 3.6.
Antipsychotics (Neuroleptics)

Name	Presumed Half-Life	Preparations	Usual Adult Daily Dose	Notes [therapeutic plasma concentration (ng/mL)]
Aripiprazole (*Abilify*®)	75–94+ hr	5, 10, 15, 20, 30 mg	15–30 mg	Usually effective at 10–20 mg qd
Chlorpromazine (*Thorazine*®)	4–5 hr	10, 25, 50, 100, 200 mg	300–800 mg	First antipsychotic developed; highly sedating aliphatic [100–300]
Clozapine (*Clozaril*®)	11 hr	25, 100 mg	200–900 mg	Low affinity for D2 receptors and displaced by endogenous DA in the striatum; may target glycine and small neutral amino-acid transporters [≥350]
Fluphenazine (*Prolixin*®)	10–20 hr	1, 2.5, 5, 10 mg	1–40 mg	IM constitution available [0.2–3] deconoate
Haloperidol (*Haldol*®)	12–36 hr	0.5, 1, 2, 3, 10, 20 mg	1–100 mg	IM constitution available [5–12] deconoate
Loxapine (*Loxitane*®)	5–15 hr	5, 10, 25, 50 mg	20–250 mg	High DA-4 blockade effect
Mesoridazine (*Serentil*®)	24–48 hr	10, 25, 50, 100 mg	30–400 mg	Piperidine similar in effect to thioridazine
Molindone (*Moban*®)	6.5 hr	5, 10, 25, 50, 75, 100 mg	50–225 mg	Older agent infrequently used in contemporary practice
Olanzapine (*Zyprexa*®)	21–50 hr	2.5, 5, 7.5, 10 mg	51–20 mg	Monitor for hyperglycemia and hypertriglyceridemia; may cause weight gain [9–20]

Drug	Half-life	Available doses	Dose range	Notes
Perphenazine (*Trilafon*®)	10–20 hr	2, 4, 8, 16 mg	12–64 mg	Antagonistic effect at DA-1 and DA-2 receptors
Pimozide (*Orap*®)	55 hr	2 mg	2–10 mg	May have more effect on refractory negative symptoms than other antipsychotics; effective for Tourette's disorder
Quetiapine (*Seroquel*®)	6–7 hr	25, 100, 200, 300 mg	50–900 mg	Mesolimbic selectivity; may increase blood pressure, so careful monitoring is needed; not as likely as other atypicals to cause weight gain; monitor for cataracts
Risperidone (*Risperdal*®, *Risperdal Consta*®)	3–20 hr; Consta longer	0.5, 1, 2, 3, 4 mg	2–8 mg	Atypical antipsychotic less likely to cause TD than other antipsychotics; may block both DA-2 and 5HT2 receptors; monitor prolactin levels
Thioridazine (*Mellaril*®)	10–20 hr	10, 15, 25, 50, 100, 150 200 mg	20–800 mg	High DA-2 blockade with high muscarinic blockage (anticholinergic effect) [200–800]
Thiothixene (*Navane*®)	10–20 hr	1, 2, 5, 10, 20 mg	6–60 mg	Unique thioxanthene [1–5]
Trifluoperazine (*Stelazine*®)	10–20 hr	1, 2, 5, 10 mg	2–40 mg	Piperazine
Ziprasidone (*Geodon*®)	7 hr	20, 40, 60, 80 mg	20–80 mg BID	Initial cardiogram needed as drug can slow electrical conduction in some patients; take with food

has not been well-studied or documented (Sagduyu, 2003). Most clinicians consider them to be "weak" anxiolytics (Llorca et al., 2002). Table 3.7 lists atypical anxiolytics.

Baclofen (*Lioresal®*), a GABA-B receptor agonist, induces sedation and muscle relaxation (Cryan et al., 2003, Cryan et al., 2004).

Verapamil (*Calan®*) is a calcium-channel blocker that may effectively prevent mania. At high doses its effect rivals that of lithium (Klein & Uhde, 1988).

More recently developed, ***azapirones*** act via serotonergic antagonism with additional dopaminergic influence. Further effects may occur on noradrenergic and dopaminergic processes.

Buspirone (*BuSpar®*), a "second generation" anxiolytic, is a serotonin receptor 5-HT1A agonist, and chronic administration down regulates 5-HT2 receptors (Khouzam & Emes, 2002). Effective in GAD, buspirone's delayed onset of effect and need for frequent dosing increases can lead to patient dissatisfaction, noncompliance, or termination (DeMartinis, Rynn, Rickels, & Mandos, 2000). Buspirone does not cause sedation, cognitive impairments, disinhibition, or motor dysfunction, but it may take 2 to 3 weeks or longer to effectively relieve anxiety. Further, although ideal for patients who cannot take antidepressants or tolerate other medications' side effects, buspirone has not been shown to effectively treat non-GAD anxiety syndromes, except perhaps in combination within other regimens, such as adjunctive in OCD or PTSD (Gobert, Rivet, Cistarelli, & Millan, 1997; Laine et al., 2003).

BETA-BLOCKERS AND ALPHA-AGONISTS

Other classes of medications can effectively subdue anxiety (Table 3.8). ***Beta-blockers*** bind to beta-adrenergic receptors and block noradrenalin reception, reducing prominent physiological symptoms of anxiety (e.g., palpitations, tremors) by preventing norepinephrine from activating the SNS.

Propranolol (Inderal) is a nonselective beta-1 (cardiac) and beta-2 (pulmonary) receptor blockade, most useful in the physical symptoms of hyperarousal, such as palpitations, tachycardia, gastrointestinal upset, or hand tremors (Khan, Liberzon, & Abelson, 2004). Although contraindicated in respiratory disease (e.g., asthma), propranolol inhibits carbohydrate and lipid metabolism, risking hypoglycemia in diabetic patients. Beta-blockers are primarily indicated for performance anxiety, with reduction of the autonomic response to anxiety (Blanco, Antia, & Liebowitz, 2002). Only mild improvements are seen in intrapsychic symptoms (Blanco, Schneier, Schmidt, & Blanco-Jerez, 2003).

The alpha-agonists ***clonidine*** (*Catapres®*) and ***guanfacine*** (*Tenex®*) can be useful in reducing overall arousal, acting as a partial agonist at norepinephrine alpha-2 receptors (Valenca et al., 2004). As alpha-2 adrenoreceptor agonists, both agents stimulate presynaptic adrenergic neurons to block norepinephrine release. Their use in attention and conduct disorders, as well as for aggression and agitation, is well established (Piletz, Ordway, Zhu, Duncan, & Halaris, 2000).

TABLE 3.7.
Atypical Anxiolytics

Name	Presumed Action	Half-life	Preparations	Usual Adult Daily Dosage	Notes
Baclofen (*Lioresal*®)	GABA-B agonist; possible DA agonist effect	2–4 hr	10, 20 mg	20–40 mg	GABA-B agonist
Buspirone (*BuSpar*®)	5-HT1A agonist; down regulates 5-HT2 receptors over time	2–11 hr	5, 10, 15 mg	15–90 mg	Effective in GAD; structurally dissimilar to benzodiazepines; no active metabolites
Diphen-hydramine (*Benadryl*®)	Blocks histamine type 1 receptor	1–4 hr	12.5, 25, 50 mg	25–200 mg	OTC antihistamine that can also be used as an anxiolytic or to combat EPS from antipsychotics
Doxylamine (*Unisom*®)	Blocks histamine receptors	1–4 hr	25 mg	25 mg QHS	An antihistamine of the ethanolamine class found in many OTC sleep aids
Hydroxyzine (*Atarax*®, *Vistaril*®)	Histamine receptor antagonist; mild anticholinergic activity	3 hr	10, 25, 50, 100 mg	10–200 mg	Sedating antihistamine
Meprobamate (*Miltown*®)	Uncertain, but perhaps works as muscle relaxant with ancillary reduction in tension anxiety; exerts CNS depressant effects	6–17 hr	200, 400 mg	400–1600 mg	Potentially lethal side effects; infrequently used in contemporary practice

TABLE 3.8.
Beta-Blockers and Alpha-Agonists

Name	Half-life	Preparations	Usual Adult Daily Dosage	Notes
Atenolol (*Tenormin*®)	6–9 hr	50, 100 mg	50–100 mg	Beta-1 action, with smaller risk of bronchospasm in pulmonary conditions than propranolol
Clonidine (*Catapres*®)	12–16 hr	0.1, 0.2, 0.3 mg tablets; transdermal batch	0.1–0.2 mg	Partial agonist at NE alpha-2 receptors; weak agonist effect on NE alpha-1 receptors
Guanfacine (*Tenex*®)	10–12 hr	1, 2 mg	1–3 mg	Used primarily as an antihypertensive; alpha agonist
Metoprolol (*Lopressor*®)	3–4 hr	50, 100 mg	50–100 mg	Cardio-selective, mainly blocks beta-1 receptors
Nadolol (*Corgard*®)	14–24 hr	20, 40, 80, 120, 160 mg	40–80 mg	Very low lipid solubility; low in CNS effects
Pindolol (*Visken*®)	2–30+ hr	5, 10 mg	10–60 mg	Blocks SE autoreceptors and increases SE at postsynaptic sites
Propanolol, propanolol-LA (*Inderal*®)	4–6 hr (10 hr for LA)	10, 20, 40, 60, 80, 90 mg	10–40 mg	Nonselectively blocks beta-1 and beta-2 receptors

BENZODIAZEPINES

To avoid the toxic and potentially lethal effects of chronic meprobamate, barbiturate, or antipsychotic treatment, researchers continued to investigate other agents as anxiolytics. In 1957, Lowell Randall continued to work with chlordiazepoxide, a drug developed in the 1930s but put aside as ineffectual, to link its effect on reducing anxiety. Thereafter, *benzodiazepines* were found to reduce anxiety (Couprie & Lacarelle, 2004; Geller & Seifter, 1960).

Structured by a benzene ring fused to a seven-member diazepine ring, benzodiazepines exert anxiolytic, sedative, anticonvulsant, and muscular relaxation effects. Indications include short-term treatment of restlessness and anxiety, GAD and mild panic symptoms, alcohol withdrawal, seizure disorders, and muscle relaxant (diazepam). The effects of these medications are generally anxiolytic rather than specifically panicogenic, with the possible exceptions of alprazolam and clonazepam in high doses (Curtin & Schulz, 2004; Joel, Ben-Amir, Doljansky, & Flaisher, 2004). Initially, their exact mechanisms of action were unclear, but subsequent cognitive researchers pinpointed benzodiazepine receptors in the brain (Skolnick et al., 1979). Competing with GABA modulin for corresponding receptors, benzodiazepines prevent GABA modulin from acting, thereby enhancing the synaptic action of GABA. These drugs potentiate the effects of GABA by increasing GABA's ability to bind to corresponding receptors, increasing the potency of GABA. Their presumed mechanisms of action are best represented as a three-stage model: (1) chloride channels close, (2) GABA binds to receptors and ion channel opens, and (3) benzodiazepine molecules bind to receptors and enhance the opening of chloride ion channels (Atack, 2003). Subsequent hyperpolarization requires a greater depolarization to trigger an action potential. Benzodiazepines augment the anti anxiety action of the GABA-stimulated chloride system, attaching to (and thus activating) key receptors whilset blocking hyperarousal (Andreasen, Paradiso, & O'Leary, 1998). Thus, benzodiazepines seem to "work" by enhancing the effect of GABA, allosterically regulating GABA-A receptors within the limbic system, including the amygdala and on SE and NE neurons within the brainstem (Siniscalchi et al., 2003). Acute administration is associated with decreased noradrenalin and serotonin turnover. Their major pathways of metabolism are hepatic microsomal oxidation and demthylation (Bailey & Toth, 2004). Table 3.9 lists benzodiazepines.

Many benzodiazepines are available by prescription, each providing strengths and weaknesses in treatment efficacy, pharmacokinetics, and biochemical properties (Klein, 2002). Benzodiazepines can be grouped into four chemical subtypes: *2-keto*, *3-hydroxy*, *triazolo*, and *7-nitro* compounds.

2-keto compounds are prodrugs that can be inactive themselves (e.g., diazepam) but have active metabolites (e.g., desmethyldiazepam). All have very long half-lives with metabolites reaching 30–200 hours.

3-hydroxy compounds (e.g., lorazepam) are active compounds with shorter half-lives; these drugs generate no active metabolites.

TABLE 3.9.
Benzodiazepines

Name	Half-life	Preparations	Usual Adult Daily Dose	Onset/Notes
Alprazolam (*Xanax*®, *Xanax XR*®, *Niravam*®)	6–20 hr; longer for sustained-release	0.25, 0.5, 1.0, 2.0 mg tablets; 0.5, 1.0, 2.0, 3.0 XR; *Niravam*® orally disintegrating tablets 0.25, 0.5, 1.0, 2.0 mg	0.5–4 mg	Intermediate; high potential for abuse/dependence
Chlordiazepoxide (*Librium*®)	15–60 hr	5, 10, 25 mg	15–60 mg	Intermediate
Clonazepam (*Klonopin*®, *Klonopin Wafers*®)	30–40 hr	0.5, 1, 2 mg	1–15 mg	Intermediate; long-acting effect
Clorazepate (*Tranxene*®)	50–100 hr	3.75, 7.5, 11.25, 15, 22.5 mg	15–45 mg	Rapid; can be used in the management of alcohol withdrawal
Diazepam (*Valium*®)	30–60 hr	2, 5, 10 mgs	5–40 mg	Rapid; TID or QID dosing
Estazolam (*ProSom*®)	10–24 hrs	1, 2 mg	1–2 (HS) mg	Intermediate
Flurazepam (*Dalmane*®)	50+ hrs	15, 30 mg	15–30 (HS) mg	Rapid

Drug (Brand)	Half-life	Tablet strengths	Dose range	Onset / Notes
Halazepam (*Paxipam*®)	50–100 hr	20, 40 mg	60–160 mg	Slow-intermediate onset
Lorazepam (*Ativan*®)	16–20 hr	0.5, 1, 2 mg; sublingual tablets: 0.5, 1, 2 mg; injection	0.5–6 mg	Intermediate; no active metabolites; metabolism not P450 dependent
Oxazepam (*Serax*®)	5–10 hr	10, 15, 30 mg	30–120 mg	Slow
Prazepam (*Centrax*®)	60–70 hr	5, 10, 20 mg	20–60 mg	Slowest speed of onset
Quazepam (*Doral*®)	40+ hr	7.5, 15 mg	7.5–15 (HS) mg	Rapid
Temazepam (*Restoril*®)	8–18 hr	15, 30 mg	15–30 (HS) mg	Intermediate
Triazolam (*Halcion*®)	2–3 hr	0.125, 0.25 mg	0.125–0.25 (HS) mg	Intermediate

Triazolo compounds (e.g., alprazolam) are active, with active metabolites, and have relatively short half-lives.

7-nitro compounds (e.g., clonazepam) are active, without active metabolites, and have long half-lives. These compounds are metabolized by nitroreduction and oxidation.

Chief differentiations rest in absorption, half-life, and side effects; the choice of one medication relative to another typically depends on safety, patient compliance, severity of symptoms, and risk of interactions and toxicity. Alprazolam, clonazepam, lorazepam, and diazepam are the most frequently prescribed. The clinical, pharmacodynamic traits of repeated dosing of both long and short half-life elimination benzodiazepines can provide direction in the determination of which benzodiazepine is best suited for or indicated for specific applications (Wolkowitz & Pickar, 1991). Generally well absorbed from the GI tract, a benzodiazepine's onset of action is determined by rate of absorption and lipid solubility (Verster & Volkerts, 2004). High-potency benzodiazepines reduce anxiety and panic quickly, but these drugs are addictive and can lead to tolerance and dependence in high-risk patients with a history of substance abuse, personality disorders, or addictive patterns (Posternak & Mueller, 2001). Long half-life benzodiazepines offer the advantages of less frequent dosing, reduced interdose rebounding of symptoms, and potentially less severe withdrawal effects but with potential accumulation or next-day sedation following their use. Although requiring more frequent dosing, the use of short half-life benzodiazepines avoids systematic accumulation and sedation yet leads to greater rebound and interdose symptomatology. For example, *clonazepam (Klonopin®)* is a long-acting benzodiazepine with diverse applications, including seizure disorders, GAD, OCD, panic, and benzodiazepine withdrawal (Arvat, Giordano, Grottoli, & Ghigo, 2002). In addition to serotonin potentiation, clonazepam binds to benzodiazepine-GABA-chloride receptors, facilitating the effect of GABA on CNS hyperarousal (Bagdy, Graf, Anheuer, Modos, & Kantor, 2001; Rosenbaum, 2004).

Benzodiazepines are effective treatments for clinical anxiety, with rapid onset of relief and good tolerability, in 60% to 70% of patients (Davidson, 2004b; Gorman, 2001). Although highly effective and well-tolerated, benzodiazepines pose unique difficulties with dependence, rebound symptoms, memory impairments, or discontinuation syndrome (Rickels, 2004). Tolerance and physiologic or psychological dependence can occur with benzodiazepines, even at low doses, when used over time (Meiran, Reus, Webster, Shafton, & Wolkowitz, 2004; Wichniak, Brunner, Ising, Pedrosa-Gil, Holsboer, & Friess, 2004). Adverse effects generally parallel relative half-lives. Short half-life agents are generally more associated with rebound and dependence. Long-acting benzodiazepines are useful for chronic conditions where a continuous effect is desired. Somnolence and dependence are the most common side effects (Stahl, 2002). Rebound anxiety, insomnia, and tremors are common. Although still widely used in clinical practice and effective in reducing diffuse symptoms, benzodiazepines pose the risks of habituation and dependence, relegating their application to second-line status. Overall, the effects of benzodiazepines vary considerably, being influenced by patient age, liver disease, neurologic disorders, and the like, as well as concurrent use of other biochemical substances that change the distribution and elimination of benzodiazepines (Davidson, 2004b).

Some benzodiazepines are used primarily to induce sleep for the short-term treatment of insomnia (Dundar et al., 2004). Benzodiazepine hypnotics generally extend the total time the patient stays asleep, but their reduction of stages three/four sleep reduces restfulness (Morin, Belanger, & Bernier, 2004). Before using hypnotics, a comprehensive evaluation of past sleep patterns is recommended: historical trends, medical and psychiatric history, medication use, family history, screening for substance abuse, and so on. (Ringdahl, Pereira, & Delzell, 2004). Their mechanisms of action are diverse, but most affect GABA receptors or biochemical conduction (Doghramji, 2000).

NOVEL HYPNOTICS

Recently, several newer hypnotics have become available for clinical use, most seeking to improve upon the side-effect profiles of already-available medicines (Table 3.10).

Zolpidem (*Ambien®*), an imidazopyridine, acts on GABA-benzodiazepine receptors (binds selectively to GABA-A$_1$ receptors in basolateral and central amygdaloid nuclei) but lacks the anxiolytic, muscle-relaxant, and anticonvulsant properties of traditional benzodiazepines (Kang-Park, Wilson, & Moore, 2004; Lee, 2004). Its major side effects include nausea, vomiting, diarrhea, headache, or dizziness.

In 1999, **zaleplon** (*Sonata®*) was released as an extremely short-acting (1–2 hr) sleep agent that targets benzodiazepine receptors (Sanger, 2004). Both zopidem and zaleplon have short half-lives and minimal side effects, and their short-term use to regulate sleep cycles can be helpful in some anxiety probands.

Eszopiclone (*Lunesta®*) is a nonbenzodiazepine agent that also targets GABA receptors and, alllosterically, benzodiazepine receptors.

Ramelteon (*Rozerem®*) is unique in its mechanism of action, being the first melatonin receptor agonist.

ANTIDEPRESSANTS

Antidepressants have been found useful in the treatment of anxiety. Drugs in this class of medications include MAOIs, cyclic antidepressants, SSRIs, and atypical antidepressants. Table 3.11 lists the side effects of MAOIs, SSRIs, and trycyclics (a type of cyclic antidepressant).

TABLE 3.10.
Nonbenzodiazepine Hypnotics

Name	Half-life	Preparations	Usual Adult Daily Dose	Onset/Notes
Eszopiclone (*Lunesta*®)	6 hr	1, 2, 3 mg	2–3 mg QHS	Rapidly absorbed hypnotic unrelated to benzodiazepines
Ramelteon (*Rozerem*®)	1–2.6 hr	8 mg tablets	8 mg, po QHS	Melatonin receptor agonist; take 30 minutes prior to desired sleep onset
Zaleplon (*Sonata*®)	1 hr	5, 10 mg	5–20 mg	Extremely short-acting hypnotic; targets GABA receptors
Zolpidem (*Ambien*®, *Ambien* CR®)	1.6 hr; longer for CR	5, 10 mg	5–10 mg QHS	Targets benzodiazepine receptors

Monoamineoxidase Inhibitors

Pharmacotherapy of depression began in 1953 when *iproniazid* was used as a "psychic energizer." Unfortunately, many users of this medication developed significant jaundice, and the medication was eventually taken off the market. In the 1950s, researchers were using **MAO inhibitors** to elevate the mood of patients with tuberculosis (Fabre & Hamon, 2003). By blocking the enzyme MAO, monoamine oxidase inhibitors (MAOIs) lower MAO activity and increase the levels of norepinephrine, epinephrine, and serotonin in the brain (Gerardy & Dresse, 1998; Koch et al., 2004; Youdim & Weinstock, 2004). **Hydrazine MAOI's**, such as **phenelzine** and **isocarboxazid**, irreversibly inhibit MAO and have actions that persist until enzyme resynthesis occurs, usually for an additional 1 to 3 weeks following cessation of drug treatment. **Nonhydrazine MAOI's**, such as **tranylcypromine**, more reversibly inhibit MAO and have faster onset therapeutics than other antidepressants. MAOIs have a lower anticholinergic effect than tricyclics. MAOIs are also used in treatment-resistant anxiety, particularly panic and social phobia (Fahlen, Nilsson, Borg, Humble, & Pauli, 1995; Schneider,

TABLE 3.11.
Antidepressant Side-Effects

Class	Potential Side-Effects
MAOIs	MAO inhibition prevents normal metabolism of many foods, which can result in toxic chemicals accumulating in the blood (e.g., aged cheese, beer, wine, chocolate, and liver can lead to excesses of tyramine, which can cause sudden increases in blood pressure and strokes). Also, nose drops and cold remedies can lead to concentrations in the blood that can induce dangerous increases in blood pressure.
SSRIs	Gastrointestinal effects (nausea, vomiting, diarrhea), sexual dysfunction, dermatological effects (rash, pruritus), insomnia or hypersomnia, serotonin syndrome (change in mental status, restlessness, myoclonus, hyperreflexia, shivering, and tremor)
Trycyclics	Anticholinergic side effects (antidepressants and antipsychotics block acetylcholine receptors at junctions between nerve fibers and internal organs—e.g., at salivary glands resulting in "dry mouth" and at iris resulting in "blurred vision"), cardiovascular side effects (especially arrhythmia), sometimes tinnitus

et al., 1998). Although well-established in efficacy, MAOIs are now considered tertiary agents in the treatment of mood and anxiety disorders, primarily due to side effects, potential lethality, and dietary restrictions (Brunello et al., 2000; Liebowitz et al., 1999; Riederer, Lahenmayer, & Laux, 2004). The main drawback of MAOIs is their toxicity if combined with foods that contain tyramine (aged cheese, aged and cured meats, spoiled meat, poultry or fish, broad bean pods, marmite concentrated yeast extract, sauerkraut, soy sauce, soy bean condiments, and tap beer), and thus patients must be on specific diets that exclude such products. Also, some nose drops and cold remedies can lead to concentrations in the blood that can induce dangerous increases in blood pressure. MAOIs inhibit hepatic metabolism of medications, such as barbiturates and atropine, and can lead to serious medical complications (Bonnet, 2003). Due to the complexity of issues involved in monitoring dosing, side effects, and dietary restrictions, the use of MAOIs should be avoided in all but the most reliable patients for whom alternative approaches have failed to sufficiently remit symptoms (Fulton & Benefield, 1996; Heimberg et al., 1998). Table 3.12 lists MAOIs.

TABLE 3.12.
MAOI Antidepressants

Name	Presumed Half-Life	Preparations	Usual Adult Daily Dose	Notes
Isocarboxazid (*Marplan*®)	1.5–3 hr	10 mg tablets	10–50 mg	Irreversibly inhibits MAO persisting until enzyme resynthesis
Moclobemide (*Manerix*®)	1–3 hr	150, 300 mg tablets	300–450 mg	Not available in USA
Phenelzine (*Nardil*®)	1.5 hr	15 mg tablets	45–60 mg	Useful in depression with panic attacks, social phobia
Selegiline (*Eldepryl*®, *Emsam Transdermal Patch*®)	18–24 hr	5 mg tablets; 6, 9, 12 mg patch per 24-hr day	5–10 mg; 1 patch applied qd	Inhibits MAO-B with weak effects on MAO-A
Tranylcypromine (*Parnate*®)	2–3 hr	10 mg tablets	20–40 mg	Associated with weight loss; can have stimulating effect

Cyclic Antidepressants

In 1957, researching *imipramine* (Tofranil®) as a potential treatment for schizophrenia, Klein found that *tricyclic*, so named for its three-carbon ring structure, improved mood (Feighner, 1999). Further study showed imipramine to be an effective antidepressant (Klein & Fink, 1962), and subsequent medications, chemical derivatives (isotopes), were developed (Ables & Baughman, 2003). Nonselective cyclic antidepressants include *tricyclics* (e.g., amitriptyline), *dibenzoxazepines* (e.g., amoxapine), *tetracyclics* (e.g., maprotiline), and *triazolopyridines* (e.g., trazodone). Heterocyclic drugs, such as maprotiline, amoxapine, trazodone, and clomipramine, are often referred to as "second-generation tricyclics" and have been developed subsequent to TCAs with differing side effect profiles.

Tricyclics block reuptake (at presynaptic terminal axon vesicles) of norepinephrine and serotonin or increase sensitivity of postsynaptic receptors for both neurotransmitters (Bourin, David, Jolliet, & Gardier, 2002; Khawaja, Xu, Liang, & Barrett, 2004). Chronic tricyclic treatment down regulates cortical alpha-1 and alpha-2 adrenoreceptors in the brain (Subhash, Nagaraja, Sharada, & Vinod, 2003). Response efficacy may be influenced by genetic variables encoding drug-metabolizing enzymes, receptor sites, transporters and second messenger processes, or gene variants in serotonin transporters (Mancama & Kerwin, 2003). Chronic antidepressant treatment via tricyclics or heterocyclics increases cyclic adenosine monophosphate response element binding protein in the amygdala—mediating physiologic responses to stress, fear, and anxiety (Wallace et al., 2004). Tricyclics and heterocyclics increase the levels of norepinephrine and serotonin in brain neural transmission or block acetylcholine receptors (Joyce, Mulder, McKenzie, Luty, & Cloninger, 2004; Mukherjee, Knisely, & Jacobson, 2004). Serotonergic antidepressants mediate transmitter systems and receptor effects expressed throughout frontal-subcortical neural circuits. Examples of cyclics used in the treatment of clinical anxiety include amitriptyline, clomipramine, imipramine, and trazodone.

Amitriptyline (*Elavil®*) inhibits the reuptake of serotonin and norepinephrine, acts as an antagonist of muscarinic acetylcholine receptors, and also has antagonistic activity at histamine H-1 and H-2 receptors (Poltyrev & Weinstock, 2004; Stanton, Bolden-Watson, Cusack, & Richelson, 1993).

Clomipramine (*Anafranil®*), used in the treatment of OCD, is a tertiary amine tricyclic with potent anticholinergic and alpha-blocking actions, blocking both 5-HT2B and 5-HT2C receptors and facilitating the release of adrenaline (Sugimoto, Inoue, & Yamada, 2003). It may also lower CRH mRNA expression within the paraventricular hypothalamus (Cordner, Herwood, Helmreich, & Parfitt, 2004).

Imipramine (*Tofranil®*) is useful in reducing panic, but its side-effect profile makes it intolerable for some patients. Nevertheless, its efficacy as an antidepressant, antipanicogen, and hypnotic is well-documented (Zahorodna, Tokarski, & Hess, 2006).

Trazodone (*Desyrel®*) can be used acutely in low doses to reduce anxiety without the cognitive dulling that can occur with other psychotropics. Peak plasma levels occur more quickly with tertiary tricyclics (e.g., amitriptyline within one to three hours) than others. Highly lipophilic, cyclic antidepressants are highly bound to plasma proteins and metabolized primarily by the liver (Guaiana, Barbui, & Hotopf, 2003).

Table 3.13 lists cyclic antidepressants. Pharmacologic side-effect profiles for cyclic agents are linked to unique affinities as well as effects on neurotransmitters and corresponding receptors. Although differing in mechanisms of action and side-effect profiles, all affect the neurotransmission of monoamines in the brain. All cyclics have significant side effects (block acetylcholine receptors at junctions between nerve fibers and internal organs, causing dry mouth or blurred vision).

TABLE 3.13.
Lists Cyclic Antidepressants

Name	Presumed Half-Life	Preparations	Usual Adult Daily Dose	Notes
Amitriptyline (*Elavil*®)	10–22 hr	10, 25, 50, 75, 100, 150 mg	50–300 mg	Inhibits the reuptake of both SE and NE; has antagonistic effect on H1, H2, 5HT2A, and NE alpha-one receptors
Amoxapine (*Asendin*®)	8–30 hr	25, 50, 100, 150 mg	50–300 mg	Large therapeutic dose range
Clomipramine (*Anafranil*®)	20–50 hr	25, 50, 75 mg	150–250 mg	Indicated for the treatment of OCD
Desipramine (*Norpramin*®)	12–24 hr	10, 25, 50, 75, 100, 150 mg	50–300 mg	Inhibits NE transporter; antagonist activity at muscarinic ACh receptors
Doxepin (*Sinequan*®)	8–24 hr	10, 15, 25, 50, 75, 100, 150 mg	25–300 mg	Also used for various dermatological conditions
Imipramine (*Tofranil*®, *Tofranil-PM*®)	5–25 hr; longer for sustained-release preparation	10, 25, 50, 75, 100, 125, 150 mg	75–300 mg	Often useful in enuresis treatment; potentially blocks panic attacks
Maprotiline (*Ludiomil*®)	21–25 hr	25, 50, 75 mg	25–200 mg	Broad therapeutic plasma level (200–950 mol/L)
Nortriptyline (*Pamelor*®)	18–44 hr	10, 25, 50, 75 mg	75–150 mg	Less sedating than other TCAs; less likely to precipitate orthostatic hypotension
Protriptyline (*Vivactil*®)	50–200 hr	5, 10 mg	10–60 mg	Less sedating than many other cyclics, but requires TID or QID dosing
Trazodone (*Desyrel*®)	10–12 hr	50, 100, 150 mg	150–600 mg	Peak concentration reached in 1/2–2 hr; sedating; hypnotic
Trimipramine (*Surmontil*®)	7–40 hr	25, 50, 100 mg	50–300 mg	BID dosing; may cause fewer NE reactions

Substances that block the action of the autonomic nervous system can lead to orthostatic hypotension (drop in blood pressure upon standing), palpitations, intracardiac conduction slowing, increased sweating, increased blood pressure, or tremor. Table 3.14 lists the specific side effects of cyclic antidepressants. Antidepressants typically require 2 to 4 weeks on a therapeutic dose before symptom relief occurs, with equal efficacy across classes for mood disorders when therapeutic doses and adequate time for effect are achieved (Mulder, Watkins, Joyce, & Luty, 2003; Thase, 2003). Between 65% and 75% of depressed patients treated via cyclic drugs report significant improvement (Kerr, McGuffie, & Wilkie, 2001). Unfortunately, cyclics have a narrow therapeutic index (small difference between therapeutic and lethal doses) and can be lethal in overdose. Well-studied plasma blood levels are available for imipramine, nortriptyline, desipramine, and amitriptyline, although plasma levels may not precisely correspond with therapeutics (Todorov, 2004).

Selective Serotonin Reuptake Inhibitors

The development of *fluoxetine* by Lilly in the mid-1970s and its FDA approval in the 1980s brought about a revolutionary advance in mental disorder treatments by creating a novel approach to controlling the symptoms of depression, anxiety, and other medical conditions. Linking serotonin with changes in emotion and mood, this new class of drugs presumably prevents the reuptake of serotonin within the synaptic cleft (Bozkurt et al., 2004). When a neuron releases serotonin, a pumplike reuptake mechanism recaptures some of the neurotrans-

TABLE 3.14.
Side Effects of Cyclic Antidepressants

Classification	Associated Side Effects
Allergic	Skin rashes (particularly with maprotiline)
Anticholinergic	Dry mouth and nasal passages, constipation, urinary hesitance, esophageal reflux
Autonomic	Orthostatic hypotension (drop in blood pressure upon standing), palpitations, intracardiac conduction slowing, increased sweating, increased blood pressure, tremor
Central nervous system	Stimulation, sedation, delirium, myoclonic twitches (generally at high doses), nausea, speech blockage, seizures (particularly with high doses of maprotiline), and extrapyramidal symptoms (particularly with amoxapine)
Other	Weight gain, impotence, decreased libido

mitters before they are received by the receptor neuron. ***Selective serotonin reuptake inhibitors*** **(SSRIs)** block this reuptake process and enable more serotonin to reach, fire, and affect the postsynaptic receptor neuron. Serotonergic antidepressants, serotonin 1A agonists, target the basolateral nucleus of the amygdala and mediate its involvement in anxiety (Smith & Lakoski, 1998). SSRIs act through the serotonin 1A receptor to reduce anxiety, increasing serotonergic neurotransmission, decreasing "conditioned freezing," and enhancing serotonin's effect within the medial prefrontal cortex (Suhara et al., 2003). Additional effects occur as desensitization of serotonergic autoreceptors takes place in key brain regions, particularly within the raphe nuclei, locus coeruleus, and neural circuits within the amygdala (Stein, Westenberg, & Liebowitz, 2002). Additional actions may include down regulation of specific norepinephrine receptors or disruption of second-messenger systems (Barros et al., 2003; Fujishiro, Imanishi, Onozawa, & Tsushima, 2002). As a class, SSRIs enhance 5HT release in the orbitofrontal cortex, but this increased release occurs only after prolonged drug therapy (Blier & de Montigny, 1998). The delayed onset of symptom relief may represent the time necessary for desensitization of 5HT terminals in the orbitofrontal cortex, suggesting that SSRIs' therapeutics with OCD differ from traditional serotonergic blockade. All SSRIs are oxidized by the CYP enzyme system (Brosen, 2004). They are better tolerated than older cyclic antidepressants, have generally benign side-effect profiles (nausea, headache, tremor), and have a reduced risk of lethality in overdose (Van Ameringen, Lane, & Walker, 2001). Gene variants within the serotonin transporter and cytochrome P450 metabolizing enzyme may influence outcomes (Belzung, 2001). Brain metabolisms to SSRIs are disorder-specific and vary according to the degree of symptomatic improvement (Vaswani, Linda, & Ramesh, 2003).

As a group, SSRI compounds are more alike than dissimilar, with differences based on kinetics, FDA-approved indications, or slightly different side effects (Bata-Garcia, Heredia-Lopez, Alvarez-Cervera, Arankowsky-Sandoval, & Gongora-Alfaro, 2002; Stein, Van Heerden, et al., 2002). Table 3.15 lists SSRIs.

Citalopram (*Celexa*®), and its s-enantiomer ***escitalopram*** (*Lexapro*®), are the newest serotonergic agents and have similar side-effect profiles as other SSRIs (Owens & Rosenbaum, 2002; Ravna, Stylte, & Dahl, 2003; Shlik, Maron, Tru, Aluoja, & Vasar, 2004). Citalopram deactivates activity in the left medial temporal cortex (Bantick et al., 2004; Seedat et al., 2004).

Fluoxetine (*Prozac*®) has a slightly higher energizing effect, with associated mild forms of agitation, and a slightly lower somnolence rate (Joliat et al., 2004; Taylor, Farr, Klinga, & Weiss, 2004). Its regular form has a longer half-life than other SSRIs and is the only agent that comes in a once-weekly preparation (Rossi, Barraco, & Donda, 2004).

Fluvoxamine (*Luvox*®), an agent used extensively in OCD, has a slightly higher rate of nausea and insomnia than other SSRIs (Yamauchi, Tatebayashi, Nagase, Kojima, & Imanishi, 2004).

TABLE 3.15.
Selective Serotonin Reuptake Inhibitors (SSRIs)

Name	Presumed Half-life	Preparations	Usual Adult Daily Dose	Notes
Citalopram (*Celexa*®)	35 hr	10, 20 mg tablets	20–60 mg	May have higher lethality in overdose than other SSRIs
Escitalopram (*Lexapro*®)	24 hr	5, 10, 20 mg tablets	10–20 mg	S-enantiomer of citalopram
Fluoxetine (*Prozac*®, *Prozac Weekly*®, *Sarafem*®)	48–72 hr; longer for weekly preparation	10, 20, 40 mg tablets; 90 mg weekly capsule	10–80 mg	Relatively nonselective SE reuptake inhibitor; may have weak antagonism of 5-HT2C receptors; potent inhibitor of II D6 enzyme
Fluvoxamine (*Luvox*®)	15 hr	25, 50, 100 mg tablets	50–300 mg	May have agonistic effect on sigma-1 receptors; may cause nausea
Paroxetine (*Paxil*®, *Paxil CR*®)	21 hr; longer for CR	10, 20, 30, 40 mg tablets	10–60 mg	At high doses, inhibits NE transporter; NO synthase inhibitor; anticholinergic effects
Sertraline (*Zoloft*®)	26 hr	25, 50, 100 mg tablets	50–200 mg	SSRI that also binds to and inhibits DA transporter; may have fewer drug-drug interactions than other SSRIs; increased (up to 25%) absorption on a full stomach

Paroxetine (*Paxil®*) has a slightly higher incidence of somnolence, anxiolytic (and potential anticholinergic) effect, and lower incidence of GI upset (Bang & Keating, 2004; Hollander, Allen, et al., 2003; Nemeroff & Owens, 2003). Its sustained-release preparation is frequently used in the treatment of social phobia (Lepola, Bergtholdt, St. Lambert, Davy, & Ruggiero, 2004; Wagner, 2003).

Sertraline (*Zoloft®*) seems to be better tolerated with minimal side effects and a low incidence of drug-drug interactions. With a linear pharmacokinetic profile, sertraline has a weak effect on the cytochrome P450 system.

Since initial development, the SSRIs have become among the most prescribed medications in the world, having applications in neurology, psychiatry, endocrinology, gynecology, urology, and a host of other medical specialties (Bouwer & Stein, 1998; Brady, Pearlstein, & Asnis, 2000). In addition to treating depressive and anxiety conditions, SSRIs have been used "off-label" in the treatment of aggression, impulsivity, paraphilia, substance cessation, chronic fatigue syndrome, developmental delays, pain management, cataplexy, premature ejaculation, and enuresis (Black, Shea, Dursun, & Kutcher, 2000; Dulawa, Holick, Gundersen, & Hen, 2004). SSRIs have essentially *taken over* the anxiolytic market—becoming a first-line medical intervention—effective in 50% to 75% of patients with adequate dose and duration (Pigott & Seay, 1999). About 75% of patients respond to initial low dosings when a steady state is reached (4 or more weeks; Birmaher et al., 2003). Possible SSRI side effects include gastrointestinal effects (nausea, vomiting, diarrhea), sexual dysfunction, dermatological effects (rash, pruritus), insomnia or hypersomnia, and serotonin syndrome (change in mental status, restlessness, myoclonus, hyperreflexia, shivering, and tremor; J. H. Meyer et al., 2004). Many compounds can help mediate the sexual side effects of SSRIs: serotonin antagonists (e.g., cyproheptadine, granisetron), alpha-2 antagonists (e.g., yohimbine, trazodone), cholinergic agonists (e.g., bethanechol), autoreceptor agonists (e.g., buspirone, pindolol), CNS stimulants (e.g., dextroamphetamine, ephedrine), and even some natural herbs, such as ginkgo biloba and L-arginine (Waldinger, Zwinderman, & Olivier, 2001). The major drawback of SSRIs is expense, ranging in cost from approximately $2 to $6 per day for treatment (Aparasu, Mort, & Brandt, 2003). However, their total cost may be significantly less than the total costs of other depression treatments with multiple side-effect profiles.

Atypical Antidepressants

In addition to MAOI's, cyclics, and SSRIs, newer medications are being developed that have unique (often combinatory) mechanisms of action (Emslie et al., 1997). The noradrenalin neurotransmitter has been linked with numerous psychiatric disorders, including anxiety (Hirschfeld & Vornik, 2004). Novel antidepressants, particularly "mixed" effects compounds that work with combinations of neurotransmitters, continue to evolve secondary to known theories of how the brain functions, neurochemistry, and impact of drugs on neural functioning (Lydiard, 2003; Makino, Baker, Smith, & Gold, 2000). For example, newer antidepressants have increased (albeit varying) selectivity for the noradrenergic system. Table 3.16 lists these antidepressants.

Atomoxetine (*Strattera*®) is a norepinephrine reuptake inhibitor that increases neurotransmitter activity within the prefrontal cortex (Bymaster et al., 2002). It may also inhibit the presynaptic norepinephrine transporter.

Bupropion (*Wellbutrin*®) is an atypical antidepressant that apparently blocks dopamine (DA) reuptake into presynaptic neurons and possibly affects norepinephrine systems (Meyer, Goudling, Wilson, Hussey, Christensen, & Houle, 2002). Bupropion suppresses NE neuron firing by activating alpha-2 adenoceptors and increases serotonin through indirect effect on noradrenergic neurons (Redolat, Gomez, Vicens, & Carrascot, 2004). Its low incidence of side effects makes it suitable for atypical depression (Miller, Sumithran, & Dwoskin, 2002; Redolat et al., 2004). Bupropion has been shown to be effective in several anxiety conditions, including OCD, panic, and social phobia (Simon et al., 2003).

Duloxetine (*Cymbalta*®) is a potent serotonin and norepinephrine reuptake inhibitor that also has weak inhibitory effects on dopaminergic reuptake (Bymaster et al., 2003; Dunner, Goldstein, Mallinckrodt, Lu, & Detke, 2003; Goldstein et al., 2004; Skinner et al., 2004).

Mirtazapine (*Remeron*®), a unique piperazinoazepine, blocks presynaptic alpha-2 auto and hetero adrenoceptors, increasing norepinephrine and serotonergic transmission (Fabricio, Tringali, Pozzoli, & Navarra, 2004). In addition to having an antagonistic effect on 5-HT2A, 5-HT2C, and 5-HT3 receptors, mirtazapine may also antagonize NE alpha-2 and histamine H1 receptors (Falkai, 1999). Peak plasma levels occur within 2 hours, and the agent is metabolized by CYP1A2, 2D6, and 3A4 enzymes (Rogoz, Wrobel, Dlaboga, Maj, & Dziedzicka-Wasylewska, 2002).

Nefazodone (*Serzone*®), a phenylpiperazine, blocks serotonin reuptake, like the SSRIs, but without the same sexual dysfunction side effects (Taylor et al., 1995). It may also block the serotonin receptor that tends to cause increased anxiety and sleeplessness (Eloubeidi, Gaede, & Swaim, 2000). Current theory presumes that nefazodone acts as both a presynaptic serotonin reuptake inhibitor and a postsynaptic 5-hydroxytryptamine 2A receptor antagonist (Eloubeidi, Gaede, & Swaim, 2000).

Reboxetine (*Vestra*®) is a selective norepinephrine reuptake inhibitor that may be particularly effective in depressed patients with atomization and anhedonia, as well as possibly for improving deficits in attention and concentration associated with depression.

Venlafaxine (*Effexor*®) presumably blocks reuptake of both serotonin and norepinephrine, with possible weak inhibition of dopamine reuptake (Altamura, Piolo, Vitto, & Mannu, 1999; Rickels, Pollack, Sheehan, & Haskins, 2000). With continued use, venlafaxine may effect down regulation of beta-receptors (Davies,

TABLE 3.16.
Atypical Antidepressants

Name	Presumed Action	Half-life	Preparations	Usual Adult Daily Dose	Notes
Atomoxetine (*Strattera*®)	NE reuptake inhibitor	5 hr	10, 18, 25, 40, 60 mg	40–60 mg	Indicated for attention disorders
Bupropion, Bupropion SR (*Wellbutrin*®, *Wellbutrin SR*®, *Wellbutrin XL*®, *Zyban*®)	Dopamine agonist; possible NE inhibitor	11–21 hr; longer for sustained-release preparations	75, 100, 150 mg; SR 100: 150 mg; XL: 150, 300 mg	200–450 mg	Stimulating antidepressant; BID dosing for SR; QD dosing for XL; low mania induction in bipolars
Duloxetine (*Cymbalta*®)	SE and NE reuptake inhibitor; weak DA reuptake inhibition	12 hrs	20, 30, 60 mg	60 mg	Effective in treating urinary stress incontinence

Drug	Mechanism	Half-life	Tablet strengths	Dose range	Notes
Mirtazapine (*Remeron*®, *Remeron Soltabs*®)	Blocks presynaptic alpha-2 auto and hetero adrenoceptors, increasing NE and SE transmission; blocks 5-HT2 and 5-HT3 receptors minimizing serotonergic side effects	20–40 hr	15, 30 mg tablets	15–45 mg	Antagonistic effect on 5HT2A, 5HT2C, 5HT3, NE alpha-2, and H1 receptors; directly blocks 5HT2 and 5HT3 receptors
Nefazodone (*Serzone*®)	Inhibits presynaptic SE reuptake and blocks postsynaptic 5-HT2A	2–18 hr	100, 150, 200, 250 mg	200–600 mg	Requires BID dosing; may increase blood level of benzodiazepines; potent III A4 inhibitor
Venlafaxine, Venlafaxine SR (*Effexor*®, *Effexor XR*®)	Blocks reuptake of SE and NE; weak inhibitor of DA reuptake	3–7 hr (9–13 hr for metabolite)	25, 37.5, 50, 75, 100 mg; SR: 37.5, 75, 150 mg	75–375 mg	Minimal effect on P450 enzyme; may increase blood pressure; low sexual side effects

Lloyd, Jones, Barnes, & Pilowsky, 2003; Gutierrez, Stimmel, & Aiso, 2003). Well-absorbed within the GI tract, this compound is metabolized by cytochrome P-450 2D6 with major elimination occurring through urine (Martin, Martin, Rai, Richardson, & Royall, 2001). Its most common side effects are nausea, drowsiness (particularly early on in treatment), and potential to significantly raise blood pressure (Hardy, Argyropoulos, & Nutt, 2002).

Overall, atypical antidepressants are particularly useful with patients who have not responded to other classes of medicines or who have significant side effects that prevent their continued use.

HERBS AND MINERALS

In addition to prescription medications, several natural herbs and minerals are available for use in reducing anxiety. Herbs, vitamins, and dietary supplements increasingly are being marketed as possible treatments for a variety of conditions and illnesses. Looking for "natural" alternatives to drugs, many people have turned to botanicals to treat chronic conditions. As some individuals attempt to find effective treatments without bothersome side effects, the herbal market has grown in leaps and bounds. However, herbal formularies are not regulated by the FDA, and thus different brands of the same herb can vary in potency and pharmacodynamics. For example, components of each herb can produce varying pharmacologic effects depending on how the substance is produced, in what quatities, and the precision of dosings (Gutierrez, Ang-Lee, Walker, & Zacny, 2004). Further, much of the research is correlational, with conficting outcomes. Although not FDA regulated, a National Institute of Health research program evaluates the effects of vitamins, minerals, and herbs on specific conditions. Their findings are posted online at www.ods.od.nih.gov, www.crnusa.org, and www.nlm.nih.gov/medlineplus/vitaminsandminerals.html.

St. John's Wort (*Hypericum perforatum*) is an herb known for its antidepressant properties and, like SAM-e, has mixed effects on anxiety (Muller, Pfeil, & Von der Driesch, 2003). For some, St. John's Wort reduces anxiety; others find it "energizing" and anxiogenic (Beijamini & Andreatini, 2003).

Kava kava (*Piper methysticum*) is a natural herb with anxiolytic properties, and some individuals respond equally or better to this herb than to pharmaceuticals (Anke & Ramzan, 2004; Clouatre, 2004; Clough, Rowley, & O'Dea, 2004). Studies suggest that kava kava may be as effective as prescription anxiolytics for treating stress and anxiety—without addiction or abuse potential, without the need for ongoing prescriptions, with better tolerability, and without significant physiologic dependence and withdrawal (Abraham, Connor, & Davidson, 2004; Boerner, Sommer, Berger, Kuhn, Schmidt, & Mannel, 2003; Geier & Konstantinowicz, 2004). Several studies suggest that kava kava extract improves baroreflex control of the heart rate, possibly decreasing the risk of fatal dysrhymias (Cote, Kor, Cohen, & Auclair, 2004; Lehrl, 2004; Strandell, Neil, & Carlin, 2004).

Another herb, *s-adenosylmethionine* (SAMe) is formed from an amino acids methionine and adenosine triphosphate. As an antidepressant, SAMe "works" by donating its methyl group to CNS receptors through transmethylation and increasing dopaminergic and serotonergic effects. SAMe improves receptor functions linked with phospholipids methylation.

Trytophan, an essential amino acid, is a precursor for the synthesis of serotonin (known to be associated with anxiety) and melatonin (important to sleep). Often given with vitamin B6 and magnesium away from meals, trytophan can be taken with a small amount of carbohydrate to facilitate uptake. Trytophan is metabolized into niacin, melatonin, and serotonin and has relaxing and calming effects. It is a natural relaxant and sleep aid found in many foods, such as turkey.

Valerian is thought to inhibit nerve impulses and block brain receptors for the neurotransmitter GABA (Gutierrez et al., 2004; Yuan et al., 2004). Valerian may potentiate GABA receptors throughout the brain, particularly within the brainstem (Cropley, Cave, Ellis, & Middleton, 2002; De Feo & Faro, 2003; Oliva, Gonzalez-Trujano, Arrieta, Enciso-Rodriguez, & Navarrete, 2004). Worldwide, this herb is known for its anxiolytic and sedative properties.

MISCELLANEOUS INTERVENTIONS

In addition to medications, the medical paradigm offers three other interventions for reducing anxiety: *biofeedback, ECT,* and *psychosurgery.*

Biofeedback provides assessment of muscle activity, brainwaves, skin temperature, heart rate, blood pressure, and respirations (Table 3.17).Using systematic data of physiological responses, an individual's body is monitored with the intention of learning voluntary control over somatic sensations in the presence of feared stimuli. ANS activation is an important issue in anxiety, and learning to

TABLE 3.17.
Biofeedback

Type	Measurement/Description
Electroencephalographic	Electrodes placed on the skull to assess the brain's electrical activity
Electromyographic	Striated muscle tension
Galvanic skin	Electrical conductance, potential of the skin
Gastrointestinal	Electrodes placed on the surface of stomach skin to assess motility
Heart rate, pulse	Action of the heart muscle
Skin temperature	Surface body temperature

reduce arousal is a key factor in successful recovery. ***Galvanic skin response*** measures the change in electrical resistance and current in the skin when a stressful stimulus is presented. The use of biofeedback to facilitate stress reduction via relaxation has provided mixed results in effectiveness. When integrated into a comprehensive treatment program, biofeedback may help reduce somatic symptoms of anxiety.

Developed in the 1930s, ***electroconvulsive therapy*** (*ECT*) is a medical procedure occasionally used for cases of prolonged major depression (and in some cases, mania, schizophrenia, or delirium). The oldest and most controversial treatment in clinical psychiatry, ECT produces a generalized seizure in the patient's brain that alters biochemical functioning thereafter (Auriacombe, Reneric, Usandizaga, Gomez, Combouriew, & Tignol, 2000). After receiving an anesthetic and muscle relaxant (to induce sleep before the procedure and prevent "flailing about"), electrodes are placed on the patient's head and a mild electrical current (usually 50–150 watts) is passed through the brain. The current causes the brain to seize or convulse for approximately 30–120 seconds, prompting biochemical changes in electrical functionality as well as changes in neuroreceptors, neurotransmitters, or second-messenger pathways (Hermann, Ettner, Dorwart, Langman-Dorwart, & Kleinman, 1999). Additional effects may occur in muscarinic, cholinergic, and dopaminergic systems (Mathe, 1999). For depressed patients, ECT is effective in reducing symptoms for 50% to 70% of subjects (Potter & Rudorfer, 1993). Its effect in clinical anxiety is unclear.

Psychosurgery is a surgical procedure that destroys and changes selected brain regions in areas believed to be involved in emotional disorders (Anderson & Arciniegas, 2004). For clinical anxiety, psychosurgical techniques are available for OCD. Three prominent surgical procedures can be used to treat anxiety: *anterior cingulotomy* (tiny cut in cingulum nerve bundle), *subcaudate tractotomy* (producing lesions in subcaudate), and *limbic leucotomy* (lesions to cingulated and orbito-medial frontal regions). In general, psychosurgery is reserved for treatment-resistant symptoms and used only as a "last resort" intervention.

SUMMARY

Multiple mechanisms produce anxiolytic effects; compounds with vastly different biochemistries can have similar anxiolysis. Since their initial development, psychotropics have evolved and become more effective in the treatment of psychopathologies, with generally fewer (and safer) side-effect profiles, providing valuable interventions for diverse clinical syndromes (Birmaher, Yelovich, & Renaud, 1998). All medications have side effects. For example, anxiolytics can produce unwanted side effects of drowsiness, physical or psychological dependence (habituation), cognitive dulling, dry mouth, or depression. Although benzodiazepines continue to be pervasively prescribed, pharmacotherapy for clinical anxiety is shifting away from their use and toward serotonergic anti-

TABLE 3.18.
Clinical Anxiety Treatments

Anxiety Disorder	First-line Interventions	Second-line Treatments or Augmentations	Possible Options*	Comments
Generalized anxiety disorder (GAD)	SSRIs (particularly paroxetine), buspirone, atypical antidepressants (particularly venlafaxine), benzodiazepines, mirtazapine	Tricyclics (particularly imipramine), heterocyclics, anticonvulsants, antipsychotics, MAOIs, trazodone	Hydroxyzine, diphenhydramine, herbs, possibly gabapentin	Psychosocial therapies seem to be be more effective (particularly in the long run) than medical interventions
Obsessive-compulsive disorder (OCD)	Clomipramine or SSRIs (particularly fluvoxamine), atypical antipsychotics	Duloxetine, alprazolam or clonazepam, desipramine, augmentation with antipsychotic or anticonvulsant, MAOIs	Augmentation or combinations of medications are sometimes useful; bromocriptine (5–30 mg/day) in combination with antidepressant; inositol, acupuncture, aromatherapy, hypnotherapy, etc., may aid relaxation and therefore complement recovery	Highly treatable, about 90% of patients respond to combined medical and psychological therapies

(continues)

TABLE 3.18.
(Continued)

Anxiety Disorder	First-line Interventions	Second-line Treatments or Augmentations	Possible Options*	Comments
Panic disorder (PD)	SSRIs, SNRIs duloxetine, imipramine, desipramine, alprazolam	Clonazepam, MAOIs, valproic acid, gabapentin	Possibly augmentation or combinations of medications	High-potency benzodiazepines are useful in controlling sudden, intense panic, but prolonged use can bring tolerance; newer SSRIs and atypical antidepressants are costly without generic equivalents (except fluoxetine)
Post traumatic stress disorder (PTSD)	SNRIs, SSRIs, nefazodone, venlafaxine, desipramine or protriptyline, hypnotics	Phenelzine, clonazepam, other MAOIs, beta-blockers, lamotrigine, tiagabine	Trazodone (to induce sleep QHS), carbamazepine, valproic acid, possibly gabapentin	Buspirone may be effective, but further research is needed
Simple phobia (SP)	Beta-blockers	SSRIs, phenelzine, benzodiazepines, imipramine	Atypical antidepressants, gabapentin possibly effective in social phobia	Behavioral, cognitive, and cognitive-behavioral treatments, including exposure therapies, are treatments of choice

*Indicates options that may be helpful based on anecdotal, correlational, or case study evidence; outcomes for these treatments are unclear or unknown.

depressants (Lagnauoi et al., 2004). Regardless of symptoms or clinical syndrome, SSRIs have become first-line treatments for anxiety (Stone, Viera, & Parman, 2003). Table 3.18 lists first-line and second-line treatments.

Since the introduction of SSRIs, atypical antipsychotics, and novel anticonvulsants, the pharmacotherapy for clinical anxiety has changed dramatically (Brawman-Mintzer & Yonkers, 2004). All antidepressants have anxiolytic properties, and the choice of medication is governed by many factors, including cost, nature and frequency of symptoms, previous trials and responses, and so on. The mechanisms of actions of serotonergic antidepressants, anxiolytics, hypnotics, and antipsychotics may partially or primarily be mediated through neurotransmitter systems and receptor effects within the frontal-subcortical neurocircuits. When severity warrants, use of psychotropic agents "off-label" provides a multifaceted gamut of treatment options for subduing symptoms of clinical anxiety. Early identification of good/poor responders can facilitate medication choice, treatment planning, and intervention options. Ongoing treatment may be needed to prevent chronic functional impairments, morbidity, or mortality.

CHAPTER 4

Generalized Anxiety Disorder

INTRODUCED INTO DIAGNOSTIC nosology in 1980, *generalized anxiety disorder (GAD)* is characterized by continuous anxiety that lasts 6 months or more, is not attributable to a physical cause, and includes motor tension, autonomic hyperarousal, apprehension, nervousness, vigilance, scanning, or the subjective experience of fear. Diagnostic criteria include two or more spheres of persistent worry, accompanied by autonomic arousal, muscle tension, easy startle, or hypervigilance. *DSM-IV-TR* (APA, 2000, p. 432) criteria define GAD as "excessive anxiety and worry (apprehensive expectation), occurring more days than not for a period of at least 6 months, about a number of events or activities." This broad, general definition is intended to be such, because more specific fears are classified as phobias. The chief features of GAD are "free-floating" uneasiness coupled with avoidance (Ballenger et al., 2001). GAD is a residual category that conceptually underlies all other anxiety disorders, given its chief nosologic features of hyperarousal and avoidant behavior. GAD is differentiated from adjustment syndromes by its absence of an identifiable emotional stressor, from panic and phobic disorders by its pervasive and diffuse nature, and from OCD by its autonomic, cardiopulmonary, neurologic, and presumed biochemical etiologies (Hoehn-Saric, McLeod, Funderbunk, & Kowalski, 2004; Noyes, 2001). GAD probands usually consider their worries to be realistic and appropriate rather than irrational.

A central characteristic of GAD is *worry*—a cognitive process marked by rumination and brooding (Alwahhabu, 2003; Ruscio, 2002). GAD worry serves several interrelated functions: (1) idiosyncratic avoidance of conflict; (2) the prompting of potential coping strategies; (3) motivation and preparation of responses; or (4) distraction (Borkovec, 1994). Additionally, worrying can reduce physiological hyperarousal, creating an impediment for experiencing such arousal and working through its implications (Belanger, Morin, Langlois, &

DSM-IV-TR CRITERIA FOR GENERALIZED ANXIETY DISORDER*

A. Excessive anxiety and worry (apprehension expectation), occurring more days than not for at least six months, about a number of events or activities (such as work or school performance).
B. The person finds it difficult to control the worry.
C. The anxiety and worry are associated with three (or more) of the following six symptoms (with at least some symptoms present for more days than not for the past six months). Note: Only one item is required in children.
   (1) restlessness or feeling keyed up or on edge
   (2) being easily fatigued
   (3) difficulty concentrating or mind going blank
   (4) irritability
   (5) muscle tension
   (6) sleep disturbance (difficulty falling or staying asleep, or restless unsatisfying sleep)
D. The focus of the anxiety and worry is not confined to features of an Axis I disorder, e.g., the anxiety or worry is not about having a Panic Attack (as in Panic Disorder), being embarrassed in public (as in social phobia), being contaminated (as in Obsessive-Compulsive Disorder), being away from home or close relatives (as in Separation Anxiety Disorder), gaining weight (as in Anorexia Nervosa), having a serious illness (as in Hypochondriasis), and the anxiety and worry do not occur exclusively during Posttraumatic Stress Disorder.
E. The anxiety, worry, or physical symptoms cause clinically significant distress or impairment in social, occupational, or other important areas of functioning.
F. The disturbance is not due to the direct physiological effects of a substance (e.g., a drug of abuse, a medication) or a general medical condition (e.g., hyperthyroidism) and does not occur exclusively during a Mood Disorder, a Psychotic Disorder, or a Pervasive Developmental Disorder.

Ladouceur, 2004). Ironically, worry can serve as a deterrent to processing and resolving latent issues. GAD probands view their worries as significantly less controllable than controls' worries, with significantly less ability to stop or control unwanted thoughts (Kendall & Pimentel, 2003). Attempts to control thoughts and worry may paradoxically lead to the increase and exacerbation of intrusive thoughts and enhance probands' beliefs in their inability to control them (Roemer & Orsillo, 2002). In its most extreme form, GAD probands may experience excessive rumination that resembles obsessive thinking.

The content of cognitive rumination has been the subject of many principal components studies, each partitioning specific factors that comprise GAD's cognitive component. McNaughton and Gray (2000) conceptualized GAD as a cognitive disorder in which probands are preoccupied with thoughts of threat, harm, or danger. GAD probands make unrealistic, silent assumptions that imply that they are in imminent danger (Antoni et al., 2000). Such thoughts lead them to experience narrow and persistent anxiety-provoking images and thoughts. GAD probands tend to worry about physical injury, illness, death, loss of control, failure and inability to cope, rejection, or negative outcomes (Ninan, 2001, 2002). Three prominent types of maladaptive thoughts are common in GAD: (1) repetitive and catastrophized thoughts about danger, in the form of "false alarms"; (2) reduced willingness or effort to reason with fearful thoughts adaptively, particularly in becoming aware of the automatic thoughts that drive perceptual and emotional responses; and (3) globalized stimulus generalization, such that even slight triggering cues often precipitate maladaptive cognitive processes. Empirical studies of GAD reflect a consistent attentional bias toward threat and minimization of coping abilities (Hazlett-Stevens & Borkovec, 2004; Matthews, Mackintosh, & Fulcher, 1997). Overall, GAD patients tend to perceive ambiguous stimuli as threatening and pay excessive attention to possible threats (Taghavi, Dalgleish, Moradi, Neshat-Doost, & Yule, 2003).

PREVALENCE

Due to subtle differences in defining "normal" anxiety versus pathological clinical anxiety, it is difficult to obtain valid estimates of GAD's prevalence and incidence (e.g., Diefenbach et al., 2003). Twice as common in women than men, most GAD probands describe their symptoms as beginning very early in life (Masi et al., 2004). The chronic nature of GAD, along with its diffuse and pervasive features, has led some researchers to reconceptualize GAD as a personality trait or characterological condition (Cloitre et al., 2004; Wenzel, Haugen, Jackson, & Robinson, 2003). Despite its prevalence, GAD seems to be one of the less common anxiety disorders in patients seeking therapy, accounting for only about 10% of anxiety patients (Wittchen, 2002). Only about a third of GAD probands seek treatment, often beginning their course of clinical interventions through general practitioners and primary-care physicians (Brawman-Mintzer & Lydiard, 1996; Katon, Roy-Byrne, Russo, & Cowley, 2002).

SYMPTOMS

People with GAD typically feel restless, have difficulty concentrating, feel irritable, experience muscle tension, or have an erratic sleep pattern with ensuing chronic fatigue (Thayer, Friedman, Borkovec, Johnsen, & Molina, 2000). Although the disorder can emerge at any age, most probands report their symptoms beginning in childhood or adolescence (Stanley et al., 2003). Emerging data suggest that GAD has a chronic pattern of symptoms and high comorbidity with other psychiatric conditions, particularly depression (Forsythe, Parker, & Finley, 2003). GAD often co-occurs with other psychological conditions, particularly other anxiety and mood syndromes. Comorbidity with social phobia and agoraphobia is common. Further, many GAD probands experience intermittent panic, subclinical in intensity, and mild depression (secondary to gloomy outlook). Substance abuse and dependence disorders are often associated with GAD, particularly when probands seek to self-medicate.

PSYCHOSOCIAL THEORIES

Psychosocial theories of the etiology of GAD have focused on latent emotional conflicts, dysfunctional interpersonal attributions, behavioral deficits, maladaptive cognitions, or existential angst (Gosselin & Laberge, 2003). Collectively, dynamic theories view GAD as a developmental condition, marked by chronic feelings of incompetence, helplessness, or impotence.

Psychoanalysis

Freud (1894) first postulated a theory based on intrapsychic conflict, defining *neurotic anxiety* as a deflection of somatic sensual excitement from the psychical field with substitute symptoms for corresponding sexual excitation and activities that would naturally occur if allowed. Generally, failure in social or sexual interactions is a precipitating factor, leading to regression to hostile and destructive impulses that quickly are repressed. When these impulses threaten to seep into consciousness, the individual feels anxious and attempts to control conflicts via defense mechanisms, particularly repression. The rigid and extreme use of primitive defenses fosters anxiety neurosis. For example, the rigid blocking of sexual energy can be transmuted into diffuse, free-floating anxiety (Fenichel, 1945).

Freud (1936) believed that anxiety serves as a signal of danger, warning of either internal or external threat. Generalized anxiety occurs secondary to conflict between id and ego functioning with subsequent demise of defense mechanisms.

For example, chronic threat of the impending break through from unconscious to conscious awareness of taboo wish may prompt a generalized state of anxiety. Prolonged tension or pervasive conflicts can overwhelm ego defenses. If they fail, the ego is flooded with anxiety. When the ego's defenses are broken down, conflict surfaces to conscious awareness (Kumin, 1996; Luborsky & Crits-Christoph, 1998). Sexual and aggressive impulses, previously blocked from conscious expression, arise and precipitate free-floating anxiety. Whereas in phobias repression and displacement are predominant, in GAD, conflicts are free-floating and globalized without conscious awareness of the true source of fears. When unresolved conflicts around anger and dependence occur, these feelings are projected (at a deep, unconscious level) onto the environment in which conscious functioning senses a hostile, threatening environment at every turn. Freud believed that fear of internal aggression, based on the death instinct, precipitates some to project their hostility onto the environment, and then denial is used to avoid "persecutory" anxiety.

Object-Relations

Interpersonal models have focused on both historical and present-moment self-object matrices. For example, Chiu's (1971) research supports the dynamic view that extreme punishment for early id-based impulses may lead to higher levels of generalized anxiety later in life. Children of overly strict or overly protective parents may develop a fear of being attacked by bad objects or of losing good objects and subsequently carry this internalized anxiety into adulthood. In object-relations theories, instead of an inability to reconcile inner impulses, individuals suffer from failure to meaningfully engage others in sustained, gratifying relationships. Object-relations theories view GAD as a broad state of fear characterized by nervous anticipation of repeated interactions with bad objects (Stolorow & Lachmann, 1980). Here, GAD is a manifestation of disturbed object-relations early in life. The lack of well-defined soothing introjects causes anxiety to be quickly aroused and intensely experienced. Subsequent difficulties in autonomy, independence, or assertiveness ensue.

Erikson and Sullivan. In Erikson's (1950) theory, the initial conflict individuals must negotiate and resolve is trust versus mistrust, beginning at birth and extending throughout the first year. The newborn is totally helpless to meet his or her own needs, resulting in complete dependency on others. If primary caregivers meet the neonate's needs for basic sustenance, the infant develops a sense of security and trust. If primitive survival needs are not met, the infant experiences the world as untrustworthy, unable to meet its needs. Throughout life, the individual struggles with an unconscious perception of basic hostility, unpredictability, or void within the environment, breeding globalized, free-floating anxiety (GAD)—a condition similar to Horney's (1937) *basic anxiety*. Fear of abandonment and helplessness ensue. Without basic trust fostered early in life, attachment and bonding with others is impeded, and further mistrust of the environment continues in a self-defeating cycle. The nature of how subsequent symptoms are experienced and expressed depends on the timing and nature of impairments in affective development.

In Sullivan's (1953) theory, psychological symptoms are created, maintained, and expressed interpersonally. Anxiety does not exist "inside" of persons. Instead, abnormality resides in the interpersonal event. Sullivan described the *inadequate person* as one who builds relationships on the basis of dependency, always requiring someone strong to tell him or her what to do. Developmentally, the individual has taken a stance of obedience to the domineering parent or of identification with the helpless parent. In social interactions, all individuals respond to the mood sensed and experienced with others. If that mood is perceived as hostile or disapproving, it is experienced as tension and anxiety. Anxiety represents insecurity, a signal of danger to self-respect, or a major disruption in social exchanges. Anxiety is maintained by a vicious cycle caused by disruptions in interpersonal interactions. Further, generalized anxiety can result from a lack of coping and adaptive skills, defined as including realistic self-preservation capabilities in addition to more advanced, interpersonal functionings. Closely associated to interpersonal models, the cultural model views GAD as resulting from societal pressures, diffusion of roles, or unclear situational demands (Mahalik, Cournoyer, DeFrank, Cherry, & Napolitano, 1998). Societal stressors, such as changing technologies, poverty, or breaches in national security, create diffuse fears that become experienced as globalized anxiety (McLeod & Kessler, 1990). Increases in sociocultural pressures may establish a climate in which globalized anxiety develops.

Kohut. Kohut's (1971, p. 152) theory views anxiety as fear of fragmentation of the self, describing it as "dedifferentiating intrusion of narcissistic structures and their energies into the ego." *Disintegration anxiety* results when selfobject needs are unmet, severe narcissistic wounding occurs, or within uncontrolled regression. Children whose parents fail to treat them in a confident, relaxed, and supportive manner may develop disintegration anxiety, subsequently experiencing the self as lacking support and setting up lifelong defensive structures to sooth and repair their damaged self (Zerbe, 1990). If an individual is unable to empathically introspect, understand, and self-soothe, multiple defenses can be mounted against the threat of being overwhelmed by rage, including projection. Thereafter, the environment is perceived as hostile and threatening—causing internal uneasiness and anxiety. Makeshift (compensatory) structures become overwhelmed by adulthood stresses, causing a state of self-fragmentation characterized by repeated outbreaks of anxiety. This sense of anxiety is a vague, diffuse malaise that cannot be expressed in detail, is not attached to a situation or event (as in phobias), and ebbs and flows with life's vicissitudes.

Behavioral and Cognitive-Behavioral Paradigms

Wolpe (1958) believed human neuroses to be classically conditioned fear responses to specified stimuli. *"Daily hassles"* are a variant on life events and are focused on everyday stressors and their impact on functioning. In GAD, this theory implicates wide-ranging, globalized fears that become enacted by muscle tension or physiological arousal. In essence, GAD represents an inability to physiologically relax. Through systematic desensitization, patients learn to countercondition themselves to feel a general state of relaxation and calm, even in light of previously feared stimuli. Over time, this sense of relaxation is generalized to everyday functioning, thus decreasing overall anxiety.

An adaptation of conditioning models, learning theories view GAD as resulting from continued exposure to societal pressures or real dangers. Through modeling or vicarious learning, an individual develops general feelings of tension, anxiety, and uneasiness that then become generalized to others settings, places, and times. Chronic inability to cope with environmental stimuli precipitates a condition similar to learned helplessness in which adaptive responses are not deployed even though appropriate mediating cues and skills are present (*mediational deficiencies*). Some GAD probands fail to respond appropriately to situations even when they have appropriate coping skills, apparently due to dysfunctional self-talk, "automatic" self-statements, or perceptional distortions about possible negative effects of assertive behaviors (Mogg, Baldwin, Brodrick, & Bradley, 2004).

Combining both attribution and contingency theories, Rotter (1954, 1966) conceptualized *locus of control* as the degree to which individuals take responsibility for their own actions or credit external sources for their cause. Rotter (1966) stressed that the impact of a reinforcer may vary according to how the individual perceives the relationship between personal actions and resulting outcome. If the event is seen as a result of luck, chance, fate, or in the control of powerful others (i.e., noncontingent on personal behavior), the belief may be labeled *external control*; perceiving permanent characteristics is termed *internal control*. Believing that the cause, reinforcement, or fate of personal actions rests outside of one's personal control provides a general vulnerability to experiencing GAD because over time a sense of futile impotence prompts feelings of fear and anxiousness in dealing with the environment.

Cognitive Models

An offshoot of the skills deficit theory, cognitive models emphasize the creation and maintenance of symptoms secondary to maladaptive cognitive processes, particularly in automatic thoughts, self-statements, and beliefs (Taylor, Pham, Rivkin, & Armor, 1998). Three prominent types of maladaptive thoughts are common in GAD: (1) repetitive and catastrophized thoughts about danger, in the form of "false alarms"; (2) reduced willingness or effort to reason with fearful thoughts adaptively, particularly in becoming aware of the automatic thoughts that drive perceptual and emotional responses; and (3) globalized stimulus generalization, such that even slight triggering cues often precipitate maladaptive cognitive processes. GAD probands make unrealistic, silent assumptions that imply that they are in imminent danger (Antoni et al., 2000). Such thoughts lead them to experience narrow and persistent anxiety-provoking images and thoughts. Meichenbaum (1977) viewed GAD as a product of counterproductive self-statements in the face of stressful stimuli. Individual's cognitive processes and contents heighten their anxiety and render coping strategies ineffectual. Subsequent fear and anxiety ensue.

Self-instructional training teaches patients to "listen with a third ear" to their self-talk and replace dysfunctional, negative statements with productive, coping assertions. Rapee, Telfer, and Barlow (1991) suggested that two key cognitive factors significantly contribute to the initiation and maintenance of GAD: overperception of threat (e.g., globalized generalization) and underestimation of controllability (e.g., belief that self-initiated efforts to cope and adapt will be futile and ineffective). These attentional biases have been well-documented in empirical studies and thus effective treatments seek to foster more realistic and veridical cognitive perception, processing, and interpretation of environmental stimuli.

A cognitive redaction of Rotter's initial theory has been proposed regarding unpredictability and environmental contingencies. Some theorists view GAD as a generalization of a past history of numerous unpredictable negative events. When negative events are unforeseen, uncontrollable, or unexpected, they generally are experienced as more unpleasant and fear-producing than aversive events that are expected. Experiencing many uncontrollable or unpredictable events (regardless of the nature of their intensity) leads some individuals to live in a chronic state of apprehension or anxiety. These individuals become fearful of the unknown and, to avoid being caught off-guard, try to predict the occurrence of novel unforeseen negative events. Thereafter, expectations evoke behavior in others that confirms the initial beliefs. These individuals begin to interpret environmental stimuli, regardless of their nature, as dangerous, which precipitates a cycle of fearful apprehension. Subsequently, patients exhibit suppressed approach behaviors and excessive avoidance.

Ellis. Ellis (1962) provided a cognitive view of GAD based on irrationality and an individual's tendency to catastrophize events. In any situation, even if benign, not only is a negative outcome expected, but the individual broods on perceiving the most extreme, negative consequence conceivable. Thereafter, this perception becomes viewed as realistic and factual, with a genuine, highly probable threat. Whereas nonanxious individuals habituate to moderately frightening thoughts and situations, GAD probands tend to catastrophize possible outcomes and thus perpetuate their anxiety. Ellis (1973) also wrote extensively on the concept of *living life in the future* when the present is all that matters. In this model, demandingness on the future, such as on how outcomes "should" be, leads to a global anxiety felt in the present. Because individuals can only respond to situations in the present moment, in the here and now, dwelling on potential future outcomes generates a sense of helplessness, impotence, and fear of being unable to adapt. As in Beck's model of depression, misattribution has been theorized to be a causal element in GAD, particularly in susceptibility to anxiety, making some cognitive processes/contents more likely once anxious or impairing subsequent cognitive functioning is experienced (Beck et al., 2003). Whereas in depression the focus of misattribution is on negative information about the self, in anxiety the focus is on negative information about the environment, coupled with the fear of being unable to cope and adapt via internal resources. Such distortions as impaired attributions in self-other valuing, enhanced processing of projected negative evaluations, or oversensitivity to potential threat maintain a sense of hyperarousal and expectation of harm.

Behavioral and cognitive-behavioral views of clinical anxiety have evolved from major theorists and parallel the particular emphases each hold in their idiographic paradigms. Collectively, some common themes emerge. First, anxious distress and other symptoms of psychopathology are largely the result of learning, impaired efficacy expectations, or cognitive processes. Second, conditioning and contingencies play key roles. Operant conditioning can explain how fears can result in the development of avoidant behaviors. Third, successful treatments for reducing anxiety increase an individual's sense of self-efficacy and competence in mastering feared situations. All effective behavioral treatments include either imagined or in vivo exposure to feared stimuli. Techniques that decrease baseline anxiety, such as relaxation and social skills training, are used to reduce symptoms and facilitate overall functioning. Behavioral theories include conditioning, attribution, and cognitive models. Early experiences of mastery and effectiveness in functioning can, in some instances, immunize individuals against the harmful effects of stress and subsequent anxiety (Parfitt et al., 2004). Thus, behavioral models tend to focus on mastery experiences and their effects on thoughts and feelings about coping and adaptation.

Existential/Humanistic Models

Existential models focus on the responsibility of life, creating meaning in the world, and the choices that must be made throughout development. Existentialists conceptualize phobias and GAD as growing out of existential anxiety, a universal human fear of the limits and responsibilities of one's existence (May, 1950, 1953). We experience existential anxiety because we know that life is finite and we fear the death that awaits us. We also know that our actions and choices may have unexpected consequences and fear hurting others unintentionally. Finally, we suspect that life in general has no purpose and that our own personal existence may ultimately lack meaning. According to existentialists, individuals can confront their existential anxiety head on by taking responsibility for their actions, making decisions, making their lives meaningful, and appreciating their own uniqueness, or they can shrink from this confrontation by living "inauthentic lives." Existential and humanistic models shifted the focus from intrapsychic conflict to more existential angst; anxiety results from "stage fright," denial of phenomenological experience, or fear of overwhelming responsibility. Phenomenal experience is the major focus of treatment, with all stimuli seen from a perceptual viewpoint (i.e., its phenomenology); even memories and impulses are thought of as perceptions. Taken collectively, humanistic paradigms state that anxiety occurs when people stop looking at themselves honestly and acceptingly and instead deny and distort their true thoughts, emotions, and behaviors. Defensive postures ultimately serve to make individuals extremely anxious and incapable of fulfilling their potential as human beings.

Caught up in the change, confusion, and strain of cultural and familial roles, some individuals adopt "inauthentic lives" in an attempt to deny their fears, freedom, choice, and responsibilities (May & Yalom, 1989). The process of denying thoughts, emotions, and behaviors eventually precipitates anxiety and impedes fulfilling ultimate human potential. Trying to conform to the standards and ideals of society can distort idiographic traits and fails to reduce existential anxiety.

Laing (1965) integrated object-relational and existential theories into a theory of schizophrenia, because, in a milder form, it can be experienced as a free-floating anxiety similar to that in GAD. Laing's concept of the *divided self* refers to the primitive splitting of the self concept induced early in life by forces beyond the child's control, such as organic and sociocultural factors. The individual feels divided with only a tenuous understanding and constancy of his or her personal sense of self and experiences a sense of "ontological insecurity" characterized by an inability to maintain a cohesive and stable identity (Laing, 1967). Experiencing ontological insecurity causes the self to feel three forms of anxiety: *engulfment* (fear of being overwhelmed), *implosion* (fear that reality will destroy the empty identity), or *petrification* (fear of becoming an automaton or object, often accompanied by depersonalization).

With diverse and clinically rich models for conceptualizing GAD, theorists continue to try to integrate medical and psychosocial paradigms to better provide comprehensive treatments. Few studies have provided definitive biological bases for GAD; a plethora of research supports its psychological etiology (Jetty, Charney, & Goddard, 2001). Prominent neurobiological models have evolved from knowledge of how benzodiazepines "work" to provide symptom relief (Clement & Chapouthier, 1998). By far, the chief focus for biological theories has been on exploring the relationship between neurotransmitters and the body's response to anxiety.

GENETICS

Some family pattern research suggests that GAD has a genetic component marked by a physiological predisposition toward the experience of symptoms (Gordon & Hen, 2004). Family studies indicate that GAD probands are more likely than controls to have a first-degree relative with GAD (Hettema et al., 2003; Kendler, 1996; Smoller et al., 2001). Twin studies reflect a moderate heritability; around 30% of variance can be attributed to genetics (Roy, Neale, Pederson, Mathe, & Kendler, 1995; Scherrer et al., 2000). The heritability of GAD for men and women is estimated at about 15% to 20%, with no clear effects of gender-specific genes detected (Bittner et al., 2004; Hettema, Prescott, Myers, Neale, & Kendler, 2005). In one study, the best-fitting model for GAD heritability showed 15% to 20% in males and females, without significant gender-unique genes noted (Gillespie et al., 2004; Hettema, Prescott, & Kendler, 2001). Familial aggregation appears to be relatively modest (Ho Pian et al., 2005).

As with other anxiety disorders, serotonergic, noradrenergic, and gabanergic transporter genes have been researched, but no definitive themes have emerged from diverse studies (Bailey & Toth, 2004; Bellivier, Laplanche, Fournier, & Wolkenstein, 2001; Hernandez, Lastra, Urbina, Carreira, & Lima, 2002). More promising are studies that link biologically based aspects of personality with GAD symptoms (Kirk et al., 2000; Klag & Bradley, 2004). There is probably an inherited predisposition toward a labile limbic or autonomic nervous system, associated with chronic overarousal and slow habituation (Finn, Rutledge-Gorman, & Crabbe, 2003; Reidy, 2004).

Temperament is the biologically based part of personality that exists at birth and "unfolds" throughout life—individual differences in reactivity and self-regulation, influenced over time by heredity, maturation, and experience (Turkheimer, 1998). *Trait theories* assume that personality can be described as continuous dimensions in which a compendium of internal characteristics describe functioning (Blass, 1977; Buss & Cantor, 1989). Traits are the more static, descriptive aspects of personality, describing individual differences in terms of global symptomatic characteristics. Some traits have higher genetic loadings than others because they are often influenced by an interaction of many genes (Nash et al., 2004). Our early temperament is the substrate from which subsequent personality develops. For example, Pedersen, Plomin, McClearn, and Fribereg (1998) have shown remarkable consistency of neurotic and extraverted traits between twins reared together and those reared apart. Initially, five basic dimensions of temperament can be identified: fearfulness, irritability, positive affect, activity level, and attentional persistence (McCrae & Costa, 1987). These five basic factors are related to adult personality, particularly three main traits: neuroticism, introversion/extraversion, and conscientiousness (Kalisch et al., 2004). Key traits may represent genetic bases for GAD (Chambers, Power, & Durham, 2004; Pailing & Segalowitz, 2004). For example, Spielberger's (1972,

1983) **trait anxiety** describes a temperamental characteristic of overall level of anxiety, and those high in trait anxiety are more likely to contract GAD (Jezova, Makatsori, Duncko, Moncek, & Jakubek, 2004; Rule & Traver, 1983). Combining both biological and environmental components, trait anxiety incorporates early childhood experience—the atmosphere of safety or insecurity—that is integrated into a worldview (Muris & Meesters, 2004).

Certain personality characteristics, genetically determined, may pose a particular vulnerability to GAD (Battaglia, Bertell, Bajo, Politi, & Bellodi, 1998). Early, inborn styles of easily aroused infants may lead to greater propensity to contract anxiety disorders later in life (Kalin, 2004). Both Spielberger's (1983) **trait anxiety** and Reiss and McNally's (1985) **anxiety sensitivity** refer to the tendency for some individuals to become preoccupied with bodily sensations and interpret arousal as potentially harmful or debilitating. As a temperament characteristic, anxiety sensitivity has shown a strong genetic basis via twin research (Stein, Jang, & Livesley, 1999). This basic tendency has been theorized to be etiological to all anxiety conditions, and its link to generalized anxiety and panic is irrefutable (Maltby, Mayers, Allen, & Tolin, 2005; Reiss, Peterson, Bursky, & McNally, 1986). The best-supported findings may be drawn from physiological and endocrinology studies, suggesting that anxious probands have a chronically overaroused CNS and are slow to habituate to noxious stimuli (Savitz & Ramesar, 2004).

Eysenck: The Ascending Reticular Activating System

One of the first attempts to link genetically determined temperament with anxiety was Eysenck's (1967) theory of the *ascending reticular activating system* (**ARAS**). The ARAS regulates higher parts of the brain within the cerebral cortex, causing changes in sensitivity, alertness, and sleep cycle. Cortical arousal differences lead to personality characteristics that exude specific diatheses for anxiety. Those with sensitive ARAS will experience anxiety easily and frequently, creating fertile ground for the development of GAD. Eysenck's (1959, 1968) research found two bipolar dimensions in personality: **neuroticism** (characterized by emotional lability and overreactivity, with difficulty returning to a normal state after an emotional experience) and **extraversion-introversion** (traits such as being talkative or silent, sociable or reclusive, adventurous or cautious, outgoing or shy). All persons can be characterized within each continuum, with the majority of persons falling along the midpoints of the two dimensions (Amirkhan, Risinger, & Swickert, 1995). Individuals who fall at the extremes of the continua are designated as neurotic or stable, and extraverted or introverted. In his model, Eysenck (1991) proposed that usual resting levels within the ARAS activity among introverts are higher than those of extroverts. Because they have higher base levels of arousal, introverts are easily overaroused and become "stimulus shy" because they are too sensitive to being overstimulated. Eysenck believed that those with phobias tended to be introverts, more neurotic in nature, and more emotionally responsive than extraverts due to "weak" nervous systems. Therefore, they respond at lower levels and with greater intensity to stimuli than extraverts (who have "strong" nervous systems). From infancy to adulthood, these two traits and activity level have been proposed as the most heritable components of personality, yielding heritability estimates of about 50%. The effect of neuroticism and extraversion on psychological distress over a 10-year period has been estimated to be four times greater than the effects of psychological interventions to reduce distress (Brody, 1997).

Eysenck's (1967) theory is based on the workings of the central nervous system. **Excitation** is the neural processes upon which the development of learned associations between stimuli and results depend. **Inhibition** is the process of the brain relaxing and becoming calm. Whenever a stimulus-response connection is made in the CNS, both positive (excitatory, facilitative) and negative (inhibitory, obstructive) changes occur in impulse transmission. **Neuroticism**, a trait marked by emotional lability, may predispose some individuals to anxiety (Hettema, Prescott, & Kendler, 2004). Associated traits include being calm or anxious, composed or excitable, or poised or nervous. Neuroticism is thought to result from lability of the limbic system, the autonomic nervous system, or specific neurotransmitter systems (Cox, MacPherson, Enns, & McWilliams, 2004). Neurotics are conceptualized as having low threshold activation of the hippocampus, amygdala, cingulum, and hypothalamus. Emotionally labile and overreactive, neurotics tend to be overly responsive and have difficulty returning to a normal state after an emotional experience. Regardless of gender, genetic factors provide substantial influence on the individual variation of neuroticism, as well as increased liability for GAD (Hettema et al., 2004).

STRUCTURAL MODELS

Research on structural abnormalities in the brains of GAD probands has not revealed consistent patterns or causal relationships (Degroot & Treit, 2004). Instead, studies link developmental factors with subsequent impairments manifested as both structural and functional aberrations (e.g., Malmo, Malmo, & Ditto, 2003). For example, chronic stress produces decreased neuropeptide-Y and corticotrophin releasing factor in several brain regions, including the paraventricular hypothalamus and arcuate nucleus (M. S. Kim et al., 2003; Merali, Khan, Michaud, Shippy, & Anisman, 2004).

The effects of hyperactivity of the mother's limbic-hypothalamic-pituitary-adrenal axis during pregnancy on the development of the fetus's limbic-hypothalamic-pituitary-adrenal axis and monoamine systems indicate that prenatal stress affects brain development and subsequent hyperfunctioning basal and limbic-hypothalamic-pituitary-adrenal axes, leading to exhaustion and an inability to adequately respond to stress (Andersson, Sundstrom-Poromaa, Wulff, Astrom, & Bixo, 2004). Effects of prenatal stress are mediated by maternal glucocorticoid secretion (Bowman et al., 2004). Acute restraint stress in late gestation has been linked to both maternal and fetal changes, such as volume changes in the hippocampus, the properties of glucocorticoid receptors, and basal and stress-dependent functioning of the pituitary-adrenal circuit (Bremner & Vermetten, 2001; Maccari et al., 2003; Soderquist, Wijma, & Wijma, 2004).

Neonatal bonding and attachment is an important impetus to brain development and growth (Bowlby, 1977, 1983; Kalinichev, Easterling, Plotsky, & Holtzman, 2002). Remarkably stable across generations, attachment has been theorized as an autonomous instinctual system rooted in genes and inherited variables. Even small differences in neonatal handling can have an effect on subsequent brain development (O'Connor, Heron, Golding, & Glover, 2003). For example, pervasive maternal separations can produce excessive cortisol levels (Brown et al., 2004; Ordyan & Pivina, 2004). Other theories associate the quality of early maternal bonding (e.g., attachment, being held, soothing) with diminished levels of anxiety thereafter (Lyons & Schatzberg, 2003).

Reduced volume or lesions within the hippocampus may cause diffuse anxiety. Brain imaging has shown that chronic exposure to stress may precipitate lesions within the hippocampal regions. Studies have implicated the amygdala, the hippocampus, the basal ganglia, or the striatum (Rauch & Savage, 1997). Further, researchers have tentatively implicated right-hemispheric dysfunction or abnormality in GAD probands (Garraghty et al., 1998). These and other subsequent structural aberrations warrant further empirical research.

FUNCTIONAL ABNORMALITIES

When faced with potential danger, the body begins an "emergency reaction" that progresses through discrete stages. Selye's (1956, 1976) three-stage model of response to stress includes (1) somatic arousal, (2) defensive behavior, and (3) adaptation. The *fight-or-flight system* is the body's response to perceived harm and enables it by either fighting the noxious stimulus or fleeing from it (Cannon, 1929; Thayer, Friedman, & Borkovec, 1996). The body responds to novel, unfamiliar, or negative stressors by increasing arousal in physiological and psychological functioning, which prompts a general state of apprehension: In the brain stem, neurons fire in the locus coeruleus and the amygdala; the hypothalamus sends hormonal messengers to the pituitary gland, which signals the adrenal glands to produce epinephrine and norepinephrine. Prominent physiological features of the fear and anxiety response, such as hyperarousal, are generated by the autonomic nervous system (ANS). The heart begins to beat faster, blood is pumped more rapidly, and the peripheral vessels widen so that more oxygen is distributed throughout the body. The spleen contracts, releasing red blood cells to carry oxygen. The liver releases sugar for the muscles to use. Sweating increases to cool off the muscles and increase tactile sensitivity. Blood content changes so that coagulation to seal potential wounds will occur rapidly and so that lymphocyte cells can repair any damage that occurs. Increased cardiac output during the stress-response process prompts increased peripheral resistance.

Neural circuits provide a comprehensive framework for understanding the anatomy, biochemistry, and pharmacology involved in the body's response to stress (Charney, 2003). Brawman-Mintzer and Lydiard (1997, p. 17) suggested that "maladaptive responses to stressful stimuli have been observed in the locus-coeruleus-norepinephrine-sympathetic nervous system, the hypothalamic-pituitary-adrenocortical axis, and the cholecystotin system." Dysfunctions in other important neural modulators, such as 5-HT and gamma-aminobutyric acid, may also be responsible for GAD. The occipital lobe has the highest concentration of benzodiazepine receptors in the brain, leading to theories of dysfunctional processes therein as being the cause of GAD. Of particular importance is the somatic processes are the functions of the *hypothalamic-pituitary-adrenal-cortical axis*, wherein complex interactions between noradrenergic and serotonergic systems occur. Both the medial prefrontal cortex and the hippocampus are involved in the negative feedback regulation of hypothalamic-pituitary-adrenal axis activity during stress. Activation of this circuit begins with the hypothalamus sending impulses to the pituitary, which then stimulates the cortical part of the adrenal glands to produce epinephrine and cortisol. Nerve cells fire rapidly and create a hyperexcitability throughout the brain and body, involving multiple biological systems that combine to sustain prolonged resistance to perceived threat. Chronic inescapable (or unpredictable) stress can lead to dysfunction of both corticotrophin releasing hormone and norepinephrine regulation (Young, Abelson, & Cameron, 2004). Gray's (1976, 1982) model largely focuses on the septohippocampal circuit, which acts as a comparison mechanism for actual and expected cues. This neural circuit becomes active, generating anxiety, whenever actual and expected stimuli are disparate or when perception of what is sensed is aversive. Supporting his theory are findings showing that certain antianxiety medications and documented sequelae of lesions to the septohippocampal region lower arousal and subjective anxiousness (Nutt, Ballenger, Sheehan, & Wittchen, 2002). Gray also has proposed that the nervous system has subsystems that serve different functions, such as arousal and inhibition, postulating a "behavioral inhibition system" that hinders behavior in certain anxiety-provoking situations (e.g., novel or aversive incidents).

Wu and colleagues (1999) have used PET scans to develop a structural, functional theory of GAD. In their research, differences were found in the metabolism of glucose deep within the basal ganglia in normal subjects versus GAD probands. Those with GAD showed a lower metabolic rate both in cortical (white) matter and deep within the basal ganglia. The relationship between these variables is unclear, and additional research is needed. However, given the numerous physiological symptoms experienced by GAD probands, it remains likely that significant differences in brain functioning exist between controls and probands.

A different focus of research has been on the functioning of the autonomic nervous system, suggesting an "autonomic inflexibility" in those with GAD versus controls (Borkovec, 1994; T. A. Brown, Chorpita, & Barlow, 1998). Physiological arousal may be mediated by low vagal tone that results in bradycardia and decreased reactivity (Thayer et al., 2000). GAD probands show higher levels of general arousal than both clinical and nonclinical samples, generally have highly arousable central nervous systems, adapt more slowly to repeated stimuli, and respond excessively to stimuli, regardless of whether they are potentially harmful or not (Andreasen, 1997; Arborelius et al., 1999)

BIOCHEMICAL THEORIES

A specific GAD neurotransmitter has been difficult to identify, with most research suggesting multiple neurotransmitters and biochemistries (Knyazev, Savostyanov, & Lewin, 2004). Neurotransmitters lead receiving neurons either to generate another electrical impulse or cease firing, depending on which neurotransmitters and which neurons are involved (Charney & Deutch, 1996; Drevets, 1998). Potentially, any of the known inhibitory substances, such as adenosine, enkephalins, and so on, could be involved in diffuse anxiety. Researchers continue to explore possible links between GAD and neurotropins, cytokines, or cellular mediators (Deckert, 1998). The pathogenic roles of GABA, serotonin, and norepinephrine are implicated in GAD, as are corticotrophin releasing hormone and the peptide cholecystokinin (Davies & MacKenzie, 2003; Rotzinger & Vaccarino, 2003; Smoller et al., 2003). The interaction among numerous neurotransmitters at various neuroanatomies provides the strongest model for GAD's neurobiology.

GABA-Producing Neurons

Neural substrates in the inferior colliculus are particularly influenced by the inhibitory GABAergic mechanisms (Nobre & Brandao, 2004). Animals exposed to threatening stimuli exhibit a decrease in benzodiazepine receptor binding in the frontal cortex and hippocampus (Mathew et al., 2004). In fear reactions, neurons throughout the brain fire more rapidly, trigger the firing of still more neurons, and create a general state of hyperexcitability. Thereafter, GABA-producing neurons release GABA throughout the brain, inducing neurons to stop firing. Excitability is reduced, and the experience of fear and anxiety subsides.

Naturally occurring clinical substrates in the brain contain specific receptors that respond to anxiolytics. Early GABA studies focused on the "benzodiazepine receptor complex" within the brain, a GAD theory still prominent today (Insel et al., 1984; Skolnick et al., 1979). Individuals with diffuse anxiety symptoms may have diminished levels of GABA, too few GABA receptors, or GABA receptors that do not readily bind site-specific neurotransmitters (Smoller & Pollack, 1996;

Thoenen, 1995). Squires and Braestrup (1977) mapped *benzodiazepine receptors* in the brain, receptors coupled functionally to a "supramolecular receptor complex" and that involve chloride ions and GABA. Especially dense in the amygdala, frontal cortex, hippocampus, and hypothalamus, further investigation revealed that these same neuroreceptors ordinarily receive GABA, inhibiting specific neurons throughout the brain (Mombereau, Kaupmann, Van der Putten, & Cryan, 2004). Once neurons stop firing, the parasympathetic nervous system decelerates arousal of systems and decreases the likelihood that neurons transmit an impulse, resulting in a calming effect on their portions of the brain (Gifkins, Greba, & Kokkinidis, 2002). These receptors exist in large numbers throughout the brain, particularly in the cerebral cortex, hippocampus, and amygdala.

Further investigation revealed that these same neuroreceptors ordinarily receive GABA, which carries inhibitory messages throughout the brain to stop the firing of specific neurons. Once neurons stop firing, the parasympathetic nervous system decelerates arousal. Overall, the GABA/benzodiazepine receptors decrease the likelihood that neurons transmit an impulse, resulting in a calming effect on the portion of the brain in which they are active (Bloom & Kupfer, 1995; Charney & Woods, 1989). Constructed in subunits, active GABA-A receptors contain at least two alpha, two beta, and a gamma or delta subunit; only those with a gamma subunit interact and respond to benzodiazepines (Sullivan et al., 2000). All benzodiazepines primarily effect the GABA-A receptors, which also contain chloride ion channels, and to which GABA binds to increase the efficacy of certain impulses.

GABA Modulin

Normally, GABA receptors are suppressed by the protein *GABA modulin*. When GABA modulin binds to receptor sites, the receptor closes and blocks GABA access to its corresponding receptor sites. Thus, the synaptic effects of GABA are reduced. GABA-A, but not necessarily GABA-B, receptor stimulation induces anxiolysis (Nemeroff, 2003; Zarrindast, Rostami, & Sadeghi-Hariri, 2001). Particularly high concentrations of GABA-A receptors are found within the limbic system and frontal/parietal regions of the cortex (Schwartz, 1988). Reduced GABA-A receptor binding capacity has been linked with diffuse anxiety, and GABA-B antagonists may mediate an antianxiety effect through autoreceptor blockade-induced release of endogenous GABA (An et al., 2004; Kosel et al., 2004). Synaptic activation of GABA heteroreceptors elicits presynaptic inhibition of glutamatergic transmission within the basolateral amygdala (Ashton & Young, 2003). Benzodiazepines prevent GABA modulin from enhancing the synaptic action of GABA. Endogenous substances that stimulate GABA modulin provoke the anxiety response, whereas benzodiazepines can block this reaction by binding to corresponding "lock-and-key" receptors (Neigh et al., 2004). By increasing the effect of GABA, benzodiazepines decrease the nerve cell's membrane excitability.

In normal fear reactions, neurons trigger rapidly and then a reduction in excitability follows. Neurons produce GABA that then binds to specific receptor sites to stop their firing. Subsequently, the fear response is curtailed. However, in GAD patients, the feedback system that causes GABA to be released is thought to malfunction, resulting in GABA deficiency that permits excessive nerve impulse traffic throughout brain circuits (An et al., 2004). Instead of parasympathetic reduction in arousal, GAD patients continue to feel the hyperexcitement of the initial fear response without tapered reduction. GABA deficiency permits excessive nerve impulse traffic throughout the brain circuits. Individuals with diffuse anxiety symptoms may have diminished levels of GABA, too few GABA receptors, or GABA receptors that do not readily bind site-specific neurotransmitters (Smoller & Pollack, 1996; Thoenen, 1995). Benzodiazepines apparently bind to a molecule that is closely associated with the GABA postsynaptic receptor and thereby change the shape of the GABA receptor. Both barbiturates and benzodiazepines alter the shape of GABA-A receptors, causing stronger affinity for GABA (T. Inada, Nozaki, Inagaki, & Furukawa, 2003; Sigel, 2002). This shape change permits the postsynaptic neuron to respond more intensely (and normally) to GABA, in turn increasing inhibition of neuronal transmission. The ability of benzodiazepines to bind to receptors is highly correlated with anxiolytic effect, augmenting the antianxiety action of the GABA-stimulated chloride system, attaching to (and thus activating) key receptors while blocking hyperarousal (Andreasen, Paradiso, & O'Leary, 1998). Endogenous substances that stimulate GABA modulin provoke the anxiety response, whereas benzodiazepines can block this reaction by binding to corresponding "lock-and-key" receptors. The benzodiazepine receptors seem to play a role in GAD; they do not appear to be affected by tricyclic antidepressants (except perhaps secondary to sedative effects and subsequent overall relaxation).

Serotonin and GAD

Based primarily on the clinical response GAD probands have shown on SSRIs, many researchers implicate *serotonin* in diffuse anxiety (Kent, Coplan, & Gorman, 1998). Interest in the potential role of 5-HT in the biochemistry of anxiety disorders has been second only to interest in the catecholamines. Yet, the wide distribution of serotonin throughout the CNS and its interaction with multiple receptors, diverse neurotransmitters, and varying biochemical substances provide ample opportunity for potential inhibitory influence on neuronal mechanisms and subsequent behavior. Corresponding pathways ascend (spinal cord, brain stem) and descend (cortical, subcortical regions) throughout the brain. Although most of the serotonin in the body is not involved in synaptic transmission, serotonergic cell bodies are scattered in distinct clusters throughout the brain stem with caudate neurons sending their axons into the spinal cord and rostral neurons projecting into the midbrain and forebrain (Chouinard et al., 1990). Serotonergic neurons in the rostral and caudal brain stem raphe nuclear groups project into most target regions throughout limbic-midbrain loops, serving multiple functions (Yamano, Ogura, Okuyama, & Ohki-Hamazaki, 2002).

Generally more involved in biologically based theories of depression, serotonin became the focus of research in clinical anxiety (Campbell & Merchant, 2003; Charney & Deutch, 1996). The response to serotonergic medications and the worsening of symptoms after administration of serotonergic agonists indicate that this neurotransmitter is involved in clinical anxiety, particularly pathways within the locus coeruleus and limbic regions (Ohara et al., 1999). In the brain (predominantly in the midline raphe nuclei, hypothalamus, and limbic system), serotonin pools in the limbic structures and is recaptured by active reuptake (Andrade & Graeff, 2001; Lowery, 2002). The inability to maintain homeostasis of serotonin in key brain regions may be the precipitant for hyperarousal and diffuse anxiety (Marco et al., 2004; Norton & Asmundson, 2004). Increased serotonin availability contributes to the normalization of both hypoactive and hypersensitive neurons throughout the brain (Englander, Dulawa, Bhansali, & Schmauss, 2005). Its effect depends upon its interaction with specific receptors; at least 15 separate receptor sites have been identified (Kroeze, Kristiansen, & Roth, 2002; Severson, Wang, Pieribone, Dohle, & Richardson, 2003). Disturbances in serotonin 1A receptors may contribute to chronic hyperarousal and other anxiety-based somatics (Neumeister et al., 2004). Most antianxiety medications exert effects through the 5-HT1A receptor, activating inhibitory G-proteins in key region-specific biochemistries (e.g., limbic system; Lanfumey & Hamon, 2004). 5-HT3 receptors have a potentially substantial role in the regulation of the hypothalamic-pituitary-adrenal axis. 5-HT6 and 5-HT7 receptors, distributed throughout the limbic system, have known affinities for antidepressant drugs (Ansorge et al., 2004).

Central serotonergic functionality can be assessed by measuring the prolactin response to serotonergic agents, such as d-fenfluramine. Studies on the effects of buspirone, a serotonin agonist, as an effective treatment for GAD constitute consistent evidence for its serotonergic link (Apter & Allen, 1999). Buspirone, a partial 5-HT1A receptor agonist, and other 5-HT2A and 5-HT2C receptor antagonists, such as nefazodone, have been shown to be effective in treating GAD and thus spurred additional theories of its etiology (Chelben, Strous, Lustig, & Baruch, 2001).

Other Potential Neurobiological Markers

Because GAD features are generally linked to the sympathetic nervous system, some theories implicate other excitatory substances as potential neurobiological markers. Cholecystokinin prompts the release of adrenocorticotropin and cortisol, both of which activate the limbic-hypothalamic-pituitary-adrenal axis (Abelson & Young, 2003; Becker et al., 2004; Erel et al., 2004). If too much *epinephrine* is released in the brain, hyperarousal of the SNS occurs, creating more diffuse arousal (e.g., symptoms of GAD). *Norepinephrine* is an inhibitory neurotransmitter that causes alertness and wakefulness. Cell bodies for noradrenergic neurons are found throughout the brain, but high concentrations have been mapped in the bilateral nuclei of the midbrain. Arising from the locus coeruleus, the norepinephrine neurotransmitter system plays a key role in fear and anxiety, affecting the cerebral cortex, hypothalamus, and brain stem. Accordingly, clinical anxiety (predominantly GAD) may be triggered by an overactivity of norepinephrine that overstimulates certain brain functionings (Blier et al., 2004). Chronic exposure to stress can produce sensitization of norepinephrine release in the forebrain, potentiated by prior chronic stress exposure (Brunello et al., 2003). Consistent research in support of this theory has shown GAD probands are more highly aroused than normals in both clinical and normal environments (Ho, Pawlak, Guor, & Schwarting, 2004; Roemer & Orsillo, 2002).

Biologically-Based Precipitants of Anxiety

In addition to biochemical theories, other biologically-based conditions can precipitate diffuse anxiety. Various other pathophysiologies, such as metabolic disorders, antigens (any foreign substance that enters the body, such as bacteria or parasites.), infections, allergies, tumors, inadequate blood supply, or physical trauma, can affect the brain and change its physiological and behavioral output. Diverse medical conditions can mimic anxiety, such as intracranial tumors, menstrual irregularities, postconcussion syndrome, epilepsy, Cushing's syndrome, and mild head injury (Lauterbach, Freeman, & Vogel, 2003). Patients with Addison's disease and Cushing's syndrome have shown higher levels of overall anxiety and higher rates of GAD than controls (Musselman & Nemeroff, 1996). Acute hyperthyroidism is known to be anxiogenic, with many studies linking T4 concentrations and GAD symptoms (Leppavuori, Pohjasvaara, Vataja, Kaste, & Erkinjuntti, 2003). Additionally, symptoms of anxiety have been linked with hypoglycemic episodes, hyperthyroidism, cardiac arrhythmias, caffeinism, pheochromocytoma, seizure disorders, migraine, central nervous system disorders, or medication reactions. Yohimbine, an alpha-2 adrenergic receptor antagonist, activates noradrenergic neurons and precipitates anxiety in some. Medication effects, even if useful in targeting other medical conditions, can precipitate diffuse anxiety, and those most likely to elicit symptoms may include antihistamines, antiasthmatics, sympathomimetics, steroids, haloperidol and primiozide (e.g., neuroleptic-induced anxiety), selective serotonin reuptake inhibitors (SSRIs; "serotonin syndrome"), antipsychotics (akathisia), and nonprescription preparations such as diet pills and cold medicines (Kimura, Tateno, & Robinson, 2003). For a more detailed listing, see the Appendix. Standard evaluation should include obtaining a complete medical history, past and current medications, blood counts, electrolytes, calcium and glucose levels, liver functioning tests, urinalysis, drug screening, and electrocardiogram.

TREATMENTS

Treatment for GAD has been most successful using a combination of medical and psychosocial interventions, particularly in the form of interpersonal and cognitive-behavioral therapies (Rouillon, 2004). Additional alternative approaches such as acupuncture, aromatherapy, herbs, and hypnotherapy may aid relaxation and complement comprehensive recovery (Bonne, Shemer, Gorali, Katz, & Shalev, 2003; Connor & Davidson, 2002). Serotonergic and atypical antidepressants can successfully reduce the intensity and incapacitation of hyperarousal and avoidant behaviors. As with all anxiety disorders, first-line pharmacological treatments include the use of SSRIs or atypical antidepressants, as well as augmentation via azapirones and atypical anxiolytics (Allgulander et al., 2003; Flynn & Chen, 2003; Rynn & Brawman-Mintzer, 2004). Many treatment regimens have been proposed, most integrating the use of benzodiazepines, hydroxyzine, buspirone, serotonergic and hybrid antidepressants, cyclics, or novel anticonvulsants (Anti-Otong, 2003; Rickels & Rynn, 2002). Table 4.1 outlines the biopsychosocial treatments for GAD.

TABLE 4.1.
Biopsychosocial Treatments for GAD

Interventions	Targets
Pharmacological approaches	SSRIs (particularly paroxetine), buspirone, duloxetine, or venlafaxine; benzodiazepines as needed; mirtazapine
Psychoeducational interventions	Educate to improve medication compliance, provide comprehensive treatment approach utilizing diverse modalities, improve coping and adaptation skills via the teaching of novel responses, relaxation, and cognitive restructuring techniques
Psychological interventions	Developmental models that foster growth and maturation in global functioning, personality structure, and emotional attunement, working through of latent conflicts, strengthening the self via increased insight and clarification, stress inoculation training, cognitive restructuring, and identification of dysfunctional beliefs
Social interventions	Enhance social support and meaningful relationships, foster greater attachment via secure bonding, clarify boundaries and limits

Benzodiazepines

Although the risks of benzodiazepines are many (including impairment of cognitive abilities and performance and withdrawal reactions), they continue to be widely used with generally positive results. Even if taken only at therapeutic doses, prolonged use of benzodiazepines can precipitate psychological or physiological dependence (Chouinard, 2004). Gould, Otto, Pollack, and Yap (1997) have demonstrated an effect size of 0.7 improvement in symptoms when treated via benzodiazepines at therapeutic levels. Unfortunately, their effectiveness may wane within several weeks, and the risk of tolerance and dependence may prohibit chronic use (Knyazev, 2004). Often, the combination of antidepressants and benzodiazepines is used, enhancing the transmission of GABA (benzodiazepines) and stimulating the 5-HT1A receptor that subsequently inhibits the postsynaptic neuronal excitability in the amygdala and prefrontal cortex (Kapczinski, Lima, Souza, & Schmitt, 2003).

Other Regimens

Buspirone has anxiolytic properties approximately equivalent to those of benzodiazepines without the sedating effect. It has both presynaptic and postsynaptic effects (particularly within the hippocampus) on multiple neurotransmitter receptors, including serotonergic, dopaminergic, and noradrenergic (Gale & Oakley-Browne, 2001; Laine et al., 2003). Compared to benzodiazepines, antidepressants (particularly SSRIs) are more effective for psychic symptoms, cognitive rumination, and hyperarousal without threat of physiological tolerance and dependence (Atack, 2003). Further, both sedating and nonsedating antidepressants have been used successfully in GAD without concomitant depressive symptoms. Clinical response is based on the selection of particular agents while considering distribution rate, half-life, and metabolic routes. Most patients relapse after cessation of the drug; given the long-term nature of GAD, other interventions are warranted within comprehensive treatment models (Goodman, 2004; Pary, Matuschka, Lewis, Caso, & Lippmann, 2003; Powers, Smits, & Telch, 2004).

Psychotherapies

Medications have been shown to effectively reduce the symptoms of GAD, but most empirical studies reflect a greater effect from psychotherapies, particularly cognitive-behavioral techniques (Arntz, 2003; Durham, Chambers, MacDonald, Power, & Major, 2003; Epstein et al., 2004). Although studies have shown generally equal effectiveness of specific paradigms, interpersonal and cognitive-behavioral interventions have been researched and supported more than other models due to their proven efficacy, time-limited nature, and ability to provide relief quickly (Ladouceur, Leger, Dugas, & Freeston, 2004). Some research has shown effect sizes approaching 0.9 for cognitive-behavioral techniques in reducing GAD symptoms (Borkovec, Newman, & Castonguay, 2003; Dugas et al., 2003). Treatment using both medications and psychosocial treatments may have an overall synergistic effect (Ballenger, 2001; Goodwin & Gorman, 2002; Gorman, 2003; Mohlman, 2004; Taylor, 2004). Table 4.2 outlines the psychotherapeutic interventions for GAD.

Most behavioral and cognitive-behavioral treatment models focus on skills and learning, emphasizing the importance of thought processes and cognitive content. *Autogenic relaxation training* is a technique that teaches patients relaxation training so that they can maintain calm during stress or when dealing with stimuli that prompt anxiety.

Problem-focused coping is a cognitive intervention intended to reduce an individual's distress by teaching problem-solving techniques via psychoeducation. Other paradigms view anxiety as a product of counterproductive self-statements when experiencing stressful stimuli. Individuals' cognitive processes and contents heighten their anxiety and render coping strategies ineffectual. Subsequent fear and anxiety ensue.

TABLE 4.2.
Psychotherapeutic Interventions for GAD

Symptom	Interventions
Excessive worry, fear	Thought-stopping and thought substitution, decreasing perfectionism and demandingness ("things must be just this way"), cognitive restructuring to extinguish irrationality, working through emotional conflicts that precipitate fear, verbalizing worries to confidants who can understand and respond with empathy, replacing negative self-statements with coping self-statements
Expectation of doom; attentional biases toward threat	Psychoeducation to balance attribution and decision-making, rigorous disputation of cognitive distortions (e.g., "the environment is harmful")
Functional impairments	Establishment of strong peer relationships, gradual exposure to stressful situations, emphasis on health, reduction of cognitive inhibitions
General somatic arousal	Relaxation, use of self-statement techniques to continually encourage coping, contentment, serenity, etc., regular exercise to reduce muscle tension, improvement of self-esteem, medications to control hyperarousal (e.g., SSRIs), deep breathing, meditation, yoga, guided imagery
Insomnia, other sleep disturbances	Teaching of sleep hygiene, possible use of hypnotics, sedating tricyclics, mirtazapine

Self-instructional training teaches patients to "listen with a third ear" to self-talk and substitute dysfunctional, negative statements with productive, coping assertions. Systematic desensitization, counterconditioning, shaping of novel behaviors, assertiveness training, social skills techniques, and exposure therapies are effective.

Stress Inoculation Training. Social skills, problem-solving algorithms, and cognitive restructuring are useful in reducing anxiety. Meichenbaum's (1977) **stress inoculation training (SIT)** teaches anxiety management skills—breathing retraining, relaxation, thought-stopping, cognitive restructuring, and guided self-dialogue—through instruction, role-playing, and modeling. Important coping skills include education about stress and fearful reactions, appropriate appraisal and coping techniques, and rehearsal of adaptation and application (testing and practicing in real situations).

Stress inoculation training involves teaching individuals to realistically consider what lies ahead, to subdivide stressful situations into manageable parts, and to think of ways to handle stressful stimuli and cope adaptively. The use of positive self-statements—the "automatic thoughts" that individuals tell themselves—provides a key foundation for eventual coping. For example, anxious patients are taught that (1) all individuals experience stress and anxious situations; (2) cognitions can engender emotions; (3) self-monitoring and self-statements can effectively control emotional functioning; (4) problem-solving and coping skills can resolve stressors; and (5) the practice and rehearsal of coping skills can make their use more "natural" in the face of stressful situations (Parker, Buckmaster, et al., 2004). Meichenbaum's model teaches a four-stage model for coping with stress: (1) preparation, (2) confrontation and effective response, (3) management of emotions and feelings, and (4) reinforcing positive self-statements.

**STRESS-INOCULATION TRAINING:
COPING SKILLS**

- Encourage realistic understanding of the seriousness, effects, and consequences of stressful crisis.
- Promote education, understanding, and insight into relevant information.
- Provide appropriate self-talk, self-reassurance, and emotional support.
- Learn situation-specific self-care.
- Create and work toward realistic, attainable goals.
- Practice, rehearse alternative outcomes.
- Maintain perspective on life goals, priorities, and so on.

SAMPLE IRRATIONAL BELIEFS

- I need to be loved and adored by others to feel good about myself.
- I should be competent and proficient in all things I attempt.
- Avoiding stressful situations is the best way of coping in life.
- The environment is basically harmful and threatening
- When things don't go well, it's catastrophic.
- Mean people will hurt me.
- Past experiences determine my activities, interests, and capabilities.
- Novelty is too frightening to explore or attempt.
- Each situation has one "right" solution, and I must find it to be "okay."

Rational Emotive Therapy. Highly action-oriented and focused on cognitive and moral functioning, Albert Ellis's **rational emotive therapy** delineates certain **irrational beliefs** that precipitate emotional turmoil. Its basic premise is that emotional suffering is due to the maladaptive ways people construe the world as a result of holding irrational beliefs. In other words, *anxiety results from irrational thinking.* This model stresses individual's ability to think on their own and change, providing a method to solve and alleviate emotional and behavioral problems by systematically challenging beliefs and cognitive processes.

When thinking and behaving rationally, individuals are effective, happy, and competent, experiencing a sense of mastery and self-esteem. Thought and emotion are not separate, different functions; rather, emotion accompanies thinking, and thinking is usually biased, personalized, and irrational. Irrational thoughts originate in early learning. Anxious individuals perpetuate their disturbance and maintain illogical behavior by their internal verbalization of irrational ideas and thoughts. Continuing states of emotional disturbance are determined not by external events but by the perceptions and attitudes toward these events that are incorporated in the internalized sentences about them.

Negative and self-defeating thoughts and emotions must be attacked by a reorganization of perceptions and thinking so that thinking becomes logical and rational rather than illogical and irrational. Ellis's model presents the **ABC paradigm** of emotional distress: the A (*activating event*) represents an external event, B (*beliefs*) signifies an individual's thoughts and beliefs, and C (*consequences*) delineates the behavioral and emotional responses. Ellis advocates adding a

---

ELLIS'S MODEL FOR INTERVENTION

Activating Event → Beliefs → Consequences → Disputation

D (*dispute*) that motivates patients to actively identify and dispute their own irrationality. The changing of irrational beliefs occurs through disconfirmation, insight, or reconceptualization.

SUMMARY

The major features of GAD include hyperarousal, cognitive worry, and avoidance. Most biological models of GAD focus on neurotransmitters, with GABA, serotonin, and norepinephrine being key culprits. As with other anxiety disorders, effective treatments include benzodiazepines, SSRIs, or other antidepressants. Nonpharmacological interventions, such as cognitive-behavioral and interpersonal therapies, can reduce symptoms and improve overall functioning.

CHAPTER 5

Obsessive-Compulsive Disorder

FIRST DESCRIBED BY ESQUIROL in 1838, *obsessive-compulsive disorder* (OCD) has remained one of the most complicated of all anxiety conditions, integrating diffuse features of GAD, panic, and phobia. The *DSM-IV-TR* defines the essential features of OCD as "recurrent obsessions or compulsions that are severe enough to be time-consuming or cause marked distress or significant impairment" (APA, 2000, p. 417). In addition to the general criteria of hyperarousal and avoidant behaviors, OCD shows two additional defining characteristics: *cognitive rumination* (brooding, repetition, obsession) and *compulsive behavior* (any action intended to reduce the discomfort of rumination).

OCD is a highly debilitating neuropsychiatric condition, yet little is known of its etiology, neural circuits and substrates, and profile. Overall, the precise nature of the interactions among various variables, their roles in OCD, and appropriate interventions are not yet fully understood. Medical models have focused primarily on neurotransmitter activity or functionality of specific brain regions, particularly within the basal ganglia, limbic system, or prefrontal cortex. The neurocircuit linking the orbital cortex, the striatum, and the thalamus is involved in OCD. Further, current theory implicates the basal ganglia—the prefrontal cortex–basal ganglia–thalamus circuit—though its exact role is still unclear (Shimizu, Hashimoto, & Iyo, 2002; Van den Heuvel et al., 2005). The biochemistry and neuropharmacology of OCD supports both neurotransmitter theories (e.g., serotonin) and the role of the orbital–basal ganglia–thalamic circuit.

Most individuals dismiss unpleasant thoughts easily without subsequent brooding. For non obsessive individuals, a disturbing event or situation may lead to disturbing images or thoughts, but the thoughts are dismissed. However, OCD probands differ in that they seem unable to habituate, dismiss, and distract themselves from unwanted thoughts (Katrin-Kuelz, Riemann, Zahn, & Voderholzer, 2004). An *obsession* is a persistent idea, thought, or image that is experienced, at least initially, as intrusive and senseless. Obsessional content may symbolize underlying conflicts that, when recognized, provoke anxiety. Obsessive content and processes differ from the generalized worry in other anxiety disorders in that they are mental experiences that are not merely excessive worries about common stressors. Frequent OCD obsessions include five basic categories: contamination, aggression, sexuality, physiological concerns, or the need for order (Denys, de Geus, van Megen, & Westenberg, 2004b; Tuna, Tekcan, & Topcuoglu, 2005).

Thought Content

The particular content of the obsessions is symbolic of underlying conflicts that, when recognized, provoke anxiety. For obsessives, the associated anxiety linked with the event and subsequent cognitions exacerbates the intensity of the unwanted thoughts, and they become progressively more difficult to dismiss (Shin, Park, et al., 2004). Efforts to control unwanted thoughts increase their saliency and the individual's attention to them, leading to greater overall anxiety. The more stressed an individual is, the more frequent and intense the cognitive processes. Recurrence of these thoughts causes intensification of anxiety, with accompanying negative affect, and they may be judged as unpredictable and uncontrollable. The vicious negative feedback loop of anxiety then develops, with attention narrowed onto the content of the unacceptable thoughts themselves (Coles, Heimberg, Frost, & Steketee, 2005). Additionally, the OCD proband may seek to substitute good thoughts in lieu of the unwanted cognitions (*neutralizing*). They may seek special reassurance from others, deliberately think good thoughts, visualize positive images, and so on, as means of compensating for undesirable thoughts (Purdon, 2004a). Eventually the neutralizing thought or act is employed so often that it becomes an obsession or compulsion. Simultaneously, when the neutralization reduces discomfort, the individual feels that its original reprehension, dangerousness, and need for its elimination is confirmed. Thus the intrusive thought becomes even more distressing and worrisome (Purdon, 2004b). This pattern of cognitive biases leading to impaired intrapsychic processing suggests possible impairments in reality-testing among some OCD probands (Bhatara, Alshari, Warhol, McMillin, & Bhatara, 2004; Einstein & Menzies, 2004). Frequently, the nature and content of the obsessions are bizarre and delusional, and these probands usually are treated with antipsychotics (Sevincok, Akoglu, Topaloglu, & Aslantas, 2004).

Corresponding Obsessions

Obsessional content links with corresponding *compulsions* (Table 5.1). Compul- *sive behaviors* are repetitive, purposeful, and intentional behaviors performed in response to an obsession, according to perceived rules or stereotyped fashions, to provide temporary relief from anxiety and subdue rumination. Rituals are a key

TABLE 5.1.
Common Obsessions and Corresponding Compulsions

Obsessions	Compulsions
Contamination	Washing
Harming self/others	Rumination
Losing control	Avoiding specific foods/drinks
Sexual thoughts	Checking/repeating
Excessive moral or religious issues	Touching/reassurance
Perfectionism	Hoarding
Somatic concerns	Ordering/counting
Occult/evil	Praying

element in the behavioral expression of OCD, providing temporary distraction or relief from latent anxiety (Ball, Baer, & Otto, 1996; Summerfeldt, 2004). Such repetitive behaviors as handwashing, counting, checking, and cleaning are performed to subdue cognitive rumination, and not completing the ritual often leads to an increase in overall arousal and subsequent anxiety. Compulsive rituals are not limited to overt behaviors; covert rituals, such as repeating or visualizing phrases, prayers, images, and so on, can also represent compulsive rituals aimed at reducing anxiety (Fairbrother, Newth, & Rachman, 2005). Behavioral rituals provide temporary relief and *not* performing them exacerbates anxiety. Compulsions can be any activity or functioning that is intended to reduce or elude obsession, with the most common compulsive behavior being washing and checking rituals (Calamari et al., 2004). Factor analytic studies have shown common themes among patients: symmetry/ordering, hoarding, and contamination/cleaning (Denys, De Geus, Van Megen, & Westenberg, 2004c).

Variations of Symptoms

OCD clinical presentation is remarkably diverse, varying both within and across probands over time. The condition involves movement, anxiety, and impulsive features, with significant heterogeneity of symptoms and multiple "subtypes" (Anderson, Louis, Stern, & Marder, 2001; Summerfeldt, Kloosterman, Antony, Richter, & Swinson, 2004). For example, as a movement disorder, OCD involves impulsive and compulsive behaviors. As an anxiety disorder, cognitive biases and distortions in thought content may suggest delusional aspects (Einstein & Menzies, 2004). Thus, some researchers subdivide syndromes under "spectrum" classifications; advances in medical technologies have provided more sophisticated neurobiological theories (Baer, 1994; Summerfeldt, 2004). Subtyping of OCD spectrum disorders may depend upon age of onset and comorbid syndromes

DSM-IV-TR CRITERIA FOR
OBSESSIVE-COMPULSIVE DISORDER*

A. Either obsessions or compulsions:

Obsessions as defined by (1), (2), (3), and (4):

   (1) recurrent and persistent thoughts, impulses, or images that are
        experienced, at some time during the disturbance, as intrusive
        and inappropriate and that cause marked anxiety and distress
   (2) the thoughts, impulses, or images are not simply excessive wor-
        ries about real-life problems
   (3) the person attempts to ignore or suppress such thoughts, im-
        pulses, or images, or to neutralize them with some other thought
        or action
   (4) the person recognizes that the obsessional thoughts, impulses,
        or images are a product of his or her own mind (not imposed
        from without as in thought insertion)

Compulsions as defined by (1) and (2):

   (1) repetitive behaviors (e.g., hand washing, ordering, checking) or
        mental acts (e.g., praying, counting, repeating words silently)
        that the person feels driven to perform in response to an obses-
        sion, or according to rules that must be applied rigidly
   (2) the behaviors or mental acts are aimed at preventing or reduc-
        ing distress or preventing some dreaded event or situation; how-
        ever, these behaviors or mental acts either are not connected in
        a realistic way with what they are designed to neutralize or pre-
        vent or are clearly excessive

B. At some point during the course of the disorder, the person has recog-
    nized that the obsessions or compulsions are excessive or unreasonable.
    Note: This does not apply to children.
C. The obsessions or compulsions cause marked distress, are time con-
    suming (take more than one hour a day), or significantly interfere with
    the person's normal routine, occupational (or academic) functioning,
    or usual social activities or relationships.
D. If another Axis I disorder is present, the content of the obsessions or
    compulsions is not restricted to it (e.g., preoccupation with food in the
    presence of an Eating Disorder; hair pulling in the presence of Tri-
    chotillomania; concern with appearance in the presence of Body Dys-

morphic Disorder; preoccupation with drugs in the presence of a Substance Use Disorder; preoccupation with having a serious illness in the presence of Hypochondriasis; preoccupation with sexual urges or fantasies in the presence of a Paraphilia; or guilty ruminations in the presence of Major Depressive Disorder).

E. The disturbance is not due to the direct physiological effects of a substance (e.g., a drug of abuse, a medication) or a general medical condition.

Specify if:

With Poor Insight: If, for most of the time during the current episode, the person does not recognize that the obsessions and compulsions are excessive or unreasonable

*Reprinted with permission from the *Diagnostic and Statistical Manual of Mental Disorders, Fourth Edition, Text Revision*. Copyright 2000 American Psychiatric Association.

(Watson, Wu, & Cutshall, 2004). Recent factor-analytic studies have identified consistent OCD dimensions, suggesting distinct latent psychogenics, associated with different biodata, comorbidities, genetics, and treatment responses (Fontenelle, Mendlowicz, Soares, & Versiani, 2004; Morer et al., 2005). The association of tic disorders with OCD may represent a unique subtype (Crespo-Facorro et al., 1999). Other subtype groupings may include early/late onset and with/without comorbid depression (Watson, et al., 2004). Certain factors appear common among diverse OCD symptoms: (1) anxiety fueling obsessions and compulsions; (2) probands' common fear that something bad will happen in their future, as well as their assumption of responsibility; and (3) compulsive behaviors reflecting attempts to reduce momentary anxiety, without long-term relief (Mataix-Cols, do Rosario-Campos, & Leckman, 2005). Principal component analyses have provided support for obsessive and compulsive factors, each with putative genetic bases (Lochner & Stein, 2003; Miguel et al., 2005; Nordstrom & Burton, 2002).

PREVALENCE

Early estimates of lifetime prevalence of OCD were estimated to be about 1%. Later epidemiological studies estimated the annual and lifetime prevalence rates to be higher, ranging from 5% to 8% when including "OCD spectrum" conditions (Angst et al., 2004; Bebbington, 1998). Its prevalence is not daunted by gender, education, intelligence, or vocation (Cillicilli et al., 2004). As the fourth most common mental disorder, its prevalence rivals that of asthma and diabetes.

Age of onset is usually during late adolescence or early adulthood. Brain mechanisms involved in OCD may differ depending on when symptoms first begin. Busatto et al. (2001) found significant differences in cerebral blood flow in the frontal-subcortical circuits between early- and late-onset probands. Early-onset OCD patients showed decrease perfusion in the right thalamus, left anterior cingulate cortex, and prefrontal cortex (Alptekin et al., 2001; Ho Pian et al., 2005).

GENDER TYPING

Gender may contribute to the clinical and biological heterogeneity, using a dimorphic pattern of genetic susceptibility for symptoms (Lochner et al., 2004). Although most patients report that symptoms began during their teenage years, some probands report earlier onset (Ulloa, Nicolini, & Fernandez-Guasti, 2004a). Among childhood onset probands, males outnumber females dramatically (with some estimates proposing a two to one ratio). Males tend to show symptoms in their mid-teens, whereas females may not exhibit features until their early twenties. In general, males have earlier onset, differing patterns of comorbid conditions, and potential diverse genetic involvement than females. Females report changes in symptoms secondary to hormonal changes, such as those associated with menstruation, pregnancy, and menopause (Ulloa, Nicolini, & Fernandez-Guasti, 2004b). Additionally, when compared to male counterparts, female probands report a higher incidence of childhood trauma, particularly sexual abuse. The disorder persists chronically with fluctuating symptoms over time (Mataix-Coles, Alonso, Pifarre, Menchon, & Vallejo, 2002). Symptom expression may be dependent upon cultural norms, but the disorder is seen worldwide (Fontenelle, Mendlowicz, Marques, & Versiani, 2004). Risk factors include traumatic childhood abuses, significant changes that inspire overwhelming anxieties, chronic illness, conflicts involving sexuality, or impaired relationships (Norton & Whittal, 2004).

ASSOCIATED COMORBIDITIES

Comorbidity of OCD with other psychiatric disorders is quite common, with some estimates of 60% or higher. It is not uncommon for OCD patients to experience severe anxiety (e.g., GAD), episodic panic, debilitating avoidance, or depression (Basso, Bornstein, Carona, & Morton, 2001; Huppert et al., 2005). Obsessional thoughts become much like discrete phobic stimuli in their capacity to elicit panic attacks or learned alarms. Comorbidity with anxiety disorders is quite high, ranging from 25% to 60%, with the highest frequencies for specific phobias, social phobia, and panic (Comer, Kendall, Franklin, Hudson, & Pimentel, 2004; Denys, Tenney, Van Megen, de Geus, & Westenberg, 2004). At least a third of OCD patients report longstanding histories of clinical depression, but whether their depression is primary or secondary remains unclear (Millet et al.,

2004). Successful treatment of OCD usually mediates depressive symptoms. Anxiety disorders, depression, substance abuse, eating disorders, Tourette's, body dysmorphic disorder, hypochondriasis, and schizophrenia have all been associated with OCD. Both OCD and *obsessive-compulsive personality disorder* **(OCPD)** include a similar process of cognitive rumination and associated compulsivity. However, OCD is more clearly defined by behavioral symptoms while OCPD is more of a usual way of life (Albert, Maina, Forner, & Bogetto, 2004). Associated syndromes closely related to OCD include body dysmorphic disorder, Tourette's syndrome, compulsive shoplifting or gambling, behavioral addictions, and trichotillomania (compulsive pulling out of one's own hair). Pediatric movement disorders, such as Tourette's, tics, and Sydenham chorea, suggest that childhood-onset OCD and pediatric movement disorders are linked (Lochner et al., 2005). OCD often leads to secondary conditions of depression, generalized anxiety, phobias, addictions, or panic disorder.

PSYCHOSOCIAL THEORIES

Over the past 30 years, theories and treatments have evolved that integrate biological variables and environmental factors (Cartwright-Hatton, Roberts, Chitsabesan, Fothergill, & Harrington, 2004; Overbeck, Michal, Russ, Lanfermann, & Roder, 2004). Contemporary theory has integrated analytic thought, cognitive and behavioral models, and growing understanding of neurobiological variables.

Psychoanalysis

Freud's theory viewed obsessive-compulsive neurosis as secondary to regression in psychosexual development. Regression is intended to increase primitive pleasures, hold onto others via dependency, or discharge impulses differently. Obsessive thoughts may represent defenses against even more intolerable and unwanted thoughts, involving displacement and substitution. An unconscious dangerous thought brings anxiety as it threatens to seep into consciousness. Aggressive impulses reflect unfulfilled needs for self-expression or efforts to overcome feelings of vulnerability or insecurity. Competition occurs between intense, aggressive impulses and the desire to control them. If shame and doubt supercede autonomy, an "anal personality" configuration that fosters selfishness, perfectionism, or compulsive behaviors occurs. Obsessional content symbolizes underlying conflict (Mathews, Jang, Hami, & Stein, 2004). Powerful, abhorrent wishes (e.g., aggressive id impulses) and conflicts (expression vs. mediation) that have been repressed and threaten to break into consciousness put an individual at risk for obsession, and adopting the defenses of displacement and substitution provides relief. The battle between anxiety-provoking id impulses and anxiety-reducing mechanisms is played out explicitly rather than at an unconscious level. The id impulses usually take the form of obsessive thoughts, and the ego defenses appear as counterthoughts or compulsive actions. Psychogenic factors include preoccupation with aggression, preoccupation with dirt, disturbed growth, and fixation within the anal-sadistic phase. During the anal stage of development, some children experience intense rage and shame that fuel conflict between id-ego functioning and therefore set the stage for OCD. These individuals are derived of psychosexual pleasure via defecation while caregivers teach control and delay of anal gratification. If parental objects are overly hostile, rageful, or too harsh in their toilet training, the child experiences aggressive id impulses that continually seek expression. If parents handle this aggressiveness by further chastisement, the child may feel further shame, rage, or guilt. The aggressive impulses are countered by a strong desire to control them, and this intense conflict may eventually blossom into OCD. In essence, OCD results from the experience of rigid and demanding parental figures throughout the anal stage.

Fear of overwhelming id impulses prompts defensive stances. When feeling fearful of retaliation from others or of loss, OCD probands intrapsychically regress and exhibit strong emotional ambivalence, representing aggressive or hostile motives. Three ego defenses are particularly important to OCD: isolation, undoing, and reaction formation. **Isolation** refers to the process in which the ego represses affective components—but not informational parts—of an experience or trauma. **Undoing** is a defense mechanism of the ego in which it atones for past bad (immoral) acts by gestures or rituals intended to "cancel out" unpleasant thoughts and feelings. In **reaction formation**, the ego reduces anxiety by attributing the opposite feeling to the experience rather than to those that cause conflict. When forbidden impulses overwhelm the defense mechanism of isolation, a primary defense, the secondary defense of undoing is utilized via compulsive behaviors to subdue the anxiety associated with the wish. The compulsive act is an attempt to prevent the consequences anticipated by fearful obsessional thoughts or images. Reaction formation traits may become part of the personality to atone for unacceptable wishes, motives, or drives (Cruz-Fuentes, Blas, Gonzalez, Camarena, & Nicolini, 2004; Fullana et al., 2004). Powerful, abhorrent wishes (e.g., aggressive id impulses) and conflicts (expression vs. mediation) that have been repressed and threaten to break into consciousness put an individual at risk for obsession, and adopting the defenses of displacement and substitution provides relief. By breaking the connection between motive-related thoughts and actions in their context, the meaning of an unacceptable wish is lost, along with its associated anxiety. Thus, thoughts and actions can be repeated over and over again, providing instinctual gratification, without arousing anxiety. Once the conscious meaning of an act has been camouflaged, anxiety is avoided. Another form of isolation involves disconnecting an action and the feelings/emotions normally associated with it, allowing expression without precipitating anxiety. Subsequently, the repressed emotions may become attached to some other action that originally had no emotional significance but now is laden with displaced feelings.

Interpersonal Paradigms

Psychodynamic theorists believe that OCD develops early in life, regardless of when it manifests, when individuals begin to fear their own id impulses and seek to use defense mechanisms against subsequent anxiety. Object-relations theories propose that disturbed relationships early in life leave some individuals with a dichotomous view of the world, marked by polar opposites, that distort conscious perception of thoughts, emotions, interactions, and so on into either all good or all bad. Ego alien obsessions are used to neutralize the negative aspects of experience. Kohut's self psychology uniquely views OCD as a manifestation of what he referred to as ***traumatic states***, an experience of intrapsychic flooding with narcissistic libido (and potentially oral sadistic rage) due to poorly internalized regulatory functions of the ego. Reactions to frustration, narcissistic wounds, or unmet needs for soothing and idealization prompt feelings of discomfort, tension, and anxiety. To restore psychic homeostasis, obsessive-compulsive behavior attempts to get all in order and bring a sense of structure, even if it is transient. Compulsive behaviors are meant to combat the inner sense of fragmentation or deadness, incohesion, or rage. Compulsiveness may take the form of a ***narcissistic behavior disorder***, any dysfunctional activity used to reduce anxiety and bring cohesion to a fragmented self (Kohut, 1971).

Behavioral Paradigms

Rachman and Hodgson (Rachman, 1978; Rachman & Hodgson, 1974, 1980) have formulated an OCD model based on both content and process of cognitive functioning. In their model all individuals experience unwanted thoughts and intrusive cognitions occasionally. Rather than recognizing intrusive thoughts as normal and meaningless, OCD probands think they can and should control all unpleasant thoughts that pop into the mind and fear loss of control over behavior (Abramowitz, Whiteside, Kalsy, & Tolin, 2003). The specific content of the obsessions is determined by learned dispositions that certain thoughts or images are unacceptable (Janeck, Calamari, Riemann, & Heffelfinger, 2003). Other information-processing dysfunctions, such as memory, categorization, attribution, or attention, have been proposed as precipitants to OCD. For example, four types of memory impairments have been proposed: memory for actions, general memory, confidence in memory, or reality-monitoring (Matthews, Mackintosh, & Fulcher, 1997). OCD probands may fail to categorize and integrate information veridically, selectively attend to stimuli, fail to inhibit irrelevant stimuli in cognitive processes, or show memory defects that foster symptoms (Airaksinen, Larsson, & Forsell, 2005). OCD probands have shown deficits in nonverbal memory—but not verbal memory—when compared to controls (Trivedi, 1996). Tallis (1997) proposed that OCD represents chronic underinclusion of important stimuli, leading to an inability to organize experience and overdefinition of categorical boundaries. OCD probands are too exclusive in their classification processes and produce too many categories, leading to massive ambivalence and indecision in organizing and integrating experiences (Williams et al., 2005).

Some theories view OCD as a habitual "what if" condition in which probands consistently focus on the future and anticipated failure to thrive (Alonso, Menchon, et al., 2004; Szechtman & Woody, 2004). A distorted perception of looming danger and rapidly rising risk generates excessive anxiety. *Apprehensive expectation* is the anticipation of disaster. Behavioral formulations focus on two key factors: (1) neutral stimuli that provoke fear based on previous pairing with aversive outcomes, and (2) compulsions (forms of avoidance) that provide relief from anxious discomfort. Specifically, intense stress-related negative affect and neurobiological reactions are triggered by negative life events. Resulting intrusive thoughts become judged unacceptable with subsequent attempts to avoid or suppress them (Radomsky & Rachman, 2004a). Recurrence of these thoughts causes intensification of anxiety, with accompanying negative affect and a sense that these thoughts are proceeding in an unpredictable and uncontrollable manner (Libby, Reynolds, Derisley, & Clark, 2004). To reduce symptoms, patients must identify, challenge, and change dysfunctional beliefs that unwanted negative thoughts are terrible, abnormal, in need of control, and so on.

Cognitive-Behavioral Models

Salkovskis (1985, 1996) proposed a cognitive-behavioral model of OCD based on two key concepts: (1) a personalized sense of hyper-responsibility, and (2) belief in the ability to shape and influence consequences of intrusive thoughts (*pivotal power*). Believing some thoughts are unacceptable and therefore must be suppressed (a specific psychological vulnerability) may put some individuals at greater risk of OCD (Amir, Cashman, & Foa, 1997). *Responsibility OCD* manifests as irrational fears of harming others and is linked to low self-esteem and a pervasive sense of guilt (Salkovskis, Shafran, Radhman, & Freeston, 1999). One behavioral hypothesis is that early experiences teach individuals that some thoughts are dangerous and unacceptable because the terrible things they are thinking might actually happen and the patient would be responsible (Abramowitz, Deacon, Woods, & Tolin, 2004). These experiences result in a specific psychological vulnerability to OCD, learned through the same process of misinformation (Berle & Starcevic, 2005). Patients with OCD equate thoughts with specific actions or activity represented by the thoughts, a process called *thought-action fusion*, caused by excessive responsibility and prompting the same guilt experienced in childhood when a bad thought is associated with evil intent (Abramowitz, Whiteside, Lynam, & Kalsy, 2003; Shafran & Rachman, 2004). This cognitive bias has become the focus of many cognitive therapies (Lee, Cougle, & Telch, 2005).

GENETICS

OCD has a genetic component, yet localizing specific genetic variables continues to be problematic. In one study of female twins, best-fit models suggested heritabilities of 33% for obsessiveness and 26% for compulsivity (Jonnal, Gardner, Prescott, & Kendler, 2000). Correlational additive effects approach 30% of symptom variation (Williams et al., 2005). Other studies have shown 70% concordance between monozygotic twins and 50% between fraternals (Hettema et al., 2003).

Family Studies

Family and twin studies have supported a strong genetic factor in OCD, although the precise mechanisms of transmission remain unclear (Pato, Schindler, & Pato, 2001). OCD probands have a 25% chance of having a relative who also exhibits the condition (Giedd, Rapoport, Garvey, Perlmutter, & Swedo, 2000). Patterns of inheritance within families imply transmission of an autosomal dominant genetic locus. A meta-analysis of 14 published studies included 80 monozygotic twins (54 concordant) and 29 dizygotic twins (9 concordant) suggests a moderate genetic heritability (Billet, Richter, & Kennedy, 1998). Family studies reveal higher rates of OCD in first-degree relatives of OCD patients than controls; about 10% of first-degree relatives have diagnosable OCD (Billett et al., 1998; Grados, Walkup, & Walford, 2003). Because of the common association between Tourette's and OCD, some researchers have speculated that these conditions may be different expressions of a similar underlying genetic vulnerability, possibly in the basal ganglia, frontal cortex region (Slattery et al., 2004). Some researchers have linked genetic variations with OCD and associated conditions, such as anorexia, Asperger's, social phobia, tics, substance abuse, or neurologically based movement disorders (Hudziak et al., 2004). There is an increased rate of OCD in patients with Tourette's syndrome, as well as some scattered studies that show a link between OCD and tics (Kurlan & Kaplan, 2004). Some forms of OCD may share common genetics with Tourette's syndrome, suggesting a facultative part of the Tourette's phenotypic spectrum (Cath, Spinhoven, Landman, & Van Kempen, 2001).

Candidate Genes

Many candidate genes have been suggested, based largely on studies linking serotonergic and dopaminergic systems (Hemmings et al., 2003; Hemmings et al., 2004; Walitza et al., 2004). Polymorphisms of genes of the serotonergic system and pathways are increasingly becoming the target of controlled studies, though providing mixed results (Chabane et al., 2004; Meira-Lima et al., 2004).

Analysis of DNA samples from OCD probands suggests association with an un-common mutant, malfunctioning gene that leads to faulty transporter function-ing (e.g., hSERT) and aberrant biochemical regulations in families with preva-lence OCD (Stengler-Wenzke, Muller, Angermeyer, Sabri, & Hesse, 2004). A second variant in the same gene has been linked with greater biochemical ef-fects and intensity of OCD symptoms (Baca-Garcia et al., 2005). A substitution of Val425 for Ile425 in the genetic variants of the hSERT has been linked with OCD (Urraca et al., 2004). This variant, correlated with increased expression and function of the serotonin transporter, may be associated with unusual sever-ity or treatment resistance in some OCD probands. The 5-HT1Dbeta receptor gene may be involved in mediating the intensity of cognitive rumination. Ca-marena, Aguilar, Loyzaga, and Nicolini (2004) found that the 5-HT1Dbeta re-ceptor gene consistently predicted severity of OCD symptoms. Polymorphisms of the dopamine DA-3 and DA-4 receptors have been associated with obsessive-compulsive personality traits but not OCD (Joyce et al., 2003; Millet et al., 2003). Van der Wee and colleagues (2004) found that OCD probands, when compared to controls, showed greater binding patterns for dopamine transporter in the left caudate and left putamen. Genes involved in the autoimmune re-sponse, such as the myelin oligodendrocyte glycoprotein (MOG) gene, may be involved in early-onset OCD (Denys, Fluitman, Kavelaars, Heijnen, & West-berg, 2004; Zai et al., 2004).

Because serotonin, glutamate, and dopamine have been associated with OCD, many transporter genes may produce genetic vulnerability (Meira-Lima et al., 2004). Theoretically, polymorphisms in genes related to tryptophan hy-droxylase, serotonin 2A receptor, serotonin 2C receptor, serotonin transporter, dopamine DA-4 receptor, dopamine transporter, and possibly NMDA receptors may be involved in creating diatheses for OCD. Variants in genes modulating monoamine metabolism contribute to OCD susceptibility, with gender-specific dimorphic patterns of OCD vulnerability (Saunders-Pullman et al., 2002). Sig-nificant links between OCD and MAO-A genes have been found (Camarena et al., 2001). GRIN2B may be associated with greater susceptibility to OCD. New and converging studies (integrating basic neuroscientific and clinical neu-roimaging findings) suggest that altered glutamatergic neurotransmission may be involved in OCD, and associated subunit receptor genes may be implicated (Carlsson, 2001; Harvey, Scheepers, Brand, & Stein, 2001). A functional poly-morphism in the coding region of the COMT gene has also been proposed (Schindler, Richter, Kennedy, Pato, & Pato, 2000). However, Erdal and col-leagues (2003) failed to find a relationship between COMT enzyme activity gov-erned by genetic polymorphism at codon 158. COMT gene polymorphism was not directly associated with OCD; further clarification is needed. Polymor-phisms in the glutamate receptor, ionotropic, N-methyl-d-aspartate 2B have been associated with OCD (Bergink, van Megen, & Westenberg, 2004). Arnold, Rosenberg, et al, (2004) found that polymorphisms in the untranslated region of glutamate receptor 2B may provide a unique vulnerability for certain subtypes of OCD. Polymorphisms in the 3' untranslated region of GRIN2B may be linked to OCD. Further study is needed, but this finding may suggest a unique role for glutamate in the pathogenesis of OCD.

Overall, apart from twin studies that compare known genetics and subsequent OCD symptoms, research provides contradictory and antagonistic outcomes. Phenotypic and genetic heterogeneity of OCD symptoms poses unique difficulties in locating susceptibility genes; subtyping and endophenotyping based on brain mechanisms may be useful in isolating genetic vulnerabilities (Wolff, Alsobrook, & Pauls, 2000). Still other research has looked at protective genetic variations that may lessen the risk of OCD or symptom intensity (Camarena et al., 2004). Unfortunately, attempts to identify genetic etiologies have produced mixed and conflicting results (Azzam & Matthews, 2003). A better understanding of internal processes, intrapsychic functionings, environmental triggers, OCD subtypes, and pathophysiologies will foster further localizing of genes that confer risk. Further research is needed to determine the exact nature of genetic contributions.

STRUCTURAL MODELS

Using imaging scans and other measures of brain functionality, researchers are exploring the link between structural abnormalities, subsequent functional impairments, and OCD symptoms. Unfortunately, research on structural abnormalities in the brains of OCD probands has provided inconsistent results (Coetzer, 2004). Nevertheless, some studies indicate abnormalities in the frontal lobes, basal ganglia, or cingulum.

Structural Research

Neurodevelopmental models have proposed that OCD results from structural irregularities initiated by disruption of normal brain maturation (Grados, 2003). Rosenberg and Keshavan (1998) cited three primary properties of OCD as pointing to a developmental aberration rather than degenerative process: (1) most probands track symptoms beginning in childhood or adolescence, (2) similarity exists between normal developmental behaviors and burgeoning OCD patterns, and (3) pathognomic neurological signs present at onset often do not show exacerbation during the fluctuating patterns of OCD symptoms. Some forms of brain damage, such as frontocaudal lesions, basal ganglia cavitations, and localized glucose metabolism impairment, have been associated with poor frontocaudal regulation within the left hemisphere of the brain (Kurup & Kurup, 2002; Pujol et al., 2004). Other neuroanatomical theories suggest that abnormalities in the cortical-striatal-thalamic-cortical circuits are involved in OCD (Evans, Lewis, & Iobst, 2004; Pujol et al., 1999). Lesions within the striato-orbito-frontal loop can produce symptomatic features of OCD (Micallef & Blin, 2001; Ogai, Iyo, Mori, &

Takei, 2005). Abnormalities in the corpus callosum have been implicated in the pathogenesis of OCD (Farchione, Lorch, & Rosenberg, 2002). OCD probands have smaller globus pallidus and amygdala volumes than healthy controls (Szezko, MacMillan, McMeniman, Chen, et al., 2004, Szesko, MacMillan, McMeniman, Lorch, et al., 2004). Because of its involvement in "primitive" emotion deep within the limbic system, the amygdala is prominent in fear conditioning and may affect the pathogenesis of OCD (Cannistraro et al., 2004). Further, case studies have shown that OCD symptoms subside after accident or illness to the orbital region or caudate nuclei (Aouizerate et al., 2004). The basal ganglia, frontal cortex, and the limbic system have been the focus of anatomical models.

Basal Ganglia

A distinct subgroup of OCD probands show enlarged basal ganglia. Within the basal ganglia, the three structures that make up the corpus striatum (caudate nucleus, putamen, and globus pallidus) have been the focus of study. Some OCD patients, particularly early-onset probands, have significantly smaller striatal volumes with larger third ventricles than controls (Rosenberg, Keshavan, Dick, et al., 1997; Rosenberg, Keshavan, O'Hearn, et al., 1997; Rosenberg et al., 2004). Striatal volumes have been inversely associated with symptom severity (Whiteside, Port, & Abramowitz, 2004). Recent studies link OCD with smaller caudate nucleus volumes but not smaller putamen volumes (Aouizerate et al., 2004). Various pathogenics have been associated with lesions within the basal nuclei, particularly OCD (Thobois, Jouanneau, Bouvard, & Sindou, 2004). OCD probands appear to have at least two compartmentalized types of basal ganglia aberration: the ritualistic compulsions and obsessions as well as impaired procedural mobilization. The volume of the caudate nucleus, measured by CT scans, appears to be smaller in OCD probands compared to controls (Robinson et al., 1995). Brain damage to the basal ganglia results in repetitive, nonsensical movements or tics (Bilgic et al., 2004).

Structural Damage

Structural damage specific to certain neural circuits may play an important psychogenic role in OCD. In a well-publicized case, an OCD proband tried to commit suicide by shooting himself in the head (McKeon, McGuffin, & Robinson, 1984). He survived the shot but significantly damaged the orbital region and caudate nuclei. Thereafter, OCD symptoms decreased dramatically, presumably secondary to structural damage. Other studies confirm this initial finding (Stengler-Wenzke, Muller, & Matthes-von-Cramon, 2003). Encephalitis, diverse head injuries (e.g., traumatic brain injuries), and tumors have been associated with the development of OCD symptoms (Berthier, Kulisevsky, Gironell, & Heras, 1996; Berthier, Kulisevsky, Gironell, & Lopez, 2001; Bilgic et al., 2004; Gamazo-Garran, Soutullo, & Ortuno, 2002). Lesions within the basal ganglia have been associated with OCD symptoms (Yaryura-Tobias & Neziroglu, 2003). Early-onset OCD has been linked with velocardiofacial syndrome (Gothelf et al., 2004). Increased regional gray matter density of frontal-subcortical circuits seems to exist in OCD probands, suggesting cerebellar dysfunction as a possible pathogenesis (Kim et al., 2001). OCD probands have been shown to have significantly less white matter than controls, as well as increased gray matter density of frontal-subcortical circuits (Breiter et al., 1994). Abnormalities in the anterior cingulated white matter may be a specific diathesis for OCD, particularly as it relates to the basal ganglia–thalamocortical neurocircuit (Szeszko et al., 2005). Additional studies have shown some support for OCD probands having significantly more gray matter and less white matter in frontal lobe than controls (Valente et al., 2005). Reduced orbital frontal and amygdala volumes in OCD probands implicate a structural abnormality of these regions in the pathophysiology of OCD (Szeszko et al., 2004). OCD probands show reduced hippocampal regions as well as enlargement in the left portions of the amygdala (Breiter & Rauch, 1996). When compared to controls, OCD probands show significantly larger anterior cingulate volumes but equal volumes in other lobes (Joel et al., 2005). A relationship between anterior cingulate volume and severity of OCD symptoms (obsessions but not compulsions) exists (Kang et al., 2004). OCD may be a product of a delay in the normal pruning processes (e.g., normal developmental reductions in the number of neural circuits throughout development) that lead to larger caudate volumes and more neural circuits (Kang et al., 2003). Because these circuits regulate purposeful behavior, aberrance could manifest as inability to mediate excessive compulsions.

FUNCTIONAL ABNORMALITIES

Because of the lack of consistency in neuroanatomical findings, researchers have turned their attention to putative abnormalities in neuroanatomical function. Morphological and functional changes closely link OCD and neurology (Chen, Xie, Han, Cui, & Zhang, 2004). Aberrant functionality—even without structural abnormalities—may occur within some brain regions, prompting symptoms. Greater activation in metabolics within certain brain regions has been correlated with specific OCD features. For example, Mataix-Cols and colleagues (2004) have linked hyperactivation of certain regions with subsequent OCD symptoms: bilateral ventromedial prefrontal lobe regions and right caudate nucleus (washing); putamen, globus pallidus, thalamus, and dorsal regions (checking); left precentral gyrus and right orbitofrontal cortex (hoarding); and left occipitotemporal regions (disgust, aversion).

Blood Flow

Positron emission tomography (PET) scanning has demonstrated characteristic changes in the cerebral metabolism of patients with OCD (Whitney, Fastenau,

Evans, & Lysaker, 2004). Hyperactivity within the anterior cingulated cortex increases with symptom provocation and normalize via treatment thereafter. In clinical trials, the right and left caudates, dorsolateral prefrontals, and cingulate have shown higher regional blood flow in OCD probands compared to controls (Diler, Kibar, & Avci, 2004; Rosenberg, Dick, O'Hearn, & Sweeney, 1997). Some OCD probands demonstrate frontotemporal dysfunction, predominantly in left-hemisphere regions (Amo et al., 2004; Tot, Ozge, Comelekoglu, Yazici, & Bal, 2002). PET scans tracking glucose and other biochemicals reveal that OCD probands metabolize glucose in these regions more rapidly than controls (Mataix-Cols et al., 2004). Neurofunctional models of OCD postulate hyperactivation of orbitofrontal, limbic, and basal ganglia circuits (Evans et al., 2004). Within cortical regions, regional cerebral blood flow within the bilateral superior frontal and bilateral parietal regions has been correlated with age of onset of OCD symptoms (Castillo et al., 2005). Pathology within the orbitofrontal cortex may lead to disruption or deregulation of serotonergic systems, manifesting in compulsive behaviors. MRI, PET, and other neuroimaging techniques link OCD with increases in blood flow and metabolics in the orbitofrontal cortex, limbic system, caudate, and thalamus, with a trend toward right-sided predominance (Maltby, Tolin, Worhunsky, O'Keefe, & Kiehl, 2005). OCD patients whose symptoms respond well to treatment show a lower rate of glucose metabolism in these brain areas than patients who are unaffected by treatment (Adler et al., 2000). Hyperfrontality (increased right and left anterior prefrontal cortex activity and increased anterior cingulate gyrus activity) and increased basal ganglia activity are associated with OCD symptoms (Bartha et al., 1998; Ciesielski, Hamalainen, Lesnik, Geller, & Ahlfors, 2005). Overall, functional neuroimaging and current neurocircuitry models of OCD implicate orbitofrontal cortex, thalamus, caudate nucleus, and anterior cingulate cortex in its pathogenesis (Neel, Stevens, & Stewart, 2002; Rosenberg et al., 2004).

Orbital Circuit

Dysfunction within the orbital region of the frontal cortex and the caudate nuclei has been linked with OCD (Evans et al., 2004; Katrin-Kuelz et al., 2004). These regions provide a neural circuit that controls and mediates the conversion of sensory input into cognitions and behavioral output (Saxena, Brody, Schwartz, & Baxter, 1998). More specifically, the circuit begins in the orbital regions that transmit impulses involving bodily excretion, sexuality, violence, and other "primitive" functions. Nerve fibers carry impulses down into the caudate nuclei for determination of corresponding behaviors. These nuclei filter impulses and allow only the most powerful to reach the thalamus, where further cognitive mediation and prompting of behavioral output occur. Current theory suggests that the orbital frontal cortex or the caudate nuclei (or both) are so active in OCD probands that numerous impulses (not just those that are potent or intense) reach the thalamus, generating obsessive thought patterns or compulsive behaviors. Once an impulse reaches the thalamus, obsessive thoughts or compulsive behaviors are generated. Theoretically, if both the orbital region and caudate nuclei are overactive or unable to partition out weak potentials, the thalamus is flooded with nerve firings resulting in subsequent breakthroughs of obsessions and compulsions. Either the orbital region or the caudate nuclei may function too actively, allowing consistent breakthrough of troublesome thoughts and subsequent compulsions into conscious awareness. Dysfunction of the thalamus may lead to unnecessary stimuli reaching the higher regions of the cerebral cortex. This "information overload" may in turn cause the brain to function inefficiently and inappropriately to other bits of stimuli received. OCD symptoms are mediated by hyperactivity in orbitofrontal-subcortical circuits, which may be attributable to an imbalance in tone between direct and indirect striato-pallidal pathways (Lacerda, Dalgalarrondo, Caetano, Camargo, et al., 2003). Hyperactivity of frontal-striatal-thalamic-frontal circuits may trigger error signals when event-processing conflicts with internalized standards or values (Papageorgiou, Rabavilas, Liappas, & Stefanis, 2003). Studies have consistently shown increased activity of probands' frontal lobe relative to control subjects—suggesting that the obsessional thinking involved in OCD may be secondary to hyperarousal in this region (Kathmann, Rupertseder, Hauke, & Zaudig, 2005). Frontotemporal paroxysmal rhythmic activity with a preferential limbic distribution may be involved in OCD, suggesting possible corticostriatal network dysfunction (Amo et al., 2004; Rauch et al., 2001).

Symptom severity has been correlated with regional blood flow within the left orbitofrontal region, with hyperactivity being associated with more intense features (Bucci et al., 2004; Shin, Ha, Kim, & Kwon, 2004). Using PET scans, the metabolic activity within the caudate nucleus for OCD probands is generally increased relative to controls (Bolton, Moore, MacMillan, Stewart, & Rosenberg, 2001). Deregulation or disruption of this feedback circuit is linked with OCD (Aylward et al., 1996). According to theory, the caudate nucleus sends erroneous inhibitory signals to the globus pallidus. The caudate nucleus malfunctions in its role of initiating and stopping certain activities and thoughts. As a result, the global pallidus fails to inhibit the thalamus from sending signals that would not have been received if the circuit operated normally. Erroneous signals from the caudate nucleus inhibit the interruption of the circuit and messages continue to reverberate.

Frontal Lobe

Other studies reveal deficits in frontal lobe functioning (Gilbert et al., 2004; Moritz et al., 2002). The mental rumination seen in OCD can be localized to the frontal lobe; prefrontal-subcortical circuits, more pronounced in the right hemisphere, are involved in the pathophysiology of OCD (Lacerda, Dalgalarrondo, Caetano, Haas, et al., 2003). Neural dysfunctions in the frontal-subcortical circuits, particularly in the right hemisphere, have been linked with OCD.

Severity of OCD symptoms have been associated with increased regional cerebral blood flow within the right thalamus (Lacerda, Dalgalarrondo, Caetano, Haas, et al., 2003). The frontal-subcortical circuits mediate not only symptomatic expression but also cognitive expression in patients with OCD (Kwon, Shin, et al., 2003). Mediating throughout, a complex dysfunctional interaction may exist among numerous cortical areas, preventing the filtration of sensations, thoughts, and normal activity (Bartha et al., 1998; Sullivan et al., 2000). When the orbital region or the caudate nuclei are hyperactive, troublesome thoughts and ruminations occur. Glucose metabolic rates within the orbito-frontal cortex were inversely correlated with subsequent SSRI response, and glucose metabolic rates within posterior cingulate cortex correlate with positive response to cingulotomy. Lower rCBF values in OFC and higher rCBF in the PCC predict better treatment response (Moritz, Hubner, & Kluwe, 2004). Abnormal hyperactivity may cause sensations, thoughts, and rituals that normally would be dampened and inhibited to "leak through" and are expressed behaviorally. The cortex prompts compulsive rituals to cope with conflicts raised by obsessive thoughts. Using PET and SPECT studies, researchers have shown OCD probands have increased metabolic activity in the frontal cortex compared to controls (Alonso et al., 2001). Increased metabolic activity in response to provocative stimulation prompts obsessional rumination, suggesting that brooding is a frontal lobe activity (Abbott & Rapee, 2004).

In addition to frontal brain regions, the basal ganglia and limbic system have been linked with OCD (Baxter, 2003; Busatto et al., 2000). As many neurological diseases of the basal ganglia are known to produce OCD-like symptoms, some researchers have proposed that OCD is essentially a basal ganglia disorder (Rossi et al., 2005). The function of the basal ganglia is to detect stimuli that activate fixed-action patterns and allow their release. These fixed-action patterns are innate species-specific responses that are motor programs for action and take the form of grooming and safety rituals. The basal ganglia store these programs and provide gating for their release. In OCD patients, basal ganglia dysfunction allows the inappropriate release of fixed-action patterns, in the form of compulsive rituals. In OCD, the basal ganglia, mediator of movement and motor script involved in routine learning, may dysfunction in its role of inhibition of behavior (Herrmann, Jacob, Unterecker, & Fallgatter, 2003).

Striatum

Bartha and colleagues (1998) link deregulation of the **striatum**, a brain region actively involved in preparing appropriate behavioral responses, with OCD — particularly the use of compulsive behaviors to avoid ongoing anxiety. The striatum serves a gating and screening function, leading to possible involvement in cognitive rumination or brooding (Pawlak, Ho, Schwarting, & Bauhofer, 2003). Other PET studies have found increased metabolic activity in the striatum during exposure among OCD cleaners, but reduced metabolic activity among

OCD checkers (Behar et al., 1994; Roth, Baribeau, Milovan, O'Connor, 2004; Roth, Baribeau, Milovan, O'Connor, & Todorov, 2004). The gating and screening activities of the striatum may fail to inhibit impulses that then lead to thoughts "leaking" into conscious awareness. Fixed-action patterns (obsessions) occur automatically and require effortful suppression and neutralization. This produces hyperactivity in the basal ganglia and frontal lobes, as well as alterations in the limbic system. Frontostriatal overactivation may disturb both procedural and declarative memories, prompting deficits in encoding and retrieval (Parker, McNally, Nakayama, & Wilhelm, 2004). Increases in blood flow within the neostriatum and thalamus are associated with urges to perform compulsive behaviors (Sturm et al., 2003).

Functional Hyperactivity

OCD is associated with functional hyperactivity of a selected neuronal network within the cingulate cortex (Ursu, Stenger, Shear, Jones, & Carter, 2003). The anterior cingulate cortex mediates cognitive detection of conflict during information-processing as well as subsequent alerting-associated systems involved in top-down control of its resolution (van Veen & Carter, 2002). *Error-related negativity* *(ERN)* is an event-related brain potential associated with monitoring and detecting errors. Enhanced ERN, a common OCD feature, may reflect abnormal functioning within the anterior cingulate cortex (Van Veen & Carter, 2002). The anterior cingulate cortex in OCD probands has been found to be hyperactive at rest, during symptom provocation, and after commission of errors on cognitive tasks (Ursu et al., 2003). Lower activity in the anterior cingulate gyrus has been found in hoarding patients compared to nonhoarding OCD probands (Mataix-Cols et al., 2004). Decreased activity within the posterior cingulate gyrus has also been shown. Neural circuits linking the orbital cortex, striatum, basal ganglia, and thalamus have been linked with OCD (Fontenelle, Mendlowicz, & Versiani, 2004).

BIOCHEMICAL THEORIES

Functional and biochemical theories may be related. If a neurotransmitter plays an active role in the operation of a specific brain region, its excess or absence may impede normal functioning. For example, neurons within the striatum (clearly implicated in OCD) require dopamine to function (Zhang et al., 2001). If adequate dopamine is not present, striatal functioning may err. As another example, a significant increase in cytosolic choline was observed in right and left medial but not lateral thalami, suggesting cytosolic choline abnormalities in the thalamus in OCD probands (Rosenberg, Amponsah, Sullivan, MacMillan, & Moore, 2001). The precise nature of structural, functional, and biochemical interactions remains unclear. Nevertheless, clinical and psychopharmacological studies have linked the serotonergic and dopaminergic systems in OCD patho-genesis (Brambilla, Perna, Bussi, & Bellodi, 2000; Denys, Zohar, & Westenberg, 2004). Other biochemical effects are likely.

Serotonin

Serotonin first was implicated in OCD when researchers discovered the reduc-tion of OCD symptoms by the antidepressant clomipramine. The efficacy of serotonergic medicines suggests potential OCD etiology via alteration in cere-bral 5-HT receptor systems, particularly within the fronto-subcortical regions (Adams et al., 2005; Castillo et al., 2005). Clomipramine, fluvoxamine, and other seretonergic agents effectively reduce OCD symptoms in about 70% of probands (Delorme et al., 2004; Gross, Sasson, Chopra, & Zohar, 1998). The *serotonin hypothesis* continues to dominate modern biochemical models of OCD, fueled predominantly by the efficacy of SSRIs (and other serotonergic agents) in reduc-ing OCD symptoms (Ackerman, Greenland, & Bystritsky, 1999). Within the or-bital circuit, serotonin plays a prominent role, with numerous target receptors, and low levels or receptor insensitivities may impede normal processes. Theorists propose that OCD may result from deregulation in the serotonergic systems, with a hypersensitivity of postsynaptic 5-HT receptors (Zohar, Kennedy, Hollander, & Koran, 2004). Serotonergic drugs may ameliorate OCD symptoms by changing the relative balance of tone through the indirect versus direct orbitofrontal-subcortical pathways, thereby decreasing activity in the overall circuit that exists in the symptomatic state. Peripheral markers of serotonin function, pharmaco-logic challenges with serotonin agonists, and drug response from SSRIs support the theory of serotonin involvement in OCD. Neuroendocrine responses to pharmacologic challenge studies suggest a hyposensitivity, whereas behavioral responses suggest a hypersensitivity. This suggests that deregulation of the sero-tonergic system is probable, although its nature remains unclear.

Research with OCD probands on biochemical variations of neurotransmit-ters has implicated serotonin and its possible activity and effects on specific brain regions (Blier & de Montigny, 1998). The discovery of the effectiveness of med-ications in reducing OCD symptoms has spurred theories and speculations con-cerning its biological etiologies. For example, naloxone rapidly exacerbates OCD symptoms while tramadol, an opioid agonist, has in some cases provided symptom reduction (Mangold, Peyrot, Giggey, & Wand, 2000). Sumatriptan, a selective ligand of the serotonin 1Dbeta autoreceptor, modifies OCD symptoms (Camarena et al., 2004). Because administration of serotonin agonists increases OCD symptoms, increased serotonin activity and increased sensitivity of certain brain regions to serotonin may combine to generate symptoms (McGrath, Campbell, Parks, & Burton, 2000). Further, administration of SE receptor an-tagonists reverses this effect. Clinical studies have measured the cerebrospinal fluid concentrations of serotonin metabolites (e.g., 5-HIAA) and the numbers of sites that bind serotonin reuptake (Greist, Jefferson, Kobak, Katzelnick, & Serlin, 1995). Several types of empirical studies have been conducted. First, concentrations of known metabolites of SE (5-HIAA) in the blood and cerebrospinal fluid provide peripheral markers of SE in the brain (Vielhaber, Riemann, Feige, Kuelz, Kirschbaum, & Voderholzer, 2005). Administration of serotonin agonists provokes symptoms in individuals whose serotonergic system is dysregulated. Unfortunately, peripheral markers have been inconsistent in establishing the role of SE in OCD (Marazziti et al., 2003). Perhaps the body compensates by masking peripheral markers that would indicate SE disruption.

Other Neurotransmitters

Although serotonergic deregulation is the leading biochemical theory, scattered studies have pointed to other systems. Improvement in OCD symptoms following treatment via clonidine, a noradrenalin alpha-2 receptor agonist, has been associated with growth hormone response to clonidine, suggesting possible norepinephrinergic mediation and defective noradrenergic functioning in OCD. Scattered animal studies link increased somatostatin with compulsive rituals (Merali, Michaud, McIntosh, Kent, & Anisman, 2003). Altered glutamatergic neurotransmission, such as excess or hyperinvolvement, may be involved in the pathogenesis of OCD, particularly within the caudate nucleus and thalamocortical-striatal circuit (Chakrabarty, Bhattacharyya, Christopher, & Khanna, 2005; Lipsky & Goldman, 2003). Based on some probands' therapeutic response to antipsychotics, some researchers have proposed dopaminergic variables in OCD (Denys, Zohar, et al., 2004). Further studies have shown that abnormalities in the binding potential of dopaminergic DA-2 receptors are linked to OCD (Denys, van der Wee, Janssen, De Geus, & Westenberg, 2004). Dopamine receptor binding within the left caudate nucleus has been shown to be lower for OCD probands than normal controls (Choi et al., 2004; Marazziti et al., 2004).

Biochemistry

Apart from neurotransmitters, many studies have tried to link other biochemicals, both endogenous to the body and otherwise, with OCD. Numerous neurochemicals in OCD probands, compared to controls, have been found to have a negative correlation between 5-HIAA concentration and symptom severity. Further, before treatment, the concentration of arginine vasopressin was negatively correlated with OCD, whereas corticotropin releasing hormone did not differentiate probands from normal controls (Atmaca, Tezcan, Kuloglu, & Ustundag, 2005). *Arginine vasopressin* (a stress-responsive neurohormone) may be related to OCD severity whereas 5-HIAA may predict treatment response (Rosenberg, MacMillan, & Moore, 2001). Another neuropeptide, *somatostatin*, has been the focus of investigation, too (Mottard & de la Sablonniere, 1999). When compared to controls, OCD probands have higher levels of CSF somatostatin (Baumgarten & Grozdanovic, 1998; Erzegovesi, Martucci, Henin, & Bellodi, 2001). Other studies have failed to replicate findings; the relationship between these neurohormones and OCD remains unclear (Arborelius et al., 1999). Neuropeptides may play an important role (albeit unclear at this time) in OCD (McDougle, Barr, Goodman, & Price, 1999). Studies examining other variables, including blood type and diet, are inconclusive (Anderson & Savage, 2004).

PANDAS

Genetic, neuroimmunologic, and neuroimaging studies have proposed the possibility of autoimmune-mediated pathophysiology in OCD. For a small proportion of children, OCD symptoms became worse following infection with the bacteria **Group A Streptococci** (beta hemolysis, S. Pyogenes; Castrogiovanni et al., 1998). Streptococci are gram-positive bacteria that characteristically form chains, are usually facultative anaerobes, and produce a zone of complete hemolysis around the bacterial colony when cultured on blood agar (Erzegovesi, Cavallini, et al., 2001). Group A Streptococcus is responsible for streptococcal pharyngitis, a common bacterial infection of school-aged children, and post-infectious syndromes of rheumatic fever and post-streptococcal glomerulonephritis (Bessen, 2001). Additional typical infections may include impetigo (small macules rapidly develop in vesicles, then become pustular and encrusted; lesions commonly affect face and leave depigmented areas) or cellulitis (Betancourt, Jimenez-Leon, Jimenez-Betancourt, & Castillo, 2003). **Pediatric Autoimmune Neuropsychiatric Disorders Associated with Streptococcal Infections (PANDAS)** refers to the onset of OCD subsequent to streptococcal infection. Although the link between PANDAS and S. Pyogenes remains unclear, evidence points to an autoimmune response to the infection causing antibodies to attack healthy as well as infected cells (Peterson et al., 2000; Singer et al., 2004). In this process, inflammation occurs in the basal ganglia; antibasal ganglia antibodies may be pathogenic to numerous brain regions. Structural and functional alterations in associated nuclei may ensue (Asbahr, Ramos, Costa, & Sassi, 2005).

For Group A bacteria, the major surface protein is M protein, occurring in over 100 antigenetically distinct types and forming the basis for treatment. **M protein** molecules are anchored in the cell wall of the host organism and away from the cell surface. As defense against these bacteria, the body generates antibodies to act against the M proteins on the surface of the Group A Streptococcus. In OCD, the strep bacteria are believed to have surface proteins very similar to those of brain cells, and the body's defensive antibodies can attack both infectious S. Pyogenes and healthy brain tissue (Dinn, Harris, McGonigal, & Raynard, 2001). In vulnerable children subgroups, the autoimmune response to the bacteria causes antibodies to mistakenly identify the basal ganglia as foreign matter or damage or affect certain neurotransmitters (Bessen, 2001). Vulnerability to developing PANDAS most likely is polygenetic, with elevated levels of

---

PANDAS CHARACTERISTICS

- Onset of symptoms is sudden and dramatic such that parents can frequently recall the date of onset; usual onset of OCD is more gradual
- An earlier age of onset of symptoms compared to the usual onset
- PANDAS children are seen to have complete remissions of symptoms between episodes of symptoms
- The presence of accompanying neurological signs such as tics, hyperactivity, or choreiform movements (irregular spasmodic involuntary movements of the limbs or facial muscles)
- Concurrent symptoms can include emotional lability, separation anxiety, nighttime fears, or oppositional behaviors
- Symptoms worsen following strep infection

D8/17 antibodies a potential marker of susceptibility (Giedd et al., 2000; Snider & Swedo, 2003a, 2003b, 2004).

Five criteria have been proposed within PANDAS: presence of OCD or tics; prepubertal onset; sudden onset and episodic course; temporal association between streptococcal infections and exacerbations; and associated neurological pathognomics. Other correlational research has linked PANDAS with early-onset OCD, typically in male children (3:1 male/female ratio) as young as 5 to 7 years old, and dramatic, sudden onset and episodic nature, in which periods of symptom worsening follow strep infections (Ackerman et al., 1999; Giulino et al., 2002). Onset may occur in adults, too (Bodner, Morshed, & Peterson, 2001). PANDAS OCD changes may be characterized by streptococcal titer elevations and episodic tics (Dale et al., 2004; Murphy et al., 2004). Subsequent bacterial infections can then exacerbate symptoms. Plasma exchange (PEX) or intravenous immunoglobulin (IVIG) may be able to relieve neuropsychiatric symptoms in this subgroup of children (Birmaher et al., 1998).

TREATMENTS

Pharmacological treatments for OCD have exhibited positive outcomes, particularly when combined interventions are integrated to target idiographic symptoms (Fineberg & Gale, 2005; Schruers, Koning, Luermans, Haack, & Griez, 2005). Although OCD is treatable, most probands do not seek clinical treatment (Besiroglu et al., 2004); those who do typically struggle with symptoms for 7 to 8 years before seeking care (Greist et al., 2003). Poor insight, usually prevalent in 25% of probands, has been associated with gloomier prognoses (Ravi-Kishore, Samar, Janardhan-Reddy, Chandrasekher, & Thennarasu, 2004). About 20% of

OCD patients become housebound or disabled (Angst et al., 2004). With treatment, 50% to 80% of patients show a marked reduction in symptoms and an increase in overall functioning (Bhui, 2004; Erzegovesi, Cavallini, et al., 2001; Kaplan & Hollander, 2003). Onset of therapeutic effect usually requires longer treatments (e.g., 10 to 12 weeks versus 3 to 4 for depressive disorders) and higher dosages (Ables & Baughman, 2003; Saxena et al., 2002). Clomipramine has shown a modest advantage in treating symptoms, compared to all SSRIs, with selective serotonergic agents showing equivalent therapeutics when steady-state trials with adequate dosings are achieved (Geller et al., 2003). Other factors (e.g., side-effect profiles, cost, etc.) influence specific medication choice (Hollander, 1996; Stewart et al., 2004). Table 5.2 outlines the biopsychosocial treatments for OCD. Table 5.3 lists symptom-specific interventions for OCD.

Psychotropic options have expanded rapidly secondary to a better understanding of the neurochemistry involved in OCD. SSRIs continue to be first-line

TABLE 5.2.
Biopsychosocial Treatments for OCD

Intervention	Targets
Pharmacological approaches	Clomipramine, SSRIs, duloxetine, atypical antipsychotics
Psychoeducational interventions	Educate to improve medication compliance, provide comprehensive treatment approach utilizing diverse modalities, improve coping and adaptation skills via the teaching of novel responses, relaxation, and cognitive restructuring techniques
Psychological interventions	Exposure and response prevention, symptom-focused therapies, dynamic interventions that reduce defense mechanisms and resolve unconscious conflicts, thought-stopping and cognitive techniques, counseling to reduce overall anxiety, working through of latent conflicts, strengthening the self via increased insight and clarification
Social interventions	Strengthen social support systems while reducing shame and guilt, encourage verbalization of feelings and emotions to others without compulsive follow-ups, enhance emotional intimacy with others

TABLE 5.3.
Symptom-Specific Interventions for OCD

Symptom	Interventions
Compulsions, repetitions	Exposure and response prevention (a form of deconditioning), find models of target adaptation, combat irrational assumptions related to undoing
Functional impairments	Establish strong peer relationships, gradual exposure to stressful situations, emphasis on health
Obsessions, obsessional thoughts	Thought-stopping and thought substitution, decreasing perfectionism and demandingness ("things must be just this way"), cognitive restructuring of irrationality, working through emotional conflicts that precipitate fear, resolving control and perfectionism traits, insight into "undoing" defense and its futility, awareness of reaction formation defense against conflictual feelings, habituation with reduced hypersensitivity to thought processes
Underlying anxiety	Developmental maturation (moving from infantile to adult coping and adaptation), enhance ability to process and resolve emotion, strengthen sense of self, blatant awareness within mastery experiences, form supportive social relationships that assist during times of crises, facilitate emotional attunement with self-empathy

agents, usually at higher doses and longer trials than with in other disorders, targeting 5-HT2A (Albert, Bergesio, Pessina, Maina, & Bogetto, 2002; Dougherty, Rauch, & Jenike, 2004). Other treatment studies have revealed a role for noradrenalin in OCD (Mancini, Van Amerigen, & Farvolden, 2002). Some probands exhibit a greater clinical improvement with a combination of serotonin and norepinephrine reuptake inhibition relative to SSRI treatment alone (Pallanti, Hollander, & Goodman, 2004). Augmentation of a noradrenalin reuptake inhibitor, such as desipramine, may enhance outcomes (Joel et al., 2004). Mirtazapine, an antagonist of alpha-2 adrenoreceptors, disinhibits noradrenalin activation of serotonergic neurons and may enhance its neurotransmission (Koran, Gamel, Choung, Smith, & Aboujaoude, 2005; Pallanti, Quercioli, & Bruscoli, 2004). Other noradrenergic or dopaminergic agents may work similarly in reducing OCD symptoms (Phelps & Cates, 2005; Szechtman, Culver, & Eilam, 1999). Antidepressant augmentation frequently occurs, as atypical antipsychotics and anticonvulsants show effect (Czlonkowska et al., 2003; Keuneman, Pokos, Weerasundera, & Castle, 2005). The use of multiple medications in the treatment of resistant OCD increases the likelihood of drug-drug interactions, either pharmacokinetically or pharmacodynamically (Castrogiovanni et al., 1998; Lee, Kim, & Kwon, 2005). Identification of psychotropic substrates, inducers, or inhibitors of hepatic cytochrome P450 isozymes requires further clinical research.

Clinical response has overwhelmingly shown that the serotonergic medications reduce the intensity of symptoms, yet their mechanisms of action in OCD remain unclear. Chronic SSRI treatment may alter serotonin turnover and associated neuropeptide expressions within the forebrain and midbrain regions. SSRI response in depressive and OCD syndromes seems to involve different neurobiological substrates. Elevated activity in the right caudate may be responsive to antiobsessional treatment, whereas lower right amygdala activity and higher midline prefrontal activity is implicated in depression (Saxena et al., 2004). SSRIs and clomipramine (a highly serotonergic cyclic) are significantly more effective than other antidepressants (e.g., desipramine). Widely known to reduce OCD symptoms, clomipramine acts to reduce platelet serotonin concentration and enhance norepinephrine in plasma (Delorme et al., 2004; Pariante, Hye, Williamson, Makoff, Lovestone, & Kerwin, 2003). Treatment with serotonergic antidepressants may "normalize" neurohormonal and neuroendocrine responses in key brain regions, such as within the limbic system, prefrontal lobe, or striatum (Mataix-Cols et al., 2003). Co-administration of an SSRI and clomipramine is common. Long-term administration of serotonergic drugs may prompt a down regulation of some receptors and not others. Thus, the immediate effect of SSRIs may be to increase serotonin levels, but in the long run these medicines may actually decrease levels. This hypothesis is supported by consistent research showing that treatments with SSRIs require longer time intervals (6 to 12 weeks compared to 2 to 4 weeks in other anxiety disorders) for reduction of OCD symptoms. Multiple SSRI compounds are effective in 30% to 60% of cases (Delgado & Moreno, 1998). Approximately 10% to 25% of SSRI-treated patients report significant side effects that preclude their continued use (Hollander, Allen, et al., 2003; Simpson et al., 2004).

In the last 10 years, several studies have tried to identify response profiles to link specific medications and OCD treatments (Brody et al., 1998; Husted & Shapira, 2004; Ownby, 1998). The early presence of SSRI-related side effects (e.g., nervousness, decreased libido) seems to be a positive predictor of overall response (Ackerman et al., 1999). Moderate intensity of symptoms, absence of comorbid mood disorders, and mixed pharmacotherapy regimens have been associated with better prognosis and effective outcomes (Greist et al., 2003). The positive response of first-degree relatives to SSRI treatment also predicts efficacy of serotonergic medications in OCD probands. Poor prognostic indicants for SSRI treatments include poor insight, the presence of somatic obsessions, and atypical underlying biology (Connor, Payne, Gadde, Zhang, & Davidson, 2005). Some theorists have tried to identify subgroups responsive to adjunctive medications, but research outcomes have been mixed, contradictory, or otherwise inconclusive (Black, Monohan, Gable, Blum, Clancy, & Baker, 1998). Mild or atypical symptoms, overall level of anxiety and arousal, and premorboid personality traits appear to predict positive treatment outcome (Cavedini, Erzegovesi, Ronchi, & Bellodi, 1997). Early onset of symptoms (particularly in males), symmetry and exactness-related features, comorbid psychotic symptoms (such as delusions and hallucinations, a family history of OCD, and the presence of tics are linked with poor outcomes (Fontenelle, Rosario-Campos, et al., 2004; Watson et al., 2004).

Treatment-Resistant Cases

Unfortunately, some OCD patients do not respond adequately to SSRI treatment, and still others show little improvement with serotonergic intervention even when combined with antipsychotics (Shapira et al., 2004). The high incidence of comorbid disorders with OCD has led some clinicians to advocate combinations of medications in the comprehensive treatment of OCD (Walsh & McDougle, 2004). For example, nicotine increases serotonin release in the cortex, striatum, hippocampus, dorsal raphe nucleus, and hypothalamus, showing some positive effects for some OCD probands (Salin-Pascual & Basanez-Villa, 2003; Seth, Cheeta, Tucci, & File, 2002). Comorbid conditions show a preferential response to an associated SSRI and low-dose dopaminergic antagonist regimens (Carson, 1996). Add-on therapies for nonresponders or inadequate initial treatments utilize antipsychotics (dopaminergic antagonists) to subdue symptoms (Keuneman et al., 2005). Dextroamphetamine mixtures have been reported to help some probands (Owley et al., 2002), whereas methylphenidate has been shown to worsen symptoms. *Inositol*, a glucose isomer, may regulate numerous cell functions and has demonstrated efficacy in reducing OCD symptoms (Carey, Warwick, Harvey, Stein, & Seedat, 2004). Intractable OCD continues to plague some probands, with as many as 30% to 40% continuing to suffer with significant symptoms even after response to multiple treatments (Eddy, Dutra, Bradley, & Westen, 2004).

Other Interventions

In recent years, practitioners have explored other biologically based interventions for severe or intractable OCD (Lopes et al., 2004). Surgery can be an option for severe, disabling or refractory conditions. Three prominent surgical procedures used within contemporary medicine are: *anterior cingulotomy* (insertion of an electrode needle to make a tiny cut in the cingulum nerve bundle), *subcaudate tractotomy* (producing lesions in the connecting tract of the subcaudate), and *limbic leukotomy* (lesions to both bilateral cingulated and orbitomedial frontal regions). Mainly capsulotomy and cingulotomy are used. In the case of OCD, psychosurgery affects some of the neural circuits between the frontal lobes and different structures within the limbic system. Bilateral lesions in the anterior cingulate cortex have been associated with reduced OCD intensity and without significant adverse sequelae. A *modified leucotomy*, a surgical procedure that cuts a small portion of the white matter in the cingulum, has been shown to effectively reduce the intensity of both obsessions and compulsions in OCD probands (Dougherty et al., 2002). Other neurosurgical interventions for OCD include anterior cingulotomy, tractotomy, and anterior capsulotomy, each with varying degrees of effectiveness (Abelson et al., 2005).

Behavioral Models

OCD has responded to structured behavioral programs that attempt to decondition latent anxiety with obsessive and compulsive symptoms. Integrating cognitive and behavioral models, *habituation theories* view OCD as impaired coping secondary to repeated avoidance and escapism. In this view, OCD symptoms reflect emotional avoidance of anxiety by cognitive rumination. In *habituation training*, the therapist seeks to repeatedly evoke the patient's obsessive thoughts, with the expectation that intensified exposure eventually causes them to lose their threatening meaning, generate less anxiety, and trigger fewer obsessive thoughts or compulsions (Moritz et al., 2004; Moritz & Von Muhlenen, 2005). This intervention reaches obsessions by blocking their resulting compulsive acts.

Particularly effective with OCD is a behavioral technique called *exposure and response prevention (ERP)* (Foa et al., 2005). In ERP, an OCD patient is exposed to cues (either directly or through imagery) that provoke obsessions and then is prevented from performing subsequent compulsive behaviors. Response prevention involves continual supervision of a patient while he or she is exposed to anxiety-producing stimuli. The patient is not allowed to ritualize, is exposed to coping models, receives instruction about appropriate ways to interact with the stimuli, and receives reinforcement for not ritualizing. These interventions are relatively successful although taxing on both the patient and the therapist. The patient requires 24-hour supervision, as exposure is in effect 24 hours a day for weeks at time.

In *covert-response prevention*, patients are taught to identify, prevent, and distract themselves from carrying out obsessive patterns or compulsive behaviors. Over the course of time, these symptoms decrease in frequency and intensity through counterconditioning, desensitization, and so on. ERP combines condi-

---

OCD PSYCHOSOCIAL OVERVIEW

- Gradual exposure is equally as effective as flooding in vivo.
- Modeling does not seem to enhance treatment effectiveness.
- Treatment can be administered by the patient in the natural environment.
- Spouse-aided exposure is about equally effective as self-controlled exposure.
- Supplementing in vivo exposure with self-instructional training does not increase therapeutic efficacy.
- Prolonged exposure sessions are superior to shorter ones.
- Both exposure to distressing stimuli and response prevention of the ritual are essential components.
- Attention-focusing on the feared stimuli may enhance habituation.
- Antidepressant drugs (clomipramine) may reduce depressed mood and enhance compliance.
- The therapist may need to address targets other than the obsessive-compulsive problem.
- The effectiveness of behavioral procedures with obsessions is less well-established than with compulsions.

---

tioning and flooding models to "disconnect" (break the conditioned link) obsessions from underlying uneasiness and eliminate rituals that prevent habituation (e.g., getting use to) of fears. Exposure reduces anxiety associated with obsessions, and response prevention deconditions "temporary relief" of anxiety to induce further desensitization. Research on predictors of success with ERP have failed to reveal consistent trends (Hembree, Riggs, Kozak, Franklin, & Foa, 2003).

SUMMARY

In contemporary theory, OCD remains controversial in its description, etiology, epidemiology, and treatment; scientific and clinical understanding of it remains poor. OCD continues to be the focus of numerous research studies, mostly investigating the link between brain functioning and symptoms. Structural, functional, and biochemical theories have been proposed, and all share the common assumption of genetic vulnerability inherited from kin. Thereafter, biochemical or functional vulnerabilities, or combinations thereof, add to basic genetic vulnerabilities to prompt symptoms. The precise nature of the interactions among various biologically based variables, their roles in OCD, and appropriate interventions are not yet fully understood. Multiple systems are involved. Successful treatments, effective in as many as 90% of cases, often combine numerous pharmacological interventions, focusing on serotonin and dopamine within the brain. Future research needs to clarify the exact mechanisms of actions, etiologies, and combinations of biologies involved in OCD. Goals include identifying and treating residual symptoms, optimizing combinations of drugs within medical regimens, and characterizing subgroups of treatment-refractory probands likely to respond to antipsychotic or neurosurgical augmentations.

CHAPTER 6

Panic Disorder

O F ALL ANXIETY CONDITIONS, panic disorder (PD) has elicited the most attention from researchers seeking biological bases and treatments. When anxiety intensifies to a smothering experience, a feeling of impending danger occurs. Terror hyperarouses the body, and the sympathetic nervous system floods the body with epinephrine. In extreme cases, the epinephrine that is produced becomes excessive and results in severe, sudden experiences of anxiety. The term *panic* refers to the sudden onset of fear or terror with feelings of impending doom; this sudden, intense fear/anxiety is characterized by the experience of hyperarousal, physiological symptoms, and behavioral subjective distress. Its roots can be traced to Greek mythology, in the god Pan's inflicting such unpleasant states on others. A *panic attack* is an episodic bout of severe, intense anxiety marked by fear, autonomic hyperarousal, or the experience of overwhelming despair, accompanied by at least four of 13 somatic or cognitive symptoms.

Panic attacks are described as sudden bursts of emotion consisting of a large number of somatic symptoms and feelings of dying and losing control. Often, attacks are accompanied by heart rate elevations of approximately 40 BPM that cannot be accounted for by physical exercise (Broman-Fulks, Berman, Rabian, & Webster, 2004). Discrete panic bouts can occur abruptly at any time (even during periods of rest), and usually reach a peak within a 10 minutes (Craske & Rowe, 1997). The attack rarely lasts longer than 20 minutes, because the body cannot sustain the intense fight-or-flight hyperarousal. A panic attack is not inherently dangerous, but its experience can prompt fears of "going crazy" or losing control of both personal and environmental functionings (Hicks et al., 2005).

The initial panic attack is unique in that it (1) occurs with sudden onset of intense fear; (2) takes place spontaneously, without apparent environmental precipitants; (3) responds to tricyclic antidepressants but not to neuroleptics or benzodiazepines; and (4) itself serves as the initiator and reinforcer of the avoidant behavior found in associated agoraphobia (Brookler, 2004).

DSM-IV-TR CRITERIA FOR PANIC ATTACK

Note: A Panic Attack is not a codable behavior. Code the specific diagnosis in which the Panic Attack occurs (e.g., 300.21 Panic Disorder with Agoraphobia).

A discrete period of intense fear or discomfort, in which four (or more) of the following symptoms developed abruptly and reached a peak within 10 minutes:

(1)   palpitations, pounding heart, or accelerated heart rate
(2)   sweating
(3)   trembling or shaking
(4)   sensations of shortness of breath or smothering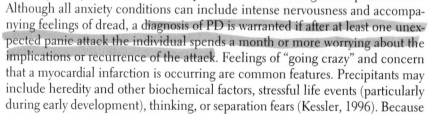
(5)   feeling of choking
(6)   chest pain or discomfort
(7)   nausea or abdominal distress
(8)   feeling dizzy, unsteady, lightheaded, or faint
(9)   derealization (feelings of unreality) or depersonalization (being detached from oneself)
(10) fear of losing control or going crazy
(11) fear of dying
(12) paresthesias (numbness or tingling sensations)
(13) chills or hot flashes

*Reprinted with permission from the *Diagnostic and Statistical Manual of Mental Disorders, Fourth Edition, Text Revision.* Copyright 2000 American Psychiatric Association.

The primary feature of PD is the persistent fear of having future panic attacks. Although all anxiety conditions can include intense nervousness and accompanying feelings of dread, a diagnosis of PD is warranted if after at least one unexpected panic attack the individual spends a month or more worrying about the implications or recurrence of the attack. Feelings of "going crazy" and concern that a myocardial infarction is occurring are common features. Precipitants may include heredity and other biochemical factors, stressful life events (particularly during early development), thinking, or separation fears (Kessler, 1996). Because of the prominence of physiological symptoms in PD, many patients are seen by primary-care physicians or specialists before being referred for therapeutic intervention. Angina and panic can share common somatic symptoms, such as feeling unable to catch one's breath, heart palpitations, pounding heart, chest pain, dizziness or lightheadedness, weakness, hot or cold flashes, shakiness, and some-times stomach upset, nausea, or diarrhea (Salkovskis & Clarke, 1993). Heart disease and thyroid dysfunction can be mistaken for PD. Probands often overemphasize physical complaints and minimize potential psychological symptoms, unless specific inquiry is initiated (Ehlers, 1995). PD is frightening because of the episodic nature of symptoms, its seeming lack of being under conscious control, and subsequent complications. As a result, many become uneasy about leaving their homes or usual surroundings for fear of recurrence. *Agoraphobia*, the intense fear of public places or open spaces, is characterized by marked fear of entering crowded or public places or leaving home. Those with PD often develop agoraphobia, and some clinicians view the two as inherently connected (Davids et al., 2002).

**DSM-IV-TR CRITERIA FOR PANIC
DISORDER WITHOUT AGORAPHOBIA***

A. Both (1) and (2)
  (1) recurrent unexpected Panic Attacks
  (2) at least one of the attacks has been followed by one month (or more) of one (or more) of the following:
      (a) persistent concern about having additional attacks
      (b) worry about the implications of the attack or its consequences (e.g., losing control, having a heart attack, "going crazy")
      (c) a significant change in behavior related to the attacks
B. Absence of Agoraphobia.
C. The Panic Attacks are not due to the direct physiological effects of a substance (e.g., a drug of abuse, a medication) or a general medical condition (e.g., hyperthyroidism)
D. The Panic Attacks are not better accounted for by another mental disorder, such as Social Phobia (e.g., occurring on exposure to feared social situations), Specific Phobia (e.g., on exposure to a specific phobic situation), Obsessive-Compulsive Disorder (e.g., on exposure to dirt in someone with an obsession about contamination), Posttraumatic Stress Disorder (e.g., in response to stimuli associated with a severe stressor), or Separation Anxiety Disorder (e.g., in response to being away from home or close relatives).

*Reprinted with permission from the *Diagnostic and Statistical Manual of Mental Disorders, Fourth Edition, Text Revision*. Copyright 2000 American Psychiatric Association.

Biological models of PD emerged in the 1960s, when benzodiazepines were found to be generally ineffective in their treatment (Roy-Byrne & Cowley, 1998). Instead, certain antidepressant medications, particularly imipramine and desipramine, were found to block symptoms (Goddard & Charney, 1997; Klein & Fink, 1962). Thus, researchers began to believe that the biological arousals involved in GAD and PD may be different in pathophysiology (e.g., brain region), activity, or process (Goddard, Brouette, & Almai, 2001; Nutt, Glue, Lawson, & Wilson, 1990). A variety of research outcomes have led theorists to hypothesize multiple models of PD implicating diverse systems. Biological bases have been linked with noradrenergic systems, particularly within the locus coeruleus, a nucleus in the pons. Other etiologies include phobic responses to anxiety ("fear of fear"), fear of separation, turmoil, emotional conflicts, conditioning, or cognitive irrationalities.

PREVALENCE

Defining the epidemiology of PD is quite difficult, because many individuals who meet diagnostic criteria are either not treated or are given medications for ancillary medical conditions that then subdue their anxiety symptoms. As with other clinical anxieties, the lack of standardized assessment instruments and measurement error clouds outcome estimates. Early studies suggested a meager 0.5% prevalence rate among the population, but subsequent estimates have continually risen. Current estimates suggest approximately 2% to 3% of the U.S. population suffers from PD, and appropriate treatment reduces or prevents symptoms in 70% to 90% of patients. Rarely beginning before puberty, panic attacks usually begin in late adolescence or early adulthood (Diler, 2003). PD typically begins in early adulthood, with roughly half of all probands developing symptoms before the age of 25 years (Craske, Poulton, Tsao, & Poltkin, 2001). Women are twice as likely as men to develop PD, with symptoms beginning in early adulthood (Kendler et al., 1995). Comorbidity with depression is quite high, with some researchers estimating that between 30% and 50% of PD probands also suffer from a mood disorder (Gorman & Coplan, 1996). PD probands generally report more complex medical histories and somatic disease, and they may be acutely more vulnerable to gastrointestinal diseases, angina, and thyroid conditions than controls (Hofmann, Nutzinger, Kotter, & Herzog, 2001).

PSYCHOLOGICAL THEORIES

Psychological theories emerged from traditional psychoanalysis and have flourished into complex, comprehensive paradigms.

Psychoanalysis

Initially, Freud viewed panic as the threat that unconscious conflict would overwhelm ego functioning, defense mechanisms, and seep into preconscious and conscious awareness (Milrod et al., 2001). This analytic theory views generalized anxiety as occurring during the oral stage of libidinal development. Infantile rage and fear are associated with or stem from fantasized ideas of swallowing, chewing up, or annihilating another. Because of the infant's total dependence on the caregiver for sustenance, this motive is repressed and can precipitate panic whenever triggers occur, or during times in which ego energies are vested elsewhere (Shear et al., 1993). The resulting emotional conflict can become expressed as panic with ensuing flooding of fear.

In its most primitive sense, this theory views panic as a subconscious defense against separation and individuation, often alternating with fear of fusion or engulfment, with conflictual intrapsychic emotion (Battaglia et al., 1998). In order to meaningfully exist, individuals must attach with others. Aloneness does not mean being without people around them, but being without selfobject experiences even in the presence of people. Psychopathology can be defined as "a feeling of badness of the self," or, more precisely, the lack of cohesion, understanding, structure, or definition of the self.

Object-Relations and Ego Psychology

Subsequent British object-relations and ego psychology models revised traditional analytic theory to emphasize *fear of separation* from primary caregivers or external sources of comfort. The potential for object loss, particularly the object's ability to guide structure, regulate affect, and organize the intrapsychic self, precipitates panic and fear secondary to the collapse of underlying ego support. Ego psychology allows for anxiety to occur at any psychosocial stage, secondary to identity or role confusion, but both Hartmann and Erikson specifically targeted old age and geriatrics as a major source of panic. Decline in physiological faculties, sensory acuity, or cognitive ability may lead to somatic arousal. Further, panic can be generated when elderly individuals' evaluation of their life fails to note purpose, meaning, or cosmological bliss. The lifespan is nearing end, and an individual may experience despair, fright, or panic in failing to significantly function.

Attachment Theory. In Bowlby's theory (1969), separation anxiety precipitates nervous uneasiness, irritability, or a sense of impending doom when the individual is thrust into autonomous functioning when isolated or separated from a significant other. *Separation anxiety disorder* is defined as a developmental condition marked by excessive and enduring anxiety in a child when apart from primary caregivers (APA, 2000). Often these children become preoccupied with morbid fears about harm to the caregiver that would prevent subsequent reunification. Physiological symptoms may include increased respiration, nausea, aches and pains, or dizziness. Anxiety intensifies into panic when the individual's distress over perceived or actual separation exacerbates into fear when apart from others.

DSM-IV-TR CRITERIA FOR SEPARATION ANXIETY DISORDER*

A. Developmentally inappropriate and excessive anxiety concerning separation from home or from those to whom the individual is attached, as evidenced by three (or more) of the following:
   (1) recurrent excessive distress when separation from home or major attachment figures occurs or is anticipated
   (2) persistent and excessive worry about losing, or about possible harm befalling, major attachment figures
   (3) persistent and excessive worry that an untoward event will lead to separation from a major attachment figure (e.g., getting lost or being kidnapped)
   (4) persistent reluctance or refusal to go to school or elsewhere because of fear of separation
   (5) persistently and excessively fearful or reluctant to be alone or without major attachment figures at home or without significant adults in other settings
   (6) persistent reluctance or refusal to go to sleep without being near a major attachment figure or to sleep away from home
   (7) repeated nightmares involving the theme of separation
   (8) repeated complaints of physical symptoms (such as headaches, stomachaches, nausea, or vomiting) when separation from major attachment figures occurs or is anticipated
B. The duration of the disturbance is at least four weeks.
C. The onset is before age 18 years.
D. The disturbance causes clinically significant distress or impairment in social, academic (occupational), or other important areas of functioning.
E. The disturbance does not occur exclusively during the course of a Pervasive Developmental Disorder, Schizophrenia, or other Psychotic Disorder and, in adolescents and adults, is not better accounted for by Panic Disorder With Agoraphobia.

Specify if:

Early Onset: If onset occurs before age 6 years

*Reprinted with permission from the *Diagnostic and Statistical Manual of Mental Disorders, Fourth Edition, Text Revision.* Copyright 2000 American Psychiatric Association.

Ainsworth expanded on Bowlby's initial theory to further describe the relationship between anxiety and infant-maternal object bonding. Sensitive, empathic responses by the mother to the infant's distress and fear comforts and fosters *secure attachment*. Unresponsive mothers produce anxious offspring. Even in individuals who appear to be well beyond the early attachment-individuation struggle, subsequent effects may still be evident (Osofsky, 1995). Closely tied to subconscious intense fear of separation, some dynamic theories view panic as secondary to unresolved conflicts with anger, rage, and hostility. Facing potential object loss, the child feels threatened and loses cohesion and integrity of the self. To avert further decompensation, the child becomes enraged and seeks to destroy any precipitant of loss. A vicious cycle begins in which distress (particularly rage) precipitates need for attachment as well as fear of its loss.

Kohut. In self psychology, panic attacks represent an intense onset of anticipatory fear of disintegration or fragmentation of the self. The resulting condition would be a psychotic disorganization of both internal and external worlds, without the appropriate self-structuring needed to cope and adapt. Thus, whenever the self feels overwhelmed and unable to respond with cohesion and strength, intense panic occurs (Najavits, 2002).

Cognitive-Behavioral Research

Biological researchers initially paved the way for neurobiological theories of panic, but in recent years cognitive and cognitive-behavioral models have offered more comprehensive paradigms. PD probands may be particularly prone to bias in their perception, processing, and understanding of stimuli and information in general. **Attribution** is the process through which individuals make decisions about the causality of behavior. Attributions of predictability and controllability seem to be a function of early developmental experiences in one's environment. If one develops a sense of control or mastery, one may be relatively immune to the onset of the cycle of anxious apprehension. Studies have consistently shown that PD probands exhibit multiple memory biases, such as superior memory for words related to anxiety and threat. This memory bias for threat appears enhanced when people are hyperaroused. Taken together, these results suggest that threat-related material may have preferential access to conscious mentation in probands.

Barlow's (2002) work in distinguishing between anxiety and fear led him to propose that panic represents an individual's false alarm to neutral stimuli that cognitively are perceived as potentially harmful. These precipitants become unconditioned stimuli for classically conditioned panic attacks, what Barlow (2002) called *learned alarms*. Internal physiological cues become conditioned stimuli for fear-based panic. The perception that these alarm reactions are unpredictable (or uncontrollable) is a risk factor that can exacerbate anxious apprehension, which then can foster panic. A functionality model, the *fear of fear* model combines both physiological hyperarousal and cognitive labeling in producing PD. A person reacts to body sensations with fear. Increased panic and related somatic symptoms are associated with enhanced ability to perceive internal physiological cues, as well as the fear of such sensations (Eley, Stirling, Ehlers, Gregory, & Clark, 2004). Sequentially, an individual overreacts to physiological arousal by labeling arousal as frightening and fearful, thus worsening original symptoms and amplifying subjective terror. Thereafter, the individual learns to fear the fear response, and a conditioned "fear of fear" state occurs. Subsequent conditioning produces PD. PD is viewed as stemming from a fear of fear, or more accurately a fear of sensations that occur during physical arousal, such as dizziness, racing heart, and breathlessness. People with PD misinterpret these benign sensations as a signal of imminent danger and, as a result, often experience panic attacks. Although the attacks seem to occur out of the blue, from a CBT perspective panic attacks are actually in response to physical feelings that people without PD might otherwise just ignore. As the frequency of panic attacks increases, people often begin to avoid situations where they fear another attack may occur or where help would not be immediately available.

A variant of fear of fear models, cognitive models implicate catastrophic misinterpretation of ordinarily benign sensations as harbingers of impending psychological or physiological harm. Panic-prone individuals are highly sensitive to misinterpreting bodily sensations and cognitively construe them to be catastrophic. Inadequate coping skills, lack of social support, or a history of unpredictability of negative events predisposes some individuals to assume that experiences and body sensations signal impending harm. Rather than understanding the probable cause as benign, PD probands worry about losing control, fear the worst, lose perspective, and rapidly deteriorate into panic. Expecting that their "dangerous" sensations may recur, PD individuals set themselves up for future misinterpretations and subsequent panic (Hiller, Leibbrand, Rief, & Fichter, 2005).

A recent cognitive theory holds that panic patients are more likely to misattribute the causes of behavior, particularly relative to their own safety. PD probands frequently engage in "safety behaviors" before or during panic attacks that they subsequently attribute as being the cause of their safety, rather than understanding the benign nature of their somatic arousal. Another cognitive model for PD focuses on general cognitive factors precipitating a vulnerability for panic. In this theory, misinterpretation of bodily sensations occurs in prone individuals who previously have developed beliefs, attitudes, and cognitive appraisals that physiological arousal is harmful or dangerous—a mild form of catastrophic thinking. *Anxiety sensitivity* refers to general cognitive beliefs that certain somatic symptoms will probably lead to harm or malaise. This trait is best described as "fear of anxiety-related sensations" (McNally, 2003). Schmidt, Lerew, and Jackson (1999) have shown that high levels of anxiety sensitivity are strongly correlated with PD. Anxiety sensitivity constitutes a risk factor for PD (Ehlers, Mayou, & Bryant, 1998; Lipsitz et al., 2004). First-degree relatives are more anxiety-sensitive than controls but less so than PD probands, suggesting that anxiety sensitivity may have a genetic basis (Simon et al., 2004).

GENETICS

There is increasing evidence that the etiology of PD has a genetic component, although the precise mode of transmission remains unclear. PD "runs in families" and has greater concordance in monozygotic twins than in fraternal siblings (Middledorp, Cath, Van Dyck, & Boomsma, 2005). Yet the precise genetic vulnerability, its exact contribution, and its etiological effect remain unclear. Rates of PD are higher in first-degree relatives of PD probands than first-degree relatives of controls (Smoller et al., 2001; Smoller et al., 2003; Smoller et al., 2005). About 20% to 25% of people with PD also have relatives with the disorder (Krystal, Niehoff-Deutsch, & Charney, 1996). Using family and genetic studies of panic, Krystal and colleagues (1996) suggested that what seems to be inherited is a "vulnerability" to develop anxiety rather than a specific clinical syndrome itself. Often there is a deficit in the protein that transports noradrenalin or serotonin, thus leading to hyperarousal or deregulation of mood (Martinez-Barrondo et al., 2005). Some probands report that family members have similar symptoms, as well as other related conditions. Studies of twins confirm the possibility of "genetic inheritance" of the condition (Reichborn-Kjennerud et al., 2004). In one study, 31% of identical twins were concordant, whereas all dizygotic twins were discordant (Tsuang, Domschke, Jerkey, & Lyons, 2004). Strong familial influences have been shown.

Based on twin concordance studies, many researchers have attempted to locate and identify specific genes or genetic transporters that create diatheses for PD (Bellodi et al., 1998). The most comprehensive review of associational studies was conducted by Maron and colleagues (2005) who investigated 90 candidate gene polymorphisms, utilizing arrayed primer extension technology, as possible precipitants to PD. Maron identified eight potential—although nominal in association (and generally not clinically significant in meaning)—genetic bases, all associated with cholecystokinin, serotonin, and dopamine systems. Each of a minor effect, their combination and subsequent expressions via neurotransmitter propagation may contribute to forms of PD. The L allele and L/L genotype has been linked to PD (Woo, Yoon, & Yu, 2002). Genes on chromosome 13q, and possibly on chromosome 22, influence the susceptibility toward a pleiotropic syndrome that includes panic, bladder problems, headaches, mitral valve prolapse, and possibly thyroid dysfunction. An inherited defect in the metabolism of CCK has been proposed, particularly in its effect in regulating digestion and endogenous opioids. Other genetic causes may include congenital insufficiency of the parasympathetic nervous system, supersensitivity of adrenergic receptors, or inherited aberrant neurotransmitter functionality, principally with norepinephrine, serotonin, or GABA.

STRUCTURAL MODELS

Most theorists conceptualize PD as a result of the aggregation of genetic predisposition, neurochemical aberrance, and psychological dysfunction. Few studies have found differences between PD probands and comparable controls. Those that have provide mixed results without significant replication. Nevertheless, in an effort to be all-inclusive, I have presented these data here.

An early structural model cited deficit structure or decreased integrity of the blood-brain barrier (Boles-Ponto et al., 2002). Compromised makeup of the blood-brain barrier can result in more rapid ingestion of amino acids, systemic hormones, or other substances that can thereafter induce hyperarousal or panic. Further, structural brain imaging studies with PD probands have implicated the temporal lobe and, more specifically, the hippocampus. The temporal lobe is particularly involved in memory processes and auditory projection, potentially accounting for exaggerated startle responses among anxious probands. Language, memory, and emotion are primary functions of the temporal cortex. Animal studies indicate that the frontal cortex and medial temporal lobe are involved in anxiety (Woods, 1992). The hippocampus, a cortical structure in the medial region of the temporal lobe, is part of the limbic system. Deterioration in information-processing in the right prefrontal cortex may be implicated in PD. Using CAT and PET scans, cortical atrophy or deregulation of cerebral blood flow produce vasoconstriction within the brain, which then may stimulate the central nervous system (Gorman, Kent, Sullivan, & Coplan, 2000). Hyperactivity of the CNS can prompt noradrenergic reactivity and subsequent panic. Brain scans have also revealed that PD probands have nearly a third less of the serotonin receptor 5-HT1A in three structures—anterior cingulate, posterior cingulated, and raphe—that straddle the center of the brain (Gonzalez, Quinonez, Rangel, Pino, & Hernandez, 2004).

FUNCTIONAL ABNORMALITIES

PD is generally viewed as resulting from noradrenergic-based processes, particularly within the locus coeruleus (Klein, Koplewicz, & Kanner, 1992). Using neuroimaging, Krystal and colleagues (1996) linked activity within the locus coeruleus with panic symptoms. Panic may be the result of endogenously occurring noradrenergic overactivation (Bourin, Baker, & Bradwejn, 1998).

An interesting line of biological research has linked panic with ***beta-adrenergic overactivity*** within the nervous system. This theory links symptoms of anxiety

L

with hypersensitivity to stimulation of beta-adrenergic receptors. The underlying neurophysiology and neurochemistry of panic implicates the overactivity of noradrenergic systems throughout the forebrain regions. The beta-adrenergic nervous system controls the organ systems in PD, and thus heart palpitations, sweating, and so on, are evidence of beta-adrenergic hyperactivity. Two types of receptors, alpha and beta, are found in the sympathetic nervous system. Beta receptors are found in the heart, skeletal muscle, blood vessels, bronchial muscle, gastrointestinal track, and bladder. Beta stimulation leads to increased heart rate, myocardial contractility, dilation of skeletal arterioles, and bronchodialation — all physiological concomitants to symptoms reported in PD/agoraphobia. Panic attacks are manifestations of massive discharges from a hyperdynamic beta-adrenergic sympathetic nervous system. Researchers have looked at the connection between these symptoms and PD, hypothesizing that PD probands may be genetically predisposed to be hypersensitive to massive stimulation of the beta-adrenergic receptors. Beta-adrenergic drugs (e.g. clonidine) can effectively control panic attacks by stopping these peripheral physiological activations. However, in panic probands, infusions of sodium lactate are not significantly alleviated by beta-blockers (Strohle, Kellner, Holsboer, & Wiedemann, 2001).

A prominent site of noradrenergic activity is at the base of the brain. Panic is viewed as being linked to the noradrenergic system and, more specifically, the locus coeruleus. The locus coeruleus (LC) is a dense cluster of neurons, a tiny nucleus in the pons, which contains 50% to 70% of all noradrenergic neurons (i.e., produces 50% to 70% of the brain neurotransmitter norepinephrine). Neurons from these nuclei project both to the limbic system and to the cortex, producing approximately 70% of the norepinephrine in the brain. Functionally, the LC responds to environmental stimuli and potential danger by triggering a response to perceived impending doom. Once activated, the LC stimulates the amygdala, thus stimulating old memories, perceptions, sensations, and emotions experienced in the past. These "primal" reactions usually trigger their own reactions, particularly via emotional response, such as a sense of helplessness or powerlessness. As with PTSD, early childhood experiences can contribute to PD (Goodwin, Ferguson, & Horwood, 2005).

In animal models, the electrical stimulation of the LC led to paniclike behaviors, suggesting that panic might be based on noradrenergic overstimulation. Prominent in the 1980s, the theory that overstimulation of the LC precipitates clinical anxiety flourished. Peripheral measures, such as CSF, NE, its principal metabolite MHPG, plasma NE and MHPG, and urinary measures of these catecholamines, have demonstrated a clear link between stimulation of the LC and the experience of panic. Hyperstimulated norepinephrine neuronal transmission produces the experience of increased arousal, physiological symptoms associated with fear, and the subjective experience (phenomenology) of clinical anxiety. The LC region also is unusual in that it has a diminished blood-brain barrier. Researchers hypothesize that PD symptoms result from endogenous excessive stimulation of the LC, leading to excessive discharge and neural firing

(Redmond, 1985). Panic, anxiety, and fear are controlled by changes in norepinephrine metabolism in the LC, which is particularly vulnerable due to its lack of a protective blood-brain barrier. Beta-adrenergic blocking drugs (e.g., clonidine) produce a decrease in anxiety. Using neuroimaging, Krystal and colleagues (1996) have linked the activity within the LC with symptoms of panic disorder. Tricyclic antidepressants (particularly imipramine and desipramine) curtail LC firing and produce a decrease in anxiety (block panic attacks).

MEDICAL CONDITIONS

Numerous medical conditions, diseases, and illicit substances can provoke the sensations of a panic attack (Table 6.1). Some researchers are investigating the link between PD and various neurological, endocrinological, and cardiological systems within the body. Current findings suggest that literally hundreds of different diseases or conditions can mimic PD symptoms; thus a thorough medical evaluation is recommended for all potential probands (Nutt & Lawson, 1992). Major associations include hyperventilation, asthma, limbic seizures, thyroid dysfunction, hypoglycemia, and cardiac irregularities. Slight physical sensations are amplified into signs of impending doom, prompting a full-blown panic.

Angina

Early on, researchers became interested in various organ systems and their relationship to the subjective experience in anxiety. **Angina**, atypical chest pain, is a frequent symptom in patients presenting for medical care and is often associated with respiratory or cardiac disease. As many as 25% of patients seeking emergency medical care for chest pain have undiagnosed PD, with even higher prevalence among patients in outpatient settings (Huffman, Pollack, & Stern, 2002). Key differentiating factors may include the absence of coronary artery disease, atypical chest pain, younger age of onset, and a high level of self-reported anxiety. Females are more likely to be diagnosed with PD than males, and thus gender may also be a discriminating variable (McLaughlin et al., 2003).

COPD, Asthma

Respiratory diseases have frequently been cited as being associated with PD, with some researchers hypothesizing their comorbidity to be attributable to similar causes. PD probands are particularly susceptible to carbon dioxide challenges, and some researchers view this increased CO_2 vulnerability to be related to respiratory pathology. **Chronic obstructive pulmonary disease (COPD)** is a generic term that refers to any condition or syndrome that interferes with normal air movement and breathing, such as chronic bronchitis, emphysema, or asthma. **Emphysema** is a chronic condition in which the bronchioles lose their

TABLE 6.1.
Medical Conditions and Anxiety

Condition	Definition
Alcoholism	Chronic alcohol abuse or dependence
Allergies, allergic reactions	An abnormal reaction by the immune system that usually includes inflammation and the release of histamine (such as in hay fever, allergic rhinitis)
Asthma	Chronic recurrent obstructive disease of the bronchial airways; spasming of the bronchioles
Cannabis abuse	Intoxication, abuse, or withdrawal symptoms of THC use
Cardiac disease	Irregular heartbeat, structural abnormalities; hyper-and hypotension; ardiac arrytrhmias; angina
Chronic obstructive pulmonary disease (COPD)	Long-term condition or disease that obstructs the airway, lungs, or the natural flow of breathing
Cocaine intoxication	Acute intoxication secondary to cocaine or its derivatives
Cytomegalovirus	Viral infection, EBV etiology
Dementias	Degenerative neurological disease that features insidious degeneration of the brain; the pathophysiology includes clumplike deposits in the brain consisting of neuritic plaques and neurofibrillary tangles; additional brain changes include neuronal loss, shrinkage, or atrophy of the brain, depletion of acetylcholine neurotransmitters involved in memory, and accumulation of foreign deposits in the cerebral vasculature (e.g., Alzheimer's disease)
Diabetes	Disorder of the pancreas (insulin deficiency)
Drug withdrawal	Symptoms secondary to the cessation of substances
Emphysema	Chronic obstructive pulmonary disease secondary to the loss of the elasticity of the bronchiole with subsequent deficits in oxygen expiration

(continues)

TABLE 6.1.
(Continued)

Condition	Definition
Encephalitis	Inflammation of the brain
Fever	Increased temperature above the normal 98.6 degrees
Folic-acid deficiency	Any condition or disease leading to a lack of folic acid
Gastrointestinal disorders	Ulcers, irritable bowel syndrome
HIV, AIDS	Human immunodeficiency virus infection; acquired immune deficiency syndrome
Huntington's disease	A neurological condition in which excessive dopamine and deficient GABA in the caudate nucleus (diencephalic-limbic structures of the brain) lead to neuronal atrophy in the caudate nucleus and frontal areas of the cortex
Hyperglycemia	High blood sugar
Hyperthyroidism	Chronic excess of thyroid hormone
Hyperventilation syndrome	Chronic hyperventilation
Internal hemorrhage	Bleeding within the body
Lead poisoning	Repeated exposure to or ingestion of lead
Miscellaneous infection	Bacterial or viral infections
Mononucleosis (MONO)	A prolonged viral disease/illness that affects the liver, spleen, or lymphatic system
Multiple sclerosis (MS)	A condition of the nervous system in which lesions, commonly called "plaques," predominate in periventricular spaces throughout the white matter of the brain and spinal cord (CNS), usually impairing muscular functioning
Neurotoxins	Any harmful substance or poison that may damage or kill parts of the body, particularly within the nervous system
Pheochromacytoma	Tumor of the adrenal glands
Pneumonia	An infectious infultrait of the lungs
Strep infection	A bacterial infection, group A streptococcus (S. pyogenes)
Temporal-lobe seizures, seizure disorders	Sudden, excessive electrical discharge of cerebral neurons within the temporal lobe
Thyrotoxicosis	Disorders of the thyroid gland
Toluene abuse	Sequelae associated with the use of toluene
Wilson's disease	Condition in which diminished levels of ceruloplasmin result in deposits of copper in the liver, brain, corneas, or kidneys

elasticity, making it more difficult to move oxygen in and out. **Asthma** is a chronic breathing condition in which airways narrows become obstructed, or irritated. Inflammation in the lungs and associated systems creates difficulty in breathing, characterized by bronchoconstriction, wheezing, coughing, shortness of breath, or "tightness" in the chest. These symptoms are often mistakenly identified as panic (Potoczek, 2005). Further, those with asthma could have higher levels of anxiety in general (e.g., greater anxiety sensitivity), which could lead to panic in those vulnerable to the condition. Finally, as another contributing factor, almost all antiasthma medications can precipitate panic attacks, as most are stimulating or belong to the xanthine class, which again would increase the likelihood for PD (Motl & Dishman, 2004).

Hyperventilation Theories

Closely linked to beta-adrenergic theories, hyperventilation theories emphasize the role of "overbreathing" in panic via stimulation of the autonomic nervous system (Gilbert, 2003). **Hyperventilation**—rapid, shallow breathing caused by an imbalance of carbon dioxide levels in the blood—frequently occurs with panic. During hyperventilation, the product of respiration rate and tidal volume exceeds metabolic needs, and more carbon dioxide is exhaled than is produced by cellular metabolism. Based on the assumption that hyperventilation is central to panic disorder, Clark, Salkovskis, and Chalkley (1985) showed patients how a mild panic attack could be created by voluntarily hyperventilating. Thereafter, subjects were taught breathing control via relaxation techniques. Within 2 weeks, most patients had benefited from this "treatment."

One early theory was that panic resulted from chronic hyperventilation, and that its associated symptoms (e.g., dizziness, arousal sensations) may be misinterpreted by patients as signifying impending doom, causing them to overbreathe and escalate their fear, until a panic attack occurs. Based on the finding that breathing air containing higher-than-usual amounts of carbon dioxide can generate a panic attack, oversensitive carbon dioxide receptors have also been proposed as a mechanism that could stimulate hyperventilation. Hyperventilation may activate the autonomic nervous system, leading to the familiar somatic aspects of panic episodes. Lactate sensitivity results from chronic hyperventilation. However, subsequent research failed to show that PD patients were more likely to chronically hyperventilate than non-PD normals (M. Brown, Smits, Powers, & Telch, 2003). Current theory holds that hyperventilation may serve to intensify panic attacks or prolong them but is not their cause.

Hypothyroidism

Thyroid functioning is vital in regulating systemic equilibrium, particularly within the central nervous system. Deficiencies may allow hyperactivity of certain substances that, in the end, prompt greater noradrenergic activity and subsequent panic.

Mitral Valve Prolapse

The most commonly diagnosed cardiovascular abnormality, ***mitral valve prolapse (MVP)*** is a medical condition in which the mitral valve between the left upper chamber and left lower chamber of the heart does not function properly. In MVP, valves are enlarged and some tissues connecting the flaps may be too long—causing the valve flaps to bulge upward to the left atrium rather than closing smoothly as the heart contracts. Blood reflux into the left atrium during the systole occurs due to the lack of adhesion between valve flaps. This medical disorder occurs when the left atrium heart valve does not close properly (left ventricle) and produces a systolic click (murmur). The disorder is usually asymptomatic but may cause headaches, giddiness, fatigue, shortness of breath, palpitations, and chest pain (***mitral valve prolapse syndrome***). Although the exact cause of MVP remains unclear, hyperadrenergic activity and magnesium deficiency have been suggested (Grimaldi, 2002). Accordingly, excessive levels of adrenalin can create the sensation of uneasiness and nervousness and, if intensified, panic. Anxiety occurs in about a third of cases (Tamam, Ozpoyraz, San, & Bozkurt, 2000). In some individuals, MVP can produce symptoms similar to those associated with panic. Table 6.2 compares the symptoms of MVP with those of panic.

TABLE 6.2.
Mitral Valve Prolapse and Panic Disorder: A Comparison

Mitral Valve Prolapse	Symptom	Panic Disorder
Occasionally present	Fatigue, chronic tiredness	Rarely present
Occasionally present	Difficulty breathing	Occasionally present
Often present	Palpitations, chest pain	Often present
Rarely present	Choking	Occasionally present
Rarely present	Vertigo (dizziness)	Often present
Rarely present	Derealization, "feeling strange," sense of acting or "being on stage"	Often present
Rarely present	Numbness, tingling (particularly in the extremities), tremor	Often present
Rarely present	Skin and kinesthetic changes	Often present, with cycling of "hot and cold flashes"
Rarely present	Sweating, fainting	Often present
Rarely present	Fear, apprehension, feeling of "going crazy"	Often present

Pheochromocytoma

Pheochromocytoma is a tumor of the chromaffin cells in the adrenal medulla or sympathetic tissues surrounding the adrenal glands. These rare (0.3% of all panic patients) tumors of catecholamine-producing chromaffin cells often lead to hypertension and other symptoms of catecholamine excess, such as headache, palpitations, tachycardia, pallor, nausea, vomiting, and weight loss. Chronic clinical anxiety can occur secondary to norepinephrine release within the central nervous system. Usual treatment includes laparoscopic adrenalectomy. Catecholamine blockade via phenoxybenzamine or metyrosine often alleviates symptoms.

Seizure Disorders

Epilepsy is a brain disorder characterized by transient disturbances in the electrical activity of the brain (*seizures*). During an episode, nearly all nerve cells within certain neurocircuits are bombarded with synaptic activity, whether it be inhibitory or excitatory, and massive depolarization occurs. Although potentially the result of diverse causes and prompting a myriad of manifestations, seizures, conceptualized as erratic or excessive electrical discharge, can produce panic via kindling or stimulation of adrenergic activity.

BIOCHEMICAL THEORIES

Data suggest that the biological etiologies of PD are related to several functional biochemistries, including serotonin, NE, GABA, DA, and cholecystokinin. PD is a heterogeneous condition that involves numerous neurotransmitter systems that combine to generate symptoms, with primary dysfunction linked to one or a few neurotransmitters. Kellner, Yassouridis, Hubner, Baker, and Weidemann (2003) found that the cholecystokinin neurotransmitter system plays a significant role in the neurobiology of PD. Cholecystokinin-tetrapeptide (CCK-4) induces panic in both PD probands and normal controls. This same panic is mediated and reduced via lorazepam, a GABA agent, and other GABAergic treatments. A possible interaction between GABA and CCK systems may be involved in PD (Zwanzger et al., 2003).

Provocation Theories

In the *biological challenge test* (BCT), biochemicals are used to stimulate bodily sensations, mimicking the intense hyperarousal that accompanies a panic attack (Gorman, Papp, & Coplan, 1994). Using between-group experimental designs, research consistently has shown that provoked symptoms incite panic attacks in PD patients more so than in those with other anxiety disorders, other medical and psychological conditions, or healthy controls (Margraf, Ehlers, & Roth, 1986). Interpretation of outcomes seeks to determine neurobiological substrates prominent in PD or understand "nonphysiological" variables in cognitive perception, appraisal, and understanding of somatic symptoms (Battaglia et al., 1998). Table 6.3 lists the substances that can precipitate anxiety.

Panicogens

Numerous substances can induce panic. A *panicogen* is any substance, such as sodium lactate, carbon dioxide, and yohimbine, used to induce the symptoms of a panic attack. Many agents can provoke anxiety: epinephrine, isoproterenol, yohimbine, lactate, and caffeine (Dews, O'Brien, & Bergman, 2002). Biological stimulants can be used to induce panic in patients and then physiological changes that occur as a result of the initial stimulation can be monitored. Using sodium lactate infusions, individuals with a history of PD tend to react with panic, but those without such history generally do not (Gurguis & Uhde, 1990). Regardless of history, the provocation of panic using this and other substances can be blocked both pharmacologically and by psychological treatments. Using this and the biological challenge test, researchers also have implicated norepinephrine, serotonin, and GABA as potential factors in panic.

The inhalation of carbon dioxide is commonly used to produce anxiety and panic in both controls and probands. Inhalation of 35% carbon dioxide activates the HPA axis, increases blood pressure, and prompts the subjective feeling of fear. The noradrenergic system, particularly regions in the brain stem (e.g., locus coeruleus) may be a key mediator of these responses. Subsequent monitoring compares incidence, likelihood, and intensity of symptoms between PD probands and normal controls. In general, PD probands are more vulnerable to its effects than "normal" controls. Two factors emerge as common across "panic provocation" studies. First, a high level of apprehension or high baseline anxiety seems a consistent predictor of panic in the laboratory across different procedures. A second factor is the elicitation of a specific somatic response that is associated with a sense of loss of control. These may eventually provide evidence for a psychobiological theory of panic that incorporates both physiological arousal and cognitive labeling (Schmidt, Forsyth, Santiago, & Trakowski, 2002).

Metabolic Paradigms

The *lactate panicogenesis hypothesis* implicates high levels of sodium lactate in the blood as the precipitant to panic (Pitts, 1969). Compared to only 13% of controls, 67% of PD patients experience a panic attack when infused with sodium lactate (Margraf et al., 1986). A variation of provocation theory, this view holds that panic attacks result from endogenously produced high levels of blood sodium lactate. If a tricyclic antidepressant is administered before the lactate in-

TABLE 6.3.
Substances That Can Precipitate Anxiety

Substance	Applications/Description/Mechanism of Action
Albuterol (as well as older bronchodilators, such as isoproterenol, metaproterenol, and isoetharine)	Asthma; COPD; emphysema
Anticholinergics, atropine	Neurological disorders
Baclofen	Muscle relaxant
Beta-carboline drugs	Benzodiazepine receptor reverse agonists
Bicarbonate	Base substance
Bromocriptine	Dopamine agonist
Bupropion	Antidepressant, smoking cessation
Caffeine	Stimulant commonly found in tea, cola, and coffee, as well as many OTC and prescription medications, such as migraine medicines
Captopril	High blood pressure medicine
Cephalosporins	Antibiotics
Carbon dioxide inhalation	Infusions precipitate panic in about two-thirds of PD probands
Cholecystokinin	A gallbladder stimulant
Cocaine	Stimulant
Cromolyn	Antiasthma medication
Cycloserine	Antibiotic used to treat tuberculosis
Dextroamphetamine	Stimulant used in the treatment of attention disorders and narcolepsy
Ephedra sinica	A Chinese herb used as a potent bronchodilator
Epinephrine	A synthetic version of the hormone adrenaline produced by the body, this substance acts as a bronchodilator
Fenfluramine	Serotonin-releasing drug used to treat obesity— removed from U.S. market because of mortality issues
Flumazenil	GABA receptor antagonist
Hypericum perforatum	Herbal substance sold usually as mood enhancer under the name of St. John's Wort
Isoproterenol (Isuprel)	Bronchodilator
Marinol	Analgesic
m-chlorophenylpiperazine (mCPP)	Serotonergic drug; excites nondopaminergic neurons in the substantial nigra and ventral tegmental area by activating serotonin

(continues)

TABLE 6.3.
(Continued)

Mefloquine	Antimalarial medicine
Methamphetamine	Synthetic stimulant
Methylphenidate	Stimulant used in the treatment of attention disorders and narcolepsy
Narcotics	Pain relief
Nicotine	Found in tobacco
Nonsteroidal anti-inflammatory drugs	Pain relief, inflammation
Pemoline	Stimulant used in the treatment of attention disorders and narcolepsy
Phenelzine	Depression (MAO inhibitor)
Phenylpropanolamine	Decongestant
Sodium lactate	Stimulant
Steroids	Prescribed for numerous medical conditions, including chronic pain, MS, inflammation, and asthma
Theophylline, terbutaline	Asthma; COPD; emphysema
Yohimbine	Alpha-2 receptor agonist

jection, a panic attack does not develop (Coplan & Lydiard, 1998). Injections of adrenaline and inhalation of carbon monoxide or yohimbine also produce anxiety attacks in PD patients. Hence, elevated blood lactate levels appear neither necessary nor sufficient for development of PD. Nevertheless, PD patients may have some special susceptibility to lactate. Some PD probands may have a defect in lactate metabolism that generates raised blood lactate levels, in turn provoking panic (De Cristofaro, Sessarego, Pupi, Biondi, & Faravelli, 1993).

Serotonergic Hypothesis

In close association with the locus coeruleus hypothesis, this theory conceptualizes PD as the result of overstimulated serotonergic neurons in the dorsal raphe nucleus (Sheehan & Harnett-Sheehan, 1996). Probands have a heightened sensitivity to subsequent somatic symptoms and thus are more susceptible to panic symptoms, such as hyperarousal. Medications that block the reuptake of serotonin, such as SSRIs, are effective in reducing both the frequency and intensity of panic attacks (Wade, Lepola, Koponen, Pedersen, Pederson, 1997). The potential role of serotonergic action as the basis for panic is supported by comparing tonic immobility as a survival mechanism in animals. Additionally, conceptualized as intensified fear, anxiety has definitively been linked with serotonin, particularly its 5-HT1A receptor (Broocks et al., 2003).

Noradrenergic Hyperactivity

Irregularities in the synthesis and release of norepinephrine have been proposed as possible causes of panic. When panicogens with known norepinephric effect are injected, subjects experience symptoms similar to those seen in PD. Hypersensitivity of known receptors may be a contributing factor to PD. Radiotracer catecholamine kinetics and clinical microneurography suggest that PD may involve faulty neuronal norepinephrine uptake, with subsequent sensitization of the heart to symptom generation. Esler and colleagues (2004) found that PD probands experience large sympathetic nerve neurograms, with large increases in cardiac norepinephrine spillover, accompanied by the adrenal medullary secretion of epinephrine.

Practically any precipitant of enhanced noradrenergic activity can prompt panic. Exertion, such as strenuous exercise, intensifies the symptoms of persons with chronic anxiety by elevating blood lactic acid levels; those vulnerable to panic generally experience mild symptoms whereas controls experience no such anxiety (Cosci, De Gooyer, Schruers, Faravelli, & Griez, 2005). Respiration-related provocation of panic can occur during exercise or carbon-dioxide inhalation.

TREATMENTS

Though less prevalent than other anxiety syndromes, PD is a common condition in patients presenting for treatment. The tremendous distress, variability of symptoms, and functional impairments that occur in PD can impaire multiple areas of functioning. Initially, secondary to Klein's work, tricyclics, particularly imipramine and desipramine, were used to stave off the symptoms of PD. Unfortunately, at therapeutic doses, many patients cannot tolerate the side effects of these medications, and thus alternatives have been researched and utilized. Later research showed potent benzodiazepines to be effective in treating panic attacks (Valenca et al., 2003).

Many agents have been shown to provide antipanic intervention, and choice of medication is usually the product of multiple variables. Atypical antidepressants are the first-line treatment for PD, and tricyclics are equally effective though frequently less well-tolerated (Lader, 2005). MAOIs and noncyclic antidepressants can effectively treat panic. Research has shown that trazadone, fluoxetine, maprotiline, fluvoxamine, and zimelidine can effectively reduce symptom frequency and intensity (Englander et al., 2005). Alprazolam and other high-potency benzodiazepines are effective. For "break-through" panic, potent benzodiazepines (e.g., alprazolam, clonazepam, lorazepam) are effective in treating symptoms with or without agoraphobia (Chouinard, 2004). When determining length of treatment, many factors are considered. First, successful treatment in the acute phase seeks to reduce the intensity and frequency of panic attacks, revise cognitive worries within the fear of fear cycle, and stabilize overall functions. SSRIs, as well as imipramine or desipramine, can be effective. Table 6.4 outlines the biopsychosocial treatments for PD.

TABLE 6.4.
Biopsychosocial Treatments for PD

Intervention	Targets
Pharmacological approaches	Atypical antidepressants, SSRIs imipramine, desipramine, or protriptyline, hypnotics (particularly eszopiclone, zaleplon, zolpidem), mirtazapine, clonazepam if needed; medical history to determine potential physiogenics, review of medications to determine possible chemical etiology; reduce caffeine intake
Psychoeducational interventions	Educate to improve medication compliance, provide comprehensive treatment approach utilizing diverse modalities, improve coping and adaptation skills via the teaching of novel responses, relaxation, and cognitive restructuring techniques; explain and discuss the fear of fear cycle and its propagation of panic
Psychological interventions	Interpersonal and dynamic therapies, cognitive-behavioral interventions for thought-stopping and restructuring, relaxation and coping skills, insight into potential separation, rage, or developmental precipitants
Social interventions	Cultivation of strong social support systems, support groups with other probands, reassurance from others that episodes will pass with time

Behavioral Models

"Pure" behavioral models focus on classical and operant conditioning as the cause and maintenance of PD. According to these paradigms, certain stimuli become paired with heightened anxiety and hyperarousal, worsening into panic secondary to unsuccessful attempts to avoid or cope with cuing stimuli. Behavioral treatments focus on counterconditioning, systematic desensitization, and shaping of behaviors via exposure or implosion techniques. Essential interventions use exposure to somatic cues to reproduce (and subsequently reattribute) bodily symptoms associated with panic. Relaxation and breathing techniques have been found to be helpful. Table 6.5 lists cognitive-behavioral interventions for PD.

Despite differences in emphasis and technique in treating panic, most cognitive-behavioral therapists treat panic as heightened anxiety sensitivity that is then misconstrued and misdefined into catastrophic experience (Heldt et al., 2005).

TABLE 6.5.
Cognitive-Behavioral Interventions for PD

Symptom	Interventions
Agoraphobia (in some cases)	Gradual desensitization via shaping, deconditioning, cognitive restructuring of dysfunctional thought processes, emotional development that fosters self-esteem, sense of mastery, and competence
Fear of fear	Understand cycle and intervene before symptoms exacerbate, appropriately interpret body functioning without catastrophizing, cognitive restructuring
Panic	Differentiate bodily symptoms from true danger, concentrate on letting feelings resolve with time, confront cognitive processes that contribute to fear (e.g., catastrophizing, looking into the future—impending doom—instead of the here and now, misinterpretation of physiological functioning, etc.), self-care and positive self-statements, concentration on supportive aspects of situation and environment, process and resolve possible separation fears
Sense of impending doom	Refocus attention on here and now, strengthen sense of self and identity, clarify and interpret emotion to prevent "hidden" issues
Somatic hyperarousal	Relaxation techniques, deep breathing, meditation, yoga, guided imagery, consult physician for possible medication
Worry about implications of attack	Cognitive training to not catastrophize events or live in the future, appropriate skills acquisition to cope with episodes to prevent significant sequelae, improve social support, conjoint and familial interventions

Exposure and desensitization are crucial parts to successful intervention. Over- all, most models are multistage paradigms that utilize both learning and conditioning principles. First, patients are introduced via psychoeducation to the main concepts in the model: the nature of anxiety and panic, the role of learning and conditioning in sustaining somatic hyperarousal, and the importance of cognitive processes in interpreting sensations. Second, cognitive techniques are used to combat the distortions in thought processes, such as catastrophizing or demandingness, so that the patient can trust that no level of panic is fatal. Third, triggers and cues are identified to offer insight into the fear of fear cycle and its negative sequelae. *Symptom alarms* are identified and treated via panic management techniques, such as respiratory control, applied relaxation, and cognitive restructuring. Finally, relaxation, coping skills, and problem-solving strategies are taught so that if panic occurs, the patient is capable of implementing appropriate responses.

SUMMARY

PD is a debilitating condition that is associated with unexpected bouts of terror, intense physiological symptoms of breathlessness, rapid heart beat, and dizziness, and the fear or expectation of impending death, doom, or destruction. The fear of "going crazy" is a prominent factor. Neurobiological theories have focused on the noradrenergic system, serotonin, and genetic factors. Successful treatments include pharmacotherapy via atypical antidepressants, dynamic paradigms exploring fears of separation and individuation, and cognitive-behavioral models that use psychoeducation to disrupt the "fear of fear" cycle. With appropriate clinical treatment, most patients significantly improve and lead productive lives.

CHAPTER 7

Phobias

W HEN THE ANXIETY REACTION is circumscribed and focused on an identifiable object or event, it constitutes a *phobia*. Derived from the Greek word meaning "fear", a phobia is anxiety and persistent fear associated with a situation, object, or activity. The fear is usually not of the object or situation itself but of potential impact of contact with it, such as the experience of harm or otherwise dire consequence. Potential exposure to or involvement with the dreaded stimulus causes a reaction that subsequently inhibits behavior; thereafter, proband seek refuge from or elude the situation, environment, or object (Beidel, Turner, & Morris, 1998). Phobic response can range from mild discomfort to severe, extreme terror, during which a proband might experience panic. In this chapter, phobias are divided into three related syndromes: specific phobias, social phobia (social anxiety disorder), and agoraphobia. Each seems to have a common basis, but their treatments and clinical conceptualization can differ greatly.

Phobias encompass numerous conditions and symptoms, including specific and generalized features. Several theories have been proposed for the biological etiology of phobias, most focusing on the dysfunction of endogenous biogenic amines. For social phobia, genetic factors seem paramount, with high intrafamilial prevalence.

SPECIFIC PHOBIAS

Specific phobias are extreme anxiety reactions to specific events, objects, or situations. Quite simply, a specific phobia is an irrational fear of a generally neutral object or experience, with hyperarousal leading to avoidant behaviors. The *DSM-IV-TR* classifies specific phobias into four major categories: animal, natural environment, blood-injection-injury, and situational. Specific phobias can

DSM-IV-TR CRITERIA
FOR SPECIFIC PHOBIA*

A. Marked and persistent fear that is excessive or unreasonable, cued by the presence or anticipation of a specific object or situation (e.g., flying, heights, animals, receiving an injection, seeing blood).
B. Exposure to the phobic stimulus almost invariably provokes an immediate anxiety response, which may take the form of a situationally bound or situationally predisposed Panic Attack. Note: In children, the anxiety may be expressed by crying, tantrums, freezing, or clinging.
C. The person recognizes that the fear is excessive or unreasonable. Note: In children, this feature may be absent.
D. The phobic situation(s) is avoided or else is endured with intense anxiety or distress.
E. The avoidance, anxious anticipation, or distress in the feared situation(s) interferes significantly with the person's normal routine, occupational (or academic) functioning, or social activities or relationships, or there is marked distress about having the phobia.
F. In individuals under age 18 years, the duration is at least six months.
G. The Anxiety, Panic Attack, or phobic avoidance associated with the specific object or situation are not better accounted for by another mental disorder, such as Obsessive-Compulsive Disorder (e.g., on exposure to dirt in someone with an obsession about contamination), Posttraumatic Stress Disorder (e.g., in response to stimuli associated with a severe stressor), Separation Anxiety Disorder (e.g., in response to being away from home or close relatives), Social Phobia (e.g., avoidance of social situations because of fear of embarrassment), Panic Disorder with Agoraphobia, or Agoraphobia Without History of Panic Disorder.

Specify type:

Animal type
Natural Environment Type (e.g., heights, storms, water)
Blood-Injection-Injury Type
Situational Type (e.g., airplanes, elevators, enclosed places)
Other Type (e.g., phobic avoidance of situations that may lead to choking, vomiting, or contracting an illness; in children, avoidance of loud sounds or costumed characters)

develop at any stage of life, although some, such as animal phobias, tend to begin during childhood. Many phobias begin with a traumatic precursor, either experienced directly or vicariously through observing others. Thereafter, the event and anything associated therein is avoided to prevent reexperiencing the feelings associated with the original trauma. A pattern develops in which both classical and operant conditioning occurs: Avoiding the feared object is reinforced by not experiencing dreaded anxiety. However, not all individuals who experience a triggering event subsequently develop phobias. Afflicting 12% to 15% of the U.S. population, phobias are the most common psychological illness in women and the second most common in men (Fredrikson, Annas, Fischer, & Wik, 1996).

Unlike other anxiety syndromes, no empirical studies have linked biological makeup with specific phobias. Instead, most theorists consider simple phobias to be "purely" psychological (Rubino, Romeo, & Siracusano, 2003). Major therapy paradigms have developed sophisticated theories about the causes and cures of specific phobias.

Psychoanalytic Theory

In the dynamic perspective, the focus of a specific phobia awakens unwanted and avoided unconscious conflicts. The psychoanalytic view of phobias consists of five central factors in its development: (1) attraction and desire for the opposite-sexed parent, (2) jealousy and hatred for the same-sexed parent, (3) intense fear of harm from the same-sexed parent in retaliation, (4) this unconscious conflict produces anxiety that is displaced onto a neutral stimulus, and (5) the phobia is resolved ("cured") when the patient gains insight into his or her underlying conflict (Ohman, 1994). Phobias result from conflicts centered on unresolved oedipal tension, displacement, and projective identification (Freud, 1909). Phobias represent a defense against anxiety that stems from repressed id impulses. Too threatening to be part of consciousness, the repressed impulse generates anxiety that is then displaced onto some external object or situation that has a symbiotic relationship to the real object of anxiety.

Behaviorism

Behavioral models focus on learning and conditioning. By the process of classical conditioning, individuals acquire fear reactions to objects or situations (Alden, Bieling, & Wallace, 1994; Alden & Wallace, 1995). Avoidant behaviours are self-reinforcing as they provide anxiety relief. Specific phobias can develop from three basic causes: direct experience, encountering a "false" alarm (e.g., having a panic attack during a situation and thereafter fearing the situation itself), or via vicarious learning or being instructed to fear something (information transmission).

Social Learning Theory

Social learning theory views both specific and social phobias as learned behaviors secondary to observation. An individual learns to fear by watching someone else act fearfully, modeling anxious apprehension or avoidance. As in other behavioral models, the development of phobias requires a cognitive expectation of threat that is then linked to a precipitating stimulus (Johnstone & Page, 2004).

SOCIAL PHOBIA

Social phobia has been identified as a fear or irrational avoidance of situations involving the possibility of scrutiny by others. *Social anxiety* is a feeling of apprehension, embarrassment, or nervousness experienced when anticipating or actually interacting with others in social settings. The individual is afraid of acting in ways that bring humiliation or embarrassment. It is a chronic, often disabling condition characterized by a phobic avoidance of social situations. Often beginning in adolescence, social phobia centers around the fear of being humiliated in public (Hofmann, 2004, 2005). Other links include the fear of social rejection, negative evaluation from others, or enduring painful criticism from peers (Chavira, Stein, & Malcarne, 2002). Social phobics report experiencing a number of somatic symptoms, including palpitations, sweating, tension, nausea, and blurred vision, as well as visible symptoms such as trembling, shaking, blushing, and twitching. Common fears include possible evaluation from others, disregard or criticism from peers, and fear that others will see their fears and shame. In social phobia, fear and avoidance typically develop into a vicious cycle that can become severely distressing, debilitating, and even demoralizing over time. Although probands are usually aware that their fears are unreasonable, they still find themselves experiencing significant malaise and dread prior to and during social encounters. Encounters are often "endured" with significant distress or, more typically, avoided. Various forms of avoidance preclude any change in core pathologic social fears and prompt impairment and malaise (Kaminer & Stein, 2003).

Subtypes of Social Phobia

Research supports are two distinct types of social phobia (Ohman & Soares, 1993). Sufferers of *non-generalized social phobia*, the less debilitating subtype, experience anxiety in only certain social situations (e.g., public speaking, performance anxiety). Individuals with nongeneralized social phobia usually have adequate interpersonal skills and function normally outside specific stressor situations. Sufferers of *generalized social phobia* experience distress in nearly all social encounters. Generalized social phobia affects females twice as often as males, typically begins in adolescence, and is not the result of "normal" shyness

DSM-IV-TR CRITERIA FOR SOCIAL PHOBIA*

A. A marked and persistent fear of one or more social or performance situations in which the person is exposed to unfamiliar people or to possible scrutiny by others. The individual fears that he or she will act in a way (or show anxiety symptoms) that will be humiliating or embarrassing. Note: In children, there must be evidence of the capacity for age-appropriate social relationships with familiar people and the anxiety must occur in peer settings, not just in interactions with adults.

B. Exposure to the feared social situation almost invariably provokes anxiety, which may take the form of a situationally bound or situationally predisposed Panic Attack. Note: In children, the anxiety may be expressed by crying, tantrums, freezing, or shrinking from social situations with unfamiliar people.

C. The person recognizes that the fear is excessive or unreasonable. Note: In children, this feature may be absent.

D. The feared social or performance situations are avoided or else are endured with intense anxiety or distress.

E. The avoidance, anxious anticipation, or distress in the feared social or performance situation(s) interferes significantly with the person's normal routine, occupational (academic) functioning, or social activities or relationships, or there is marked distress about having the phobia.

F. In individuals under age 18 years, the duration is at least six months.

G. The fear or avoidance is not due to the direct physiological effects of a substance (e.g., a drug of abuse, a medication) or a general medical condition and is not better accounted for by another mental disorder (e.g., Panic Disorder With or Without Agoraphobia, Separation Anxiety Disorder, Body Dysmorphic Disorder, a Pervasive Developmental Disorder, or Schizoid Personality Disorder).

H. If a general medical condition or another mental disorder is present, the fear in Criterion A is unrelated to it, e.g., the fear is not of Stuttering, trembling in Parkinson's disease, or exhibiting abnormal eating behavior in Anorexia Nervosa or Bulimia Nervosa.

Specify if:

Generalized: if the fears include most social situations (also consider the additional diagnosis of Avoidant Personality Disorder)

*Reprinted with permission from the *Diagnostic and Statistical Manual of Mental Disorders, Fourth Edition, Text Revision.* Copyright 2000 American Psychiatric Association.

(Jefferson, 2001a). Generalized social phobia impedes normal development of psychosocial interactions with peers, assertiveness, and optimal functioning, due to fear of negative reactions from others (Hofman, 2005). Treatment focuses on attenuating pathological fears and reducing avoidant behaviors.

Epidemiologic studies report that social phobia has a lifetime prevalence rate of 13.3% and a one-year prevalence rate of 7.9% in community samples (Hofman & Barlow, 2002). In clinical samples, generalized fears of social interactions are primary. Onset of social phobia is typically between 11 and 19 years of age. Onset after age 25 years is rare. Social phobia appears to be a chronic condition, with most probands reporting symptoms for "as long as they can remember." Probands with generalized social phobia are more likely to develop comorbid psychological syndromes than those with nongeneralized social phobia, conferring functional impairment similar to that of mood disorders. Comorbidity with other anxiety disorders, depression, and personality disorders is common and associated with higher degrees of impairment levels and poorer long-term prognoses (Ilomaki et al., 2004). Theoretically, early detection and treatment of generalized social phobia may prevent the development of other disorders (Horley, Williams, Gonzalvez, & Gordon, 2004).

Dynamic theorists emphasize both developmental and relational variables. From an object-relations perspective, social phobia can occur secondary to early negative interactions with important caregivers. These introjected negative object representations thereafter become the guiding template through which the individual perceives the environment, and more specifically interpersonal relationships. Withdrawal and avoidance are used to elude the recapitulation of early traumatic negative interactions (Stern, 1985). As with GAD, some researchers propose that social phobia results from defects in mediating cognitive processes, particularly related to perception, appraisal, and interpretation of environmental stimuli (Foa, Franklin, Perry, & Herbert, 1996). Ellis (1962) hypothesized that social phobics are preoccupied with negative evaluations from others, and that they then catastrophize this possibility to alarming levels that evoke fear strong enough to create a phobic response. Cognitive-behavioral paradigms focus on irrational beliefs, dysfunctional thought processes, or errors in cognition, and on learning, conditioning, and skills deficits.

AGORAPHOBIA

As an exaggerated form of fear of negative evaluation in social situations, social phobia can generate such intense anxiety that agoraphobia develops. The use of agoraphobia as a distinct subcategory in the diagnostic nomenclature did not occur until 1980, in the *DSM-III*, in which it was included as part of PD. Contemporary thought brought changes to its features, conceptualization, causes, and treatments. Thereafter, agoraphobia was included in the diagnostic criteria to include categories of with and without panic.

Although most texts review agoraphobia within the PD literature, it is more appropriate to view this condition and constellation of symptoms as being an intense form of social phobia with clinical anxiety features. Agoraphobia, the fear of open or public places, was first introduced by Westphall in 1871, and its contemporary conceptualization includes the general fear of being away from home or in unfamiliar territory. Probands usually fear or avoid situations in which if they were to become overwhelmed by anxiety, obtaining help from others might be difficult, awkward, or embarrassing. The growing realization that agoraphobic avoidance is basically a compilation of anxiety about fear of panic is supported by reasonably strong evidence (Latas, Starcevic, & Vucinic, 2004). There is, however, both physiological and phenomenological evidence that panic attacks are descriptively and functionally unique events (Hofman & Barlow, 2002). Panic attacks present differently from generalized anticipatory anxiety and are experienced differently by patients. Panic attacks are also functionally related to subsequent anticipatory anxiety and avoidance. Barlow (2002) suggested that agoraphobic avoidance is simply one associated feature of severe unexpected panic. This avoidance behavior is multiply determined and maintained, but it is closely associated, at least initially, with escape tendencies of the basic emotion of fear (panic). Eventually, agoraphobic avoidance, if it is feasible, becomes one way of coping with anxiety over the possibility of additional unexpected attacks. The term **Agoraphobia** today describes severe and pervasive anxiety about being in situations from which escape might be difficult, or avoidance of situations such as being alone outside of the home, traveling in a car, bus, or airplane, or being in a crowded area. When they do leave the house, agoraphobics usually plan for the possible need for rapid escape.

DSM-IV-TR CRITERIA FOR AGORAPHOBIA WITHOUT HISTORY OF PANIC DISORDER*

A. The presence of Agoraphobia related to fear of developing panic-like symptoms (e.g., dizziness or diarrhea)
B. Criteria have never been met for Panic Disorder
C. The disturbance is not due to the direct physiological effects of a substance (e.g., a drug of abuse, a medication) or a general medical condition.
D. If an associated general medical condition is present, the fear described in Criteria A is clearly in excess of that usually associated with the condition.

*Reprinted with permission from the *Diagnostic and Statistical Manual of Mental Disorders, Fourth Edition, Text Revision.* Copyright 2000 American Psychiatric Association.

Measuring agoraphobia's epidemiology is difficult, as most patients avoid treatment secondary to their fears of leaving the house. Early prevalence rates have ranged from 3% to 6%; actual prevalence is approximately 2.5% (Magee, Eaton, Wittchen, McGonagle, & Kessler, 1996). Regardless of prevalence, the disorder is much more common in women than men, with an estimated ratio of three to one. The etiology of this vast discrepancy in gender morbidity may also be influenced by social norms, cultural mores, or familial expectations of the male being the chief breadwinner. Onset usually occurs in the mid-twentys, with a mean age of 28 (Argyropolous, Fenney, & Nutt, 2002). As a more severe form than other phobias, agoraphobia has higher rates of comorbidity with other psychological illnesses, including substance abuse, hypochondriasis, somatization disorder, and personality disorders (Latas, Starcevic, Trajkovic, & Bogojevic, 2000). Agoraphobia is often associated with the fear of intensely distressing anxiety attacks that may occur when leaving home, and often the fear-of-fear cycle exacerbates the condition. Some probands restrict their lives pervasively, sometimes to the point of remaining housebound, to avoid experiencing an anxiety attack. Untreated, the condition tends to follow a predictable pattern of cycling between attempts to overcome the fear to intense exacerbation of symptoms at its mere thought. Accompanying syndromes are common, particularly depression, panic, generalized anxiety, obsessive and compulsive patterns, and substance abuse.

Psychodynamic Theories

As conflict theories, dynamic models focus on latent forces and intrapsychic functionings that determine overt behavior. Early childhood experiences, impaired object relations, or fear of incohesion and fragmentation of the sense of self can create a sense of panic that prompts probands to withdraw safely in their abode. The meaning of objects in the environment mediates the impact of rising anxiety. Projection plays a key role in these theories, as probands attribute to the environment (and its associations) the latent conflicts and emotions that they have been unable to resolve. These typically include the inability to cope with anger and dependence. The ego responds with anxiety to the arousal of physiological response and the potential seeping into awareness of unresolved feelings and emotions. Other dynamic theories focus on fear of bad objects (e.g., conflictual relationships), exacerbation of latent shame, and generalized lack of safety attributed to anything outside the house.

Behaviorism

In the 1950s, Wolpe began to apply behavioral principles to agoraphobia via systematic desensitization, shaping, and counterconditioning. According to behavioral views, previously innocuous stimuli become paired with noxious events and subsequent emotional discomfort. Conditioning occurs as the individual continues to avoid potential cues, and through overgeneralization agoraphobia is born. By pairing distress-producing stimuli and generalization, certain stimuli in the immediate environment become conditioned fear-producing stimuli that prompt avoidant behavior. Once fear is acquired, avoiding the feared situations (e.g., the environment, unfamiliar surroundings) in itself becomes rewarding as anxiety is reduced and avoided. Behavioral treatments focus on shaping, systematic desensitization, and exposure therapies that decondition these prior classical and operant conditionings.

Cognitive and Cognitive-Behavioral Views

Cognitive models incorporate many behavioral techniques but add thought processes, cognitive appraisals, and learned schemata to explain agoraphobia. Beck's cognitive therapy rests upon the proband's faulty appraisal of the environment, his or her ability to cope therein, and the resources for adaptation immediately available if needed. Ellis's paradigm seeks to confront the automatic thought processes that are irrational, dysfunctional, and likely to lead to malaise. These and interpersonal theories have been combined by Safran into a model that incorporates social relationships, cognitive processes, and learning in agoraphobia.

A clearly defined biological basis for phobias has yet yet to be discovered, but there is probably an inherited predisposition that creates unique vulnerability. Social phobia may be a potential outcome for predisposed individuals who are exposed to environmental insult in childhood. Behavioral inhibition may be an early expression of this predisposition, with natural progression to social phobia secondary to aberrant neurochemical homeostasis. Most individuals who develop agoraphobia do so as a result of their fear of feeling panic once outside their immediate surroundings, particularly their home, and it is rare that agoraphobia occurs without the proband's first having a panic attack in public (Hayward, Killen, & Taylor, 2003). Some researchers posit "fear of a panic attack" as the chief characteristic of the disorder (Kohl, 2001). General consensus posits an inherited predisposition toward lability within the limbic and nervous systems, associated with chronic overarousal and slow habituation.

Genetics

As with other anxiety disorders, research into the genetic bases of phobias has provided mixed, inconsistent results. Family and twin studies have indicated that genes influence susceptibility to phobic anxiety, but the location and nature of the genes remains unknown. Genetic factors underlying specific fears tend to be of a general nature such that what is inherited is a trait that predisposes to anxiety in general rather than vulnerability to a specific fear. The gene encoding the norepinephrine transporter protein (SLC6A2) may influence social phobia risk (Gelernter, Page, Stein, & Woods, 2004). Fyer and colleagues (1990) showed that about 30% of first-degree relatives of phobic probands also have phobias, compared to about 10% of normal controls. The estimated morbidity risk of agoraphobia in first-degree relatives has been estimated to be 30% to 35%, with concordance rates in twin research higher when the condition is accompanied by panic (Middeldorp et al., 2005). In one study, concordance for monozygotic twins was 31%, whereas fraternal twins showed none whatsoever (Gelernter et al., 2003).

Preparedness Hypothesis

As a species, humans have a predisposition to develop certain fears. This idea is referred to as **preparedness**, because human beings, theoretically, are "prepared" to acquire some phobias and not others (Ohman & Soares, 1993). This theory of specific phobia holds that evolutionary processes precipitate the learning of avoidance behaviors that serve to protect individuals from harm and possible extinction (Ader & Cohen, 1993). Specific phobias involve stimuli that over the course of early history might have been dangerous to humanity, such as snakes and fire, and contemporary reactions are manifestations of genetically based self-preservation behaviors. Certain stressor stimuli are hardwired to produce fear responses that then lead to avoidant behaviors. Some vulnerable individuals become anxious or depressed or both when subjected to negative life events. Certain individuals are susceptible to stress produced by negative life events because of constitutional factors, relatively low social support, or some combination of personality and cognitive dispositions. These individuals react to negative life events in much the same way as they might react to physical threats from wild animals or snakes. The learning of some responses occurs more easily than the learning of others due to their inherent or intrinsic potential to harm the human race and thus inhibit the species. Some data indicate that for at least some stressor stimuli there is a built-in readiness to experience fear during exposure (Insel, 2002).

Specifically, for reasons of evolutionary significance, we seem to be sensitive to anger, criticism, or other means of social disapproval (Bailey, 1987). Therefore, most of us are socially fearful at one time or another, particularly in adolescence, but few develop social phobia. To develop social phobia, one must be biologically and psychologically vulnerable to anxious apprehension. If so, relatively minor negative life events involving performance or social interactions can lead to anxiety, particularly if an alarm is associated with these social events. Another pathway to the acquisition of social phobia is probably based on the specific and unique quality of performance deficits. Individuals experiencing social anxiety may occasionally experience some deficits in performance during a task without an encounter with an alarm, true or false. Performance deficits may then be apprehensively expected in future circumstances. This may set up the vicious cycle of anxious apprehension.

The most promising research on the genetic links with agoraphobia has centered around personality traits, as in other anxiety disorders, such as neuroticism, emotionality, and trait anxiety. Inasmuch as they are genetically based, personality and temperament variables may affect the acquisition of certain phobias—particularly social phobia (Schwartz, Snidman, & Kagan, 1999).

Eysenck's Activation Model

Eysenck (1959) viewed idiographic traits as dependent upon physiology and genetics, with individual differences resulting from biologically based inheritances. Arousal of the visceral brain system (hippocampus, amygdala, cingulum, hypothalamus) is assumed to lead to arousal of the reticular activating system, linking excitation and behavior. *Excitation* is the neural processes upon which the development of learned associations between stimuli and results depends' *inhibition* is the process of the brain relaxing and becoming calm. Whenever a stimulus-response connection is made in the CNS, both positive (excitatory, facilitative) and negative (inhibitory, obstructive) changes occur in the neural media responsible for impulse transmission. The inhibitory impulse is responsible for unlearning and extinction, and makes more difficult the passage of the neural impulse linking stimulus and response.

Eysenck believed that those with phobias tended to be introverts, more neurotic in nature, and more emotionally responsive than extraverts due to "weak" nervous systems. Therefore, they respond at lower levels and with greater intensity to stimuli than extraverts (who have "strong" nervous systems). From infancy to adulthood, these two traits and activity levels have been proposed as the most heritable components of personality, yielding heritability estimates of about 50%. The effect of neuroticism and extraversion on psychological distress over a 10-year period has been estimated to be four times greater than the effects of psychological interventions to reduce distress.

FUNCTIONAL ABNORMALITIES

The biological basis of social fear is found in the action of the amygdala and hippocampus. The amygdala appears to associate specific stimuli with fear. Contextual conditioning involves the hippocampus, crucial in spatial learning and memory, as well as the amygdala. The bed nucleus of the striate terminals also functions in arousal and extends to the hypothalamus and brain stem. Decreased activity of the right prefrontal cortex, within the right middle and inferior frontal gyri, may be involved in panic, whereas phobic fear appears to be linked to the right dorsolateral region (Paquette et al., 2003).

BIOCHEMICAL THEORIES

The neurobiology of social phobia has linked symptoms with noradrenergic, adrenergic or serotonergic neurotransmitter systems, highlighting their interaction and subsequent effects on brain functioning. Because simple phobias, including social phobias, precipitate symptoms of anxiety during exposure, researchers have hypothesized that similar neurotransmitters are involved in eliciting these symptoms as in other anxiety disorders (Nutt, Bell, & Malizia, 1998). As in GAD, epinephrine is a prime focus of research (Papp et al., 1988). For example, when in social interactions perceived to be evaluative, 50% of social phobics show a surge in epinephrine, whereas those with PD generally do not experience adrenergic flooding (Schneider, 2001). Paroxetine, a serotonin agonist, has also been shown to effectively treat GAD as well as social anxiety, a condition often thought to be a variant of GAD. Another line of thought links social disapproval to neurotransmitter activity, sensitivity, or functionality (Katzelnick et al., 1995). Both groups of probands benefit from MAO inhibitors that purportedly reduce patients' sensitivity to rejection. MAOIs work by inhibiting neurotransmitter metabolism. Beta-adrenergic blockers, such as clonidine and atenolol, can effectively reduce associated phobic physiological arousal.

TREATMENTS

Since 1980, when social phobia entered the *DSM-III* nomenclature, significant gains have occurred in pharmacologic and psychotherapeutic interventions (Table 7.1). For specific phobias, behavioral and cognitive-behavioral treatments have been most effective, but the use of beta-blockers for some phobias has also been efficacious (Hirvonen, Lindeman, Matti, & Huttunen, 2002). For social anxiety (social phobia), combined treatments show positive outcomes. Treatment recommendations are straightforward and require structured, consistent, exposure-based exercises. Cognitive restructuring, relaxation, and drug treatment (benzodiazepines and beta-blockers) have generally not provided increased gains over basic exposure. The one exception may be blood-and-injury phobia, which has been treated successfully by teaching subjects to increase blood pressure through tightening muscles at the first sign of faintness. Controlled studies are required to determine if this technique is as efficacious as in vivo exposure.

Table 7.2 outlines the biopsychosocial treatments for phobia.

Biological treatments have been most successful for performance phobia and social anxiety. Beta-blockers can effectively subdue the hyperarousal associated with performance anxiety (Birk, 2004). Beta-blockers have been reported to be most effective in reducing performance anxiety, binding to beta-adrenergic receptors and blocking the reception of norepinephrine and epinephrine. Beta-blockers can reduce physiological symptoms of anxiety, such as palpitations and tremors, because they prevent norepinephrine from activating the SNS. Gener-

TABLE 7.1.
Interventions for Phobia

Symptom	Intervention
Avoidance of stressful stimulus	Systematic desensitization with shaping of target behavior, relaxation techniques, confronting irrational thoughts
Functional impairments	Establish strong peer relationships, gradual exposure to stressful situations, emphasis on health
Intense fear	Confront catastrophizing thoughts, relaxation and breathing techniques for somatic arousal, focus on present moment to avoid "impending doom" fears
Social phobia	Practice social skills, use relaxation and breathing techniques to control anxiety and reduce self-consciousness, understand early attachment style and effect on present relationships

TABLE 7.2.
Biopsychosocial Treatment for Phobia

Intervention	Targets
Pharmacological approaches	SNRIs, SSRIs, beta-blockers for performance anxiety
Psychoeducational interventions	Educate to improve medication compliance, provide comprehensive treatment approach utilizing diverse modalities; improve coping and adaptation skills via the teaching of novel responses, relaxation, and cognitive restructuring techniques; social skills, assertiveness, and problem-solving techniques
Psychological interventions	Interpersonal and dynamic therapies, cognitive-behavioral interventions, counterconditioning, relaxation training
Social interventions	Cultivation of strong social support systems, support groups

alized social phobia is less predictable than nongeneralized social phobia and often needs different interventions.

As with all other anxieties, atypical antidepressants and SSRIs have shown significant effect in reducing the symptoms of social anxiety disorder, and they are the first-line treatments with 50% to 75% response (Lydiard, 2001). Other options include MAOIs, tricyclics, benzodiazepines, or anticonvulsants. The first antidepressant shown to be useful for social phobia was phenelzine, an MAOI. Tranylcypromine, another MAOIs, also appears to be effective, but the risk of serious side effects, such as death, often preclude their use. The anticonvulsant gabapentin, a GABA agonist, has been found to be more effective than placebo (Pande Davidson, & Jefferson, 1999). Other anticonvulsants with GABA potentiation may be helpful in patients with mood lability, dual diagnoses, or head trauma. The newer antidepressants venlafaxine and nefazodone (recently removed from the market in the U.S.) show promise in the treatment of social phobia.

Overwhelmingly, treatment of phobias has shown the most success when using psychological techniques. The most effective treatments tend to be largely behavioral, with exposure in vivo being the most effective and efficient intervention (Table 7.3). Radical behaviorism concentrates on behavior itself rather than on some presumed underlying cause. Thus, behavioral interventions focus on reducing avoidant behavior and concrete, measurable indicants of anxiety. *Systematic desensitization* is Wolpe's (1958) term for the alleviation of maladaptive anxiety by counterconditioning. Pairing relaxation with imagined scenes depicting situations in which the patient feels anxious, this technique essentially is an

TABLE 7.3.
Behavioral interventions for Phobia

Intervention	Description
Assertiveness training	Straightforward expression of feelings taking into account impact and social appropriateness
Counterconditioning	Conditioning relaxation and peaceful imagery with feared object
Flooding	Rapid exposure to feared stimulus, over an extended period of time, without opportunity to escape
In vivo	Real life, in the real world
Simulated exposures	Imagined or fantasized exposure to object
Social skills training	Techniques to build social networks that provide support when in crises
Thought restructuring	Changing irrationality of view regarding object

extinction process where the patient is presented with a conditioned stimulus (e.g., phobic object) in the absence of a reinforcer (aversive stimulation). Wolpian models emphasize reducing maladaptive anxiety, whereas Skinnerian paradigms seek to modify operant conditioning and shape novel behaviors. Participant modeling can be used to expose the phobic individual to alternative responses to their maladaptive symptoms, such as adaptation skills, problem-solving, assertiveness, and cognitive restructuring.

For social phobia, as with all phobias, some variant of exposure forms the heart of psychosocial interventions. The psychological treatment of agoraphobic avoidance has been extensively researched, and evidence for its efficacy has been well documented. In vivo exposure is of major benefit for the fear and avoidance exhibited by agoraphobics. As with all phobic disorders, some variant of exposure forms the heart of any psychosocial treatment for social phobia. Cognitive restructuring aimed specifically at the fear of negative evaluation is considered essential by some researchers.

SUMMARY

Phobias are the most common anxiety condition, but the research supporting their biological basis is sparse. Specific phobias can develop at any time throughout the lifespan, and they are most effectively treated via behavioral methods. Numerous biological markers have been proposed for social phobia, but empirical research continues to lag behind proposed models. With agoraphobia, the fear-of-fear cycle seems most appropriate in describing its etiology, with combined pharmacological and behavioral methods used throughout treatment.

CHAPTER 8

Posttraumatic Stress Disorder

MOST INDIVIDUALS WHO experience stress are affected acutely, but most readily recover over time. However, following cataclysmic events, many individuals become highly anxious and depressed with symptoms that continue well after the situation or experience is over. Stress reaction disorders are extreme forms of maladaptive stress responses that can prompt severe psychological and physiological disability. In *acute posttraumatic stress disorder* (APTSD), symptoms associated with *posttraumatic stress disorder* (PTSD) occur within 1 to 3 months of exposure to the traumatizing event or combination of events. An acute or posttraumatic stress reaction can occur at any age, even in childhood, and can significantly affect personal, familial, social, and occupational functioning (Dalgleish & Power, 2004). The *DSM-IV-TR* criteria defines PTSD as an "anxiety disorder marked by symptoms subsequent to the experience or witnessing of severe trauma, usually defined by reexperiencing the event (flashbacks), avoidant behavior, and physiological hyper arousal" (p. 424). PTSD is characterized by several essential, symptomatic features, including recurrent dreams and intrusive thoughts, sleep disturbances, emotional and responsive numbing, anxiety, dissociation, intermittent aggression, mood lability, hyperarousal, and exaggerated startle response. Heightened reactivity to reminiscent stimuli ("cues") occurs (Elsesser, Sartory, & Tackenberg, 2004). The disorder is also characterized by a chronic reliving of the trauma, rather than habituation to it, that usually persists indefinitely and is marked by exaggerated and prolonged effects of stress. Brewin, Andrews, and Rose (2003) found a high level of overlap between PTSD and APTSD diagnoses, with both equally predictive of prognosis 6 months later. The high level of overlap suggests that they refer to the same condition or disorder (Clayton, 2004; Taylor, Asmindson, & Carleton, 2005). Aside from diverse onsets and durations, the two anxiety conditions are almost identical (Elklit & Brink, 2004), and thus these terms are used interchangeably hereafter.

DSM-IV-TR CRITERIA FOR ACUTE
STRESS DISORDER*

A. The person has been exposed to a traumatic event in which both of the following were present:
   (1) the person experienced, witnessed, or was confronted with an event or events that involved actual or threatened death or serious injury, or a threat to the physical integrity of self or others
   (2) the person's response involved intense fear, helplessness, or horror
B. Either while experiencing or after experiencing the distressing event, the individual has three (or more) of the following dissociative symptoms:
   (1) a subjective sense of numbing, detachment, or absence of emotional responsiveness
   (2) a reduction in awareness of his or her surroundings (e.g., "being in a daze")
   (3) derealization
   (4) depersonalization
   (5) dissociative amnesia (i.e., inability to recall an important aspect of the trauma
C. The traumatic event is persistently reexperienced in at least one of the following ways: recurrent images, thoughts, dreams, illusions, flashback episodes, or a sense of reliving the experience; or distress on exposure to reminders of the traumatic event
D. Marked avoidance of stimuli that arouse recollections of the trauma (e.g., thoughts, feelings, conversations, activities, places, people).
E. Marked symptoms of anxiety or increased arousal (e.g., difficulty sleeping, irritability, poor concentration, hypervigilance, exaggerated startle response, motor restlessness).
F. The disturbance causes clinically significant distress or impairment in social, occupational, or other important areas of functioning or impairs the individual's ability to pursue some necessary task, such as obtaining necessary assistance or mobilizing personal resources by telling family members about the traumatic event.
G. The disturbance lasts for a minimum of two days and a maximum of four weeks and occurs within four weeks of the traumatic event.
H. The disturbance is not due to the direct physiological effects of a substance (e.g., a drug of abuse, a medication) or a general medical condition, is not better accounted for by Brief Psychotic Disorder, and is not merely an exacerbation of a preexisting Axis I or Axis II disorder.

DSM-IV-TR CRITERIA FOR
POSTTRAUMATIC STRESS DISORDER*

A. The person has been exposed to a traumatic event in which both of the following were present:
  (1) the person experienced, witnessed, or was confronted with an event or events that involved actual or threatened death or serious injury, or a threat to the physical integrity of self or others
  (2) the person's response involved intense fear, helplessness, or horror. Note: In children, this may be expressed instead by disorganized or agitated behavior.
B. The traumatic event is persistently reexperienced in one (or more) of the following ways:
  (1) recurrent and intrusive distressing recollections of the event, including images, thoughts, or perceptions. Note: In young children, repetitive play may occur in which themes or aspects of the trauma are expressed.
  (2) recurrent distressing dreams of the event. Note: In children, there may be frightening dreams without recognizable content.
  (3) acting or feeling as if the traumatic event were recurring (includes a sense of reliving the experience, illusions, hallucinations, and dissociative flashback episodes, including those that occur on awakening or when intoxicated). Note: In young children, trauma-specific reenactment may occur.
  (4) intense psychological distress at exposure to internal or external cues that symbolize or resemble an aspect of the traumatic event
  (5) physiological reactivity on exposure to internal or external cues that symbolize or resemble an aspect of the traumatic event
C. Persistent avoidance of stimuli associated with the trauma and numbing of general responsiveness (not present before the trauma), as indicated by three (or more) of the following:
  (1) efforts to avoid thoughts, feelings, or conversations associated with the trauma
  (2) efforts to avoid activities, places, or people that arouse recollections of the trauma
  (3) inability to recall an important aspect of the trauma
  (4) markedly diminished interest or participation in significant activities
  (5) feeling of detachment or estrangement from others
  (6) restricted range of affect (e.g., does not expect to have loving feelings)
  (7) sense of a foreshortened future (e.g., does not expect to have a career, marriage, children, or a normal life span)

D. Persistent symptoms of increased arousal (not present before the trauma), as indicated by two (or more) of the following:
   (1) difficulty falling or staying asleep
   (2) irritability or outbursts of anger
   (3) difficulty concentrating
   (4) hypervigilence
   (5) exaggerated startle response
E. Duration of the disturbance (symptoms in Criteria B, C, and D) is more than one month.
F. The disturbance causes clinically significant distress or impairment in social, occupational, or other important areas of functioning.

Specify if:

Acute: if duration of symptoms is less than three months
Chronic: if duration of symptoms is three months or more

Specify if:

With Delayed Onset: if onset of symptoms is at least six months after the stressor

*Reprinted with permission from the *Diagnostic and Statistical Manual of Mental Disorders, Fourth Edition, Text Revision.* Copyright 2000 American Psychiatric Association.

THE TRAUMATIC PRECIPITANTS OF PTSD

Persons suffering from PTSD have experienced a traumatic event that is usually outside the range of normal human experience. *Trauma* can be defined as any event, experienced either in vivo or via observation, in which the threat of death, injury, or physical harm produces feelings of terror, horror, or helplessness. Subsequent symptoms can include a myriad of hyperarousal and avoidant issues, as well as cognitive, emotional, and interpersonal sequelae. Traumatized individuals not only exhibit anxiety, but also may experience depression, substance abuse, dissociation, or multiple physical health concerns (Akechi et al., 2004; O'Donnell, Creamer, & Pattison, 2004). The proband has great difficulty keeping the traumatic experience out of his or her consciousness, despite trying to do so. Intrusive memories are usually of warning stimuli signaling the moments with the greatest emotional arousal (Beshai, 2004). The term *reexperiencing* refers to any form of reliving the traumatic event, such as in a daydream, nightmare, intrusive thought, or flashback. *Flashbacks* are vivid, painful, intrusive recollections of a painful event or experience, often recurring in dreams via nightmares. Flashbacks and "ordinary" memories of traumatic events or situations differ and seem to be based on divergent mental representations (Kardinerr, 1941). Flashbacks generally involve greater detail, more aversive connotation, and heightened emotional experience, particularly feelings of fear, helplessness, or horror (Hellawell & Brewin, 2004; Salomons, Osterman, Gagliese, & Katz, 2004). Janet (1889) first proposed that exposure to severe trauma leads to an overwhelming plethora of intense thoughts and feelings, too numerous or intense to integrate, leading some individuals to selectively attend away from the trauma to irrelevant thoughts and feelings. *Dissociation* is an ego defense mechanism that reduces conflict by separating incompatible or contradictory attitudes (and concomitant feelings) by maintaining a compartmentalization in which the two attitudes (and feelings) never occur simultaneously. Dissociation involves greater activation of specific neural networks within the brain involved in representing emotional states (Lanius et al., 2005).

ONSET

PTSD is the only anxiety disorder where there is a clearly identified onset. The disorder appears to be directly related to the intensity and severity of the personal experience with the catastrophe or trauma. Additive genetic, common environmental, and unique situational effects best explain variance in responses to trauma (Frans, Rimmo, Aberg, & Fredrikson, 2005). More specifically, a proximal event prompts a constellation of symptoms in vulnerable individuals. Severe trauma, such as war, rape, or life-threatening incidents, can result in the development of debilitating symptoms, such as an intrapsychic reexperiencing of the trauma or significant hyperarousal (Asmundson, Bonin, Frombach, & Norton, 2000). Acute and chronic stress reactions can emerge in response to any cataclysmic event, when perceived as horrifying in nature, and have been most associated with studies secondary to active combat conditions (as in war). Further, these syndromes can occur in the wake of natural disasters or subsequent to the experience of intentional abuse, harm, or torture.

Unlike other anxiety disorders, which typically are cued by objects or situations most people would not find threatening, situations that cause PTSD—combat, rape, earthquake, natural disaster—would be traumatic for anyone. Although approximately 50% of all individuals will be exposed to severe trauma throughout their lifetime, only a small percentage will contract PTSD (Karl, Malta, & Maercker, 2005). Following the event occurrence, victims experience anxiety characterized by elevated activity, and such cognitive symptoms as difficulty concentrating and memory impairment (Flouri, 2005). This is accompanied by symptoms of reexperiencing the traumatic event and suppression or numbing of emotional responsiveness. Detachment, emotional unresponsiveness, and reduction of environmental surroundings ("being in a daze") are frequent features (Macy, 2002). PTSD patients exhibit similarities in numerous biological and psychological arenas. PTSD probands manifest greater changes in heart rate, blood pressure, and plasma epinephrine relative to normal controls when exposed to traumatic stressors (McEwen, 2000, 2002). However, tonic sympathetic nervous system activity in PTSD patients may not differ from that of healthy controls (Weber & Reynolds, 2004). Psychological commonalities include chronic reexperiencing of the traumatic even, avoidant behaviors, reduced overall responsiveness, and increased arousal, anxiety, or depression (Young, Rosen, & Finney, 2005). Guilt and shame are frequent concomitants. Sleep is a major concern among PTSD probands (Neylan et al., 2003; Neylan et al., 2005). Studies show that PTSD patients experience significantly less sleep than controls (Otte et al., 2005). Overall, development of symptoms is generally linked with the intensity of exposure (Maercker, Michael, Fehm, Becker, & Margraf, 2004).

REPEATED EXPOSURE
TO PERCEIVED THREATS

Repeated exposure to perceived threats without controllability can be as incapacitating as a single exposure to an event or situation that far exceeds "the range of normal human experience." Trauma intensity is related to duration of symptoms (Perkonigg et al., 2005). Yet, being present during a catastrophe or trauma is not sufficient by itself to produce PTSD. PTSD develops on only a subset of those exposed to trauma, suggesting the existence of stressor and individual differences that affect vulnerability (Creamer, McFarlane, & Burgess, 2005). Key mediating variables seem to be the nature of childhood experiences (and their effects on both biological and psychological makeup), personality traits and temperament, and the nature and extent of social support relationships (Olff, Langeland, & Gersons, 2005).

SYMPTOMS AND RECOVERY

Once PTSD develops, symptoms vary greatly, and treatment outcomes are closely related to intensity of trauma, premorbid functioning, and patient compliance. Recovery is greatly affected by self-system factors, social support, coping style, personality traits, and treatment compliance (Raskind et al, 2003). Blocks to adequate recovery include dissociation, negative reactions (e.g., blame) from others, and excessive anger and guilt (Roy-Byrne et al., 2004). Many continue to experience stress long after the conclusion of the precipitous trauma. Almost half of PTSD probands whose symptoms began during wartime continued to experience significant impairment from their symptoms decades later (D'ardenne,

Capuzzo, Fakhoury, Jankovic-Gavrilovic, & Priebe, 2005). Somewhat more than a third of persons with PTSD fail to respond to treatment even after many years (Cloitre, Chase Stovall-McClough, Miranda, & Chemtob, 2004; Davidson, 2000a, 2004c). The general course and prognosis of PTSD is highly variable, being subject to the influence of multiple factors, such as the nature of the initial trauma and resiliency. Most individuals who experience severe trauma recover without intervention, emerging as sadder but more sophisticated persons. If, however, the natural process of mastery is blocked in some way or is not properly paced, the condition can become chronic. Those with more intense physiologic reactions immediately following the trauma are more likely to struggle with chronic PTSD features than those who are able to better control their initial reactions (Beck, 2004). Other posttrauma factors, such as debriefing and perceived social support, can greatly influence the intensity and longevity of PTSD symptoms (Pawlyk, Jha, Brennan, Morrison, & Ross, 2005).

PREVALENCE

Clearly measuring and describing the prevalence of PTSD is difficult, as often varying degrees of the disorder can confuse its diagnosis. That said, it is estimated that approximately 4% to 9% of the U.S. population will have the condition in any given year, with as many as a third of these probands having been exposed to war and battle zones (Almedom, 2004). The estimated lifetime prevalence of PTSD among adult Americans is about 8%, with women twice as likely as men to contract PTSD when exposed to the same trauma (Hughes et al., 2005). About 3.6% of U.S. adults ages 18 to 54 have PTSD in a given year, and, among trauma victims, the estimated prevalence is 25% to 35% (Maren, 2005). Lifetime prevalence of PTSD in the general population is estimated at 9%, with up to half of these probands showing chronic symptoms (Mol et al, 2005). Other studies suggest that 10% to 15% of the population experience scattered symptoms of posttraumatic reaction syndromes not necessarily intense or pervasive enough to warrant clinical diagnosis (Olszewski & Varrasse, 2005). Among trauma victims, the rate is much higher, ranging from 20% to 25%, and between 35% to 95% of victims of violent assaults manifest PTSD (Brewin et al., 2003).

Certain occupations are at risk for developing PTSD by virtue of increased exposure to trauma. For example, between 9% to 26% of police, nurses, and firefighters develop symptoms in response to stressors experienced on the job (Dirkzwager, Bramsen, Ader, & Van der Ploeg, 2005). Estimates of lifetime prevalence of trauma exposure are that more than 60% of men and more than 50% of women experienced at least one traumatic event in their life, with the majority actually experiencing multiple traumas (Pico-Alfonso et al., 2004). The probability of a trauma leading to PTSD varies substantially across trauma types, with research suggesting that rape for women and combat for men are the most likely precipitants (Korinthenberg, Shreck, Weser, & Lehmkuhl, 2004). Women are somewhat more likely to manifest symptoms than men following exposure to the same trauma (Jaycox & Foa, 1998). Based on this finding, some researchers hypothesize a hormonal or distinctly female-oriented endocrine etiology, with its exact cause unclear (Keane & Barlow, 2002).

As with other anxiety disorders, PTSD is a complex syndrome that shares similarities with other conditions. Comorbid anxiety disorders are common, with 21% of females and 8% of males reporting co-occurring panic and 10% to 15% of all patients reporting obsessive-compulsive symptoms (Dinn, Harris, & Raynard, 1999). Even though PTSD is a reactive disorder to the exposure to or experience of severe trauma, because of its diffuse link with other anxiety reactions, some researchers believe PTSD is an exacerbation (or amalgamation) of other clinical anxieties (Elzinga & Bremner, 2002; Huppert et al., 2005). PTSD can share common features of GAD, PD, and phobias, and thus each separate component of the PTSD reaction may involve separate biochemical processes (Packard & Cahill, 2001).

PREDISPOSING FACTORS

Studies have provided profiles or characteristics of individuals that may put them at risk to contract PTSD. Childhood experiences, personality characteristics, and the nature and strength of social support systems are key factors. People whose childhoods have been characterized by poverty, parental separation, or divorce before their 10th birthday, whose family members suffered from chronic physical or mental disorders, or who have experienced assault, abuse, or catastrophe at an early age appear more likely to develop PTSD in the face of later trauma than people without such predisposing variables (Davidson, 2004c). The inability to debrief subsequent to the trauma, such as with soldiers who remain on the combat field after witnessing traumatic deaths of their colleagues, has been linked to higher susceptibility (Boris, Ou & Singh, 2005). Further, the extent of the dissociation during and immediately after traumatization is associated with diathesis, with more dissociation linked to higher levels of PTSD and more intense symptoms. The tendency to dissociate or psychologically separate experiences from the experience and memory of abuse may become a habitual mode of dealing with traumatic events in life, leading to a pattern of "walling off" later traumas and subsequent PTSD (Johnson, Sheehan, & Chard, 2003). The experience of childhood abuse (regardless of nature) has been linked with higher probability of contracting PTSD when individuals are exposed to comparable traumas than those without such history (Kassam-Adams & Winston, 2004). Those with a family history of psychopathology are more likely to develop PTSD than those without familial bases (Gill, Szanton, & Page, 2005). Diatheses can include autonomic hyperactivity stemming from years of child abuse, imprisonment, or torture (Arnsten, Matthews, Ubriani, Taylor, & Li, 1991).

PTSD PREDISPOSING FACTORS

- Childhood trauma
- Concomitant personality disorder
- Lack of social support, erratic interpersonal relationships, poor bonding
- Physiological vulnerability to psychiatric illness
- Recent life stressors
- External locus of control
- History of substance abuse

PSYCHOLOGICAL THEORIES

Most models of PTSD etiology have focused on psychological and developmental factors, particularly on learning and cognitive variables. Dynamic theories focus on development, maturation, and maintenance of the self system.

Freud

Psychosocial theories of PTSD began with the original work of Freud, who originally viewed postreactive stress conditions as forms of dissociation (Freud, 1894; Palyo & Beck, 2005). Later, he abandoned this view and proposed that persistent trauma reactions reflect the conflicts between the traumatic event and the latent childhood repressed conflicts, ideas, and impulses it recapitulated. The ongoing reexperiencing of trauma, usually through cognition, is defensive behavior that maintains its associated affect in the present moment rather than as a memory of actual experience. This derealized, depersonalized defensive posture attempts to blunt the overwhelming force of the traumatic experience against the individual's ego strength.

The term *repetition compulsion* refers to interactional factors in perpetuating repetitive maladaptive patterns, such as recurrent trauma flashbacks and dreams, repeating aspects of the trauma as a present-moment event rather than a historical experience. Thereafter, Freud referred to *traumatic neurosis* as the emotional upheaval generated by severe trauma. Because of the intensity of the trauma, and the inability of the ego to resolve its associated conflicts, its associated emotional intensity overwhelms defense mechanisms and seeps into conscious awareness. Analytic therapists focus on the patient's need to bear the trauma and subsequent intrapsychic damage while developing adequate coping and defense mechanisms to maintain personality integrity and allow continued daily functioning.

Self Psychology

Kohut's (1977) model of trauma, and subsequent PTSD, focuses less on exposure to external catastrophes and more on the nature and quality of interpersonal interactions with others. *Trauma* is defined as empathic failure by the selfobject. When intense, severe, or occurring at a critical developmental stage, the experience of selfobject failure becomes so overbearing and incapacitating to the self system that fragmentation and incohesion occurs. Subsequent sequelae depend on when the self system suffered the significant empathy failure trauma, the individual's basic vulnerability and self system makeup, and the nature of intrapsychic defenses. Traumatic sequelae represent an intense onset of anticipatory fear of disintegration or fragmentation of the self. The resulting condition would be a psychotic disorganization of both internal and external worlds, without the appropriate self structuring needed to cope and adapt. Thus, whenever the self feels overwhelmed and unable to respond with cohesion and strength, intense anxiety occurs (Najavits, 2002).

Behavioral and Cognitive-Behavioral Paradigms

Behavioral and cognitive-behavioral models focus on learning, conditioning, and cognitive processes. Radical behaviorists view PTSD as secondary to instrumental and classical conditioning. Fear is acquired via conditioning in which a neutral stimulus comes to evoke (or cue) fear through its association or pairing with the aversive traumatic experience. Generalization can occur to other potential triggers. Neutral stimuli that were present during the trauma become precipitating factors in prompting the reexperiencing of the emotional upheaval associated with the original experience. Avoidant behavior is established through operant conditioning, in which the individual learns to elude reminding (overgeneralized) stimuli to defend against the possibility of reexperiencing the emotion associated with the original trauma. Cognitive theorists conceptualize the emotional pain and upheaval of experiencing severe trauma as secondary to the cognitive processes associated with it, particularly the beliefs, views, and values associated therein. The interpretation of events and their meaning are the precipitants to subsequent symptoms, not the experience of the trauma itself.

Existential Models

Humanistic paradigms and other third-force views have contributed little to the understanding of PTSD, inasmuch as their bases rely on foundational precepts that become invalidated during extreme trauma. Thereafter, individuals struggle with the basic core aspects of finding meaning for their lives, negotiating purpose and drive, and working with ontological anxiety that creeps into awareness whenever triggering cues of the traumatic experience are perceived (Brody & Ehrlichman, 1998). Existential views have contributed enormously to treatment models that combine symptom reduction with philosophical structures, internal schemata, and life purpose (McAdams, 2001).

NEUROBIOLOGICAL MODELS

Biological models have flourished with greater understanding of PTSD and its subsequent effects, more sophisticated knowledge of molecular biology and neurochemistry, and greater capabilities in neuroimaging. Most psychobiological approaches to PTSD focus on the failure to regulate the autonomic reactions to stimuli such that probands experience hyperarousal and emotional numbing. Psychophysiological, neurohormonal, and neuroanatomical changes have been observed in trauma victims who develop PTSD, and these changes are thought to deregulate responses to incoming stimuli and inhibit successful pruning and processing of traumatic memories. Specific brain regions, particularly the amygdala, locus coeruleus, thalamus, and hippocampus, have consistently shown aberrant functioning in PTSD (Protopopescu et al., 2005). Learned helplessness, kindling, and allostatic sensitization models have led to biogenic theories involving norepinephrine, dopamine, endogenous opiates, and benzodiazepine receptors within the limbic-hypothalamic-pituitary-adrenal axis. Alterations in the regulation of the noradrenergic systems and the hypothalamic-pituitary-adrenal axis have been shown (Bush, Luu, & Posner, 2000). Neuroendocrinological research on the physiological systems involved in stress evidenced hyperfunctioning of the sympatho-adrenal axis together with reduced activity, through enhanced negative feedback, of the hypothalamic-pituitary-adrenal axis in patients with PTSD (Otte et al., 2005). An impaired corticoid response to stressors seems to be associated with enhanced vulnerability to PTSD (Pine et al., 2005). Excess catecholamines, unchecked by corticoids, promote overconsolidation of traumatic memories and undue generalization to other stressful situations (Pillar, Malhotra, & Lavie, 2000). Symptoms such as numbing and flashbacks have been related to endogenous opioids (Hoistad et al., 2005). Neuroimaging studies evidenced a reduction of hippocampal volume in PTSD patients, which has been related to both cognitive changes and abnormalities of the limbic-hypothalamic-pituitary-adrenal axis (Olszewski & Varrasse, 2005). Further, PTSD arousal symptoms are associated with increased activity in the right side of the parietal lobe (Fanselow, 2000). Overall, PTSD involves numerous neurobiological substrates, symptom chronicity and recovery, risk and resilience factors, and critical time points for etiology and interventions.

GENETICS

Psychogenetic research has focused on identifying subsets of heritability and genetic factors that may predispose some individuals to PTSD symptoms following exposure to severe trauma. Broadly defined phenotypes, the necessity of environmental exposure to trauma, and comorbid psychiatric illnesses complicate genetic studies. Nevertheless, family and twin studies suggest a substantial genetic contribution to the susceptibility to contract PTSD (Bryant et al., 2005). For example, a large-scale twin study of Vietnam veterans demonstrated a significant genetic contribution to chronic PTSD upon exposure to combat trauma (Segman et al., 2002). Genetic predisposition has been shown in PTSD, with higher rates of symptoms in monozygotic twins relative to dizygotic twins (Koenen 2002; Koenen et al., 2003). Additive genetic influences specific to PTSD account for 13.6% of variance (Segman & Shalev, 2003). Genetically determined changes in dopaminergic reactivity may contribute to the occurrence of PTSD symptoms among trauma survivors (Lawford et al., 2003; Segman et al., 2002). Additional studies have suggested that genetic abnormalities may lead to enhanced secretion of epinephrine and norepinephrine (Bachmann et al., 2005).

Genetic factors can influence the outcome of exposure to some forms of trauma, perhaps through personality traits, temperaments, or childhood environments. The association of familial psychopathology and PTSD may be mediated by increased risk of traumatic exposure and by known, preexisting psychological illness. The heritability of trauma exposure and PTSD symptoms in male and female twin pairs shows moderate genetic influences (Stein, Jang, Taylor, Vernon, & Livesley, 2002).

STRUCTURAL MODELS

Neuroimaging studies have provided detailed accounts of the wide-ranging neurobiological changes that occur in trauma victims and their continuing effect on overall functioning. Exposure to specific psychological traumas can damage brain regions that subsequently prompt symptoms of PTSD (Hull, 2002). Fear-conditioned activation of the amygdala and associated structures, such as the hypothalamus, locus coeruleus, periaqueductal gray, and parabrachial nucleus, have been linked with symptoms (Bremner & Vermetten, 2004). The limbic system, vital to memory and emotional reactions to incoming stimuli, has been implicated in PTSD. Three brain regions appear to differ in PTSD probands relative to controls: the hippocampus, amygdala, and medial frontal cortex (Nutt & Malizia, 2004).

Experience and behavior affect gene expression and brain structure, and genes and brain structure have reciprocal effects on behavior and experience (Bhatnagar et al., 2004; Joels, Verkuyl, & Van Riel, 2003; Read, Perry, Moskowitz, & Connolly, 2001). Prenatal, perinatal, and postnatal factors can substantially mediate genetic unfoldings on CNS maturation (Koehl et al., 2004). During prenatal development, peak growth rates can exceed 250,000 nerve cell generations per minute to form over 100 trillion neural connections in the human brain at birth (Field et al., 2003). Only parts of the limbic system (e.g., hypothalamus, amygdala) are fully developed at birth; other brain structures continue to mature throughout childhood and adolescence (Giedd, 2004). Further growth and maturation occurs throughout development and subsides at about 20 years of age.

Prenatal Pathophysiologies

Various pathophysiologies can take place during prenatal development and affect the fetus, such as metabolic disorders, antigens (any foreign substance that triggers the immune system, such as bacteria or parasites), infections, allergies, tumors, inadequate blood supply, or physical trauma. Any of these can affect the brain and change its physiological and behavioral output (Alfonso et al., 2004). For example, iron deficiency in early life alters the course of cognitive and neuroanatomical development, causing patterns of decreased activity and responsiveness to external stimuli. Its effect has been linked to central dopaminergic pathways, particularly those involved in withdrawal and isolation. Iron concentrations in dopaminergic regions and densities of associated receptors and transporters are intimately involved in activity and reactivity. Significant deficiencies can affect functional activity in the corpus striatum, prefrontal cortex, and midbrain (Beard, Erikson, & Jones, 2002).

Chronic prenatal exposure to neurotoxins can have dramatic effects on the developing fetus, as well as induce long-lasting changes in structure and function of postnatal physiological maturation (Christensen, Gonzalez, & Rayburn, 2003; Oberlander, Misri, Fitzgerald, Kostaras, Rurak, & Riggs, 2004). The mother's emotions activate the autonomic nervous system, which in turn stimulates the endocrine glands and the secretion of hormones. *Anoxia* during perinatal/postnatal experiences can clearly affect development during critical periods in which the individual is acutely sensitive to particular influences (Kaufman, Plotsky, Nemeroff, & Charney, 2000).

Studies have linked early developmental patterns during critical periods of development with genetic expression of inherited traits (Allen, West, Chen, & Earnest, 2004; Bannerman et al., 2004). Traumatization in childhood increases the risk for both anxiety and mood disorders (Nicolson, 2004).

Fetal origins theory states that early environmental variables can affect vulnerability to neuropsychiatric diseases later in life. For example, early maternal separation can have chronic effects on stress-responsive substrates, including both brain functionality and neurochemical processes (Zimmerberg & Kajunski, 2004). Exposure to chronic stress can precipitate increased neurotransmitter concentrations (e.g., CRF), catecholamine depletion within the CNS, and reduced hippocampal volume (Daniels, Pietersen, Carstens, & Stein, 2004). These and other cognitive variables are involved in PTSD.

Extensive research has linked prenatal stress with subsequent defects in brain development, such as brain morphology, receptor density and sensitivity, CNS function, and the activation of certain neurocircuits (Barr et al., 2004). Prenatal stress, anxiety, and psychological malaise of the mother has been associated with numerous biochemical and hormone changes both in the mother and in the neurobiobehavioral development of the fetus (Darnaudery et al., 2004; Gorman, Mathew, & Coplan, 2002). Maternal and fetal autonomic systems and their limbic-hypothalamic-pituitary-adrenal axis are affected by prenatal maternal stress and associated with long-term reductions in the size of the fetal hippocampus, the density and sensitivity of glucocorticoid receptors, and basal and stress-induced responses of pituitary-adrenal activity (Fonseca, Massoco, & Palermo-Neto, 2002; Mulder et al., 2002). Prenatal anxiety can elevate the levels of corticotropin releasing hormone within the mother's nervous system and lead to preterm delivery (Davies & MacKenzie, 2003; Mancuso, Schetter, Rini, Roesch, & Hobel, 2004). Maternal stress, infection, and obstetric complications can trigger cytokine signaling and other neurobiological dysfunctions. Further, ongoing exposure to stressful stimuli can produce immunosuppression leading to increased susceptibility to infection, disease, or autoimmune dysfunction (Bachman et al., 2005). Prenatal brain structure can be shaped by epigenetic factors, such as the mother's neuroendocrine responses to social and environmental stressors (Tohmi, Tsuda, Watanabe, Kakita, & Nawa, 2004). Subtle but significant effects on locomotion, motor skills, muscle coordination, and hyperarousal (similar to that in anxiety) have been linked to prenatal exposure to barbiturates. The mother's prenatal use of marijuana or alcohol has been associated with the child's poor academic performance, increased emotional lability, and general vulnerabilities for psychiatric illnesses (Allen et al., 2004; Goldschmidt, Richardson, Cornelius, & Day, 2004).

Maltreatment in Childhood

Developmental considerations are vital to subsequent somatic and emotional functioning. The experience of maltreatment or other forms of trauma impinges upon normal brain development and creates unique vulnerabilities for psychopathologies, especially anxiety (Davidson, 2000b; Yamada, Santo-Yamada, & Wada, 2002). Psychological trauma can have detrimental effects on brain function that can alter patterns of subsequent neurodevelopment. Early stress and traumatic maltreatment can produce neurobiological changes in the developing brain within numerous substrates, pathways, and neural circuits (Gross & Hen, 2004). Childhood stress affects the brain's response to trauma and factors that mediate subsequent responses (Bremner, 2003a). For example, functional hyperactivity within the limbic-hypothalamic-pituitary-adrenal axis in PTSD probands has been linked to the experience of adversity in childhood and the development of subsequent adult psychopathology (Alexander et al., 2005). Overall, prenatal, perinatal, and postnatal variables can influence an individual's unique susceptibility or diathesis to PTSD.

A *neurodevelopmental deficit* is an age-specific structural or functional impediment in the maturing CNS. Childhood experiences occurring during critical developmental periods leave some individuals vulnerable to anxiety (Gilbertson et al., 2002). The term *brain plasticity* refers to the ability and process of the

central nervous system to make physiological adaptations to changing environmental influences throughout development (Kolb & Whishaw, 1998). In one
animal model, the development of certain neurocircuits was linked with neonatal rearing and determination of genetic-environmental interactions on brain
development (Parfitt et al., 2004). Early stress can precipitate attenuated development in the left neocortex (the parts of the brain that apply thought to emotion),
hippocampus, or amygdala (Teicher et al., 2003). Psychological trauma can produce anatomical and neurofunctional changes in the developing brain (Fennema-
Notestine, Stein, Kennedy, Archibald, & Jernigan, 2002). For example, maltreated
subjects with subsequent PTSD had 7% smaller intracranial and 8% smaller cerebral volumes than normal controls (Kitayama, Vaccarino, Kutner, Weiss, & Bremner, 2005). The total midsagittal area and the middle and posterior regions of the
corpus callosum were smaller in abused subjects. Symptoms of intrusive
thoughts, avoidance, and dissociation have been negatively linked with intracranial volume (Paulus, Feinstein, Simmons, & Stein, 2004). Smaller brain volumes
are associated with earlier onset of trauma (Lanius et al., 2002).

Failure to Regulate Biophysiological Functioning

Researchers have proposed that the effects of experiencing severe trauma may,
in those predisposed, bring pathophysiological changes similar to those seen in
crowding or animal models of inescapable shock (Pynoos, Steinberg, & Wraith,
1995; Yehuda, 1999a, 1999b). These biobehavioral changes precipitate down
regulation of subsequent bodily functioning, cognition, and emotional processes
(Davidson, 2000a). Theorists propose that PTSD results from a chronic failure
to regulate biophysiological functioning (*kindling*), reactions to stress, or cognitive cues such that the individual experiences ongoing hyperarousal, reactive
emotional numbing, or psychological (intrapsychic) fragmentation/incohesion
(Anisman et al., 1998). Several studies have shown that PTSD probands show
higher overall levels of galvanic skin response functioning relative to normal
controls, particularly in response to cuing stimuli of stressful experiences (Good
& Peterson, 2001; Yehuda, Boisoneau, & Lowry, 1995). These posttrauma changes
may lead to a loss in stimulus discrimination; neutral or approximate ("cuing")
stimuli trigger spiraling emotional sequelae. The repeated replaying of intrusive,
distressing recollections following a traumatic experience can modify the structure of neural networks involved in the processing of memory (Dalgleish &
Power, 2004). Animal models have shown that repeated exposure to stress produces enhanced physiological reactivity, heightened startle responses, and over-
production of endogenous opioids that act as analgesics (Hernandez-Avila,
Wand, Luo, Gelernter, & Kranzler, 2003). Depletion of serotonin has been
implicated in the PTSD symptoms of hyperirritability and failure to mediate
arousal (Marshall et al., 2001).

Exaggerated startle and flashback symptoms may be the result of the failure
of higher brain regions, such as the hippocampus and medial frontal cortex, to

mediate and reduce symptoms and distress that are regulated through the amygdala in response to triggers or cues of the initial trauma (Fanselow, 2000). The presence of an abnormally large cavum septum pellucidum may be a neurobiological vulnerability for PTSD (Smith, 2005). In one study, pairs of twins were compared for overt symptoms of PTSD and volume of their cavum septum pellucidum, with larger volumes associated with PTSD expression (May, Chen, Gilbertson, Shenton, & Pitman, 2004). However, the most consistent finding among neuroimaging studies has linked hippocampal volume with PTSD. A region within the limbic system, the hippocampus records spatial and temporal aspects of experiences into memory. Changes in the hippocampus are thought to be responsible for intrusive memories and flashbacks that occur in PTSD probands. Using PET neuroimaging, Shin and colleagues (2004) have shown abnormal regional cerebral blood flow response in the hippocampus and parahippocampal gyrus during explicit recollection of traumatic memories.

Research has shown decreased hippocampal volume in PTSD probands when compared to normal controls, which may effect limbic-hypothalamic-pituitary-adrenal axis dysfunction in PTSD (Wignall et al., 2004). Structural brain-imaging studies have linked smaller volumes of the hippocampus relative to controls in PTSD, with subsequent limits on proper evaluation and categorization of experience (Daniels, Richter, & Stein, 2004). Extensive research using magnetic imaging has shown a relationship between PTSD and the hippocampus, in both war and sexual abuse trauma survivors (Villarreal & King, 2001). Diminished hippocampal volume, via decreased neuronal density or general atrophy, may result from chronic amygdaloid hyperarousal. Lindauer and colleagues (2004) linked smaller hippocampal volumes with increased incidence, prevalence, and severity of PTSD symptoms. In their studies, the volumes of the amygdala, parahippocampal gyrus, gray and white matter, and other brain regions were not significantly different in PTSD probands versus controls (Klumpers et al., 2004). Brain regions involved in memory function have been linked with PTSD, particularly in the recall of stressful imagery. Neural processes relevant to the effects of stress on memory, such as fear conditioning, stress sensitization, and extinction, are implicated in PTSD (Bremner et al., 2005).

FUNCTIONAL ABNORMALITIES

As with other conditions, brain structure and function may be linked in precipitating certain conditions. All functions of the brain are susceptible to nonphysiological influences, such as social factors, that mediate genotypic influences on present operation (Teicher, 2002). For PTSD, functional brain imaging studies have revealed altered cerebral function (activation and deactivation) in the amygdala, hippocampus, prefrontal cortex, and anterior cingulate (Pawlak, Magarinos, Melchor, McEwen, & Strickland, 2003). Overall hyperarousal in key brain regions, including the nucleus accumbens, striatum, amygdala, and hypothalamus, have been linked with PTSD. Cingulate hypoperfusion has consistently been linked with PTSD (Gilboa et al., 2004). Aggregately, studies indicate the involvement of temporal and prefrontal cortical dysfunction, particularly serotonergic enervation therein (Jatzko et al., 2005). Additional findings have implicated activation of the rostral and dorsal anterior cingulate, amygdala, and posterior parietal neurocircuits (Bryant et al., 2005).

Early stress and traumatic maltreatment produce neurobiological changes in the developing nervous system through numerous substrates, pathways, and neural circuits (Mulder et al., 2002). For example, exposure to traumatic stressors can lead to a fear-conditioned activation of the amygdala and associated structures, such as the hypothalamus, locus coeruleus, periaqueductal gray, and parabrachial nucleus. Symptomatic PTSD features, such as flashbacks, may result from a failure of the hippocampus and frontal cortex to dampen the exaggerated arousal and distress that are mediated via the amygdala in response to reminders of traumatic events (Sakamoto et al., 2005). Other possible sequelae include variations in endocrine, autonomic, and behavioral stress responses as a result of a permanent sensitivity in corticotrophin releasing factor and other neurotransmitter systems (Bayatti, Zschocke, & Behl, 2003; Fennema-Notestine et al., 2002). Accompanying autonomic, neurotransmitter, and endocrine effects ensue.

Chronic stress increases serotonin neurotransmission within the medial prefrontal cortex and amygdala, yet some studies suggest that prolonged exposure to stressors can inhibit serotonin production (Senkowski, Linden, Zubragel, Bar, & Gallinat, 2003; Stein, Westenberg, & Liebowitz, 2002). For those who have experienced severe trauma in childhood, the cooccurrence of PTSD and borderline personality disorder is quite high (Golier et al., 2003; Modestin, Furrer, & Malti, 2005). Traumatic childhood experiences occurring during critical developmental periods leave some individuals vulnerable to PTSD and other anxiety-related syndromes (Kobasa & Courington, 1981). Bremner and colleagues (1995) identified several characteristics or traits of those most likely to develop PTSD: poverty, children of divorce, familial history of mental illness, recurrent trauma or unexpected pressures, and the experience of severe catastrophic events (Pynoos et al., 1995). The tendency of children who experience these events to psychologically separate themselves from the experience and memory of the event may make them prone to further habituation of dissociation as a primary means of dealing with trauma.

Failure to Regulate Autonomic Reactions

Some theories propose that PTSD results from a failure to regulate autonomic reactions to stressful stimuli, leading to hyperreactivity and emotional numbing. This dysregulation of the emotional and physiological responsiveness occurs with specific reminders of the initial trauma as well as in reaction to misinterpreted neutral stimuli—signifying a loss of stimulus discrimination. In addition, the individual learns to fear his or her own emotional responses, associating them with helplessness, hopelessness, or lack of control. Functional activation studies have implicated hyperaroused functioning within the amygdala and insula combined with a failure to engage the emotional regulatory processes of the medial prefrontal, anterior cingulate cortex, and hippocampus (Kimble & Kaufman, 2004). Persistent, intrusive reexperiencing commonly occurring in PTSD is construed as a failure of cingulate inhibition of hyperresponsive amygdaloid processes. When the amygdala is hyperactivated due to stress and fear, the prefrontal cortex serves to inhibit its activity. When decreased or inefficient prefrontal cortex functioning occurs, the amygdala continues to generate significant feelings of fear (Debiec & Ledoux, 2004; Protopopescu et al., 2005). Thereafter, decreased benzodiazepine receptor binding throughout the prefrontal cortex occurs, metabolism and blood flow slows within the hippocampus (and surrounding thalamus and cingulate gyrus), and heightened sensitivity to norepinephrine occurs. The inability of the prefrontal cortex to "rein in" the amygdala and associated structures leads to sporadic symptoms (Heim & Nemeroff, 2001).

There has been support of this model in significant imaging studies comparing probands with controls for key areas of the brain, such as the amygdala, hippocampus, and prefrontal cortex (Martin, Wright, McMullin, Shin, & Rauch, 2004). PTSD patients show a relative increase in regional cerebral perfusion in the anterior and posterior cingulate, the right temporal and parietal regions, the putamen, and the left hippocampal areas (Shin, Orr, et al., 2004). Symptomatic features of hyperarousal, exaggerated startle, and flashbacks may be related to dysfunction within the hippocampus and medial prefrontal cortex to dampen exaggerated symptoms that are then mediated through the amygdala in response to potential environmental triggers or reminding cues of the original traumatic experience (Nutt & Malizia, 2004).

Another area of interest in brain functionality and PTSD concerns the amygdala. Known for its involvement in the acquisition of fear responses, many empirical studies have looked at the role of the amygdala in "overlearned" fear responses involved in PTSD (Bremner et al., 2005; Britton, Phan, Taylor, Fig, & Liberzon, 2005). Shin and colleagues (2005) compared controls and PTSD probands, finding exaggerated amygdaloid reactivity, diminished prefrontal cortex responsivity, and a significant interaction between these two regions during the fear response. These studies suggest the influence of the amygdala over regions involved in autonomic and higher-order memories (Gilboa et al., 2004).

Other studies of war-related PTSD have shown that some probands show damaged functioning of the hippocampus (Bremner et al., 1995). Abnormal cerebral blood flow responses within the hippocampus occur during explicit recall of traumatic memories (Shin, Shin, et al., 2004). As vital parts to the limbic system, both the hippocampus and amygdala play key roles in the initiation, experience, and regulation of emotion. Functional activation studies implicate hyperactive amygdala and insula, as well as a failure to engage mediational structures in the medial prefrontal and anterior cingulate cortex.

BIOCHEMICAL THEORIES

Exposure to traumatic stress involves a complex neurohormonal response, precipitating the release of catecholamines, neurotransmitters, hormones of the hypothalamus, pituitary, and adrenal gland (e.g., cortisol, vasopressin, oxytocin), and other biochemicals. Underlying both structural and functional aberrations are neuromodulatory systems involving diverse biochemicals that interact to prompt symptoms. Recent advances in research methodologies, neurobiological testing, and technology have afforded greater investigation of biochemical theories. Cross-system research now includes neuroendocrine (e.g., limbic-hypothalamic-pituitary-adrenal axis), neurochemical (e.g., CRF, neurotransmitters), and neuro-immunologic (e.g., cellular immunity) variables to be investigated and linked with PTSD (Segmen et al., 2002). The locus coeruleus noradrenergic system, prefrontal cortex dopamine system, endogenous opiates, limbic-hypothalamic-pituitary-adrenal axis and corticosteroid releasing factors, and kindling theories may play psychogenic roles (Friedman, Wang, Jalowiec, McHugo, & McDonagh-Coyle, 2005).

Cathecholamines

Catecholamines are prime factors in all anxiety disorders, and PTSD is no exception. Neurotransmitters and other neuroactive agents have linked PTSD symptoms to increased levels of certain catecholamines. As with PD, one theory of PTSD focuses on the role of norepinephrine within the brain (Brady et al., 2000). Down regulation of alpha-2 adrenergic receptors promotes increased locus coeruleus activity, causing greater production and release of norepinephrine (Friedman, 2000). This model hypothesizes that increased or excessive release of norepinephrine from the locus coeruleus, in response to trauma, projects into the hippocampus and amygdala, facilitating encoding of fear-related memories (Strawn, Ekhator, Horn, Baker, & Geracioti, 2004). Thereafter, greater responses from the sympathetic nervous system occur in response to cues reminiscent of the traumatic events. Dysfunction in central noradrenergic function has been shown to be related to both selective attention and abnormality in PTSD (Neylan et al., 2004). Hyperresponsive peripheral and central nervous system noradrenergic activity may prompt PTSD symptoms, such as hyperarousal and intrusive thoughts.

Chronic adrenergic activation is associated with down regulation of noradrenergic receptors, sustaining increases in output. The noradrenergic neurons play a central role in coordinating multiple brain regions. Alterations in the regulation of the noradrenergic systems and the limbic-hypothalamic-pituitary-adrenal axis produce elevations in epinephrine, norepinephrine, and related metabolites. Disturbances in norepinephrine systems are likely to manifest in aberrant modulation of working memory, involuntary recollection of traumatic experiences, arousal, and sleep patterns. Modification of associated neural networks may also have a secondary effect of kindling within the hippocampus that then further modulates sensitivity to stressors (Kellett & Kokkinidis, 2004). High levels of norepinephrine may inhibit the release of corticotrophin releasing hormone and thereby inhibit the hypothalamic-pituitary-adrenal axis. Subsequent deficiencies in endogenous opioids can occur. An impaired corticoid response to stressors seems to provide an enhanced diathesis to PTSD. Excess catecholamines, unmediated by corticoids, promote consolidation of traumatic memories and foster undue generalization to other environmental stressors.

Neuromodulatory Systems

Neuromodulatory systems involving GABA and possibly opioids may underlie PTSD (Liberzon & Phan, 2003). Facing danger, the body produces high levels of GABA and natural opiates, which can temporarily mask pain. Neuromodulatory systems focus on GABA. Scientists have found that PTSD probands produce higher levels of GABA even after the danger passes, which may lead to blunted emotional effects. Endogenous opiates have a known effect on pain and sensory sensitivity, and some theories have focused their connection to PTSD. Opioid-mediated analgesia develops in animal experiments following exposure to traumatic stress, leading to the hypothesis that increased CNS opioidergic activity occurs in PTSD. As a hallmark feature of PTSD, emotional numbing and decreased responsivity may result from overactive opiate tracts that cause general numbing throughout emotional experience and expression. Hyperactivity of noradrenergic and endogenous opiate circuits may prompt PTSD symptoms, such as numbing and flashbacks (Hoistad et al., 2005).

The central nervous system is linked to the endocrine glands by the effects of the hypothalamus on the pituitary gland. Consisting of ductless glands (with no external excretion), the neuroendocrine system secretes hormones that are circulated throughout the blood and lymph systems. Target organs (and associated cells) have receptors that respond to particular hormones. **Adrenocorticotropic hormone (ACTH)** is a pituitary hormone that stimulates the release of hormones from the adrenal cortex during the experience of stress. Another pituitary hormone, **beta-lipotropin** incorporates many of the same amino acid sequences found in neuropeptides involved in the stress response. The **sympathetic adrenal medullary system (SAM)** releases adrenalin (epinephrine) into the bloodstream. In response to stress, the hypothalamus releases corticotropin releasing factor that travels to the pituitary gland, where it triggers the release of ACTH. ACTH released into the bloodstream causes the cortex of the adrenal gland to release stress hormones, such as corticosteroids.

Cortisol, a corticosteroid synthesized by the adrenal cortex, is released to increase blood pressure and sodium uptake (Raison & Miller, 2003). Cortisol affects the availability of carbohydrates, fats, and glucose metabolism, possibly having trophic effects on specific brain regions (Neylan, Schuff, et al., 2003). If cortisol levels remain elevated for too long, muscle breakdown, decreased inflammatory response, and suppression of the immune system can occur (Frye & Walf, 2004; Melamed, Shirom, Toker, Berliner, & Shapira, 2004). Hormones, stress, learning experiences, or social interactions can produce changes in neural circuits by influencing gene expression (Carrasco & Van de Kar, 2003; Hettema et al., 2003; Rondo, Vaz, Moraes, & Tomkins, 2004). Other studies have linked abnormally low levels of cortisol in PTSD probands relative to controls (Aerni, Traber, Hock, Roozendaal, Schelling, Papassotiropoulos, et al., 2004). These findings remain unclear.

Neuroendocrinological research on the physiological processes involved in the stress response have shown hyperfunctioning of the sympatho-adrenal axis together with reduced activity of the limbic-hypothalamic-pituitary-adrenal axis in PTSD (Sahar, Shalev, & Porges, 2001). Extensive research suggests that memory formation is enhanced by endogenous systems mediated by stress hormones and the functions of the limbic system (Birmes, Escande, Gourdy, & Schmitt, 2000; Bonne et al., 2005; Bonne, Gilboa, et al., 2003). The amygdala is integrally involved in memory processes that occur throughout the limbic system and associated brain regions. Emotional arousal on memory consolidation is regulated by the release of adrenal hormones, particularly epinephrine and glucocorticoids, as well as other neurotransmitters that converge in mediating noradrenalin within the amygdala (Bachmann et al., 2005). Under severe stress, the memory-modulatory system promotes the formation of vivid, chronic memories, such as flashbacks. These memory modulation systems propagated by the amygdala may be involved in the formation of painful flashback memories involved in PTSD (Kellet & Kokkinidis, 2004; Rasmusson et al., 2004).

Resting levels of glucocorticoids have been shown to be decreased in PTSD probands when compared to controls (Karlovic, Martinac, Buljan, & Zoricic, 2004). The endocrine system releases certain hormones into the extracellular fluids surrounding capillary beds. Thereafter, they find their way into general circulation. The endocrine glands include the adrenal medulla, which secretes epinephrine and norepinephrine, and the adrenal cortex, which produces steroids (Karlovic, Marusic, & Martinac, 2004). The outer layer of the adrenal cortex, the zona glomerulosa, manufactures mineralocorticoids. The next layer of cells, the zona fasciculata, produces cortical hormones, such as the glucocorticoids cortisone and hydrocortisone. These hormones facilitate the breakdown of proteins that provide metabolic energy, as well as prepare the body to handle stress and reduce inflammation (Kasckow, Baker, & Geracioti, 2001). When dysfunction of the limbic-hypothalamic-pituitary-adrenal axis occurs, glucocorticoids are suppressed. Normally, the hypothalamus releases corticotrophin releasing factor that acts on the pituitary to release ACTH and other hormones to stimulate the adrenal cortex to release cortisol. However, in PTSD, the pituitary exhibits a blunted ACTH response, resulting in less cortisol production (Rauch, Shin, et al., 2003). At the same time, there is an up regulation of glucocorticoid receptors on lymphocytes secondary to low circulating levels of cortisol. Research has shown that PTSD patients, relative to controls, may have move lymphocyte glucocorticoid receptors (Ouimette et al., 2004).

Neurohormonal changes in PTSD probands have been found. First, prolonged stress causes depletion of the noradrenergic system, leading to hypersensitivity of receptors to subsequent new release of norepinephrine. The neuroendocrinology of PTSD appears to be the result of hyperactive central CRH systems with underactivity of the pituitary-adrenal axis (Bleiberg & Markowitz, 2005). PTSD probands tend to have abnormal levels of key hormones involved in response to stress. Some studies have shown that their cortisol levels are lower than controls and epinephrine and norepinephrine levels are higher than controls (Kellner et al., 2003). The expression of myelin basic protein in cerebrospinal fluid, hypothalamus and hippocampus, and temporoparietal cortex may be involved in PTSD. The level of myelin basic protein in cerebrospinal fluid may be a sensitive biological marker for damage within specific brain regions involved in PTSD (Kellner et al., 2002).

Based on male/female prevalence, some researchers hypothesize a hormonal or distinctly endocrine etiology, with its exact cause unclear (Keane & Barlow, 2002; Young & Breslau, 2004). Hypersecretion of CRF within the CNS has been linked with PTSD, as well as increased adrenal cortisol responses to ACTH and increased pituitary ACTH and adrenal cortisol responses to corticotropin releasing factor (Newport et al., 2003). Comparing PTSD probands to normal controls, PTSD individuals have exaggerated cortisol responses to stress but lower baseline levels prior to exposure to trauma. In the areas of stress and stress response, the hypothalamic-pituitary-gonadal (HPG) system circulates testosterone throughout the body, which may be suppressed by physical or psychological stress (Spivak, Maayan, Mester, & Weizman, 2003). Veterans with PTSD have been shown to have higher levels of corticotrophin releasing factor in their cerebrospinal fluid relative to controls (Britton et al., 2005). The effects of enhanced CRF on subsequent functioning remain unclear. More research is needed to clarify the nature and impact of these variables in prompting or intensifying PTSD symptoms.

TREATMENTS

The inclusion of APTSD and PTSD as diagnostic categories has spurred a wealth of putative treatments, all primarily focusing on reducing associated symptoms, gaining perspective of the traumatic experience, and reaffirming basic beliefs and philosophies that seemingly were marred via exposure (Ballenger et al., 2004). Practice guidelines include psychoeducation, coping skills training, experiential trust, and medication management (Gray, Elhai, & Frueh, 2004). Biopsychosocial models incorporate multiple variables into comprehensive treatment programs (Lombardo & Gray, 2005). Anxiolytics can reduce tension, hyperarousal, and exaggerated startle responses while antidepressants can often lessen the intensity of flashbacks, nightmares, intrusive recollections, or associated mood lability (Cooper, Carty, & Creamer, 2005). Psychological treatments utilize relationship-based paradigms that reaffirm interpersonal connections (Daldrup et al., 1994; Loveland-Cook et al., 2004). Psychosocial therapies focus on enhancing social functioning, extinction of symptoms, and improved functioning. Overall, PTSD is most effectively treated via psychotherapy, although intermittent medical interventions can be used to alleviate functional impairments secondary to symptoms (Redgrave, 2003). Table 8.1 outlines the biopsychosocial treatments for PTSD. Table 8.2 lists interventions.

Medications

Many medications have been used in the treatment of PTSD, most with male combat veterans without proper matching or controls. The positive symptoms of PTSD (reexperiencing the past, increased arousal) generally respond better than negative symptoms (avoidance, withdrawal). As in all other anxiety conditions,

TABLE 8.1.
Biopsychosocial Treatments for PTSD

Intervention	Targets
Pharmacological approaches	Atypical antidepressants, SSRI's, desipramine or protriptyline, hypnotics to induce sleep (particularly eszopiclone, zaleplon, zolpidem), mirtazapine, bupropion, clonazepam if needed; check (and treat if needed) testosterone level (Baker et al., 2005)
Psychoeducational interventions	Educate to improve medication compliance; provide comprehensive treatment approach utilizing diverse modalities; improve coping and adaptation skills via the teaching of novel responses; relaxation and cognitive restructuring techniques; debriefing, validation of experiences, bibliotherapy focusing on coping and adaptation; sleep hygiene instruction
Psychological interventions	Interpersonal and dynamic therapies, cognitive-behavioral interventions for thought-stopping and restructuring of the "reliving" experience, a strong therapeutic relationship with a trained therapist that reaffirms basic philosophies of life
Social interventions	Cultivation of strong social support systems, support groups with other trauma victims (particularly if theme-based); referral to state agencies for case management and assistance

TABLE 8.2.
Interventions for PTSD

Symptom	Intervention
Exposure to traumatic event	Debrief: As soon as possible following exposure to trauma, victims need to confide in trustworthy others who can empathically validate feelings, help process and resolve underlying emotions; and normalize response to trauma while diffusing anxiety; revalidate basic beliefs that were violated by the trauma; relaxation training with subsequent exposure therapy (in vivo or imaginary); control victim's exposure to unnecessary situations that remind the person of his or her initial trauma
Disillusionment	Reaffirm basic beliefs that were violated by the trauma, particularly if able to discuss with empathic peers; teach self-helping skills; seek referral to resources (e.g., clergy, crisis counselors, therapists.)
Nightmares, dreams of event	Improve sleep hygiene; verbalize feelings and emotions related to trauma within empathic response of peers; begin a journal of dreams and review with trustworthy others, linking specific emotions with each part of event; use guided imagery to purposefully process events
Numbing of emotional response	Improve awareness and contact with internal affective processes; verbalize feelings within empathic relationships, pairing parts (stages) of event with corresponding emotions
Recurrent intrusive thoughts, images	Thought-stopping and thought-restructuring techniques, process and resolve underlying emotions that prompt recurrent images
Reexperiencing event	Verbalize experience within empathic relationships, pair parts of the event with corresponding emotions; allow confidants to affirm and validate associated feelings and sequelae
Social discomfort	Practice relating with others, social skills, and empathic bonding; cognitive restructuring; verbalize fears in the present moment while being receptive to empathic feedback

first-line pharmacotherapy for PTSD has utilized SSRIs, particularly those that have sedating or calming effects (Pitman & Delahanty, 2005). Sertraline, paroxetine, and escitalopram have been successfully used to alleviate associated anxiety, improve sleep cycles, and reduce overall arousal (Seedat et al., 2004). Additionally, tricyclics, particularly those with heavy noradrenergic effects, have been used to regulate norepinephrine dysfunction or down regulation. Desipramine and protriptyline have the strongest noradrenergic effects within the heterocyclic drugs, and they are commonly used to improve sleep (via their sedating effects) and enhance attention and concentration in PTSD probands (Mellman, Clark, & Peacock, 2003).

Medical attempts to alleviate PTSD have tried just about all psychotropics, including antidepressants, benzodiazepines, antipsychotics, and anticonvulsants (Berlant, 2004; L. L. Davis et al., 2004). Tricyclic antidepressants have been used to reduce putative locus coeruleus overactivity, as well as mediate noradrenergic regulation. Prazosin is a centrally acting alpha-1 adrenergic antagonist that may be effective in PTSD (Raskind et al., 2003). Benzodiazepines have been widely used and are believed to reduce limbic system kindling and neurochemical changes in the locus coeruleus and hypothalamus. Severe affective lability may warrant treatment via a mood stabilizer. Valproic acid, carbamazepine, and lamotrigine have been effective in reducing hyperarousal, aggression, impulsivity, and explosiveness associated with PTSD, though with mixed outcomes (Citrome et al., 2004). Adrenergic agents, such as beta-blockers, used either alone or in combination with an SSRI can target hyperarousal and impulsivity (Kant, Chalansani, Chengappa, & Dieringer, 2004). Beta-adrenergic blockers such as propanolol have shown promise in reducing aggression and arousal. Alpha-2 adrenergic agents, such as clonidine, appear to be effective through suppression of activity in the locus coeruleus. In cases of severe self-injurious behavior, dissociation, psychosis, or aggression, antipsychotics may be useful. Atypical agents can effectively reduce associated aggression and agitation (Carson & Kitagawa, 2004).

Overall, many medications have been used to treat the symptoms of PTSD, but few have systematic studies supporting their long-term efficacy (Kinrys et al., 2003). Pharmacotherapy may be more effective in treating concomitant depression, anxiety, and hyperarousal than in affecting avoidance, denial, or emotional numbing (Agid, Shalev, & Lerer, 2001). Further research is needed to hone treatment regimens and better tailor intervention to targeted symptoms. Table 8.3 outlines medication augmentation strategies for PTSD.

Exposure-Based Combination Interventions

Mainstay therapies include exposure-based and pharmacological interventions, particularly via atypical antidepressants (Yehuda, Golier, Halligan, et al., 2004; Yehuda, Golier, Yang, & Tischler, 2004). About 50% of cases of PTSD remit

TABLE 8.3.
Medication Augmentation Strategies

Symptom	SSRI or Atypical Antidepressants
Dissociation	Valproic acid or carbamazepine
Hyperarousal	Benzodiazepine or buspirone
Insomnia	Trazodone or atypical antipsychotic
Mood lability, explosiveness	Anticonvulsant or lithium
Psychotic features	Antipsychotics or atypical antipsychotics
Startle	Clonidine or propranolol

within 6 months (Asnis, Kohn, Henderson, & Brown, 2004). For the remainder, the disorder typically persists for years and can dominate the sufferer's life. A longitudinal study of Vietnam veterans, for example, found 15% of veterans to be suffering from PTSD 19 years after combat exposure (Berthier, Posada, & Puentes, 2001).

Although symptomatic relief can occur via medications, full recovery from PTSD requires the development of insight and perspective into the nature of the trauma, its origin, and its continuing impact on daily functioning (Janoff-Bulman, 1992). Therapy requires significant emotional counterexperiences (such as establishing trusting relationships with others, beginning with the therapist and generalizing thereafter and intellectual confrontation of basic philosophical issues in living (Fontana & Rosenheck, 2004). Key issues include (1) the nature of good and evil, (2) the inherent conflict between relatedness and autonomy, and (3) the problem of leading a meaningful and reasonably secure life in a capricious and uncaring world (Brewin, 2001; Joseph, 2004).

Psychodynamic Interventions

Inherently relationship-focused, psychodynamic therapy helps individuals recover from trauma, focusing on intrapsychic conflict about the trauma (Brett, 1993). Traditional dynamic treatments utilize clarification and interpretation of feelings and emotion to bring latent conflicts, recapitulated by the precipitating trauma, into conscious awareness and to integrate them in the personality structure. *Catharsis*, an emotional release, is a process in which feelings are experienced and openly expressed verbally, leading to relief of inner emotional tension. Within the therapeutic context, catharsis coupled with the therapist's empathic response leads to a sense of relief and validation (Purves & Erwin, 2004). Working through unconscious conflict tapped by the experience of trauma promotes recovery.

Kohut's (1977) model of trauma, and subsequent PTSD, focuses less on exposure to external catastrophes and more on the subsequent nature and quality of interpersonal interactions with others. Trauma is defined as *empathic failure by the selfobject*. When trauma is intense, severe, or occurs at a critical developmental stage, the experience of selfobject failure becomes so overwhelming and incapacitating to the self system that fragmentation and incohesion occurs. Subsequent sequelae depend upon when the self system suffered the significant empathy failure trauma, the individual's basic vulnerability and self system makeup, and the nature of intrapsychic defenses (Schore, 2003). The relationships among early ontogenic attachment disorganization, graded traumatic experience, and PTSD is well documented (Ballenger et al., 2004).

The empathic attunement and therapeutic ambience experienced within the relationship between patient and therapist mends broken schemata via the process and transmuting internalization of the empathic response from the selfobject. Combining object-relations and self psychology theories, the presence or absence of strong interpersonal support has a definitive link with PTSD (Kobasa & Puccetti, 1983). Regardless of the nature of catastrophic trauma, those with strong social supports are less likely to develop PTSD (Bleiberg & Markowitz, 2005). Evidence of the therapeutic role of social support in facilitating recovery is widespread and unequivocal (Bandelow, Zohar, Hollander, Kasper, & Moller, 2002).

Behavioral Therapies

Behavioral models focus on conditioning and learning models, implementing counterconditioning, and systematic desensitization interventions to alleviate symptoms. Social skills, cognitive restructuring, and novel learning are usually included in successful behavioral treatments. Key factors include psychoeducation, sustained exposure to trigger cues and memories until habituation occurs, coping-skills training, and resilience-bolstering. Cognitive-behavioral interventions include prolonged exposure, stress-inoculation training, cognitive restructuring, active disputation of irrational beliefs, and confrontation of attributional biases. Near unanimity of agreement on the utility of exposure-based treatment procedures has been reached in the treatment of PTSD (Bisson & Andrew, 2005). This includes imaginal exposure in which the contextual and emotional experiences of the trauma are worked through systematically. Vaughan and Tarrier's (1992) *image habituation training* treatment model for PTSD uses an imaginal exposure presented via tape-recorded descriptions of recurrent trauma-related images followed by silence, in which the patient is instructed to imagine the event as vividly as possible, while applying cognitive restructuring, relaxation, and so on. At its heart is counterconditioning and desensitization (Krakow et al., 2004). Devilly and Spence's (1999) cognitive-behavioral *trauma treatment protocol* model for PTSD utilizes prolonged imagery and in vivo exposure mixed with traditional cognitive therapy interventions.

Shapiro's (1989) *eye movement desensitization and reprocessing* **(EMDR)** is an alternative treatment for PTSD in which the patient is asked to concentrate on the traumatic event, the negative cognitions associated with it, and the associated emotions while focusing on the therapist's finger as it moves from side to side. After each set of movements, the patient reports any new feelings or forgotten memories. In theory, this technique induces lateral eye movements that accelerate the processing of affective-cognitive data. Many clinicians believe that the effectiveness of EMDR to reduce PTSD symptoms rests on its utilization of exposure and cognitive-restructuring therapies (Lamprecht et al., 2004; Levin, Lazrove, & van der Kolk, 1999). Further sound research is needed to clarify its "active ingredients" and "mechanisms of action."

Existential Paradigms

At the heart of third-force theories rests the basic assumption that given free will and personal responsibility to create and maintain one's own life and its progression toward meaningful existence, individuals will be continually faced with making sense of a sometimes capricious world. The environment, therefore, can present traumatic experiences that must be infused into a sense of self by providing a sense of meaning and purpose therein. Given these bases, humanistic models strike at the core of the shattered world views of PTSD probands, yet their theory provides little with regard to actual implementation of meaningful recovery.

Intervention from humanistic paradigms for PTSD focuses on the recreation of authenticity, courage, and persistence in living in an unpredictable world with experiences of unimaginable trauma (Herman, 1992). Horowitz (1999) conceptualized PTSD as annihilation or extreme invalidation of basic core beliefs concerning self and others. These basic schemata form the template through which reality is perceived, interpreted, and assimilated. Treatment must occur within a supportive therapeutic relationship that reaffirms basic tenets of life, validates the patient's world view, and creates meaning from otherwise senseless traumatic experience (Schiralde, 2000). Recovery occurs when the originally unassimilable traumatic experience is assimilated by working through the implications of the trauma via appropriate modification of the individual's conceptual system. Normally, the traumatic neurosis will heal by itself and the individual will emerge a sadder but more sophisticated person. If, however, the natural process of mastery is blocked in some way or is not properly paced, the condition can become chronic. Then, treatment is needed to provide appropriate intervention to bolster the courage to face existential responsibility, create ongoing meaning in life, and reaffirm basic assumptions about the nature of existence (Horowitz, 1997). Therapy will often require significant emotional counterexperiences (such as establishing trusting relationships with people) and intellectual confrontation of basic philosophical issues in living, such as the nature of good and evil, the inherent conflict between relatedness and autonomy, and the problem of leading a meaningful and reasonably secure life in the world (LeDoux & Gorman, 2001).

SUMMARY

PTSD is a complex reaction of mixed anxiety symptoms, often including generalized anxiety, obsessive and compulsive features, and panic. Current research on the causes and successful treatments has focused on neurodevelopmental variables, neurotransmitter systems, and brain functionality, integrating learning and philosophical factors. Effective treatments include atypical antidepressants, long-acting and potent benzodiazepines (e.g., clonazepam), atypical antipsychotics, and anticonvulsants. Dynamic, interpersonal, cognitive-behavioral, and humanistic psychotherapies can reduce symptoms and promote adaptation.

Commonly Used
Psychotropic Medications

Drug (generic available?)	Predominant Indications	Presumed Mechanism of Action (Pharmacodynamics)	Available Preparations	Half-life	Usual Daily Dose	Potential Side Effects
Acamprosate calcium *Campral®* (no)	Alcohol dependence	Unclear; may interact with glutamate and GABA	333 mg tablets	20–33 hr	666 mg TID	Somulence, rash, rhinitis, abnormal vision, decreased libido
Alprazolam *Xanax®*, *Xanax XR®*, (yes, except XR)	PD; anxiety with depression; social phobia	Benzodiazepines relieve anxiety by a three-stage model: (1) the chloride channel closes, (2) GABA binds to receptors and ion channel opens, (3) benzodiazepine molecules bind to receptors and enhance opening of chloride ion channel; binds to a molecule that is closely associated with the GABA postsynaptic receptor, thereby permitting the postsynaptic neuron to respond more intensely (and normally) to GABA, increasing inhibition of neuronal-message transmission; may have some effects on the noradrenergic system, causing postsynaptic down regulation of beta receptors and increasing the activity of N-protein, which couples post synaptic receptors to the interneuronal energy system in the CNS; mediates GABA actions	0.25, 0.5, 1.0, 2.0 mg tablets; 0.5, 1.0, 2.0, 3.0 XR; *Niravam®* orally disintegrating tablets 0.25, 0.5, 1.0, 2.0 mg	11–14 hr; longer for XR (rapid absorption)	0.5–4 mg; higher in the treatment of panic disorder (up to 10 mg)	Somulence, weight gain, impaired attention and concentration, potential abuse and dependence
Amantadine *Symmetrel®* (yes)	Parkinson's disease; antiviral	Presumably increases dopamine in the brain; dopamine agonist	100 mg capsules	30–50 hr	100–300 mg	Insomnia, nervousness, agitation

Drug	Indication	Mechanism	Available forms	Half-life	Dose	Side effects
Amitriptyline *Elavil*® (yes)	Depression; chronic pain; insomnia; myalgia; ADHD	Inhibits the reuptake mechanism for norepinephrine and the indoleamine 5-HT (serotonin)	10, 25, 50, 75, 100, 150 mg tablets	10–22 hr	50–300 mg	Hypersomulence, weight gain, dry mouth, constipation
Amoxapine *Ascendin*® (yes)	Depression	Inhibits the reuptake mechanism for norepinephrine and the indoleamine 5-HT (serotonin)	25, 50, 100, 150 mg tablets	8–30 hr	50–600 mg	Hypersomulence, weight gain, dry mouth, constipation
Aripiprazole *Abilify*® (no)	Schizophrenia; psychosis; angry outbursts; anxiety; bipolar disorder	Partial DA-2 and 5-HT1A receptor agonist and 5-HT2A receptor antagonist	5, 10, 15, 20, 30 mg tablets	75–94+ hr	15–30 mg	Cognitive impairment, weight gain, hyper-somulence, decreased libido, confusion, increased risk for diabetes
Atenolol *Tenormin*® (yes)	Hypertension (HTN); to treat side effects of Lithium	Alpha-adrenergic receptor agonist that may cause a decrease in neurotransmitter amount released from presynaptic nerve terminals	25, 50, 100 mg tablets and 5 mg/10 ml IM	16–27 hr	25–100 mg	Fatigue, decreased blood pressure, sexual dysfunction
Atomoxetine *Strattera*® (no)	Attention disorders; possibly depression	Selective norepinephrine reuptake inhibitor	10, 18, 25, 40, 60 mg capsules	5 hr	40–100 mg	Increased blood pressure, changes in sleep pattern, possible liver damage
Benztropine *Cogentin*® (yes)	Antihistamine; anticholinergic; antipsychotic-induced extrapyramidal symptoms	Anticholinergic, antihistamine	0.5, 1, 2 mg tablets	3–6 hr	1–2 mg BID	Memory impairment, dry mouth, blurred vision, constipation, nausea

(continues)

Drug (generic available?)	Predominant Indications	Presumed Mechanism of Action (Pharmacodynamics)	Available Preparations	Half-life	Usual Daily Dose	Potential Side Effects
Biperiden *Akineton®* (yes)	Anticholinergic; antipsychotic-induced extra-pyramidal symptoms	Anticholinergic, antihistamine	2 mg tablets	4–6 hr	2–8 mg	Memory impairment, dry mouth, blurred vision, constipation, nausea
Bromocriptine *Parlodel®* (yes)	Hyperprolactinemia-associated dysfunctions; acromegaly; Parkinson's disease	Dopamine receptor agonist	2.5, 5 mg tablets	80–100+ hr	2.5–5 mg	Fatigue, somnolence, sexual dysfunction
Bupropion *Wellbutrin®* (yes), *Wellbutrin SR* (yes), *Wellbutrin XL* (no), *Zyban®* (no)	Depression; attention disorders; smoking cessation; chronic pain; fatigue	Dopamine agonist; possible NE inhibitor	Tablets: 75, 100, 150 mg; SR 100, 150 mg, XL 150, 300 mg	11–14 hr	200–450 mg	Headache, agitation, constipation, insomnia, anxiety
Buspirone *BuSpar®* (no)	Anxiety; GAD	SE-1A agonist; chemically similar to sertraline	5, 7.5, 10, 15 mg tablets	2–3 hr (slow absorption)	15–60 mg	Nausea, decreased libido, increased appetite, headache, vision disturbance
Butabarbital *Butisol®* (yes)	Seizure disorder; insomnia; hypnotic	Enhances the effect of GABA on corresponding receptors; may also inhibit the release of calcium ions into presynaptic vesicles, potentially reducing neurotransmitter release or effect	15, 30, 50, 100 mg tablets & 30 mg/5 ml Elixir	34–42 hr	15–120 mg	Somnolence, weight gain, impaired attention and concentration, potential abuse and dependence

Drug	Indication	Action	Forms	Half-life	Dose	Side effects
Carbamazepine *Tegretol*® (yes) *Carbatrol*® (no) *Equetro*® (no)	Seizure disorder; bipolar I; schizoaffective disorder; mood disorders; impulse-control disorders	Uncertain as to the exact therapeutic effect; may stabilize mood by decreasing kindling effect in the limbic area of the brain; thus, a system that was initially barely responsive to a low-dose stimulus can ultimately spontaneously discharge; carbamazepine works by preventing the easily provoked electrical and biological changes seen when a particular stress is experienced	100, 200 mg tablets & 100 mg/5 ml elixir	15–35 hr initially; varies thereafter	400–1600 mg	Rashes, ataxia, incoordination, dizziness, weakness, blood dyscrasias, liver dysfunction, kidney and liver toxicity
Chloral hydrate *Noctec*® (yes)	Insomnia	CNS depressant	Capsules: 250, 500 mg; concentrate: 500 mg/ml	8–12 hr	500–1500 mg	Hypersomulence, daytime fatigue
Chlordiazepoxide *Librium*® (yes)	Anxiety; alcohol withdrawal	Mediates GABA action	5, 10, 25 mg tablets; 5, 10, 25 mg capsules; 100 mg/2 ml (Amp) parenteral form	15–60 hr (rapid absorption)	15–100 mg	Somulence, weight gain, impaired attention and concentration, potential abuse and dependence
Chlorpromazine *thorazine*® (yes)	Psychosis; agitation	Inhibits dopaminergic neurotransmission	10, 25, 50, 100, 200 mg tablets	4–5 hr	300–800 mg	Anticholinergic effects, dry mouth, dystonia, tardive dyskinesia
Citalopram *Celexa*® (no)	Depression; OCD; GAD; panic; social anxiety	Selective serotonin reuptake inhibitor (SSRI)	10, 20, 40 mg tablets	35 hr	10–60 mg	Nausea, impaired vision, decreased libido, somulence, headache, restlessness

(continues)

Drug (generic available?)	Predominant Indications	Presumed Mechanism of Action (Pharmacodynamics)	Available Preparations	Half-life	Usual Daily Dose	Potential Side Effects
Clomipramine *Anafranil®* (yes)	OCD; depression	Inhibits the reuptake mechanism for norepinephrine and the indoleamine 5-HT (serotonin)	25, 50, 75 mg tablets	18–38 hr	150–250 mg	Hypersomulence, weight gain, dry mouth, constipation
Clonazepam *Klonopin®* (yes), Klonopin Wafers® (no)	GAD; PTSD; OCD; seizure disorder; hypnotic; benzo-diazepine with-drawal; angry outbursts	Mediates GABA action; has some 5-HT potentiating properties	0.5, 1.0, 2.0 mg tablets; 0.125, 0.25., 0.5, 1, 2 mg wafers	30–40 hr (very rapid absorption)	0.125–4 mg	Somulence, weight gain, impaired attention and concentration, potential abuse and dependence
Clonidine *Catapres®* (yes), *Catapres®* Transdermal Patch (no)	Hypertension (HTN); opioid withdrawal; impulse-control disorders; ADHD	Binds to beta-adrenergic receptors and blocks reception of NE	0.1, 0.2, 0.3 mg tablets; patch: 0.1, 0.2, 0.3 QD	12–16 hr	0.1–0.2 mg BID to TID (tablets)	Fatigue, amotivational syndrome, hypersomulence
Clorazepate *Tranxene®* (yes)	Hypnotic; anxiety; GAD	Mediates GABA action; binds to a molecule that is closely associated with the GABA postsynaptic receptor, thereby permitting the postsynaptic neuron to respond more intensely (and normally) to GABA, increasing inhibition of neuronal-message transmission	3.75, 7.5, 15 mg tablets; 3.75, 7.5 mg capsules; 11.25, 22.5 mg sustained-release	50–100 hr (very rapid absorption)	15–60 mg	Somulence, weight gain, impaired attention and concentration, potential abuse and dependence
Clozapine *Clozaril®* (yes)	Schizophrenia (particularly treatment-resistant psychosis)	Affects at least nine neurotransmitter receptors but does not block the dopamine receptor, DA-2, to the degree of the older antipsychotics; also has serotonin-blocking properties	25, 100 mg tablets	11 hr	200–900 mg	Agranulocytosis

Drug	Uses	Mechanism	Forms	Duration	Dose	Side effects
Cyproheptadine *Periactin®* (yes)	Nausea	SE and histamine antagonist; some anticholinergic effects	4 mg tablets	Unclear	4–20 mg	Fatigue, somulence, sexual dysfunction
Desipramine *Norpramin®* (yes)	Depression; attention disorders; possibly cocaine withdrawal	Inhibits the reuptake mechanism for norepinephrine and the indoleamine 5-HT (serotonin)	10, 25, 50, 75, 100, 150 mg tablets	12–24 hr	75–300 mg	Hypersomulence, weight gain, dry mouth, constipation
Desmopressin acetate *DDAVP®* (no)	Enuresis	Synthetic form of vasopressin, an antidiuretic hormone that reduces urine production	0.1, 0.2 mg tablets; nasal spray	Unclear	0.1–0.6 mg	Headache, nausea, flushing, cramping
Dexmethylphenidate HCl *Focalin®*, *Focalin XR®* (no)	Attention disorders; narcolepsy	Blocks reuptake of NE and DA (CNS stimulant)	2.5, 5, 10 mg tablets; 5, 10, 20 mg XR capsules	2–4.5 hrs; longer for XR	5–20 mg	Agitation, headache, loss of appetite, insomnia, mood lability, potential for abuse
Dextroamphetamine *Dexedrine®*, *Dexedrine Spansules®*, *DextroStat* (yes)	Attention disorders; narcolepsy; obesity	Precipitates the release of NE; at high doses, causes SE and DA release; inhibits CNS MAO activity	5, 10, mg tablets; 15 mg spansule	8–12 hr	5–30 mg	Agitation, headache, loss of appetite, insomnia, mood lability, potential for abuse
Dextroamphetamine aspartate + dextroamphetamine sulphate + amphetamine sulphate + amphetamine saccarate *Adderall®*, *Adderall XR®* (yes, except XR)	Attention deficit disorder; narcolepsy; impulse-control disorders; oppositional defiant disorder	Noncatecholamine sympathomimetic amine with CNS stimulant activity	5, 7.5, 10, 12.5, 15, 20, 30 mg tablets; 5, 10, 15, 20, 25, 30 mg XR capsules	6–8 hr; longer for XR	5–30 mg	Agitation, headache, loss of appetite, insomnia, mood lability, potential for abuse

(continues)

Drug (generic available?)	Predominant Indications	Presumed Mechanism of Action (Pharmacodynamics)	Available Preparations	Half-life	Usual Daily Dose	Potential Side Effects
Diazepam *Valium*® (yes)	Anxiety; muscle relaxant; headaches (particularly tension-based H/A); separation anxiety; PTSD; insomnia	Mediates GABA action; muscle relaxant	2, 5, 10 mg tablets; 15 mg sustained-release tablets; 10 mg/2 ml (Amp or Syr), 50 mg/10 ml (vial) parenteral form	30–60 hr (very rapid absorption)	4–40 mg	Somulence, weight gain, impaired attention and concentration, potential abuse and dependence
Diltiazem *Cardizem*® (yes)	HTN; angry outbursts	Relaxes smooth muscles with resultant decrease in peripheral vascular resistance	30, 60, 90, 120, 180, 240, 300, 360, 420 mg; SR now available	20 hr	30–240 mg	Fatigue, decreased blood pressure, somulence, sexual dysfunction
Diphenhydramine *Benadryl*® (yes)	Antihistamine; hypnotic; antipsychotic-induced extrapyramidal symptoms	Blocks histamine-1 receptor	12.5, 25, 50 mg tablets	1–4 hr	25–100 mg	Somulence, weight gain, impaired attention and concentration
Disulfiram *Antabuse*® (yes)	Alcohol dependence	Precipitates elevated levels of acetaldehyde when combined with ethanol; blocks oxidation of alcohol at acetaldehyde stage; inhibits metabolism of alcohol at acetaldehyde level	250, 500 mg tablets	60–120 hr	250–500 mg	Drowsiness, fatigue, body odor, headache, tremor, dizziness

Drug	Indication	Mechanism	Dosage forms	Half-life	Dose range	Side effects
d-methamphetamine hydrochloride *Desoxyn®* (yes)	Attention disorders; narcolepsy; possibly to improve cognitive function in AIDS	Sympathomimetic amine, CNS stimulant	Tablet: 5 mg; SR tablet: 5, 10, 15 mg	4–5 hr	5–20 mg	Agitation, headache, loss of appetite. insomnia, mood lability, potential for abuse
Donepezil hydrochloride *Aricept®* (no)	Dementia	Cholinesterase inhibitor, increasing acetylcholine in the cortex	5, 10 mg tablets	70–80 hrs	5–10 mg	Flulike symptoms, nausea, diarrhea, dyspepsia, myalgia
Doxepin *Adapin®*, *Sinequan®* (yes)	Depression; skin disorders	Inhibits the reuptake mechanism for norepinephrine and the indoleamine 5-HT (serotonin)	10, 25, 50, 75, 100, 150 mg capsules	11–23 hr	75–300 mg	Weight gain, increase in appetite, orthostatic hypotension, dry mouth, fatigue, loss of libido
Duloxetine *Cymbalta®* (no)	Depression; chronic fatigue; urinary incontinence; chronic pain; diabetic neuropathy	SE and NE reuptake inhibitor	20, 30, 60 mg capsules	12 hr	30–60 mg	Nausea, urinary hesitancy, impaired vision, decreased libido, somnolence, headache, restlessness, retarded ejaculation
Estazolam *ProSom®* (yes)	Insomnia	Mediates GABA action	1, 2 mg capsules	10–24 hr	0.5–2.0 mg	Somnolence, weight gain, impaired attention and concentration, potential abuse and dependence
Eszopiclone *Lunesta®* (no)	Insomnia	Unclear; interacts with GABA-receptor complexes coupled to benzodiazepine receptors	1, 2, 3, mg tablets	6 hr (rapid absorption)	1–3 mg	Somnolence, weight gain, impaired attention and concentration, potential abuse and dependence

(continues)

Drug (generic available?)	Predominant Indications	Presumed Mechanism of Action (Pharmacodynamics)	Available Preparations	Half-life	Usual Daily Dose	Potential Side Effects
Ethchlorvynol *Placidyl®* (yes)	Insomnia	Unclear; may suppress reticular formation of the midbrain	100, 200, 500, 750 mg capsules	5 hr	500–750 mg	Somulence, weight gain, impaired attention and concentration, potential abuse and dependence
Ethinamate *Valmid®* (yes)	Insomnia	Unclear	500 mg capsules	10–20 hr	500–1000 mg	Somulence, weight gain, impaired attention and concentration, potential abuse and dependence
Fluoxetine *Prozac®*, *Sarafem®* (yes)	Mood disorders; postpartum depression; anxiety; PMS; premature ejaculation	Selective serotonin reuptake inhibitor (SSRI)	Puvules: 10, 20, 40 mg; syrup 20 mg/5 ml	24–72 hr	10–80 mg	Nausea, impaired vision, decreased libido, somulence, headache, restlessness
Fluphenazine *Prolixin®* (yes)	Psychosis; severe agitation	Blockade of DA-2 receptors	1, 2.5, 5, 10 mg tablets; decanoate	10–20 hr	1–40 mg	Anticholinergic effects, dry mouth, dystonia, tardive dyskinesia
Flurazepam *Dalmane®* (yes)	Hypnotic	Benzodiazepine; binds to GABA receptors and changes their shape; mediates GABA action	15, 30 mg capsules	50+ hr (intermediate absorption)	15–30 mg	Somulence, weight gain, impaired attention and concentration, potential abuse and dependence

Fluvoxamine Luvox® (yes)	OCD; depression; anxiety; insomnia	Selective serotonin reuptake inhibitor (SSRI)	25, 50, 100 mg tablets	15–16 hr	50–300 mg	Nausea, impaired vision, decreased libido, somulence, headache, restlessness
Gabapentin Neurontin® (no)	Seizures; bipolar disorder	Exact mechanism of action unclear, but may act by enhancing GABA turnover	100, 300, 400 mg capsules; 600, 800 mg tablets; 250 mg/5 ml oral solution	5–7 hr	300–3600 mg	Postherpetic neuralgia, dizziness, somulence, peripheral edema
Galantamine hydrobromide Reminyl® (no)	Alzheimer's disease	Reversible inhibitor of acetylcholinesterase	4, 8, 12 mg tablets	7 hr	16–24 mg BID	Flulike symptoms, nausea, diarrhea, dyspepsia, myalgia
Glutethimide Doriden® (yes)	Insomnia	Unclear	250, 500 mg tablets	4 hr	250–500 mg	Somulence, weight gain, impaired attention and concentration, potential abuse and dependence
Guanfacine Tenex® (yes)	Hypertension; agitation; ADHD; mood lability	Alpha-2 adrenoreceptor agonist	1, 2 mg tablets	17 hr	1–3 mg QHS	Dry mouth, somnolence, vertigo, constipation
Halazepam Paxipam® (yes)	Anxiety; agitation	Mediates GABA action	20, 40 mg tablets	50–100 hr	60–160 mg	Somulence, weight gain, impaired attention and concentration, potential abuse and dependence

(continues)

Drug (generic available?)	Predominant Indications	Presumed Mechanism of Action (Pharmacodynamics)	Available Preparations	Half-life	Usual Daily Dose	Potential Side Effects
Haloperidol *Haldol®* (yes)	Psychosis; insomnia	Inhibits dopaminergic neurotransmission	0.5, 1, 2, 5, 10, 20, mg tablets; 2 mg/ml oral concentrate; decanoate	10–20 hr	1–100 mg	Anticholinergic effects, dry mouth, dystonia, tardive dyskinesia
Hydroxyzine *Atarax®, Vistaril®* (yes)	Allergic rhinitis; itching; anxiety	Histamine receptor antagonist	10, 25, 50, 100 mg tablets	2–4 hr	10–300 mg	Dry mouth, hypersomnulence, impaired attention and concentration
Imipramine *Tofranil®, Tofranil PM®* (yes)	Depression; enuresis; panic disorder	Inhibits the reuptake mechanism for norepinephrine and the indoleamine 5-HT (serotonin)	10, 25, 50, 75, 100, 125, 150 mg tablets; sustained-release capsules	5–25 hr	75–300 mg	Hypersomnulence, weight gain, dry mouth, constipation
Isocarboxazid *Marplan®* (yes)	Depression; anxiety	When MAO interacts chemically with molecules of norepinephrine, it removes the nitrogen, or amine, component from it by oxidation and destroys its effectiveness as a neurotransmitter—MAO inhibitors block this destructive activity of the enzyme MAO and thus stop the destruction of norepinephrine	10 mg tablet	1–3 hr	10–50 mg	Hypotension, weight gain, ankle edema, sexual dysfunction, transient hypertension, urinary hesitation

Drug	Uses	Mechanism	Forms	Half-life	Dosage	Side effects
Lamotrigine *Lamictal*® (yes)	Bipolar disorder; mood lability; depression; seizures	Uncertain; may effect sodium channels that affect glutamate and aspartate; may have inhibitory effect on SE receptors	25, 100, 150, 200 mg tablets	25 hr	50–250 mg	Rash, depression
Levetiracetam *Keppra*® (no)	Seizure disorder; possibly bipolar or intermittent explosive disorder	Unclear	250, 500, 750 mg tablets; 100 mg/ml oral suspension	7 hr	500–3000 mg	Rashes, ataxia, incoordination, dizziness, weakness, blood dyscrasias, liver dysfunction, kidney and liver toxicity
Lithium carbonate *Eskalith*®, *Lithobid*® (yes)	Bipolar disorder; depression; schizoaffective disorder	Thought to alter synaptic activity in neurons that use norepinephrine and serotonin, but not in the same way as antidepressant drugs; may effectively treat bipolar functioning by directly altering sodium ion activity in neurons; affects the balance of both norepinephrine and serotonin transmitters binding to postsynaptic receptors, perhaps by stabilizing the receptor membrane—in turn, correcting both super- and subsensitivity; may stabilize catecholamine receptors	150, 300 mg tablets; SR 300, 450, 600 mg tablets	8–35; hr longer for SR	900–1600 mg	Weight gain, diaphoresis, hair loss, thirst, lethargy, widening of QRS complex, arrhythmias, edema, thyroid abnormalities
Lorazepam *Ativan*® (yes)	Anxiety; agitation; alcohol withdrawal	Mediates GABA action	0.5, 1, 2 mg tablets	10–20 hr (intermediate absorption)	2–6 mg	Somnulence, weight gain, impaired attention and concentration, potential abuse and dependence

(continues)

Drug (generic available?)	Predominant Indications	Presumed Mechanism of Action (Pharmacodynamics)	Available Preparations	Half-life	Usual Daily Dose	Potential Side Effects
Loxapine *Loxitane*® (yes)	Psychosis; schizoaffective disorder	Inhibits dopaminergic neurotransmission	5, 10, 25, 50 mg tablets	5–15 hr	20–250 mg	Hypersomulence, weight gain, dry mouth, constipation
Maprotiline *Ludiomil*® (yes)	Depression	Inhibits the reuptake mechanism for norepinephrine and the indoleamine 5-HT (serotonin)	25, 50, 75 mg tablets	21–25 hr	75–225 mg	Hypersomulence, weight gain, dry mouth, constipation
Memantine *Namenda*® (no)	Alzheimer's disease	NMDA receptor antagonist	5, 10 mg tablets; oral suspension	60–80 hr	20 mg	Flulike symptoms, nausea, diarrhea, dyspepsia, myalgia
Meprobamate *Miltown*® (yes)	Psychosis; agitation; anxiety	Uncertain, but perhaps works as muscle relaxant with ancillary reduction in tension anxiety; exerts CNS depressant effects	200, 400 mg capsules	6–17 hr	400–1600 mg	Anticholinergic effects, dry mouth, dystonia, tardive dyskinesia
Mesoridazine *Serenti*® (yes)	Schizophrenia; psychosis	Unclear	10, 25, 50, 100 mg tablets	24–48 hr	30–400 mg	Anticholinergic effects, dry mouth, dystonia, tardive dyskinesia
Methamphetamine *Desoxyn*® (yes)	ADD; ADHD; impulse-control disorders	CNS stimulant, sympathomimetic amine	Tablet: 5 mg; SR tablet: 5, 10, 15 mg	4–5 hr	5–20 mg	Agitation, headache, loss of appetite, insomnia, mood lability, potential for abuse
Methylphenidate *Ritalin*®, *Ritalin LA*®, *Ritalin LA*®, *Concerta*® *Metadate ER*®, *Metadate CD*® (yes, but not newer formulations)	ADD, narcolepsy; depression (especially in the elderly)	Mild CNS stimulant; may activate brain stem and cortex	Tablet: 5, 10, 20 mg; SR: 20 mg; LA: 10, 20, 30, 40 mg; Concerta: 18, 27, 36, 54 mg OROS	2 hr; longer for sustained-release	20–30 mg	Agitation, headache, loss of appetite, insomnia, mood lability, potential for abuse

Methyprylon Noludar® (yes)	Insomnia	Unclear	Tablet: 50, 200 mg; capsule: 300 mg	10–20 hr	200–400 mg	Somulence, weight gain, impaired attention and concentration, potential abuse and dependence
Midazolam Versed® (yes)	Insomnia	Unclear; probable benzodiazepine receptor agonist	20 mg/10 ml, 40 mg/10 ml (vial), 2 mg/ml, 4 mg/ml (Syr), 1 mg/ml, 5 mg/ml (vial)	1–12 hr	Varies; IV only	Somulence, weight gain, impaired attention and concentration, potential abuse and dependence
Mirtazapine Remeron® (yes), Remeron Soltabs® (no)	Depression; agitated mood disorders; insomnia	Blocks presynaptic alpha-2 auto and hetero adrenoceptors, increasing norepinephrine and serotonergic transmission; blocks 5-HT2 and 5-HT3 receptors (minimizing serotonergic side effects)	15, 30, 45 mg tablets	20–40 hr	15–45 mg	Hypersomnolence, weight gain, dry mouth, constipation
Modafinil Provigil® (no)	Narcolepsy; hypopnea syndrome; obstructive sleep apnea; possibly ADHD	Mild stimulant that increases neuronal activity throughout the brain	100, 200 mg tablets; patch soon to be available	40 hr	200–400 mg	Headache, hyperkinesis, potential for abuse
Molindone Moban® (yes)	Schizophrenia; psychosis	Inhibits dopaminergic neurotransmission	5, 10, 25, 50, 100 mg tablets; 20 mg/ml oral suspension	10–20 hr	50–225 mg	Anticholinergic effects, dry mouth, dystonia, tardive dyskinesia
Nadolol Corgard® (yes)	HTN; angry outbursts	Nonselective blocks beta-adrenergic receptors	20, 40, 80, 120, 160 mg tablets	14–24 hr	40–80 mg	Fatigue, decreased blood pressure, somulence, sexual dysfunction

(continues)

Drug (generic available?)	Predominant Indications	Presumed Mechanism of Action (Pharmacodynamics)	Available Preparations	Half-life	Usual Daily Dose	Potential Side Effects
Naltrexone ReVia® (no), Vivitrol® (no)	Substance dependence	Long-acting antagonist of opiate receptors	50 mg capsule; 4 ml vials	96 hr	25–50 mg	Abdominal pain, anxiety, headache, nausea
Nefazodone Serzone® (yes)	Depression	Blocks serotonin reuptake, plus blocks serotonin receptor	100, 150, 200, 250 mg tablets	2.6–7.4 hr	200–600 mg	Nausea, impaired vision, liver damage, somnolence, headache, restlessness
Nortriptyline Pamelor® (yes)	Depression; chronic pain; insomnia	Inhibits the reuptake mechanism for norepinephrine and the indoleamine 5-HT (serotonin)	10, 25, 50, 75 mg capsules; 10 mg/5 ml oral suspension	18–44 hr	75–150 mg	Hypersomnulence, weight gain, dry mouth, constipation
Olanzapine Zyprexa® (no)	Schizophrenia; psychosis	Blocks a variety of different receptors, especially specific serotonin receptors	2.5, 5, 7.5, 10, 15, 20 mg tablets	21–50 hr	2.5–20 mg	Weight gain, decreased libido
Oxazepam Serax® (yes)	Anxiety; alcohol withdrawal	Mediates GABA action	15 mg tablets; 10, 15, 30 mg capsules	5–10 hr (slow absorption)	30–120 mg	Somnulence, weight gain, impaired attention and concentration, potential abuse and dependence
Oxcarbazepine Trileptal® (no)	Seizure disorders; possibly bipolar disorder	May reduce kindling within the brain; may block sodium channels	150, 300, 600 mg tablets; oral suspension	2–9 hr	600–2400 mg	Rashes, ataxia, incoordination, dizziness, weakness, blood dyscrasias, liver dysfunction, kidney and liver toxicity

(continues)

Drug	Used for	Action	Forms	Half-life	Dosage	Side effects
Paroxetine Paxil® (yes), Paxil CR® (no)	Depression; anxiety; social anxiety; panic disorder	Selective serotonin reuptake inhibitor (SSRI)	10, 20, 30, 40 mg tablets; CR: 12.5, 25, 37.5 mg capsules	21–26 hr	10–60 mg	Nausea, impaired vision, decreased libido, somulence, headache, restlessness, fatigue
Pemoline Cylert® (yes)	ADHD	Mild CNS stimulant	18.75, 37.5, 75 mg tablets	12 hr	56.25–75 mg	Agitation, headache, loss of appetite, insomnia, mood lability, liver damage
Pentobarbital Nembutal® (yes)	Anxiety; seizure disorder	CNS alteration	50, 100 mg capsules	15–48 hr	60–80 mg	Somulence, weight gain, impaired attention and concentration, potential abuse and dependence
Perphenazine Trilafon® (yes)	Schizophrenia; psychosis; possibly eating disorders	Inhibits dopaminergic neurotransmission	2, 4, 8, 16 mg tablets	10–20 hr	12–64 mg	Anticholinergic effects, dry mouth, dystonia, tardive dyskinesia
Phenelzine Nardil® (yes)	Depression; anxiety	When MAO interacts chemically with molecules of norepinephrine, it removes the nitrogen, or amine, component from it by oxidation and destroys its effectiveness as a neurotransmitter—MAO inhibitors block this destructive activity of the enzyme MAO and thus stop the destruction of norepinephrine	15 mg tablets	1.5 hr	15–90 mg	Anticholinergic effects, hypotension, weight gain, ankle edema, sexual dysfunction

Drug (generic available?)	Predominant Indications	Presumed Mechanism of Action (Pharmacodynamics)	Available Preparations	Half-life	Usual Daily Dose	Potential Side Effects
Phenobarbital *Luminal*® (yes)	Anxiety; seizure disorder; agitation	Barbiturate with CNS alteration	15, 16, 30, 32, 60, 65, 100 mg tablets	80–120 hr	30–600 mg	Somnulence, weight gain, impaired attention and concentration, potential abuse and dependence
Pimozide *Orap*® (yes)	Schizophrenia; psychosis; tics	Inhibits dopaminergic neurotransmission	1, 2 mg tablets	55 hr	2–10 mg	Anticholinergic effects, dry mouth, dystonia, tardive dyskinesia
Prazepam *Centrax*® (yes)	Anxiety	Mediates GABA action	5, 10 mg capsules (now discontinued in U.S.)	60–70 hr	20–60 mg	Somnulence, weight gain, impaired attention and concentration, potential abuse and dependence
Propranolol *Inderal*® (yes)	HTN; social phobia	Blocks beta-adrenergic receptors	10, 20, 40, 60, 80, 90 mg tablets	3–6 hr	10–240 mg	Decreased blood pressure, sexual dysfunction, somnulence, fatigue
Protriptyline *Vivactil*® (yes)	Depression	Blocks NE and SE reuptake	5, 10 mg tablets	50–200 hr	10–60 mg	Hypersomulence, weight gain, dry mouth, constipation
Quazepam *Doral*® (yes)	Insomnia	Mediates GABA action	7.5, 15, 30 mg capsules	40+ hr (intermediate absorption)	7.5–15 mg	Somnulence, weight gain, impaired attention and concentration, potential abuse and dependence

Drug	Uses	Mechanism of action	Forms	Half-life	Dose	Side effects
Quetiapine Seroquel® (no)	Schizophrenia; psychosis; bipolar disorder	Exhibits affinity for both serotonin and dopamine receptors; targets neurons in the prefrontal cortex, striatum, limbic system, and anterior pituitary	25, 100, 200, 300 mg tablets	6 hr	50–750 mg	Hypertension, somnolence, sedation, fatigue, increased risk for diabetes
Ramelteon Rozerem® (no)	Insomnia	Melatonin receptor agonist	8 mg tablets	1–2.6 hrs	8 mg, po QHS	Somnulence, weight gain, impaired attention and concentration, "hangover effect"
Risperidone Risperdal®, Risperdal Consta® (no)	Schizophrenia; psychosis; angry outbursts; oppositional defiant disorder	Primarily blocks the DA-2 receptor	0.25, 0.5, 1, 2, 3, 4 mg tablets; decanoate available	3–20 hr	2–16 mg	Hypersomnolence, weight gain, dry mouth, constipation, dystonia, cognitive confusion, increased risk for diabetes
Rivastigmine tartrate Exelon® (no)	Alzheimer's disease	Enhances cholinergic functioning	1.5, 3, 4.5, 6 mg capsules	1.5 hr	3–6 mg BID	Flulike symptoms, nausea, diarrhea, dyspepsia, myalgia
Ropinirole hydrochloride Requip® (no)	Restless legs syndrome	Dopaminergic agonist	0.25, 0.5, 1, 2, 3, 4, 5 mg tablets	6 hr	1–2 mg	Sudden sleep episodes, syncope, hypotension, orthostatic hypotension
Selegiline Eldepryl® Emsam Transdermal Patch® (no)	Depression	Irreversible inhibitor of MAO, particularly MAO-B	5 mg tablets; 6, 9, 12 mg transdermal patch	18–25 hr	6–12 mg QD	Potentially lethal when dietary restrictions are violated
Sertraline Zoloft® (no)	Depression; anxiety, PMS	Selective serotonin reuptake inhibitor (SSRI)	25, 50, 100 mg tablets	15–26 hr	50–200 mg	Nausea, impaired vision, decreased libido, somnolence, headache, restlessness

(continues)

Drug (generic available?)	Predominant Indications	Presumed Mechanism of Action (Pharmacodynamics)	Available Preparations	Half-life	Usual Daily Dose	Potential Side Effects
Tacrine *Cognex®* (no)	Dementia	Cholinesterase inhibitor	10, 20, 30, 40 mg capsules	2–4 hr	10–20 mg	Flulike symptoms, nausea, diarrhea, dyspepsia, myalgia
Temazepam *Restoril®* (yes)	Insomnia	Mediates GABA action	7.5, 15, 30 mg capsules	8–18 hr (slow absorption)	15–30 mg	Somnlence, weight gain, impaired attention and concentration, potential abuse and dependence
Thioridazine *Mellaril®* (yes)	Agitation; anxiety; psychosis; schizophrenia; mania	Inhibits dopaminergic neurotransmission	10, 15, 25, 50, 100, 150, 200 mg tablets	9–30 hr	20–800 mg	Anticholinergic effects, dry mouth, dystonia, tardive dyskinesia
Thiothixene *Navane®* (yes)	Agitation; psychosis; schizophrenia; mania; anxiety	Inhibits dopaminergic neurotransmission	1, 2, 5, 10, 20 mg tablets	34 hr	6–60 mg	Anticholinergic effects, dry mouth, dystonia, tardive dyskinesia
Tiagabine hydrochloride *Gabitril®* (no)	Anticonvulsant; bipolar disorder; anxiety	Unclear, but possibly through enhancing GABA effect	2, 4, 12, 16, 20 mg tablets	7–9 hr	4–32 mg	Hypersomnulence, weight gain, decreased libido
Topiramate *Topamax®* (no)	Anticonvulsant; mood stabilizer	Unknown; may inhibit electrical stimulation	15, 25, 100, 200 mg tablets	21 hr	25–200 mg	Weight loss, impaired memory and other cognitive impairments

Drug	Use	Mechanism	Form	Half-life	Dose	Side effects
Tranylcypromine Parnate® (yes)	Depression; anxiety; panic disorder	When MAO interacts chemically with molecules of norepinephrine, it removes the nitrogen, or amine, component from it by oxidation and destroys its effectiveness as a neurotransmitter—MAO inhibitors block this destructive activity of the enzyme MAO and thus stop the destruction of norepinephrine	10 mg tablet	2.5 hr	30–50 mg	Anticholinergic effects, hypotension, weight gain, ankle edema, sexual dysfunction
Trazodone Desyrel® (yes)	Depression; hypnotic; anxiety	Inhibits the reuptake mechanism for norepinephrine and the indoleamine 5-HT (serotonin)	50, 100, 150, 300 mg tablets	10–12 hr	150–600 mg	Hypersomulence, priapism, dry mouth, fatigue
Triazolam Halcion® (yes)	Anxiety; hypnotic	Mediates GABA action	0.125, .25 mg tablets	2–3 hr (rapid absorption)	0.125–0.50 mg	Somulence, weight gain, impaired attention and concentration, potential abuse and dependence
Trifluoperazine Stelazine® (yes)	Psychosis; schizophrenia	Inhibits dopaminergic neurotransmission	1, 2, 5, 10 mg tablets	10–20 hr	2–40 mg	Anticholinergic effects, dry mouth, dystonia, tardive dyskinesia
Trihexyphenidyl Artane® (yes)	Parkinson's disease; EPS	ACh and antihistamine effects	2, 5 mg tablets	4–6 hr	4–15 mg	Insomnia, nervousness, agitation
Trimipramine Surmontil® (yes)	Depression	Inhibits the reuptake mechanism for norepinephrine and the indoleamine 5-HT (serotonin)	25, 50, 100 mg capsules	7–40 hr	50–300 mg	Hypersomulence, weight gain, dry mouth, constipation

(continues)

Drug (generic available?)	Predominant Indications	Presumed Mechanism of Action (Pharmacodynamics)	Available Preparations	Halflife	Usual Daily Dose	Potential Side Effects
Valproate, valproic acid *Depakene*®, *Depakote*®, *Depakote ER*® (no)	Bipolar disorder; seizure disorder; impulse-control disorder; possibly mood and anxiety disorders	Potentiates the effects of GABA, decreasing both electrical activity (explaining its antiseizure effect) and biochemical activity (similar to the effect of lithium); may block voltage-dependent sodium channels	250, 500 mg capsules & 250 mg/5 ml; ER: 250, 500 mg tablets	5–20 hr; longer for ER	750–4000 mg	Weight gain, somulence, fatigue
Venlafaxine, Venlafaxine XR *Effexor*® (yes), *Effexor XR*® (no)	Depression; anxiety; insomnia; attention disorders	Blocks reuptake of both serotonin and norepinephrine	25, 37.5, 50, 75, 100 mg tablets; XR: 37.5, 75, 150 mg capsules	3–7 hr; longer for sustained-release	75–375 mg	Increased blood pressure, possible liver damage, severe withdrawal syndrome
Zaleplon *Sonata*® (no)	Insomnia	Targets benzodiazepine receptor sites	5, 10 mg capsules	1–2 hr	5–10 mg	Somulence, weight gain, impaired attention and concentration, potential abuse and dependence
Ziprasidone *Geodon*® (no)	Schizophrenia; possibly bipolar disorder; intermittent explosive disorder	Targets serotonergic and dopaminergic receptors; DA-2 and 5HT2 antagonist	20, 40, 60, 80 mg capsules	7 hr	20–80 mg BID with food	Cardiac dysfunction, weight gain, hypersomulence
Zolpidem *Ambien*®, *Ambien CR*® (no)	Insomnia	Targets benzodiazepine receptor sites	5, 10 mg tablets; CR: 6.25, 12.5 mg tablets	2–3 hr; longer for sustained-release forumation	5–10 mg IR; 6.25–12.5 CR	Somulence, weight gain, impaired attention and concentration, potential abuse and dependence

APPENDIX B

Professional Organizations and Resources

Agoraphobic Foundation of Canada, P.O. Box 132, Chomedey, Laval, Quebec, H7W 4K2, Canada.

Agoraphobics in Action, Inc., P.O. Box 1662, Antioch, Tennessee 37011-1662. (615) 831-2383.

Agoraphobics in Motion—AIM, 605 West 11th Mile Road, Royal Oaks, Michigan 48067. (313) 547-0400.

American Academy of Child and Adolescent Psychiatry, 3615 Wisconsin Avenue NW, Washington, D.C. 20016. (800) 333-7636. www.aacap.org

American Association of Pastoral Counselors, 9504-A Lee Highway, Fairfax, Virginia 22031. (703) 385-6967. www.aapc.org

American Psychiatric Association, 1400 K Street NW, Suite 1101, Washington, D.C. 20005. (800) 368-5777, (202) 682-6000. www.psych.org

American Psychological Association (APA), 750 First Street NE, Washington, D.C. 20002-4242. (800) 964-2000. www.apa.org

Anxiety Disorders Association of America (ADAA), 11900 Parklawn Drive, Suite 100, Rockville, Maryland 20852. (310) 231-9350. www.adaa.org

Association for the Advancement of Behavior Therapy (AABT), 305 Seventh Avenue, Suite 16A, New York, New York 10001. (212) 279-7970.

CHAANGE, 128 Country Club Drive, Chula Vista, California 91911. (619) 425-3992.

Encourage Newsletter, 13610 North Scottsdale Road, Suite 10-126, Scottsdale, Arizona 85254.

Freedom from Fear, 308 Seaview Avenue, Staten Island, New York 10305. (888) 442-2022, (718) 351-1717. www.freedomfromfear.org

International Society for Traumatic Stress Studies (ISTSS), 60 Revere Drive, Suite 500, Northbrook, Illinois 60062. (847) 480-9028. www.istss.org

National Alliance for the Mentally Ill (NAMI), 2107 Wilson Boulevard, Suite 300, Arlington, Virginia 22201-3042. (703) 524-7600. www.nami.org

National Anxiety Foundation, 3135 Cluster Drive, Lexington, Kentucky 40517. www.lexington-on-line.com/naf.html

National Institute of Mental Health (NIMH), 6001 Executive Boulevard, Room 8184, MSC 9663, Bethesda, Maryland 20892-9663. (301) 443-4513. www.nimh.nih.gov/anxiety

National Mental Health Association (NMHA), 2001 N. Beauregard Street, 12th Floor, Alexandria, Virginia 22311. (703) 684-7722. Fax: (703) 684-5968. www.nmha.org/infoctr/factsheets/index.cfm

National Mental Health Consumer Self-Help Clearinghouse, 1211 Chestnut St., 11th Floor, Philadelphia, Pennsylvania 19107. (800) 688-4226. www.mentalhelp.net

National Panic and Anxiety Disorders Newsletter, 1718 Burgundy Place, Suite B, Santa Rosa, California 95403. (707) 527-5738.

National Phobics Society, The Anxiety Disorders Charity, Zion Community Resource Center, 339 Stretford Road, Hulme, Manchester M15 4ZY. (0870) 7700-456.

New Beginnings Foundation for Agoraphobia, P.O. Box 9327, Glendale, California 91227. (818) 549-9966.

Obsessive Compulsive Anonymous, P.O. Box 215, New Hyde Park, New York 11040. (516) 741-4901.

Obsessive-Compulsive Foundation, P.O. Box 70, Milford, Connecticut 06460. (203) 878-5669. www.ocfoundation.org

Obsessive Compulsive Information Center, 8000 Excelsior Drive, Suite 203, Madison, Wisconsin 53717. (608) 836-8070.

Phobics Anonymous, P.O. Box 1180, Palm Springs, California 92263. (619) 322-2673.

Post-Traumatic Stress Disorder Alliance, www.PTSDAlliance.org

Sidran Traumatic Stress Foundation, 200 E. Joppa Road, Suite 207, Baltimore, Maryland 21286. (410) 825-8888. www.sidran.org

Trauma Survivors Anonymous, 2022 Fifteenth Avenue, Columbus, Ohio 31901. (706) 649-6500.

APPENDIX C

Abbreviations Used in Treatment Settings

Abbreviation	Description
a.c.	Ante cibum (before meals)
Ach	Acetylcholine
ADHD	Attention deficit hyperactivity disorder
ADD	Attention deficit disorder
ADLs	Activities of daily living
ADR	Adverse drug reaction
AFP	Alpha-fetoprotein
AIMS	Abnormal Involuntary Movement Scale
ANS	Autonomic nervous system
APE	Acute psychiatric emergency
APA	American Psychological Association, American Psychiatric Association
a.q.	aqua (water)
AWS	Alcohol withdrawal syndrome
BDI	Beck Depression Inventory
BDZ	Benzodiazepine
BID	Bis in die (twice a day)
BPD	Borderline personality disorder
BPRS	Brief Psychiatric Rating Scale
bp	Blood pressure
CBC	Complete blood count
CBZ	Carbamazepine
CGI	Clinical global impression
CNS	Central nervous system

CO_2	Carbon dioxide
CPZ	Chlorpromazine
CSM	Committee on the Safety of Medicines
CVA	Cerebralvascular accident
D1	Dopamine-1 receptor
D2	Dopamine-2 receptor
DA; D	Dopamine
d/b	Double-blind study
D/K	Don't know
DSM	*Diagnostic and Statistical Manual of Mental Disorders*
DT	Delirium tremens
Dx	Diagnosis
e/c	Enteric-coated
EC50	Effective concentration 50%
ECG	Electrocardiogram
ECT	Electroconvulsive therapy
EEG	Electroencephalogram
EMDR	Eye movement desensitization and reprocessing
EMS	Emergency medical services
EPS	Extrapyramidal side effects
EPSP	Excitatory postsynaptic potential
FBC	Full blood count
GABA	Gamma-aminobutyric acid
G/I	Gastrointestinal
GTC	Generalized tonic-clonic seizure
GTP	Guanosine triphosphate
5HT	Serotonin
7-HT	7-hydroxytryptamine
HCL	Hydrochloride
HD	High dose
h.s.	Hora somni (at bedtime)
Hx	History
ICD	International classification of disease
IPSP	Inhibitory postsynaptic potential
IV	Intravenous
IM	Intramuscular
kg	Killogram
L/A	Long-acting
LD	Low dose
LD50	Lethal dose 50
LFT	Liver function test
MAOI	Monoamine oxidase inhibitor
MDI	Metered dose inhaler
Mgs	Milligrams
MHA	Mental Health Act (1983)

MHPG	3-methoxy-4-hydroxyphenylglycol
MW	Molecular weight
NE	Norepinephrine
NA	Noradrenalin
N/K	Not known
NMS	Neuroleptic malignant syndrome
NT	Neurotransmitter
O_2	Oxygen
OCD	Obsessive-compulsive disorder
O/C	Oral contraceptive
OD	Overdose
OTC	Over-the-counter
PD	Panic disorder
PG	Prostaglandin
PMH	Previous medical history
p.o.	Per ost (by mouth)
PR	Rectal administration
PRN	Pro re nata (as needed)
pt	Patient
PTSD	Posttraumatic stress disorder
q.	Every
q.d.; QD	Every day
q.i.d.; QID	Quarter in die (four times a day)
REM	Rapid eye movement
RT	Rapid tranquillization
Rx	Take thou a recipe (by prescription)
SA	Short-acting
s/c; SubQ	Subcutaneous
SF	Sugar-free
SIB	Self-injurious behavior
Sig.	Signa (directions)
SR	Sustained-release
SSRI	Serotonin selective reuptake inhibitor
Statim; STAT	Immediately
t; ½	Half-life
TBI	Traumatic brain injury
TCA	Tricyclic antidepressant
TD	Tardive dyskinesia
TDM	Therapeutic drug monitoring
t.i.d.; TID	Ter in die (three times a day)
UAD	Use as directed
Ut Dict.	As directed
Vd	Volume of distribution
Wt	Weight
yo	Year-old

References

Abbott, M. J., & Rapee, R. M. (2004). Post-event rumination and negative self-appraisal in social phobia before and after treatment. *Journal of Abnormal Psychology, 113*(1), 136–144.

Abelson, J. L., Curtis, G. C., Sagher, O., Albucher, R. C., Harrigan, M., Taylor, S. F., Martis, B., & Giodani, B. (2005). Deep brain stimulation for refractory obsessive-compulsive disorder. *Biological Psychiatry, 57*(5), 510–516.

Abelson, J. L., & Young, E. A. (2003). Hypothalamic-pituitary adrenal response to cholescystokinin-B receptor agonism is resistant to cortisol feedback inhibition. *Psychoneuroendocrinology, 28*(2), 169–180.

Ables, A. Z., & Baughman, O. L. (2003). Antidepressants: Update on new agents and indications. *American Family Physician, 6*(3), 547–554.

Abraham, K. C., Connor, K. M., & Davidson, J. R. (2004). Explanatory attributions of anxiety and recovery in a study of kava. *Journal of Alternative Complementary Medicine, 10*(3), 556–559.

Abramov, U., Raud, S., Koks, S., Innos, J., Kurrikoff, K., Matsui, T., & Vasar, E. (2004). Targeted mutation of CCK(2) receptor gene antagonises behavioral changes induced by social isolation in female, but not in male mice. *Behavioural Brain Research, 155*(1), 1–11.

Abramowitz, J. S., Deacon, B. J., Woods, C. M., & Tolin, D. F. (2004). Association between Protestant religiosity and obsessive-compulsive symptoms and cognitions. *Depression and Anxiety, 20*(2), 70–76.

Abramowitz, J. S., Foa, E. B., & Franklin, M. E. (2003). Exposure and ritual prevention for Obsessive-compulsive disorder: Effects of intensive versus twice-weekly sessions. *Journal of Consulting and Clinical Psychology, 71*(2), 394–398.

Abramowitz, J. S., Whiteside, S., Kalsy, S. A., & Tolin, D. F. (2003). Thought control strategies in obsessive-compulsive disorder: A replication and extension. *Behaviour Research and Therapy, 41*(5), 529–540.

Abramowitz, J. S., Whiteside, S., Lynam, D., & Kalsy, S. (2003). Is thought-action fusion specific to obsessive-compulsive disorder? A mediating role of negative affect. *Behaviour Research and Therapy, 41*(9), 1069–1079.

Abrams, J. K., Johnson, P. L., Hollis, J. H., & Lowery, C. A. (2004). Anatomic and functional tomography of the dorsal raphe nucleus. *Annals of the New York Academy of Sciences, 1018*, 46–57.

Abramson, L. Y., Seligman, M. E. P., & Teasdale, J. (1978). Learned helplessness in humans: Critique and reformulation. *Journal of Abnormal Psychology, 87*, 32–48.

Ackerman, D. L., Greenland, S., & Bystritsky, A. (1999). Side effects as predictors of drug response in obsessive-compulsive disorder. *Journal of Clinical Psychopharmacology,* 19(5), 459–465.

Adamec, R. E., Blundell, J., & Burton, P. (2003). Phosphorylated cyclic AMP response element binding protein expression induced in the periaqueductal gray by predator stress: Its relationship to the stress experience, behavior, and limbic neural plasticity. *Progress in Neuro-psychopharmacology & Biological Psychiatry,* 27(8), 1243–1267.

Adams, K. H., Hansen, E. S., Pinborg, L. H., Hasselbalch, S. G., Svarer, C., Holm, S., Bolwig, T. G., & Knudsen, G. M. (2005). Patients with obsessive-compulsive disorder have increased 5HT2A receptor binding in the caudate nuclei. *International Journal of Neuropsychopharmacology,* 8(3), 391–401.

Adell, A. (2004). Antidepressant properties of substance P antagonists: Relationship to monoaminergic mechanisms? *Current Drug Targets. CNS and Neurological Disorders,* 3(2), 113–121.

Ader, R., & Cohen, N. (1993). Psychoneuroimmunology: Conditioning and stress. *Annual Review of Psychology,* 44, 53–85.

Adler, C. M., McDonough-Ryan, P., Sax, K. W., Holland, S. K., Arndt, S., & Strakowski, S. M. (2000). fMRI of neural activation with symptom provocation in un-medicated patients with obsessive- compulsive disorder. *Journal of Psychiatric Research,* 34(4–5), 317–324.

Adolphs, R., Tranel, D., & Damasio, A. R. (1998). The human amygdala in social judgment. *Nature,* 393, 470–474.

Aerni, A., Traber, R., Hock, C., Roozendaal, B., Schelling, G., Papassotiropoulos, A., et al. (2004). Low-dose cortisol for symptoms of posttraumatic stress disorder. *American Journal of Psychiatry,* 161(8), 1488–1490.

Agid, O., Shalev, A. Y., & Lerer, B. (2001). Triiodothyronin augmentation of selective serotonin reuptake inhibitors in posttraumatic stress disorder. *Journal of Clinical Psychiatry,* 62(3), 169–173.

Ahsan, H., Hodge, S. E., Heiman, G. A., Begg, M. D., & Susser, E. S. (2002). Relative risk for genetic associations: The case-parent triad as a variant of case-cohort design. *International Journal of Epidemiology,* 31(3), 669–678.

Aihara, K., Shimada, J., Miwa, T., Tottori, K., Burris, K. D., Yocca, F. D., Horie, M., & Kikuchi, T. (2004). The novel antipsychotic aripiprazole is a partial agonist at short and long isoforms of D2 receptors linked to the regulation of adenylyl cyclase activity and prolactin release. *Brain Research,* 1003(1–2), 9–17.

Ainsworth, M. D. S. (1962). The effects of maternal deprivation: A review of findings and controversy in the context of research strategy. In *Deprivation of Maternal Care: A Reassessment of Its Effects.* Public Health Papers, 14. Geneva: World Health Organization.

Ainsworth, M. D. S. (1969). Object relations, dependency, and attachment: A theoretical review of the infant-mother relationship. *Child Development,* 40, 969–1025.

Airaksinen, E., Larsson, M., & Forsell, Y. (2005). Neuropsychological functions in anxiety disorders in population-based samples: Evidence of episodic memory dysfunction. *Journal of Psychiatric Research,* 39(2), 207–214.

Akechi, T., Okuyama, T., Sugawara, Y., Nakano, T., Shima, Y., & Uchitomi, Y. (2004). Major depression, adjustment disorders, and posttraumatic stress disorder in terminally ill cancer patients: Associated and predictive factors. *Journal of Clinical Oncology,* 22(10), 1957–1965.

Alban, J. P., Hopson, M. M., Ly, V., & Whyte, J. (2004). Effect of methylphenidate on vital signs and adverse effects in adults with traumatic brain injury. *American Journal of Physical Medicine and Rehabilitation,* 83(2), 131–137.

Albert, U., Bergesio, C., Pessina, E., Maina, G., & Bogetto, F. (2002). Management of treatment resistant obsessive-compulsive disorder: Algorithms for pharmacotherapy. *Pan-minerva Medicine,* 44(2), 83–91.

Albert, U., Maina, G., Forner, F., & Bogetto, F. (2004). DSM-IV obsessive-compulsive personality disorder: Prevalence in patients with anxiety disorders and in healthy comparison subjects. *Comprehensive Psychiatry, 45*(5), 325–332.

Alcalay, R. N., Giladi, E., Pick, C. G., & Gozes, I. (2004). Intranasal administration of NAP, a neuroprotective peptide, decreases anxiety-like behavior in aging mice in the elevated plus maze. *Neuroscience Letter, 361*(1–3), 128–131.

Alden, L. E., Bieling, P. J., & Wallace, S. T. (1994). Perfectionism in an interpersonal context: A self-regulation analysis of dysphoria and social anxiety. *Cognitive Therapy and Research, 33*, 497–506.

Alden, L. E., & Wallace, S. T. (1995). Social phobia and social appraisal in successful and unsuccessful social interactions. *Behavioural Research and Therapy, 33*, 497–506.

Alescio-Lautier, B., Paban, V., & Soumireu-Mourat, B. (2000). Neuromodulation of memory in the hippocampus by vasopressin. *European Journal of Pharmacology, 405*(1–3), 63–72.

Alexander, K. W., Quas, J. A., Goodman, G. S., Ghetti, S., Edelstein, R. S., Redlich, A. D., Cordon, I. M., & Jones, D. P. (2005). Traumatic impact predicts long-term memory for documented child sexual abuse. *Psychological Sciences, 16*(1), 33–40.

Alexopoulos, G. S., Streim, J., Carpenter, D., & Docherty, J. P. (2004). Using antipsychotic agents in older patients. *Journal of Clinical Psychiatry, 65*(2), 5–99.

Alfonso, J., Pollevick, G. D., van der Hart, M. G., Flugge, G., Fuchs, E., & Frasch, A. C. (2004). Identification of genes regulated by chronic psychosocial stress and antidepressant treatment in the hippocampus. *European Journal of Neuroscience, 19*(3), 659–666.

Allen, G. C., West, J. R., Chen, W. J., & Earnest, D. J. (2004). Developmental alcohol exposure disrupts circadian regulation on BDNF in the rat suprachiasmatic nucleus. *Neurotoxicology and Teratology, 26*(3), 353–358.

Allgulander, C., Bandelow, B., Hollander, E., Montgomery, S. A., Nutt, D. J., Okasha, A., Pollack, M. H., Stein, D. J., & Swinson, R. P. (2003). WCA recommendations for the long-term treatment of generalized anxiety disorder. *CNS Spectrum, 8*(8), 53–61.

Allgulander, C., Hirschfeld, R. M., & Nutt, D. J. (2002). Long-term treatment strategies in anxiety disorders. *Psychopharmacology Bulletin, 36*(2), 72–92.

Alloy, L. B., Peterson, C., Abramson, L. Y., & Seligman, M. E. P. (1984). Attributional style and the generality of learned helplessness. *Journal of Personality and Social Psychology, 46*, 681–687.

Almedom, A. M. (2004). Factors that mitigate war-induced anxiety and mental distress. *Journal of Biosocial Science, 36*(4), 445–461.

Alonso, P., Menchon, J., Mataix-Cols, D., Pifarre, J., Urretavizcaya, M., Crespo, J. M., Jimenez, S., Vallejo, G., & Vallejo, J. (2004b). Perceived parental rearing style in obsessive-compulsive disorder: Relation to symptom dimensions. *Psychiatry Research, 127*(3), 267–278.

Alonso, P., Pujol, J., Cardoner, N., Benlloch, L., Deus, J., Menchon, J. M., Capdevila, A., & Vallejo, J. (2001). Right prefrontal repetitive transcranial magnetic stimulation in obsessive-compulsive disorder: A double-blind, placebo-controlled study. *American Journal of Psychiatry, 158*, 1143–1145.

Alptekin, K., Degirmenci, B., Kivircik, B., Durak, H., Yemez, B., Derebek, E., & Tunca, Z. (2001). Tc-99m HMPAO brain perfusion SPECT in drug-free obsessive-compulsive patients without depression. *Psychiatry Research, 107*(1), 51–56.

Altamura, A. C., Piolo, R., Vitto, M., & Mannu, P. (1999). Venlafaxine in social phobia: A study in selective serotonin reuptake inhibitor non-responders. *International Journal of Clinical Psycholopharmacology, 14*(4), 239–245.

Altar, C. A. (1999). Neurotropins and depression. *Trends in Pharmacological Sciences, 20*(2), 59–61.

Alvarez-Silva, S., Alvarez-Rodriguez, J., Perez-Echeverria, M. J., & Alvarez-Silva, I. (2005). Panic and epilepsy. *Journal of Anxiety Disorders, 6*, 1–7.

Alves, S. H., Pinheiro, G., Motta, V., Landeira-Fernandez, J., & Cruz, A. P. (2004). Anxiogenic effects in the rat elevated plus-maze of 5HT2C agonists into ventral but not dorsal hippocampus. *Behavioural Pharmacology, 15*(1), 37–43.

Alwahhabu, F. (2003). Anxiety symptoms and generalized anxiety disorder in the elderly: A review. *Harvard Review of Psychiatry, 11*(4), 180–193.

Amaral, D. G. (2002). The primate amygdala and the neurobiology of social behavior: Implications for understanding social anxiety. *Biological Psychiatry, 51*(1), 11–17.

Amaral, D. G. (2003). The amygdala, social behavior, and danger detection. *Annals of the New York Academy of Sciences, 1000,* 337–347.

American Psychiatric Association (2000). *Diagnostic and Statistical Manual of Mental Disorders* (4th Ed., Revised). Washington D.C.: Author.

Amick, B. C., Kawachi, I., Coakley, E. H., Lerner, S., Levine, S., & Colditz, G. A. (1998). Relationship of job strain and isostrain to health status in a cohort of women in the United States. *Scandinavian Journal of Work and Environmental Health, 24,* 54–61.

Amico, J. A., Mantella, R. C., Vollmer, R. R., & Li, X. (2004). Anxiety and stress responses in female oxytocin deficient mice. *Journal of Neuroendocrinology, 16*(4), 319–324.

Amir, N., Cashman, L., & Foa, E. B. (1997). Strategies of thought control in obsessive-compulsive disorder. *Behavior Research and Therapy, 35*(8), 775–777.

Amirkhan, J. H., Risinger, R. T., & Swickert, R. J. (1995). Extraversion: A "hidden" personality factor in coping? *Journal of Personality, 63,* 189–212.

Amital, D., Fostick, L., Sasson, Kindler, S., Amital, H., & Zohar, J. (2005). Anxiogenic effects of sumatriptan in panic disorders: A double-blind, placebo-controlled study. *European Neuropsychopharmacology, 15*(3), 279–282.

Amo, C., Quesney, L. F., Ortiz, T., Maestu, F., Fernandez, A., Lopez-Ibor, M. I., & Lopez-Ibor, J. J. (2004). Limbic paroxysmal magnetoencephalographic activity in 12 obsessive-compulsive disorder patients: A new diagnostic finding. *Journal of Clinical Psychiatry, 65*(2), 156–162.

An, J. J., Bae, M. H., Cho, S. R., Lee, S. H., Choi, S. H., Lee, B. H., Shin, H. S., Kim, Y. N., Park, K. W., Borrelli, E., & Baik, J. H. (2004). Altered GABAergic neurotransmission in mice lacking dopamine D2 receptors. *Molecular and Cellular Neurosciences, 25*(4), 732–741.

Anderson, C. A., & Arciniegas, D. B. (2004). Neurosurgical interventions for neuropsychiatric syndromes. *Current Psychiatry Reports, 6*(5), 355–363.

Anderson, K. E., Louis, E. D., Stern, Y., & Marder, K. S. (2001). Cognitive correlates of obsessive and compulsive symptoms in Huntington's Disease. *American Journal of Psychiatry, 158,* 799–801.

Anderson, K. E., & Savage, C. R. (2004). Cognitive and neurobiological findings in obsessive-compulsive disorder. *Psychiatric Clinics of North America, 27*(1), 37–47.

Andersson, L., Sundstrom-Poromaa, I., Bixo, M., Wulff, M., Bondestam, K., & Strom, M. (2003). Point prevalence of psychiatric disorders during the second trimester of pregnancy: A population-based study. *American Journal of Obstetrics and Gynecology, 189*(1), 148–154.

Andersson, L., Sundstrom-Poromaa, I., Wulff, M., Astrom, M., & Bixo, M. (2004). Implications of antenatal depression and anxiety for obstetric outcome. *Obstetrics and Gynecology, 104*(3), 467–476.

Andrade, C. S., & Guimaraes, F. S. (2003). Anxiolytic-like effect of group housing on stress-induced behavior in rats. *Depression and Anxiety, 18*(3), 149–152.

Andrade, T. G., & Graeff, F. G. (2001). Effect of electrolytic and neurotoxic lesions of the median raphe nucleus on anxiety and stress. *Pharmacology, Biochemistry, and Behavior, 70*(1), 1–14.

Andreasen, N. C. (1997). Linking mind and brain in the study of mental illnesses: A project for a scientific psychopathology. *Science, 275,* 1586–1593.

Andreasen, N. C., Paradiso, S., & O'Leary, D. S. (1998). "Cognitive dysmetria" as an integrative theory of schizophrenia: A dysfunction in corical-subcorital-cerebellar circuitry? *Schizophrenia Bulletin, 24,* 203–218.

Andrews, G., & Slade, T. (2002). Agoraphobia without a history of panic disorder may be part of the panic disorder syndrome. *Journal of Nervous and Mental Disorder, 190*(9), 624–630.

Angst, J., Gamma, A., Endrass, J., Goodwin, R., Ajdacic, V., Eich, D., & Rossler, W. (2004). Obsessive- compulsive severity spectrum in the community: Prevalence, comorbidity, and course. *European Archives of Psychiatry and Clinical Neuroscience, 254*(3), 156–164.

Anisman, H., Zaharia, M. D., Meaney, M. J., & Merali, Z. (1998). Do early life events permanently alter behavioral and hormonal responses to stressors? *International Journal of Developmental Neuroscience, 16*(3–4), 149–164.

Anke, J., & Ramzan, I. (2004). Pharmacokinetic and pharmacodynamic drug interactions with kava (piper methysticum). *Journal of Ethnopharmacology, 93*(2–3), 153–160.

Ansorge, M., Tanneberger, C., Davies, B., Theuring, F., & Kusserow, H. (2004). Analysis of the murine 5HT receptor gene promoter in vitro and vivo. *European Journal of Neuroscience, 20*(2), 363–374.

Antai-Otong, D. (2003). Current treatments of generalized anxiety disorder. *Journal of Psychosocial Nursing and Mental Health Services, 41*(12), 20–29.

Antoni, M. H., Cruess, D. G., Cruess, S., Lutgendorf, S., Kumar, M., Ironson, G., Klimas, N., Fletcher, M. A., & Schneiderman, N. (2000). Cognitive-behavioral stress management intervention effects on anxiety, 24–hr. urinary norepinephrine output, and T-cytotoxic suppressor cells over time among symptomatic HIV-infected gay men. *Journal of Consulting and Clinical Psychology, 68,* 31–45.

Aouizerate, B., Cuny, E., Martin-Guehl, C., Guehl, D., Amieva, H., Benazzouz, A., Fabrigoule, C., Allard, M., Rougier, A., Bioulac, B., Tignol, J., & Burbaud, P. (2004). Deep brain stimulation of the ventral caudate nucleus in the treatment of obsessive-compulsive disorder and major depression: Case report. *Journal of Neurosurgery, 101*(4), 682–686.

Aparasu, R., Mort, J., & Brandt, H. (2003). Psychotropic medication expenditures for community- dwelling elderly persons. *Psychiatric Services, 54,* 739–742.

Apter, J., & Allen, L. A. (1999). Buspirone: Future directions. *Journal of Clinical Psychopharmacology, 19*(1), 86–93.

Arbelle, S., Benjamin, J., Golin, M., Kremer, I., Belmaker, R. H., & Ebstein, R. P. (2003). Relation of shyness in grade school children to the genotype for the long form of the serotonin transporter promoter region polymorphism. *American Journal of Psychiatry, 160*(4), 671–676.

Arborelius, L., Owens, M. J., Plotsky, P. M., & Nemeroff, C. B. (1999). The role of corticotrophin- releasing factor in depression and anxiety disorders. *Journal of Endocrinology, 160,* 1–12.

Arevalo, C., De Miguel, R., & Hernandez-Tristan, R. (2001). Cannabinoid effects on anxiety-related behaviors and hypothalamic neurotransmitters. *Pharmacology, Biochemistry, and Behavior, 70*(1), 123–131.

Argyropoulos, S. V., Bell, C. J., & Nutt, D. J. (2001). Brain function in social anxiety disorder. *Psychiatric Clinics of North America, 24*(4), 707–722.

Argyropolous, S. V., Fenney, A., & Nutt, D. J. (2002). *Anxiety Disorders Comorbid with Depression: Panic Disorder with Agoraphobia.* New York: Martin Dunitz Publishers.

Aricioglu, F., & Altunbas, H. (2003). Harmane induces anxiolysis and antidepressant-like effects in rats. *Annals of the New York Academy of Sciences, 1009,* 196–201.

Arinami, T., Itokawa, M., Aoki, J., Shibuya, H., Ookubo, Y., Iwawaki, A., Ota, K., Shimizu, H., Hamaguchi, H., & Toru, M. (1996). Further association study on dopamine D2 receptor variant S311C in schizophrenia and affective disorders. *American Journal of Medical Genetics, 67,* 133–138.

Armstrong, D., & Earnshaw, G. (2004). What constructs do GPs use when diagnosing psychological problems? *British Journal of General Practice: The Journal of the Royal College of General Practitioners, 54*(505), 580–583.

Arnold, P., Banerjee, S. P., Bhandari, R., Lorch, E., Ivey, J., Rose, M., & Rosenberg, D. R. (2003). Childhood anxiety disorders and developmental issues in anxiety. *Current Psychiatry Report, 5*(4), 252–265.

Arnold, P. D., Rosenberg, D. R., Mundo, E., Tharmalingam, S., Kennedy, J. L., & Richter, M. A. (2004). Association of a glutamate (NMDA) subunit receptor gene (GRIN2B) with obsessive-compulsive disorder: A preliminary study. *Psychopharmacology, 174*(4), 530–538.

Arnold, P. D., Zai, G., & Richter, M. A. (2004). Genetics of anxiety disorders. *Current Psychiatry Reports, 6*(4), 243–254.

Arnsten, A., Matthew, R., Ubriani, R., Taylor, J., & Li, B. (1991). Alpha-1 noradrenergic receptor stimulation impairs prefrontal cortical cognitive function. *Biological Psychiatry, 45,* 26–31.

Arntz, A. (2003). Cognitive therapy versus applied relaxation as treatment of generalized anxiety disorder. *Behaviour Research and Therapy, 41*(6), 633–646.

Arvat, E., Giordano, R., Grottoli, S., & Ghigo, E. (2002). Benzodiazepines and anterior pituitary function. *Journal of Endocrinology Investigation, 25*(8), 735–747.

Asakawa, A., Inui, A., Momose, K., Ueno, N., Fujino, M. A., & Kasuga, M. (1998). Endomorphins have orexigenic and anxiolytic activities in mice. *Neuroreport, 9*(10), 2265–2267.

Asarnow, J. R., Thompson, M., Hamilton, E. B., Goldstein, M. J., & Guthrie, D. (1994). Family-expressed emotion, childhood-onset depression, and childhood-onset schizophrenia spectrum disorders: Is expressed emotion a nonspecific correlate of child psychopathology or a specific risk factor for depression? *Journal of Abnormal Child Psychology, 22,* 129–146.

Asbahr, F. R., Ramos, R. T., Costa, A. N., & Sassi, R. B. (2005). Obsessive-compulsive symptoms in adults with history of rheumatic fever, Sydenham's chorea, and type I diabetes mellitus: Preliminary results. *Acta Psychiatrica Scandinavica, 111*(2), 159–161.

Asch, S. E. (1946). Forming impressions of personality. *Journal of Abnormal and Social Psychology, 41,* 258–290.

Ashe, J. H., & Aramakis, V. B. (1998). Brain development and plasticity. In H. S. Friedman (Ed.), *Encyclopedia of Mental Health I* (pp. 305–317). San Diego, California: Academic Press.

Ashton, H., & Young, A. H. (2003). GABAergic drugs: Exit stage left, enter stage right. *Journal of Psychopharmacology, 17*(2), 174–178.

Asmundson, G. J., Bonin, M. F., Frombach, I. K., & Norton, G. R. (2000). Evidence of a disposition toward fearfulness and vulnerability to posttraumatic stress in dysfunctional pain patients. *Behaviour Research and Therapy, 38*(8), 801–812.

Asnis, G. M., Kohn, S. R., Henderson, M., & Brown, N. L. (2004). SSRIs versus non-SSRIs in posttraumatic stress disorder: An update with recommendations. *Drugs, 64*(4), 383–404.

Assal, F., Alarcon, M., Solomon, E. C., Masterman, D., Geschwind, D. H., & Cummings, J. L. (2004). Association of the serotonin transporter and receptor gene polymorphisms in neuropsychiatric symptoms in Alzheimer disease. *Archives of Neurology, 61*(8), 1249–1253.

Atack, J. R. (2003). Anxioselective compounds acting at the GABAA receptor benzodiazepine binding site. *Current Drug Targets. CNS and Neurological Disorders, 2*(4), 213–232.

Atanackovic, D., Kroger, H., Serke, S., & Deter, H. C. (2004). Immune parameters in patients with anxiety or depression during psychotherapy. *Journal of Affective Disorders, 81*(3), 201–209.

Atmaca, M., Tezcan, E., Kuloglu, M., & Ustundag, B. (2005). Serum levels in obsessive-compulsive disorder. *Psychiatrty and Clinical Neuroscience, 59*(2), 189–193.

Auld, F., & Hyman, M. (1991). *Resolution of Inner Conflict: An Introduction to Psychoanalytic Therapy.* Washington, D. C.: American Psychological Association.

Auriacombe, M., Reneric, J. P., Usandizaga, D., Gomez, F., Combourieu, I., & Tignol, J. (2000). Post-ECT agitation and plasma lactate concentrations. *Journal of ECT, 16*(3), 263–267.

Austin, A. A., & Chorpita, B. F. (2004). Temperament, anxiety, and depression: Comparisons across five ethnic groups of children. *Journal of Clinical Child and Adolescent Psychology, 33*(2), 216–226.

Aylward, E. H., Harris, G. J., Hoehn-Saric, R., Barta, P. E., Machlin, S. R., & Pearlson, G. D. (1996). Normal caudate nucleus in obsessive-compulsive disorder assessed by quantitative neuroimaging. *Archives of General Psychiatry, 53*, 577–584.

Azzam, A., & Mathews, C. A. (2003). Meta-analysis of the association between the catecholamine- o-methyltransferase gene and obsessive-compulsive disorder. *American Journal of Medical Genetics, 123*(1), 64–69.

Baca-Garcia, E., Salgado, B. R., Segal, H. D., Lorenzo, C. V., Acosta, M. N., Romero, M. A., Hernandez, M. D., Saiz-Ruiz, J., Fernandex-Piqueras, J., & de Leon, J. (2005). A pilot study of the continuum between compulsivity and impulsivity in females: The serotonin transporter promoter polymorphism. *Progress in Neuropsychopharmacology and Biological Psychiatry, 29*(5), 713–717.

Bachmann, A. W., Sedgley, T. L., Jackson, R. V., Gibson, J. N., Young, R. M., & Torpy, D. J. (2005). Glucocorticoid receptor polymorphisms and posttraumatic stress disorder. *Psychoneuroendocrinology, 30*(3), 297–306.

Baer, L. (1994). Factor analysis of symptom subtypes of obsessive-compulsive disorder and their relation to personality and tic disorders. *Journal of Clinical Psychiatry, 55*, 18–23.

Bagdy, G., Graf, M., Anheuer, Z. E., Modos, E. A., & Kantor, S. (2001). Anxiety-like effects induced by fluoxetine, sertraline, or m-CPP treatment are reversed by pretreatment with the 5HT2C receptor antagonist SB-242084 but not the 5HT1A receptor antagonist WAY-100635. *International Journal of Neuropsychopharmacology, 4*(4), 399–408.

Bailey, K. G. (1987). *Human Paleopsychology: Aggression and Pathological Processes.* Hillsdale, New Jersey: Lawrence Erlbaum.

Bailey, S. J., & Toth, M. (2004). Variability in the benzodiazepine response of serotonin 5–HT1A receptor null mice displaying anxiety-like phenotype: Evidence for genetic modifiers in the 5–HT-mediated regulation of GABA(A) receptors. *Journal of Neuroscience, 24*(28), 6343–6351.

Baker, D. G., Ekhator, N. N., Kasckow, J. W., Dashevsky, B., Horn, P. S., Bednarik, L., & Geracioti, T. D. (2005). Higher levels of basal serial CSF cortisol in combat veterans with posttraumatic stress disorder. *American Journal of Psychiatry, 162*(5), 992–994.

Balasubramaniam, A. (2002). Clinical potentials of neuropeptide Y family of hormones. *American Journal of Surgery, 183*(4), 430–434.

Bale, T. L., & Vale, W. W. (2004). CRF and CRF receptors: Role in stress responsivity and other behaviors. *Annual Review of Pharmacology and Toxicology, 44*, 525–557.

Ball, S. G., Baer, L., & Otto, M. W. (1996). Symptom subtypes of obsessive-compulsive disorder in behavioral treatment studies: A quantitative review. *Behaviour Research and Therapy, 34*, 47–51.

Ballenger, J. C. (2001). Overview of different pharmacotherapies for attaining remission in generalized anxiety disorder. *Journal of Clinical Psychiatry, 62*, 11–19.

Ballenger, J. C., Davidson, J. R., Lecrubier, Y., Nutt, D. J., Bobes, J., Beidel, D. C., Ono, Y., & Westberg, H. G. (2001). Consensus statement on generalized anxiety disorder. *Journal of Clinical Psychiatry, 62*(11), 53–58.

Ballenger, J. C., Davidson, J. R., Lecrubier, Y., Nutt, D. J., Marshall, R. D., Nemeroff, C. B., Shalev, A. Y., & Yehuda, R. (2004). Consensus statement on posttraumatic stress disorder from the International Consensus Group on Depression and Anxiety. *Journal of Clinical Psychiatry, 65*(1), 55–62.

Bandelow, B., Zohar, J., Hollander, E., Kasper, S., & Moller, H. J. (2002). World Federation of Societies of Biological Psychiatry guidelines for the pharmacological treatment of anxiety, obsessive-compulsive, and posttraumatic stress disorders. *World Journal of Biological Psychiatry, 3*(4), 171–199.

Bandura, A. (1965). Vicarious processes: A case of no-trial learning. In L. Berkowitz (Ed.), *Advances in Experimental Social Psychology (Vol. II)*. New York: Academic Press.

Bandura, A. (1988). Self-efficacy conception of anxiety. *Anxiety Research, 1,* 77–98.

Bandura, A., & Kupers, C. J. (1964). Transmission of patterns of self-reinforcement through modeling. *Journal of Abnormal Social Psychology, 69,* 1–9.

Bang, L. M., & Keating, G. M. (2004). Paroxetine controlled release. *CNS Drugs, 18*(6), 365–366.

Bannerman, D. M., Rawlins, J. N., McHugh, S. B., Deacon, R. M., Yee, B. K., Bast, T., Zhang, W. N., Pothuizen, H. H., & Feldon, J. (2004). Regional dissociations within the hippocampus-memory and anxiety. *Neuroscience and Biobehavioral Reviews, 28*(3), 273–283.

Bannister, D. (Ed.). (1985). *Issues and Approaches in Personal Construct Theory.* Florida: Academic Press.

Bannister, D., & Mair, J. M. (1988). *The Evaluation of Personal Constructs.* London, England: Academic Press.

Bantick, R. A., Rabiner, E. A., Hirani, E., de Vries, M. H., Hume, S. P., & Grasby, P. M. (2004). Occupancy of agonist drugs at the 5–HT1A receptor. *Neuropsychopharmacology, 29*(5), 847–859.

Barlow, D. H. (2002). *Anxiety and Its Disorders: The Nature and Treatment of Anxiety & Panic (2nd Ed.)*. New York: Guilford Press.

Barlow, D. H., Gorman, J. M., Shear, K. M., & Woods, S. W. (2000). Cognitive-behavioral therapy, imipramine, or their combination for panic disorder: A randomized controlled trial. *Journal of the American Medical Association, 283*(19), 2529–2536.

Barnes, T. R., & McPhillips, M. A. (1998). Novel antipsychotics, extrapyradmidal side effects and tardive dyskinesia. *International Clinical Psychopharmacology, 13*(3), S49–S57.

Barr, C. S., Newman, T. K., Becker, M. L., Parker, C. C., Champoux, M., Lesch, K. P., Goldman, D., Suomi, S. J., & Higley, J. D. (2003). The utility of the non-human primate: Model for studying gene by environment interactions in behaviour research. *Genes, Brain, and Behavior, 2*(6), 336–340.

Barr, C. S., Newman, T. K., Shannon, C., Parker, C., Dvoskin, R. I., Becker, M. L., Schwandt, M., Champoux, M., Lesch, K. P., Goldman, D., Suomi, S. J., & Higley, J. D. (2004). Rearing condition and rh5–HTTLPR interact to influence limbic-hypothalamic-pituitary-adrenal axis response to stress in infant maraques. *Biological Psychiatry, 55*(7), 733–738.

Barros, M., Mello, E. L., Maior, R. S., Muller, C. P., De Souza-Silva, M. A., Carey, R. J., Huston, J. P., & Tomaz, C. (2003). Anxiolytic-like effects of the selective 5HT1A receptor antagonist WAY100635 in non-human primates. *European Journal of Pharmacology, 482*(1–3), 197–203.

Barry, J. J., Lembke, A., & Bullock, K. D. (2004). Current status of the utilization of antiepileptic treatments in mood, anxiety, and aggression: Drugs and devices. *Clinical EEG and Neuroscience, 35*(1), 4–13.

Bartha, R., Stein, M. B., Williamson, P. C., Drost, D. J., Neufeld, R. W. J., Carr, T. J., Canaran, G., Densmore, M., Anderson, G., & Siddiqui, A. (1998). A short echo H spectroscopy and volumetric MRI study of the corpus striatum in patients with obsessive-compulsive disorder and comparison subjects. *American Journal of Psychiatry, 155,* 1584–1591.

Basch, M. F. (1981). *Doing Psychotherapy*. New York: Basic Books.

Basso, M. R., Bornstein, R. A., Carona, F., & Morton, R. (2001). Depression accounts for executive function deficits in obsessive-compulsive disorder. *Neuropsychiatry, Neuropsychology, and Behavioral Neurology, 14*(4), 241–245.

Bast, T., & Feldon, J. (2003). Hippocampal modulation of sensorimotor processes. *Progress in Neurobiology, 70*(4), 319–345.

Bata-Garcia, J. L., Heredia-Lopez, F. J., Alvarez-Cervera, F. J., Arankowsky-Sandoval, G., & Gongora-Alfaro, J. L. (2002). Circling behavior induced by microinjection of serotonin reuptake inhibitors in the substantia nigra. *Pharmacology, Biochemistry, and Behavior, 71*(1–2), 353–363.

Battaglia, M., Bertell, S., Bajo, S., Politi, E., & Bellodi, L. (1998). An investigation of the co-occurrence of panic and somatization disorders through temperamental variables. *Psychosomatic Medicine, 60*(6), 726–729.

Baxter, L. R. (2003). Basal ganglia systems in ritualistic social displays: Reptiles and humans; function and illness. *Physiological Behavior, 79*(3), 451–460.

Bayatti, N., Zschocke, J., & Behl, C. (2003). Brain region-specific neuroprotective action and signaling of corticotropin-releasing hormone in primary neurons. *Endocrinology, 144*(9), 4051–4060.

Beard, J. L., Erikson, K. M., & Jones, B. C. (2002). Neurobehavioral analysis of developmental iron deficiency in rats. *Behavioural Brain Research, 134*(1–2), 517–524.

Bebbington, P. E. (1998). Epidemiology of obsessive-compulsive disorder. *British Journal of Psychiatry, 35*, 2–6.

Beck, A. T. (1976). *Cognitive Therapy and the Emotional Disorders*. New York: International Universities Press.

Beck, A. T. (1991). Cognitive therapy: A 30–year retrospective. *American Psychologist, 46*(4), 368–375.

Beck, A. T., & Clark, D. A. (1988). Anxiety and depression: An information processing perspective. *Anxiety Research, 1*, 23–36.

Beck, A. T., & Emery, G. (1985). *Anxiety Disorders and Phobias: A Cognitive Perspective*. New York: Basic Books.

Beck, C. T. (2004). Posttraumatic stress disorder due to childbirth: The aftermath. *Nursing Research, 53*(4), 216–224.

Beck, J. G., Novy, D. M., Diefenbach, G. J., Stanley, M. A., Averill, P. M., & Swann, A. C. (2003). Differentiating anxiety and depression in older adults with generalized anxiety disorder. *Psychological Assessment, 15*(2), 184–192.

Becker, C., Andre, J., Zeau, B., Rettori, M. C., Guardiola-Lemaitre, B., Hamon, M., & Benoliel, J. J. (2004). Melatonin MT(1/2) receptor stimulation reduces cortical overflow of cholecystokinin-like material in a model of anticipation of social defeat in the rat. *Neuropharmacology, 46*(8), 1158–1167.

Behar, D., Rapoport, J. L., Berg, C. J., Denckla, M. B., Mann, L., Cox, C., Fedio, P., Zahn, T., & Wolfman, M. G. (1994). Computerized tomography and neuropsychological test measures in adolescents with obsessive-compulsive disorder. *American Journal of Psychiatry, 141*, 363–369.

Beidel, D. C., & Turner, S. M. (1998). *Shy Children, Phobic Adults: Nature and Treatment of Social Phobia*. Washington, DC: American Psychological Association.

Beijamini, V., & Andreatini, R. (2003). Effects of hypericum perforatum and paroxetine in the mouse defense test battery. *Pharmacology, Biochemistry, and Behavior, 74*(4), 1015–1024.

Belanger, L., Morin, C. M., Langlois, F., & Ladouceur, R. (2004). Insomnia and generalized anxiety disorder: Effects of cognitive behavior therapy for GAD on insomnia symptoms. *Journal of Anxiety Disorders, 18*(4), 561–571.

Bellivier, F., Laplanche, J. L., Fournier, G., & Wolkenstein, P. (2001). Serotonin transporter gene polymorphism and psychiatric disorders in NF1 patients. *American Journal of Medical Genetics, 105*(8), 758–760.

Bellodi, L., Perna, G., Caldirola, D., Arancio, C., Bertani, A., & Di Bella, D. (1998). CO2–induced panic attacks: A twin study. *American Journal of Psychiatry, 155*(9), 1184–1188.

Belzung, C. (2001). The genetic basis of the pharmacological effects of anxiolytics: A review based on rodent models. *Behavioural Pharmacology, 12*(6–7), 451–460.

Benjamin, J., Gulman, R., Osher, Y., Segman, R., & Ebstein, R. (1997). Dopamine D4 receptor polymorphism associated with panic disorder. *American Journal of Medical Genetics (Neuropsychiatric Genetics), 74,* 613.

Benkelfat, C., Bradwejn, J., Meyer, E., Ellenbogen, M., Milot, S., Gjedde, A., & Evans, A. (1995). Functional neuroanatomy of CCK4–induced anxiety in normal healthy volunteers. *American Journal of Psychiatry, 152*(8), 1180–1184.

Bergink, V., van Megen, H. J., & Westenberg, H. G. (2004). Glutamate and anxiety. *European Neuropsychopharmacology, 14*(3), 175–183.

Berlant, J. L. (2004). Prospective open-label study of add-on and monotherapy topiramate in civilians with chronic nonhallucinatory posttraumatic stress disorder. *BMC Psychiatry, 4*(1), 24.

Berle, D., & Starcevic, V. (2005). Thought-action fusion: Review of the literature and future directions. *Clinical Psychology Review, 25*(3), 263–284.

Bernardo, M., Parellada, E., Lomena, F., Catafau, A. M., Font, M., Gomez, J. C., Lopez-Carrero, C., Gutierrez, F., Pavia, J., & Salamero, M. (2001). Double-blind olanzapine vs. haloperidol D2 dopamine receptor blockade in schizophrenic patients: A baseline-endpoint. *Psychiatry Research, 107*(2), 87–97.

Bernstein, G. A., Borchardt, C. M., & Perwien, A. R. (1996). Anxiety disorders in children and adolescents: A review of the past 10 years. *Journal of the American Academy of Child and Adolescent Psychiatry, 35*(9), 1110–1119.

Berridge, C. W., & Waterhouse, B. D. (2003). The locus coeruleus-noradrenergic system: Modulation of behavioral state and state-dependent cognitive processes. *Brain Research, 42*(1), 33–84.

Berthier, M. L., Kulisevsky, J. J., Gironell, A., & Heras, J. A. (1996). Obsessive-compulsive disorder associated with brain lesions: Clinical phenomenology, cognitive function, and anatomic correlates. *Neurology, 47*(2), 353–361.

Berthier, M. L., Kulisevsky, J. J., Gironell, A., & Lopez, O. L. (2001). Obsessive-compulsive disorder and traumatic brain injury: Behavioral, cognitive, and neuroimaging findings. *Neuropsychiatry, Neuropsychology, and Behavioral Neurology, 14*(1), 23–31.

Berthier, M. L., Posada, A., & Puentes, C. (2001). Dissociative flashbacks after right frontal injury in a Vietnam veteran with combat-related posttraumatic stress disorder. *Journal of Neuropsychiatry and Clinical Neuroscience, 13*(1), 101–105.

Bertoglio, L. J., & Carobrez, A. P. (2003). Anxiolytic-like effets of NMDA/glycine-B receptor ligands are abolished during the elevated plus-maze trial 2 in rats. *Psychopharmacology, 170*(4), 335–342.

Beshai, J. A. (2004). Toward a phenomenology of trance logic in posttraumatic stress disorder. *Psychological Reports, 94*(2), 649–654.

Besiroglu, L., Cillis, A. S., & Askin, R. (2004). The predictors of health care seeking behavior in obsessive-compulsive disorder. *Comprehensive Psychiatry, 45*(2), 99–108.

Bessen, D. E. (2001). Genetics of childhood disorders: Autoimmune disorders: Streptococcal infection and autoimmunity, an epidemiological perspective. *Journal of the American Academy of Child and Adolescent Psychiatry, 40*(11), 1346–1348.

Betancourt, Y. M., Jimenez-Leon, J. C., Jimenez-Betancourt, C. S., & Castillo, V. E. (2003). Autoimmune neuropsychiatric disorders associated to infection by streptococcus in the pediatric age: PANDAS. *Review of Neurology, 36*(1), 95–107.

Bhagwanjee, A., Parekh, A., Paruk, Z., Peterson, I., & Subedar, H. (1998). Prevalence of minor psychiatric disorders in an adult African rural community in South Africa. *Psychological Medicine, 28,* 1137–1147.

Bhatara, V., Alshari, M. G., Warhol, P., McMillin, J. M., & Bhatara, A. (2004). Coexistent hypothyroidism, psychosis, and severe obsessions in an adolescent: A 10-year follow-up. *Journal of Child and Adolescent Psychopharmacology, 14*(2), 315–323.

Bhatnagar, S., Sun, L. M., Raber, J., Maren, S., Julius, D., & Dallman, M. F. (2004). Changes in anxiety-related behaviors and hypothalamic-pituitary-adrenal activity in mice lacking the 5HT3A receptor. *Psychological Behavior, 81*(4), 545–555.

Bhui, K. (2004). Switching serotonin reuptake inhibitors may be of benefit in people with obsessive-compulsive disorder. *Evidence Based Mental Health, 7*(4), 114.

Bilgic, B., Baral-Kulaksizoglu, I., Hanagasi, H., Saylan, M., Aykutlu, E., Gurvit, H., & Emre, M. (2004). Obsessive-compulsive disorder secondary to bilateral frontal damage due to a closed head injury. *Cognition, Behavior, and Neurology, 17*(2), 118–120.

Billett, E., Richter, J., & Kennedy, J. (1998). Genetics of obsessive-compulsive disorder. In R. Swinson, M. Antony, S. Rachman, & M. Richter (Eds.), *Obsessive-Compulsive Disorder: Theory, Research, and Treatment* (pp. 181–206). New York: Guilford.

Birk, L. (2004). Pharmacotherapy for performance anxiety disorders: Occasionally useful but typically contraindicated. *Journal of Clinical Psychology, 60*(8), 867–879.

Birmaher, B., Axelson, D. A., Monk, K., Kalas, C., Clark, D. B., Ehmann, M., Bridge, J., Heo, J., & Brent, D. A. (2003). Fluoxetine for the treatment of childhood anxiety disorders. *Journal of the American Academy of Child and Adolescent Psychiatry, 42*(4), 415–423.

Birmaher, B., Yelovich A. K., & Renaud, J. (1998). Pharmacologic treatment for children and adolescents with anxiety disorders. *Pediatric Clinics of North America, 45*(5), 1187–1204.

Birmes, P., Escande, M., Gourdy, P., & Schmitt, L. (2000). Biological factors of posttraumatic stress: Neuroendocrine aspects. *Encephale, 26*(6), 55–61.

Bisson, J., & Andrew, M. (2005). Psychological treatment of posttraumatic stress disorder (PTSD). *Cochrane Database System Review, 18*(2), 3388.

Black, D. W., Monohan, P., Gable, J., Blum, N., Clancy, G., & Baker, P. (1998). Hoarding and treatment response in 38 nondepressed subjects with obsessive-compulsive disorder. *Journal of Clinical Psychiatry, 5*, 420–425.

Black, K., Shea, C., Dursun, S., & Kutcher, S. (2000). Selective serotonin reuptake inhibitor discontinuation syndrome: Proposed diagnostic criteria. *Journal of Psychiatry and Neurosciences, 25*(3), 255–261.

Blanco, C., Antia, S. X., & Liebowitz, M. R. (2002). Pharmacotherapy of social anxiety disorder. *Biological Psychiatry, 51*(1), 109–120.

Blanco, C., Schneier, F. R., Schmidt, S., & Blanco-Jerez, C. R. (2003). Pharmacological treatment of social anxiety disorder: A meta-analysis. *Depression and Anxiety, 18*(1), 29–40.

Blass, T. (Ed.). (1977). *Personality Variables in Social Behavior.* New York: John Wiley & Sons.

Bleiberg, K. L., & Markowitz, J. C. (2005). A pilot study of interpersonal psychotherapy for posttraumatic stress disorder. *American Journal of Psychiatry, 162*(1), 181–183.

Blier, P., Gobbi, G., Haddjeri, N., Santarelli, L., Mathew, G., & Hen, R. (2004). Impact of substance P receptor antagonism on the serotonin and norepinephrine systems: Relevance to the antidepressant anxiolytic response. *Journal of Psychiatry and Neurosciences, 29*(3), 208–218.

Blier, R., & de Montigny, C. (1998). Possible serotonergic mechanisms underlying the antidepressant and anti-obsessive-compulsive disorder responses. *Society of Biological Psychiatry, 44*, 313–323.

Bloom, F. E., & Kupfer, D. J. (1995). *Psychopharmacology: The Fourth Generation of Progress.* New York: Raven Press.

Bodner, S. M., Morshed, S. A., & Peterson, B. S. (2001). The question of PANDAS in adults. *Biological Psychiatry, 49*(9), 807–810.

Boehm, S. L., Reed, C. L., McKinnon, C. S., & Phillips, T. J. (2002). Shared genes influence sensitivity to the effects of ethanol on locomotor and anxiety-like behaviors and the stress axis. *Psychopharmacology, 161*(1), 54–63.

Boerner, R. J., Sommer, H., Berger, W., Kuhn, U., Schmidt, U., & Mannel, M. (2003). Kava-kava extract LI 150 is as effective as opipramol and buspirone in generalized anxiety disorder: An eight-week randomized, double-blind multi-centre clinical trial in 129 outpatients. *Phytomedicine, 10*(4), 38–49.

Boles-Ponto, L. L., Kathol, R. G., Kettelkamp, R., Watkins, G. L., Richmond, J. C. W., Clark, J., & Hichwa, R. D. (2002). Global cerebral blood flow after CO_2 inhalation in normal subjects and Patients with panic disorder determined with [^{15}O) water and PET. *Journal of Anxiety Disorders, 16*, 247–258.

Bolton, J., Moore, G. J., MacMillan, S., Stewart, C. M., & Rosenberg, D. R. (2001). Case study: Caudate glutamatergic changes with paroxetine persist after medication discontinuation in pediatric OCD. *Journal of American Academy of Child and Adolescent Psychiatry, 40*(8), 903–906.

Bonavita, C., Ferrero, A., Cereseto, M., Velardez, M., Rubio, M., & Wikinski, S. (2003). Adaptive changes in the rat hippocampal glutamatergic neurotransmission are observed during long-term treatment with lorazepam. *Psychopharmacology, 166*(2), 163–167.

Bond, M., & Perry, J. C. (2004). Long-term changes in defense styles with psychodynamic psychotherapy for depressive, anxiety, and personality disorders. *The American Journal of Psychiatry, 161*(9), 1665–1671.

Bonne, O., Bain, E., Neumeister, A., Nugent, A. C., Vythilingam, M., Carson, R. E., Luckenbaugh, D. A., Eckelman, W., Herscovitch, P., Drevets, W. C., & Charney, D. S. (2005). No change in serotonin type 1A receptor binding in patients with posttraumatic stress disorder. *American Journal of Psychiatry, 162*(2), 383–385.

Bonne, O., Gilboa, A., Louzoun, Y., Brandes, D., Yona, I., Lester, H., Barkai, G., Freedman, N., Chisin, R., & Shalev, A. Y. (2003). Resting regional cerebral perfusion in recent posttraumatic stress disorder. *Biological Psychiatry, 54*(10), 1077–1086.

Bonne, O., Shemer, Y., Gorali, Y., Katz, M., & Shalev, A. Y. (2003). A randomized, double-blind, placebo-controlled study of classical homeopathy in generalized anxiety disorder. *Journal of Clinical Psychiatry, 64*(3), 282–287.

Bonnet, U. (2003). Moclobemide: Therapeutic use and clinical studies. *CNS Drug Review, 9*(1), 97–140.

Borden, L. A., Murali-Dhar, T. G., Smith, K. E., Weinshank, R. L., Branchek, T. A., & Gluchowski, C. (1994). Tiagabine, SK&F 89976-A, CI-966, and NNC-711 are selective for the cloned GABA transporter GAT-1. *European Journal of Pharmacology, 269*(2), 219–224.

Boris, N. W., Ou, A. C., & Singh, R. (2005). Preventing posttraumatic stress disorder after mass exposure to violence. *Biosecurity and Bioterrorism: Biodefense Strategy, Practice, and Science, 3*(2), 154–163.

Borkovec, T. D. (1994). The nature, functions, and origins of worry. In G. L. Davey & F. Tallis (Eds.), *Worrying: Perspectives on Theory, Assessment, and Treatment* (pp. 5–34). England: Wiley.

Borkovec, T. D., & Castonguay, L. G. (1998). What is the scientific meaning of empirically supported therapy? *Journal of Consulting and Clinical Psychology, 66*(1), 136–142.

Borkovec, T. D., & Costello, E. (1993). Efficacy of applied relaxation and cognitive-behavioral therapy in the treatment of generalized anxiety disorder. *Journal of Consulting and Clinical Psychology, 61*(4), 611–619.

Borkovec, T. D., Newman, M. G., & Castonguay, L. G. (2003). Cognitive-behavioral therapy for generalized anxiety disorder with integrations from interpersonal and experiential therapies. *CNS Spectrum, 8*(5), 382–389.

Bourin, M., Baker, G. B., & Bradwejn, J. (1998). Neurobiology of panic disorder. *Journal of Psychosomatic Research, 44*, 163–180.

Bourin, M., David, D. J., Jolliet, P., & Gardier, A. (2002). Mechanism of action of antidepressants and therapeutic perspectives. *Therapie, 57*(4), 385–396.

Bourin, M., & Hascoet, M. (2001). Drug mechanisms in anxiety. *Current Opinion in Investigational Drugs, 2*(2), 259–265.

Bourin, M., Malinge, M., Vasar, E., & Bradwejn, J. (1996). Two faces of choilecystokinin: Anxiety and schizophrenia. *Fundamental & Clinical Pharmacology, 10*(2), 116–126.

Bouwer, C., & Stein, D. J. (1998). Use of the selective serotonin reuptake inhibitor citalopram in the treatment of generalized social phobia. *Journal of Affective Disorders, 49*(1), 79–82.

Bowlby, J. (1969). *Attachment Vol. I: Attachment and Loss*. New York: Basic Books.

Bowlby, J. (1977). The making and breaking of affectionate bonds. *British Journal of Psychiatry, 130*, 201–210.

Bowlby, J. (1983). Developmental psychiatry comes of age. *American Journal of Psychiatry, 145*, 1–10.

Bowman, R. E., MacLusky, N. J., Sarmiento, Y., Frankfurt, M., Gordon, M., & Luine, V. N. (2004). Sexually dimorphic effects of prenatal stress on cognition, hormonal responses, and central neurotransmitters. *Endocrinology, 145*(8), 3778–3787.

Bozkurt, G., Abay, E., Ates, I., Karabogaz, G., Ture, M., Savran, F. O., Palanduz, S., Temocin, K., & Algunes, C. (2004). Clastogenicity of selective serotonin-reuptake inhibitors. *Mutation Research, 558*(1–2), 137–144.

Brady, K., Pearlstein, T., & Asnis, G. M. (2000). Efficacy and safety of sertraline treatment of posttraumatic stress disorder: A randomized controlled trial. *Journal of the American Medical Association, 283*(14), 1837–1844.

Brambilla, F., Biggio, G., Pisu, M. G., Purdy, R. H., Gerra, G., Zaimovich, A., & Serra, M. (2004). Plasma concentrations of anxiolytic neurosteroids in men with normal anxiety scores: A correlation analysis. *Neuropsychobiology, 50*(1), 6–9.

Brambilla, F., Mellado, C., Alciati, A., Pisu, M. G., Purdy, R. H., Zanone, S., Perini, G., Serra, M., & Biggio, G. (2005). Plasma concentration of anxiolytic neuroactive steroids in men with panic disorder. *Psychiatry Research, 135*(3), 185–190.

Brawman-Mintzer, O., & Lydiard, R. B. (1996). Generalized anxiety disorder: Issues in epidemiology. *Journal of Clinical Psychiatry, 57*(7), 3–8.

Brawman-Mintzer, O., & Lydiard, R. B. (1997). Biological basis of generalized anxiety disorder. *Journal of Clinical Psychiatry, 58*(3), 16–25.

Brawman-Mintzer, O., & Yonkers, K. A. (2004). New trends in the treatment of anxiety disorders. *CNS Spectrums, 9*(8 Suppl 7), 19–27.

Breiter, H. C., Etcoff, N. L., Whalen, P. J., Kennedy, W. A., Rauch, S. L., Buckner, R. L., Strauss, M. M., Hyman, S. E., & Rosen, B. R. (1996). Response and habituation of the human amygdala during visual processing of facial expression. *Neuron, 17*, 875–887.

Breiter, H. C., Filipek, P. A., Kennedy, D. N., Baer, L., Pticher, D. A., Olivares, M. J., Rensha, W. P. F., & Caviness, V. S. (1994). Retrocallosal white matter abnormalities in patients with obsessive- compulsive disorder. *Archives of General Psychiatry, 51*, 663–664.

Breiter, H. C., & Rauch, S. L. (1996). Functional MRI and the study of OCD: From symptom provocation to cognitive-behavioral probes of cortico-striatal systems and the amygdala. *Neuroimaging, 4*(3, 3), 127–138.

Bremner, J. D. (1999). Does stress damage the brain? *Biological Psychiatry, 45*, 797–805.

Bremner, J. D. (2003). Long-term effects of childhood abuse on brain and neurobiology. *Child and Adolescent Psychiatric Clinics of North America, 12*(2), 271–292.

Bremner, J. D. (2003b). Functional neuroanatomical correlates of tramatic stress revisited seven years later, this time with data. *Psychopharmacology Bulletin, 37*(2), 6–25.

Bremner, J. D., Randall, P. R., Scott, T. M., Bronen, E. A., Seibyl, J. P., Southwick, S. M., Delaney, R. C., McCarthy, G., Charney, D. S., & Innis, R. B. (1995). MRI-based measurement of hippocampal volume in patients with combat-related posttraumatic stress disorder. *American Journal of Psychiatry, 152*(7), 973–981.

Bremner, J. D., & Vermetten, E. (2001). Stress and development: Behavioral and biological consequences. *Developmental Psychopathology, 13*(3), 473–489.

Bremner, J. D., & Vermetten, E. (2004). Neuroanatomical changes associated with pharmacotherapy in posttraumatic stress disorder. *Annals of the New York Academy of Sciences, 1032,* 154–157.

Bremner, J. D., Vermetten, E., Schmahl, C., Vaccarino, V., Vythilingam, M., Afzal, N., Grillon, C., & Charney, D. S. (2005). Positron emission tomographic imaging of neural correlates of a fear acquisition and extinction paradigm in women with childhood sexual-abuse-related posttraumatic stress disorder. *Psychological Medicine, 35*(6), 791–806.

Brett, E. A. (1993). Psychoanalytic contributions to a theory of traumatic stress. In J. P. Wilson & B. Raphael (Eds.), *International Handbook of Traumatic Stress Syndromes* (pp. 61–68). New York: Plenum.

Brewin, C. R. (2001). A cognitive neuroscience account of posttraumatic stress disorder and its treatment. *Behaviour Research and Therapy, 39*(4), 373–393.

Brewin, C. R., Andrews, B., & Rose, S. (2003). Diagnostic overlap between acute stress disorder and PTSD in victims of violent crime. *American Journal of Psychiatry, 160,* 783–785.

Britton, J. C., Phan, K. L., Taylor, S. F., Fig, L. M., & Liberzon, I. (2005). Corticolimbic blood flow in posttraumatic stress disorder during script-driven imagery. *Biological Psychiatry, 57*(8), 832–840.

Brody, A. L., Saxena, S., Schwartz, J. M., Stoessel, P. W., Maidment, K., Phelps, M. E., & Baxter, L. R. (1998). FDG-PET predictors of response to behavioral therapy and pharmacotherapy in obsessive-compulsive disorder. *Psychiatry Research, 84*(1), 1–6.

Brody, N. (1997). Dispositional paradigms: Comment on Eysenck (1997) and the biosocial science of individual differences. *Journal of Personality and Social Psychology, 73,* 1242–1245.

Brody, N., & Ehrlichman, H. (1998). *Personality Psychology: The Science of Individuality.* Upper Saddle River, NJ: Prentice Hall.

Broman-Fulks, J. J., Berman, M. E., Rabian, B. A., & Webster, M. J. (2004). Effects of aerobic exercise on anxiety sensitivity. *Behaviour Research and Therapy, 42*(2), 125–136.

Broocks, A., Meyer, T., Opitz, M., Bartmann, U., Hillmer-Vogel, U., George, A., Pekrun, G., Wedekind, D., Ruther, E., & Bandelow, B. (2003). 5HT1A responsivity in patients with panic disorder before and after treatment with aerobic exercise, clomipramine, or placebo. *European Neuropsychopharmacology, 13*(3), 153–164.

Brookler, K. H. (2004). Vestibular ENG findings in a patient with agoraphobia. *Ear, Nose, and Throat Journal, 83*(6), 387.

Brosen, K. (2004). Some aspects of genetic polymorphism in the biotransformation of antidepressants. *Therapie, 59*(1), 5–12.

Brown, E. S., Varghese, F. P., & McEwen, B. S. (2004). Association of depression with medical illness: Does cortisol play a role? *Biological Psychiatry, 55*(1), 1–9.

Brown, M., Smits, J. A., Powers, M. B., & Telch, M. J. (2003). Differential sensitivity of the three ASI factors in predicting panic disorder patients' subjective and behavioral response to hyperventilation challenge. *Journal of Anxiety Disorders, 17*(5), 583–591.

Brown, T. A., Campbell, L. A., Lehman, C. L., Grisham, J. R., & Mancill, R. B. (2001). Current and lifetime comorbidity of the DSM-IV anxiety and mood disorders in a large clinical sample. *Journal of Abnormal Psychology, 110*(4), 49–58.

Brown, T. A., Chorpita, B. F., & Barlow, D. H. (1998). Structural relationships among dimensions of the DSM-IV anxiety and mood disorders and dimensions of negative affect, positive affect, and autonomic arousal. *Journal of Abnormal Psychology, 107,* 179–192.

Brunello, N., Blier, P., Judd, L. L., Mendlewicz, J., Nelson, C. J., Souery, D., Zohar, J., & Racagni, G. (2003). Noradrenaline in mood and anxiety disorders: Basic and clinical studies. *International Clinical Psychopharmacology, 18*(4), 191–202.

Brunello, N., den Boer, J. A., & Judd, L. L. (2000). Social phobia: Diagnosis and epidemiology, neurobiology and pharmacology, Comorbidity and treatment. *Journal of Affective Disorders, 60*(1), 61–74.

Bryant, R. A., Felmingham, K. L., Kemp, A. H., Barton, M., Peduto, A. S., Rennie, C., Gordon, E., & Williams, L. M. (2005). Neural networks of information processing in posttraumatic stress disorder: A functional magnetic resonance imaging study. *Biological Psychiatry, 58*(2), 111–118.

Bucci, P., Mucci, A., Volpe, U., Merlotti, E., Galderisi, S., & Maj, M. (2004). Executive hypercontrol in obsessive-compulsive disorder: Electrophysiological and neuropsychological indices. *Clinical Neurophysiology, 115*(6), 1340–1348.

Bugenthal, J. F. T. (1965). *The Search or Authenticity*. New York: Holt, Rinehart, & Winston.

Bugenthal, J. F. T. (1976). *The Search for Existential Identity*. San Francisco, California: Jossey-Bass.

Busatto, G. F., Buchpiguel, C. A., Zamignani, D. R., Garrido, G. E., Glabus, M. F., Rosario-Campos, M. C., Castro, M. C., Maia, A., Rocha, E. T., McGuire, P. K., & Miguel, E. C. (2001). Regional cerebral blood flow abnormalities in early-onset obsessive-compulsive disorder: An exploratory SPECT study. *Journal of American Academy of Child and Adolescent Psychiatry, 40*(3), 347–354.

Busatto, G. F., Zamignani, D. R., Buchpiguel, C. A., Garrido, G. E., Glabus, M. F., Rocha, E. T., Maia, A. F., Rosario-Campos, M. C., Castro, C., Furuie, S. S., Gutierrez, M. A., McGuire, P. K., & Miguel, E. C. (2000). A voxel-based investigation of regional cerebral blood flow abnormalities in obsessive-compulsive disorder using single photon emission computed tomography (SPECT). *Psychiatry Research, 99*(1), 15–27.

Bush, G., Luu, P., & Posner, M. I. (2000). Cognitive and emotional influences in anterior cingulate cortex. *Trends in Cognitive Science, 4*, 215–222.

Buss, D. M., & Cantor, N. (Eds.). (1989). *Personality Psychology: Recent Trends and Emerging Directions*. New York: Springer-Verlag.

Bymaster, F. P., Beedle, E. E., Findlay, J., Gallagher, P. T., Krushinski, J. H., Mitchell, S., Robertson, D. W., Thompson, D. C., Wallace, L., & Wong, D. T. (2003). Duloxetine (Cymbalta), a dual inhibitor of serotonin and norepinephrine reuptake. *Bioorganic & Medicinal Chemistry Letters, 13*(24), 4477–4480.

Bymaster, F. P., Katner, J. S., Nelson, D. L., Hemrick-Luecke, S. K., Threlkeld, P. G., Heilgenstein, J. H., Morin, S. M., Gehlert, D. R., & Perry, K. W. (2002). Atomoxetine increases extracellular levels of norepinephrine and dopamine in prefrontal cortex of rat: A potential mechanism of efficacy in attention deficit hyperactivity disorder. *Neuropsychopharmacology, 27*(5), 699–711.

Bymaster, F. P., Rasmussen, K., Calligaro, D. O., Nelson, D. L., DeLapp, N. W., Wong, D. T., & Moore, N. A. (1997). In vitro and in vivo biochemistry of olanzapine: A novel, atypical antipsychotic drug. *Journal of Clinical Psychiatry, 55*(A), 42–52.

Caccia, S. (2004). Metabolism of the newest antidepressants: Comparisons with related predecessors. *IDrugs, 7*(2), 143–150.

Calamari, J. E., Wiegartz, P. S., Rieman, B. C., Cohen, R. J., Greer, A., Jacobi, D. M., Jahn, S. C., & Carmin, C. (2004). Obsessive-compulsive disorder subtypes: An attempted replication and extension of a symptom-based taxonomy. *Behaviour Research and Therapy, 42*(6), 647–670.

Calixto, A. V., Vandresen, N., de Nucci, G., Moreno, H., & Faria, M. S. (2001). Nitric oxide may underlie learned fear in the elevated T-maze. *Brain Research Bulletin, 55*(1), 37–42.

Camarena, B., Aguilar, A., Loyzaga, C., & Nicolini, H. (2004). A family-based association study of the 5HT1Dbeta receptor gene in obsessive-compulsive disorder. *International Journal of Neuropsychopharmacology, 7*(1), 49–53.

Camarena, B., Rinetti, G., Cruz, C., Gomez, A., de la Fuente, J. R., & Nicolini, H. (2001). Additional evidence that genetic variation of MAO-A gene supports a gender subtype in obsessive-compulsive disorder. *American Journal of Medical Genetics, 105*(3), 279–282.

Campbell, B. M., & Merchant, K. M. (2003). Serotonin 2C receptors within the basolateral amygdala induces acute fear-like responses in an open-field environment. *Brain Research, 993*(1–2), 1–9.

Campisi, A., Caccamo, D., Raciti, G., Cannavo, G., Macaione, V., Curro, M., Macaione, S., Vanella, A., & Ientile, R. (2003). Glutamate-induced increases in transglutaminase activity in primary cultures of astroglial cells. *Brain Research, 978*(1–2), 24–30.

Cannistraro, P. A., & Rauch, S. L. (2003). Neural circuitry of anxiety: Evidence from structural and functrional neuroimaging studies. *Psychological Bulletin, 37*(4), 8–25.

Cannistraro, P. A., Wright, C. I., Wedig, M. M., Martis, B., Shin, L. M., Wilhelm, S., & Rauch, S. L. (2004). Amygdala responses to human faces in obsessive-compulsive disorder. *Biological Psychiatry, 56*(12), 916–920.

Cannon, W. B. (1929). *Bodily Changes in Pain, Hunger, Fear, and Rage.* Boston: Branford.

Carey, P. D., Warwick, J., Harvey, B. H., Stein, D. J., & Seedat, S. (2004). Single photon emission computed tomography (SPECT) in obsessive-compulsive disorder before and after treatment with inositol. *Metabolic Brain Disorders, 19*(1–2), 125–134.

Carlini, V. P., Varas, M. M., Cragnolini, A. B., Schioth, H. B., Scimonelli, T. N., & De Barioglio, S. R. (2004). Differential role of the hippocampus, amygdala, and dorsal raphe nucleus in regulating feeding, memory, and anxiety-like behavioral responses to ghrelin. *Biochemical and Biophysical Research Communications, 313*(3), 635–641.

Carlsson, M. L. (2001). On the role of prefrontal cortex glutamate for the antithetical phenomenology of obsessive-compulsive disorder and attention deficit hyperactivity disorder. *Progress in Neuropsychopharmacology & Biological Psychiatry, 25*(1), 5–26.

Carlsson, M. L., Calsson, A., & Nilsson, M. (2004). Schizophrenia: From dopamine to glutamate and back. *Current Medicinal Chemistry, 11*(3), 267–277.

Carpenter, L. L., Tyrka, A. R., McDougle, C. J., Malison, R. T., Owens, M. J., Nemeroff, C. B., & Price, L. H. (2004). Cerebrospinal fluid corticotrophin-releasing factor and perceived early-life stress in depressed patients and healthy control subjects. *Neuropsychopharmacology, 29*(4), 777–784.

Carrasco, G. A., & Van de Kar, L. D. (2003). Neuroendocrine pharmacology of stress. *European Journal of Pharmacology, 463*(1–3), 235–272.

Carson, S. W. (1996). Pharmacokinetic and psychodynamic drug interactions with polypharmacotherapy of treatment-resistant affective and obsessive-compulsive disorders. *Psychopharmacology Bulletin, 32*(4), 555–568.

Carson, W. H., & Kitagawa, H. (2004). Drug development for anxiety disorders: New roles for atypical antipsychotics. *Psychopharmacology Bulletin, 38*(1), 38–45.

Cartwright-Hatton, S., Roberts, C., Chitsabesan, P., Fothergill, C., & Harrington, R. (2005). Systematic review of the efficacy of cognitive behaviour therapies for childhood and adolescent anxiety disorders. *British Journal of Clinical Psychology, 43*(4), 421–436.

Carvajal, C. C., Vercauteren, F., Dumont, Y., Michalkiewicz, M., & Quirion, R. (2004). Aged neuropeptide Y transgenic rats are resistant to acute stress but maintain spatial and non-spatial learning. *Behavioural Brain Research, 153*(2), 471–480.

Cashdan, S. (1988). *Object relations therapy: Using the relationship.* New York: Norton.

Castillo, A. R., Buchpiguel, C. A., de Araujo, L. A., Castillo, J. C., Asbahr, F. R., Maia, A. K., & de Oliveira Latorre, M. R. (2005). Brain SPECT imaging in children and adolescents with obsessive-compulsive disorder. *Journal of Neural Transmission, 24*, 1–8.

Castrogiovanni, P., Iapichino, S., Pacchierotti, C., & Pieraccini, F. (1998). Season of birth in psychiatry: A review. *Neuropsychobiology, 37*, 175–181.

Cath, D. C., Spinhoven, P., Landman, A. D., & Van Kempen, G. M. (2001). Psychopathology and personality characteristics in relation to blood serotonin in Tourette's syndrome and obsessive- compulsive disorder. *Journal of Psychopharmacology, 15*(2), 111–119.

Cavedini, P., Erzegovesi, S., Ronchi, P., & Bellodi, L. (1997). Predictive value of obsessive-compulsive personality disorder in antiobsessional pharmacological treatment. *European Neuropsychopharmacology, 7*(1), 45–49.

Cavedini, R., Cavedini, P., Mistretta, P., Bassi, T., Angelone, S. M., Ubbiali, A., & Bellodi, L. (2003). Basal-corticofrontal circuits in schizophrenia and obsessive-compulsive disorder: A controlled, double dissociation study. *Biological Psychiatry, 54*(4), 437–443.

Chabane, N., Millet, B., Delorme, R., Lichtermann, D., Mathieu, F., Laplanche, J. L., Roy, I., Mouren, M. C., Hankard, R., Maier, W., Launay, J. M., & Leboyer, M. (2004). Lack of evidence for association between serotonin transporter gene (5–HTTLPR) and obsessive-compulsive disorder by case control and family association in humans. *Neuroscience, 363*(2), 154–156.

Chakrabarty, K., Bhattacharyya, S., Christopher, R., & Khanna, S. (2005). Glutamatergic dysfunction in OCD. *Neuropsychopharmacology, 4*, 1–7.

Chambers, J. A., Power, K. G., & Durham, R. C. (2004). The relationship between trait vulnerability and anxiety and depressive diagnoses at long-term follow-up of generalized anxiety disorder. *Journal of Anxiety Disorders, 18*(5), 587–607.

Charney, D. S. (2003). Neuroanatomical circuits modulating fear and anxiety behaviors. *Acta Psychiatrica Scandinavica Supplement, 417*, 38–50.

Charney, D. S., & Deutch, A. Y. (1996). A functional neuroanatomy of anxiety and fear: Implications for the pathophysiology and treatment of anxiety disorders. *Critical Reviews in Neurobiology, 10*, 419–446.

Charney, D. S., & Woods, S. W. (1989). Benzodiazepine treatment of panic disorder: A comparison of alprazolam and lorazepam. *Journal of Clinical Psychiatry, 40*, 1129–1132.

Chavira, D. A., Stein, M. B., & Malcarne, V. L. (2002). Scrutinizing the relationship between shyness and social phobia. *Journal of Anxiety Disorders, 16*, 585–598.

Chelben, J., Strous, R. D., Lustig, M., & Baruch, Y. (2001). Remission of SSRI-induced akathisia after switch to nefazodone. *Journal of Clinical Psychiatry, 62*(7), 570–571.

Chen, K., Holschneider, D. P., Wu, W., Rebrin, I., & Shih, J. C. (2004). A spontaneous point mutation produces MAO A/B knock-out mice with greatly elevated monoamines and anxiety- like behavior. *Journal of Biological Chemistry, 7*, 7–14.

Chen, X. L., Xie, J. X., Han, H. B., Cui, Y. H., & Zhang, B. Q. (2004). MR perfusion-weighted imaging and quantitative analysis of cerebral hemodynamics with symptom provocation in unmedicated patients with obsessive-compulsive disorder. *Neuroscience Letter, 370*(2–3), 206–211.

Chiu, L. H. (1971). Manifest anxiety in Chinese and American children. *Journal of Psychology, 79*(2), 273–284.

Choi, J. S., Kang, D. H., Kim, J. J., Ha, T. H., Lee, J. M., Youn, T., Kim, I. Y., Kim, S. I., & Kwon, J. S. (2004). Left anterior subregion of orbitofrontal cortex volume reduction and impaired organizational strategies in obsessive-compulsive disorder. *Journal of Psychiatric Research, 38*(2), 193–199.

Chorpita, B. F. (2002). The tripartite model and dimensions of anxiety and depression: An examination structure in a large school sample. *Journal of Abnormal Child Psychology, 30*(2), 177–190.

Chouinard, G. (2004). Issues in the clinical use of benzodiazepines: Potency, withdrawal, and rebound. *Journal of Clinical Psychiatry, 65*(5), 7–12.

Chouinard, G., Goodman, W., Greist, J., Jenike, M., Rasmussen, S., White, K., Hackett, E., Gaffney, M., & Brick, P. A. (1990). Results of a double0–blind placebo controlled trial of a new serotonin uptake inhibitor, sertraline, in the treatment of obsessive-compulsive disorder. *Psychopharmacology Bulletin*, 26(3), 78–94.

Christensen, H. D., Gonzalez, C. L., & Rayburn, W. F. (2003). Effects from prenatal exposure to alprazolam on the social behavior of mice offspring. *American Journal of Obstetrics and Gynecology*, 189(5), 1452–1457.

Cialdini, R. B. (2001). *Influence: Science and Practice* (4th Ed.). Boston: Allyn & Bacon.

Ciesielski, K. T., Hamalainen, M. S., Lesnik, P. G., Geller, D. A., & Ahlfors, S. P. (2005). Increased MEG activation in OCD reflects a compensatory mechanism specific to the phase of a visual working memory task. *Neuroimaging*, 24(4), 1180–1191.

Cillicilli, A. S., Telcioglu, M., Askin, R., Kaya, N., Bodur, S., & Kucur, R. (2004). Twelve-month prevalence of obsessive-compulsive disorder in Konya, Turkey. *Comprehensive Psychiatry*, 45(5), 367–374.

Citrome, L., Casey, D. E., Daniel, D. G., Wozniak, P., Kochan, L. D., & Tracy, K. A. (2004). Adjunctive divalproex and hostility among patients with schizophrenia receiving olanzapine or risperidone. *Psychiatric Services*, 55, 290–294.

Clark, D. M., Salkovskis, P. M., & Chalkley, A. J. (1985). Respiratory control as a treatment for panic attacks. *Journal of Behavior Therapy and Experimental Psychiatry*, 16, 23–30.

Clayton, P. J. (2004). PSTD, acute stress disorder, and DSM-V. *American Journal of Psychiatry*, 161(3), 584.

Clement, Y., Calatayud, F., & Belzung, C. (2002). Genetic basis of anxiety-like behavior: A critical review. *Brain Research Bulletin*, 57(1), 57–71.

Clement, Y., & Chapouthier, G. (1998). Biological bases of anxiety. *Neuroscience and Biobehavioural Reviews*, 22, 623–633.

Cloitre, M., Chase Stovall-McClough, K., Miranda, R., & Chemtob, C. M. (2004). Therapeutic alliance, negative mood regulation, and treatment outcome in child abuse-related posttraumatic stress disorder. *Journal of Consulting and Clinical Psychology*, 72(3), 411–416.

Cloitre, M., Yonkers, K. A., Pearlstein, T., Altemus, M., Davidson, K. W., Pigott, T. A., Shear, M. K., Pine, D., Ross, J., Howell, H., Brogan, K., Rieckmann, N., & Clemow, L. (2004). Women and anxiety disorders: Implications for diagnosis and treatment. *CNS Spectrums*, 9(9 Suppl 8), 1–16.

Clouatre, D. L. (2004). Kava kava: Examining new reports of toxicity. *Toxicology Letters*, 150(1), 85–96.

Clough, A. R., Rowley, K., & O'Dea, K. (2004). Kava use, dyslipidaemia, and biomarkers of dietary quality in Aboriginal people in Arnhem Land in the Northern Territory (NT), Australia. *European Journal of Clinical Nutrition*, 58(7), 1090–1093.

Coetzer, B. R. (2004). Obsessive-compulsive disorder following brain injury: A review. *International Journal of Psychiatry and Medicine*, 34(4), 363–377.

Coles, M. E., Heimberg, R. G., Frost, R. O., & Steketee, G. (2005). Not just right experiences and obsessive-compulsive features: Experimental and self-monitoring perspectives. *Behaviour Research and Therapy*, 43(2), 153–167.

Comer, J. S., Kendall, P. C., Franklin, M. E., Hudson, J. L., & Pimentel, S. S. (2004). Obsessing/worrying about the overlap between obsessive-compulsive disorder and generalized anxiety disorder in youth. *Clinical Psychology Review*, 24(6), 663–683.

Comings, D. E., Gonzalez, N. S., Cheng Li, S. C., & MacMurray, J. (2003). A "line item" approach to the identification of genes involved in polygenic behavioral disorders: The adrenergic alpha2A gene. *American Journal of Medical Genetics*, 118(1), 110–114.

Commons, K. G., & Valentino, R. J. (2002). Cellular basis for the effects of substance P in the periaqueductal gray and dorsal raphe nucleus. *Journal of Comparative Neurology*, 447(1), 82–97.

Connor, K. M., & Davidson, J. R. (2002). A placebo-controlled study of kava kava in generalized anxiety disorder. *International Clinical Psychopharmacology, 17*(4), 185–188.

Connor, K. M., Payne, V. M., Gadde, K. M., Zhang, W., & Davidson, J. R. (2005). The use of aripiprazole in obsessive-compulsive disorder: Preliminary observations in eight patients. *Journal of Clinical Psychiatry, 66*(1), 49–51.

Conti, L. H., Jirout, M., Breen, L., Vanella, J. J., Schork, N. J., & Printz, M. P. (2004). Identification of quantitative trait loci for anxiety and locomotion phenotypes in rat recombinant inbred strains. *Behavior Genetics, 34*(1), 93–103.

Cooper, J., Carty, J., & Creamer, M. (2005). Pharmacotherapy for posttraumatic stress disorder: Empirical review and clinical recommendations. *The Australian New Zealand Journal of Psychiatry, 39*(8), 674–682.

Coplan, J. D., & Lydiard, R. B. (1998). Brain circuits in panic disorder. *Biological Psychiatry, 44,* 1264–1276.

Coplan, J. D., Pine, D. S., Papp, L. A., & Gorman, J. M. (1997). A view of noradrenergic, hypothalamic-pituitary-adrenal axis and extrahypothalamic corticotrophin-releasing factor function in anxiety and affective disorders: The reduced growth hormone response to clonidine. *Psychopharmacology Bulletin, 33,* 193–204.

Cordner, A. P., Herwood, M. B., Helmreich, D. L., & Parfitt, D. B. (2004). Antidepressants blunt the effects of inescapable stress on male mating behavior and decrease corticotropin-releasing hormone mRNA expression in the hypothalamic paracentricular nucleus of the Syrian hamster (mesocricetus auratus). *Journal of Neuroendocrinology, 16*(7), 628–636.

Correll, C. U., Leucht, S., & Kane, J. M. (2004). Lower risk for tardive dyskinesia associated with second-generation antipsychotics: A systematic review of one-year studies. *American Journal of Psychiatry, 161,* 414–425.

Cosci, F., Gooyer, T., Schruers, K., Faravelli, C., & Griez, E. (2005). The influence of ethanol infusion on the effects of 35% CO2 challenge: A study in panic disorder patients and healthy volunteers. *European Psychiatry, 20*(3), 299–303.

Cote, C. S., Kor, C., Cohen, J., & Auclair, K. (2004). Composition and biological activity of traditional and commercial kava extracts. *Biochemical and Biophysical Research Communications, 322*(1), 147–152.

Coupey, S. M. (1997). Barbiturates. *Pediatric Review, 18*(8), 260–264.

Couprie, C., & Lacarelle, B. (2004). Bioequivalence and therapeutic equivalence in psychiatry. *Encephale, 30*(2), 167–170.

Cox, B. J., MacPherson, P. S., Enns, M. W., & McWilliams, L. A. (2004). Neuroticism and self-criticism associated with posttraumatic stress disorder in a nationally representative sample. *Behavioral Research and Therapy, 42*(1), 105–114.

Craske, M. G., Poulton, R., Tsao, J. C., & Poltkin, D. (2001). Paths to panic disorder/agoraphobia: An exploratory analysis from age three to 21 in an unselected birth cohort. *Journal of the American Academy of Child and Adolescent Psychiatry, 40*(5), 556–563.

Craske, M. G., & Rowe, M. K. (1997). Nocturnal panic. *Clinical Psychology: Science & Practice, 4,* 153–174.

Crawford, R. (2004). Risk ritual and the management of control and anxiety in medical culture. *Health, 8*(4), 505–528.

Creamer, M., McFarlane, A. C., & Burgess, P. (2005). Psychopathology following trauma: The role of subjective experience. *Journal of Affective Disorders, 86*(2–3), 175–182.

Crespo-Facorro, B., Cabranes, J. A., Lopez-Ibor Alcocer, M. I., Paya, B., Fernandez-Perez, C., Encinas, M., Ayuso-Mateos, J. L., & Lopez-Ibor, J. J. (1999). Regional cerebral blood flow in obsessive-compulsive patients with and without a chronic tic disorder: A SPECT study. *European Archives of Psychiatry and Clinical Neuroscience, 249*(3), 156–161.

Cronin, N. B., O'Reilly, A., Duclohier, H., & Wallace, B. A. (2003). Binding of the anticonvulsant drug lamotrigine and the neurotoxin batrachotoxin to voltage-gated sodium channels induces conformational changes associated with block and steady-state activation. *Journal of Biological Chemistry, 278*(12), 10675–10682.

Cropley, M., Cave, Z., Ellis, J., & Middleton, R. W. (2002). Effect of kava and valerian on human physiological and psychological responses to mental stress assessed under laboratory conditions. *Phytotherapy Research, 16*(1), 23–27.

Cruz-Fuentes, C., Blas, C., Gonzalez, L., Camarena, B., & Nicolini, H. (2004). Severity of obsessive- compulsive symptoms is related to self-directedness character traits in obsessive-compulsive disorder. *CNS Spectrums, 9*(8), 607–612.

Cryan, J. F., Kelly, P. H., Chaperon, F., Gentsch, C., Mombereau, C., Lingenhoehl, K., Froestl, W., Bettler, B., Kaupmann, K., & Spooren, W. P. (2004). Behavioral characterization of the novel GABA(B) receptor-positive modulator GS39783 (N, N'-dicyclopentyl-2-methylsulfanyl-5-nitro-pyrimidine-4,6- diamine): Anxiolytic-like activity without side effects associated with baclofen or benzodiazepines. *Journal of Pharmacology and Experimental Therapies, 310*(3), 952–963.

Cryan, J. F., Kelly, P. H., Neijt, H. C., Sansig, G., Flor, P. J., & Van der Putten, H. (2003). Antidepressant and anxiolytic-like effects in mice lacking the group III metabotropic glutamate receptor mGluR7. *European Journal of Neuroscience, 17*(11), 2409–2417.

Curtin, F., & Schulz, P. (2004). Clonazepam and lorazepam in acute mania: A Bayesian meta-analysis. *Journal of Affective Disorders, 78*(3), 201–208.

Czlonkowska, A. I., Zienowicz, M., Bidzinski, A., Maciejak, P., Lehner, M., Taracha, E., Wislowska, A., & Plaznik, A. (2003). The role of neurosteroids in the anxiolytic, antidepressive-, and anticonvulsive effects of selective serotonin reuptake inhibitors. *Medical Science Monitor, 9*(11), 270–275.

Dadds, M. R., & Roth, J. H. (2001). Family processes in the development of anxiety problems. In M. W. Vasey & M. R. Dadds (Eds.), *The Developmental Psychopathology of Anxiety* (pp. 278–303). New York: Oxford University Press.

Daldrup, R. J., Engle, D., Holiman, M., & Beutler, L. E. (1994). The intensification and resolution of blocked affect in an experiential psychotherapy. *British Journal of Clinical Psychology, 33*(2), 129–141.

Dale, R. C., Heyman, I., Surtees, R. A., Church, A. J., Giovannoni, G., Goodman, R., & Neville, B. G. (2004). Dyskinesias and associated psychiatric disorders following streptococcal infections. *Archives of Disorders in Children, 89*(7), 604–610.

Dalgleish, T., & Power, M. J. (2004). Emotion-specific and emotion-non-specific components of posttraumatic stress disorder (PTSD): Implications for a taxonomy of related psychopathology. *Behaviour Research and Therapy, 42*(9), 1069–1088.

Daniels, W. M., Pietersen, C. Y., Carstens, M. E., & Stein, D. J. (2004). Maternal separation in rats leads to anxiety-like behavior and a blunted ACTH response and altered neurotransmitter levels in response to a subsequent stressor. *Metabolic Brain Disorders, 19*(1–2), 3–14.

Daniels, W. M., Richter, L., & Stein, D. J. (2004). The effects of repeated intra-amygdala CRF injections on rat behavior and HPA axis function after stress. *Metabolic Brain Disorders, 19*(1–2), 15–23.

D'ardenne, P., Capuzzo, N., Fakhoury, W. K., Jankovic-Gavrilovic, J., & Priebe, S. (2005). Subjective quality of life and posttraumatic stress disorder. *Journal of Nervous and Mental Disorders, 193*(1), 62–65.

Darnaudery, M., Dutriez, I., Viltart, O., Morley-Fletcher, S., & Maccari, S. (2004). Stress during gestation induces lasting effects on emotional reactivity of the dam rat. *Behavioural Brain Research, 153*(1), 211–216.

Davids, E., Muller, M. J., Rollman, N., Burkart, M., Regier-Klein, E., Szegedi, A., Benkert, O., & Maier, W. (2002). Syndrome profiles in alcoholism and panic disorder with or without agoraphobia: An explorative family study. *Progress in Neuro-psychopharmacology & Biological Psychiatry, 26*(6), 1079–1087.

Davidson, J. R. (1998). Pharmacotherapy of social anxiety disorder. *Journal of Clinical Psychiatry, 59*(17), 47–52.

Davidson, J. R. (2000a). Pharmacotherapy of posttraumatic stress disorder: Treatment options, long-term follow-up, and predictors of outcome. *Journal of Clinical Psychiatry, 61*(5), 52–56.

Davidson, J. R. (2000b). Trauma: The impact of post-traumatic stress disorder. *Journal of Psychopharmacology, 14*(1), 5–12.

Davidson, J. R. (2004b). Use of benzodiazepines in social anxiety disorder, generalized anxiety disorder, and posttraumatic stress disorder. *Journal of Clinical Psychiatry, 65*(5), 29–33.

Davidson, J. R. (2004c). Long-term treatment and prevention of posttraumatic stress disorder. *Journal of Clinical Psychiatry, 65*(1), 44–48.

Davies, E., & MacKenzie, S. M. (2003). Extra-adrenal production of corticosteroids. *Clinical and Experimental Pharmacology & Physiology, 30*(7), 437–445.

Davies, J., Lloyd, K. R., Jones, I. K., Barnes, A., & Pilowsky, L. S. (2003). Changes in regional cerebral blood flow with venlafaxine in the treatment of major depression. *American Journal of Psychiatry, 160*(2), 374–376.

Davis, L. L., Jewell, M. E., Ambrose, S., Farley, J., English, B., Bartolucci, A., & Petty, F. (2004). A placebo-controlled study of nefazodone for the treatment of chronic posttraumatic stress disorder: A preliminary study. *Journal of Clinical Psychopharmacology, 24*(3), 291–297.

Davis, M., & Shi, C. (1999). The extended amygdala: Are the central nucleus of the amygdala and the bed nucleus of the stria terminalis differentially involved in fear versus anxiety? *Annals of the New York Academy of Sciences, 877,* 281–291.

De Bellis, M. D., & Keshavan, M. S. (2003). Sex differences in the brain maturation in maltreatment- related pediatric posttraumatic stress disorder. *Neuroscience and Biobehavioral Review, 27*(1–2), 103–117.

De Cristofaro, M. T., Sessarego, A., Pupi, A., Biondi, F., & Faravelli, C. (1993). Brain perfusion abnormalities in drug-naive, lactate sensitive panic patients: A SPECT study. *Biological Psychiatry, 33*(7), 505–512.

De Feo, V., & Faro, C. (2003). Pharmacological effects of extracts from valeriana adscendens: Effects on GABA uptake and amino acids. *Phytotherapy Research, 17*(6), 661–664.

De Gucht, V. (2003). Stability of neuroticism and alexithymia in somatization. *Comprehensive Psychiatry, 44*(6), 466–471.

De Jong, M. J., Moser, D. K., An, K., & Chung, M. L. (2004). Anxiety is not manifested by elevated heart rate and blood pressure in acutely ill cardiac patients. *European Journal of Cardiovascular Nursing, 3*(3), 247–253.

De Kloet, E. R., Sibug, R. M., Helmerhorst, F. M., & Schmidt, M. (2005). Stress, genes, and the mechanism of programming the brain for later life. *Neuroscience Biobehavioral Review, 29*(2), 271–281.

De Kloet, R. E. (2003). Hormones, brain, and stress. *Endocrinology Regulation, 37*(2), 51–68.

De Paula-Soares, V., & Zangrossi, H. (2004). Involvement of 5HT1A and 5HT2 receptors of the dorsal periaqueductal gray in the regulation of the defensive behaviors generated by the elevated T-maze. *Brain Research Bulletin, 64*(2), 181–188.

Deacon, R. M., Penny, C., & Rawlins, J. N. (2003). Effects of medial prefrontal cortex cytotoxic lesions in mice. *Behavioural Brain Research, 139*(1–2), 139–155.

Debiec, J., & Ledoux, J. E. (2004). Disruption of reconsolidation but not consolidation of auditory fear conditioning by noradrenergic blockade in the amygdala. *Neuroscience, 129*(2), 267–272.

Deckert, J. (1998). The adenosine A(2A) receptor knockout mouse: A model for anxiety? *International Journal of Neuropsychopharmacology, 1*(2), 187–190.

Degroot, A., & Nomikos, G. G. (2004). Genetic deletion and pharmacological blockade of CB1 receptor modulates anxiety in the shock-probe burying test. *European Journal of Neuroscience, 20*(4), 1059–1064.

Degroot, A., & Treit, D. (2004). Anxiety is functionally segregated within the septohippocampal system. *Brain Research, 1001*(1–2), 60–71.

Delagrange, P., Atkinson, J., Boutin, J. A., Casteilla, L., Lesieur, D., Misslin, R., Pellissier, S., Penicaud, L., & Renard, P. (2003). Therapeutic perspectives for melatonin agonists and antagonists. *Journal of Neuroendocrinology, 15*(4), 442–448.

Delgado, P. L., & Moreno, F. A. (1998). Different roles for serotonin in anti-obsessional drug action and the pathophysiology of obsessive-compulsive disorder. *British Journal of Psychiatry, 35,* 21–25.

Delorme, R., Krebs, M. O., Chabane, N., Roy, I., Millet, B., Mouren-Simeoni, M. C., Maier, W., Bourgeron, T., & Leboyer, M. (2004). Frequency and transmission of glutamate receptors GRIK2 and GRIK3 polymorphisms in patients with obsessive-compulsive disorder. *Neuroreport, 15*(4), 699–702.

DeMartinis, N., Rynn, M., Rickels, K., & Mandos, L. (2000). Prior benzodiazepine use and buspirone response in the treatment of generalized anxiety disorder. *Journal of Clinical Psychiatry, 61,* 91–94.

Denys, D., De Geus, F., Van Megen, H. J., & Westenberg, H. G. (2004). A double-blind, randomized, placebo-controlled trial of quetiapine addition in patients with obsessive-compulsive disorder refractory to serotonin reuptake inhibitors. *Journal of Clinical Psychiatry, 65*(8), 1040–1048.

Denys, D., De Geus, F., Van Megen, H. J., & Westenberg, H. G. (2004b). Symptom dimensions in obsessive-compulsive disorder: Factor analysis on a clinician-rated scale and a self-report measure. *Psychopathology, 37*(4), 181–189.

Denys, D., De Geus, F., Van Megen, H. J., & Westenberg, H. G. (2004c). Use of factor analysis to detect potential phenotypes in obsessive-compulsive disorder. *Psychiatry Research, 128*(3), 273–280.

Denys, D., Fluitman, S., Kavelaars, A., Heijnen, C., & Westenberg, H. (2004). Decreased TNF-alpha and NK activity in obsessive-compulsive disorder. *Psychoneuroendocrinology, 29*(7), 945–952.

Denys, D., Tenney, N., van Megen, H. J., de Geus, F., & Westenberg, H. G. (2004). Axis I and II comorbidity in a large sample of patients with obsessive-compulsive disorder. *Journal of Affective Disorders, 80*(2–3), 155–162.

Denys, D., van der Wee, N., Janssen, J., De Geus, F., & Westenberg, H. G. (2004). Low level of dopaminergic D2 receptor binding in obsessive-compulsive disorder. *Biological Psychiatry, 55*(10), 1041–1045.

Denys, D., Zohar, J., & Westenberg, H. G. (2004). The role of dopamine in obsessive-compulsive disorder: Preclinical and clinical evidence. *Journal of Clinical Psychiatry, 65*(14), 11–17.

De-Paris, F., Sant-Anna, M. K., Vianna, M. R., Barichello, T., Busnello, J. V., Kapczinski, F., Quevedo, J., & Izquierdo, I. (2003). Effects of gabapentin on anxiety induced by simulated public speaking. *Journal of Psychopharmacology, 17*(2), 184–188.

Devilly, G. L., & Spence, S. H. (1999). The relative efficacy and treatment distress of EMDR and a cognitive-behavioral trauma treatment protocol in the amelioration of post-traumatic stress disorder. *Journal of Anxiety Disorders, 13*(1–2), 131–157.

Dews, P. B., O'Brien, C. P., & Bergman, J. (2002). Caffeine: Behavioral effects of withdrawal and related issues. *Food, Chemistry, and Toxicology, 40*(9), 1257–1261.

Diefenbach, G. J., Hopko, D. R., Feigon, S., Stanley, M. A., Novy, D. M., Beck, J. G., & Averill, P. M. (2003). 'Minor GAD': Characteristics of subsyndromal GAD in older adults. *Behaviour Research and Therapy, 41*(4), 481–487.

Diler, R. S. (2003). Panic disorder in children and adolescents. *Yonsei Medical Journal*, *44*(1), 174–179.

Diler, R. S., Kibar, M., & Avci, A. (2004). Pharmacotherapy and regional cerebral blood flow in children with obsessive-compulsive disorder. *Yonsei Medical Journal*, *45*(1), 90–99.

Dinn, W. M., Harris, C. L., McGonigal, K. M., & Raynard, R. C. (2001). Obsessive-compulsive disorder and immunocompetence. *International Journal of Psychiatry Medicine*, *31*(3), 311–320.

Dinn, W. M., Harris, C. L., & Raynard, R. C. (1999). Posttraumatic obsessive-compulsive disorder: A three-factor model. *Psychiatry*, *62*(4), 313–324.

Dirkzwager, A. J., Bramsen, I., Ader, H., & Van der Ploeg, H. M. (2005). Secondary traumatization in partners and parents of Dutch peacekeeping soldiers. *Journal of Family Psychology*, *19*(2), 217–226.

Doghramji, K. (2000). The need for flexibility in dosing of hypnotic agents. *Sleep*, *23*(1), 16–20.

Dougherty, D. D., Baer, L., Cosgrove, G. R., Cassem, E. H., Price, B. H., Nierenberg, A. A., Jenike, M. A., & Rauch, S. L. (2002). Prospective long-term follow-up of 44 patients who received cingulotomy for treatment-refractory obsessive-compulsive disorder. *American Journal of Psychiatry*, *159*, 269–275.

Dougherty, D. D., Rauch, S. L., & Jenike, M. A. (2004). Pharmacotherapy for obsessive-compulsive disorder. *Journal of Clinical Psychology*, *60*(11), 1195–1202.

Doyle, A. C., & Pollack, M. H. (2003). Establishment of remission criteria for anxiety disorders. *The Journal of Clinical Psychiatry*, *64*(15), 40–45.

Dremencov, E., Gispan-Herman, I., Rosenstein, M., Mendelman, A., Overstreet, D. H., Zohar, J., & Yadid, G. (2004). The serotonin-dopamine interaction is critical for fast-onset action of antidepressant treatment: In vivo studies in an animal model of depression. *Progress in Neuropsychopharmacology & Biological Psychiatry*, *28*(1), 141–147.

Drevets, W. C. (1998). Functional neuroimaging studies of depression: The anatomy of melancholia. *Annual Review of Medicine*, *49*, 341–361.

Dugas, M. J., Ladouceur, R., Leger, E., Freeston, M. H., Langlois, F., Provenchen, M. D., & Boisvert, J. M. (2003). Group cognitive-behavioral therapy for generalized anxiety disorder: Treatment outcome and long-term follow-up. *Journal of Consulting and Clinical Psychology*, *71*(4), 821–825.

Dulawa, S. C., Holick, K. A., Gundersen, B., & Hen, R. (2004). Effects of chronic fluoxetine in animal models of anxiety and depression. *Neuropsychopharmacology*, *29*(7), 1321–1330.

Dundar, Y., Dodd, S., Strobl, J., Boland, A., Dickson, R., & Walley, T. (2004). Comparative efficacy of newer hypnotic drugs for the short-term management of insomnia: A systematic review and meta-analysis. *Human Psychopharmacology*, *19*(5), 305–322.

Dunner, D. L., Goldstein, D. J., Mallinckrodt, C., Lu, Y., & Detke, M. J. (2003). Duloxetine in treatment of anxiety symptoms associated with depression. *Depression and Anxiety*, *18*(2), 53–61.

Durand, V. M., & Barlow, D. H. (2003). *Essentials of Abnormal Psychology* (3rd Ed.). Pacific Grove, California: Wadsworth.

Durham, R. C., Chambers, J. A., MacDonald, R. R., Power, K. G., & Major, K. (2003). Does cognitive-behavioral therapy influence the long-term outcome of generalized anxiety disorder? An 8–14 year follow-up of two clinical trials. *Psychological Medicine*, *33*(3), 499–509.

Eaves, L., Heath, A., Martin, N., Maes, H., Neale, M., Kendler, K., Kirk, K., & Corey, L. (1999). Comparing the biological and cultural inheritance of personality and social attitudes in the Virginia 30,000 study of twins and their relatives. *Twin Research: The Official Journal of the International Society for Twin Studies*, *2*(2), 62–80.

Eddy, K. T., Dutra, L., Bradley, R., & Westen, D. (2004). A multidimensional meta-analysis of psychotherapy and pharmacotherapy for obsessive-compulsive disorder. *Clinical Psychology Review, 24*(8), 1011–1030.

Ehlers, A. (1995). A 1–year prospective study of panic attacks: Clinical course and factors associated with maintenance. *Journal of Abnormal Psychology, 104*, 164–172.

Einstein, D. A., & Menzies, R. G. (2004). Role of magical thinking in obsessive-compulsive symptoms in an undergraduate sample. *Depression and Anxiety, 19*(3), 174–179.

Eley, T. C., Bolton, D., O'Connor, T. G., Perrin, S., Smith, P., & Plomin, R. (2003). A twin study of anxiety-related behaviors in preschool children. *Journal of Child Psychology and Psychiatry and Other Allied Disciplines, 44*(7), 945–960.

Eley, T. C., Stirling, I., Ehlers, A., Gregory, A. M., & Clark, D. M. (2004). Heart-beat perception, panic somatic symptoms and anxiety sensitivity in children. *Behaviour Research and Therapy, 42*(4), 439–448.

Eley, T. C., Tahir, E., Angleitner, A., Harriss, K., McClay, J., Plomin, R., Riemann, R., Spinath, F., & Craig, I. (2003). Association analysis of MAOA and COMT with neuroticism assessed by peers. *American Journal of Medical Genetics, 120B* (1), 90–96.

Elklit, A., & Brink, O. (2004). Acute stress disorder as a predictor of posttraumatic stress disorder in physical assault victims. *Journal of Interpersonal Violence, 19*(6), 709–726.

Ellis, A. E. (1962). *Reason and Emotion in Psychotherapy.* New York: Lyle Stuart.

Ellis, A. E. (1971). *Growth through Reason.* Palo Alto, California: Science & Behavior Books.

Ellis, A. E. (1972). *How to Master your Fear of Flying.* New York: Curtis Books.

Ellis, A. E. (1973). *Humanistic Psychotherapy: The Rational-Emotive Approach.* New York: Julian.

Eloubeidi, M. A., Gaede, J. T., & Swaim, M. W. (2000). Reversible nefazodone-induced liver failure. *Science, 45*(5), 1036–1038.

Elsesser, K., Sartory, G., & Tackenberg, A. (2004). Attention, heart rate, and startle response during exposure to trauma-relevant pictures: A comparison of recent trauma victim and patients with posttraumatic stress disorder. *Journal of Abnormal Psychology, 113*(2), 289–301.

Ely, T. C. (1997). General genes: A new theme in developmental psychopathology. *Current Directions in Psychological Science, 6*, 90–95.

Elzinga, B. M., & Bremner, J. D. (2002). Are the neural substrates of memory the final common pathway in posttraumatic stress disorder? *Journal of Affective Disorders, 70*(1), 1–17.

Emslie, G. J., Weinberg, W. A., Kowatch, R. A., Hughes, C. W., Carmody, T. J., & Rush, A. J. (1997). Fluoxetine treatment of depressed children and adolescents. *Archives of General Psychiatry, 54*, 1031–1037.

Englander, M. T., Dulawa, S. C., Bhansali, P., & Schmauss, C. (2005). How stress and fluoxetine modulate serotonin 2C receptor pre-mRNA editing. *Journal of Neurosciences, 25*(3), 648–651.

Engle, D., & Holiman, M. (2004). A gestalt-experiential perspective on resistance. *Journal of Clinical Psychology, 58*(2), 175–183.

Enoch, M. A., Xu, K., Ferro, E., Harris, C. R., & Goldman, D. (2003). Genetic origins of anxiety in women: A role for a functional catechol-o-methyltransferase polymorphism. *Psychiatric Genetics, 13*(1), 33–41.

Epstein, G. N., Halper, J. P., Barrett, E. A., Birdsall, C., McGee, M., Baron, K. P., & Lowenstein, S. (2004). A pilot study of mind-body changes in adults with asthma who practice mental imagery. *Alternative Therapies, Health, and Medicine, 10*(4), 66–71.

Epting, F. R. (1984). *Personal Construct Counseling and Psychotherapy.* Chichester, England: Wiley Books.

Erdal, M. E., Tot, S., Yazici, K., Yazici, A., Herken, H., Erdem, P., Derici, E., & Camdeviren, H. (2003). Lack of association of catechol-o-methyltransferase gene polymorphism in obsessive-compulsive disorder. *Depression and Anxiety, 18*(1), 41–45.

Erel, U., Arborelius, L., & Brodin, E. (2004). Increased cholecystokinin release in the rat anterior cingulate cortex during carrageenan-induced arthritis. *Brain Research, 1022*(1–2), 39–46.

Erikson, E. H. (1950). *Childhood and Society.* New York: Norton.

Erzegovesi, S., Cavallini, M. C., & Cavedini, P. (2001). Clinical predictors of drug response in obsessive-compulsive disorder. *Journal of Clinical Psychopharmacology, 21*(5), 488–492.

Erzegovesi, S., Martucci, L., Henin, M., & Bellodi, L. (2001). Low versus standard dose mCPP challenge in obsessive-compulsive patients. *Neuropsychopharmacology, 24*(1), 31–36.

Esler, M., Alvarenga, M., Lambert, G., Kaye, D., Hastings, J., Jennings, G., Morris, M., Schwqarz, R., & Richards, J. (2004). Cardiac sympathetic nerve biology and brain monoamine turnover in panic disorder. *Annals of the New York Academy of Sciences, 1018,* 505–514.

Evans, D. W., Lewis, M. D., & Iobst, E. (2004). The role of the orbitofrontal cortex in normally developing compulsive-like behaviors and obsessive-compulsive disorder. *Brain Cognition, 55*(1), 220–234.

Eysenck, H. J. (1957). *The Dynamics of Anxiety and Hysteria.* London, England: Routledge & Kegan Paul.

Eysenck, H. J. (1959). Learning theory and behaviour therapy. *Journal of Mental Science, 105,* 61–75.

Eysenck, H. J. (1967). *The Biological Basis of Personality.* Springfield, Illinois: Thomas.

Eysenck, H. J. (1968). A theory of the incubation of anxiety/fear responses. *Behaviour Research and Therapy, 6,* 309–322.

Eysenck, H. J. (1991). Dimensions of personality: 16, 5, or 3—Criteria for a taxonomic paradigm. *Personality and Individual Differences, 12,* 773–790.

Fabre, V., & Hamon, M. (2003). Mechanisms of actions of antidepressants: New data from escitalopram. *Encephale, 29*(3), 259–265.

Fabricio, A. S., Tringali, G., Pozzoli, G., & Navarra, P. (2004). Mirtazapine acutely inhibits basal and K(+)–stimulated release of corticotropin-releaasing hormone from the rat hypothalamus via a non-genomic mechanism. *Psychopharmacology, 8*(1), 7–14.

Fahlen, T., Nilsson, H. L., Borg, K., Humble, M., & Pauli, U. (1995). Social phobia: The clinical efficacy and tolerability of the monoamine oxidase-A and serotonin uptake inhibitor brofaromine. *Acta Psychiatrica Scandinavica, 92,* 351–358.

Fairbairn, W. R. D. (1954). *An Object-Relations Theory of Personality.* New York: Basic Books.

Fairbrother, N., Newth, S. J., & Rachman, S. (2005). Mental pollution: Feelings of dirtiness without physical contact. *Behaviour Research and Therapy, 43*(1), 121–130.

Falkai, P. (1999). Mirtazapine: Other indications. *Journal of Clinical Psychiatry, 60*(17), 36–40.

Fanselow, M. S. (2000). Contextual fear, gestalt memories, and the hippocampus. *Behavior and Brain Research, 110,* 73–81.

Farchione, T. R., Lorch, E., & Rosenberg, D. R. (2002). Hypoplasia of the corpus callosum and obsessive-compulsive symptoms. *Journal of Child Neurology, 17*(7), 535–537.

Fehr, C., Grintschuk, N., Szegedi, A., Anghelescu, I., Klawe, C., Singer, P., Hiemke, C., & Dahmen, N. (2000). The HTR1B 861G>C receptor polymorphism among patients suffering from alcoholism, major depression, anxiety disorders, and narcolepsy. *Psychiatry Research, 97*(1), 1–10.

Fehr, C., Szegedi, A., Anghelescu, I., Klawe, C., Hiemke, C., & Dahmen, N. (2000). Sex differences in allelic frequencies of the 5–HT2C Cys23Ser polymorphism in psychiatric patients and healthy volunteers: Findings from an association study. *Psychiatric Genetics, 10*(2), 59–65.

Feighner, J. P. (1999). Mechanism of action of antidepressant medications. *Journal of Clinical Psychiatry, 60*(4), 4–11.

Fenichel, O. (1945). *The Psychoanalytic Theory of Neurosis*. New York: Norton.

Fennema-Notestine, C., Stein, M. B., Kennedy, C. M., Archibald, S. L., & Jernigan, T. L. (2002). Brain morphometry in female victims of intimate partner violence with and without posttraumatic stress disorder. *Biological Psychiatry*, 52(11), 1089–1101.

Field, T., Diego, M., Hernandez-Reif, M., Salman, F., Schanberg, S., Kuhn, C., Yando, R., & Bendell, D. (2003). Prenatal anger effects on the fetus and neonate. *Journal of Obstetrics and Gynecology*, 22(3), 260–266.

Findling, R. L., Aman, M. G., Eerdekens, M., Derivan, A., & Lyons, B. (2004). Long-term, open-label study of risperidone in children with severe disruptive behaviors and below-average IQ. *American Journal of Psychiatry*, 161, 677–684.

Fineberg, N. A., & Gale, T. M. (2005). Evidence-based pharmacotherapy of obsessive-compulsive disorder. *International Journal of Neuropsychopharmacology*, 8(1), 107–129.

Finn, D. A., Rutledge-Gorman, M. T., & Crabbe, J. C. (2003). Genetic animal models of anxiety. *Neurogenetics*, 4(3), 109–135.

First, M. B., & Tasman, A. (2006). *DSM-IV-TR Mental Disorders: Diagnosis, Etiology, and Treatment*. New York: Wiley.

Flouri, E. (2005). Posttraumatic stress disorder (PTSD): What we have learned and what we still have not found out. *Journal of Interpersonal Violence*, 20(4), 373–379.

Floyd, D. W., Jung, K. Y., & McCool, B. A. (2003). Chronic ethanol ingestion facilitates N-methyl-D- aspartate receptor function and expression in rat lateral/basolateral amygdala neurons. *Journal of Pharmacology and Experimental Therapeutics*, 307(3), 1020–1029.

Floyd, M., McKendree-Smith, N., Bailey, E., Stump, J., Scogin, F., & Bowman, D. (2002). Two-year follow-up of self-examination therapy for generalized anxiety disorder. *Journal of Anxiety Disorder*, 16(4), 369–375.

Flynn, C. A., & Chen, Y. C. (2003). Antidepressants for generalized anxiety disorder. *American Family Physician*, 68(9), 1757–1758.

Foa, E. B., Franklin, M. E., Perry, K. J., & Herbert, J. D. (1996). Cognitive biases in social phobia. *Journal of Abnormal Psychology*, 105, 433–439.

Foa, E. B., Liebowitz, M. R., Kozak, M. J., Davies, S., Campeas, R., Franklin, M. E., Huppert, J. D., Kjernisted, K., Rowan, V., Schmidt, A. B., Simpson, H. B., & Tu, X. (2005). Randomized, placebo- controlled trial of exposure and ritual precention, clomipramine, and their combination in the treatment of obsessive-compulsive disorder. *American Journal of Psychiatry*, 162(1), 151–161.

Follette, W. C., & Houts, A. C. (1996). Models of scientific progress and the role of theory in taxonomy development: A case study of the DSM. *Journal of Consulting and Clinical Psychology*, 64, 1120–1132.

Fonseca, E. S., Massoco, C. O., & Palermo-Neto, J. (2002). Effects of prenatal stress on stress-induced changes in behavior and macrophage activity of mice. *Physiology & Behavior*, 77(2–3), 205–215.

Fontana, A., & Rosenheck, R. (2004). Trauma, change in strength of religious faith, and mental health service use among veterans treated for PTSD. *Journal of Mental and Nervous Disorders*, 192(9), 579–584.

Fontana, D., & Abouserie, R. (1993). Stress levels, gender, and personality factors in teachers. *British Journal of Educational Psychology*, 63(2), 261–270.

Fontenelle, L. F., Mendlowicz, M. V., Marques, C., & Versiani, M. (2004). Trans-cultural aspects of obsessive-compulsive disorder: A description of a Brazillian sample and a systematic review of international clinical studies. *Journal of Psychiatric Research*, 38(4), 403–411.

Fontenelle, L. F., Mendlowicz, M. V., Soares, I. D., & Versiani, M. (2004). Patients with obsessive-compulsive disorder and hoarding symptoms: A distinctive clinical sub-type? *Comprehensive Psychiatry*, 45(5), 375–383.

Fontenelle, L. F., Mendlowicz, M. V., & Versiani, M. (2004). Patients with obsessive-compulsive disorder (OCD) displayed cognitive deficits consistent with a dysfunction of the dorsolateral-striatal circuit. *Psychological Medicine*, 34(1), 181.

Fontenelle, L. F., Rosario-Campos, M. C., Mendlowicz, M. V., Ferrao, Y. A., Versiani, M., & Miguel, E. C. (2004). Treatment-response by age at onset in obsessive-compulsive disorder. *Journal of Affective Disorders*, 83(2–3), 283–284.

Forsyth, D. R. (1995). *Our Social World*. Pacific Grove, CA: Brooks-Cole.

Forsyth, J. P., Parker, J. D., & Finlay, C. G. (2003). Anxiety sensitivity, controllability, and experiential avoidance and their relation to drug of choice and addiction severity in a residential sample of substance-abusing veterans. *Addictive Behaviors*, 28(5), 851–870.

Foster, R. H., & Goa, K. L. (1998). Risperidone: A pharmacoeconomic review of its use in schizophrenia. *Pharmacoeconomics*, 14, 97–133.

Fountoulakis, K. N., Nimatoudis, I., Iacovides, A., & Kaprinis, G. (2004). Off-label indications for atypical antipsychotics: A systematic review. *Annals of General Hospital Psychiatry*, 3(1), 4.

Fowles, D. C. (2001). Biological variables in psychopathology: A psychobiological perspective. In H. E. Adams & P. B. Sutker (Eds.), *Comprehensive Handbook of Psychopathology* (3rd Ed.) (pp. 85–104). New York: Plenum Publishers.

Fox, N. A., Henderson, H. A., Marshall, P. J., Nichols, K. E., & Ghera, M. M. (2004). Behavioral inhibition: Linking biology and behavior within a developmental framework. *Annual Review of Psychology*, 8, 12–17.

Frankl, V. (1963). *Man's Search for Meaning*. Boston: Beacon.

Frankl, V. (1965). *The Doctor and the Soul*. New York: Knopf.

Frankl, V. (1969). *The Will to Meaning: Foundations and Applications of Logotherapy*. New York: New American Library.

Frans, O., Rimmo, P. A., Aberg, L., & Fredrikson, M. (2005). Trauma exposure and posttraumatic stress disorder in the general population. *Acta Psychiatrica Scandanavica*, 111(4), 291–299.

Fredrikson, M., Annas, P., Fischer, H., & Wik, G. (1996). Gender and age differences in the prevalence of specific fears and phobias. *Behaviour Research and Therapy*, 34, 33–39.

Fredrikson, M., & Furmark, T. (2003). Amygdaloid regional cerebral blood flow and subjective fear during symptom provocation in anxiety disorders. *Annals of the New York Academy of Sciences*, 985, 341–347.

Freud, A. (1946). *The Ego and the Mechanism of Defense*. New York: International Universities Press.

Freud, S. (1894). The neuropsychoses of defense. In J. Strachey (Ed.), *The Standard Edition of the Complete Psychological Works of Sigmund Freud* (Vol. 3, pp. 41–61). London: Hogarth Press.

Freud, S. (1901). Psychopathology of everyday life. In J. Strachey (Ed.), *The Standard Edition of the Complete Psychological Works of Sigmund Freud* (Vol. 6). London: Hogarth Press.

Freud, S. (1909). Five lectures on psychoanalysis. In J. Strachey (Ed.), *The Standard Edition of the Complete Psychological Works of Sigmund Freud* (Vol. 11, pp. 7–55). London: Hogarth Press.

Freud, S. (1936). *The Problem of Anxiety*. New York: Norton.

Frey, B. N., Mabilde, L. C., & Eizirik, C. L. (2004). The integration of psychopharmacology and psychoanalytic psychotherapy: A critical review. *Revista Brasileira de Psiquiatria*, 26(2), 118–123.

Friedman, M. J. (2000). What might the psychobiology of posttraumatic stress disorder teach us about future approaches to pharmacotherapy. *Journal of Clinical Psychiatry*, 61(7), 44–51.

Friedman, M. J., Wang, S., Jalowiec, J. E., McHugo, G. J., & McDonagh-Coyle, A. (2005). Thyroid hormone alterations among women with posttraumatic stress disorder due to childhood sexual abuse. *Biological Psychiatry, 57*(10), 1186–1192.

Frost, R. O., & Steketee, G. (Eds.). (2002). *Cognitive Approaches to Obsessions and Compulsions: Theory, Assessment, and Treatment.* Oxford, United Kingdom: Pergamon.

Frye, C. A., & Walf, A. A. (2004). Estrogen and/or progesterone administered systemically or to the amygdala can have anxiety-, fear-, and pain-reducing effects in ovariectomized rats. *Behavioral Neuroscience, 118*(2), 306–313.

Fujishiro, J., Imanishi, T., Onozawa, K., & Tsushima, M. (2002). Comparison of the anticholinergic effects of the serotonergic antidepressants, paroxetine, fluvoxamine, and clomipramine. *European Journal of Pharmacology, 454*(2–3), 183–188.

Fullana, M. A., Mataix-Cols, D., Trujillo, J. L., Caseras, X., Serrano, F., Alonso, P., Menchon, J. M., Vallejo, J., & Torrubia, R. (2004). Personality characteristics in obsessive-compulsive disorder and individuals with subclinical obsessive-compulsive problems. *British Journal of Clinical Psychology, 43*(4), 387–398.

Fulton, B., & Benfield, P. (1996). Meclobemide: An update of its pharmacological properties and therapeutic use. *Drugs, 52*(3), 450–474.

Fyer, A. J., Mannuzza, S., Gallops, M. S., Martin, L. Y., Aaronson, C., Gorman, J. M., Liebowitz, M. R., & Klein, D. F. (1990). Familial transmission of simple phobia and fears: A preliminary report. *Archives of General Psychiatry, 47,* 252–256.

Gadd, C. A., Murtra, P., De Felipe, C., & Hunt, S. P. (2003). Neurokinin-1 receptor-expressing neurons in the amygdala modulate morphine reward and anxiety behaviors in the mouse. *Journal of Neuroscience, 23*(23), 8271–8280.

Gaillard, W. D., Zeffiro, T., Fazilat, S., DeCarli, C., & Theodore, W. H. (1996). Effect of valproate on cerebral metabolism and blood flow: An 18F-2–deoxyglucose and 15O water positron emission tomography study. *Epilepsia, 37*(6), 515–521.

Gale, C., & Oakley-Browne, M. (2001). Generalized anxiety disorder. In *Clinical Evidence: Mental Health* (pp. 90–102). Tennessee: BMJ Publishing Group.

Gall, F. (1835). *Works: On the Functions of the Brain and Each of Its Parts.* Boston: Marsh, Capen, & Lyon.

Gallagher, B. J. (2001). *The Sociology of Mental Illness* (4th Ed.). New York: Prentice Hall.

Gallagher, H. M., Rabian, B. A., & McCloskey, M. S. (2004). A brief group cognitive-behavioral intervention for social phobia in childhood. *Journal of Affective Disorders, 18*(4), 459–479.

Gamazo-Garran, P., Soutullo, C. A., & Ortuno, F. (2002). Obsessive-compulsive disorder secondary to brain dysgerminoma in an adolescent boy: A positron emission tomography case report. *Journal of Child and Adolescent Psychopharmacology, 12*(3), 259–263.

Garcia, R. (2002). Stress, synaptic plasticity, and psychopathology. *Review of Neuroscience, 13*(3), 195–208.

Gardner, R. A. (1993). *Psychotherapy with Children.* New Jersey: Jason Aronson.

Garraghty, P. E., Churchill, J. D., & Banks, M. K. (1998). Adult neural plasticity: Similarities between two paradigms. *Current Directions in Psychological Science, 7,* 87–91.

Geier, F. P., & Konstantinowicz, T. (2004). Kava treatment in patients with anxiety. *Phytotherapy Research, 18*(4), 297–300.

Gelenberg, A. J., & Pies, R. (2003). Matching the bipolar patient and the mood stabilizer. *Annals of Clinical Psychiatry, 15*(3–4), 203–216.

Gelernter, J., Page, G. P., Bonvicini, K., Woods, S. W., Pauls, D. L., & Kruger, S. (2003). A chromosome 14 risk locus for simple phobia: Results from a genomewide linkage scan. *Molecular Psychiatry, 8*(1), 71–82.

Gelernter, J., Page, G. P., Stein, M. B., & Woods, S. W. (2004). Genome-wide linkage scan for loci predisposing to social phobia evidence for a chromosome 16 risk locus. *American Journal of Psychiatry, 161*(1), 59–66.

Geller, D. A., Biederman, J., Stewart, S. E., Mullin, B., Martin, A., Spencer, T., & Faraone, S. V. (2003). Which SSRI? A meta-analysis of pharmacotherapy trials in pediatric obsessive-compulsive disorder. *American Journal of Psychiatry, 160*(11), 1919–1928.

Geller, I., & Seifter, J. (1960). The effects of meprobamate, barbiturates, d-amphetamine, and promazine on experimentally induced conflict in the rat. *Psychopharmacologia, 1,* 382–492.

Gerardy, J., & Dresse, A. (1998). Regional action of brofaromine on rat brain MAO-A and MAO-B. *Progress in Neuro-Psychopharmacology & Biological Psychiatry, 22*(7), 1141–1155.

Ghelardoni, S., Tomita, Y. A., Bell, J. M., Rapoport, S. I., & Bosetti, F. (2004). Chronic carbamazepine selectively downregulates cytosolic phospholipase A(2) expression and cyclooxygenase activity in rat brain. *Biological Psychiatry, 56*(4), 248–254.

Giedd, J. N. (2004). Structural magnetic resonance imaging of the adolescent brain. *Annals of the New York Academy of Sciences, 1021,* 77–85.

Giedd, J. N., Rapoport, J. L., Garvey, M. A., Perlmutter, S., & Swedo, S. E. (2000). MRI assessment of children with obsessive-compulsive disorder or tics associated with streptococcal infection. *American Journal of Psychiatry, 157,* 281–283.

Gifkins, A., Greba, Q., & Kokkinidis, L. (2002). Ventral tegmental area dopamine neurons mediate the shock sensitization of acoustic startle: A potential site of action for benzodiazepine anxiolytics. *Behavioral Neuroscience, 116*(5), 785–794.

Gilbert, C. (2003). Clinical applications of breathing regulation: Beyond anxiety management. *Behavior Modification, 27*(5), 692–709.

Gilbert, D. L., Bansal, A. S., Sethuraman, G., Sallee, F. R., Zhang, J., Lipps, T., & Wassermann, E. M. (2004). Association of cortical disinhibition with tic, ADHD, and OCD severity in Tourette syndrome. *Movement Disorders, 19*(4), 416–425.

Gilbertson, M. W., Shenton, M. E., Ciszewski, A., Kasai, K., Lasko, N. B., Orr, S. P., & Pitman, R. K. (2002). Smaller hippocampal volume predicts pathologic vulnerability to psychological trauma. *National Neuroscience, 5*(11), 1242–1247.

Gilboa, A., Shalev, A. Y., Laor, L., Lester, H., Louzoun, Y., Chisin, R., & Bonne, O. (2004). Functional connectivity of the prefrontal cortex and the amygdala in posttraumatic stress disorder. *Biological Psychiatry, 55*(3), 263–272.

Gill, J. M., Szanton, S. L., & Page, G. G. (2005). Biological underpinnings of health alterations in women with PTSD: A sex disparity. *Biological Research in Nursing, 7*(1), 44–54.

Gillespie, N. A., Kirk, K. M., Evans, D. M., Heath, A. C., Hickie, I. B., & Martin, N. G. (2004). Do the genetic or environmental determinants of anxiety and depression change with age? A longitudinal study of Australian twins. *Twin Research, 7*(1), 39–53.

Gillett, E. (1996). Learning theory and intrapsychic conflict. *International Journal of Psychoanalysis, 77*(4), 689–707.

Gilligan, P. J., & Li, Y. W. (2004). Corticotropin-releasing factor antagonists: Recent advances and exciting prospects for the treatment of human diseases. *Current Opinion in Drug Discovery & Development, 7*(4), 487–497.

Giulino, L., Gammon, P., Sullivan, K., Franklin, M., Foa, E., Maid, R., & March, J. S. (2002). Is parental report of upper respiratory infection at the onset of obsessive-compulsive disorder suggestive of pediatric autoimmune neuropsychiatric disorder associated with streptococcal infection? *Journal of Child and Adolescent Psychopharmacology, 12*(2), 157–164.

Gobert, A., Rivet, J. M., Cistarelli, J. M., & Millan, M. J. (1997). Buspirone enhances duloxetine- and fluoxetine-induced increases in dialysate levels of dopamine and noradrenaline, but not serotonin, in the fontal cortex of feely moving rats. *Journal of Neurochemistry, 68*(3), 1326–1329.

Goddard, A. W., Brouette, T., & Almai, A. (2001). Early coadministration of clonazepam with sertraline for panic disorder. *Archives of General Psychiatry, 58*(7), 681–686.

Goddard, A. W., & Charney, D. S. (1997). Toward an integrated neurobiology of panic disorder. *Journal of Clinical Psychiatry, 58*(2), 4–11.

Golden, R. N. (2004). Making advances where it matters: Improving outcomes in mood and anxiety disorders. *CNS Spectrums, 9*(6 Suppl 4), 14–22.

Goldschmidt, L., Richardson, G. A., Cornelius, M. D., & Day, N. L. (2004). Prenatal marijuana and alcohol exposure and academic achievement at age 10. *Neurotoxicology and Teratology, 26*(4), 521–532.

Goldstein, D. J., Lu, Y., Detke, M. J., Wiltse, C., Mallinckrodt, C., & Demitrack, M. A. (2004). Duloxetine in the treatment of depression: A double-blind, placebo-controlled comparison with paroxetine. *Journal of Clinical Psychopharmacology, 24*(4), 389–399.

Golier, J. A., Yehuda, R., Bierer, L. M., Mitropoulous, V., New, A. S., Schmeidler, J., Silverman, J. M., & Siever, L. J. (2003). The relationship of borderline personality disorder and posttraumatic stress disorder and traumatic events. *American Journal of Psychiatry, 160*, 2018–2024.

Gonul, A. S., Kula, M., Sofuoglo, S., Tutus, A., & Esel, E. (2003). Tc-99 HMPAO SPECT study of regional cerebral blood flow in olanzapine-treated schizophrenic patients. *European Archives of Psychiatry and Clinical Neuroscience, 253*(1), 29–33.

Gonzalez, L. E., Quinonez, B., Rangel, A., Pino, S., & Hernandez, L. (2004). Tonic and phasic alteration in amygdala 5HT, glutamate, and GABA transmission after prefrontal cortex damage in rats. *Brain Research, 1005*(1–2), 154–163.

Good, C., & Petersen, C. (2001). SSRI and mirtazapine in PTSD. *Journal of the American Academy of Child and Adolescent Psychiatry, 40*(3), 263–264.

Goodman, W. K. (2004). Selecting pharmacotherapy for generalized anxiety disorder. *Journal of Clinical Psychiatry, 65*(13), 8–13.

Goodwin, R. D., Ferguson, D. M., & Horwood, L. J. (2005). Childhood abuse and familial violence and the risk of panic attacks and panic disorder in young adulthood. *Psychological Medicine, 35*(6), 881–890.

Goodwin, R. D., & Gorman, J. M. (2002). Psychopharmacologic treatment of generalized anxiety disorder and the risk of major depression. *American Journal of Psychiatry, 159*(11), 1935–1937.

Gordon, J. A., & Hen, R. (2004). Genetic approaches to the study of anxiety. *Annual Review of Neuroscience, 27*, 193–222.

Gorman, J. M. (2001). A 28–year-old woman with panic disorder. *Journal of the American Medical Association, 286*(4), 450–457.

Gorman, J. M. (2003a). Treating generalized anxiety disorder. *Journal of Clinical Psychiatry, 64*(2), 24–29.

Gorman, J. M., & Coplan, J. D. (1996). Comorbidity of depression and panic disorder. *Journal of Clinical Psychiatry, 57*(10), 34–43.

Gorman, J. M., Hirschfeld, R. M., & Ninan, P. T. (2002). New developments in the neurobiological basis of anxiety disorders. *Psychopharmacology Bulletin, 36*(2), 49–67.

Gorman, J. M., Kent, J. M., Sullivan, G. M., & Coplan, J. D. (2000). Neuroanatomical hypothesis of panic disorder, revised. *American Journal of Psychiatry, 157*, 493–505.

Gorman, J. M., Mathew, S., & Coplan, J. (2002). Neurobiology of early life stress: Nonhuman primate models. *Seminars in Clinical Neuropsychiatry, 7*(2), 96–103.

Gorman, J. M., Papp, L. A., & Coplan, J. D. (1994). Anxiogenic effects of CO_2 and hyperventilation in patients with panic disorder. *American Journal of Psychiatry, 151*, 547–553.

Gorwood, P. H. (2004). Generalized anxiety disorder and major depressive disorder comorbidity: An example of genetic pleiotropy? *European Psychiatry, 19*(1), 27–33.

Gosselin, P., & Laberge, B. (2003). Etiological factors of generalized anxiety disorder. *Encephale, 29*(4, 1), 351–361.

Gothelf, D., Presburger, G., Zohar, A. H., Burg, M., Nahmani, A., Frydman, M., Shohat, M., Inbar, D., Aviram-Goldring, A., Yeshaya, J., Steinberg, T., Finkelstein, Y.,

Frisch, A., Weizman, A., & Apter, A. (2004). Obsessive-compulsive disorder in patients with velocardiofacial syndrome. *American Journal of Medical Genetics, 126B*(1), 99–105.

Gould, R. A., Otto, M. W., Pollack, M. H., & Yap, L. (1997). Cognitive behavioral and pharmacological treatment of generalized anxiety disorder: A preliminary meta-analysis. *Behavior Therapy, 28*, 285–305.

Grabe, H. J., Lange, M., Wolff, B., Volzke, H., Lucht, M., Freyberger, H. J., John, U., & Cascorbi, I. (2004). Mental and physical distress is modulated by a polymorphism in the 5HT transporter gene interacting with social stressors and chronic disease burden. *Molecular Psychiatry, 7*, 7–9.

Grados, M. A. (2003). Obsessive-compulsive disorder after traumatic brain injury. *International Review of Psychiatry, 15*(4), 350–358.

Grados, M. A., Walkup, J., & Walford, S. (2003). Genetics of obsessive-compulsive disorders: New findings and challenges. *Brain Development, 25*(1), 55–61.

Gray, J. A. (1976). The behavioural inhibition system: A possible substrate for anxiety. In M. P. Feldman & A. Broadhurst (Eds.), *Theoretical and Experimental Bases of the Behaviour Therapies* (pp. 3–41). London: John Wiley & Sons.

Gray, J. A. (1982). *The Neuropsychology of Anxiety.* New York: Oxford University Press.

Gray, J. A., & McNaughton, N. (1996). The neuropsychology of anxiety: Reprise. In D. A. Hope (Ed.), *Perspectives on Anxiety, Panic, and Fear* (43rd Annual Nebraska Symposium on Motivation) (pp. 61–134). Lincoln, Nebraska: University of Nebraska Press.

Gray, J. A., & McNaughton, N. (1998). What's where in the neuropsychology of anxiety. Paper presented at a *Workshop on Arousal and Anxiety*, National Institute of Mental Health: Rockville, Maryland.

Gray, M. J., Elhai, J. D., & Frueh, B. C. (2004). Enhancing patient satisfaction and increasing treatment compliance: Patient education as a fundamental component of PTSD treatment. *Psychiatric Quarterly, 75*(4), 321–332.

Greba, Q., Gifkins, A., & Kokkinidis, L. (2001). Inhibition of amygdaloid dopamine D2 receptors impairs emotional learning measured with fear-potentiated startle. *Brain Research, 899*(1–2), 218–226.

Greenberg, L. S., & Malcolm, W. (2002). Resolving unfinished business: Relating process to outcome. *Journal of Consulting and Clinical Psychology, 70*(2), 406–416.

Greist, J. H., Bandelow, B., Hollander, E., Marazziti, D., Montgomery, S. A., Nutt, D. J., Okasha, A., Swinson, R. P., & Zohar, J. (2003). WCA recommendations for the long-term treatment of obsessive-compulsive disorder in adults. *CNS Spectrums, 8*(8), 7–16.

Greist, J. H., Jefferson, J. W., Kobak, K. A., Katzelnick, D. J., & Serlin, R. C. (1995). Efficacy and tolerability of serotonin transport inhibitors in obsessive-compulsive disorder: A meta-analysis. *Archives of General Psychiatry, 52*(1), 53–60.

Grimaldi, B. L. (2002). The central role of magnesium deficiency in Tourette's syndrome: Causal relationships between magnesium deficiency, altered biochemical pathways and symptoms relating to Tourette's syndrome and several reported comorbid conditions. *Medical Hypotheses, 58*(1), 47–60.

Groenink, L., Joordens, R. J., Hijzen, T. H., Dirks, A., & Olivier, B. (2000). Infusion of flesinoxan into the amygdala blocks the fear-potentiated startle. *Neuroreport, 11*(10), 2285–2288.

Groenink, L., Van Bogaert, M. J., Van der Gugten, J., Oosting, R. S., & Olivier, B. (2003). 5–HT1A receptor and 5–HT1B receptor knockout mice in stress and anxiety paradigms. *Behavioural Pharmacology, 14*(5–6), 369–383.

Gross, C., & Hen, R. (2004). The developmental origins of anxiety. *National Review of Neuroscience, 5*(7), 545–552.

Gross, C., Zhuang, X., Stark, K., Ramboz, S., Oosting, R., Kirby, L., Santarelli, L., Beck, S., & Hen, R. (2002). Serotonin 1A receptor acts during development to establish normal anxiety-like behavior in the adult. *Nature, 416*(6879), 396–400.

Gross, R., Sasson, Y., Chopra, J., & Zohar, J. (1998). Biological models of obsessive-compulsive disorder: The serotonin hypothesis. In R. P. Swinson, M. M. Anthony, S.

Rachman, & M. A. Richter (Eds.), *Obsessive-compulsive disorder: Theory, Research, and Treatment* (pp. 3–32). New York: Guilford.

Guaiana, G., Barbui, C., & Hotopf, M. (2003). Amitriptyline versus other types of pharmacotherapy for depression. *Cochrane Database of Systematic Reviews, 2*, 4186.

Gunasekara, N. A., & Spencer, C. M. (1998). Quetiapine—A review of its use in schizophrenia. *CNS Drugs, 9*, 325–340.

Gundel, H., O'Connor, M. F., Littrell, L., Fort, C., & Lane, R. D. (2003). Functional neuroanatomy of grief: An fMRI study. *American Journal of Psychiatry, 160*, 1946–1953.

Gurguis, G. N. M., & Uhde, T. W. (1990). Plasma 3–methoxy-4–hydroxyphenylethylene (MHPG) and growth hormone responses to yohimbine in panic disorder patients and normal controls. *Psychoneuroendocrinology, 15*, 217–224.

Gutierrez, M. A., Stimmel, G. L., & Aiso, J. Y. (2003). Venlafaxine: A 2003 update. *Clinical Therapeutics, 25*(8), 2138–2154.

Gutierrez, S., Ang-Lee, M. K., Walker, D. J., & Zacny, J. P. (2004). Assessing subjective and psychomotor effects of the herbal medication valerian in healthy volunteers. *Pharmacology, Biochemistry, and Behavior, 78*(1), 57–64.

Haapasalo-Pesu, K. M., Saarijarvi, S., & Sorvaniemi, M. (2003). National prescribing practices of adolescent psychiatrists for psychotropic medications in outpatient care in Finland. *Nordic Journal of Psychiatry, 57*(6), 405–409.

Haddjeri, N., & Blier, P. (2001). Sustained blockade of neurokinin-1 receptors enhances serotonin neurotransmission. *Biological Psychiatry, 50*(3), 191–199.

Hahn, C. G., Gyulai, L., Baldassano, C. F., & Lenox, R. H. (2004). The current understanding of lamotrigine as a mood stabilizer. *Journal of Clinical Psychiatry, 65*(6), 791–804.

Haier, R. J. (1998). Brain scanning and neuroimaging. In H. S. Friedman (Ed.), *Encyclopedia of Mental Health I* (pp. 317–330). San Diego, California: Academic Press.

Haller, J., Varga, B., Ledent, C., & Freund, T. F. (2004). CB1 cannabinoid receptors mediate anxiolytic effects: Convergent genetic and pharmacological evidence with CB1–specific agents. *Behavioural Pharmacology, 15*(4), 299–304.

Hameg, A., Bayle, F., Nuss, P., Dupuis, P., Garay, R. P., & Dib, M. (2003). Affinity of cyamemazine, an anxiolytic antipsychotic drug, for human recombinant dopamine versus serotonin receptor subtypes. *Biochemistry and Pharmacology, 65*(3), 435–440.

Hammond, D. C. (2005). Neurofeedback with anxiety and affective disorders. *Child and Adolescent Psychiatric Clinics of North America, 14*(1), 105–123.

Hardy, J., Argyropoulos, S., & Nutt, D. J. (2002). Venlafaxine: A new class of antidepressant. *Hospital Medicine, 63*(9), 549–552.

Hariri, A. R., Mattay, V. S., Tessitore, A., Kolachana, B., Fera, F., Goldman, D., Egan, M. F., & Weinberger, D. R. (2002). Serotonin transporter genetic variation and the response of the human amygdala. *Science, 297*(5580), 400–403.

Hariri, A. R., & Weinberger, D. R. (2003). Functional neuroimaging of genetic variation in serotonergic neurotransmission. *Genes, Brain, and Behavior, 2*(6), 341–349.

Harkany, T., Hartig, W., Berghuis, P., Dobszay, M. B., Zilberter, Y., Edwards, R. H., Mackie, K., & Ernfors, P. (2003). Complementary distribution of type 1 cannabinoid receptors and vesicular glutamate transporter 3 in basal forebrain suggests input-specific retrograde signalling by cholinergic neurons. *European Journal of Neurosciences, 18*(7), 1979–1992.

Harman, J. S., Rollman, B. L., Hanusa, B. H., Lenze, E. J., & Shear, M. K. (2002). Physician office visits of adults for anxiety disorders in the United States, 1985–1998. *Journal of General Internal Medicine, 17*(3), 165–172.

Harmer, C. J., Shelley, N. C., Cowen, P. J., & Goodwin, G. M. (2004). Increased positive versus negative affective perception and memory in healthy volunteers following selective serotonin and norepinephrine reuptake inhibition. *American Journal of Psychiatry, 161*(7), 1256–1263.

Hart, J. T., & Tomlinson, T. M. (Eds.).(1970). *New Directions in Client-Centered Therapy*. Boston: Houghton Mifflin.

Harter, M. C., Conway, K. P., & Merikangas, K. R. (2003). Associations between anxiety disorders and physical illness. *European Archives of Psychiatry and Clinical Neuroscience, 253*(6), 313–320.

Hartmann, H. (1950). Comments on the psychoanalytic theory of the ego. In Heinz Hartmann's (Ed.), *Essays On Ego Psychology* (pp.113–141). New York: International Universities Press.

Hartmann, H. (1964). *Essays on Ego Psychology: Selected Problems in Psychoanalytic Theory*. New York: International Universities Press.

Hartz, R. A., Nanda, K. K., Ingalls, C. L., Ahuja, V. T., Moleski, T. F., Zhang, G., Wong, H., Peng, Y., Kelley, M., Lodge, N. J., Zaczek, R., Gilligan, P. J., & Trainor, G. L. (2004). Design, synthesis, and biological evaluation of 1,2,3,7–tetrahyro-6H-purin-6–one and 3,7–dihydro-1H-purine-2,6–dione derivatives as corticotropin-releasing factor(1) receptor antagonists. *Journal of Medical Chemistry, 47*(19), 4741–4754.

Harvey, B. H., Oosthuizen, F., Brand, L., Wegener, G., & Stein, D. J. (2004). Stress-restress evokes iNOS activity and altered GABA levels and NMDA receptors in rat hippocampus. *Psychopharmacology, 166*(1), 235–245.

Harvey, B. H., Scheepers, A., Brand, L., & Stein, D. J. (2001). Chronic inositol increases striatal D(2) receptors but does not modify dexamphetamine-induced motor behavior: Relevance to obsessive compulsive disorder. *Pharmacology, Biochemistry, and Behavior, 68*(2), 245–253.

Haslam, N. (2003). Categorical versus dimensional models of mental disorder: The taxometric evidence. *The Australian New Zealand Journal of Psychiatry, 37*(6), 696–704.

Hayry, M. (2004). Prescribing cannabis: Freedom, autonomy, and values. *Journal of Medical Ethics, 30*(4), 333–336.

Hayward, C., Killen, J. D., & Taylor, C. B. (2003). The relationship between agoraphobia symptoms and panic disorder in a non-clinical sample of adolescents. *Psychological Medicine, 33*(4), 733–738.

Hazlett-Stevens, H., & Borkovec, T. D. (2004). Interpretive cues and ambiguity in generalized anxiety disorder. *Behaviour Research and Therapy, 42*(8), 881–892.

Hedges, L. E. (1994). *In Search of the Lost Mother of Infancy*. New Jersey: Aronson.

Heider, F. (1958). *The Psychology of Interpersonal Relations*. New York: John Wiley & Sons.

Heilig, M. (2004). The NPY system in stress, anxiety, and depression. *Neuropeptides, 38*(4), 213–224.

Heim, C., & Nemeroff, C. B. (2001). The role of childhood trauma in the neurobiology of mood and anxiety disorders: Preclinical and clinical studies. *Biological Psychiatry, 49*, 1023–1039.

Heimberg, R. G., Liebowitz, M. R., Hope, D. A., Schneier, F. R., Holt, C. S., Welkowitz, L., Juster, H. R., Campeas, R., Bruch, M. A., Cloitre, M., Fallon, B., & Klein, D. F. (1998). Cognitive- behavioral group therapy versus phenelzine in social phobia: 12–week outcome. *Archives of General Psychiatry, 55*, 1133–1141.

Heldt, E., Manfro, G. G., Kipper, L., Blaya, C., Maltz, S., Isolan, L., & Otto, M. W. (2005). One-year follow-up of pharmacotherapy-resistant patients with panic disorder treated with cognitive-behavioral therapy: Outcome and predictors of remission. *Behaviour Research and Therapy, 7*, 1–9.

Hellawell, S. J., & Brewin, C. R. (2004). A comparison of flashbacks and ordinary autobiographical memories of trauma: Content and language. *Behaviour Research and Therapy, 42*(1), 1–12.

Hembree, E. A., Riggs, D. S., Kozak, M. J., Franklin, M. E., & Foa, E. B. (2003). Long-term efficacy of exposure and ritual prevention therapy and serotonergic medications for obsessive-compulsive disorder. *CNS Spectrums, 8*(5), 363–371.

Hemmings, S. M., Kinnear, C. J., Lochner, C., Niehaus, D. J., Knowles, J. A., Moolman-Smook, J. C., Cordield, V. A., & Stein, D. J. (2004). Early- versus late-onset obsessive-compulsive disorder: Investigating genetic and clinical correlates. *Psychiatry Research, 128(2),* 175–182.

Hemmings, S. M., Kinnear, C. J., Niehaus, D. J., Moolman-Smook, J. C., Lochner, C., Knowles, J. A., Corfield, V. A., & Stein, D. J. (2003). Investigating the role of dopaminergic and serotonergic candidate genes in obsessive-compulsive disorder. *European Neuropsychopharmacology, 13(2),* 93–98.

Herman, J. (1992). *Trauma and Recovery.* New York: Basic Books.

Hermann, N., Mamdani, M., & Lanctot, K. L. (2004). Atypical antipsychotics and risk of cerebrovascular accidents. *American Journal of Psychiatry, 161,* 1113–1115.

Hermann, R. C., Ettner, S. L., Dorwart, R. A., Langman-Dorwart, N., & Kleinman, S. (1999). Diagnoses of patients treated with ECT: A comparison of evidence-based standards with reported use. *Psychiatric Services, 50,* 1059–1065.

Hernandez-Avila, C. A., Wand, G., Luo, X., Gelernter, J., & Kranzler, H. R. (2003). Association between the cortisol response to opioid blockade and Asn40Asp polymorphism at the mu-opioid receptor locus. *American Journal of Medical Genetics, 118(1),* 60–65.

Hernandez-Gomez, A. M., Aguilar-Roblero, R., & Perez de la Mora, M. (2002). Role of cholecystokinin-B receptors in anxiety. *Amino Acids, 23(1–3),* 283–290.

Hernandez, E., Lastra, S., Urbina, M., Carreira, I., & Lima, L. (2002). Serotonin, 5-hydroxyindoleacetic acid, and serotonin transporter in blood peripheral lymphocytes of patients with generalized anxiety disorder. *International Immunopharmacology, 2(7),* 893–900.

Herrero, A. I., Del Olmo, N., Gonzalez-Escalada, J. R., & Solis, J. M. (2002). Two new actions of topiramate: Inhibition of depolarizing GABAA-mediated responses and activation of a potassium conductance. *Neuropharmacology, 42(2),* 210–220.

Herrmann, M. J., Jacob, C., Unterecker, S., & Fallgatter, A. J. (2003). Reduced response-inhibition in obsessive-compulsive disorder measured with topographic evoked potential mapping. *Psychiatry Research, 120(3),* 265–271.

Hettema, J. M., Annas, P., Neale, M. C., Kendler, K. S., & Fredrikson, M. (2003). A twin study of the genetics of fear conditioning. *Archives of General Psychiatry, 60(7),* 702–708.

Hettema, J. M., Neale, M. C., & Kendler, K. S. (2001). A review and meta-analysis of the genetic epidemiology of anxiety disorders. *American Journal of Psychiatry, 158(10),* 1568–1578.

Hettema, J. M., Prescott, C. A., & Kendler, K. S. (2001). A population-based twin study of generalized anxiety disorder in men and women. *Journal of Nervous and Mental Disorders, 189(7),* 413–420.

Hettema, J. M., Prescott, C. A., & Kendler, K. S. (2004). Genetic and environmental sources of covariation between generalized anxiety disorder and neuroticism. *American Journal of Psychiatry, 161(9),* 1581–1587.

Hettema, J. M., Prescott, C. A., Myers, J. M., Neale, M. C., & Kendler, K. S. (2005). The structure of genetic and environmental risk factors for anxiety disorders in men and women. *Archives of General Psychiatry, 62(2),* 182–189.

Heuzenroeder, L., Donnelly, M., Haby, M. M., Mihalopoulos, C., Rossell, R., Carter, R., Andrews, G., & Vos, T. (2004). Cost-effectiveness of psychological and pharmacological interventions for generalized anxiety disorder and panic disorder. *Australian and New Zealand Journal of Psychiatry, 38(8),* 602–612.

Hicks, T. V., Leitenberg, H., Barlow, D. H., Gorman, J. M., Shear, M. K., & Woods, S. W. (2005). Physical, mental, and social catastrophic cognitions as prognostic factors in cognitive-behavioral and pharmacological treatments for panic disorder. *Journal of Consulting and Clinical Psychology, 73(3),* 506–514.

Higgins, L. T. (2004). Cultural effects on the expression of some fears by Chinese and British female students. *The Journal of Genetic Psychology, 165(1),* 37–49.

Hill, C. E., & Nakayama, E. Y. (2000). Client-centered therapy: Where has it been and where is it going? *Journal of Clinical Psychology, 56*(7), 861–875.

Hiller, W., Leibbrand, R., Rief, W., & Fichter, M. M. (2005). Differentiating hypochondriasis fom panic disorder. *Journal of Anxiety Disorders, 19*(1), 29–49.

Hindmarch, I. (2002). Beyond the monoamine hypothesis: Mechanisms, molecules, and methods. *European Psychiatry, 17*(3), 294–299.

Hirschfeld, R. M., & Vornik, L. A. (2004). Newer antidepressants: Review of efficacy and safety of escitalopram and duloxetine. *Journal of Clinical Psychiatry, 65*(4), 46–52.

Hirvonen, J., Lindeman, S., Matti, J., & Huttunen, P. (2002). Plasma catecholamines, serotonin, and their metabolites and beta-endorphin of winter swimmers during one winter: Possible correlations to psychological traits. *International Journal of Circumpolar Health, 61*(4), 363–372.

Ho, Y. J., Pawlak, C. R., Guo, L., & Schwarting, R. K. (2004). Acute and long-term consequences of single MDMA administration in relation to individual anxiety levels in the rat. *Behavior and Brain Research, 149*(2), 135–144.

Ho Pian, K. L., Van Megen, H. J., Ramsey, N. F., Mandl, R., Van Rijk, P. P., Wynne, H. J., & Westenberg, H. G. (2005). Decreased thalamic blood flow in obsessive-compulsive disorder patients responding to fluvoxamine. *Psychiatry Research, 138*(2), 89–97.

Hoehn-Saric, R., Harris, G. J., Pearlson, G. D., Cox, C. S., Machlin, S. R., & Camargo, E. E. (1991). A fluoxetine-induced frontal lobe syndrome in an obsessive-compulsive patient. *Journal of Clinical Psychiatry, 52*(3), 131–133.

Hoehn-Saric, R., McLeod, D. R., Funderbunk, F., & Kowalski, P. (2004). Somatic symptoms and physiologic responses in generalized anxiety disorder and panic disorder: An ambulatory monitor study. *Archives of General Psychiatry, 61*(9), 913–921.

Hofmann, P. J., Nutzinger, D. O., Kotter, M. R., & Herzog, G. (2001). The hypothalamic-pituitary- thyroid axis in agoraphobia, panic disorder, major depression, and normal controls. *Journal of Affective Disorders, 66*(1), 75–77.

Hoffmann, S. G. (2004). Cognitive mediation of treatment change in social phobia. *Journal of Consulting and Clinical Psychology, 72*(3), 393–399.

Hoffmann, S. G. (2005). Perception of control over anxiety mediates the relation between catastrophic thinking and social anxiety in social phobia. *Behaviour Research and Therapy, 43*(7), 885–895.

Hofmann, S. G., & Barlow, D. H. (2002). Social phobia (social anxiety disorder). In D. H. Barlow, *Anxiety and Its Disorders: The Nature and Treatment of Anxiety and Panic* (2nd Ed.) (pp. 454–476). New York: Guilford Press.

Hoistad, M., Samskog, J., Jacobsen, K. X., Olsson, A., Hansson, H. A., Brodin, E., & Fuxe, K. (2005). Detection of beta-endorphin in the cerebrospinal fluid after intrastriatal microinjection into the rat brain. *Brain Research, 1041*(2), 167–180.

Hollander, E. (1996). Obsessive-compulsive disorder-related disorders: The role of selective serotonergic reuptake inhibitors. *International Clinical Psychopharmacology, 11*(5), 75–87.

Hollander, E., Allen, A., Steiner, M., Wheadon, D. E., Oakes, R., & Burnham, D. B. (2003). Acute and long-term treatment and prevention of relapse of obsessive-compulsive disorder with paroxetine. *Journal of Clinical Psychiatry, 64*(9), 1113–1121.

Hollander, E., Baldini-Rossi, N., Sood, E., & Pallanti, S. (2003). Risperidone augmentation in treatment-resistant obsessive-compulsive disorder: A double-blind, placebo-controlled study. *International Journal of Neuropsychopharmacology, 6*(4), 397–401.

Holmes, A., Heilig, M., Rupniak, N. M., Steckler, T., & Griebel, G. (2003). Neuropeptide systems as novel therapeutic agents for depression and anxiety disorders. *Trends in Pharmacological Science, 24*(11), 580–588.

Holmes, A., Kinney, J. W., Wrenn, C. C., Li, Q., Yang, R. J., Ma, L., Vishwanath, J., Saavedra, M. C., Innerfield, C. E., Jacoby, A. S., Shine, J., Iismaa, T. P., & Crawley, J. N. (2003). Galanin GAL-R1 receptor null mutant mice display increased anxiety-like behavior specific to the elevated plus-maze. *Neuropsychopharmacology, 28*(6), 1031–1044.

Horinouchi, Y., Akiyoshi, J., Nagata, A., Matsushita, H., Tsutsumi, T., Isogawa, K., Noda, T., & Nagayama, H. (2004). Reduced anxious behavior in mice lacking the CCK2 receptor gene. *European Neuropsychopharmacology, 14*(2), 157–161.

Horley, K., Williams, L. M., Gonsalvez, C., & Gordon, E. (2004). Face to face: Visual scanpath evidence for abnormal processing of facial expressions in social phobia. *Psychiatry Research, 127*(1–2), 43–53.

Horney, K. (1937). *The Neurotic Personality of Our Time.* New York: Norton.

Horowitz, M. J. (1979). *Stress Response Syndromes.* New York: Jason Aronson.

Horowitz, M. J. (1986). Stress-response syndromes: A review of posttraumatic and adjustment disorders. *Hospital and Community Psychiatry, 37,* 241–249.

Horowitz, M. J. (1988). *Introduction to Psychodynamics: A New Synthesis.* Northvale, New Jersey: Jason Aronson.

Horowitz, M. J. (1999). *Essential Papers on Posttraumatic Stress Disorder.* New York: New York University Press.

Huber, D., & Henrich, G. (2003). Personality traits and stress sensitivity in migraine patients. *Behavioral Medicine, 29*(1), 4–13.

Hudziak, J. J., Van Beijsterveldt, C. E., Althoff, R. R., Stanger, C., Rettew, D. C., Nelson, E. C., Todd, R. D., Bartels, M., & Boomsma, D. I. (2004). Genetic and environmental contributions to the Child Behavior Checklist Obsessive-compulsive Scale: A cross-cultural twin study. *Archives of General Psychiatry, 61*(6), 608–616.

Huffman, J. C., Pollack, M. H., & Stern, T. A. (2002). Panic disorder and chest pain: Mechanisms, morbidity, and management. *Primary Care Companion Journal of Clinical Psychiatry, 4*(2), 54–62.

Hughes, J. W., Feldman, M. E., & Beckham, J. C. (2005). Posttraumatic stress disorder is associated with attenuated baroreceptor sensitivity among female, but not male, smokers. *Biological Psychiatry, 7,* 1–7.

Hull, A. M. (2002). Neuroimaging findings in posttraumatic stress disorder: Systematic review. *British Journal of Psychiatry, 181,* 102–110.

Hull, C. L. (1943). *Principles of Behavior.* New York: Appleton-Century-Crofts.

Huot, R. L., Gonzalez, M. E., Ladd, C. O., Thrivikraman, K. V., & Plotsky, P. M. (2004). Foster litters prevent hypothalamic-pituitary-adrenal axis sensitization mediated by neonatal maternal separation. *Psychoneuroendocrinology, 29*(2), 279–289.

Huppert, J. D., Franklin, M. E., Foa, E. B., & Davidson, J. R. (2003). Study refusal and exclusion from a randomized treatment study of generalized social phobia. *Journal of Anxiety Disorders, 17*(6), 683–693.

Huppert, J. D., Moser, J. S., Gershuny, B. S., Riggs, D. S., Spokas, M., Filip, J., Hajcak, G., Parker, H. A., Baer, L., & Foa, E. B. (2005). The relationship between obsessive-compulsive and posttraumatic stress symptoms in clinical and non-clinical samples. *Journal of Anxiety Disorders, 19*(1), 127–136.

Husted, D. S., & Shapira, N. A. (2004). A review of the tretment for refractory obsessive-compulsive disorder: From medicine to deep brain stimulation. *CNS Spectrum, 9*(11), 833–847.

Hwang, B. H., Stewart, R., Zhang, J. K., Lumeng, L., & Li, T. K. (2004). Corticotropin-releasing factor gene expression is down-regulated in the central nucleus of the amygdala of alcohol-preferring rats which exhibit high anxiety: A comparison between rat lines selectively bred for high and low alcohol preference. *Brain Research, 1026*(1), 143–150.

Ilomaki, R., Hakko, H., Timonrn, M., Lappalainen, J., Makikyro, T., & Rasamen, P. (2004). Temporal relationship between the age of onset of phobic disorders and development of substance dependence in adolescent psychiatric patients. *Drug and Alcohol Dependence, 75*(3), 327–330.

Inada, T., Nozaki, S., Inagaki, A., & Furukawa, T. A. (2003). Efficacy of diazepam as an anti-anxiety agent: Meta-analysis of double-blind, randomized controlled trials carried out in Japan. *Human Psychopharmacology, 18*(6), 483–487.

Insel T. R. (2002). Social anxiety: from laboratory studies to clinical practice. *Biological Psychiatry, 51*(1), 1–3.

Insel, T. R., Ninan, P. T., Aloi, J., Jimerson, D. C., Skolnick, P., & Paul, S. M. (1984). A benzodiazepine receptor-mediated model of anxiety. *Archives of General Psychiatry, 41,* 741–750.

Issakidis, C., Sanderson, K., Corry, J., Andrews, G., & Lapsley, H. (2004). Modelling the population cost-effectiveness of current and evidence-based optimal treatment for anxiety disorders. *Psychological Medicine, 34*(1), 19–35.

Jacob, C. P., Strobel, A., Hohenberger, K., Ringel, T., Gutknecht, L., Reif, A., Brocke, B., & Lesch, K. P. (2004). Association between allelic variation of serotonin transporter function and neuroticism in anxious cluster C personality disorders. *American Journal of Psychiatry, 161*(3), 569–572.

Jacobson, L., & Sapolsky, R. (1991). The role of the hippocampus in feedback regulation of the hypothalamic-pituitary-adrenocortical axis. *Endocrine Reviews, 12,* 118–134.

Janeck, A. S., Calamari, J. E., Riemann, B. C., & Heffelfinger, S. K. (2003). Too much thinking about thinking?: Metacognitive differences in obsessive-compulsive disorder. *Journal of Anxiety Disorders, 17*(2), 181–195.

Janet, P. (1889). *L'automatisme Psychologique.* Paris: Felix Alcan.

Janoff-Bulman, R. (1992). *Shattered Assumptions: Towards a New Psychology of Trauma.* New York: Free Press.

Jatzko, A., Schmitt, A., Kordon, A., & Braus, D. F. (2005). Neuroimaging findings in posttraumatic stress disorder: Review of the literature. *Fortschr Neurol Psychiatr, 73*(7), 377–391.

Javitt, D. C. (2004). Glutamate as a therapeutic target in psychiatric disorders. *Molecular Psychiatry, 7,* 27–31.

Jaycox, L. H., & Foa, E. B. (1998). Posttraumatic stress. In H. S. Friedman (Ed.), *Encyclopedia of Mental Health* (Vol. III, pp. 209–218). San Diego: Academic Press.

Jedema, H. P., & Grace, A. A. (2004). Corticotropin-releasing hormone directly activates noradrenergic neurons of the locus coeruleus recorded in vitro. *Journal of Neurosciences, 24*(43), 9703–9713.

Jefferson, J. W. (2001). Benzodiazepines and anticonvulsants for social phobia (social anxiety disorder). *Journal of Clinical Psychiatry, 62*(1), 50–53.

Jefferson, J. W. (2001a). Social anxiety disorder: More than just a little shyness. *Primary Care Companion Journal of Clinical Psychiatry, 3*(1), 4–9.

Jetty, P. V., Charney, D. S., & Goddard, A. W. (2001). Neurobiology of generalized anxiety disorder. *Psychiatric Clinics of North America, 24*(1), 75–97.

Jezova, D., Makatsori, A., Duncko, R., Moncek, F., & Jakubek, M. (2004). High trait anxiety in healthy subjects is associated with low neuroendocrine activity during psychosocial stress. *Progress in Neuro-psychopharmacology & Biological Psychiatry, 28*(8), 1331–1336.

Joel, D., Ben-Amir, E., Doljansky, J., & Flaisher, S. (2004). Compulsive lever-pressing in rats is attenuated by the serotonin reuptake inhibitors paroxetine and fluvoxamine but not by the tricyclic antidepressant desipramine or the anxiolytic diazepam. *Behavioural Pharmacology, 15*(3), 241–252.

Joel, D., Doljansky, J., Roz, N., & Rehavi, M. (2005). Role of the orbital cortex and of the serotonergic system in a rat model of obsessive-compulsive disorder. *Neuroscience, 130*(1), 25–36.

Joels, M., Verkuyl, J. M., & Van Riel, E. (2003). Hippocampal and hypothalamic function after chronic stress. *Annals of the New York Academy of Sciences, 1007,* 367–378.

Joffe, R. T., Swinson, R. P., & Levitt, A. J. (1991). Acute psychostimulant challenge in primary obsessive-compulsive disorder. *Journal of Clinical Psychopharmacology, 11,* 237–241.

Johnson, D. M., Sheahan, T. C., & Chard, K. M. (2003). Personality disorders, coping strategies, and posttraumatic stress disorder in women with histories of childhood sexual abuse. *Journal of Child Sexual Abuse, 12*(2), 19–39.

Johnstone, K. A., & Page, A. C. (2004). Attention to phobic stimuli during exposure: The effect of distraction on anxiety reduction, self-efficacy, and perceived control. *Behaviour Research and Therapy, 42*(3), 249–275.

Joliat, M. J., Schmidt, M. E., Fava, M., Zhang, S., Michelson, D., Trapp, N. J., & Miner, C. M. (2004). Long-term treatment outcomes of depression with associated anxiety: Efficacy of continuation treatment with fluoxetine. *Journal of Clinical Psychiatry, 65*(3), 373–378.

Jones, E. E., & Davis, K. E. (1965). The attribution process in person perception. In L. Berkowitz (Ed.), *Advances in Experimental Social Psychology* (pp. 219–266). New York: Academic Press.

Jones, N., Duxon, M. S., & King, S. M. (2002). 5HT2C receptor mediation of unconditioned escape behavior in the unstable elevated exposed plus maze. *Psychopharmacology, 164*(2), 214–220.

Jonnal, A. H., Gardner, C. O., Prescott, C. A., & Kendler, K. S. (2000). Obsessive and compulsive symptoms in a general population of female twins. *American Journal of Medical Genetics, 96*(6), 791–796.

Jorm, A. F., Christensen, H., Griffiths, K. M., Rodgers, B., & Blewitt, K. A. (2004). Effectiveness of complementary and self-help treatments for anxiety disorders. *Medical Journal of Australia, 181*(7), 29–46.

Joseph, R. (1998). The limbic system. In H. S. Friedman (Ed.), *Encyclopedia of Mental Health II* (pp. 555–569). San Diego: Academic Press.

Joseph, S. (2004). Client-centered therapy, posttraumatic stress disorder, and posttraumatic growth: Theoretical perspectives and practical implications. *Psychology and Psychotherapy, 77*(1), 101–119.

Joyce, P. R., Mulder, R. T., McKenzie, J. M., Luty, S. E., & Cloninger, C. R. (2004). Atypical depression, atypical temperament, and a differential antidepressant response to fluoxetine and nortriptyline. *Depression and Anxiety, 19*(3), 180–186.

Joyce, P. R., Rogers, G. R., Miller, A. L., Mulder, R. T., Luty, S. E., & Kennedy, M. A. (2003). Polymorphisms of DRD4 and DRD3 and risk of avoidant and obsessive personality traits and disorders. *Psychiatry Research, 119*(1–2), 1–10.

Kalin, N. H. (2004). Studying non-human primates: A gateway to understanding anxiety disorders. *Psychopharmacology Bulletin, 38*(1), 8–13.

Kalin, N. H., Shelton, S. E., & Davidson, R. J. (2004). The role of the central nucleus of the amygdala in mediating fear and anxiety in the primate. *Journal of Neuroscience, 24*(24), 5506–5515.

Kalinichev, M., Easterling, K. W., Plotsky, P. M., & Holtzman, S. G. (2002). Long-lasting changes in stress-induced corticosterone response and anxiety-like behaviors as a consequence of neonatal maternal separation in Long-Evan rats. *Pharmacology, Biochemistry, and Behavior, 73*(1), 131–140.

Kalisch, R., Salome, N., Platzer, S., Wigger, A., Czisch, M., Sommer, W., Singewald, N., Heilig, M., Berthele, A., Holsboer, F., Landgraf, R., & Auer, D. P. (2004). High trait anxiety and hyporeactivity to stress of the dorsomedial prefrontal cortex: A combined phMRI and Fos study in rats. *Neuroimaging, 23*(1), 382–391.

Kaminer, D., & Stein, D. J. (2003). Social anxiety disorder. *World Journal of Biological Psychiatry, 4*(3), 103–110.

Kandel, E. R. (1999). Biology and the future of psychoanalysis: A new intellectual framework for psychiatry revisited. *American Journal of Psychiatry, 156*, 505–524.

Kang, D. H., Kim, J. J., Choi, J. S., Kim, Y. I., Kim, C. W., Youn, T., Han, M. H., Chang, K. H., & Kwon, J. S. (2004). Volumetric investigation of the frontal-subcortical circuitry in patients with obsessive-compulsive disorder. *Journal of Neuropsychiatry and Clinical Neurosciences, 16*(3), 342–349.

Kang, D. H., Kwon, J. S., Kim, J. J., Youn, T., Park, H. J., Kim, M. S., Lee, D. S., & Lee, M. (2003). Brain glucose metabolic changes associated with neuropsychology improvements after four months of treatment in patients with obsessive-compulsive disorder. *Acta Psychiatrica Scandinavica*, 107(4), 291–297.

Kang-Park, M. H., Wilson, W. A., & Moore, S. D. (2004). Differential actions of diazepam and zolpidem in basolateral and central amygdala nuclei. *Neuropharmacology*, 46(1), 1–9.

Kant, R., Chalansani, R., Chengappa, K. N., & Dieringer, M. F. (2004). The off-label use of clozapine in adolescents with bipolar disorder, intermittent explosive disorder, or posttraumatic stress disorder. *Journal of Child and Adolescent Psychopharmacology*, 14(1), 57–63.

Kapczinski, F., Lima, M. S., Souza, J. S., & Schmitt, R. (2003). Antidepressants for generalized anxiety disorder. *Cochrane Database System Review*, 2, 3592.

Kaplan, A., & Hollander, E. (2003). A review of pharmacologic treatments for obsessive-compulsive disorder. *Psychiatric Services*, 54(8), 1111–1118.

Kapur, S., & Seeman, P. (2001). Does fast dissociation from the dopamine D2 receptor explain the action of atypical antipsychotics?: A new hypothesis. *American Journal of Psychiatry*, 158, 360–369.

Kardiner, A. (1941). *The Traumatic Neuroses of War*. New York: Hoeber.

Karl, A., Malta, L. S., & Maercker, A. (2005). Meta-analytic review of event-related potential studies in posttraumatic stress disorder. *Biological Psychiatry*, 6, 1–7.

Karlovic, D., Martinac, M., Buljan, D., & Zoricic, Z. (2004). Relationship between serum lipid concentrations and posttraumatic stress disorder symptoms in soldiers with combat experiences. *Acta Medicine Okayama*, 58(1), 23–27.

Karlovic, D., Marusic, S., & Martinac, M. (2004). Increase of serum triiodothyronine concentration in soldiers with combat-related chronic post-traumatic stress disorder with or without alcohol dependence. *Wien Klin Wochenschr*, 116(11–12), 385–390.

Karpiak, C. P., & Benjamin, L. S. (2004). Therapist affirmation and the process and outcome of psychotherapy: Two sequential analytic studies. *Journal of Clinical Psychology*, 60(6), 659–676.

Kasckow, J. W., Baker, D., & Geracioti, T. D. (2001). Corticotropin-releasing hormone in depression and posttraumatic stress disorder. *Peptides*, 22(5), 845–851.

Kassam-Adams, N., & Winston, F. K. (2004). Predicting child PTSD: The relationship between acute stress disorder and PTSD in injured children. *Journal of the American Academy of Child and Adolescent Psychiatry*, 43(4), 403–411.

Kassed, C. A., & Herkenham, M. (2004). NF-kappaB p50–deficient mice show reduced anxiety-like behaviors in tests of exploratory drive and anxiety. *Behavioural Brain Research*, 154(2), 577–584.

Katerndahl, D., & Ferrer, R. L. (2004). Knowledge about recommended treatment and management of major depressive disorder, panic disorder, and generalized anxiety disorder among family physicians. *Primary Care Companion of Journal of Clinical Psychiatry*, 6(4), 147–151.

Kathmann, N., Rupertseder, C., Hauke, W., & Zaudig, M. (2005). Implicit sequence learning in obsessive-compulsive disorder: Further support for the frontal-striatal dysfunction model. *Biological Psychiatry*, 6, 1–7.

Katon, W., & Walker, E. A. (1998). Medically unexplained symptoms in primary care. *The Journal of Clinical Psychiatry*, 59(20), 15–20.

Katon, W. J., Roy-Byrne, P., Russo, J., & Cowley, D. (2002). Cost-effectiveness and cost onset of a collaborative care intervention for primary care patients with panic disorder. *Archives of General Psychiatry*, 59(12), 1098–1104.

Katrin-Kuelz, A., Riemann, D., Zahn, R., & Voderholzer, U. (2004). Object alternation test: Is it sensitive enough to detect cognitive dysfunction in obsessive-compulsive disorder? *European Psychiatry*, 19(7), 441–443.

Katzelnick, D. J., Kobak, K. A., Greist, J. H., Jefferson, J. W., Mantle, J. M., & Serlin, R. C. (1995). Sertraline for social phobia: A double-blind, placebo-controlled crossover study. *American Journal of Psychiatry, 152,* 1368–1371.

Kaufman, J., & Charney, D. (2000). Comorbidity of mood and anxiety disorders. *Depression and Anxiety, 12*(1), 69–76.

Kaufman, J., Plotsky, P. M., Nemeroff, C. B., & Charney, D. S. (2000). Effects of early adverse experiences on brain structures and function: Clinical implications. *Biological Psychiatry, 48,* 778–790.

Kaufmann, W. A., Humpel, C., Alheid, G. F., & Marksteiner, J. (2003). Compartmentation of alpha 1 and alpha 2 GABAA receptor subunits within rat extended amygdala: Implications for benzodiazepine action. *Brain Research, 964*(1), 91–99.

Keane, T. M., & Barlow, D. H. (2002). Posttraumatic stress disorder. In D. H. Barlow, *Anxiety and Its Disorders: The Nature and Treatment of Anxiety and Panic* (2nd Ed.). New York: Guilford Press.

Keefe, R., Seidman, L. J., Christensen, B. K., Hamer, R. M., Sharma, T., Sitskoorn, M. M., Lewine, R., Yurgelun-Todd, D. A., Gur, R. C., Tohen, M., Tollefson, G. D., Sanger, T. M., & Lieberman, J. A. (2004). Comparative effect of atypical and conventional antipsychotic drugs on neurocognition in first-episode psychosis: A randomized, double-blind trial of olanzapine versus low doses of haloperidol. *American Journal of Psychiatry, 161,* 985–995.

Keen, E. (1970). *Three Faces of Being: Toward an Existential Clinical Psychology.* New York: Appleton-Century-Crofts.

Kellett, J., & Kokkinidis, L. (2004). Extinction deficit and fear reinstatement after electrical stimulation of the amygdala: Implications for kindling-associated fear and anxiety. *Neuroscience, 127*(2), 277–287.

Kelleu, S. P., Bratt, A. M., & Hodge, C. W. (2003). Targeted gene deletion of the 5HT3A receptor subunit produces an anxiolytic phenotype in mice. *European Journal of Pharmacology, 461*(1), 19–25.

Kelley, H. H. (1971). *Attribution in Social Interaction.* Morristown, New Jersey: General Learning Press.

Kellner, M., Baker, D. G., Yassouridis, A., Bettinger, S., Otte, C., Naber, D., & Widemann, K. (2002). Mineralocorticoid receptor function in patients with posttraumatic stress disorder. *American Journal of Psychiatry, 159,* 1938–1940.

Kellner, M., Yassouridis, A., Hubner, R., Baker, D. G., & Weidemann, K. (2003). Endocrine and cardiovascular responses to corticotropin-releasing hormone in patients with posttraumatic stress disorder: A role for atrial natriuretic peptide? *Neuropsychobiology, 47*(2), 102–108.

Kelly, F. D. (1997). *The Assessment of Object Relations Phenomena in Adolescents: TAT and Rorschach Measures.* New Jersey: Lawrence Erlbaum.

Kelly, G. A. (1955). *The Psychology of Personal Constructs.* New York: Norton.

Kendall, P. C., & Pimentel, S. S. (2003). On the physiological symptom constellation in youth with generalized anxiety disorder (GAD). *Journal of Anxiety Disorders, 17*(2), 211–221.

Kendall, P. C., Safford, S., Flannery-Schroeder, E., & Webb, A. (2004). Child anxiety treatment: Outcomes in adolescence and impact on substance use and depression at 7.4-year follow-up. *Journal of Consulting and Clinical Psychology, 72*(2), 276–287.

Kendler, K. S. (1996). Major depression and generalized anxiety disorder: Same genes, (partly) different environments—revisited. *British Journal of Psychiatry, 30,* 68–75.

Kendler, K. S., Hettema, J. M., Butera, F., Gardner, C. O., & Prescott, C. A. (2003). Life event dimensions of loss, humiliation, entrapment, and danger in the prediction of onsets of major depression and generalized anxiety. *Archives of General Psychiatry, 60*(8), 789–796.

Kendler, K. S., Neale, M. C., Kessler, R. C., Heath, A. C., & Eaves, L. J. (1992). The genetic epidemiology of phobias in women. The interrelationship of agoraphobia, social phobia, situational phobia, and simple phobia. *Archives of General Psychiatry, 49*(4), 273–281.

Kendler, K. S., Walters, E. E., Neale, M. C., Kessler, R. C., Heath, A. C., & Eaves, L. J. (1995). The structure of the genetic and environmental risk factors for six major psychiatric disorders in women: Phobia, generalized anxiety disorder, panic disorder, bulimia, major depression, and alcoholism. *Archives of General Psychiatry, 52*, 374–383.

Kennedy, S. H., & Lam, R. W. (2003). Enhancing outcomes in the management of treatment resistant depression: A focus on atypical antipsychotics. *Bipolar Disorder, 5*(2), 36–47.

Kent, J. M., Coplan, J. D., & Gorman, J. M. (1998). Clinical utility of the selective serotonin reuptake inhibitors in the spectrum of anxiety. *Biological Psychiatry, 44*, 812–824.

Kent, J. M., Mathew, S. J., & Gorman, J. M. (2002). Molecular targets in the treatment of anxiety. *Biological Psychiatry, 52*(10), 1008–1030.

Kent, J. M., & Rauch, S. L. (2003). Neurocircuitry of anxiety disorders. *Current Psychiatry Report, 5*(4), 266–273.

Kerr, G. W., McGuffie, A. C., & Wilkie, S. (2001). Tricyclic antidepressant overdose: A review. *Journal of Emergency Medicine, 18*, 236–241.

Kessler, R. J. (1996). Panic disorder and the retreat from meaning. *Journal of Clinical Psychoanalysis, 5*(4), 505–528.

Kessler, R. C., (2003). The impairments caused by social phobia in the general population: Implications for intervention. *Acta Psychiatrica Scandinavica Supplement, 417*, 19–27.

Ketter, T. A., Wang, P. W., Nowakowska, C., & Marsh, W. K. (2004). New medication treatment options for bipolar disorder. *Acta Psychiatrica Scandinavica Supplement, 9*(422), 18–33.

Khan, S., Liberzon, I., & Abelson, J. L. (2004). Effects of propranolol on symptom and endocrine responses to pentagastrin. *Psychoneuroendocrinology, 29*(9), 1163–1171.

Khawaja, X., Xu, J., Liang, J. J., & Barrett, J. E. (2004). Proteomic analysis of protein changes developing in rat hippocampus after chronic antidepressant treatment: Implications for depressive disorders and future therapies. *Journal of Neuroscience Research, 75*(4), 451–460.

Khouzam, H. R., & Emes, R. (2002). The use of buspirone in primary care. *Journal of Psychosocial Nursing and Mental Health Services, 40*(7), 34–41.

Kierkegaard, S. (1954). *The Sickness Unto Death.* Garden City, New York: Doubleday.

Kikuchi, M., Komuro, R., Oka, H., Kidani, T., Hanaoka, A., & Koshino, Y. (2005). Relationship between anxiety and thyroid function in patients with panic disorder. *Progress in Neuro-psychopharmacology & Biological Psychiatry, 29*(1), 77–81.

Kim, J. J., Lee, M. C., Kim, J., Kim, I. Y., Kim, S. I., Han, M. H., Chang, K. H., & Kwon, J. S. (2001). Grey matter abnormalities in obsessive-compulsive disorder: Statistical parametric mapping of segmented magnetic resonance images. *British Journal of Psychiatry, 179*, 330–334.

Kim, M. S., Kang, S. S., Youn, T., Kang, D. H., Kim, J. J., & Kwon, J. S. (2003). Neuropsychological correlates of P300 abnormalities in patients with schizophrenia and obsessive-compulsive disorder. *Psychiatry Research, 123*(2), 109–123.

Kim, Y. R., Min, S. K., & Yu, B. H. (2004). Differences in beta-adrenergic receptor sensitivity between women and men with panic disorder. *European Neuropsychopharmacology, 14*(6), 515–520.

Kimble, M., & Kaufman, M. (2004). Clinical correlates of neurological change in posttraumatic stress disorder: An overview of critical systems. *Psychiatric Clinics of North America, 27*(1), 49–65.

Kimura, M., Tateno, A., & Robinson, R. G. (2003). Treatment of poststroke generalized anxiety disorder comorbid with poststroke depression: Merged analysis of nortriptyline trials. *American Journal Geriatric Psychiatry, 11*(3), 320–327.

Kinrys, G., Pollack, M. H., Simon, N. M., Worthington, J. J., Nardi, A. E., & Versiani, M. (2003). Valproic acid for the treatment of social anxiety disorder. *International Clinical Psychopharmacology, 18*(3), 169–172.

Kinzig, K. P., D'Alessio, D. A., Herman, J. P., Sakai, R. R., Vahl, T. P., Figueiredo, H. F., Murphy, E. K., & Seeley, R. J. (2003). CNS glucagon-like peptide-1 receptors mediate endocrine and anxiety responses to interoceptive and psychogenic stressors. *Journal of Neuroscience, 23*(15), 6163–6170.

Kirk, K. M., Birley, A. J., Statham, D. J., Haddon, B., Lake, R. I., Andrews, J. G., & Martin, N. G. (2000). Anxiety and depression in twin and sib pairs extremely discordant and concordant for neuroticism: Prodromus to a linkage study. *Twin Research, 3*(4), 299–309.

Kirmayer, L. J. (1991). The place of culture in psychiatric nosology: Taijin kyofusho and DSM-IIIR. *The Journal of Nervous and Mental Disease, 179*, 19–28.

Kiropoulos, L. A., Klimidis, S., & Minas, H. (2004). Depression and anxiety: A comparison of older- aged Greek-born immigrants and Anglo-Australians. *The Australian and New Zealand Journal of Psychiatry, 38*(9), 714–724.

Kitayama, N., Vaccarino, V., Kutner, M., Weiss, P., & Bremner, J. D. (2005). Magnetic resonance imaging (MRI) measurement of hippocampal volume in posttraumatic stress disorder: A meta-analysis. *Journal of Affective Disorders, 6*, 1–7.

Kjernisted, K. D., & Bleau, P. (2004). Long-term goals in the management of acute and chronic anxiety disorders. *Canadian Journal of Psychiatry, 49*(3), 51–63.

Klag, S., & Bradley, G. (2004). The role of hardiness in stress and illness: An exploration of the effect of negative affectivity and gender. *British Journal of Health Psychology, 9*(2), 137–161.

Klein, D. F., & Fink, M. (1962). Psychiatric reaction patterns to imipramine. *American Journal of General Psychiatry, 50*, 306–317.

Klein, E. (2002). The role of extended-release benzodiazepines in the treatment of anxiety: A risk-benefit evaluation with a focus on extended-release alprazolam. *Journal of Clinical Psychiatry, 63*(14), 27–33.

Klein, E., & Uhde, T. W. (1988). Controlled study of verapamil for treatment of panic disorder. *Journal of American Psychiatry, 143*, 235–236.

Klein, M. (1932). *The Psychoanalysis of Children*. New York: Delacorte Press.

Klein, R. G., Koplewicz, H. S., & Kanner, A. (1992). Imipramine treatment of children with separation anxiety disorder. *Journal of the American Academy of Child and Adolescent Psychiatry, 31*, 21–28.

Klodzinska, A., Tatarczynska, E., Chojnacka-Wojcik, E., Nowak, G., Cosford, N. D., & Pilc, A. (2004). Anxiolytic-like effects of MTEP, a potent and selective mGlu5 receptor agonist does not involve GABA(A) signaling. *Neuropharmacology, 47*(3), 342–350.

Klumpers, U. M., Tulen, J. H., Timmerman, L., Fekkes, D., Loonen, A. J., & Boomsma, F. (2004). Responsivity to stress in chronic posttraumatic stress disorder due to childhood sexual abuse. *Psychological Reports, 94*(2), 408–410.

Knapp, D. J., Overstreet, D. H., Moy, S. S., & Breese, G. R. (2004). SB242084, flumazenil, and CRA1000 block ethanol withdrawal-induced anxiety in rats. *Alcoholism, 32*(2), 101–111.

Knyazev, G. G., Savostyanov, A. N., & Levin, E. A. (2004). Alpha oscillations as a correlate of trait anxiety. *International Journal of Psychophysiology, 53*(2), 147–160.

Kobasa, S. C. (1979). Stressful life events, personality, and health: An inquiry into hardiness. *Journal of Personality and Social Psychology, 37*, 1–11.

Kobasa, S. C., & Courington, S. (1981). Personality and constitution as mediators in the stress-illness relationship. *Journal of Health and Social Behavior, 22*, 368–378.

Kobasa, S. C., & Puccetti, M. C. (1983). Personality and social resources in stress-resistance. *Journal of Personality and Social Psychology, 45*, 839–850.

Kobayashi, K., Shimizu, E., Hashimoto, K., Mitsumori, M., Koike, K., Okamura, N., Koizumi, H., Ohgake, S., Matsuzawa, D., Zhang, L., Nakazato, M., & Iyo, M. (2005). Serum brain-derived neurotrophic factor (BDNF) levels in patients with panic disorder: As a biological predictor of response to group cognitive behavioral therapy. *Progress in Neuropsychopharmacology and Biological Psychiatry, 29*(5), 658–663.

Koch, S., Hemrick-Luecke, S. K., Thompson, L. K., Evans, D. C., Threlkeld, P. G., Nelson, D. L., Perry, K. W., & Bymaster, F. P. (2004). Comparison of effects of dual transporter inhibitors on monoamine transporters and extracellular levels in rats. *Neuropharmacology, 45*(7), 935–944.

Koehl, M., Lemaire, V., Vallee, M., Abrous, N., Piazza, P. V., Mayo, W., Maccari, S., & Le Moal, M. (2004). Long term neurodevelopmental and behavioral effects of perinatal life events in rats. *Neurotoxicology Research, 3*(1), 65–83.

Koenen, K. C., Harley, R., Lyons, M. J., Wolfe, J., Simpson, J. C., Goldberg, J., Eisen, S. A., & Tsuang, M. (2002). A twin registry study of familial and individual risk factors for trauma exposure and posttraumatic stress disorder. *Journal of Nervous and Mental Disorders, 190*(4), 209–218.

Koenen, K. C., Lyons, M. J., Goldberg, J., Simpson, J., Williams, W. M., Toomey, R., Eisen, S. A., True, W. R., Cloitre, M., Wolfe, J., & Tsuang, M. T. (2003). A high risk twin study of combat-related PTSD comorbidity. *Twin Research, 6*(3), 218–226.

Kohl, F. (2001). Agoraphobia—place anxiety/place fear—place-related vertigo: The classical description of place anxiety by Carl Westphal and Emil Cordes and its significance for the history of the concept and current discussion of anxiety disorders. *Psychiatric Practice, 28*(1), 3–9.

Kohut, H. (1971). *The Analysis of the Self*. New York: International Universities Press.

Kohut, H. (1977). *The Restoration of the Self*. New York: International Universities Press.

Kolb, B., & Whishaw, I. Q. (1998). Brain plasticity and behavior. *Annual Review of Psychology, 49*, 43–64.

Korb, M. P., Gorrell, J., & DeRiet, V. V. (1989). *Gestalt Therapy: Practice and Theory* (2nd ed.). Boston: Allyn and Bacon.

Korinthenberg, R., Shreck, J., Weser, J., & Lehmkuhl, G. (2004). Posttraumatic syndrome after minor head injury cannot be predicted by neurological investigations. *Brain Development, 26*(2), 113–117.

Kosel, M., Rudolph, U., Wielepp, P., Luginbuhl, M., Schmitt, W., Fisch, H. U., & Schlaepfer, T. E. (2004). Diminished GABA(A) receptor-binding capacity and a DNA base substitution in a patient with treatment-resistant depression and anxiety. *Neuropsychopharmacology, 29*(2), 347–350.

Krakow, B., Haynes, P. L., Warner, T. D., Santana, E., Melendrez, D., Johnston, L., Hollifield, M., Sisley, B. N., Koss, M., & Shafer, L. (2004). Nightmares, insomnia, and sleep-disordered breathing in fire evacuees seeking treatment for posttraumatic sleep disturbance. *Journal of Traumatic Stress, 17*(3), 257–268.

Krezel, W., Dupont, S., Krust, A., Chambon, P., & Chapman, P. F. (2001). Increased anxiety and synaptic plasticity in estrogen receptor beta-deficient mice. *Proceedings of the National Academy of Sciences of the United States of America, 98*(21), 12278–12282.

Kroeze, W. K., Kristiansen, K., & Roth, B. L. (2002). Molecular biology of serotonin receptors structure and function at the molecular level. *Current Topics in Medicinal Chemistry, 2*(6), 507–528.

Krystal, J. H., Niehoff-Deutsch, D. N., & Charney, D. S. (1996). The biological basis of panic disorder. *Journal of Clinical Psychiatry, 57*, 23–31.

Kudryavtseva, N. N., Gerrits, M. A., Avgustinovich, D. F., Tenditnik, M. V., & Van Ree, J. M. (2004). Modulation of anxiety-related behaviors by micro- and kappa-opioid receptor agonists depends on the social status of mice. *Peptides, 25*(8), 1355–1363.

Kumin, I. (1996). *Preobject Relatedness: Early Attachment and the Psychoanalytic Situation*. New York: The Guilford Press.

Kunzle, H. (2004). The hippocampal continuation (indusium griseum): Its connectivity in the hedgehog tenrec and its status within the hippocampal formation of higher vertebrates. *Anatomy and Embryology, 208(3)*, 183–213.

Kurup, R. K., & Kurup, P. A. (2002). Hypothalamic digoxin deficiency in obsessive-compulsive disorder and la Tourette's syndrome. *International Journal of Neuroscience, 112(7)*, 797–816.

Kushner, M. G., Abrams, K., & Borchardt, C. M. (2000). The relationship between anxiety disorders and alcohol use disorders: A review of major perspectives and findings. *Clinical Psychology Review, 20*, 149–171.

Kuzma, J. M., & Black, D. W. (2004). Integrating pharmacotherapy and psychotherapy in the management of anxiety disorders. *Current Psychiatry Reports, 6(4)*, 268–273.

Kwon, J. S., Shin, Y. W., Kim, C. W., Kim, Y. I., Youn, T., Han, M. H., Chang, K. H., & Kim, J. J. (2003b). Similarity and disparity of obsessive-compulsive disorder and schizophrenia in MR volumetric abnormalities of the hippocampus-amaygdala complex. *Journal of Neurology and Neurosurgical Psychiatry, 74(7)*, 962–964.

Laakso, A., Wallius, E., Kajander, J., Bergman, J., Eskola, O., Solin, O., Ilonen, T., Salokangas, R. K., Syvalahti, E., & Hietala, J. (2003). Personality traits and striatal dopamine synthesis capacity in healthy subjects. *American Journal of Psychiatry, 160(5)*, 904–910.

Lacerda, A. L., Dalgalarrondo, P., Caetano, D., Camargo, E. E., Etchebehere, E. C., & Soares, J. C. (2003). Elevated thalamic and prefrontal regional cerebral blood flow in obsessive-compulsive disorder: A SPECT study. *Psychiatry Research, 123(2)*, 125–134.

Lacerda, A. L., Dalgalarrondo, P.,Caetano, D., Haas, G. L., Camargo, E. E., & Keshavan, M. S. (2003). Neuropsychological performance and regional cerebral blood flow in obsessive-compulsive disorder. *Progress in Neuro-psychopharmacology & Biological Psychiatry, 27(4)*, 657–665.

Lader, M. L. (2005). Management of panic disorder. *Expert Review of Neurotherapics, 5(2)*, 259–266.

Ladouceur, R., Leger, E., Dugas, M., & Freeston, M. H. (2004). Cognitive-behavioral treatment of generalized anxiety disorder (GAD) for older adults. *International Psychogeriatrics, 16(2)*, 195–207.

Lagnauoi, R., Depont, F., Fourrier, A., Abouelelfath, A., Begaud, B., Verdoux, H., & Moore, N. (2004). Patterns and correlates of benzodiazepine use in the French general population. *European Journal of Clinical Pharmacology, 60(8)*, 1–9.

Laine, K., Ahokoski, O., Huopponen, R., Hanninen, J., Palovaara, S., Ruuskanen, J., Bjorklund, H., Anttila, M., & Rouru, J. (2003). Effect of the novel anxiolytic drug deramciclane on the pharmacokinetics and pharmacodynamics of the CYP3A4 probe drug buspirone. *European Journal of Clinical Pharmacology, 59(10)*, 761–766.

Laing, R. D. (1965). *The Divided Self.* Baltimore: Pelican.

Laing, R. D. (1967). *The Politics of Experience.* New York: Ballantine.

Lamberty, Y., Falter, U., Gower, A. J., & Klitgaard, H. (2003). Anxiolytic profile of the antiepileptic drug levetiracetam in the Vogel conflict test in the rat. *European Journal of Pharmacology, 469(1–3)*, 97–102.

Lamprecht, F., Kohnke, C., Lempa, W., Sack, M., Matzke, M., & Munte, T. F. (2004). Event-related potentials and EMDR treatment of posttraumatic stress disorder. *Neuroscience Research, 49(2)*, 267–272.

Landgraf, R. (2001). Neuropeptides and anxiety-related behavior. *Endocrinology Journal, 48(5)*, 517–533.

Lane, H. Y., Lin, C. C., Huang, C. H., Chang, Y. C., Hsu, S. K., & Chang, W. H. (2004). Risperidone response and 5HT6 receptor gene variance: Genetic association analysis with adjustment for nongenetic confounders. *Schizophrenia Research, 67(1)*, 63–70.

Lanfumey, L., & Hamon, M. (2004). 5HT1 receptors. *Current Drug Targets. CNS Neurological Disorders, 3(1)*, 1–10.

Lang, P. J., Bradley, M. M., & Cuthbert, B. N. (1998). Emotion, motivation, and anxiety: Brain mechanisms and psychophysiology. *Biological Psychiatry, 44*, 1248–1263.

Lanius, R. A., Williamson, P. C., Bluhm, R. L., Densmore, M., Boksman, K., Neufeld, R. W., Gati, J. S., & Menon, R. S. (2005). Functional connectivity of dissociative responses in posttraumatic stress disorder: A functional magnetic resonance imaging investigation. *Biological Psychiatry, 57*(8), 873–884.

Lanius, R., Williamson, P., Boksman, K., Densmore, M., et al. (2002). Brain activation during script-driven imagery induced dissociative responses in PTSD: A functional magnetic resonance imaging investigation. *Biological Psychiatry, 52*, 305–311.

Lapin, I. P. (2003). Neurokynurenines (NEKY) as common neurochemical links of stress and anxiety. *Advances in Experimental Medicine and Biology, 527*, 121–125.

Larsen, M. B., Elfving, B., & Wiborg, O. (2004). The chicken serotonin transporter discriminates between serotonin selective reuptake inhibitors: A species-scanning mutagenesis study. *Journal of Biological Chemistry, 7*, 21–27.

Lasaite, L., Bunevicius, R., Lasiene, D., & Lasas, L. (2004). Psychological functioning after growth hormone therapy in adult growth hormone deficient patients: Endocrine and body composition correlates. *Medicina, 40*(8), 740–744.

Latas, M., Starcevic, V., & Vucinic, D. (2004). Predictors of work disabilities in patients with panic disorder with agoraphobia. *European Psychiatry, 19*(5), 280–284.

Lauterbach, E. C., Freeman, A., & Vogel, R. L. (2003). Correlates of generalized anxiety and panic attacks in dystonia and Parkinson disease. *Cognition, Behavior, and Neurology, 16*(4), 225–233.

Lawford, B. R., McD-Young, R., Noble, E. P., Kann, B., Arnold, L., Rowell, J., & Ritchie, T. L. (2003). D2 dopamine receptor gene polymorphism: Paroxetine and social functioning in posttraumatic stress disorder. *European Neuropsychopharmacology, 13*(5), 313–320.

Lazarus, A. A. (1971). *Behavior Therapy and Beyond.* New York: McGraw-Hill.

Lazarus, A. A. (1976). *Multimodal Behavior Therapy.* New York: Springer.

Leary, T. (1957). *Interpersonal Diagnosis of Personality.* New York: Ronald.

Lecrubier, Y. (2001a). The burden of depression and anxiety in general medicine. *Journal of Clinical Psychiatry, 62*(8), 4–9.

Lecrubier, Y. (2001b). Prescribing patterns for depression and anxiety worldwide. *Journal of Clinical Psychiatry, 62*(13), 31–36.

LeDoux, J. E. (1998). Fear and the brain: Where have we been, and where are we going? *Biological Psychiatry, 46*, 1167–1180.

LeDoux, J. E., & Gorman, J. M. (2001). A call to action: Overcoming anxiety through active coping. *American Journal of Psychiatry, 158*, 1953–1955.

Lee, H. J., Cougle, J. R., & Telch, M. J. (2005). Thought-action fusion and its relationship to schizotypy and OCD symptoms. *Behaviour Research and Therapy, 43*(1), 29–41.

Lee, H. J., Kim, Z. S., & Kwon, S. M. (2005). Thought disorder in patients with obsessive-compulsive disorder. *Journal of Clinical Psychology, 61*(4), 401–413.

Lee, Y. J. (2004). Overview of the therapeutic management of insomnia with zolpidem. *CNS Drugs, 18*(1), 17–23.

Leiderman, D. B., Balish, M., Bromfield, E. B., & Theodore, W. H. (1991). Effect of valproate on human cerebral glucose metabolism. *Epilepsia, 32*(3), 417–422.

Leonard, H. L., Swedo, S. E., Garvey, M., Beer, D., Perlmutter, S., Lougee, L., Karitani, M., & Dubbert, B. (1999). Postinfectious and other forms of obsessive-compulsive disorder. *Child and Adolescent Psychiatric Clinics of North America, 8*(3), 497–511.

Lepine, J. P. (2002). The epidemiology of anxiety disorders: Prevalence and societal costs. *The Journal of Clinical Psychiatry, 63*(14), 4–8.

Lepkifker, E., Sverdlik, A., Iancu, I., Ziv, R., Segev, S., & Kotler, M. (2004). Renal insufficiency in long-term lithium treatment. *Journal of Clinical Psychiatry, 65*(6), 850–856.

Lepola, U., Bergtholdt, B., St. Lambert, J., Davy, K. L., & Ruggiero, L. (2004). Controlled-release paroxetine in the treatment of patients with social anxiety disorder. *Journal of Clinical Psychiatry, 65*(2), 222–229.

Leppavuori, A., Pohjasvaara, T., Vataja, R., Kaste, M., & Erkinjuntti, T. (2003). Generalized anxiety disorders three to four months after ischemic stroke. *Cerebrovascular Disease, 16(3)*, 257–264.

Leslie, J. C., Shaw, D., McCabe, C., Reynolds, D. S., & Dawson, G. R. (2004). Effects of drugs that potentiate GABA on extinction of positively-reinforced operant behavior. *Neuroscience and Biobehavioral Review, 28(3)*, 229–238.

Levin, P., Lazrove, S., & van der Kolk, B. (1999). What psychological testing and neuroimaging tell us about the treatment of posttraumatic stress disorder by Eye Movement Desensitization and Reprocessing. *Journal of Anxiety Disorders, 13(1–2)*, 159–172.

Lewejohann, L., Skryabin, B. V., Sachser, N., Prehn, C., Heiduschka, P., Thano, S., Jordan, U., Dell'Omo, G., Vyssotski, A. L., Pleskacheva, M. G., Lipp, H. P., Tiedge, H., Brosius, J., & Prior, H. (2004). Role of a neuronal small non-messenger RNA: Behavioral alterations in BC1 RNA-deleted mice. *Behavioural Brain Research, 154(1)*, 273–289.

Lewin, K. (1935). *A Dynamic Theory of Personality*. New York: McGraw-Hill.

Lewin, K. (1951). *Field Theory in Social Science*. New York: Harper.

Lezak, M. D., Howieson, D. B., Loring, D. W., Hannay, H. J., & Fischer, J. S. (2004). *Neuropsychological Assessment* (4th Ed.). New York: Oxford University Press.

Libby, S., Reynolds, S., Derisley, J., & Clark, S. (2004). Cognitive appraisals in young people with obsessive-compulsive disorder. *Journal of Child Psychology and Psychiatry, 45(6)*, 1076–1084.

Liberzon, I., & Phan, K. L. (2003). Brain-imaging studies of posttraumatic stress disorder. *CNS Spectrum, 8(9)*, 641–650.

Licinio, J., O'Kirwan, F., Irizarry, K., Merriman, B., Thakur, S., Jepson, R., Lake, S., Tantisira, K. G., Weiss, S. T., & Wong, M. L. (2004). Association of a corticotropin-releasing hormone receptor 1 haplotype and antidepressant treatment response in Mexican-Americans. *Molecular Psychiatry, 9*, 7–12.

Lieberman, J. A. (2004). Dopamine partial agonists: A new class of antipsychotic. *CNS Drugs, 18(4)*, 251–267.

Liebowitz, M. R., Heimberg, R. G., Schneier, F. R., Hope, D. A., Davies, S., Holt, C. S., Goetz, D., Juster, H. R., Lin, S. L., Brunch, M. A., Marshall, R., & Klein, D. F. (1999). Cognitive-behavioral group therapy versus phenelzine in social phobia: Long-term outcome. *Depression and Anxiety, 10*, 89–98.

Lindauer, R. J., Vlieger, E. J., Jalink, M., Olff, M., Carlier, I. V., Majoie, C. B., Den Heeten, G. J., & Gersons, B. P. (2004). Smaller hippocampal volume in Dutch police officers with posttraumatic stress disorder. *Biological Psychiatry, 56(5)*, 356–363.

Linden, A. M., Johnson, B. G., Peters, S. C., Shannon, H. E., Tian, M., Wang, Y., Yu, J. L., Koster, A., Baez, M., & Schoepp, D. D. (2002). Increased anxiety-related behavior in mice deficient for metabotropic glutamate 8 (mGlu8) receptor. *Neuropharmacology, 43(2)*, 251–259.

Lindenmayer, J. P., Czobor, P., Volavka, J., Lieberman, J. A., Citrome, L., Sheitman, B., McEvoy, J. P., Cooper, T. B., & Chakos, M. (2004). Effects of atypical antipsychotics on the syndromal profile in treatment-resistant schizophrenia. *Journal of Clinical Psychiatry, 65(4)*, 551–556.

Lipsitz, J. D., Masia-Warner, C., Apfel, H., Marans, Z., Hellstern, B., Forand, N., Levenbraun, Y., & Fyer, A. J. (2004). Anxiety and depressive symptoms and anxiety sensitivity in youngsters with noncardiac chest pain and benign heart murmurs. *Journal of Pediatric Psychology, 29(8)*, 607–612.

Lipsitz, J. D., & Schneier, F. R. (2000). Social phobia: Epidemiology and cost of illness. *Pharacoeconomics, 18(1)*, 23–32.

Lipsky, R. H., & Goldman, D. (2003). Genomics and variation of ionotropic glutamate receptors. *Annals of the New York Academy of Sciences, 1003*, 22–35.

Liu, Y. F., Bertram, K., Perides, G., McEwen, B. S., & Wang, D. (2004). Stress induces activation of stress-activated kinases in the mouse brain. *Journal of Neurochemistry, 89(4)*, 1034–1043.

Llorca, P. M., Spadone, C., Sol, O., Danniau, A., Bougerol, T., Corruble, E., Faruch, M., Macher, J. P., Sermet, E., & Servant, D. (2002). Efficacy and safety of hydroxyzine in the treatment of generalized anxiety disorder: A three-month double-blind study. *Journal of Clinical Psychiatry, 63*(11), 1020–1027.

Lochner, C., Seedat, S., du Toit, P. L., Nel, D. G., Niehaus, D. J., Sandler, R., & Stein, D. J. (2005). Obsessive-compulsive disorder and trichotillomania: A phenomenological comparison. *BMC Psychiatry, 5*(1), 2.

Lochner, C., & Stein, D. J. (2003). Heterogeneity of obsessive-compulsive disorder: A literature review. *Harvard Review of Psychiatry, 11*(3), 113–132.

Loebel, A. D., Botts, S. R., & Feldman, B. I. (1998). Atypical antipsychotics in the managed care era. *American Journal of Managed Care, 4,* S37–S59.

Lombardo, T. W., & Gray, M. J. (2005). Beyond exposure for posttraumatic stress disorder (PTSD) symptoms: Broad-spectrum PTSD treatment strategies. *Behavior Modification, 29*(1), 3–9.

Loscher, W. (2002). Basic pharmacology of valproate: A review after 35 years of clinical use for the treatment of epilepsy. *CNS Drugs, 16*(10), 669–6994.

Loveland-Cook, C. A., Flick, L. H., Homan, S. M., Campbell, C., McSweeney, M., & Gallagher, M. E. (2004). Posttraumatic stress disorder in pregnancy: Prevalence, risk factors, and treatment. *Obstetrics and Gynecology, 103*(4), 710–717.

Lowery, C. A. (2002). Functional subtests of serotonergic neurones: Implications for control of the hypothalamic-pituitary-adrenal axis. *Journal of Neuroendocrinology, 14*(11), 911–923.

Luborsky, L. (1996). Theories of cure in psychoanalytic psychotherapies and the evidence for them. *Psychoanalytic Inquiry, 16,* 257–264.

Luborsky, L., & Crits-Christoph, P. (1998). *Understanding Transference: The Core Conflictual Relationship Theme Method* (2nd Ed.). Washington, DC: American Psychological Association.

Luo, N., Fones, C. S., Thumboo, J., & Li, S. C. (2004). Factors influencing health-related quality of life of Asians with anxiety disorders in Singapore. *Quality of Life Research: An International Journal of Quality of Life Aspects of Treatment, Care and Rehabilitation, 13*(2), 557–565.

Lydiard, R. B. (2001). Social anxiety disorder treatment: Role of SSRIs. In S. A. Montgomery & J. A. den Boer (Eds.), *Perspectives in Psychiatry, Volume 8: SSRIs in Depression and Anxiety* (2nd Ed.) (pp. 129–150). New York, John Wiley & Sons.

Lydiard, R. B. (2003). The role of GABA in anxiety disorders. *Journal of Clinical Psychiatry, 64*(3), 21–27.

Lyons, D. M., & Schatzberg, A. F. (2003). Early maternal availability and prefrontal correlates of reward-related memory. *Neurobiology of Learning and Memory, 80*(2), 97–104.

Maccari, S., Darnaudery, M., Morley-Fletcher, S., Zuena, A. R., Cinque, C., & Van Reeth, O. (2003). Prenatal stress and long-term consequences: Implications of glucocorticoid hormones. *Neuroscience and Biobehavioral Reviews, 27*(1–2), 119–127.

MacLean, P. (1990). *The Triune Brain in Evolution.* New York: Plenum.

Macy, R. D. (2002). Prevalence rates for PTSD and utilization of behavioral health services for an adult Medicaid population (Ph.D. dissertation). Union College, Ohio.

Maddi, S. R. (2001). *Personality Theories: A Comparative Analysis* (6th Ed.). Prospect Heights, Illinois: Waveland.

Maddock, C., Baita, A., Orru, M. G., Sitzia, R., Costa, A., Muntoni, E., Farci, M. G., Carpiniello, B., & Pariante, C. M. (2004). Psychopharmacological treatment of depression, anxiety, irritability, and insomnia in patients receiving interferon-alpha: Prospective case series and a discussion of biological mechanisms. *Journal of Psychopharmacology, 18*(1), 41–46.

Maercker, A., Michael, T., Fehm, L., Becker, E. S., & Margraf, J. (2004). Age of traumatization as a predictor of posttraumatic stress disorder or major depression in young women. *British Journal of Psychiatry, 184,* 482–487.

Magee, W. J., Eaton, W. W., Wittchen, H. U., McGonagle, K. A., & Kessler, R. C. (1996). Agoraphobia, simple phobia, and social phobia in the National Comorbidity Survey. *Archives of General Psychiatry, 53*, 159–168.

Mahalik, J. R., Cournoyer, R. J., DeFrank, W., Cherry, M., & Napolitano, J. M. (1998). Men's gender role conflict and use of psychological defenses. *Journal of Counseling Psychology, 45*, 247–255.

Maier, S. F., Laudenslager, M., & Ryan, S. M. (1985). Stressor controllability, immune function, and endogenous opiates. In F. R. Brush and J. B. Overneier (Eds.), *Affect, Conditioning, and Cognition: Essays on the Determinants of Behavior* (pp. 203–210). Hillsdale, New Jersey: Erlbaum.

Makino, S., Baker, R. A., Smith, M. A., & Gold, P. W. (2000). Differential regulation of neuropeptide YmRNA expression in the arcuate nucleur and locus coeruleus by stress and antidepressants. *Journal of Neuroendocrinology, 12(5)*, 387–395.

Malhotra, A. K., Murphy, G. M., & Kennedy, J. L. (2004). Pharmacogenetics of psychotropic drug response. *American Journal of Psychiatry, 161*, 780–796.

Maltby, N., Mayers, M. F.., Allen, G. J., & Tolin, D. F. (2005). Anxiety sensitivity: Stability in prospective research. *Journal of Anxiety Disorders, 19(6)*, 708–716.

Maltby, N., Tolin, D. F., Worhunsky, P., O'Keefe, T. M., & Kiehl, K. A. (2005). Dysfunctional action monitoring hyperactivates frontal-striatal circuits in obsessive-compulsive disorder: An event-related fMRI study. *Neuroimaging, 24(2)*, 495–503.

Mamo, D., Kapur, S., Shammi, C. M., Papatheodorou, G., Mann, S., Therrien, F., & Remington, G. (2004). A PET study of dopamine D2 and serotonin 5HT2 receptor occupancy in patients with schizophrenia treated with therapeutic doses of ziprasidone. *American Journal of Psychiatry, 161*, 818–825.

Mancama, D., & Kerwin, R. W. (2003). Role of pharmacogenomics in individualizing treatment with SSRIs. *CNS Drugs, 17(3)*, 143–151.

Mancini, C., Van Ameringen, M., & Farvolden, P. (2002). Does SSRI augmentation with antidepressants that influence noradrenergic function resolve depression in obsessive-compulsive disorder? *Journal of Affective Disorders, 68(1)*, 59–65.

Mancuso, R. A., Schetter, C. D., Rini, C. M., Roesch, S. C., & Hobel, C. J. (2004). Maternal prenatal anxiety and corticotropin-releasing hormone associated with timing of delivery. *Psychosomatic Medicine, 66(5)*, 762–769.

Maneuf, Y. P., Gonzalez, M. I., Sutton, K. S., Chung, F. Z., Pinnock, R. D., & Lee, K. (2003). Cellular and molecular action of the putative GABA-mimetic, gabapentin. *Cellular and Molecular Life Sciences, 60(4)*, 742–750.

Mangold, D. L., Peyrot, M., Giggey, P., & Wand, G. S. (2000). Endogenous opioid activity is associated with obsessive-compulsive symptomology in individuals with a family history of alcoholism. *Neuropsychopharmacology, 22(6)*, 595–607.

Mantino, D., Church, A. J., Dale, R. C., & Giovannoni, G. (2005). Antibasal ganglia antibodies and PANDAS. *Movement Disorders, 20(1)*, 116–117.

Manzanares, J., Uriguen, L., Rubio, G., & Palomo, T. (2004). Role of endocannabinoid system in mental diseases. *Neurotoxin Research, 6(3)*, 213–224.

Marais, E., Klugbauer, N., & Hofmann, F. (2001). Calcium channel alphas(2)delta subunits-structure and gabapentin binding. *Molecular Pharmacology, 59(5)*, 1243–1248.

Marazziti, D., Baroni, S., Masala, I., Giannaccini, G., Mungai, F., Di Nasso, E., & Cassano, G. B. (2003). Decreased lymphocyte 3H-paroxetine binding in obsessive-compulsive disorder. *Neuropsychobiology, 47(3)*, 128–130.

Marco, E. M., Perez-Alvarez, L., Borcel, E., Rubio, M., Guaza, C., Ambrosio, E., File, S. E., & Viveros, M. P. (2004). Involvement of 5HT1A receptors in behavioral effects of the cannabinoid receptor agonist CP55,940 in male rats. *Behavioural Pharmacology, 15(1)*, 21–27.

Maren, S. (2005). Building and burying fear memories in the brain. *Neuroscientist, 11(1)*, 89–99.

Margraf, J., Ehlers, A., & Roth, W. T. (1986). Sodium lactate infusions and panic attacks: A review and critique. *Psychosomatic Medicine, 48,* 23–51.

Markianos, M., Hatzimanolis, J., Lykouras, L., & Christodoulou, G. N. (2002). Prolactin responses to acute clomipramine and haloperidol of male schizophrenic patients in a drug-free state and after treatment with clozapine or with olanzapine. *Schizophrenia Research, 56*(1–2), 11–17.

Maron, E., Nikopensius, T., Koks, S., Altmae, S., Heinaste, E., Vabrit, K., Tammekivi, V., Hallast, P., Koido, K., Kurg, A., Metspalu, A., Vasar, E., Vasar, V., & Shlik, J. (2005). Association study of 90 candidate gene polymorphisms in panic disorder. *Psychiatric Genetics, 15*(1), 17–24.

Marowsky, A., Fritschy, J. M., & Vogt, K. E. (2004). Functional mapping of GABA receptor subtypes in the amygdala. *European Journal of Neuroscience, 20*(5), 1281–1289.

Marshall, R. D., Beebe, K. L., Oldham, M., et al. (2001). Efficacy and safety of paroxetine treatment for chronic PTSD: A fixed-dose, placebo-controlled study. *American Journal of Psychiatry, 158,* 1982–1988.

Martin, B., Wright, C. I., McMullin, K. G., Shin, L. M., & Rauch, S. L. (2004). Functional magnetic resonance imaging evidence for a lack of striatal dysfunction during implicit sequence learning in individuals with animal phobia. *American Journal of Psychiatry, 161*(1), 67–71.

Martin, S. D., Martin, E., Rai, S. S., Richardson, M. A., & Royall, R. (2001). Brain blood flow changes in depressed patients treated with interpersonal psychotherapy or venlafaxine hydrochloride: Preliminary findings. *Archives of General Psychiatry, 58*(7), 641–648.

Martinez, G., Ropero, C., Funes, A., Blotta, C., Landa, A. I., & Gargiulo, P. A. (2002). Effects of selective NMDA and non-NMDA blockade in the nucleus accumbens on the plus-maze test. *Physiology & Behavior, 76*(2), 219–224.

Martinez-Barrondo, S., Saiz, P., Morales, B., Garcia-Portilla, M., Coto, E., Alvarez, M., Bascaran, M. T., Bousono, M., & Bobes, J. (2005). Negative evidence in association between apolipoprotein E polymorphism and panic disorder. *European Psychiatry, 6,* 1–7.

Martinez-Barrondo, S., Saiz, P., Morales, B., Garcia-Portilla, M., Coto, E., Alvarez, M., & Bobes, J. (2005). Serotonin gene polymorphisms in patients with panic disorder. *Actas Esp Psiquiatr, 33*(4), 210–215.

Masi, G., Millepiedi, S., Mucci, M., Poli, P., Bertini, N., & Milantoni, L. (2004). Generalized anxiety disorder in referred children and adolescents. *Journal of the American Academy of Child and Adolescent Psychiatry, 43*(6), 752–760.

Masi, G., Perugi, G., Toni, C., Millepiedi, S., Mucci, M., Bertini, N., & Akiskal, H. S. (2004). Obsessive-compulsive bipolar comorbidity: Focus on children and adolescents. *Journal of Affective Disorders, 78*(3), 175–183.

Masling, J. M., & Bornstein, R. F. (Eds.). (1993). *Psychoanalytic Perspectives on Psychopathology.* Washington, D. C.: American Psychological Association.

Masling, J. M., & Bornstein, R. F. (Eds.). (1994). *Empirical Perspectives on Object-Relations Theory.* Washington, D. C.: American Psychological Association.

Masling, J. M., & Bornstein, R. F. (Eds.). (1996). *Psychoanalytic Perspectives on Developmental Psychology.* Washington, D. C.: American Psychological Association.

Maslow, A. H. (1968). *Toward a Psychology of Being.* Princeton: Van Nostrand.

Maslow, A. H. (1970). *Motivation and Personality* (2nd Ed.). New York: Harper & Row.

Massana, G., Serra-Grabulosa, J. M., Salgado-Pineda, P., Gasto, C., Junque, C., Massana, J., & Mercader, J. M. (2003). Parahippocampal gray matter density in panic disorder: A voxel-base morphometric study. *American Journal of Psychiatry, 160*(3), 566–568.

Mataix-Cols, D., Alonso, P., Hernandez, R., Deckersbach, T., Savage, C. R., Menchon, J., & Vallejo, J. (2003). Relation of neurological soft signs to nonverbal memory performance in obsessive-compulsive disorder. *Journal of Clinical and Experimental Neuropsychology, 25*(6), 842–851.

Mataix-Cols, D., Alonso, P., Pifarre, J., Menchon, J. M., & Vallejo, J. (2002). Neuropsychological performance in medicated versus unmedicated patients with obsessive-compulsive disorder. *Psychiatry Research, 109(3),* 255–264.

Mataix-Cols, D., do Rosario-Campos, M. C., & Leckman, J. F. (2005). A multidimensional model of obsessive-compulsive disorder. *American Journal of Psychiatry, 162(2),* 228–238.

Mataix-Cols, D., Wooderson, S., Lawrence, N., Brammer, M. J., Speckens, A., & Phillips, M. L. (2004). Distinct neural correlates of washing, checking, and hoarding symptom dimensions in obsessive-compulsive disorder. *Archives of General Psychiatry, 61(6),* 564–574.

Mathe, A. A. (1999). Neuropeptides and electroconvulsive treatment. *Journal of Electroconvulsive Therapy, 15(1),* 60–75.

Mathew, S. J., Mao, X., Coplan, J. D., Smith, E., Sackeim, H. A., Gorman, J. M., & Shungu, D. C. (2004). Dorsolateral prefrontal cortical pathology in generalized anxiety disorder: A photon magnetic resonance spectroscopic imaging study. *American Journal of Psychiatry, 161,* 1119–1121.

Mathews, C. A., Jang, K. L., Hami, S., & Stein, M. B. (2004). The structure of obsessionality among young adults. *Depression and Anxiety, 20(2),* 77–85.

Matthews, A., Mackintosh, B., & Fulcher, E. P. (1997). Cognitive biases in anxiety and attention to threat. *Trends in Cognitive Sciences, 1,* 340–355.

May, F. S., Chen, Q. C., Gilbertson, M. W., Shenton, M. E., & Pitman, R. K. (2004). Cavum septum pellucidum in monozygotic twins discordant for combat exposure: Relationship to posttraumatic stress disorder. *Biological Psychiatry, 55(6),* 656–658.

May, R. (1950). *The Meaning of Anxiety.* New York: Ronald Press.

May, R. (1953). *Man's Search for Himself.* New York: Delta.

May, R. (1967). *Psychology and the Human Dilemma.* New York: Van Nostrand-Reinhold.

May, R. (Ed.)(1969). *Existential Psychology* (2nd ed.). New York: Random House.

May, R. (1977). *The Meaning of Anxiety* (2nd Edition). New York: Norton.

May, R. (1981). *Freedom and Destiny.* New York: Norton.

May, R., & Yalom, I. (1989). Existential psychotherapy. In R. J. Corsini & D. Wedding (Eds.), *Current Psychotherapies* (pp. xx–xx). Itasca, Illinois: Peacock.

McAdams, D. P. (2001). *The Person: An Integrated Introduction to Personality Psychology* (3rd Ed.). Fort Worth, TX: Harcourt Brace.

McClelland, D. C. (1951). *Personality.* New York: Dryden.

McClelland, D. C. (1961). *The Achieving Society.* New Jersey: Van Nostrand.

McCrae, R. R., & Costa, P. T. Jr. (1987). Validation of the five-factor model of personality across instruments and observers. *Journal of Personality and Social Psychology, 52,* 81–90.

McDougle, C. J., Barr, L. C., Goodman, W. K., & Price, L. H. (1999). Possible role of neuropeptides in obsessive-compulsive disorder. *Psychoneuroendocrinology, 24(1),* 1–24.

McEwen, B. S. (2000). The neurobiology of stress: From serendipity to clinical relevance. *Brain Research, 886(1–2),* 172–189.

McEwen, B. S. (2002). The neurobiology and neuroendocrinology of stress: Implications for posttraumatic stress disorder from a basic science perspective. *Psychiatric Clinics of North America, 25(2),* 469–494.

McEwen, B. S. (2003). Mood disorders and allostatic load. *Biological Psychiatry, 54(3),* 200–207.

McEwen, B. S., & Magarinos, A. M. (1997). Stress effects on morphology and function of the hippocampus. *Annals of the New York Academy of Sciences, 821,* 271–284.

McGrath, M. J., Campbell, K. M., Parks, C. R., & Burton, F. H. (2000). Glutamatergic drugs exacerbate symptomatic behavior in a transgenic model of comorbid Tourette's syndrome and obsessive-compulsive disorder. *Brain Research, 877(1),* 23–30.

McHugh, S. B., Deacon, R. M., Rawlins, J. N., & Bannerman, D. M. (2004). Amygdala and ventral hippocampus contribute differentially to mechanisms of fear and anxiety. *Behavioral Neuroscience, 118(1)*, 63–78.

McKeon, J., McGuffin, P., & Robinson, P. (1984). Obsessive-compulsive neurosis following head injury: A report of four cases. *British Journal of Psychiatry, 144*, 190–192.

McLaughlin, T., Geissler, E. C., & Wan, G. J. (2003). Comorbidities and associated treatment charges in patients with anxiety disorders. *Pharmacotherapy, 23(10)*, 1251–1256.

McLeod, J. D., & Kessler, R. C. (1990). Socioeconomic status differences in vulnerability to undesirable lfe events. *Journal of Health and Social Behavior, 31(2)*, 162–172.

McNally, R. J. (1994). *Panic Disorder: A Critical Analysis*. New York: Guilford Press.

McNally, R. J. (2003). *Remembering Trauma*. Cambridge, Massachusetts: Harvard University Press.

McNaughton, N., & Gray, J. (2000). Anxiolytic action on the behavioral inhibition system implies multiple types of arousal contribute to anxiety. *Journal of Affective Disorders, 61*, 161–179.

McWilliams, N. (1994). *Psychoanalytic Diagnosis: Understanding Personality Structure in the Clinical Process*. New York: Guilford Press.

Meares, R. (2004). The conversational model: An outline. *American Journal of Psychotherapy, 58(1)*, 51–66.

Meichenbaum, D. (1974). *Cognitive Behavior Modification*. Morristown, New Jersey: General Learning Press.

Meichenbaum, D. (1977). *Cognitive-Behavior Modification*. New York: Plenum.

Meichenbaum, D. (1985). *Stress Inoculation Training*. New York: Plenum Press.

Meira-Lima, I., Shavitt, R. G., Miguita, K., Ikenaga, E., Miguel, E. C., & Vallada, H. (2004). Association analysis of the catechol-o-methyltransferase (COMT), serotonin transporter (5-HTT), and serotonin 2A receptor (5HT2A) gene polymorphisms with obsessive-compulsive disorder. *Genes, Brain, and Behavior, 3(2)*, 75–79.

Meiran, S. E., Reus, V. I., Webster, R., Shafton, R., & Wolkowitz, O. M. (2004). Chronic pregnenolone effects in normal humans: Attenuation of benzodiazepine-induced sedation. *Psychoneuroendocrinology, 29(4)*, 486–500.

Meissner, W. W. (1988). *Treatment of Patients in the Borderline Spectrum*. New York: Aronson.

Melamed, S., Shirom, A., Toker, S., Berliner, S., & Shapira, I. (2004). Association of fear of terror with low-grade inflammation among apparently healthy employed adults. *Psychosomatic Medicine, 66(4)*, 484–491.

Mellman, T. A., Clark, R. E., & Peacock, W. J. (2003). Prescribing patterns for patients with posttraumatic stress disorder. *Psychiatric Services, 54*, 1618–1621.

Meltzer, H. Y., Arvanitis, L., Bauer, D., & Rein, W. (2004). Placebo-controlled evaluation of four novel compounds for the treatment of schizophrenia and schizoaffective disorder. *American Journal of Psychiatry, 161*, 975–984.

Mendlowicz, M. V., & Stein, M. B. (2000). Quality of life in individuals with anxiety disorders. *The American Journal of Psychiatry, 157*, 669–682.

Merali, Z., Khan, S., Michaud, D. S., Shippy, S. A., & Anisman, H. (2004). Does amygdaloid corticotropin-releasing hormone (CRH) mediate anxiety-like behaviors? Dissociation of anxiogenic effects and CRH release. *European Journal of Neuroscience, 20(1)*, 229–239.

Merali, Z., Michaud, D., McIntosh, J., Kent, P., & Anisman, H. (2003). Differential involvement of amygdaloid CRH system(s) in the salience and valence of the stimuli. *Progress in Neuro-Psychopharmacology & Biological Psychiatry, 27(8)*, 1201–1212.

Merritt, T. C. (2000). Recognition and acute management of patients with panic attacks in the emergency department. *Emergency Medicine Clinics of North America, 18(2)*, 289–300.

Meyer, J. H., Wilson, A. A., Sagrati, S., Hussey, D., Carella, A., Potter, W. Z., Gino-vart, N., Spencer, E. P., Cheok, A., & Houle, S. (2004). Serotonin transporter occupancy of five selective serotonin reuptake inhibitors at different doses: An [11C]DASB positron emission tomography study. *American Journal of Psychiatry, 161*(5), 826–835.

Micallef, J., & Blin, O. (2001). Neurobiology and clinical pharmacology of obsessive-compulsive disorder. *Clinical Neuropharmacology, 24*(4), 191–207.

Michael, T., Ehlers, A., Halligan, S. L., & Clark, D. M. (2005). Unwanted memories of assault: What intrusion characteristics are associated with PTSD? *Behavior Research and Therapy, 43*(5), 613–628.

Middeldorp, C. M., Cath, D. C., Van Dyck, R., & Boomsma, D. I. (2005). The co-morbidity of anxiety and depression in the perspective of genetic epidemiology: A review of twin and family studies. *Psychological Medicine, 35*(5), 611–624.

Miguel, E. C., Leckman, J. F., Rauch, S., do Rosario-Campos, M. C., Hounie, A. G., Mercadante, M. T., Chacon, P., & Pauls, D. L. (2005). Obsessive-compulsive disorder phenotypes: Implications for genetic studies. *Molecular Psychiatry, 10*(3), 258–275.

Miller, D. B., & O'Callaghan, J. P. (2003). Effects of aging and stress on hippocampal structure and function. *Metabolism: Clinical and Experimental, 52*(10, 2), 17–21.

Miller, D. K., Sumithran, S. P., & Dwoskin, L. P. (2002). Bupropion inhibits nico-tine-evoked [(3)H] overflow from rat striatal slices preloaded with [(3)H] dopamine and from rat hippocampal slices preloaded with [(3)H] norepinephrine. *Journal of Pharmacology and Experimental Therapeutics, 302*(3), 1113–1122.

Millet, B., Chabane, N., Delorme, R., Leboyer, M., Leroy, S., Poirier, M. F., Bourdel, M. C., Mouren- Simeoni, M. C., Rouillon, F., Loo, H., & Krebs, M. O. (2003). Association between the dopamine receptor D4(DRD4) gene and obsessive-compulsive disorder. *American Journal of Medical Genetics, 116*(1), 55–59.

Millet, B., Kochman, F., Gallarda, T., Krebs, M. O., Demonfaucon, F., Barrot, I., Bourdel, M. C., Olie, J. P., Loo, H., & Hantouche, E. G. (2004). Phenomenological and comorbid features associated in obsessive-compulsive disorder: Influence of age on onset. *Journal of Affective Disorders, 79*(1–3), 241–246.

Milrod, B. L., Busch, F., Leon, A. C., Aronson, A., Roiphe, J., Rudden, M., Singer, M., Shapiro, T., Goldman, H., Richter, D., & Shear, M. K. (2001). A pilot open trial of brief psychodynamic psychotherapy for panic disorder. *Journal of Psychotherapy Practice and Research, 10*(4), 239–245.

Milrod, B. L., & Shear, M. K. (1991). Dynamic treatment of panic disorder: A review. *Journal of Nervous and Mental Disorders, 179*(12), 741–743.

Mineka, S., Watson, D., & Clark, L. A. (1998). Comorbidity of anxiety and unipolar mood disorders. *Annual Review of Psychology, 49*, 377–412.

Modestin, J., Furrer, R., & Malti, T. (2005). Different traumatic experiences are associated with different pathologies. *Psychiatric Quarterly, 76*(1), 19–32.

Mogg, K., Baldwin, D. S., Brodrick, P., & Bradley, B. P. (2004). Effect of short-term SSRI treatment on cognitive bias in generalized anxiety disorder. *Psychopharmacology, 5*, 7–12.

Mohlman, J. (2004). Psychosocial treatment of late-life generalized anxiety disorder: Current status and future directions. *Clinical Psychology Review, 24*(2), 149–169.

Mol, S. S., Arntz, A., Metsemakers, J. F., Dinant, G. J., Vilters-van Montfort, P. A., & Knottnerus, J. A. (2005). Symptoms of posttraumatic stress disorder after non-traumatic events: Evidence from an open population study. *British Journal of Psychiatry, 186*, 494–499.

Mombereau, C., Kaupmann, K., Van der Putten, H., & Cryan, J. F. (2004). Altered response to benzodiazepine anxiolytics in mice lacking GABAB1 receptors. *European Journal of Pharmacology, 497*(1), 119–120.

Montezinho, L. P., Duarte, C., Fonseca, C. P., Glinka, Y., Layden, B., Mota de Fre-itas, D., Geraldes, C. F., & Castro, M. M. (2004). Intracellular lithium and cyclic AMP levels are mutually regulated in neuronal cells. *Journal of Neurochemistry, 90*(4), 920–930.

Moore, R. Y., & Bloom, F. E. (1979). Central catecholamine neuron systems: Anatomy and physiology of the norepinephrine and epinephrine systems. *Annual Review of Neuroscience, 2,* 113–168.

Morer, A., Vinas, O., Lazaro, L., Calvo, R., Andres, S., Bosch, J., Gasto, C., Massana, J., & Castro, J. (2005). Subtyping obsessive-compulsive disorder: Clinical and immunological findings in child and adult onset. *Journal of Psychiatric Research, 7,* 1–7.

Morin, C. M., Belanger, L., & Bernier, F. (2004). Correlates of benzodiazepine use in individuals with insomnia. *Sleep Medicine, 5*(5), 457–462.

Moritz, S., Birkner, C., Kloss, M., Jahn, H., Hand, I., Haasen, C., & Krausz, M. (2002). Executive functioning in obsessive-compulsive disorder, unipolar depression, and schizophrenia. *Archives of Clinical Neuropsychology, 17*(5), 477–483.

Moritz, S., Hubner, M., & Kluwe, R. (2004). Task switching and backward inhibition in obsessive-compulsive disorder. *Journal of Clinical & Experimental Neuropsychology, 26*(5), 677–683.

Moritz, S., & Von Muhlenen, A. (2005). Inhibition of return in patients with obsessive-compulsive disorder. *Journal of Anxiety Disorders, 19*(1), 117–126.

Moroz, G. (2004). High-potency benzodiazepines: Recent clinical results. *Journal of Clinical Psychiatry, 65*(5), 13–18.

Motl, R. W., & Dishman, R. K. (2004). Effects of acute exercise on the soleus H-reflex and self-reported anxiety after caffeine ingestion. *Physiological Behavior, 80*(4), 577–585.

Mottard, J. P., & de la Sablonniere, J. F. (1999). Olanzapine-induced obsessive-compulsive disorder. *American Journal of Psychiatry, 156*(5), 799–800.

Mukherjee, K., Knisely, A., & Jacobson, L. (2004). Partial glucocorticoid agonist-like effects of imipramine on hypothalamic-pituitary-adrenocortical activity, thymus weight, and hippocampal glucocorticoid receptors in male C57BL/6 mice. *Endocrinology, 145*(9), 4185–4191.

Mulder, E. J., Robles de Medina, P. G., Huizink, A. C., Van den Bergh, B. R., Buitelaar, J. K., & Visser, G. H. (2002). Prenatal maternal stress: Effects on pregnancy and the (unborn) child. *Early Human Development, 70*(1–2), 3–14.

Mulder, R. T., Watkins, W. G., Joyce, P. R., & Luty, S. E. (2003). Age may affect response to antidepressants with serotonergic and noradrenergic actions. *Journal of Affective Disorders, 76*(1–3), 143–149.

Muller, D., Pfeil, T., & Von Den Driesch, V. (2003). Treating depression comorbid with anxiety—results of an open, practice-oriented study with St. John's Wort WS5572 and valerian extract in high doses. *Phytomedicine, 10*(4), 25–30.

Mundo, E., Zai, G., Lee, L., Parikh, S. V., & Kennedy, J. L. (2001). The 5HT1Dbeta receptor gene in bipolar disorder: A family-based association study. *Neuropsychopharmacology, 25*(4), 608–613.

Muris, P., & Meesters, C. (2004). Children's somatization symptoms: Correlations with trait anxiety, anxiety sensitivity, and learning experiences. *Psychological Reports, 94*(3, 2), 1269–1275.

Musselman, D. L., & Nemeroff, C. B. (1996). Depression and endocrine disorders: Focus on the thyroid and adrenal system. *British Journal of Psychiatry Supplement, 30,* 123–128.

Muzina, D. J., & Calabrese, J. R. (2005). Maintenance therapies in bipolar disorder: Focus on randomized controlled trials. *The Australian New Zealand Journal of Psychiatry, 39*(8), 652–661.

Najavits, L. M. (2002). *Seeking Safety: A Treatment Manual for PTSD and Substance Abuse.* New York: Guilford.

Nash, M. W., Huezo-Diaz, P., Williamson, R. J., Sterne, A., Purcell, S., Hoda, F., Cherny, S. S., Abecasis, G. R., Prince, M., Gray, J. A., Ball, D., Asherson, P., Mann, A.,

Goldberg, D., McGuffin, P., Farmer, A., Plomin, A., Plomin, R., Craig, I. W., & Sham, P. C. (2004). Genome-wide linkage analysis of a composite index of neuroticism and mood-related scales in extreme selected sibships. *Human Molecular Genetics, 9,* 7–12.

Natelson, B. H. (2004). Stress, hormones, and disease. *Physiological Behavior, 82*(1), 139–143.

Neel, J. L., Stevens, V. M., & Stewart, J. E. (2002). Obsessive-compulsive disorder: Identification, neurobiology, and treatment. *Journal of the American Osteopathic Association, 102*(2), 81–86.

Neigh, G. N., Kofler, J., Meyers, J. L., Bergdall, V., La Perle, K. M., Traystman, R. J., & DeVries, A. C. (2004). Cardiac arrest/cardiopulmonary resuscitation increases anxiety-like behavior and decreases social interaction. *Journal of Cerebral Blood Flow and Metabolism, 24*(4), 372–382.

Nemeroff, C. B. (2003). The role of GABA in the pathophysiology and treatment of anxiety disorders. *Psychopharmacology Bulletin, 37*(4), 133–146.

Nemeroff, C. B. (2004). Advancing the treatment of anxiety disorders: New findings and novel uses for atypical antipsychotics. *Psychopharmacology Bulletin, 38*(1), 6–7.

Nemeroff, C. B., & Owens, M. J. (2003). Neuropharmacology of paroxetine. *Psychopharmacology Bulletin, 37*(1), 8–18.

Netto, C. F., & Guimaraes, F. S. (2004). Anxiogenic effect of cholecystokinin in the dorsal periaqueductal gray. *Neuropsychopharmacology, 29*(1), 101–107.

Neumeister, A., Bain, E., Nugent, A. C., Carson, R. E., Bonne, O., Luckenbaugh, D. A., Eckelman, W., Herscovitch, P., Charney, D. S., & Drevets, W. C. (2004). Reduced serotonin type 1A receptor binding in panic disorder. *Journal of Neuroscience, 24*(3), 589–591.

Newport, D. J., Heim, C., Owens, M. J., Ritchie, J. C., Ramsey, C. H., Bonsall, R., Miller, A. H., & Nemeroff, C. B. (2003). Cerebrospinal fluid corticotrophin-releasing factor (CRF) and vasopressin concentrations predict pituitary response in the CRF stimulation test: A multiple regression analysis. *Neuropsychopharmacology, 28*(3), 569–576.

Neylan, T. C., Brunet, A., Pole, N., Best, S. R., Metzler, T. J., Yehuda, R., & Marmar, C. R. (2005). PTSD symptoms predict waking salivary cortisol levels in police officers. *Psychoneuroendocrinology, 30*(4), 373–381.

Neylan, T. C., Jasiukaitis, P. A., Lenoci, M., Scott, J. C., Metzler, T. J., Weiss, D. S., Schoenfeld, F. B., & Marmar, C. R. (2003). Temporal instability of auditory and visual event-related potential in posttraumatic stress disorder. *Biological Psychiatry, 53*(3), 216–225.

Neylan, T. C., Lenoci, M., Rothlind, J., Metzler, T. J., Schuff, N., Du, A. T., Franklin, K. W., Weiss, D. S., Weiner, M. W., & Marmar, C. R. (2004). Attention, learning, and memory in posttraumatic stress disorder. *Journal of Traumatic Stress, 17*(1), 41–46.

Neylan, T. C., Schuff, N., Lenoci, M., Yehuda, R., Weiner, M. W., & Marmar, C. R. (2003). Cortisol levels are positively correlated with hippocampal N-acetylaspartate. *Biological Psychiatry, 54*(10), 1118–1121.

Ngan, E. T., Lane, C. J., Ruth, T. J., & Liddle, P. F. (2002). Immediate and delayed effects of risperidone on cerebral metabolism in neuroleptic naive schizophrenic patients: Correlations with symptom change. *Journal of Neurology and Neurosurgical Psychiatry, 72*(1), 106–110.

Nicolson, N. A. (2004). Childhood parental loss and cortisol levels in adult men. *Psychoneuroendocrinology, 29*(8), 1012–1018.

Niemeyer, R. A. (1985). Personal constructs in clinical practice. In P. C. Kendall (Ed.), *Advances in Cognitive-Behavioral Research and Therapy* (Vol. IV, pp. 275–339). Orlando, Florida: Academic Press.

Niemeyer, R. A. (1985b). *The Development of Personal Construct Psychology.* Lincoln, Nebraska: University of Nebraska Press.

Ninan, P. T. (2001). Recent perspectives on the diagnosis and treatment of generalized anxiety disorder. *American Journal of Managed Care, 7*(11), 367–376.

Ninan, P. T. (2002). New insights into the diagnosis and pharmacologic management of generalized anxiety disorder. *Psychopharmacology Bulletin, 36*(2), 105–122.

Nobler, M. S., Roose, S. P., Prohovnik, I., Moeller, J. R., Louie, J., Van Heertum, R. L., & Sackeim, H. A. (2000). Regional blood flow in mood disorders: Effects of antidepressant medication in late-life depression. *American Journal of Geriatric Psychiatry, 8*(4), 289–296.

Nobre, M. J., & Brandao, M. L. (2004). Analysis of freezing behavior and ultrasonic vocalization in response to foot-shocks, ultrasound signals and GABAergic inhibition in the inferior colliculus: Effects of muscimol and midazolam. *European Neuropsychopharmacology, 14*(1), 45–52.

Nolte, J. (2002). *The Human Brain: An Introduction to Its Functional Anatomy* (5th Ed.). St. Louis: Mosby.

Nordstrom, E. J., & Burton, F. H. (2002). A transgenic model of comorbid Tourette's syndrome and obsessive-compulsive disorder circuitry. *Molecular Psychiatry, 7*(6), 617–625.

Norton, P. J., & Asmundson, G. J. (2004). Anxiety sensitivity, fear, and avoidance behavior in headache pain. *Pain, 111*(1–2), 218–223.

Norton, P. J., & Whittal, M. L. (2004). Thematic similarity and clinical outcome in obsessive-compulsive disorder group treatment. *Depression and Anxiety, 20*(4), 195–197.

Noyes, R. (2001). Comorbidity in generalized anxiety disorder. *Psychiatric Clinics of North America, 24*(1), 41–55.

Nutt, D. J. (2005). Overview of diagnosis and drug treatments of anxiety disorders. *CNS Spectrums, 10*(1), 49–56.

Nutt, D. J., Ballenger, J. C., Sheehan, D., & Wittchen, H. U. (2002). Generalized anxiety disorder: Comorbidity, comparative biology, and treatment. *International Journal of Neuropsychopharmacology, 5*(4), 315–325.

Nutt, D. J., Bell, C. J., & Malizia, A. L. (1998). Brain mechanisms of social anxiety disorder. *Journal of Clinical Psychiatry, 59*(17), 4–11.

Nutt, D. J., Glue, P., Lawson, C., & Wilson, S. (1990). Flumazenil provocation of panic attacks: Evidence for altered benzodiazepines receptor sensitivity in panic disorder. *Archives of General Psychiatry, 47*, 917–925.

Nutt, D. J., & Lawson, C. (1992). Panic attacks: A neurochemical overview of models and mechanisms. *British Journal of Psychiatry, 160*, 165–178.

Nutt, D. J., & Malizia, A. L. (2004). Structural and functional brain changes in posttraumatic stress disorder. *Journal of Clinical Psychiatry, 65*(1), 11–17.

Oberlander, T. F., Misri, S., Fitzgerald, C. E., Kostaras, X., Rurak, D., & Riggs, W. (2004). Pharmacologic factors associated with transient neonatal symptoms following prenatal psychotropic medication exposure. *Journal of Clinical Psychiatry, 65*(2), 230–237.

O'Connor, T. G., Heron, J., Golding, J., & Glover, V. (2003). Maternal antenatal anxiety and behavioral/emotional problems in children: A test of a programming hypothesis. *Journal of Child Psychology and Psychiatry, 44*(7), 1025–1036.

O'Donnell, M. L., Creamer, M., & Pattison, P. (2004). Posttraumatic stress disorder and depression following trauma: Understanding comorbidity. *American Journal of Psychiatry, 161*(8), 1390–1396.

Ogai, M., Iyo, M., Mori, N., & Takei, N. (2005). A right orbitofrontal region and OCD symptoms: A case report. *Acta Psychiatrica Scandanavica, 111*(1), 74–76.

Ohara, K., Suzuki, Y., Ochiai, M., Tsukamoto, T., Tani, K., & Ohara, K. (1999). A variable- number-tandem-repeat of the serotonin transporter gene and anxiety disorders. *Progress in Neuro-psychopharmacology & Biological Psychiatry, 23*(1), 55–65.

Ohman, A. (1994). "Unconscious anxiety": Phobic responses to masked stimuli. *Journal of Abnormal Psychology, 103*, 231–240.

Ohman, A., & Soares, J. (1993). On the automatic nature of phobia fear: Conditioned electrodermal responses to masked fear-relevant stimuli. *Journal of Abnormal Psychology, 102*, 121–132.

Okada, M., Zhu, G., Yoshida, S., Kanai, S., Hirose, S., & Kaneko, S. (2002). Exocytosis mechanism as a new targeting site for mechanisms of action of antiepileptic drugs. *Life Science, 72*(4–5), 435–440.

Olff, M., Langeland, W., & Gersons, B. P. (2005). The psychobiology of PTSD: Coping with trauma. *Psychoneuroendocrinology, 30*(10), 974–982.

Oliva, I., Gonzalez-Trujano, M. E., Arrieta, J., Enciso-Rodriguez, R., & Navarrete, A. (2004). Neuropharmacological profile of hydroalcohol extract of valerian edulis ssp. procera roots in mice. *Phytotherapy Research, 18*(4), 290–296.

Olszewski, T. M., & Varrasse, J. F. (2005). The neurobiology of PTSD: Implications for nurses. *Journal of Psychosocial Nursing and Mental Health Services, 43*(6), 40–47.

Ordyan, N. E., & Pivina, S. G. (2004). Characteristics of the behavior and stress-reactivity of the hypophyseal-adrenal system in prenatally stressed rats. *Neuroscience and Behavioral Physiology, 34*(6), 569–574.

Orosco, M., Rouch, C., Beslot, F., Feurte, S., Regnault, A., & Dauge, V. (2004). Alpha-lactalbumin- enriched diets enhance serotonin release and induce anxiolytic and rewarding effects in the rat. *Behavioural Brain Research, 148*(1–2), 1–10.

Osofsky, J. D. (1995). Perspectives on attachment and psychoanalysis. *Psychoanalytic Psychology, 12*, 347–362.

Otte, C., Lenoci, M., Metzler, T., Yehuda, R., Marmar, C. R., & Neylan, T. C. (2005). Hypothalamic-pituitary-adrenal axis activity and sleep in posttraumatic stress disorder. *Neuropsychpharmacology, 30*(6), 1173–1180.

Ouimette, P., Cronkite, R., Henson, B. R., Prins, A., Gima, K., & Moos, R. H. (2004). Posttraumatic stress disorder and health status among female and male medical patients. *Journal of Traumatic Stress, 17*(1), 1–9.

Overbeck, G., Michal, M., Russ, M. O., Lanfermann, H., & Roder, C. H. (2004). Convergence of psychotherapeutic and neurobiological outcome measures in a patient with OCD. *Psychotherapy and Psychosomatic Medical Psychology, 54*(2), 73–81.

Owens, M. J., & Rosenbaum, J. F. (2002). Escitalopram: A second-generation SSRI. *CNS Spectrums, 7*(4), 34–39.

Owley, T., Owley, S., Leventhal, B., & Cook, E. H. (2002). Case series: Adderall augmentation of serotonin reuptake inhibitors in childhood-onset obsessive-compulsive disorder. *Journal of Child and Adolescent Psychopharmacology, 12*, 165–171.

Ownby, R. L. (1998). Computational model of obsessive-compulsive disorder: Examination of etiologic hypothesis and treatment strategies. *Depression and Anxiety, 8*(3), 91–103.

Packard, M. G., & Cahill, L. (2001). Affective modulation of multiple memory systems. *Current Opinion in Neurobiology, 11*, 752–756.

Pailing, P. E., & Segalowitz, S. J. (2004). The error-related negativity as a state and trait measure: Motivation, personality, and ERP's in response to errors. *Psychophysiology, 41*(1), 84–95.

Pallanti, S., Hollander, E., & Goodman, W. K. (2004). A qualitative analysis of nonresponse: Management of treatment-refractory obsessive-compulsive disorder. *Journal of Clinical Psychiatry, 65*(14), 6–10.

Pallanti, S., Quercioli, L., & Bruscoli, M. (2004). Response acceleration with mirtazapine augmentation of citalopram in obsessive-compulsive patients without comorbid depression: A pilot study. *Journal of Clinical Psychiatry, 65*(10), 1394–1399.

Palyo, S. A., & Beck, J. G. (2005). Is the concept of "repression" useful for the understanding of chronic PTSD? *Behaviour Research and Therapy, 43*(1), 55–68.

Papageorgiou, C. C., & Rabavilas, A. D. (2003). Abnormal P600 in obsessive-compulsive disorder: A comparison with healthy controls. *Psychiatry Research, 119*(1–2), 133–143.

Papageorgiou, C. C., Rabavilas, A. D., Liappas, I., & Stefanis, C. (2003). Do obsessive-compulsive patients and abstinent heroin addicts share a common psychophysiological mechanism? *Neuropsychobiology, 47*(1), 1–11.

Papp, L. A., Gorman, J. M., Liebowitz, M. R., Fyer, A. J., Cohen, B., & Klein, D. F. (1988). Epinephrine infusions in patients with social phobia. *American Journal of Psychiatry, 145*, 733–736.

Paquette, V., Levesque, J., Mensour, B., Leroux, J. M., Beaudoin, G., Bourgouin, P., et al. (2003). "Change the mind and you change the brain": Effects of cognitive-behavioral therapy on the neural correlates of spider phobia. *Neuroimage, 18(2)*, 401–409.

Parada, A., & Soares-da-Silva, P. (2002). The novel anticonvulsant BIA 2–093 inhibits transmitter release during opening of voltage-gated sodium channels: A comparison with carbamazepine and oxcarbazepine. *Neurochemistry International, 40(5)*, 435–440.

Parfitt, D. B., Levin, J. K., Saltstein, K. P., Klayman, A. S., Greer, L. M., & Helmreich, D. L. (2004). Differential early rearing environments can accentuate or attenuate the responses to stress in male C57BL/6 mice. *Brain Research, 1016(1)*, 111–118.

Pariante, C. M., Hye, A., Williamson, R., Makoff, A., Lovestone, S., & Kerwin, R. W. (2003). The antidepressant clomipramine regulates cortisol intracellular concentrations and glucocorticoid receptor expression in fibroblasts and rat primary neurones. *Neuropsychopharmacology, 28(9)*, 1553–1561.

Parker, H. A., McNally, R. J., Nakayama, K., & Wilhelm, S. (2004). No disgust recognition deficit in obsessive-compulsive disorder. *Journal of Behavior Therapy and Experimental Psychiatry, 35(2)*, 183–192.

Parker, K. J., Buckmaster, C. L., Schatzberg, A. F., & Lyons, D. M. (2004). Prospective investigation of stress inoculation in young monkeys. *Archives of General Psychiatry, 61(9)*, 933–941.

Pary, R., Matuschka, P. R., Lewis, S., Caso, W., & Lippmann, S. (2003). Generalized anxiety disorder. *Southern Medical Journal, 96(6)*, 581–586.

Passons, W. R. (1975). *Gestalt Approaches in Counseling.* New York: Holt, Rinehart & Winston.

Patel, S., Roelke, C. T., Rademacher, D. J., Cullinan, W. E., & Hillard, C. J. (2004). Endocannabinoid signaling negatively modulates stress-induced activation of the hypothalamic-pituitary-adrenal axis. *Endocrinology, 8*, 2–9.

Pato, M. T., Schindler, K. M., & Pato, C. N. (2001). The genetics of obsessive-compulsive disorder. *Current Psychiatry Reports, 3(2)*, 163–168.

Paulus, M. P., Feinstein, J. S., Simmons, A., & Stein, M. B. (2004). Anterior cingulate activation in high trait anxious subjects is related to altered error processing during decision making. *Biological Psychiatry, 55(12)*, 1179–1187.

Pavlov, I. (1927). *Conditioned Reflexes.* Oxford: Oxford University Press.

Pawlak, C. R., Ho, Y. J., Schwarting, R. K., & Bauhofer, A. (2003). Relationship between striatal levels of interleukin-2 mRNA and plus-maze behavior in the rat. *Neuroscience Letters, 341(3)*, 205–208.

Pawlak, R., Magarinos, A. M., Melchor, J., McEwen, B., & Strickland, S. (2003). Tissue plasminogen in the amygdala is critical for stress-induced anxiety-like behavior. *Nature Neuroscience, 6(2)*, 168–174.

Pawlyk, A. C., Jha, S. K., Brennan, F. X., Morrison, A. R., & Ross, R. J. (2005). A rodent model of sleep disturbances in posttraumatic stress disorder: The role of context after fear conditioning. *Biological Psychiatry, 57(3)*, 268–277.

Pedersen, N. L., Plomin, R., McClearn, G. E., & Fribereg, L. (1998). Neuroticism, Extraversion, and related traits in adult twins reared apart and reared together. *Journal of Personality and Social Psychology, 55*, 950–957.

Pelissolo, A., Andre, C., Chignon, J. M., Dutoit, D., Martin, P., Richard-Berthe, C., & Tignol, J. (2002). Anxiety disorders in private practice psychiatric outpatients: Prevalence, comorbidity, and burden (DELTA study). *L'encephale, 28(6)*, 510–519.

Penalva, R. G., Flachskamm, C., Zimmermann, S., Wurst, W., Holsboer, F., Reul, J. M., & Linthorst, A. C. (2002). Corticotropin-releasing hormone receptor type 1–deficiency enhances hippocampal serotonergic neurotransmission: An in vivo microdialysis study in mutant mice. *Neuroscience, 109*(2), 253–266.

Perkonigg, A., Pfister, H., Stein, M. B., Hofler, M., Lieb, R., Maercker, A., & Wittchen, H. U. (2005). Longitudinal course of posttraumatic stress disorder and posttraumatic stress disorder symptoms in a community sample of adolescents and young adults. *American Journal of Psychiatry, 162*(7), 1320–1327.

Perls, F. S. (1969). *In and Out of the Garbage Pail*. Lafayette, CA: Real People Press.

Perls, F. S., Hefferline, R. F., & Goodman, P. (1951). *Gestalt Therapy*. New York: Julian Press.

Peterson, B. S., Leckman, J. F., Tucker, D., Scahill, L., Staib, L., Zhang, H., et al., (2000). Preliminary findings of antistreptococcal antibody titers and basal ganglia volumes in tic, obsessive-compulsive, and attention deficit hyperactivity disorders. *Archives of General Psychiatry, 57*(4), 364–372.

Pickering, A. D. (1997). The conceptual nervous system and personality: From Pavlov to neural networks. *European Psychologist, 2*, 139–163.

Pico-Alfonso, M. A., Garcia-Linares, M. I., Celda-Navarro, N., Herbert, J., & Martinez, M. (2004). Changes in cortisol and dehydroepiandrosterone in women victims of physical and psychological intimate partner violence. *Biological Psychiatry, 56*(4), 233–240.

Pigott, T. A., & Seay, S. M. (1999). A review of the efficacy of selective serotonin reuptake inhibitors in obsessive-compulsive disorder. *Journal of Clinical Psychiatry, 60*(2), 101–106.

Piletz, J. E., Ordway, G. A., Zhu, H., Duncan, B. J., & Halaris, A. (2000). Autoradiographic comparison of [2H]–clonidine binding to non-adrenergic sites and alpha(2)–adrenergic receptors in human brain. *Neuropsychopharmacology, 23*(6), 697–708.

Pillar, G., Malhotra, A., & Lavie, P. (2000). Posttraumatic stress disorder and sleep: What a nightmare! *Sleep Medicine Review, 4*(2), 183–200.

Pine, D. S., Mogg, K., Bradley, B. P., Montgomery, L., Monk, C. S., McClure, E., Guyer, A. E., Ernst, M., Charney, D. S., & Kaufman, J. (2005). Attention bias to threat in maltreated children: Implications for vulnerability to stress-related psychopathology. *American Journal of Psychiatry, 162*(2), 291–296.

Pitman, R. K., & Delahanty, D. L. (2005). Conceptually driven pharmacologic approaches to acute trauma. *CNS Spectrums, 10*(2), 99–106.

Pitts, F. N. (1969). The biochemistry of anxiety. *Scientific American, 69*, 220.

Pollack, M. H. (2004). Unmet needs in the treatment of anxiety disorders. *Psychopharmacology Bulletin, 38*(1), 31–37.

Polster, E., & Polster, M. (1973). *Gestalt Therapy Integrated: Contours of Theory and Practice*. New York: Brunner/Mazel.

Poltyrev, T., & Weinstock, M. (2004). Gender difference in the prevention of hyperanxiety in adult prenatally stressed rats by chronic treatment with amitriptyline. *Psychopharmacology, 171*(3), 270–276.

Posserud, I., Agerforz, P., Ekman, R., Bjornsson, E. S., Abrahamsson, H., & Simren, M. (2004). Altered viceral perceptual and neuroendocrine response in patients with irritable bowel syndrome during mental stress. *Gut, 53*(8), 1102–1108.

Post, R. M. (2004). Neurobiology of seizures and behavioral abnormalities. *Epilepsia, 45*(2), 5–14.

Posternak, M., & Mueller, T. (2001). Assessing the risks and benefits of benzodiazepines for anxiety disorders in patients with a history of substance abuse or dependence. *American Journal of Addictions, 10*, 48–68.

Potoczek, A. (2005). Difficult asthma, stress, and panic disorder. *Psychiatria Polska, 39*(1), 51–66.

Potter, W. Z., & Rudorfer, M. V. (1993). Electroconvulsive therapy: A modern medical procedure. *New England Journal of Medicine, 328*, 882.

Powers, M. B., Smits, J. A., & Telch, M. J. (2004). Disentangling the effects of safety-behavior utilization and safety-behavior availability during exposure-based treatment: A placebo-controlled trial. *Journal of Consulting and Clinical Psychology, 72*(3), 448–454.

Protopopescu, X., Pan, H., Tuescher, O., Cloitre, M., Goldstein, M., Engelien, W., Epstein, J., Yang, Y., Gorman, J., LeDoux, J., Silbersweig, D., & Stern, E. (2005). Differential time courses and specificity of amygdala activity in posttraumatic stress disorder subjects and normal control subjects. *Biological Psychiatry, 57*(5), 464–473.

Pujol, J., Soriano-Mas, C., Alonso, P., Cardoner, N., Menchon, J. M., Deus, J., & Vallejo, J. (2004). Mapping structural brain alterations in obsessive-compulsive disorder. *Archives of General Psychiatry, 61*(7), 720–730.

Pujol, J., Torres, L., Deus, J., Cardoner, N., Pifarre, J., Capdevila, A., & Vallejo, J. (1999). Functional magnetic resonance imaging study of frontal lobe activation during word generation in obsessive-compulsive disorder. *Biological Psychiatry, 45*(7), 891–897.

Purdon, C. (2004a). Cognitive-behavioral treatment of repugnant obsessions. *Journal of Clinical Psychology, 60*(11), 1169–1180.

Purdon, C. (2004b). Empirical investigations of thought suppression in OCD. *Journal of Behavior Therapy and Experimental Psychiatry, 35*(2), 121–136.

Purves, D. G., & Erwin, P. G. (2004). Posttraumatic stress and self-disclosure. *Journal of Psychology, 138*(1), 23–33.

Pynoos, R. S., Steinberg, A. M., & Wraith, R. (1995). A developmental model of childhood traumatic stress. In D. Cocchetti & D. J. Cohen (Eds.), *Developmental Psychopathology, Vol. 2: Risk, Disorder, and Adaptation* (pp. 72–95). New York: John Wiley and Sons.

Quick, M. W. (2003). Regulating the conducting states of a mammalian serotonin transporter. *Neuron, 40*(3), 537–549.

Quilty, L. C., Van Ameringen, M., Mancini, C., Oakman, J., & Farvolden, P. (2003). Quality of life and the anxiety disorders. *Journal of Anxiety Disorders, 17*(4), 405–426.

Rabbani, M., Sajjadi, S. E., Jafarian, A., & Vaseghi, G. (2005). Anxiolytic effects of salvia reuterana boiss on the elevated plus-maze model of anxiety in mice. *Journal of Ethnopharmacology, 101*(1–3), 100–103.

Rachman, S. (1978). *Fear and Courage.* San Francisco: W. H. Freeman.

Rachman, S., & Hodgson, R. I. (1974). Synchrony and desynchrony in fear and avoidance. *Behavior Research and Therapy, 12*, 311–318.

Rachman, S., & Hodgson, R. I. (1980). *Obsessions and Compulsions.* Englewood Cliffs, New Jersey: Prentice Hall.

Radley, J. J., Sisti, H. M., Hao, J., Rocher, A. B., McCall, T., Hof, P. R., McEwen, B. S., & Morrison, J. H. (2004). Chronic behavioral stress induces apical dendritic reorganization in pyramidal neurons of the medial prefrontal cortex. *Neuroscience, 125*(1), 1–6.

Raison, C. L., & Miller, A. H. (2003). When not enough is too much: The role of insufficient glucocorticoid signaling in the pathophysiology of stress-related disorders. *American Journal of Psychiatry, 160*, 1554–1565.

Rapaport, M. H., Clary, C., Fayyad, R., & Endicott, J. (2005). Quality-of-life impairment in depressive and anxiety disorders. *American Journal of Psychiatry, 162*(2), 1171–1178.

Rapee, R. M., Telfer, L. A., & Barlow, D. H. (1991). The role of safety cues in mediating the response to inhalations of CO_2 in agoraphobics. *Behavior Research and Therapy, 29*(4), 353–355.

Raskind, M. A., Peskind, E. R., Kanter, E. D., Petrie, E. C., Radant, A., Thompson, C. E., et al. (2003). Reduction of nightmares and other PTSD symptoms in combat veterans by prazosin: A placebo-controlled study. *American Journal of Psychiatry, 160*, 371–373.

Rasmusson, A. M., Vasek, J., Lipschitz, D. S., Vojvoda, D., Mustone, M. E., Shi, Q., Gudmundsen, G., Morgan, C. A., Wolfe, J., & Charney, D. S. (2004). An increased capacity for adrenal DHEA release is associated with decreased avoidance and negative mood symptoms in women with PTSD. *Neuropsychopharmacology, 29*(8), 1546–1557.

Rasmusson, A. M., Vythilingam, M., & Morgan, C. A. (2003). The neuroendocrinology of posttraumatic stress disorder: New directions. *CNS Spectrums, 8*(9), 665–667.

Rauch, S. L., & Savage, C. R. (1997). Neuroimaging and neuropsychology of the striatum: Bridging basic science and clinical practice. *Psychiatric Clinics of North America, 20*, 741–768.

Rauch, S. L., Shin, L. M., Segal, E., Pitman, R. K., Carson, M. A., McMullin, K., Whalen, P. J., & Makris, N. (2003). Selectively reduced regional cortical volumes in posttraumatic stress disorder. *Neuroreport, 14*(7), 913–916.

Rauch, S. L., Shin, L. M., & Wright, C. I. (2003). Neuroimaging studies of amygdala function in anxiety disorders. *Annals of the New York Academy of Sciences, 985*, 389–410.

Rauch, S. L., Whalen, P. J., Curran, T., Shin, L. M., Coffey, B. J., Savage, C. R., et al. (2001). Probing striato-thalamic function in obsessive-compulsive disorder and Tourette syndrome using neuroimaging methods. *Advances in Neurology, 85*, 207–224.

Ravi-Kishore, V., Samar, R., Janardhan-Reddy, Y. C., Chandrasekhar, C. R., & Thennarasu, K. (2004). Clinical characteristics and treatment response in poor and good insight obsessive-compulsive disorder. *European Psychiatry, 19*(4), 202–208.

Ravna, A. W., Stylte, I., & Dahl, S. G. (2003). Molecular mechanism of citalopram and cocaine interactions with neurotransmitter transporter. *Journal of Pharmacology and Experimental Therapeutics, 307*(1), 34–41.

Read, J., Perry, B. D., Moskowitz, A., & Connolly, J. (2001). The contribution of early traumatic events to schizophrenia in some patients: A tramagenic neurodevelopmental model. *Psychiatry, 64*(4), 319–345.

Redgrave, K. (2003). Brain function and conditioning in posttraumatic stress disorder. *Journal of Social Health, 123*(2), 120–123.

Redmond, D. E. (1985). Neurochemical basis for anxiety and anxiety disorders: Evidence from drugs which decrease human fear or anxiety. In A. H. Tuma & J. D. Maser (Eds.), *Anxiety and the Anxiety Disorders*. Hillsdale, New Jersey: Lawrence Erlbaum.

Redolat, R., Gomez, M. C., Vicens, P., & Carrasco, M. C. (2004). Bupropion effects on aggressiveness and anxiety in OF1 male mice. *Psychopharmacology, 7*, 1–7.

Redrobe, J. P., Dumont, Y., Herzog, H., & Quirion, R. (2003). Neuropeptide Y (NPY) Y2 receptors mediate behavior in two animal models of anxiety: Evidence from Y2 receptor knockout mice. *Behavioural Brain Research, 141*(2), 251–255.

Reichborn-Kjennerud, T., Roysamb, E., Tambs, K., Torgersen, S., Kringlen, E., Magnus, P., & Harris, J. R. (2004). Genetic and environmental influences on the association between smoking and panic attacks in females: a population-based twin study. *Psychological Medicine, 34*(7), 1271–1277.

Reidy, J. (2004). Trait anxiety, trait depression, worry, and memory. *Behaviour Research and Therapy, 42*(8), 937–948.

Reiss, S., & McNally, R. J. (1985). Expectancy model of anxiety. In S. Reiss & R. R. Bootzin (Eds.), *Theoretical Issues in Behavior Therapy* (pp. 107–121). San Diego: Academic Press.

Reiss, S., Peterson, R. A., Bursky, D. M., & McNally, R. J. (1986). Anxiety sensitivity, anxiety frequency, and the prediction of fearfulness. *Behaviour Research and Therapy, 1*, 1–8.

Renik, O. (2000). Subjectivity and unconsciousness. *Journal of Analytic Psychology, 45*(1), 3–20.

Renik, O. (2001). The patient's experience of therapeutic benefit. *Psychoanalytic Quarterly, 70*(1), 231–241.

Reznik, I., Yavin, I., Stryjer, R., Spivak, B., Gonen, N., Strous, R., Mester, R., et al. (2004). Clozapine in the treatment of obsessive-compulsive symptoms in schizophrenia patients: A case series study. *Pharmacopsychiatry, 37*(2), 52–56.

Rickels, K., & Rynn, M. (2002). Pharmacotherapy of generalized anxiety disorder. *Journal of Clinical Psychiatry, 63*(14), 9–16.

Rickels, K., Zaninelli, R., McCafferty, J., Bellew, K., Iyangar, M., & Sheehan, D. (2003). Paroxetine treatment of generalized anxiety disorder: A double-blind, placebo-controlled study. *American Journal of Psychiatry, 160*(4), 749–756.

Riederer, P., Lachenmayer, L., & Laux, G. (2004). Clinical applications of MAO-inhibitors. *Current Medicinal Chemistry, 11*(15), 2033–2043.

Ringdahl, E. N., Pereira, S. L., & Delzell, J. E. (2004). Treatment of primary imsomnia. *Journal of the American Board of Family Practice, 17*(3), 212–219.

Risbrough, V. B., Hauger, R. L., Roberts, A. L., Vale, W. W., & Geyer, M. A. (2004). Corticotropin- releasing factor receptors CRF1 and CRF2 exert both additive and opposing influences on defensive startle behavior. *Journal of Neuroscience, 24*(29), 6545–6552.

Rizk, A., Curley, J., Robertson, J., & Raber, J. (2004). Anxiety and cognition in histamine H3 receptor –/– mice. *European Journal of Neuroscience, 19*(7), 1992–1996.

Robinson, D., Wu, H., Munne, R. A., Ashtari, M., Alvir, J. M., Lerner, G., Koreen-Cole, K., & Bogerts, B. (1995). Reduced caudate nucleus volume in obsessive-compulsive disorder. *Archives of General Psychiatry, 52*(5), 393–398.

Rodriguez, B. F., Weisberg, R. B., Pagano, M. E., Machan, J. T., Culpepper, L., & Keller, M. B. (2004). Frequency and patterns of psychiatric comorbidity in a sample of primary care patients with anxiety disorders. *Comprehensive Psychiatry, 45*(2), 129–137.

Rodriguez, G., Vitali, P., Canfora, M., Calvini, P., Girtler, N., De Leo, C., Piccardo, A., & Nobili, F. (2004). Quantitative EEG and perfusional single photon emission computed tomography correlation during long-term donepezil therapy in Alzheimer's disease. *Clinical Neurophysiology, 115*(1), 39–49.

Roemer, L., & Orsillo, S. M. (2002). Expanding our conceptualization of and treatment for generalized anxiety disorder: Integrating mindfulness/acceptance-based approaches with existing cognitive-behavioral models. *Clinical Psychology: Science and Practice*.

Rogers, C. R. (1942). *Counseling and Psychotherapy: Newer Concepts in Practice*. Boston, Massachusetts: Houghton-Mifflin.

Rogers, C. R. (1951). *Client-Centered Therapy: Its Current Practice, Implications, and Theory*. Boston, Massachusetts: Houghton-Mifflin.

Rogers, C. R. (1955). The phenomenological theory of personality. In W. S. Sahakian (Ed.), *Psychology of Personality: Readings in Theory* (pp. 473–494). Chicago: Rand-McNally.

Rogers, C. R. (1959). A theory of therapy, personality, and interpersonal relationships, as developed in the client-centered framework. In S. Koch (Ed.), *Psychology: A Study of Science* (Vol. 3, pp. 184–256). New York: McGraw-Hill.

Rogers, C. R. (1969). *Freedom to Learn*. Columbus, Ohio: Charles E. Merrill.

Rogers, C. (1987). Rogers, Kohut, and Erikson: A personal perspective on some similarities and differences. In J. Zeig's (Ed.), *Evolution of Psychotherapy* (pp. 179–188), New York: Brunner.

Rogoz, Z., Wrobel, A., Dlaboga, D., Maj, J., & Dziedzicka-Wasylewska, M. (2002). Effect of repeated treatment with mirtazapine on the central alpha1–adrenergic receptors. *Journal of Physiological Pharmacology, 53*(1), 105–116.

Rondo, P. H., Vaz, A. J., Moraes, F., & Tomkins, A. (2004). The relationship between salivary cortisol concentrations and anxiety in adolescent and non-adolescent pregnant women. *Brazilian Journal of Medical Biology Research, 37*(9), 1403–1409.

Rosen, J. B. (2004). The neurobiology of conditioned and unconditioned fear: A neurobehavioral system analysis of the amygdala. *Behavioral and Cognitive Neuroscience Reviews, 3*(1), 23–41.

Rosenbaum, J. F. (2004). The development of clonazepam as a psychotropic: The Massachusetts General Hospital experience. *Journal of Clinical Psychiatry, 65*(5), 3–6.

Rosenberg, D. R., Amponsah, A., Sullivan, A., MacMillan, S., & Moore, G. J. (2001). Increased medial thalamic choline in pediatric obsessive-compulsive disorder as detected by quantitative in vivo spectroscopic imaging. _Journal of Child Neurology, 16_(9), 636–641.

Rosenberg, D. R., Dick, E. L., O'Hearn, K. M., & Sweeney, J. A. (1997). Response-inhibition deficits in obsessive-compulsive disorder: An indicator of dysfunction in frontostriatal circuits. _Journal of Psychiatry and Neuroscience, 22_(1), 29–38.

Rosenberg, D. R., & Keshavan, M. S. (1998). Toward a neurodevelopmental model of obsessive- compulsive disorder. _Archives of General Psychiatry, 52_, 393–398.

Rosenberg, D. R., MacMillan, S. N., & Moore, G. J. (2001). Brain anatomy and chemistry may predict treatment response in pediatric obsessive-compulsive disorder. _International Journal of Neuropsychopharmacology, 4_(2), 179–190.

Rosenberg, D. R., Mirza, Y., Russell, A., Tang, J., Smith, J. M., Banerjee, S. P., Bhandari, R., Rose, M., Ivey, J., Boyd, C., & Moore, G. J. (2004). Reduced anterior cingulate glutamatergic concentrations in childhood OCD and major depression versus healthy controls. _Journal of the American Academy of Child and Adolescent Psychiatry, 43_(9), 1146–1153.

Rossi, A., Barraco, A., & Donda, P. (2004). Fluoxetine: A review on evidence based medicine. _Annals of General Hospital Psychiatry, 3_(1), 2.

Rossi, A., Bartalini, S., Ulivelli, M., Mantovani, A., Di Muro, A., Goracci, A., Castrogiovanni, P., Battistini, N., & Passero, S. (2005). Hypofunctioning of sensory gating mechanisms in patients with obsessive-compulsive disorder. _Biological Psychiatry, 57_(1), 16–20.

Roth, R. M., Baribeau, J., Milovan, D. L., & O'Connor, K. (2004). Speed and accuracy on tests of executive function in obsessive-compulsive disorder. _Brain Cognition, 54_(3), 263–265.

Roth, R. M., Baribeau, J., Milovan, D. L., O'Connor, K., & Todorov, C. (2004b). Procedural and declarative memory in obsessive-compulsive disorder. _Journal of International Neuropsychology and Sociology, 10_(5), 647–654.

Rotter, J. B. (1954). _Social Learning and Clinical Psychology._ Englewoods Cliffs, New Jersey: Prentice-Hall.

Rotter, J. B. (1966). Generalized expectancies for internal versus external control of reinforcement. _Psychological Monographs, 80_, (Whole No. 609).

Rotter, J. B. (1967). Beliefs, social attitudes and behavior: A social learning analysis. In R. Jessor & S. Feschbach (Eds.), _Cognition, Personality and Clinical Psychology_ (pp. 112–140). San Francisco, California: Jossey-Bass.

Rotzinger, S., & Vaccarino, F. J. (2003). Cholecystokinin receptor subtypes: Role in the modulation of anxiety-related and reward-related behaviors in animal models. _Journal of Psychiatry and Neuroscience, 28_(3), 171–181.

Rouillon, F. (2004). Long-term therapy of generalized anxiety disorder. _European Psychiatry, 19_(2), 96–101.

Roy, M. A., Neale, M. C., Pederson, N. L., Mathe, A. A., & Kendler, K. S. (1995). A twin study of generalized anxiety disorder and major depression. _Psychological Medicine, 25_, 1037–1049.

Roy-Byrne, P. P., & Cowley, D. S. (1998). Search for pathophysiology of panic disorder. _Lancet, 352_, 1646–1647.

Roy-Byrne, P. P., Russo, J., Michelson, E., Zatzick, D., Pitman, R. K., & Berliner, L. (2004). Risk factors and outcome in ambulatory assault victims presenting to the acute emergency department setting: Implications for secondary prevention studies in PTSD. _Depression and Anxiety, 19_(2), 77–84.

Roy-Byrne, P. P., & Wagner, A. (2004). Primary care perspectives on generalized anxiety disorder. _Journal of Clinical Psychiatry, 65_(13), 20–26.

Rubino, I. A., Romeo, D., & Siracusano, A. (2003). Styles of adaptation in panic disorder with and without agoraphobia. _Perception and Motor Skills, 97_(3 Pt 2), 1223–1230.

Rudolph, U., & Mohler, H. (2004). Analysis of GABA(A) receptor function and dissection of the pharmacology of benzodiazepines and general anesthetics through mouse genetics. _Annual Review of Pharmacology and Toxicology, 44_, 475–498.

Rule, W. R., & Traver, M. D. (1983). Test-retest reliabilities of state-trait anxiety inventory in a stressful social analogue situation. *Journal of Personality Assessment, 47*(3), 276–277.

Ruscio, A. M. (2002). Delimiting the boundaries of generalized anxiety disorder: Differentiating high worriers with and without GAD. *Journal of Anxiety Disorder, 16*(4), 377–400.

Rynn, M. A., & Brawman-Mintzer, O. (2004). Generalized anxiety disorder: Acute and chronic treatment. *CNS Spectrums, 9*(10), 716–723.

Safran, J. D., & Segal, Z. V. (1990). *Interpersonal Process in Cognitive Therapy.* Basic Books: New York.

Sahar, T., Shalev, A., & Porges, S. (2001). Vagal modulation of responses to mental challenge in posttraumatic stress disorder. *Biological Psychiatry, 49,* 637–643.

Sajdyk, T. J., Shekhar, A., & Gehlert, D. R. (2004). Interactions between NPY and CRF in the amygdala to regulate emotionality. *Neuropeptides, 38*(4), 225–234.

Sakamoto, H., Fukuda, R., Okuaki, T., Rogers, M., Kasai, K., Machida, T., Shirouzu, I., Yamasue, H., Akiyama, T., & Kato, N. (2005). Parahippocampal activation evoked by masked traumatic images in posttraumatic stress disorder: A functional MRI study. *Neurimaging, 26*(3), 813–821.

Salin-Pascual, R. J., & Basanez-Villa, E. (2003). Changes in compulsion and anxiety symptoms with nicotine transdermal patches in non-smoking obsessive-compulsive disorder patients. *Review in Investigating of Clinics, 55*(6), 650–654.

Salkovskis, P. M. (1985). Obsessional-compulsive symptoms: A cognitive-behavioral analysis. *Behaviour Research and Therapy, 25,* 571–583.

Salkovskis, P. M. (Ed.). (1996). *Frontiers in Cognitive Therapy.* New York: Guilford Press.

Salkovskis, P. M., & Clark, D. M. (1993). Panic disorder and hypochondriasis. Special issue: Panic, cognitions and sensations. *Advances in Behaviour Research and Therapy, 5,* 23–48.

Salkovskis, P. M., Shafran, R., Radhman, S., & Freeston, M. H. (1999). Multiple pathways to inflated responsibility beliefs in obsessional problems: Possible origins and implications for therapy and research. *Behaviour Therapy and Research, 37,* 1055–1072.

Salomons, T. V., Osterman, J. E., Gagliese, L., & Katz, J. (2004). Pain flashbacks in posttraumatic stress disorder. *Clinical Journal of Pain, 20*(2), 83–87.

Salzman, C. (2004). Late-life anxiety disorders. *Psychopharmacology Bulletin, 38*(1), 25–30.

Sanger, D. J. (2004). The pharmacology and mechanisms of action of new generation non-benzodiazepine hypnotic agents. *CNS Drugs, 18*(1), 9–15.

Sansone, R. A., Hendricks, C. M., Gaither, G. A., & Reddington, A. (2004). Prevalence of anxiety symptoms among a sample of outpatients in an internal medicine clinic: A pilot study. *Depression and Anxiety, 19*(2), 133–136.

Santini, E., Ge, H., Ren, K., Pena de Ortiz, S., & Quirk, G. J. (2004). Consolidation of fear extinction requires protein synthesis in the medial prefrontal cortex. *Journal of Neuroscience, 24*(25), 5704–5710.

Sapolsky, R. M. (1996). Stress, glucocorticoids, and damage to the nervous system: The current state of confusion. *Stress, 1,* 1–19.

Sarbin, T. R. (1997). On the futility of psychiatric diagnostic manuals and the return of personal agency. *Applied and Preventive Psychology, 6,* 233–243.

Sareen, J., Kirschner, A., Lander, M., Kjernisted, K. D., Eleff, M. K., & Reiss, J. P. (2004). Do Antipsychotics ameliorate or exacerbate obsessive-compulsive symptoms: A systematic review. *Journal of Affective Disorders, 82*(2), 167–174.

Sartre, J. P. (1947). *Existentialism.* New York: Associated Book Publishers, Ltd.

Sartre, J. P. (1956). *Being and Nothingness.* New York: Philosophical Library.

Satishchandra, P., Krishnamoorthy, E. S., van Elst, L. T., Lemieux, L., Koepp, M., Brown, R. J., & Trimble, M. R. (2003). Mesial temporal structures and comorbid anxiety disorders in refractory partial epilepsy. *Journal of Neuropsychiatry and Clinical Neuro-sciences, 15,* 450–452.

Saunders-Pullman, R., Shriberg, J., Heiman, G., Raymond, D., Wendt, K., Kramer, P., Schilling, K., Kurlan, R., Klein, C., Ozelius, L. J., Risch, N. J., & Bressman, S. B. (2002). Myoclonus dystonia: Possible association with obsessive-compulsive disorder and alcohol dependence. *Neurology, 58*(2), 242–245.

Savitz, J. B., & Ramesar, R. S. (2004). Genetic variants implicated in personality: A review of the more promising candidates. *American Journal of Medical Genetics, 131B* (1), 20–32.

Saxena, S., Brody, A. L., Maidment, K. M., Smith, E. C., Zohrabi, N., Katz, E., Baker, S. K., & Baxter, L. P. (2004). Cerebral glucose metabolism in obsessive-compulsive hoarding. *American Journal of Psychiatry, 161*(6), 1038–1048.

Saxena, S., Brody, A. L., Schwartz, J. M., & Baxter, L. R. (1998). Neuroimaging and frontal-subcortical circuitry in obsessive-compulsive disorder. *British Journal of Psychia-try, 35,* 26–37.

Saxena, S., Body, A. L., Ho, M. L., Alborzian, S., Maidment, K. M., Zohrabi, N., Ho, M. K., Huang, S. C., Wu, H. M., & Baxter, L. R. (2002). Differential cerebral metabolic changes with paroxetine treatment of obsessive-compulsive disorder vs. major depression. *Archives of General Psychiatry, 59*(3), 250–261.

Saxena, S., Brody, A. L., Maidment, K. M., Smith, E. C., Zohrabi, N., Katz, E., Baker, S. K., & Baxter, L. R. (2004). Cerebral glucose metabolism in obsessive-compulsive hoarding. *American Journal of Psychiatry, 161*(6), 1038–1048.

Scaccianoce, S., Mattei, V., Del Bianco, P., Gizzi, C., Sorice, M., Hiraiwa, M., & Misasi, R. (2004). Hippocampal prosaposin changes during stress: A glucocorticoid-independent event. *Hippocampus, 14*(3), 275–280.

Scapillato, D., & Manassis, K. (2002). Cognitive-behavioral interpersonal group treat-ment for anxious adolescents. *Journal of the American Academy of Child and Adolescent Psychiatry, 41*(6), 739–741.

Schell, T. L., Marshall, G. N., & Jaycox, L. H. (2004). All symptoms are not created equal: The prominent role of hyperarousal in the natural course of posttraumatic psycho-logical distress. *Journal of Abnormal Psychology, 113*(2), 189–197.

Scherrer, J. F., True, W. R., Xian, H., Lyons, M. J., Eisen, S. A., Goldberg, J., Lin, N., & Tsuang, M. T. (2000). Evidence for genetic influences common and specific to symp-toms of generalized anxiety and panic. *Journal of Affective Disorders, 57*(1–3), 25–35.

Schindler, K. M., Richter, M. A., Kennedy, J. L., Pato, M. T., & Pato, C. N. (2000). Association between homozygosity at the COMT gene locus and obsessive-compulsive disorder. *American Journal of Medical Genetics, 96*(6), 721–724.

Schinka, J. A., Busch, R. M., & Robichaux-Keene, N. (2004). A meta-analysis of the association between the serotonin transporter gene polymorphism (5–HTTLPR) and trait anxiety. *Molecular Psychiatry, 9*(2), 197–202.

Schiralde, G. R. (2000). *The Posttraumatic Stress Disorder Sourcebook.* New York: Contemporary Press.

Schmidt, N. B., Forsyth, J. P., Santiago, H. T., & Trakowski, J. H. (2002). Classifica-tion of panic attack subtypes in patients and normal controls in response to biological challenge: Implications for assessment and treatment. *Journal of Anxiety Disorders, 16,* 625–638.

Schmidt, N. B., Lerew, D. R., & Jackson R. J. (1999). Prospective evaluation of anxi-ety sensitivity in the pathogenesis of panic: Replication and extension. *Journal of Abnor-mal Psychology, 108,* 532–537.

Schmitt, U., Luddens, H., & Hiemke, C. (2002). Anxiolytic-like effects of acute and chronic GABA transporter inhibition in rats. *Journal of Neural Transmission, 109*(5–6), 871–880.

Schneider, F. R. (2001). Treatment of social phobia with antidepressants. *Journal of Clinical Psychiatry, 62*(1), 43–48.

Schneider, F. R., Goetz, D., Campreas, R., Fallon, B., Marshall, R., & Liebowitz, M. R. (1998). Placebo-controlled trial of moclobemide in social phobia. *British Journal of Psychiatry, 173,* 70–77.

Schore, A. (2003). *Affect Regulation and the Repair of the Self.* New York: W. W. Norton.

Schruers, K., Koning, K., Leurmans, J., Haack, M. J., & Griez, E. (2005). Obsessive-compulsive disorder: A critical review of therapeutic perspectives. *Acta Psychiatrica Scandanavica, 111*(4), 261–271.

Schwartz, C. E., Snidman, N., & Kagan, J. (1999). Adolescent social anxiety as an outcome of inhibited temperament in childhood. *Journal of the American Academy of Child and Adolescent Psychiatry, 38*(8), 1008–1015.

Schwartz, R. D. (1988). The GABA-A receptor-gated ion channel: Biochemical and pharmacological studies structure and function. *Biochemical Pharmacology, 37,* 3369.

Seedat, S., Warwick, J., van Heerden, B., Hugo, C., Zungu-Dirwayi, N., Van Kradenburg, J., & Stein, D. J. (2004). Single photon emission computed tomography in post-traumatic stress disorder before and after treatment with a selective serotonin reuptake inhibitor. *Journal of Affective Disorders, 80*(1), 45–53.

Seeman, M. V. (1997). Psychopathology in women and men: Focus on female hormones. *American Journal of Psychiatry, 154,* 1641–1647.

Segman, R. H., Cooper-Kazaz, R., Macciardi, F., Goltser, T., Halfon, Y., Dobroborski, T., & Shalev, A. Y. (2002). Association between the dopamine transporter gene and post-traumatic stress disorder. *Molecular Psychiatry, 7*(8), 903–907.

Segman, R. H., & Shalev, A. Y. (2003). Genetics of posttraumatic stress disorder. *CNS Spectrums, 8*(9), 693–698.

Seligman, M. E. P. (1968). Chronic fear produced by unpredictable shock. *Journal of Comparative and Physiological Psychology, 66,* 402–411.

Seligman, M. E. P. (1970). On the generality of the laws of learning. *Psychological Review, 77,* 406–418.

Seligman, M. E. P. (1995). The effectiveness of psychotherapy: The Consumer Reports study. *American Psychologist, 50,* 965–974.

Seligman, M. E. P., Schulman, P., DeRubeis, R. J., & Hollon, S. D. (1999). The prevention of depression and anxiety. *Prevention and Treatment, 2,* 8.

Selye, H. (1956). *The Stress of Life.* New York: McGraw-Hill.

Selye, H. (1976). *The Stress of Life* (2nd Ed.). New York: McGraw-Hill.

Sen, S., Villafuerte, S., Nesse, R., Stoltenberg, S. F., Hopcian, J., Gleiberman, L., Weder, A., & Burmeister, M. (2004). Serotonin transporter and GABA(A) alpha-6 receptor variants are associated with neuroticism. *Biological Psychiatry, 55*(3), 244–249.

Sena, L. M., Bueno, C., Pobbe, R. L., Andrade, T. G., Zangrossi, H., & Viana, M. B. (2003). The dorsal raphe nucleus exerts opposed control on generalized anxiety and panic-related defensive responses in rats. *Behavioural Brain Research, 142*(1–2), 125–133.

Senkowski, D., Linden, M., Zubragel, D., Bar, T., & Gallinat, J. (2003). Evidence for disturbed cortical signal processing and altered serotonergic neurotransmission in generalized anxiety disorder. *Biological Psychiatry, 53*(4), 304–314.

Serby, M. (2003). Methylphenidate-induced obsessive-compulsive symptoms in an elderly man. *CNS Spectrums, 8*(8), 612–613.

Seth, P., Cheeta, S., Tucci, S., & File, S. E. (2002). Nicotinic-serotonergic interactions in brain and behavior. *Pharmacology, Biochemistry, and Behavior, 71*(4), 795–805.

Severson, C. A., Wang, W., Pieribone, V. A., Dohle, C. I., & Richardson, G. B. (2003). Midbrain serotonergic neurons are central pH chemoreceptors. *Nature Neuroscience, 6*(11), 1139–1140.

Sevincok, L., Akoglu, A., Topaloglu, B., & Aslantas, H. (2004). Neurological soft signs in schizophrenic patients with obsessive-compulsive disorder. *Psychiatry and Clinical Neuroscience, 58(3),* 274–279.

Shafran, R., & Rachman, S. (2004). Thought-action fusion: A review. *Journal of Behavior Therapy and Experimental Psychiatry, 35(2),* 87–107.

Shapira, N. A., Ward, H. E., Mandoki, M., Murphy, T. K., Yang, M. C., Blier, P., & Goodman, W. K. (2004). A double-blind, placebo-controlled trial of olanzapine addition in fluoxetine-refractory obsessive-compulsive disorder. *Biological Psychiatry, 55(5),* 553–555.

Shapiro, F. (1989). Efficacy of the eye movement desensitization procedure in the treatment of traumatic memories. *Journal of Trauma and Stress, 2(2),* 199–223.

Shapiro, T. (1989). The psychodynamic formulation in child and adolescent psychiatry. *Journal of the American Academy of Child and Adolescent Psychiatry, 28,* 675–680.

Sharma, V. (2003). Atypical antipsychotics and suicide in mood and anxiety disorders. *Bipolar Disorder, 5(2),* 48–52.

Shear, M. K., Cassano, G. B., Frank, E., Rucci, P., Rotondo, A., & Fagiolini, A. (2002). The panic- agoraphobic spectrum: Development, description, and clinical significance. *Psychiatric Clinics of North America, 25(4),* 739–756.

Shear, M. K., Cooper, A. M., & Klerman, G. L. (1993). A psychodynamic model of panic disorder. *American Journal of Psychiatry, 150(6),* 859–866.

Sheehan, D. V., & Harnett-Sheehan, K. (1996). The role of SSRIs in panic disorder. *Journal of Clinical Psychiatry, 57,* 51–58.

Sheline, Y. I., Mittler, B. L., & Mintun, M. A. (2002). The hippocampus and depression. *European Psychiatry, 17(3),* 300–305.

Shelton, C. I. (2004). Diagnosis and management of anxiety disorders. *Journal of the American Osteopathic Association, 104(3),* 2–5.

Shimizu, E., Hashimoto, K., & Iyo, M. (2002). The neurobiological approaches to obsessive-compulsive disorder. *Japanese Journal of Psychopharmacology, 22(4),* 111–119.

Shin, L. M., Orr, S. P., Carson, M. A., Rauch, S. L., Macklin, M. L., Lasko, N. B., Peters, P. M., Metzger, L. J., Dougherty, D. D., Cannistraro, P. A., Alpert, N. M., Fischman, A. J., & Pitman, R. K. (2004). Regional cerebral blood flow in the amygdala and medial prefrontal cortex during traumatic imagery in male and female Vietnam veterans with PTSD. *Archives of General Psychiatry, 61(2),* 168–176.

Shin, L. M., Shin, P. S., Heckers, S., Krangel, T. S., Macklin, M. L., Orr, S. P., Lasko, N., Segal, E., Makris, N., Richert, K., Levering J., Schacter, D. L., Alpert, N. M., Fischman, A. J., Pitman, R. K., & Rauch, S. L. (2004). Hippocampal function in posttraumatic stress disorder. *Hippocampus, 14(3),* 292–300.

Shin, L. M., Wright, C. L., Cannistraro, P. A., Wedig, M. M., McMullin, K., Martis, B., Macklin, M. L., Lasko, N. B., Cavanagh, S. R., Krangel, T. S., Orr, S. P., Pitman, R. K., Whalen, P. J., & Rauch, S. L. (2005). A functional magnetic resonance imaging study of amygdala and medial prefrontal cortex responses to overtly presented fearful faces in posttraumatic stress disorder. *Archives of General Psychiatry, 62(3),* 273–281.

Shin, M. S., Park, S. J., Kim, M. S., Lee, Y. H., Ha, T. H., & Kwon, J. S. (2004). Deficits of organizational strategy and visual memory in obsessive-compulsive disorder. *Neuropsychology, 18(4),* 665–672.

Shin, Y. W., Ha, T. H., Kim, S. Y., & Kwon, J. S. (2004). Association between EEG alpha power and visuospatial function in obsessive-compulsive disorder. *Psychiatry and Clinical Neuroscience, 58(1),* 16–20.

Shinnick-Gallagher, P., McKernan, M. G., Xie, J., & Zinebi, F. (2003). L-type voltage-gated calcium channels are involved in the in vivo and in vitro expression of fear conditioning. *Annals of the New York Academy of Sciences, 985,* 135–149.

Shlik, J., Maron, E., Tru, I., Aluoja, A., & Vasar, V. (2004). Citalopram challenge in social anxiety disorder. *International Journal of Neuropsychopharmacology, 7(2),* 177–182.

Sickle, B. J., Xiang, K., & Tietz, E. I. (2004). Transient plasticity of hippocampal CA1 neuron glutamate receptors contributes to benzodiazepine withdrawal anxiety. *Neuropsychopharmacology, 7*(1), 7–12.

Sigel, E. (2002). Mapping of the benzodiazepine recognition site on GABA-A receptors. *Current Topics in Medical Chemistry, 2*(8), 833–839.

Silverstein, M. L. (1999). *Self Psychology and Diagnostic Assessment.* New Jersey: Lawrence Erlbaum.

Silverstein, S. M., & Uhlhaas, P. J. (2004). Gestalt psychology: The forgotten paradigm in abnormal psychology. *American Journal of Psychology, 117*(2), 259–277.

Simon, N. M., Emmanuel, N., Ballanger, J., Worthington, J. J., Kinrys, G., Korbly, N. B., Farach, F. J., & Pollack, M. H. (2003). Bupropion sustained release for panic disorder. *Psychopharmacology Bulletin, 37*(4), 66–72.

Simon, N. M., Otto, M. W., Smits, J. A., Nicolaou, D. C., Reese, H. E., & Pollack, M. H. (2004). Changes in anxiety sensitivity with pharmacotherapy for panic disorder. *Journal of Psychiatry Research, 38*(5), 491–495.

Simpson, H. B., Liebowitz, M. R., Foa, E. B., Kozak, M. J., Schmidt, A. B., Rowan, V., Petkova, E., Kjernisted, K., Huppert, J. D., Franklin, M. E., Davies, S. O., & Campeas, R. (2004). Post- treatment effects of exposure therapy and clomipramine in obsessive-compulsive disorder. *Depression and Anxiety, 19*(4), 225–233.

Singer, H. S., Loiselle, C. R., Lee, O., Minzer, K., Swedo, S., & Gris, F. H. (2004). Anti-basal ganglia antibodies in PANDAS. *Movement Disorders, 19*(4), 406–415.

Singewald, N., & Sharp, T. (2000). Neuroanatomical targets of anxiogenic drugs in the hindbrain as revealed by Fos immunocytochemistry. *Neuroscience, 98*(4), 759–770.

Siniscalchi, A., Rodi, D., Cavallini, S., Marino, S., Ferraro, L., Beani, L., & Bianchi, C. (2003). Effects of cholecystokinin tetrapeptide (CCK4) and of anxiolytic drugs on GABA outflow from the cerebral cortex of freely moving rats. *Neurochemistry International, 42*(1), 87–92.

Skinner, B. F. (1953). *Science and Human Behavior.* New York: Macmillan.

Skinner, B. F. (1974). *About Behaviorism.* New York: Knopf.

Skinner, M. H., Kuan, H. Y., Skerjanec, A., Seger, M. E., Heathman, M., O'Brien, L., Reddy, S., & Knadler, M. P. (2004). Effect of age on the pharmacokinetics of duloxetine in women. *British Journal of Clinical Pharmacology, 57*(1), 54–61.

Skolnick, P., Syapin, P. J., Paugh, B. A., Monacada, V., Marangoes, P. J., & Paul, S. M. (1979). Inosine, an endogeneous ligand of the brain benzodiazepine receptor, antagonizes pentylenetetrazole-evoked seizures. *Proceedings of the National Academy of Sciences of the United States of America, 76,* 1515–1518.

Slade, T., & Andrews, G. (2001). DSM-IV and ICD-10 generalized anxiety disorder: Discrepant diagnoses and associated disability. *Social Psychiatry and Psychiatric Epidemiology, 36*(1), 45–51.

Slattery, M. J., Dubbert, B. K., Allen, A. J., Loenard, H. L., Swedo, S. E., & Gourley, M. F. (2004). Prevalence of obsessive-compulsive disorder in patients with systemic lupus erythematosus. *Journal of Clinical Psychiatry, 65*(3), 301–306.

Smith, J. E., & Lakoski, J. M. (1998). Cellular eletrophysiological effects of chronic flouxetine and duloxetine administration on serotonergic responses in the aging hippocampus. *Synapse, 30*(3), 318–328.

Smith, M. E. (2005). Bilateral hippocampal volume reduction in adults with posttraumatic stress disorder: A meta-analysis of structural MRI studies. *Hippocampus, 6,* 1–7.

Smith, M. V., Rosenheck, R. A., Cavaleri, M. A., Howell, H. B., Poschman, K., & Yonkers, K. A. (2004). Screening for and detection of depression, panic disorder, and PTSD in public-sector obstetric clinics. *Psychiatric Services, 55*(4), 407–414.

Smoller, J. W., Acierno, J. S., Rosenbaum, J. F., Biederman, J., Pollack, M. H., Meninger, S., Pava, J. A., Chadwick, L. H., White, C., Bulzacchelli, M., & Slaugenhaupt, S. A. (2001). Targeted genome screen of panic disorder and anxiety disorder proneness using homology to murine QTL regions. *American Journal of Medical Genetics, 105*(2), 195–206.

Smoller, J. W., & Pollack, M. H. (1996). Pharmacologic approaches to treatment-resistant social phobia and generalized anxiety disorder. In M. H. Pollack, M. W. Otto, & J. F. Rosenbaum (Eds.), *Challenges in Clinical Practice: Pharmacologic and Psychosocial Strategies* (pp. 141–170). New York: Guilford Press.

Smoller, J. W., Rosenbaum, J. F., Biederman, J., Kennedy, J., Dai, D., Racette, S. R., Laird, N. M., Kagan, J., Snidman, N., Hirschfeld-Becker, D., Tsuang, M. T., Sklar, P. B., & Slaugenhaupt, S. A. (2003). Association of a genetic marker at the corticotropin-releasing hormone locus with behavioral inhibition. *Biological Psychiatry, 54*(12), 1376–1381.

Smoller, J. W., Yamaki, L. H., Biederman, J., Racette, S., Laird, N. M., Kagan, J., Snidman, N., Faraone, S. V., Hirschfeld-Becker, D., Tsuang, M. T., Slaugenhaupt, S. A., Rosenbaum, J. F., & Sklar, P. B. (2005). The corticotrophin-releasing hormone gene and behavioral inhibition in children at risk for panic disorder. *Biological Psychiatry, 57*(12), 1485–1492.

Snider, L. A., & Swedo, S. E. (2003). Childhood onset obsessive-compulsive disorder and tic disorders: Case report and literature review. *Journal of Child and Adolescent Psychopharmacology, 13*(1), 81–88.

Snider, L. A., & Swedo, S. E. (2003b). Post-streptococcal autoimmune disorders of the central nervous system. *Current Opinions in Neurology, 16*(3), 359–365.

Snider, L. A., & Swedo, S. E. (2004). PANDAS: Current status and directions for research. *Molecular Psychiatry, 9*(10), 900–907.

Sodhi, M. S., & Saunders-Bush, E. (2004). Serotonin and brain development. *International Review of Neurobiology, 59*, 111–174.

Sorensen, G., Lindberg, C., Wortwein, G., Bolwig, T. G., & Woldbye, D. P. (2004). Differential roles for neuropeptide Y Y1 and Y5 receptors in anxiety and sedation. *Journal of Neuroscience Research, 77*(5), 723–729.

Spano, D., Branchi, I., Rosica, A., Pirro, M. T., Riccio, A., Mithbaokar, P., Affuse-Arra, C., Campolongo, P., Terracciano, D., Macchia, V., Bernal, J., Alleva, E., & De Lauro, R. (2004). RHES is involved in striatal function. *Molecular Cell Biology, 24*(13), 5788–5796.

Spielberger, C. D. (Ed.). (1972). *Anxiety: Current Trends in Theory and Research* (Vol. 2). Orlando, FL: Academic Press.

Spielberger, C. D. (1983). *Manual for the State-Trait Anxiety Inventory (STAI, Form Y)*. Palo Alto, CA: Consulting Psychologists Press.

Spivak, B., Maayan, R., Mester, R., & Weizman, A. (2003). Plasma testosterone levels in patients with combat-related posttraumatic stress disorder. *Neuropsychobiology, 47*(2), 57–60.

Squires, R. F., & Braestrup, C. (1977). Benzodiazepine receptors in rat brain. *Nature, 226*, 732–734.

Sramek, J. J., Zarotsky, V., & Cutler, N. R. (2002). Generalized anxiety disorder: Treatment options. *Drugs, 62*(11), 1635–1648.

Stahl, S. M. (2002). Don't ask, don't tell, but benzodiazepines are still the leading treatments for anxiety disorders. *Journal of Clinical Psychiatry, 63*(9), 756–757.

Stahl, S. M. (2004). Anticonvulsants as anxiolytics, part 1: Tiagabine and other anticonvulsants with actions on GABA. *Journal of Clinical Psychiatry, 65*(3), 291–292.

Stahl, S. M. (2004b). Anticonvulsants as anxiolytics, part 2: Pregabalin and gabapentin as alpha(2)delta ligands at voltage-gated calcium channels. *Journal of Clinical Psychiatry, 65*(4), 460–461.

Stanley, M. A., Beck, J. G., Novy, D. M., Averill, P. M., Swann, A. C., Diefenbach, G., & Hopko, D. R. (2003). Cognitive-behavioral treatment of late-life generalized anxiety disorder. *Journal of Consulting and Clinical Psychology, 71*(2), 309–319.

Stanton, T., Bolden-Watson, C., Cusack, B., & Richelson, E. (1993). Antagonism of the five cloned human muscarinic cholinergic receptors expressed in CHO-K1 cells by antidepressants and antihistamines. *Biochemical Pharmacology, 45*(11), 2352–2354.

Stein, D. J., Van Heerden, B., Hugo, C., Van Kradenburg, J., Warwick, J., Zungu-Dirwayi, N., & Seedat, S. (2002). Functional brain imaging and pharmacotherapy in trichotillomania: Single photon emission computed tomography before and after treatment with the selective serotonin reuptake inhibitor citalopram. *Progress in Neuro-psychopharmacology & Biological Psychiatry, 26*(5), 885–890.

Stein, D. J., Westenberg, H. G., & Liebowitz, M. R. (2002). Social anxiety disorder and generalized anxiety disorder: Serotonergic and dopaminergic neurocircuitry. *Journal of Clinical Psychiatry, 63*(6), 12–19.

Stein, M. B., Jang, K. L., & Livesley, W. J. (1999). Heritability of anxiety sensitivity: A twin study. *American Journal of Psychiatry, 156*(2), 246–251.

Stein, M. B., Jang, K. L., Taylor, S., Vernon, P. A., & Livesley, W. J. (2002). Genetic and environmental influences on trauma exposure and posttraumatic stress disorder symptoms: A twin study. *American Journal of Psychiatry, 159*, 1675–1681.

Stengler-Wenzke, K., Muller, U., Angermeyer, M. C., Sabri, O., & Hesse, S. (2004). Reduced serotonin transporter-availability in obsessive-compulsive disorder. *European Archives of Psychiatry and Clinical Neuroscience, 254*(4), 252–255.

Stengler-Wenzke, K., Trosbach, J., Dietrich, S., & Angermeyer, M. C. (2004b). Experience of stigmatization by relatives of patients with obsessive-compulsive disorder. *Archives of Psychiatric Nursing, 18*(3), 88–96.

Stern, D. N. (1985). *The Interpersonal World of the Infant: A View From Psychoanalysis and Developmental Psychology*. New York: Basic Books.

Stewart, S. E., Geller, D. A., Jenike, M., Pauls, D., Shaw, D., Mullin, B., & Faraone, S. V. (2004). Long-term outcome of pediatric obsessive-compulsive disorder: A meta-analysis and qualitative review of the literature. *Acta Psychiatrica Scandinavica, 110*(1), 4–13.

Stolorow, R., & Lachmann, F. (1980). *The Psychoanalysis of Developmental Arrests*. New York: International Universities Press.

Stone, K. J., Viera, A. J., & Parman, C. L. (2003). Off-label applications for SSRI's. *American Family Physician, 68*(3), 498–504.

Strandell, J., Neil, A., & Carlin, G. (2004). An approach to the in vitro evaluation of potential for cytochrome P450 enzyme inhibition from herbals and other natural remedies. *Phytomedicine, 11*(2–3), 98–104.

Strawn, J. R., Ekhator, N. N., Horn, P. S., Baker, D. G., & Geracioti, T. D. (2004). Blood pressure and cerebrospinal fluid norepinephrine in combat-related posttraumatic stress disorder. *Psychosomatic Medicine, 66*(5), 757–759.

Strohle, A., Kellner, M., Holsboer, F., & Wiedemann, K. (2001). Anxiolytic activity of atrial natriuretic peptide in patients with panic disorder. *American Journal of Psychiatry, 158*(9), 1514–1516.

Strupp, H. H. (1973). On the basic ingredients of psychotherapy. *Journal of Consulting and Clinical Psychology, 41*, 1–8.

Strupp, H. H. (1993). The Vanderbilt psychotherapy studies: Synopsis. *Journal of Consulting and Clinical Psychology, 61*(3), 431–433.

Sturm, V., Lenartz, D., Koulousakis, A., Treuer, H., Herholz, K., Klein, J. C., & Klosterkotter, J. (2003). The nucleus accumbens: A target for deep brain stimulation in obsessive-compulsive and anxiety disorders. *Journal of Chemical Neuroanatomy, 26*(4), 293–299.

Sugimoto, Y., Inoue, K., & Yamada, J. (2003). The tricyclic antidepressant clomipramine increases plasma glucose levels of mice. *Journal of Pharmacological Science, 93*(1), 74–79.

Suhara, T., Takano, A., Sudo, Y., Ichimiya, T., Inoue, M., Yasuno, F., Ikoma, Y., & Okubo, Y. (2003). High levels of serotonin transporter occupany with low-dose clomipramine in comparative occupancy study with fluvoxamine using positron emission tomography. *Archives of General Psychiatry, 60*(4), 386–391.

Sullivan, H. S. (1953). *The Interpersonal Theory of Psychiatry*. New York: Norton.

Sullivan, H. S. (1954). *The Psychiatric Interview*. New York: Norton.

Sullivan, G. M., Kent, J. M., & Coplan, J. D. (2000). The neurobiology of stress and anxiety. In D. I. Mostofsky & D. H. Barlow (Eds.), *The Management of Stress and Anxiety in Medical Disorders* (pp. 15–35). Needham Heights, MA: Allyn & Bacon.

Summerfeldt, L. J. (2004). Understanding and treating incompleteness in obsessive-compulsive disorder. *Journal of Clinical Psychology, 60*(11), 1155–1168.

Summerfeldt, L. J., Kloosterman, P. H., Antony, M. M., Richter, M. A., & Swinson, R. P. (2004). The relationship between miscellaneous symptoms and major symptom factors in obsessive-compulsive disorder. *Behaviour Research and Therapy, 42*(12), 1453–1467.

Sundet, J. M., Skre, I., Okkenhaug, J. J., & Tambs, K. (2003). Genetic and environmental causes of the interrelationships between self-reported fears: A study of a non-clinical sample of Norwegian identical twins and their families. *Scandinavian Journal of Psychology, 44*(2), 97–106.

Suzuki, R., Lumeng, L., McBride, W. J., Li, T. K., & Hwang, B. H. (2004). Reduced neuropeptide Y mRNA expression in the central nucleus of amygdala of alcohol preferring (P) rats: Its potential involvement in alcohol preference and anxiety. *Brain Research, 1014*(1–2), 251–254.

Szabo, S. T., & Blier, P. (2002). Effects of serotonin reuptake inhibition plus 5HT2A receptor antagonism on the firing activity of norepinephrine neurons. *Journal of Pharmacology and Experimental Therapeutics, 302*(3), 983–991.

Szechtman, H., Culver, K., & Eilam, D. (1999). Role of dopamine systems in obsessive-compulsive disorder (OCD): Implications from a novel psychostimulant-induced animal model. *Polish Journal of Pharmacology, 51*(1), 55–61.

Szechtman, H., & Woody, E. (2004). Obsessive-compulsive disorder as a disturbance of security motivation. *Psychological Review, 111*(1), 111–127.

Szeszko, P. R., Ardekani, B. A., Ashtari, M., Malhotra, A. K., Robinson, D. G., Bilder, R. M., & Lim, K. O. (2005). Whiat matter abnormalities in obsessive-compulsive disorder: A diffusion tensor imaging study. *Archives of General Psychiatry, 62*(7), 782–790.

Szeszko, P. R., MacMillan, S., McMeniman, M., Chen, S., Baribault, K., Lim, K. O., Ivey, J., Rose, M., Banerjee, S. P., Bhandari, R., Moore, G. J., & Rosenberg, D. R. (2004). Brain structural abnormalities in psychotropic drug-naive pediatrics patients with obsessive-compulsive disorder. *American Journal of Psychiatry, 161*(6), 1049–1056.

Szeszko, P. R., MacMillan, S., McMeniman, M., Lorch, E., Madden, R., Ivey, J., Banerjee, S. P., Moore, G. J., & Rosenberg, D. R. (2004b). Amygdala volume reductions in pediatric patients with obsessive-compulsive disorder treated with paroxetine: Preliminary findings. *Neuropsychopharmacology, 29*(4), 826–832.

Taghavi, M. R., Dalgleish, T., Moradi, A. R., Neshat-Doost, H. T., & Yule, W. (2003). Selective processing of negative emotional information in children and adolescents with generalized anxiety disorder. *British Journal of Clinical Psychology, 42*(3), 221–230.

Talbot, N. L., Duberstein, P. R., Butzel, J. S., Cox, C., & Giles, D. E. (2003). Personality traits and symptom reduction in a group treatment for women with histories of childhood sexual abuse. *Comprehensive Psychiatry, 44*(6), 448–453.

Tallis, F. (1997). The neuropsychology of obsessive-compulsive disorder: A review and consideration of clinical implications. *British Journal of Clinical Psychology, 36*, 3–20.

Tamam, L., Ozpoyraz, N., San, M., & Bozkurt, A. (2000). Association between idiopathic mitral valve prolapse and panic disorder. *Croatian Medical Journal, 41*(4), 410–416.

Tamminga, C. A. (2003). Similarities and differences among antipsychotics. *Journal of Clinical Psychiatry*, 64(17), 7–10.

Taylor, D. P., Carter, R. B., Eison, A. S., Mullins, U. L., Smith, H. L., Torrente, J. R., Wright, R. N., & Yocca, F. D. (1995). Pharmacology and neurochemistry of nefazodone, a novel antidepressant drug. *Journal of Clinical Psychiatry*, 56(6), 3–11.

Taylor, G. T., Farr, S., Klinga, K., & Weiss, J. (2004). Chronic fluoxetine suppresses circulating estrogen and the enhanced spatial learning of estrogen-treated ovariectomized rats. *Psychoneuroendocrinology*, 29(10), 1241–1249.

Taylor, S. E. (2004). Cognitive therapy is more effective than fluoxetine in people with generalized social phobia. *Evidence Based Mental Health*, 7(3), 75.

Taylor, S. E., Asmundson, G. J., & Carleton, R. N. (2005). Simple versus complex PTSD: A cluster analytic investigation. *Journal of Anxiety Disorders*, 6, 1–7.

Taylor, S. E., Pham, L. B., Rivkin, I. D., & Armor, D. A. (1998). Harnessing the imagination: Mental simulation, self-regulation, and coping. *American Psychologist*, 53(4), 429–439.

Teicher, M. H. (2002). Scars that won't heal: The neurobiology of child abuse. *Scientific American*, 286(3), 68–75.

Teicher, M. H., Andersen, S. L., Polcari, A., Anderson, C. M., Navalta, C. P., & Kim, D. M. (2003). The neurobiological consequences of early stress and childhood maltreatment. *Neuroscience and Biobehavioral Review*, 27(1–2), 33–44.

Thakker, J., & Ward, T. (1998). Culture and classification: The cross-cultural application of the DSM-IV. *Clinical Psychology Review*, 18, 501–529.

Thase, M. E. (2003). Effectiveness of antidepressants: Comparative remission rates. *Journal of Clinical Psychiatry*, 64(2), 3–7.

Thase, M. E., & Trivedi, M. (2002). Optimizing treatment outcomes for patients with depression and generalized anxiety disorder. *Psychopharmacology Bulletin*, 36(2), 93–102.

Thayer, J. F., Friedman, B. H., & Borkovec, T. D. (1996). Autonomic characteristics of generalized anxiety disorder and worry. *Biological Psychiatry*, 39, 255–266.

Thayer, J. F., Friedman, B. H., Borkovec, T. D., Johnsen, B. H., & Molina, S. (2000). Phasic heart period reactions to cued threat and nonthreat stimuli in generalized anxiety disorder. *Psychophysiology*, 37(3), 361–368.

Thobois, S., Jouanneau, E., Bouvard, M., & Sindou, M. (2004). Obsessive-compulsive disorder after unilateral caudate nucleus bleeding. *Acta Neurochirurgica*, 146(9), 1027–1031.

Thoenen, H. (1995). Neurotropins and neuronal plasticity. *Science*, 270, 593–598.

Thomas, E., Pernar, L., Lucki, I., & Valentino, R. J. (2003). Corticotropin-releasing factor in the dorsal raphe nucleus regulates activity of lateral septal neurons. *Brain Research*, 960(1–2), 201–208.

Tillich, P. (1952). *The Courage to Be*. New Haven: McGraw-Hill.

Todorov, C. (2004). Is there a specific pharmacological treatment for anxiety disorders? Summary of a controversy. *Sante Mentale au Quebec*, 29(1), 127–136.

Tohmi, M., Tsuda, N., Watanabe, Y., Kakita, A., & Nawa, H. (2004). Perinatal inflammatory cytokine challenge results in distinct neurobiological alterations in rats: Implication in psychiatric disorders of developmental origin. *Neuroscience Research*, 50(1), 67–75.

Tot, S., Ozge, A., Comelekoglu, U., Yazici, K., & Bal, N. (2002). Association of QEEG findings with clinical characteristics of OCD evidence of left frontotemporal dysfunction. *Canadian Journal of Psychiatry*, 47(6), 538–545.

Trichard, C., Paillere-Martinot, M. L., Attar-Levy, D., Recassens, C., Monnet, F., & Martinot, J. L. (1998). Binding of antipsychotic drugs to cortical 5HT2A receptors: A PET study of chlorpromazine, clozapine, and amisulpride in schizophrenic patients. *American Journal of Psychiatry*, 155(4), 505–508.

Trivedi, M. H. (1996). Functional neuroanatomy of obsessive-compulsive disorder. *Journal of Clinical Psychiatry, 57*(8), 26–35.

Tsai, W. Y., Heiman, G. A., & Hodge, S. E. (2005). New simple tests for age-at-onset anticipation: Application to panic disorder. *Genetic Epidemiology, 6,* 1–8.

Tsaltas, E., Kontis, D., Chrysikakou, S., Giannou, H., Biba, A., Pallidi, S., Christodoulou, A., Maillis, A., & Rabavilas, A. (2005). Reinforced spatial alternation as an animal model of obsessive-compulsive disorder (OCD): Investigation of 5HT2C and 5HT1D receptor involvement in OCD pathophysiology. *Biological Psychiatry, 57*(10), 1176–1185.

Tsao, J. C., Myers, C. D., Craske, M. G., Bursch, B., Kim, S. C., & Zeltzer, L. K. (2004). Role of anticipatory anxiety and anxiety sensitivity in children's and adolescents' laboratory pain responses. *Journal of Pediatric Psychology, 29*(5), 379–388.

Tsao, S. D., & McKay, D. (2004). Behavioral avoidance tests and disgust in contamination fears: Distinctions from trait anxiety. *Behaviour Research and Therapy, 42*(2), 207–216.

Tschenett, A., Singewald, N., Carli, M., Balducci, C., Salchner, P., Vezzani, A., Herzog, H., & Sperk, G. (2003). Reduced anxiety and improved stress coping ability in mice lacking NPY-Y2 receptors. *European Journal of Neuroscience, 18*(1), 143–148.

Tse, W. S., & Bond, A. J. (2001). Serotonergic involvement in the psychosocial dimension of personality. *Journal of Psychopharmacology, 15*(3), 195–198.

Tsiouris, J. A., & Brown, W. T. (2004). Neuropsychiatric symptoms of fragile x syndrome: pathophysiology and pharmacotherapy. *CNS Drugs, 18*(11), 687–703.

Tsuang, M., Domschke, K., Jerkey, B. A., & Lyons, M. J. (2004). Agoraphobic behavior and panic attack: A study of male twins. *Journal of Anxiety Disorders, 18*(6), 799–807.

Tucker, P., Beebe, K. L., Burgin, C., Wyatt, D. B., Parker, D. E., Masters, B. K., & Nawar, O. (2004). Paroxetine treatment of depression with posttraumatic stress disorder: Effects on autonomic reactivity and cortisol secretion. *Journal of Clinical Psychopharmacology, 24*(2), 131–140.

Tucker, P., Ruwe, W. D., Masters, B., Parker, D. E., Hossain, A., Trautman, R. P., & Wyatt, D. B. (2004). Neuroimmune and cortisol changes in selective serotonin reuptake inhibitor and placebo treatment of chronic posttraumatic stress disorder. *Biological Psychiatry, 56*(2), 121–128.

Tukel, R., Polat, A., Gene, A., Bozkurt, O., & Atli, H. (2004). Gender-related differences among Turkish patients with obsessive-compulsive disorder. *Comprehensive Psychiatry, 45*(5), 362–366.

Tuna, S., Tekcan, A. I., & Topcuoglu, V. (2005). Memory and metamemory in obsessive-compulsive disorder. *Behaviour Research and Therapy, 43*(1), 15–27.

Tupler, L. A., Davidson, J. R., Smith, R. D., Lazeyras, F., Charles, H. C., & Krishnan, K. R. (1997). A repeat proton magnetic resonance spectroscopy study in social phobia. *Biological Psychiatry, 42*(6), 419–424.

Turkheimer, E. (1998). Heritability and biological explanation. *Psychological Review, 105,* 782–791.

Turner, S. M., Beidel, D. C., & Jacob, R. G. (1994). Social phobia: A comparison of behavior therapy and atenolol. *Journal of Consulting and Clinical Psychology, 62,* 350–358.

Ulloa, R. E., Nicolini, H., & Fernandez-Guasti, A. (2004). Age differences in an animal model of obsessive-compulsive disorder: Participation of dopamine in an animal model of OCD. *Pharmacology, Biochemistry, and Behavior, 78*(4), 661–666.

Ulloa, R. E., Nicolini, H., & Fernandez-Guasti, A. (2004b). Sex differences on spontaneous alternation in prepubertal rats: Implications for an animal model of obsessive-compulsive disorder. *Progress in Neuropsychopharmacology & Biological Psychiatry, 28*(4), 687–692.

Urraca, N., Camarena, B., Gomez-Caudillo, L., Esmer, M. C., & Nicolini, H. (2004). Mu opioid receptor gene as a candidate for the study of obsessive-compulsive disorder with and without tics. *American Journal of Medical Genetics, 127*(1), 94–96.

Ursu, S., Stenger, V. A., Shear, M. K., Jones, M. R., & Carter, C. S. (2003). Overactive action monitoring in obsessive-compulsive disorder: Evidence from functional magnetic resonance imaging. *Psychological Science, 14*(4), 347–353.

Valenca, A. M., Mezzasalma, M. A., Nascimento, I., Lopes, F. L., Zin, W. A., & Nardi, A. E. (2004). Respiratory panic disorder treatment with clonidine. *Canadian Journal of Psychiatry, 49*(2), 154.

Valenca, A. M., Nardi, A. E., Mezzasalma, I., Zin, W. A., Lopes, F. L., & Versiani, M. (2003). Therapeutic response to benzodiazepine in panic disorder subtypes. *Sao Paulo Medical Journal, 121*(2), 77–80.

Valente, A. A., Miguel, E. C., Castro, C. C., Amaro, E., Duran, F. L., Buchpiguel, C. A., Chitnis, X., McGuire, P. K., & Busatto, G. F. (2005). Regional gray matter abnormalities in obsessive-compulsive disorder: A voxel-based morphometry study. *Biological Psychiatry, 6,* 1–7.

Van Ameringen, M. A., Lane, R. M., & Walker, J. R. (2001). Sertraline treatment of generalized social phobia: A 20–week, double blind, placebo-controlled study. *American Journal of Psychiatry, 158*(2), 275–281.

Van den Bergh, B. R., & Marcoen, A. (2004). High antenatal maternal anxiety is related to ADHD symptoms, externalizing problems, and anxiety in 8– and 9–year-olds. *Child Development, 75*(4), 1085–1097.

Van den Heuvel, O. A., Van de Wetering, B. J., Veltman, D. J., & Paul, D. L. (2000). Genetic studies of panic disorder: A review. *Journal of Clinical Psychiatry, 61*(10), 756–766.

Van den Heuvel, O. A., Veltman, D. J., Groenewegen, H. J., Cath, D. C., Van Balkom, A. J., Van Hartskamp, J., Barkhof, & Van Dyck, R. (2005). Frontal-striatal dysfunction during planning in obsessive-compulsive disorder. *Archives of General Psychiatry, 62*(3), 301–309.

Van der Wee, N. J., Stevens, H., Hardeman, J. A., Mandl, R. C., Denys, D. A., Van Megen, H. J., Kahn, R. S., & Westenberg, H. M. (2004). Enhanced dopamine transporter density in psychotropic-naïve patients with obsessive-compulsive disorder shown by [1231]–CIT SPECT. *American Journal of Psychiatry, 161*(12), 2201–2206.

Van Veen, V., & Carter, C. S. (2002). The anterior cingulate as a conflict monitor: fMRI and ERP studies. *Physiology and Behavior, 77*(4–5), 477–482.

Vance, A. L., & Luk, E. S. (1998). Attention deficit hyperactivity disorder and anxiety: Is there an association with neurodevelopmental deficits. *Australian New Zealand Journal of Psychiatry, 32*(5), 650–657.

Vandel, P., Haffen, E., Nezelof, S., Broly, F., Kantelip, J. P., & Sechter, D. (2004). Clomipramine, fluoxetine, and CYP2D6 metabolic capacity in depressed patients. *Human Psychopharmacology, 19*(5), 293–298.

Vaswani, M., Linda, F. K., & Ramesh, S. (2003). Role of selective serotonin reuptake inhibitors in psychiatric disorders: A comprehensive review. *Progress in Neuropsychopharmacology & Biological Psychiatry, 27*(1), 85–102.

Vaughan, K., & Tarrier, N. (1992). The use of image habituation training with posttraumatic stress disorders. *British Journal of Psychiatry, 161,* 658–664.

Verster, J. C., & Volkerts, E. R. (2004). Clinical pharmacology, clinical efficacy, and behavioral toxicity of alprazolam: A review of the literature. *CNS Drug Reviews, 10*(1), 45–76.

Vielhaber, K., Riemann, D., Feige, B., Kuelz, A., Kirschbaum, C., & Voderholzer, U. (2005). Impact of experimentally induced serotonin deficiency by tryptophan depletion on saliva cortisol concentrations. *Pharmacopsychiatry, 38*(2), 87–94.

Villarreal, G., & King, C. Y. (2001). Brain imaging in posttraumatic stress disorder. *Seminal Clinical Neuropsychiatry, 6*(2), 131–145.

Wade, A. G., Lepola, U., Koponen, H. J., Pedersen, V., & Pederson, T. (1997). The effect of citalopram in panic disorder. *British Journal of Psychiatry, 170,* 549–553.

Wagner, K. D. (2003). Paroxetine treatment of mood and anxiety disorders in children and adolescents. *Psychopharmacology Bulletin, 37*(1), 167–175.

Waldinger, M. D., Zwinderman, A. H., & Olivier, B. (2001). Antidepressants and ejaculation: A double-blind, randomized, placebo-controlled, fixed-dose with paroxetine, sertraline, and nefazodone. *Journal of Clinical Psychopharmacology, 21*(3), 293–297.

Walitza, S., Wewetzer, C., Gerlach, M., Klampfi, K., Geller, F., Barth, N., Hahn, F., Herpertz- Dahlmann, B., Gossler, M., Fleishhaker, C., Schulz, E., Hebebrand, J., Warnke, A., & Hinney, A. (2004). Transmission disequilibrium studies in children and adolescents with obsessive- compulsive disorders pertaining to polymorphisms of genes of the serotonergic pathway. *Journal of Neural Transmission, 111*(7), 817–825.

Walker, D. L., & Davis, M. (2002). The role of amygdala glutamate receptors in fear learning, fear-potentiated startle, and extinction. *Pharmacology, Biochemistry, and Behavior, 71*(3), 379–392.

Walker, D. L., Rattiner, L. M., & Davis, M. (2002). Group II metabotropic glutamate receptors within the amygdala regulate fear as assessed with potentiated startle in rats. *Behavioral Neuroscience, 116*(6), 1075–1083.

Walker, D. L., Toufexis, D. J., & Davis, M. (2003). Role of the bed nucleus of the stria terminalis versus the amygdala in fear, stress, and anxiety. *European Journal of Psychopharmacology, 463*(1–3), 199–216.

Wallace, T. L., Stellitano, K. E., Neve, R. L., & Duman, R. S. (2004). Effects of cyclic adenosine monophosphate response element binding protein overexpression in the basolateral amygdala on behavioral models of depression and anxiety. *Biological Psychiatry, 56*(3), 151–160.

Walsh, K. H., & McDougle, C. J. (2004). Pharmacological augmentation strategies for treatment-resistant obsessive-compulsive disorder. *Expert Opinion on Pharmacotherapy, 5*(10), 2059–2067.

Watson, D., Wu, K. D., & Cutshall, C. (2004). Symptom subtypes of obsessive-compulsive disorder and their relation to dissociation. *Journal of Anxiety Disorders, 18*(4), 435–458.

Watson, J. B. (1913). Psychology as the behaviorist views it. *Psychological Review, 20,* 158–177.

Watson, J. B. (1916). The place of the conditioned reflex in psychology. *Psychological Review, 23,* 89–116.

Weber, D. A., & Reynolds, C. R. (2004). Clinical perspectives on neurobiological effects of psychological trauma. *Neuropsychology Review, 14*(2), 115–129.

Weiner, B. (1974). *Achievement Motivation and Attribution Theory.* Morristown: New Jersey: General Learning Press.

Weiss, E. L., Potenza, M. N., McDougle, C. J., & Epperson, C. N. (1999). Olanzepine addition in obsessive-compulsive disorder refractory to selective serotonin reuptake inhibitors: An open-label case series. *Journal of Clinical Psychiatry, 60*(8), 524–527.

Weitzdoerfer, R., Gerstl, N., Pollack, D., Hoeger, H., Dreher, W., & Lubec, G. (2004). Long-term influence of perinatal asphyxia on the social behavior in aging rats. *Gerontology, 50*(4), 200–205.

Weitzdoerfer, R., Hoeger, H., Engidawork, E., Engelmann, M., Singewald, N., Lubec, G., & Lubec, B. (2004). Neuronal nitric oxide synthase knock-out mice show impaired cognitive performance. *Nitric Oxide: Biology and Chemistry, 10*(3), 130–140.

Wenzel, A., Haugen, E. N., Jackson, L. C., & Robinson, K. (2003). Prevalence of generalized anxiety at eight weeks postpartum. *Archives of Women's Mental Health, 6*(1), 43–49.

Whiteside, S. P., Port, J. D., & Abramowitz, J. S. (2004). A meta-analysis of functional neuroimaging in obsessive-compulsive disorder. *Psychiatry Research, 132*(1), 69–79.

Whitney, K. A., Fastenau, P. S., Evans, J. D., & Lysaker, P. H. (2004). Comparative neuropsychological function in obsessive-compulsive disorder and schizophrenia with and without obsessive-compulsive symptoms. *Schizophrenia Research, 69*(1), 75–83.

Wichniak, A., Brunner, H., Ising, M., Pedrosa-Gil, F., Holsboer, F., & Friess, E. (2004). Impaired hypothalamic-pituitary-adrenocortical (HPA) system is related to severity of benzodiazepine withdrawal in patients with depression. *Psychoneuroendocrinology,* 29(9), 1101–1108.

Wigger, A., Sanchez, M. M., Mathys, K. C., Ebner, K., Frank, E., Liu, D., Kresse, A., Neumann, I. D., Holsboer, F., Plotsky, P. M., & Landgraf, R. (2004). Alterations in central neuropeptide expression, release, and receptor binding in rats bred for high anxiety: Critical role of vasopressin. *Neuropsychopharmacology,* 29(1), 1–14.

Wignall, E. L., Dickson, J. M., Vaughan, P., Farrow, T. F., Wilkinson, I. D., Hunter, M. D., & Woodruff, P. W. (2004). Smaller hippocampal volume in patients with recent-onset posttraumatic stress disorder. *Biological Psychiatry,* 56(11), 832–836.

Williams, N. L., Shahar, G., Riskind, J. H., & Joiner, T. E. (2005). The looming maladaptive style predicts shared variance in anxiety disorder symptoms: Further support for a cognitive model of vulnerability to anxiety. *Journal of Anxiety Disorders,* 19(2), 157–175.

Winnicott, D. W. (1965). *The Maturational Process and the Facilitating Environment: Studies in the Theory of Emotional Development.* New York: International Universities Press.

Wittchen, H. U. (2002). Generalized anxiety disorder: Prevalence, burden, and cost to society. *Depression and Anxiety,* 16(4), 162–171.

Wolff, M., Alsobrook, J. P., & Pauls, D. L. (2000). Genetic aspects of obsessive-compulsive disorder. *Psychiatric Clinics of North America,* 23(3), 535–544.

Wolkowitz, O. M., & Pickar, D. (1991). Benzodiazepines in the treatment of schizophrenia: A review and reappraisal. *American Journal of Psychiatry,* 148, 714–726.

Wolpe, J. (1958). *Psychotherapy by Reciprocal Inhibition.* Stanford: Stanford University Press.

Wolpe, J., & Lazarus, A. A. (1969). *The Practice of Behavior Therapy.* New York: Pergamon.

Woo, J. M., Yoon, K. S., & Yu, B. H. (2002). Catechol O-methyltransferase genetic polymorphism in panic disorder. *American Journal of Psychiatry,* 159, 1785–1787.

Woods, S. W. (1992). Regional cerebral blood flow imaging with SPECT in psychiatric disease: Focus on schizophrenia, anxiety disorders, and substance abuse. *Journal of Clinical Psychiatry,* 53, 20–25.

World Health Organization (1992). *The ICD-10 Classification of Mental and Behavioral Disorders: Clinical Descriptions and Diagnostic Guidelines.* Geneva: Author.

Wu, J. C., Buchsbaum, M. S., Gillin, J. C., Tang, C., Cadwell, S., Wiegand, M., Najafi, A., Klein, E., Hazen, K., Bunney, W. E., Fallon, J. H., & Keator, D. (1999). Prediction of antidepressant effects of sleep deprication by metabolic rates in the ventral anterior cingulate and medial prefrontal cortex. *American Journal of Psychiatry,* 156(8), 1149–1158.

Wunderlich, G. R., Raymond, R., DeSousa, N. J., Nobrega, J. N., & Vaccarino, F. J. (2002). Decreased CCK(B) receptor binding in rat amygdala in animals demonstrating greater anxiety-like behavior. *Psychopharmacology,* 164(2), 193–199.

Xu, Y. L., Reinscheid, R. K., Huitron-Resendiz, S., Clark, S. D., Wang, Z., Lin, S. H., Brucher, F. A., Zeng, J., Ly, N. K., Henriksen, S. J., De Lecea, L., & Civelli, O. (2004). Neuropeptide S: A neuropeptide promoting arousal and anxiolytic-like effects. *Neuron,* 43(4), 487–497.

Yalcin, B., Fullerton, J., Miller, S., Keays, D. A., Brady, S., Bhomra, A., Jefferson, A., Volpi, E., Copley, R. R., Flint, J., & Mott, R. (2004). Unexpected complexity in the haplotypes of commonly used inbred strains of laboratory mice. *Proceedings of the National Academy of Sciences of the United States of America,* 101(26), 9734–9739.

Yamada, K., Santo-Yamada, Y., & Wada, K. (2002). Restraint stress impaired maternal behavior in female mice lacking the neuromedin B receptor (NMB-R) gene. *Neuroscience Letters,* 330(2), 163–166.

Yamano, M., Ogura, H., Okuyama, S., & Ohki-Hamazaki, H. (2002). Modulation of 5HT system in mice with a targeted disruption of neuromedin B receptor. *Journal of Neuroscience Research,* 68(1), 59–64.

Yamauchi, M., Tatebayashi, T., Nagase, K., Kojima, M., & Imanishi, T. (2004). Chronic treatment with fluvoxamine desensitizes 5–HT(2C) receptor-mediated hypolocomotion in rats. *Pharmacology, Biochemistry, and Behavior, 78*(4), 683–689.

Yaryura-Tobias, J. A., & Neziroglu, F. A. (2003). Basal ganglia hemorrhagic ablation association with temporary suppression of obsessive-compulsive symptoms. *Rev Bras Psiquiatr, 25*(1), 40–42.

Yasuno, F., Suhara, T., Ichimiya, T., Takano, A., Ando, T., & Okubo, Y. (2004). Decreased 5HT1A receptor binding in amygdala of schizophrenia. *Biological Psychiatry, 55*(5), 439–444.

Yatham, L. N. (2004). Newer anticonvulsants in the treatment of bipolar disorder. *Journal of Clinical Psychiatry, 65*(10), 28–35.

Yehuda, R. (1999a). Biological factors associated with susceptibility to posttraumatic stress disorder. *Canadian Journal of Psychiatry, 44,* 34–39.

Yehuda, R. (1999b). Linking the neuroendocrinology of posttraumatic stress disorder with recent neuroanatomic findings. *Seminal Clinical Neuropsychiatry, 4*(4), 256–265.

Yehuda, R., Boisoneau, D., & Lowry, M. T. (1995). Dose-response changes in plasma cortisol and lymphocyte glucorticoid receptors following dexamethasone administration in combat veterans with and without posttraumatic stress disorder. *Archives of General Psychiatry, 52*(7), 583–593.

Yehunda, R., Golier, J. A., Halligan, S. L., Meaney, M., & Bierer, L. M. (2004). The ACTH response to dexamethasone in PTSD. *American Journal of Psychiatry, 161*(8), 1397–1403.

Yehunda, R., Golier, J. A., Yang, R. K., & Tischler, L. (2004). Enhanced sensitivity to glucocorticoids in peripheral mononuclear leukocytes in posttraumatic stress disorder. *Biological Psychiatry, 55*(11), 1110–1116.

Yerkes, R. M., & Dodson, J. D. (1908). The relation of strength of stimulus to rapidity of habit formation. *Journal of Comparative Neurology and Psychology, 18,* 459–482.

Yoo, J. H., Lee, S. Y., Loh, H. H., Ho, I. K., & Jang, C. G. (2004). Altered emotional behaviors and the expression of 5HT(1A) and M(1) muscarinic receptors in micro-opioid knockout in mice. *Synapse, 54*(2), 72–82.

Yoshimura, R., Nakamura, J., Shinkai, K., & Ueda, N. (2004). Clinical response to antidepressant treatment and 3–methoxy-4–hydroxyphenylglycol levels: Mini review. *Progress in Neuro-psychopharmacology & Biological Psychiatry, 28*(4), 611–616.

Youdim, M. B., & Weinstock, M. (2004). Therapeutic applications of selective and non-selective inhibitors of monoamine oxidase A and B that do not cause significant tyramine potentiation. *Neurotoxicology, 25*(1–2), 243–250.

Young, A. S., Klap, R., Sherbourne, C. D., & Wells, K. B. (2001). The quality of care for depressive and anxiety disorders in the United States. *Archives of General Psychiatry, 58*(1), 55–61.

Young, E. A., Abelson, J. L., & Cameron, O. G. (2004). Effect of comorbid anxiety disorders on the hypothalamic-pituitary-adrenal axis response to a social stressor in major depression. *Biological Psychiatry, 56*(2), 113–120.

Young, E. A., & Breslau, N. (2004). Cortisol and catecholamines in posttraumatic stress disorder: An epidemiologic community study. *Archives of General Psychiatry, 61*(4), 394–401.

Young, H. E., Rosen, C. S., & Finney, J. W. (2005). A survey of PTSD screening and referral practices in VA addiction treatment programs. *Journal of Substance Abuse and Treatment, 28*(4), 313–319.

Yuan, C. S., Mehendale, S., Xiao, Y., Aung, H. H., Xie, J. T., & Ang-Lee, M. K. (2004). The gamma- aminobutyric acidergic effects of valarian and valerenic acid on rat brainstem neuronal activity. *Anesthesia and Analgesia, 98*(2), 353–358.

Zahorodna, A., Tokarski, K., & Hess, G. (2006). Imipramine treatment ameliorates corticosterone induced alterations in the effects of 5–HT1 and 5–HT4 receptor activation in the CA1 area of the rat hippocampus. *European Psychopharmacology, 16*(5), 383–390.

Zai, G., Bezchlibnyk, Y. B., Richter, M. A., Arnold, P., Burroughs, E., Barr, C. L., & Kennedy, J. L. (2004). Myelin oligodendrocyte glycoprotein (MOG) gene is associated with obsessive-compulsive disorder. *American Journal of Medical Genetics, 129*(1), 64–68.

Zarrindast, M. R., Bakhsha, A., Rostami, P., & Shafaghi, B. (2002). Effects of intrahippocampal injection of GABAergic drugs on memory retention of passive avoidance learning in rats. *Journal of Psychopharmacology, 16*(4), 313–319.

Zarrindast, M. R., Rostami, P., & Sadeghi-Hariri, M. (2001). GABA(A) but not GABA(B) receptor stimulation induces antianxiety profile in rats. *Pharmacology, Biochemistry, and Behavior, 69*(1–2), 9–15.

Zerbe, M. (1990). Clinical management of the pregnant trauma victim. *AACN Clinical Issues in Critical Care Nursing, 1*(3), 479–494.

Zhang, C., Steiner, J. P., Hamilton, G. S., Hicks, T. P., & Poulter, M. O. (2001). Regeneration of dopaminergic function in 6–hydroxydopamine-lesioned rats by neuroimmunophilin ligand treatment. *Journal of Neuroscience, 21*(15), 156.

Zimmerberg, B., & Kajunski, E. W. (2004). Sexually dimorphic effects of postnatal allopregnanolone on the development of anxiety behavior after early deprivation. *Pharmacology, Biochemistry, and Behavior, 78*(3), 465–471.

Zimmerman, M., & Chelminski, I. (2003). Generalized anxiety disorder in patients with major depression: Is DSM-IV's hierarchy correct? *American Journal of Psychiatry, 160*(3), 504–512.

Zink, C. F., Pagnoni, G., Martin-Skurski, M. E., Chappelow, J. C., & Berns, G. S. (2004). Human striatal responses to monetary reward depend on saliency. *Neuron, 42*, 509–517.

Zinker, J. C. (1978). *Creative Process in Gestalt Therapy*. New York: Random House.

Zinker, J. C. (1994). *In Search of Good Form: Gestalt Therapy with Couples and Families*. San Francisco: Jossey-Bass Publishers.

Zohar, J., Kennedy, J. L., Hollander, E., & Koran, L. M. (2004). Serotonin-1D hypothesis of obsessive- compulsive disorder: An update. *Journal of Clinical Psychiatry, 65*(14), 18–21.

Zorrilla, E. P., & Koob, G. F. (2004). The therapeutic potential of CRF(1) antagonists for anxiety. *Expert Opinion on Investigational Drugs, 13*(7), 799–828.

Zvolensky, M. J., Kotov, R., Antipova, A. V., & Schmidt, N. B. (2005). Diathesis stress model for panic-related distress: A test in a Russian epidemiological sample. *Behavior Research and Therapy, 43*(4), 521–532.

Zwanzger, P., Eser, D., Aicher, S., Schule, C., Baghai, T. C., Padberg, F., Ella, R., Moller, H. J., & Rupprecht, R. (2003). Effects of alprazolam on cholecystokinin-tetrapeptid-induced panic and hypothalamic-pituitary-adrenal-axis activity: A placebo-controlled study. *Neuropsychopharmacology, 28*(5), 979–984.

Zwanzger, P., Jarry, H., Eser, D., Padberg, F., Baghai, T., Schule, C., Ella, R., Moller, H. J., & Rupprecht, R. (2003). Plasma gamma-aminobutyric acid (GABA) levels in cholecystokinine-tetrapeptide (CCK4) induced anxiety. *Journal of Neural Transmission, 110*(3), 313–316.

Index

Page numbers followed by *t* refer to tables.